# Canada Today

**Daniel J. McDevitt**
Head of History
Glenforest Secondary School
Mississauga, Ontario

**Angus L. Scully**
Head of History
Morning Star Secondary School
Mississauga, Ontario

**Carl F. Smith**
Assistant Head of History
Port Credit Secondary School
Mississauga, Ontario

Prentice-Hall of Canada, Ltd., Scarborough, Ontario

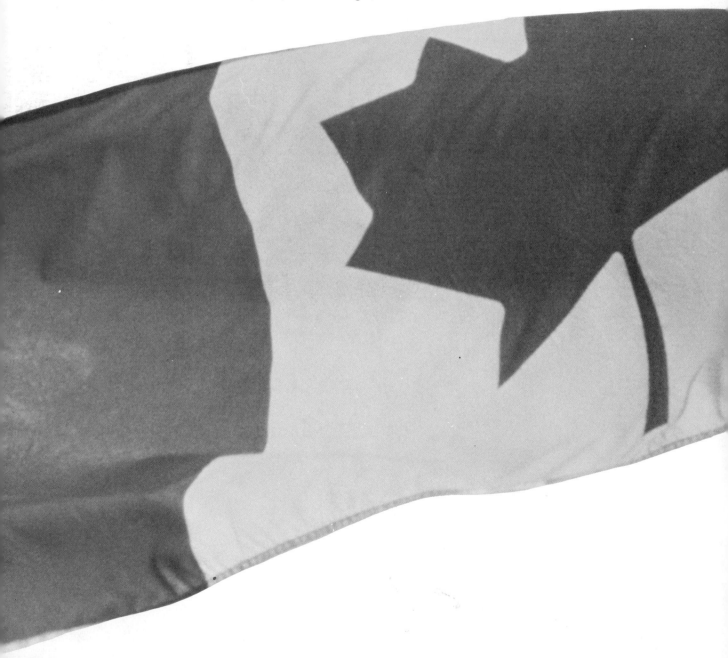

# Canada Today

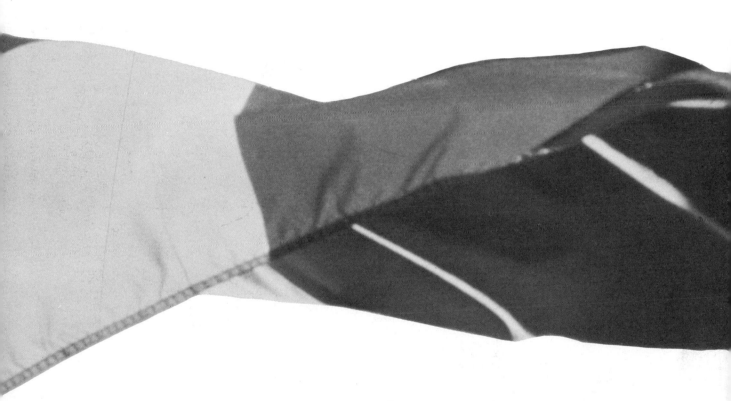

Canadian Cataloguing in Publication Data

McDevitt, Daniel J.
   Canada today

For use in schools.

Includes index.
ISBN 0-13-112847-7

1. Canada—History.   2. Canada—English-
French relations.   3. Canada—Relations (General)
with foreign countries.   I. Scully, Angus L.
II. Smith, Carl F., 1943-      III. Title.

FC164.M32                971              C79-094100-7
F1026.M32

Prentice-Hall, Inc., Englewood Cliffs,
New Jersey
Prentice-Hall of Australia, Pty., Ltd.,
Sydney
Prentice-Hall of India Pvt., Ltd.,
New Delhi
Prentice-Hall International, Inc., London
Prentice-Hall of Japan, Inc., Tokyo
Prentice-Hall of Southeast Asia (Pte.) Ltd.,
Singapore


ISBN 0-13-112847-7

Production Editor: MaryLynne Meschino
Design: John Zehethofer
Illustrations: Samuel Daniel/James Loates Illustrating/Colin Gillies

Composition: CompuScreen Typesetting Ltd.
Printed and bound in Canada by The Bryant Press Limited

 2 3 4 5   BP   83 82 81 80 79

# Contents

# Acknowledgements

This book is a product of teamwork. When we started our work, we did not realize how much we would come to depend on the help of others.

We were supported from the beginning by the talented personnel at Prentice-Hall. Rob Greenaway nourished our belief that the book might gain a wide audience across Canada. He helped us tailor our work to fit the needs of our readers, and encouraged us to complete the book in the relatively short time at our disposal. MaryLynne Meschino, the production editor, assisted us in writing the book with her constructive criticism and diplomacy. She encouraged us to make cuts to the manuscript that were necessary but painful, yet she offered clear, simple alternatives to the cut material. Beth Burgess was of great help in arranging for the illustrations and photos.

Many other people made this a team effort. Frank Sambells had practical suggestions for communicating the importance of geography in the tensions facing our country. Hazel McCallion patiently pointed out the issues confronting our governments each day. Other friends, colleagues, and specialists, too numerous to name, directed us in preparing the other sections of the text.

The final members of the team were our families: Emily McDevitt and children Danny, Laura, Monica, and Maureen; Jill Scully and children Kimberley and Jeffrey; and Gloria Smith and son Aaron Tyler. Our wives were of great help. They offered ingenious explanations to the children old enough to ask why we spent so much time writing, and devised distractions for those who were too young to understand why we were so busy. For over a year they also explained to friends and relatives why we could not visit them on weekends. Our families motivated us to try to make our work good enough for students today. They inspired us to try to write a book that our own children will be proud of when they are old enough to understand what we have written.

# Preface

*Canada Today* is a book about flesh and blood people facing the challenges of life in Canada. In the past, Canadians have had to deal with issues and find solutions to problems. Canadians today are faced with many of these past concerns, as well as with new ones. You, as Canadians, have a say in these issues. You have a role to play in shaping Canada's future. This is why it is important for you to understand the issues in Canada's past and in modern Canadian society.

This text will help you to understand your country. The book describes key areas of conflict in our history. It shows that solutions were found by Canadians in the past. The text also provides information about present-day tensions, and asks you to try and resolve these issues.

*Canada Today* focuses on five main Canadian issues: geography, government, French-English relations, relations with the US, and world concerns.

As you look through the book, you will notice that *Canada Today* is unique in many ways. Information is presented to you through short stories, case studies, biographies, letters, newspaper-style articles, maps, and diagrams. We hope that this approach will make the issues come alive for you.

Quite often, fictional (made-up) people and situations are used to present real issues and attitudes. The fiction helps recreate the drama and excitement of Canada's past and present. It should also make clear the facts, concepts, and issues you are studying by making them personal to you. Many experts have checked the fictional materials to make sure that the facts and the tone in them are accurate. All fictional accounts are clearly identified in the book.

Another feature of *Canada Today* is its wide range of exercises and activities. They are designed to involve you, as thinking people, in your country's history and in its future. Seven different types of activities help you to think about and understand the material in the book. These exercises also encourage you to develop different skills such as organizing facts and solving problems. The purpose of each type of activity is described more fully in the introductory section of the book, "Countdown Canada".

Several other features of *Canada Today* will make your learning easier. The content has been carefully selected, organized, and written, and the reading level has been strictly controlled. The design of the text will also assist you in your studies. A short table of contents appears at the beginning of each chapter. It tells you which issues are discussed in that section of the book. At the end of each chapter there is a glossary of new or difficult words and phrases. Words listed in the glossary appear in coloured print the first time they are used in the book. Also, as you work through the book, do not pass lightly over the photos and illustrations. They have been chosen to provide new information, explain a new concept, or get you to think about an issue.

No book can possibly teach you all there is to know about Canada. However, we hope that *Canada Today* will give you a better understanding of the country. We hope, too, that the skills you will learn will encourage you to learn more and do more as involved citizens of Canada.

Daniel McDevitt
Angus Scully
Carl Smith
Toronto, 1979

# Countdown Canada: The end of a country

## Introduction

Is it possible that Canada will one day cease to exist? Imagine this situation: sometime in the future, Canada is faced with serious problems. No solutions can be found. The prime minister signs a treaty that makes the country part of the United States. The independent nation of Canada then no longer exists.

To most Canadians, such an end to Canada seems impossible. They think that Canada is an independent nation now, and has been since 1867. They also think that Canada has gained and kept its independence easily. This is not quite true. Canadians have had to meet many challenges to gain and keep their independence.

Canada has survived as a nation because each generation has been able to answer the challenges facing it. To remain independent, Canadians must continue to find solutions to their problems. Many of the problems are the same as the ones faced by past generations. Here are some of these challenges:

1. Can Canadians from different geographic regions feel that they belong to one country?
2. Can both English-speaking and French-speaking people live in harmony in one nation?
3. What kind of government and laws are best for a vast country?
4. Can Canada survive the influence of its extremely powerful neighbour, the United States?

The following newscast deals with the idea of Canada becoming a part of the United States of America. It is a fictional (made-up) story. However, it brings out some important challenges facing Canadians today. It also introduces you to issues that will be looked at in the text.

**A CBC Special Report**
**Countdown Canada**

---

| | |
|---|---|
| **Part one** | **Canada: The end of a nation** |
| *The scene:* | *CBC studios, Ottawa. July 4, 1995.* |
| *Time:* | *Zero hour minus sixty minutes.* |

---

Julian Cleva

**Margaret Kandal, news commentator** Good morning. This is
Margaret Kandal speaking to you from Ottawa. At noon today—
zero hour—Canada will cease to exist as a nation. In about one
hour Jack Southfield, President of the United States of America,
and Prime Minister Brad Portland will sign a treaty. With this
agreement, Canada will become part of the United States. We will
be bringing you live coverage of the signing. We will also talk to
Canadians across the country to see how they feel about the treaty.
But first, we'll have a recap of the events leading up to this
important day.

During the 1980s Canada had serious economic problems. These
problems grew worse after January 1990, when Quebec declared its
independence. Relations between Quebec and Canada were not
good. Foreign companies stopped investing in the country. They
felt Canada was becoming too unstable. Many companies
pulled out of Canada. This increased the nation's political and
social problems. In December of 1992; the Union party was
formed. It saw union with the United States as the only solution to
Canada's problems. It promised to work toward achieving this
union. The party steadily won support. In the federal election of

3

1994, the Union party was voted into power. The screen behind me shows the election results. The Union party won 142 of the 207 seats in the House of Commons.

Since then delegations from Canada have been meeting with President Southfield and his advisers. Their purpose is to arrange for the union. They have been discussing issues such as the banks, money, citizenship, and law. All the details of joining one huge country to another are being worked out. Today, July 4, 1995, at noon, the union will become official. Canadians will become citizens of the United States of North America. The map on the screen shows that five new states will be added to the US.

**Fig. I-1   The United States of North America**

| Party | Seats |
|-------|-------|
| Union Party .......................................... | 142 seats |
| National Party (formerly the Conservative and Liberal Parties) ........................................ | 46 seats |
| Other Parties ........................................ | 19 seats |

After Quebec separation, 282 seats in Canadian House of Commons reduced to 207. No elections possible in breakaway nation. Quebec's 75 seats held vacant

**Fig. I-2 Election results for total seats in Commons**

## Countdown Canada time line

In news reports, events are often discussed out of their time sequence. It is usually easier to understand history if we have a clear idea of the order of events. A time line helps us get a good picture. The fictional time line below shows the events of the last six years of Canada's existence. The most important events appear in italics.

| YEAR | | EVENT |
|------|------|-------|
| February | 1989 | *Serious economic troubles.* Foreign countries reduce their **investments** in Canada. |
| June | 1989 | *Quebec provincial* **referendum.** *Quebec voters say "yes" to separation.* |
| January | 1990 | *Quebec proclaims its independence.* Quebec and Canada agree to negotiate (work out) details of separation. |
| Summer | 1990 | **Economic slowdown** *in Quebec and Canada.* Canadian dollar falls in value. Atlantic provinces seriously affected—high unemployment, inflation. |
| November | 1990 | *Meetings between Quebec and Canada break down.* Government leaders from Canada and Quebec are unable to work out a trade agreement. |
| February | 1991 | *Quebec claims federal buildings and property located in Quebec.* *Canadian Armed Forces occupy federal territory in Quebec.* La Police Nationale du Québec (PNQ—formerly the Quebec Provincial Police) and militia start defence training. |
| May | 1991 | *Quebec claims Labrador.* The governments of Newfoundland and Labrador cut off hydroelectricity from Churchill Falls to Quebec. Canada imposes oil **blockade** on Quebec. Sarnia to Montreal pipeline closed. |
| Summer | 1991 | *Economic decline continues.* Crisis in manufacturing and automotive industries. General Motors cuts back auto production and begins major layoffs. Quebec withdraws claim to Labrador. |

| | | |
|---|---|---|
| November | 1991 | *Racial tension increases.* |
| | | Some people blame immigration policy for high unemployment. |
| | | "Canada for Canadians" group formed. Over 17 000 active members by year's end. |
| Spring | 1992 | *Unemployment increases across country.* |
| | | *Canadian dollar hits low of 71 cents US.* |
| | | Federal government criticized for its lack of action. |
| | | Protests against three main political parties. |
| July | 1992 | Unemployment riots in Vancouver and St. John's. |
| December | 1992 | *New political party formed, the Union party.* |
| | | It favours joining Canada to US. Brad Portland elected leader. |
| Spring | 1993 | *Race riots in Toronto and Vancouver.* |
| | | Manitoba and Saskatchewan declared **depressed areas.** |
| | | Number of requests to emigrate to the United States hits 250 000. The US continues to refuse Canadians entry. |
| Summer | 1993 | Public opinion poll shows that Union party is gaining favour. |
| September | 1993 | *Conservatives and Liberal parties join to form "National party".* This party wants independence for Canada. |
| | | New Democratic party remains independent. |
| January | 1994 | Unemployment relief camps started in Saskatchewan and Manitoba. |
| Spring and Summer | 1994 | Bank of Canada forced to borrow from US to support sagging Canadian dollar. |
| | | *Unemployment riots in Vancouver, Toronto, Regina, Sydney, Hamilton, Fredericton.* |
| November | 1994 | *Canadian election on issue of union with US.* |
| | | *Union party elected by a large majority.* |
| April | 1995 | Over 100 000 Canadians march on US Consulate in Toronto. |
| | | American Embassy in Ottawa bombed. |
| July 4 | 1995 | *Signing of Treaty of Union.* |

How are Canadians reacting to the union? Feelings are mixed. Throughout history, Canadians have prided themselves on building a North American country different from the US. For some, the signing of the treaty is a bitter event. Most people, though, welcome the chance to join the States. The election results show this general feeling. Let's look at the reactions of people across the country. First from Halifax.

Test your understanding of the basic facts in
Part one of the newscast. Each question requires
a short answer. You may look back at the story
to find the answers. Quick quizzes are tests of
understanding, not memory. Answers to all
Quick quizzes in this book are found at the back
of the text.

1. In general, what is this newscast about?

2. What happened to the economies of Canada
   and the new state of Quebec after Quebec's
   separation?
3. What was the name of the political party
   formed in 1992? What was its aim?
4. How did Canadians show that they wanted
   union with the US?
5. What is to happen to the provinces of Canada
   after union with the US?

**Part two**     **Canadians react to union**
*The scene:*     *Halifax, Nova Scotia.*
*Time:*     *Zero hour minus 50 minutes.*

John McQueen

**Bill Mackenzie, CBC correspondent** This is Bill Mackenzie reporting from Halifax. In less than one hour the Atlantic provinces
will become the new state of Eastsea. People here are sad that
Canada will no longer exist as a nation. However, they see union
as a way of solving their many problems. This is Jim Hennessy,
a businessman in the Halifax area. What are your feelings about
the union of Canada and the States?

**Jim Hennessy** I'm against the union. I think that it is going to
wipe out a lot of businesses in the area. I own a company that
makes woodburning stoves. Business isn't too bad right now. My
stoves cost less than the American ones imported from New
England. But once we join the States, **tariffs** will be eliminated
and the New England stoves will cost much less. I'll never be

able to compete with the big American factories. They can turn out stoves faster and more cheaply than I can. This union will finish my business.

**Bill Mackenzie** Jim Hennessy is worried about the economic problems that union may create. People like Josie White express other concerns. Why are you opposed to union?

**Josie White** I'm upset at the idea of leaving behind our British traditions. I don't want to pick up the American way of life. To me, Britain is our mother country. Our nation is based on a **parliamentary system of government,** like Britain's. I don't like the idea of becoming part of a **republic!** That's what the US is.

---

*The scene:*     *Toronto, Ontario.*

---

John McQueen

**Anna Ferrara, CBC correspondent** Many Torontonians feel that union with the United States will improve economic conditions. But they are looking to this union to solve other problems as well. There has been conflict between Canadians and immigrant groups here in Toronto in the past few years. Protests and riots have brought fear to people like Willie Cook. He belongs to the Immigrants for Canada Society, a group that supports union. Mr. Cook, why was your society formed? How do you think union with the United States will help immigrants?

**Willie Cook** It is always hard to be a stranger in a new land. Quite often immigrants have to learn a whole new way of life. Lately, it has been harder than usual for immigrants. Some Canadian-born people have been blaming us for the unemployment in the country. They say we are stealing jobs that belong to people born in Canada. Some groups have marched against us....There have even been riots! We have feared for our lives. Our society was formed to help immigrants cope with this conflict. But it isn't easy. Our society decided that we will be better protected if Canada becomes part of the US. Canada has always had racial trouble—just look at the country's history. Remember how badly the Japanese living in British Columbia were treated during the Second World War? Sure, the United States has its share of racial conflict. But we think that the US government will protect immigrants. Maybe we are wrong. But we are willing to take a chance. Anything is better than having to live with things the way they are now!

**Anna Ferrara** Racial trouble is only one of the many problems facing Canadians. Yet this issue has been serious enough to influence voters. The racial problem has led people like Willie Cook to vote for the Union party. This is Anna Ferrara in Toronto, Ontario.

*The scene:     Winnipeg, Manitoba.*

John McQueen

**Roger Monty, CBC correspondent** This is Roger Monty in Winnipeg. At noon today Manitoba, Saskatchewan, and Alberta will form the new US state Almansask. Westerners do not seem to be upset about this. Many of them welcome the chance to be part of the United States. I have with me Jack Rankin, president of Local 445 of the Sewers' Union. He is here to tell viewers about the reaction of workers in his union.

**Jack Rankin**  Most of our people seem happy about joining the United States. For the past few years, there have been plenty of jobs in the oil and gas industries. But workers in mining and manufacturing have been laid off. I've fought to have as many workers kept on as possible. But management has had to cut production and jobs. Because of this, lots of people have gone south to the States to look for work. Once we become part of the States the economy will be more stable. There will be more jobs right here. Another thing—when Canada joins the States, tariffs will disappear. This will open up the whole US market to our industries. And without tariffs, prices on a lot of US goods will drop. I really think union with the States is a good thing. We'll get a new start. We'll be a strong state in a strong country!

**Roger Monty**  Jack Rankin has pointed out some important benefits of union with the States. Other westerners often give another reason for joining the States. When Canada joins the States, Almansask will have close ties with the states south of here, Montana and North Dakota. These states are similar to the western provinces geographically. They also share many of the same advantages and problems. Westerners, therefore, feel that these western states are natural partners for them. This is Roger Monty in Winnipeg.

---

*The scene:*    *Vancouver, British Columbia.*

---

John McQueen

10

**Della Stern, CBC correspondent**  This is Della Stern in Vancouver. The atmosphere here today is light-hearted. People seem to be happy. British Columbians are looking to union with the States to solve many problems. In the last six years, the economy of the province has suffered greatly. Unemployment in key industries such as mining and forestry has increased. Foreign companies have been afraid to invest in BC. Labour unrest has rocked the province. Some British Columbians thought the province should follow Quebec's example and separate from Canada. But in the 1994 election, more than 90% of all British Columbians voted for the Union party. They clearly felt that union with the States was the best answer to their problems. With me is the Honourable Jacob Merriweather, a member of the BC Legislature. Sir, why does British Columbia favour union with the United States?

**Jacob Merriweather**  We in British Columbia feel that Confederation has nothing to offer us. For over a hundred years we have paid taxes. This money has gone to help support the poorer provinces. When Quebec left Canada, our economy was hit hard. People began to protest. It has been difficult to keep law and order in some cities. Confederation was an experiment, and it's time we realized that the experiment has failed. It's time to move on to something new. Union with the States will give us stability and more jobs. We'll be able to get back on our feet.

**Della Stern**  To most British Columbians, union is the best answer to the problems of the last hundred years. The next hundred will tell them whether or not this was the right choice. This is Della Stern in Vancouver.

---

*The scene:*   CBC studios, Ottawa, Ontario.
*Time:*   Zero hour minus 25 minutes.

---

**Margaret Kandal**  To those of you who have just tuned in, welcome. We have been asking Canadians how they feel about union with the United States. There is another question being asked today: What will happen to Quebec now? Some observers are predicting that Quebec, too, will one day become part of the States. Others say that Quebec values its independence and won't give it up easily. For an analysis of the situation in Quebec we go to René Turcot.

*The scene:* *National Assembly Building in Quebec City.*

**René Turcot, CBC correspondent** Good morning. I'm here in the **National Assembly Building.** The question being asked today is very simple: How long will it be before Quebec joins the United States? It has only been a few years since Quebec realized its dream—to be an independent nation. But now economic and social trouble is threatening this independence.

| | *Before Separation* | *After Separation* |
|---|---|---|
| Trade | In 1974, Quebec sold 6.7 billion dollars in goods to other provinces. It bought 5.6 billion dollars in goods. Its trade surplus was therefore 1.1 billion dollars. | In 1994, Quebec manufacturing declined. Quebec sold 4.5 billion dollars in goods to Canada. It bought 4.9 billion dollars in goods. |
| Unemployment | From 1953 to 1975 Quebec had one of the worst unemployment rates in Canada. The average for this period was 7%. | After separation unemployment reached an average of 12%. Some regions of Quebec, such as Gaspé and the northwest, hit 25% - 30%. |
| Income | Quebec workers were paid less than the average Canadian worker in the period 1953–75. The average income was roughly 93% of what the average worker elsewhere in Canada received. | Quebec workers received even less in wages than they got while in Confederation. The Quebec average income slipped to about 87% of the Canadian average income. |

Source of statistics "Before Separation": *Living Together*, Economic Council of Canada, (Ottawa, 1977); also *Financial Post* 1978 6 11.

**Fig. I-3 Quebec before and after Separation: Some statistics**

Quebec has many serious problems. This chart shows that economic depression has hit this new country hard. Quebec and Canada were unable to come to a free trade agreement. Trade in Quebec has therefore decreased. Unemployment has gone up. Workers are making less money now than when Quebec was a part of Canada.

Quebec succeeded in breaking away from Canada. But to solve its problems it may have to follow in Canada's footsteps. Quebeckers are looking to the US for answers to their problems. This is René Turcot in Quebec City.

Here is another Quick quiz to test your understanding of the basic facts of Countdown Canada. These questions require short answers.

1. Name at least two cities in which CBC reporters interviewed Canadians about union.
2. What new state was to be formed by Newfoundland, Nova Scotia, Prince Edward Island, and New Brunswick?
3. What would happen to tariffs on goods as a result of union?
4. What effect would this have on some Canadian businesses?
5. How would Canada's system of government change?
6. Why did trouble develop between Canadian-born people and immigrants?
7. Did the labour union leader, Jack Rankin, approve of the idea of union?
8. In the elections of 1994, did British Columbia generally favour union?
9. What did some experts predict would happen to Quebec if Canada joined the US?
10. Fig. I-3 shows that Quebec's economy suffered after separation. Name one problem in Quebec's economy.

---

| Part three | At the border crossing |
| --- | --- |
| *The scene:* | *CBC studios, Ottawa, Ontario.* |
| *Time:* | *Zero hour minus 20 minutes.* |

Julian Cleva

**Margaret Kandal** A large crowd has gathered outside the Parliament Buildings in Ottawa. The people are waiting quietly for the signing of the treaty. However, all is not peaceful across the country. Protest groups are creating disturbances at points along the entire Canada-US border. Igor Melnik has this report from the Rainbow Bridge, which links Ontario and New York State at Niagara Falls.

John McQueen

**Igor Melnik, CBC correspondent** People of all ages are here to protest against union with the United States. They are trying to create as much noise and confusion as they can. Large groups of people are lying on the roads approaching the bridge. This is tying up traffic for several kilometres in all directions. The Ontario Provincial Police have been on the scene since early morning. They have been trying to maintain order and prevent injuries. Police have blocked the bridge with police cars to keep people from crossing to the American side. A number of people near the bridge have been chanting "We won't join!" for over an hour. Some of the people blocking traffic are singing "O Canada". With me are two students who have been watching the morning's activities.

I noticed that you haven't joined in the protest. Do you agree with these people who don't want union with the States?

**First student** I think these people are crazy. They're over-reacting. I like Americans. The way things are going in Canada, we need them. Americans are really no different from us, so why not join them?

**Second student** I agree. We're just like Americans. We listen to American groups, watch American TV programmes, see American movies. Even though we call ourselves Canadians, we are like part of the States. This treaty will just make it official.

**Igor Melnik** Many people feel that Canada has no identity of its own. Yet hundreds of Canadians are here today protesting against union. (He goes up to a woman sitting on road.) Why are you demonstrating against union?

**Woman**  I love my country, and I want to see it remain independent!

**Igor Melnik**  What do you think of the comment that Canada has no identity?

**Woman**  People who say that are wrong! Sure there are a lot of different cultures in Canada—American, European, Asian, African .... The list goes on and on. And there are many different life styles in Canada too. But Canada is a society that accepts these different life styles. And to me, that is the Canadian identity. Canada is a nation that accepts many cultures and ways of life. Canadians should be proud of the different cultures within it. If they were, then the differences could *unite* people rather than divide them! I'm proud of Canada and I'm protesting against the people who have given away our independence.

**Igor Melnik**  Our studios have reports that huge crowds like this one are protesting at many border points. Many people today are upset at the idea of union with the States. This is Igor Melnik at the Rainbow Bridge, Niagara Falls, Ontario.

---

| Part four | President Southfield's press release on the union |
|---|---|
| *The scene:* | *CBC studios, Ottawa, Ontario.* |
| *Time:* | *Zero hour minus 15 minutes.* |

---

**Margaret Kandal**  In a few moments, President Southfield and Prime Minister Portland will sign the Treaty of Union. After the signing, the prime minister will be retiring from public life. He gave his farewell speech to the Canadian people last night. The prime minister spoke of the dream of freedom and happiness that the founders of the nation had. He said that Canadians today have not given up the dream. Rather, they are looking to the United States for help in achieving their goals.

President Southfield also made a press statement last night. The president was in the press room of the Parliament Buildings in Ottawa speaking to reporters.

**President Southfield (a videotape of press release)**  Canada and the United States have been friends for many years. Tomorrow, the ties between our two countries will become even closer. I am proud to have Canada as part of our nation. I know I speak for all US citizens when I say this.

I want to make it clear that the United States did not try to take over Canada. Washington knew that Canada had been in trouble for some time. But the US government did not offer Canada a place in the

Union. The Canadian government made the first move. Soon after the November 1994 election, a team of officials from Ottawa was sent to Washington. Their purpose was to discuss a possible union of our two countries.

You may well ask why the United States would accept a troubled country like Canada into the Union. Let me say this: we wanted to help our neighbour. As I said earlier, Canada is a good friend. It needed help. The US was there to give it. Also, a troubled Canada was a threat to the United States. The US has a lot of money tied up in Canada. To protect our interests, we need a stable Canadian society. Union is a way to improve the situation. Lastly, Canada is rich in resources—oil, wood, minerals. It has highly trained people. These human and natural resources must be used. The United States can use them to the benefit of everyone—the United States, Canada, and the world.

| Part five | The signing of the treaty |
|---|---|
| *The scene:* | *First, CBC studios, Ottawa. Then, a large platform in front of the Parliament Buildings.* |
| *Time:* | *Zero hour minus one minute.* |

**Margaret Kandal** It is almost noon. The signing of the treaty will take place in front of the Parliament Buildings. CBC reporter Mary Orme is outside waiting for the prime minister and the president to arrive.

**Mary Orme, reporter** I am standing directly in front of the platform where the signing will take place. A huge crowd has gathered

John McQueen

silently to witness this historic event. In the distance you can hear the cries of people demonstrating against the treaty. Members of the RCMP are holding the protesters back, away from the area.

Many important officials are standing on the platform. To the left of the table are the premiers of the nine provinces. With them are the governors of border states such as New York. To the right stand members of the Canadian federal cabinet, Canada's last cabinet.

Here comes President Southfield! The prime minister and the **Governor General of Canada** are with him. They make their way slowly through the crowd. The prime minister is stopping along the way to shake hands with people. The leaders of the two countries now mount the stairs to the platform. They approach the table on which the treaty is placed. The crowd is hushed. Everyone stands at attention as the Canadian Armed Forces band plays "O Canada" for the last time. It is a truly moving moment.

President Southfield signs the treaty. The prime minister now approaches the table. He looks up for a long moment at the Peace Tower, where the Canadian flag is moving softly in the July breeze. He is now bending down to sign the treaty. The two leaders shake hands and smile as the crowd applauds. The band is playing the first bars of the American national anthem. The United States of North America now officially exists as one nation from the Arctic to the Mexican border. We return you now to Margaret Kandal for a wrap-up of the broadcast.

---

**QUICK QUIZ**

Test your understanding of the whole newscast. These questions require short answers.

1. In the newscast, what is the importance of July 4, 1995?
2. What is meant by "Quebec separation"?
3. How was it decided that Canada would join the United States?
4. What did the woman at the Rainbow Bridge say about Canada's identity?
5. According to President Southfield why did Canada decide to join the United States?

**READING BETTER**

1. Reading is a key way to get information. You are introduced to facts and ideas. You also learn about people's opinions and beliefs. It is therefore important to understand what you read. "Reading better" exercises will help you develop reading skills.

   In this exercise, you are asked to find important details. This is a key reading skill. It is especially helpful in history and social science classes. Answer the following questions about important details in the news broadcast. You may have to refer back to the text for the answers.

1. *The president's press release*
   Why did the United States want to join up with Canada? Give two reasons.
2. *Rainbow Bridge scene*
   What did the woman interviewed say about the variety of Canada's peoples?
3. *Report from Quebec City*
   What prediction about Quebec is made at the end of this report?

**ORGANIZING BETTER**

1. These activities are slightly more complicated than "Reading better" exercises. You will often be asked to list the main ideas in stories, articles, charts, and even pictures. When ideas are organized, they are easier to learn and remember. You get a clear picture of what is going on.

   All the people interviewed in the programme have opinions about union with the US. Look back over the story. List the opinions of the following people. You should put these opinions in your own words. Be sure to explain the reasons the people give for their opinions.

1. Jim Hennessy (Halifax)
2. Josie White (Halifax)
3. Willie Cook (Toronto)
4. Jack Rankin (Winnipeg)
5. Jacob Merriweather (Vancouver)

USING YOUR KNOWLEDGE

1. If you were a reporter interviewing people across the country on July 4, 1995, what questions would you ask? Here are some issues you could ask about:

schools travel citizenship immigration job chances in the United States hospitals health care

SOLVING PROBLEMS

1. In this book you will often be required to solve problems. You will be asked for practical suggestions on how to meet Canada's challenges. It is sometimes hard to do this. Social scientists have tried to come up with methods of problem-solving. These methods do not work all of the time. However in general, they do help students make better decisions about problems. Here is a problem-solving model that you can use throughout this text. There are six steps in the model.

1. Write down the nature of the problem. Before you can solve a problem, you must understand it. You will find out how well you understand a problem as you try to explain it on paper.
2. Make a list of goals that the problem is interfering with. Problems usually prevent people or nations from achieving certain goals. Try to think of what these goals may be.
3. Make a list of things that can be done to solve the problem. Put down anything that comes to mind.
4. Decide what the results of each of your solutions may be.
5. Compare the results of your different solutions with the goals you wrote out in step 2.
6. Choose the solution that matches your goals most closely.

NOTE: This model is adapted from *The Policy-Making Process*, Charles Lindblom, Prentice-Hall Inc., (Englewood Cliffs, New Jersey, 1968).

This first question will give you practice in performing step 1 of the problem-solving model. Look back at Countdown Canada. Describe the main problems that Canada could not solve on its own. Use the following headings to help you.
Political problems
Economic problems
Social and racial problems

TAKING A STAND

1. The other activities in the text help you to understand issues. Once you understand them, you should be able to form a reasoned opinion about them. "Taking a stand" activities ask you to decide your position on certain issues.

In the summer of 1993, a public opinion poll was taken. Canadians were asked about union with the US. They were also asked many other questions related to Canada. Here are the questions found in the poll. Decide how you feel about the various issues, and answer the questions.

1. If you were given a chance to vote for union with the United States today, what would you do?
   a) Favour union
   b) Reject union
   c) No opinion
2. If Canada were to join the United States, how would you feel about it?
   a) Very happy
   b) A little happy
   c) A little sad
   d) Very sad
   e) Do not care
   f) Do not know
3. How do you feel about immigrants in Canada?
   a) They help Canada a lot
   b) They help Canada a little
   c) They neither help nor harm Canada
   d) They harm Canada a little
   e) They harm Canada a lot
   f) Do not know
4. Which do you think is the best word to describe the United States in relation to Canada?
   a) A partner
   b) A neighbour
   c) An enemy
   d) A bully
   e) Do not know
5. If it became very costly to live in Canada, what would you do?
   a) Stay in Canada

b) Move to the United States or some other country
c) Do not know

6. Do you think of yourself as a Canadian?
a) Often
b) Seldom
c) Never

7. Do you think of yourself as a Maritimer, Ontarian, Manitoban, etc.?
a) Often
b) Seldom
c) Never

8. How do you feel about keeping Canada together?
a) Very interested
b) Moderately interested
c) Slightly interested
d) Not interested at all
e) Do not know

9. How important to Canada's future is a Quebec that is part of the nation?
a) Very important
b) A little important
c) Not very important
d) Not important at all
e) Do not know

10. If you think that a united Canada is important, what would you do to show your viewpoint?

a) Join a protest march
b) Give money or time to support the idea
c) Talk with others to understand the problem better
d) Support a group to promote your opinions

## RESEARCHING

1. Countdown Canada brings out many topics that are of interest to us in the text. Use your library to find out more about them. Look up these headings in the card catalogue. Your teacher and librarian can help you from there to find more information.

| Canada and the US: | Foreign ownership |
| | Trade and industry |
| Quebec: | Industry |
| | Confederation |
| | Politics |
| | Separatism |
| Canada: | Regions |
| | Bilingualism |
| | Multiculturalism |
| | Immigration |
| | Economy |
| | Political parties, Government |
| | Culture |

## GLOSSARY

**Blockade.** An official break-off in trade between two or more countries.

**Depressed areas.** Areas of a country that are in poor economic condition.

**Economic slowdown.** A drop in business activity.

**Governor General of Canada.** The Canadian representative of the British monarchy.

**Investments.** Money given to a business to help it operate. Some of the profits are given to the investor in return for this help.

**National Assembly Building.** The building in which the Quebec Legislature meets.

**Parliamentary system of government.** A democratic system of government in which the leader must be a member of the elected legislature.

**Referendum.** A vote taken to see whether or not the people of a country accept certain government laws.

**Republic.** A democratic system of government that has a president elected separately from the legislature.

**Tariffs.** A tax placed on imports.

# PART ONE
# The land, the law, and the government of Canada

# UNIT ONE:
# The land that shapes us

What does the future hold for Canada? In Countdown Canada we saw just one of many possible courses of action. Indeed, the question about Canada's future is hard to answer. But we do know one thing for sure. The future depends on how we meet our country's challenges today. We can meet these challenges only if we understand the issues involved. This is why it is so important to know our country well.

One of the main challenges facing Canada is geography. Canada is a vast land made up of many distinct regions. Each region has its own history, **physical features,** and **climate.** People tend to make their living in different ways, depending on the region. The people in one region may be better off financially than people in another. This can create problems in the country.

Geography makes Canadians different. Yet we should realize that it can also unify us. Our ways of life are affected to a certain extent by the areas we live in. The land helps to shape us into what we are. This is one thing that Canadians have in common.

In this unit we examine Canada's geography. We try to find answers to the following questions.

**1** What are the different regions of Canada?

**2** How do these regions help make people different?

**3** How can Canadians meet the challenge that geography presents to them?

# 1/The people and the land

## Contents

### Introduction

Canada stretches almost 6 000 km from Newfoundland to the Yukon-Alaska border. The distance from the shores of Lake Erie to the tip of Ellesmere Island is about 5 000 km.

This huge land has many distinct physical features. The major physical features roughly divide the country into six regions. They are:

1. The Appalachian region
2. The Great Lakes-St. Lawrence Lowlands
3. The Canadian Shield
4. The Prairies
5. The Cordilleras-British Columbia region
6. The Canadian Arctic

In this chapter, we look at the major regions of Canada. This study will increase our understanding of the challenges facing the country. We will get to know the advantages and problems of each region.

The chapter takes the form of a CBC special report. Reporters are based in each region of the country. They will tell us basic facts about the different regions. The chapter attempts to answer the following questions:

1. **What are the physical features of each region?**
2. **What is the climate of each region?**
3. **What peoples have lived in the different regions? How do people make their living?**
4. **What are the challenges facing Canadians in each region?**

**A CBC Special Report**
**Canada: From sea to sea**

*The scene:*     *CBC studios, Toronto, Ontario.*

Julian Cleva

**Peter Holstrom, host and commentator**   Good evening. This is Peter
Holstrom for CBC Special Report. Today we hear a lot about
regional differences in Canada. Some parts of the country are
poorer than others. In some areas most people can find jobs, while
in others, many people are jobless. People from the east often feel
isolated from people in the west. People in the north resent
developers from the south. We hear about these issues every day,
but not many people really understand them. They don't know
why differences exist. They're not even sure of the different regions
in the country.

Canada can be divided into six regions. On the screen behind me
is a map of these areas. Tonight CBC Special Report takes a close
look at each of Canada's regions.

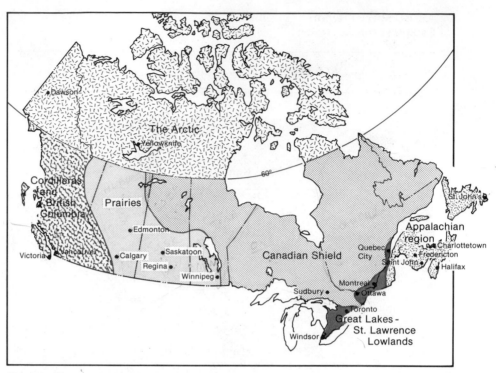

**Fig. 1-1   The physical regions of Canada**

## ORGANIZING BETTER

| Physical region | Major cities | Provinces in the region |
|---|---|---|
| Appalachian region | Halifax, St. John's | Newfoundland, New Brunswick Nova Scotia, PEI, parts of Quebec |
| Great Lakes-St. Lawrence Lowlands | | |
| Canadian Shield | | |
| Prairies | | |
| Cordilleras and British Columbia | | |
| The Arctic | | |

1. Copy this chart in your notebook. In the first column, write the names of some major cities found in each region. Refer to Fig. 1-1 for help. The first region is done for you.

2. Which provinces are part of each region? Write your answers on the chart. Again the first region is done for you.

26

**The Appalachian Report**

**Bill Mackenzie, CBC correspondent**  This is Bill Mackenzie in St. John's, the capital of Newfoundland. The Appalachian region makes up about 5% of Canada's land mass. This area consists of the Atlantic provinces—Newfoundland, Nova Scotia, New Brunswick, and Prince Edward Island. Some sections of Quebec—the Eastern Townships and the Gaspé Peninsula—are also part of the region.

### Physical features

If we take a general survey we find that the landscape of Appalachian Canada is varied. In most places it is rugged, with great expanses of forest. There are **outcroppings** of rock in Nova Scotia and Newfoundland. Yet, lush green fields and sandy beaches are found in PEI.

The map behind me (Fig. 1-2) shows that there are three major land types in Appalachian Canada. The *lowlands* are formed of rocks such as shale and sandstone. These rocks are easily worn away by water, wind and frost. The *uplands* consist of harder rocks such as slate and limestone. The upland areas are, in general, high but fairly level. The *highlands* are made of the oldest, hardest rocks in the region. Mountains and valleys have been carved into the highlands through the years by the forces of erosion. The highlands are quite rugged.

The seas along the coasts of the land are shallow. These areas are actually parts of the mainland and islands that have been submerged. These submerged areas are called the *continental shelf*. The higher parts of the shelf are called the *Banks*.

### Climate

In Appalachian Canada, the Atlantic Ocean moderates the climate. Summers are cooler and winters are slightly warmer than on the Prairies or in the Canadian Shield. Average winter temperatures are about $-5^\circ$ C, while in the summer, the average temperature is about $17^\circ$ C.

The Appalachian region is fairly wet. It gets about 1 500 mm of **precipitation** a year. This precipitation results when warm air from the Atlantic Ocean collides with cold air from the northwest.

### The people and the economy

The Appalachian region was originally inhabited by Native Peoples. Indian tribes like the Beothuk, a group that is now extinct, lived in Newfoundland. The Micmacs were the first people to settle in Nova Scotia, New Brunswick, and PEI. Today their descendants live in the area.

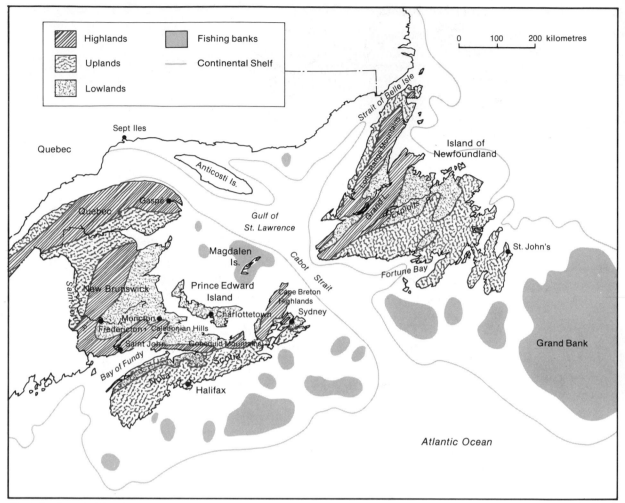

**Fig. 1-2   Appalachian Canada**

The French were the first Europeans to settle in Appalachian Canada. Samuel de Champlain founded Port Royal (near present-day Annapolis Royal) in 1605.

The area of Nova Scotia and Newfoundland came under English control in 1713, and Halifax was founded in 1749. These events began a long history of English settlement in the area. After the American Revolution, Loyalists settled there, adding to the English population in the region. By 1800 Nova Scotia and New Brunswick were the largest English-speaking colonies in British North America. However, only about 10% of Canada's people live in the Appalachian region today.

The region enjoyed a great period of wealth from 1800 to 1860. It sold great quantities of fish and wood products to Europe. Its wooden ships were known all over the world. Trade flourished with the New England states and the West Indies.

After 1860, Appalachian Canada began to suffer setbacks. Free trade with the US (reciprocity) stopped in 1866. Other parts of Canada began to compete with the region as a source of lumber for Europe. Iron ships and steam power came of age, so the region's shipbuilding industry suffered. Appalachian Canada settled into a pattern of slow economic growth and high unemployment.

For many years the economy of Appalachian Canada was based on agriculture, fishing, and forestry. However, more industry is coming into the region. This industry is necessary for the growth of the economy.

The chart on the screen shows the major economic activities in the region today (Fig. 1-3).

| Province or area | Major economic activities |
| --- | --- |
| Prince Edward Island | Fishing, agriculture (potatoes), tourism |
| New Brunswick | Forestry, mining, tourism |
| Newfoundland | Forestry, mining, hydroelectricity |
| Nova Scotia | Manufacturing, mining (coal), steel production, tourism |
| Gaspé and Eastern Townships | Forestry, mining (asbestos), tourism, agriculture, fishing |

Fig. 1-3  Economic activities of the Appalachian region

*Future challenges*

The challenges facing the Appalachian region are great. Will the region be able to develop a healthy economy? As the economy grows will the traditional ways of life disappear?

The future of Appalachian Canada is promising. Major centres are well linked by roads and railways along river valleys and around the coast. Rivers provide transportation for the flourishing timber industry.

The fishing industry has benefited from recent developments. Canada recently laid claim to waters 200 nautical miles (about 370 km) off its coast. The 200-mile limit will prevent foreign fleets from overfishing the coastal waters. This will help boost the Appalachian fishing industry. Fish exports are expected to double in the coming years.

There may be deposits of oil and gas off the coasts of the region. If countries need to turn to other fuel sources, Cape Breton's coal reserves will be important. Newfoundland continues to develop its hydroelectric resources. The iron ore industry is being built up in Labrador. In New Brunswick, potash discoveries have been made. Such hydroelectric and mineral developments add strength to the resource industries.

Both federal and provincial governments have programmes to encourage economic growth in the region. These will likely work

**Fishing in Appalachian Canada. What might happen to wages if exports doubled?**

better if the resource-based industries are healthy. Appalachian Canada expects to see less unemployment and higher income figures as more jobs become available. Because of recent developments it appears that this goal may be reached.

Bill Mackenzie, reporting from St. John's.

Here is a series of questions that require short answers.

1. Name the four provinces and the areas of Quebec that make up Appalachian Canada.
2. What are the three major land types of the region?
3. What is the continental shelf?
4. Describe the temperatures and precipitation typical of this climate.
5. What percentage of Canada's population lives in this region?
6. Name two important mineral resources in the area.
7. Which is the most northern of the Atlantic provinces?
8. Name one reason for the decline of the economy of the area after 1860.
9. Name two economic activities that are being developed to boost the economy.
10. How is the 200-mile limit expected to improve fishing in the region?

ORGANIZING BETTER

1. Fig. 1-4 is a table of statistics about the regions of Canada. Read the table and answer the questions that follow.

|  | Index of wages and salaries per worker | Unemployment rate in percentages | |
|---|---|---|---|
| Atlantic region | 83 | 9.9 | 11.6 |
| Quebec | 93 | 8.1 | 8.8 |
| Ontario | 109 | 6.3 | 6.0 |
| Prairie region | 95 | 3.4 | |
| BC | 105 | 8.3 | |
| Canada | 100 | 6.9 | 7.1 |

Source: *Living Together: A Study of Regional Disparities*. Economic Council of Canada, 1977.

**Fig. 1-4   Wages and salaries, unemployment in Canada, by region, 1975**

*How to read this table*

Wages differ from job to job and from region to region. Quite often statisticians want to compare wages. They have, therefore, figured out how to take statistics and work them out to numbers called indexes. They can use these index numbers to compare wages. (Index numbers can be used to compare many other things. Some of these are temperatures, ages, or the number of people without a job.) Index numbers are calculated in a very complex way. We will not concern ourselves here with the way indexes are found.

In Fig. 1-4, the first column of numbers shows wages in some regions of Canada. Figures for the country as a whole are also given. All these figures are index numbers. The wage of the average worker in Canada is rated at 100. Figures above or below 100 mean that wages are above or below the average.

How can we understand these index numbers better? Let us say that a worker from Ontario went to a store. The worker wanted to buy an item for $1.00. He or she would have $1.09 available to pay for it. A person from Quebec would have only 93 cents. How much would the worker from the Atlantic Provinces have? What is the result? The Ontario worker would be able to buy the article. The worker from Quebec or the Atlantic provinces would not.

The second column of numbers in the table are unemployment rates. These rates tell us what percentage of Canadians are without jobs. The figures refer only to those Canadians who are *looking* for a job, but who cannot find one. In 1975, for example, 6.9% of Canadian workers were jobless.

1. Does the average worker in Atlantic Canada make more or less than the average worker in Canada?
2. What is the unemployment rate in the Atlantic provinces? How does it compare with the rate for Canada?
3. Write a sentence describing the wage and unemployment picture of Atlantic Canada in 1975.

**Great Lakes-St. Lawrence Lowlands Report**

**Ted Hominiuk, CBC correspondent**  This is Ted Hominiuk in
Toronto, Ontario. The Great Lakes-St. Lawrence Lowlands area is
one of the most prosperous in the country. This region stretches
from Quebec City in the northeast, to Windsor in the southwest, a
distance of about 960 km.

*Physical features*

Most of the land in the area is lowland. An arm of the Canadian
Shield, called the Frontenac Axis, slices through this lowland
region between Cornwall and Kingston. It cuts the area in two.
Montreal is the centre of one part of the region and Toronto is the
centre of the other. Another rocky formation, the Niagara
Escarpment, runs north from Niagara Falls to Tobermory,
Ontario.

   The region consists of **bedrock** covered with layers of **clayey
soils,** sandy soils, and gravel. Because of the good farming soil,
agriculture in the region has flourished.

*Climate*

We know that the Atlantic Ocean moderates the climate of the
Appalachian region. In the Great Lakes-St. Lawrence Lowlands
region, the Great Lakes moderate the climate. Summers tend to be

**Mechanized farming in Ontario's Niagara region.
Can you give one reason for using such expensive machinery?**

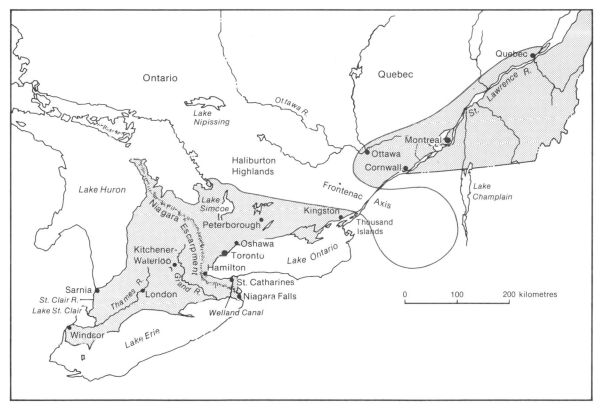

**Fig. 1-5   The Great Lakes-St. Lawrence Lowlands**

Ontario Ministry of Industry and Tourism

warm and humid. There are about 150 to 190 **frost-free days** a year. This gives the area a long **growing season.** The winters are often colder than the winters in Appalachian Canada. However, they are warmer than winters in the Shield or Prairie regions. About 875 mm of precipitation fall each year. Winds tend to blow from west to east.

### *The people and the economy*

This region was first inhabited by two groups of Native Peoples, the Algonkians and the Iroquoians. The first European settlers in the area were the French. They settled the lower part of the St. Lawrence River valley (the part nearer the ocean) in the seventeenth century. Settlement in the region grew after the British conquered New France and after the American Revolution. British and American settlers came to what is now Ontario.

The Great Lakes-St. Lawrence Lowlands region still attracts newcomers from all over the world. People from many different ethnic groups live in this area. It is, in fact, the most populated region in the country.

**Montreal harbour. What transportation systems can you see in this photo?**

The region was once made up mostly of farms. Today most people live in densely populated towns and cities. Only 10% of the people still live on farms.

The farms in the area have become highly mechanized. They produce most of the poultry, dairy products, and meat used in the region. A large food-processing industry also ships products to other parts of Canada or exports them.

Manufacturing began in the pioneer days. The region has since become the manufacturing hub of the country. Key products in the area are cars and car parts, steel and iron items, textiles and clothing, industrial and farm chemicals, and hundreds of other **secondary manufacturing** products.

Why is the region so successful as a manufacturing centre? There are many reasons. It has access to many resources. The timber, minerals, and hydroelectric energy of the Shield are near at hand. The air, land, and water transportation systems are excellent. For example, the Macdonald-Cartier Freeway (the 401) runs almost the length of the region. It is the busiest highway in the country.

There are other important factors in the growth of manufacturing. There is a supply of fresh water from the Great Lakes and from the area's many rivers. The US provides a huge market for the region's products. There is also a dense population. This population supplies a skilled work force as well as a market for products.

*Future challenges*

This is a thriving region. The unemployment rate is low. Family incomes are the highest in the country. People have many job and education opportunities. Population growth in the area is high.

This growth does bring problems, however. There are conflicts over how the land should be used. Both factories and farms need land. Also, as the population increases, its needs grow. These needs include housing, roads, schools, water supplies, and pollution controls. These problems put a strain on government. Local governments, in particular, are affected by these problems. However, both local and provincial governments must learn to respond effectively to the needs of the region.

Other regions in Canada are seeing a growth in their industries and cities. They can look to the Great Lakes-St. Lawrence Lowlands for guidance. They can perhaps learn from the region's mistakes.

Ted Hominiuk in Toronto.

---

**QUICK QUIZ**
**Copy the following sentences in your notebook.**
**Fill in the blanks with the correct answer.**

1. The two chief physical features that give this region its name are the _____ and _____. (six words)
2. An arm of the _____ divides the Lowlands near Kingston. This arm is called the _____ Axis. (three words)
3. Summers in this region tend to be hot and _____. (one word)
4. The climate is an aid to farming. There is a long _____ of about 150 to 190 frost-free days. (two words)
5. The _____ were Indians who lived in the area. (one word)
6. This region is sometimes referred to as the _____ centre of Canada. (one word)
7. Manufacturing has grown because of the nearness of natural _____ in the Canadian Shield. Another reason is the excellent land, water, and air _____ systems. (two words)
8. Both farms and industries need room to

expand. This creates a problem over
_____ use. (one word)

9. The growth of the region has created certain
problems. These problems put a special
strain on _____ government. (one
word)

10. Agriculture has become highly _____
in almost all sectors of the farming industry.
(one word)

## RESEARCHING

1. Do an in-depth study of one of the industries
of the Great Lakes-St. Lawrence Lowlands. In
your study look at topics such as product,
amount of money and equipment needed,
market, transportation systems, and type of
labour needed.

## READING BETTER

1. A key reading skill is the ability to compare
ideas, events, or areas. Compare the two
regions studied so far in this chapter. Base
your comparison on these points:
   1. At least two physical features
   2. Two points about climate
   3. Key products of the region
   4. Problems facing the region

---

### The Canadian Shield Report

**Bud Kestern, CBC correspondent**  This is Bud Kestern in Sudbury.
The Canadian Shield is a storehouse of mineral and timber
resources. Much hydroelectricity is produced here also. Canadians
need natural resources such as these. They look to the Shield to fill
this need.

#### Physical features

The Canadian Shield is a giant area of rock and lakes. It curves
around Hudson Bay and the Hudson Bay Lowlands. The Shield
makes up over half of Canada's land mass. It stretches from the
Arctic Ocean to the south shores of the Great Lakes. To the east of
it is the Appalachian region; to the west lie the Prairies.

The Shield consists of hard **Precambrian rock.** This rock is so
hard that soil has not yet developed in many areas. There are many
rivers and lakes in the region. Much of the area is covered in
forests. Many people consider the Shield, with its lakes, rocks, and
trees, to be Canada's distinctive **landform.**

#### Climate

The Shield covers a huge area of Canada. Therefore it is hard to
talk in general terms about the climate. The climate will vary from
place to place.

There are some general trends to note, however. The Shield is
colder and drier than Appalachian Canada or the Lowlands. The
region has barely 80 frost-free days, so the climate does not favour
agriculture. This climate does not favour construction, either. The
low temperatures make building hard in the fall, winter, and early
spring. Roads, pipelines, and foundations of structures are
affected.

**Fig. 1-6   The Canadian Shield**

**Mine shaft, Cobalt. What two challenges might face this mine?**

**Gorge, the Shield. What physical features do you see?**

37

Precipitation in the region increases from west to east. In northern Manitoba the yearly average is 380 mm. Quebec gets about 1 000 mm of precipitation.

### The people and the economy

The first settlers of the Shield region were the Algonkian Indians and the Inuit. These people led nomadic lives as hunters and trappers. Today, Indian groups in the area include the Cree, Ojibway, Naskapi, and Montagnais. Some live on reserves and follow the traditional way of life, while others work in cities and towns.

Some Europeans settled in the area in the nineteenth century. However, the rugged landscape of the region did not attract farmers from the rich St. Lawrence Lowlands. The Shield was also hard to cross through, and therefore delayed the settlement of the West.

The coming of the railway opened up the region. Forest and mining industries began to grow. Today, airplanes and good roads make transportation easier. Even still, the Shield is home to less than two million people. These people tend to live in resource-based towns.

The Canadian Shield is rich in natural resources. Hydroelectric development, mining, and forestry are its key industries. Giant plants at Churchill Falls and James Bay generate hydroelectric power, while other rivers in the area produce smaller amounts of electricity. Some of these rivers are the Ottawa, the St. Maurice, and the Manicouagan.

Pulp and paper production is also important in the Shield. There are many lumbering and pulp and paper centres. They are found mostly along the rivers and on the shores of the Great Lakes. From them comes the linerboard, newsprint, and cardboard used in our industrial society.

The most important industry in the Shield is mining. Minerals such as iron ore, copper, nickel, zinc, and lead are found in great quantities. There are also supplies of uranium. This mineral has gained importance because of the energy crisis.

There are many mining towns in the region. Among the most important are Sudbury, Noranda-Rouyn, Elliott Lake, Thompson, and Schefferville. The mining industry provides all kinds of jobs. There is, of course, work in the mines themselves. But for every miner there are twelve other people working in other jobs related to mining. This includes work in the processing and manufacturing of metals.

### Future challenges

The Canadian Shield is still a largely untouched region. Its resources will be used in the future to build up Canada's economy.

**Fig. 1-7  Minerals in the Canadian Shield**

As these resources are developed, certain questions must be answered. How much development should take place? Who should resources be sold to? How will development affect the region's peoples and environment?

There are many untouched mineral resources in the area. These will be developed in the coming years. Also, the region's waterways will be used to generate more and more hydroelectricity. One hydroelectric project being built at present is the James Bay Project. This development will cost more than any other hydroelectric project undertaken by Canada. Vast communication and transportation systems are also being built in the area. The people living in the James Bay region are concerned about the project. The Cree and Inuit, fearing that their hunting and fishing grounds would be destroyed, took their case to court. The Quebec government finally transferred some land to these people. Major changes were also made to the project itself.

Pollution is also a problem in the Shield region. Water quality is affected by industries such as pulp and paper. The air is also polluted as a result of industrial development. In the Sudbury

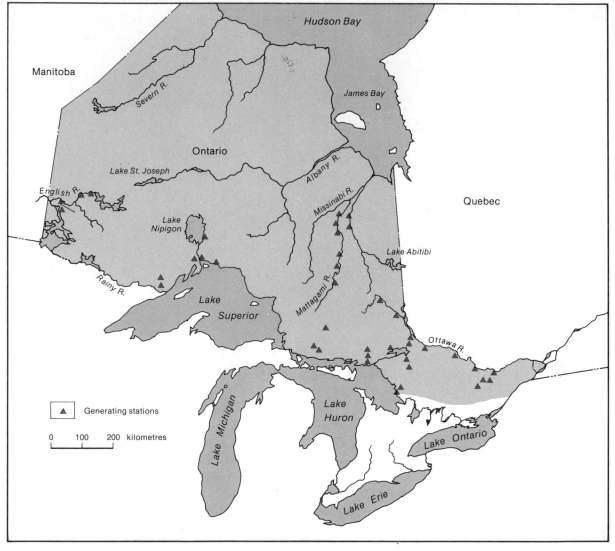

**Fig. 1-8 Hydroelectric-generating stations in the Shield area of Ontario**

region, for example, there are high levels of sulphur dioxide in the air.

Finally, the daily problems of people living in the area must be dealt with. For example, the cost of living is high in the Canadian Shield. The land does not allow much agriculture. Food must therefore be brought in from other regions at high costs.

People who have jobs in mining can also suffer. Markets for certain minerals may disappear. Mines then close and jobs are lost. When this happens, miners, their families, and the whole mining community suffer.

The resources of the Canadian Shield can be used to benefit many. However, the needs of the region's people and of the environment must always be kept in mind.

This is Bud Kestern in Sudbury.

1. Here are some topics mentioned in the Canadian Shield report. Write each of them in your book. Then find the parts of the report that deal with them. Write one sentence about each topic, using your own words.

   Pulp and paper         Cost of living
   Precambrian rock       Noranda-Rouyn
   Hydroelectricity       Precipitation

SOLVING PROBLEMS

1. In Countdown Canada, you looked at a problem-solving model. The first step of the model requires you to explain the problem. In problem-solving, it is very important to know what the problem is. This exercise will give you practice at explaining problems.

   One problem in the Canadian Shield region is the high cost of living. This is the problem you are asked to explain. Your class should be divided into two groups. The first group should consist of about one third of the class. The remaining students will make up the second group. The smaller group will act as reporters. Students in the larger group are residents of the Shield. Reporters should interview residents to find out why the cost of living is so high. Afterward, reporters can share their findings with the class.

## The Canadian Prairies Report

**Marjorie Jackson, CBC correspondent** This is Marjorie Jackson in Calgary, Alberta. Alberta, Saskatchewan, and Manitoba make up the Canadian Prairie region. The Prairie provinces were once among the poorest in the country. In the 1970s, though, they have enjoyed economic growth. The minerals and oil found in the region are two reasons for the Prairies' wealth.

### Physical features

The Prairie provinces are part of a huge plain that goes from the Mexican border to the Arctic. Although many people think the Prairies are one long stretch of flatlands, there are also rolling hills. Rivers like the Qu'Appelle and North Saskatchewan have cut deep valleys through the region. There are also areas in Alberta and Saskatchewan that could almost be described as desert.

In general, Prairie soil is very fertile. Thick humus covers much of the land. This humus is the result of centuries of decay of Prairie grass.

### Climate

The Prairie region is one of extreme temperatures. This is because there are no large bodies of water to act as a moderating influence. Winters are very cold. Summers, on the other hand, are very hot.

The Prairies get less precipitation than the Atlantic coast does. The amount of moisture increases from west to east. On the average, there is about 300 mm to 500 mm a year. This is enough moisture to support the grain crops of wheat, barley, and rapeseed.

There are several dry areas in southern Alberta and Saskatchewan. Irrigation projects have opened up large amounts of land for farming. Yet water supplies will likely remain a problem in areas that get less than 400 mm of moisture a year.

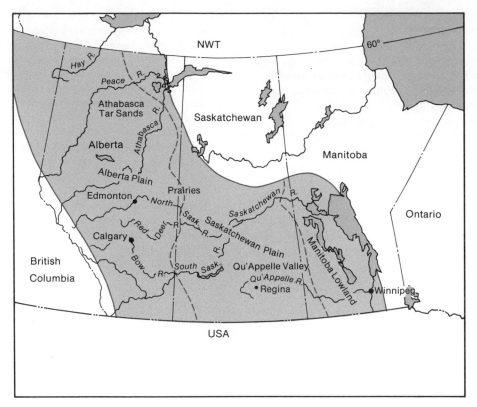

**Fig. 1-9   The Canadian Prairies**

*The people and the economy*

The Plains Indians were the first known inhabitants of the region. After the seventeenth century, the Métis also lived in the area. (Métis are people of both Indian and European blood.) Until the 1890s, there were only a few isolated European settlements. In the 1890s, though, great numbers of settlers started to come into the region. Many came from the United States, Britain and other parts of Canada. Ukrainians, Germans, Poles, and others from central

**Wheat fields and storage buildings on the Prairies. How can you tell from this picture that exports are important to farmers here?**

and eastern Europe settled the area, too. Today the Prairies are still home to people from many ethnic groups.

Farming and ranching are important economic activities in the region. Wheat is the main grain crop. It is a principal export, since Canada consumes only a quarter of the amount grown. About 40% of Canada's beef-breeding herd is found in Alberta. The meat-packing industry is important and much of Alberta's meat is sold outside the province. The Prairies are trying to export more of their agricultural products. Much of the region's manufacturing growth may occur in the food-processing industry.

Oil and natural gas reserves were discovered in Alberta after World War II. These supplies have become important in the 1970s because of the world oil crisis and high world oil prices. In 1976 Alberta produced 82% of Canada's petroleum. In 1978 the Alberta government was able to set aside 3.5 billion dollars in oil royalties. This money was put into a special fund. It will be used to keep Alberta's economy healthy when the **non-renewable resources** are gone.

The Athabasca Tar Sands are also being developed. They probably hold some of the world's largest supplies of crude oil. These tar sands and other new discoveries mean that the Prairies' oil and gas production could continue to grow.

The oil and gas boom tends to overshadow other mining activity. Coal and potash provide other sources of wealth for the region. Potash is a valuable fertilizer; the Prairie region sells it to agricultural countries around the world.

### Future challenges

In recent years the Prairies have seen great economic growth. If the region maintains this growth, any economic gaps between the West and Ontario will disappear.

As we have seen, the area has large supplies of oil and gas. These will continue to be a source of wealth for the region. The Prairies

also have vast coal supplies which cannot be ignored. Coal production has grown in recent years, due partly to a concern about future supplies of oil and gas. Most of the growth comes from sales of coal to Japan, where it is needed for the steel industry. Japan therefore invests large sums of money in coal mining in the Prairies.

The Prairie region will also play a larger role in feeding the world. The area produces great surpluses of wheat and other grains. It will be able to increase its output in the future.

The prospects for the Prairies are good. There are, however, certain problems that must be solved. More and more young people are leaving the small towns for the big cities. Because people leave, the small towns do not grow and prosper. All across the region these "dying" towns can be found.

The region will have to diversify its economy. This means that income should come from many sources. Right now, a large amount of the region's money comes from oil and gas. These non-renewable resources will one day run out. If the region has other sources of income, however, the economy will not suffer.

Marjory Jackson, Calgary.

---

## QUICK QUIZ
**These questions require an answer of a few words.**

1. What is the central province of the Prairies region?
2. As a physical region in North America, the Prairies start at what southern line?
3. The Prairies are completely flat. True or false?
4. Why is the Prairie region one of extreme temperatures?
5. What is the average yearly amount of precipitation in the region?
6. What Indians were the original inhabitants of the Prairies?
7. What device is used to increase arable land (land suitable for growing crops) on the Prairies?
8. Name one location of oil deposits in this region.
9. Name one river valley in the Prairie region.
10. When did great numbers of immigrants settle in the Prairies?

## ORGANIZING BETTER

1. We can understand the economy of the Prairies through statistics (Fig. 1-10). Look at these statistics for the years 1976 and 1977.

Compare the figures for Ontario and the Prairies.

## POPULATION

1. Which Prairie province has the largest population?
2. By how much did Alberta's population increase in this period? By what percentage did it increase? Why is this increase impressive?

## MINERAL PRODUCTION

1. Which province has the highest value in mineral production?

## VALUE OF FARM PRODUCTS

1. Which Prairie province brings in the most money from farm production?
2. In which two Prairie provinces do farm products bring in more money than mineral production does?

## USING YOUR KNOWLEDGE

1. Suppose you were interviewing ranchers from an Alberta cattle ranch. You wanted to find out whether or not the ranch was thriving. What questions about climate and soil conditions would you ask them?

| Province | Estimated population | Value of mineral production (dollars) | Value of farm products (dollars) |
|---|---|---|---|
| Ontario | 1977 8 384 000 | 2.7 billion | 2.8 billion |
| | 1976 8 278 000 | 2.5 billion | 2.7 billion |
| Alberta | 1977 1 904 000 | 8.5 billion | 1.9 billion |
| | 1976 1 844 000 | 6.9 billion | 1.8 billion |
| Saskatchewan | 1977 938 000 | 1.1 billion | 2.0 billion |
| | 1976 923 000 | 0.9 billion | 2.2 billion |
| Manitoba | 1977 1 032 000 | 0.5 billion | 0.8 billion |
| | 1976 1 022 000 | 0.5 billion | 0.8 billion |

Source: *Globe and Mail*, Report on Business, section B. Issues from 1978, January 13, 17, 18, 20.

**Fig. 1-10   Some statistics for Ontario and the Prairie provinces**

### The Cordilleras-British Columbia Report

**Melita Russo, CBC correspondent**  This is Melita Russo in Vancouver. This beautiful and thriving city is the largest in the Cordilleras-British Columbia area. Indeed, this entire western region of Canada is prosperous. There are huge amounts of natural resources here. Minerals are found in the mountains. The sea provides a wealth of fish. There are vast stretches of forest. As well, there is much fertile land for agriculture. For these and other reasons, the region is attracting more and more people.

*Physical features*

The region has a varied landscape. Mountains, valleys, and flatlands are found here.

**Aerial view of Vancouver, BC. What features of city life can you see in this picture?**

45

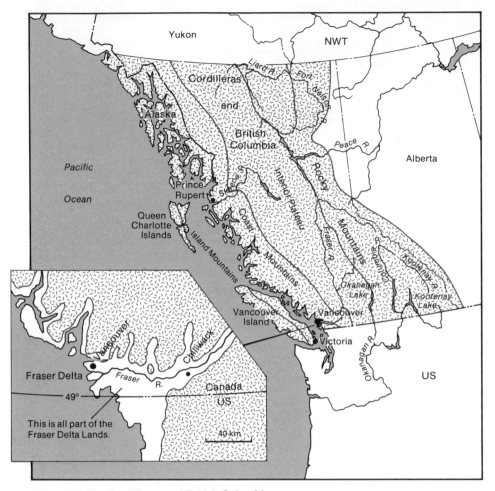

**Fig. 1-11  The Cordilleras and British Columbia**

The *Cordilleras* is the name given to all the different mountain ranges in the region. These mountains make up over 90% of British Columbia's land surface. They are actually part of a huge mountain system which starts at the tip of South America. It runs up the Pacific coast of South and North America, and extends into the Yukon. The mountains also run east into Alberta and west into the Pacific.

To get a clear picture of the physical features, we can divide the region into areas. In general, there are two mountainous areas. The first runs along the east side of the region. It includes the Rockies and the Columbia Mountains.

The second is found along the west coast. In this area are the Coast Mountains and the Island Mountains. The Island Mountains lie off the coast of the mainland. They actually form an arc of islands off the west coast. Among these are Vancouver Island and, further north, the Queen Charlotte Islands. Between these two mountainous areas is a region of plateaus. This area is called the

Interior Plateau. The southern part of it is the Fraser Plateau. Also in the area is the Okanagan Valley.

The Fraser Delta, on the west coast, is an area of flat land and rich soil. It is the most productive agricultural region in British Columbia.

### Climate

The climate of the Cordilleras-British Columbia region is varied. The Pacific Ocean moderates the climate of the coastal region. This means that summers are cool and winters are mild. The interior regions, however, do not fall under this moderating influence. Temperatures are therefore extreme. The summer temperature in Kamloops, for example, may reach 37°C.

Fig. 1-12 shows some basic information about the climate of different areas in the Cordilleras-British Columbia region. Notice that the coastal region is very wet. This is because the westerly winds pick up moisture as they pass over the ocean. The moist air is carried inland, and precipitation occurs on the west side of the mountains.

| Area | Temperature | | Yearly precipitation | Frost-free days |
|------|------|------|------|------|
| | July | January | | |
| Coastal region | 18°C | 0°C | 2 500 mm | 240 |
| Interior Plateau | 23°C | –8°C | 500–600 mm | 140 |
| Peace River | 16°C | –16°C | 450 mm | 80 |

**Fig. 1-12   The climate of the Cordilleras-British Columbia region**

### The people and the economy

Two and a half million people live in British Columbia today. About three quarters of them occupy the Fraser Delta.

Indian people were the first to live in the area. Seven main language groups have been recognized; among them are the Haida, Tlingit, and Kootenay groups. These people did not farm or keep animals. Instead, they lived mostly on the coast or near large rivers, where other types of food were readily available.

Great numbers of non-native people came to the Cordilleras-British Columbia region during the gold rush of 1858. The population grew as the region's great resources became known. People were attracted by the mines, forests, fish, and farmland. The CPR was completed in the region by 1885, bringing new immigrants to the area.

Today, the region's population is a mirror of Canada's ethnic variety. The Indian population here is the largest in the country.

People of British background make up about 45% of British Columbia's population. Germans are the second-largest ethnic group. About 100 000 French live in the area. British Columbia also has the largest number of Chinese in Canada and ranks only behind Ontario in its Japanese population.

In general, the region's economy is based on its natural resources. Of all the economic activities, forestry brings the most wealth to the region. The area contains only 2% of Canada's forests. Yet it accounts for 25% of Canada's sales in forest products. About three quarters of the region's forest products are sold to the US. The other quarter is sold to the rest of Canada, Europe, and Japan.

Mineral production is important, too. Zinc, lead, and coal are major minerals. Natural gas is a valuable resource as well. British Columbia ranks second to Alberta in the production of this fuel. Large amounts of money are being spent in natural gas exploration. In 1978, half a billion dollars was set aside for this purpose.

Farming in the region is limited by the terrain. Only 10% of the land is suitable for agriculture. The dark black soils of the Fraser, Okanagan, and Peace valleys produce excellent vegetables, fruits, and **market crops.** Most of the food produced is used in the province. Agriculture ranks in importance behind forestry, mining, and tourism.

Fishing is another growing industry. Over-fishing has been a problem here, as on the Atlantic, so the fishing industry has adopted stricter measures to conserve fish. The limits to offshore fishing have also been extended. These two measures are designed to help the growth of this important industry.

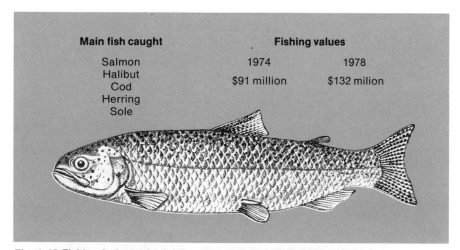

| Main fish caught | Fishing values | |
|---|---|---|
| Salmon | 1974 | 1978 |
| Halibut | $91 million | $132 milion |
| Cod | | |
| Herring | | |
| Sole | | |

**Fig. 1-13 Fishing industry in the Cordilleras-British Columbia region**

**The BC forest industry.
A giant cedar tree felled
on Moresby Island, BC.**

## Future challenges

The future of the Cordilleras-British Columbia region looks good.
The economy, which is based on natural resources, is thriving.
Growing trade makes Vancouver Canada's most important Pacific
port, with exports to and from the Orient.

The region has its problems. These problems generally result
from the area's growth. Because of the growing population,
housing in Vancouver is scarce and costly. There is also conflict
over land use. Vancouver, for example, needs room to expand, but
the flat land is needed for agriculture. Also, as it becomes
industrialized, the region must cope with problems such as
pollution.

Another of the region's problems concerns foreign investment.
The Cordilleras-British Columbia area needs investment to develop
its resources fully. Foreign countries often invest in Canadian
resources. Japan, for example, has invested heavily in the West
Coast fishing industry. If this investment continues, Canada could
lose control of the industry. The people in the region must
therefore keep an eye on foreign investment.

The Cordilleras-British Columbia region is rich in resources. It
must learn to manage these resources, and cope with the problems
of growth. If it does this, the region's increasing prosperity will
continue.

Melita Russo, Vancouver.

These questions require a short answer.

1. A mountain system makes up 90% of British Columbia's land surface. What is the name of this system?
2. Name two mountain ranges within this system.
3. What is the name of the river delta on which most British Columbians live?
4. How much moisture can the coastal region receive each year?
5. What are the three most important industries in British Columbia?
6. What development in transportation in 1885 made British Columbia easier to reach from the east?
7. What is one problem facing the fishing industry?
8. Where does BC rank in Canada's natural gas production?
9. Name some agricultural activities in British Columbia.
10. What factor gives British Columbia a good trade location?

## READING BETTER

1. Here are a number of words that appear in the Cordilleras-British Columbia report. Write one or two sentences about each. You may want to refer back to the text for information.

| | | |
|---|---|---|
| Cordilleras | forest industry | Vancouver |
| Fraser Delta | natural gas | land use |
| ethnic population | overfishing | foreign investment |

2. One of the more important reading skills is the ability to read critically. This type of reading is done *after* you have read for understanding. In it you *think about* what you have read. You ask yourself questions.

    Here is a statement about the Cordilleras-British Columbia region. "The valleys of the Kootenay, Peace, and Laird rivers are suitable for farming." A person reading critically will want to know why the author makes this statement. The reader will ask several questions. "What makes this statement true? What soils are found in these regions? How does the climate affect farming?" Once you have read critically, you can start looking for the answers to questions. You have thus begun to learn for yourself.

    Select some statements made in the reading. Write some questions about them that show you are reading critically.

## USING YOUR KNOWLEDGE

1. Imagine you live in British Columbia. Imagine also that you have the skills to do any of the following work: commercial fishing, farming, forestry, mining, or a job of your choice in the city. Which work would you select? Why?

| | |
|---|---|
| Population (estimated 1977) | 2 501 000 |
| Work force | 1 159 000 |
| Electric power generated | 34 billion kilowatt hours |
| Value of mineral production | $1.9 billion |
| Value of fish landings | $132 million |
| Value of farm products | $502 million |

Source: *Globe and Mail*, Report on Business, section B, 1978, 1 11 and 1978, 7 18.

**Fig. 1-14   An economic profile of British Columbia**

## SOLVING PROBLEMS

1. What is the problem?
    Part of understanding a problem is understanding facts about the problem and being able to use facts to back up statements. Which statements made in the text are supported by figures in Fig. 1-14? Which statements using figures are not included in this chart?
2. Asking questions
    Suppose you want to show trends in the following important sections of the British Columbian economy. What questions would you ask to get the information you need? (Ask two or three questions for each topic.)
    a) Tourism
    b) Housing
    c) Relations between employers and workers
    d) Income of residents
3. Researching
    Take the questions you have made up. Appoint members of the class to research answers to them. Class members can then give a report on the information they have found.

**The Canadian Arctic Report**

**Arna Morse, CBC correspondent**  This is Arna Morse in Inuvik. The Arctic region is Canada's last frontier. It is difficult to set down boundaries to the area. In general, though, the Arctic can be defined as the region north of the 60th parallel of latitude. This includes the great number of islands off the mainland. Canada has laid claim to all this vast area. The Canadian Arctic makes up about 40% of Canada's land surface.

The region is huge, yet only about 60 000 people live in it. Sounds of cars, chain saws, rock music, and earth-moving equipment can sometimes be heard. But in general, the Arctic is a silent land, much of it untouched by developers.

The region will probably not be untouched for much longer. It has been found to be rich in minerals and oil. However before these riches can be used, certain decisions must be made. Developers who want to move in should think about problems caused by northern development. How will development affect the lives of the Native Peoples in the region? How much should the Arctic be developed? How quickly should development take place? These are some of the issues facing not only developers, but all Canadians.

**Arctic transportation. This truck's fuel costs have climbed since 1973.**

## Physical features

The eastern part of the Arctic region consists of mountains covered with glaciers. In the west there are flat lowlands.

The region has some unique physical features. One of these is *permafrost*. Permafrost is land whose **subsoil** is permanently frozen. The map on the screen behind me shows the permafrost line. North of this line the land can be frozen to a depth of 300 m. The top few inches of this land can thaw in the summer. The few inches that do thaw permit small plants to grow.

The map also shows a tree line. No trees grow north of this line. The tree line also marks the start of the *tundra*, which is treeless plain. It consists of black mucky soil that lies on top of permanently frozen soil. This land supports a growth of small bushes, **lichens,** and mosses.

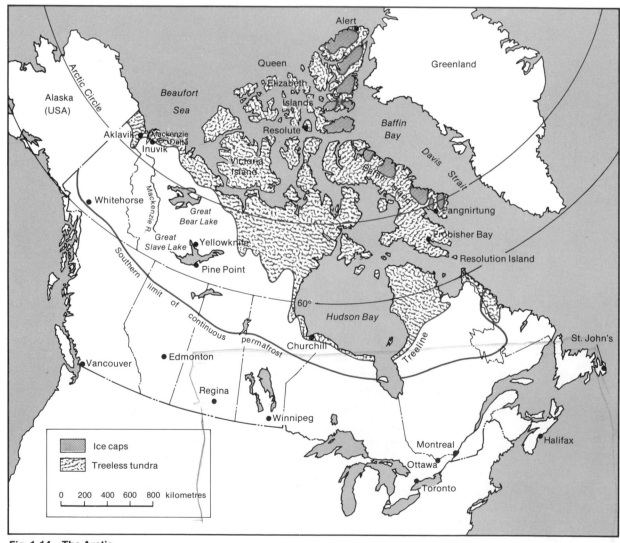

**Fig. 1-14  The Arctic**

**The Arctic tundra. Describe characteristics of the land and vegetation.**

In regions farthest to the north, the land is permanently covered with ice. In these areas, nothing grows.

### Climate

In general, the climate of the Arctic is very cold and dry. The warmest month in the region is July. In many areas temperatures average about 9° C. The temperature has gone as high as 17° C in Alert. However, temperatures are below freezing for most of the year, and winters are long and dark. Because temperatures are so low, ice forms over the water surface of most of the region. The farther north you go, the earlier the ice forms. The ice along the coast of Hudson Bay begins to break up in June. During August, September, and October, the route into the bay is ice-free. Ships can come and go freely during this period. Farther north, the ice may last even during the summer months. There is no ice-free season beyond King William Island. In some channels, however, the ice may be loose. Ships can therefore travel through.

The Canadian Arctic is very dry, receiving less than 180 mm of precipitation. Parts of the region are drier than the Sahara Desert! Why then, is the snow so deep? Because temperatures are so low, the snow never melts away. Each new snowfall adds to what is already on the ground.

### The people and the economy

The Canadian Arctic has always been sparsely settled. It is believed that people first came to the region about 20 000 years ago. These people were the ancestors of the Inuit and Indian groups of today. (See Fig. 1-15 for the names of these groups.)

53

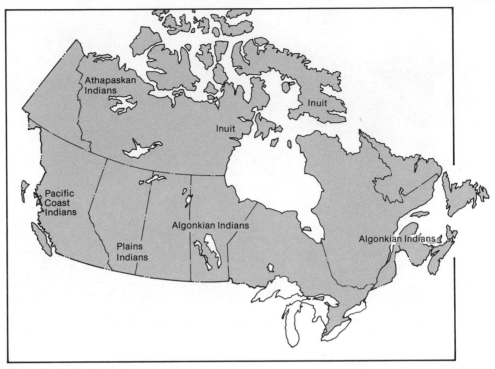

**Fig. 1-15  Native Peoples**

The Inuit groups led a semi-nomadic life. This means that they moved from place to place fairly often. Food was scarce in the region because of the climate. Therefore the Inuit survived mainly by hunting and fishing. The Arctic is rich in wildlife. Among the animals hunted by the Inuit were caribou, musk oxen, polar bears, seals, whales, and walruses.

Non-natives first ventured into the region in search of the Northwest Passage. The earliest European settlements were fur trading posts. While white fox was the main object of trade, other animals such as muskrat, mink, and beaver were also trapped.

Mineral discoveries also helped open up Arctic Canada. In 1897 gold was discovered in the **tributaries** of the Klondike River. Dawson City sprang up at the junction (point of crossing) of the Klondike and Yukon rivers. The city thrived during the gold rush.

Other important mineral discoveries were made during the 1930s. Gold was found at Yellowknife on Great Slave Lake. Silver-radium was found on Great Bear Lake. These discoveries brought people into the region.

Several other factors helped open up the Canadian Arctic. During World War II, wartime activity resulted in another boom in the Yukon. The building of airports and the Alaska Highway brought about 15000 people to Whitehorse. Airfields were also constructed in the eastern Arctic region. In the 1950s, the Distant Early Warning (DEW) line was built. This is a network of radar

**Inuvik, NWT. How might this photo correct mistaken ideas about Arctic life?**

stations across the 70th parallel, whose purpose is to warn North America of attack from over the pole. The building of the DEW line brought people to the region. Finally in recent years, oil and gas discoveries have stirred up interest in the Arctic.

One of the principal industries in the Arctic today is mining. Lead and zinc are important minerals. Large lead and zinc mines are located at Pine Point. Other minerals found in the region include silver, cadmium, iron ore, copper, and nickel. Gold is still mined at Yellowknife. Silver, lead, zinc, and cadmium are mined at Keno Hill. There are large iron ore reserves at Mary River Iron Mountain, on Baffin Island.

The Canadian Arctic has also been found to be rich in oil and natural gas. Reserves are found in the Mackenzie Delta. There are also major drilling sites in the Beaufort Sea and among the Arctic Islands. It is also possible that oil and natural gas underlie much of Hudson Bay.

There are other economic activities in the region. For example, the traditional fur trading continues. Commercial fishing on Great Slave Lake is also important. Tourism is a growing industry, especially as aircraft service to the region improves.

## Future challenges

Along with the Canadian Shield, the Arctic is Canada's main future source of economic wealth. The region is a storehouse of minerals and energy sources. Development of these resources has barely started. It is expected to increase greatly in the coming years. As development increases, certain issues will be taken into account.

### ISSUE 1: THE PLACE OF NATIVE PEOPLES

Much of the land in the region was taken over by Europeans. They did not sign treaties with the Native Peoples over how the land and its wealth would be used. Today it is agreed that the Native Peoples should be paid in some way. These people are laying claim to large areas of the north.

Land claims are only one concern of the Native Peoples. They are also worried about preserving their culture. Their life style changed as the non-native population in the region grew. Many Indians and Inuit have given up their nomadic life. They have settled down in towns to work in mining projects and other activities. The Native Peoples have been learning the skills and values of industrial society. A new way of life is open to them.

The Native Peoples are increasingly concerned with the loss of their traditional life style. They are also questioning the values of the new industrial society.

### ISSUE 2: THE PROBLEMS OF CLIMATE

It is hard to develop the resources in the region because of the climate. People working in the Arctic suffer many physical strains. The climate also makes construction difficult. For example, the ice and darkness of the region make drilling in the Beaufort Sea costly; the cost of drilling a single hole can rise to $3 000 000.

The climate creates other problems, too. The land is always freezing and thawing. Because of this, roads crack and buckle.

**Arctic transportation. How has the airplane changed life in the Arctic?**

Water supply and sewage disposal problems arise because pipes cannot be placed underground. The Arctic's resources are being developed, but money is needed to overcome the problems caused by the climate.

### ISSUE 3: THE PROBLEMS OF DISTANCE

The Arctic is Canada's longest and widest region. Its size creates many problems. To carry oil down the pipeline routes, huge lengths of pipe must be made. This is expensive. Also, food and other items have to be imported. Because of the vast distances these items travel, shipping costs are high. Shipping costs are also high because it is costly to build and maintain transportation systems. Once again, if the Arctic is to be developed, certain prices must be paid.

### ISSUE 4: PROTECTING THE ENVIRONMENT

As the Arctic region is developed, attention must be given to the environment and resources. In the past, people have cut down trees and hunted wildlife without thinking of the future. Governments and people today realize that resources should be conserved and used wisely.

Development can also disturb the life systems of the region. In a life system, one living thing depends on another to survive. If, for example, plant life is destroyed, then the animals that feed on it are affected.

The environment also needs to be protected against pollution. An oil spill may affect wildlife for hundreds of miles around.

These are just some of the problems to be faced as development increases. Canadians can use the Arctic wealth to their own advantage. However they must always be ready to meet the cost involved. And they should also take into account the peoples and environment of the region.

This is Arna Morse in Inuvik.

## Mineral production in the Arctic

The figures below show mineral production in the Yukon and Northwest Territories. These areas make up most of the Canadian Arctic. Do the figures show an increase in the value of mineral production since 1954? If you were in the mining industry, would you be interested in these figures? What questions would you ask about them?

### Value of mineral production in the Yukon and Northwest Territories

| (Figures are in thousands of dollars) | | | |
| --- | --- | --- | --- |
| | *1954* | *1969* | *1974* | *1976* |
| Yukon | 16 559 | 37 656 | 185 194 | 131 069 |
| NWT | 26 414 | 116 456 | 228 393 | 213 100 |

About 28 million dollars in oil and natural gas was recovered in the Northwest Territories in 1976. The prospects for oil in the Beaufort Sea and Arctic Islands appear good. Many companies are spending a great deal of time and money on the search for oil and gas in the region. Imperial Oil, for example, expects to spend 150 million dollars in Arctic exploration from 1977 to 1982. The federal government says that "frontier" oil will probably not be in production until the late 1980s.

Sources: *Quick Canadian Facts*, 32nd edition, pp. 64, 65, 108; also *Energy: The Task Ahead*, Report E177-1, Department of Energy, Mines and Resources, 1977, p. 16.

---

## QUICK QUIZ

These questions require short answers.

1. What is the southern boundary of the Canadian Arctic?
2. What is the population of the Arctic?
3. Name two factors that may influence decisions to develop the Arctic.
4. What are the physical features of the eastern and western parts of the region?
5. In general, what is the climate of the region like?
6. Name an important economic activity in the region.
7. Why is the Arctic so sparsely settled?
8. How does the climate make construction difficult?
9. What type of vegetation occurs above the tree line?
10. Explain the meaning of the term permafrost.

## SOLVING PROBLEMS

1. There are many problems that could arise in the Canadian Arctic. We should think about these possible problems, and try to come up with solutions now. We will therefore be ready for difficulties as they come. We may even be able to prevent the difficult situations from arising.

   What may happen if the needs of the environment are not taken into account? Some possible problems are listed below. Explain how each problem could occur. Then, suggest a possible solution to each problem.
   a) Natural vegetation may be damaged.
   b) Oil spills from pipelines or tankers may harm wildlife.
   c) Housing will not be available for persons in Arctic towns.
   d) Companies in the region may pollute the environment.
   e) Native Peoples will lose their identity.

Julian Cleva

**Peter Holstrom, host and commentator**  Canada is indeed a land of
variety. In each region, the economic activities and life styles of the
people are different. These differences exist to a certain extent
because of the landforms and physical features of each region. For
example, lumbering and the pulp and paper industry tend to be
important in a heavily-forested region. In an area with good soil
and a long growing season, people will often make their living by
farming. People are influenced, to some degree, by the physical
region they live in.

It has been said that because of the different physical regions, the
ties among Canadians from coast to coast tend to be weak. People
across the country will have different concerns. The BC miner will
have little in common with the fisher from Newfoundland. East-
west ties may appear to be weak.

The regions of Canada do, however, seem to have strong ties
with the US areas south of them. The Nova Scotia fisher has
something in common with a fisher from the US eastern sea coast.
This is largely because the physical regions they live in are similar.
Their life styles and concerns will therefore be much the same. This
north-south pull is visible all across the country. In North America,
physical features tend to run north-south. The forests of BC
continue down into the US. The prairies in Canada go down into
the US midwest. Because of physical regions, then, Canadians
sometimes appear to have stronger ties with their US neighbours
than with fellow Canadians.

Do physical regions have to be a dividing force in Canada? Many people answer with a strong "no". Many Canadians have been proud to belong to a country of such great variety. They have, of course, seen the problems created by the country's regional differences. But they have tried to overcome the lack of geographical unity. They have done this by creating other ties that bind the country together.

A great number of transportation lines tie the country together physically. The Trans-Canada Highway system stretches from Victoria, BC, to St. John's, Newfoundland. There are complex air and rail links between urban centres and remote settlements. The St. Lawrence Seaway allows ships to travel from the Atlantic to the Great Lakes. Pipelines carry oil and natural gas from one region to another.

Communication systems allow Canadians from all regions to know each other and share ideas. The CBC, for example, reaches Canadians from coast to coast through radio and television. Such communication systems are important to the development of a Canadian identity.

Government programmes are another link. Through the programmes, wealthy regions give aid to less prosperous ones. All these different ties have helped make Canada a strong and unified country. Canadians in the past have fought together against problems caused by the country's different physical regions. They learned to value the variety of the country. Canadians today can do the same. They can continue to solve the problems that are caused by regional differences. Canadians will then face the future with a common goal.

---

### Conclusion

Canada is a land of distinct regions. Each region has its own physical features, climate, history, and economic activities. Regional differences have created problems in the country. However, Canadians in the past have been able to meet the challenges presented by the physical diversity of the land. People in Canada have created ties that hold the country together.

One challenge still facing Canadians is economic inequality. Some regions have many advantages, such as large supplies of natural resources. These regions are able to offer a variety of jobs and good incomes to their people. Other regions are not as wealthy.

In the next chapter, we are going to study the question of economic opportunity. We will see what can be done to give Canadians across the land a chance for decent housing, good wages . . . a better life.

**READING BETTER**

**1. Below is a series of facts about Canada's regions. Copy the facts down in your notebook. Then match each fact with the correct region. You may use the code supplied to show the region.**

| | |
|---|---|
| **Appalachian Canada** | AP |
| **Canadian Shield** | S |
| **Arctic** | AR |
| **St. Lawrence-Great Lakes Lowlands** | L |
| **Prairies** | P |
| **Cordilleras-British Columbia** | C |

a) This region has a very small percentage of Canada's population.
b) The highest mountains in the land will be found here.
c) This region includes the Province of Nova Scotia.
d) The Frontenac Axis cuts this region in two.
e) This is the smallest physical region of Canada.
f) This region is the coldest and driest of them all.
g) This region consists of hard Precambrian rock.
h) Three provinces make up this region.
i) Several mountain ranges make up 90% of this region.
j) This region has experienced increasing prosperity since the energy crisis.

## ORGANIZING BETTER

1. Make a poster that shows all the regions of Canada. Under each region mark the dominant economic activities. Also, write on the poster a few words about each activity.

## USING YOUR KNOWLEDGE

1. Make up a short quiz about the different regions of Canada. "True or false" questions are good for this type of quiz. Include questions about landforms, climate, and the economy of the regions. Then give your quiz to another student in the class.

## SOLVING PROBLEMS

1. Problems often make it impossible for us to achieve our goals. It is important to know which goals are being interfered with when a problem comes up. Turn back to the problem-solving model in Countdown Canada. The second step asks you to list goals that are not being achieved because of the problem. This exercise will give you practice in the second step of problem-solving.

   Briefly look through the chapter. Choose three problems that are found in Canada.

## TAKING A STAND

1. Each of the regions has a contribution to make to the Canadian economy. Which region do you think is the most important? Be ready to give reasons for your point of view.

## RESEARCHING

1. Current magazines and newspaper articles contain much information about the regions of Canada. Make up a scrapbook from newspaper and magazine clippings about Canada's regions.
(You may, for example, choose one problem from the Prairies, one from the Arctic, and one from BC.) Make a list of all the goals that each problem is interfering with.

## GLOSSARY

**Bedrock.** The layer of rock under the soil.

**Clayey soils.** Earth that has a large amount of clay in it.

**Climate.** The record of weather for an area over a long period of time.

**Frost-free days.** The period of time between the last freeze of one season and the first freeze of another.

**Growing season.** The period during which crops normally grow.

**Landforms.** Different features of the earth's surface, such as hills and valleys.

**Lichen.** Moss-like wild plant life.

**Market crops.** Vegetables and other crops used as food.

**Non-renewable resources.** Natural resources that are of limited supply.

**Outcroppings.** Portions of rock showing through the surface of the earth.

**Physical features.** All aspects of the landscape.

**Precambrian rock.** Rock formations that are at least 600 million years old.

**Precipitation.** Moisture that falls to the earth. It can take the form of rain, hail, or snow.

**Secondary manufacturing.** The processing of raw materials into a more finished form.

**Subsoil.** The layer of soil underneath the surface soil.

**Tributaries.** Smaller streams that flow into a large river.

# 2/Regions that divide us

## Contents

### Introduction

We have seen that Canada is a land of many distinct regions. From coast to coast, areas differ in landscape, climate, and population.

There are also economic differences among regions in Canada. Some provinces in certain regions are richer than others. Ontario, Alberta, and British Columbia are wealthy provinces. In wealthy areas, people receive high pay for their jobs. They may be able to find jobs more easily than in the less wealthy regions. Richer areas may offer more public services, such as hospitals, good roads, and schools.

In this chapter, we take a close look at Canada's economic differences. We will attempt to find answers to these main questions:

1. **What is regional disparity? What are the signs of this disparity?**

2. **What are the reasons for the differences?**
3. **How does regional disparity affect Canadians?**
4. **What should be done to close the gap between the richer and less wealthy regions of Canada?**

### What does regional disparity mean?

Disparity means inequality or difference. You are already familiar with this concept. All people are different in one way or another. Some people you know may be shy, while others are outgoing. Or some people are better off financially than others. These people have better clothes, nicer homes, and more spending money than many others. This last type of difference is related to money, or finance. It is called financial or economic disparity. This is the type of disparity discussed in this chapter.

There are economic differences among people in various parts of Canada. *Regional disparity* means that from region to region there are differences in how well-off people are. The region people live in will affect how well-off they are. Below are profiles of people from wealthy and less wealthy parts of Canada. These profiles will point out the economic differences or disparity between regions.

**Teenage profile**

WEALTHY REGION OF CANADA

LESS WEALTHY REGION OF CANADA

*Jacqueline Borden*

*Jack Ozzawa*

| | *Education* | |
|---|---|---|
| She has a good chance of completing high school. She will probably get more education after high school. | | He does not have the same chance of finishing high school as Jacqueline has. He will probably not get more education after high school. |
| Jacqueline probably lives in a well-furnished house or apartment. She may have a room to study in. | *Housing* | Jack's home isn't as large or as comfortable as Jacqueline's. He may not have a room to study in. His home is crowded. |
| Jacqueline finds it easy to get a good-paying part-time job. She can probably spend all she makes on herself. | *Part-time job* | Jack's part-time job is low-paying and was hard to find. Some of his wages may go to support the family. |

**Worker profile**

John McQueen

WEALTHY REGION

*Nanine Broquet*

Nanine is well paid. She may receive about $220 per week. She has more types of jobs to choose from.

*Wages*

Ernst may work at the same type of job as Nanine. However, he receives less money for it. His pay may be $166 per week. Most often he will not have the same variety of jobs to choose from.

She has a good chance of keeping her job. If she loses it, she will quickly find another job. The new job may even be better than the old one.

*Unemployment*

Ernst is more likely than Nanine to be unemployed. If he loses his job, he will have to spend more time finding another one. He may have to take a low-paying job until his luck changes.

Nanine will likely stay where she is because economic conditions are good.

*Location*

Ernst is likely to look for a better place to live. He may move to another place in the province. He may even go outside the province to richer areas like Ontario, Alberta, or British Columbia.

LESS WEALTHY REGION

*Ernst Browder*

## Some signposts of regional disparity

A signpost is an indicator or a clue. There are certain signposts, or indicators of regional disparity. These signposts show us that economic differences do exist among Canada's regions. They also show us which regions are rich, and which are less wealthy.

### Signpost 1: Wages

Workers in one region of Canada are paid more than workers in another. This is one signpost of regional disparity. Fig. 2-1

| | |
|---|---|
| Atlantic region | 83 |
| Quebec | 93 |
| Ontario | 109 |
| Prairies | 95 |
| British Columbia | 105 |

Source: *Living Together: A Study of Regional Disparities*, Economic Council of Canada, (Ottawa, 1977), p. 39.

**Fig. 2-1 Index numbers for wages across Canada**

shows index numbers for wages of Canadian workers. We can note certain **general trends.** Workers in the Atlantic provinces make less than people in Quebec and the Prairies. These Atlantic workers receive much less than people in Ontario and British Columbia do.

### Signpost 2: Unemployment and job opportunities

Let us say that Ernst Browder works in Quebec. The Quebec unemployment rate in 1975 was 8.8%. Nanine Broquet works in the Prairies, where the unemployment rate was only 3.4% in 1975. This means that a higher percentage of people were jobless in Quebec than on the Prairies. Thus Ernst would have a harder time finding a job than Nanine would. This is a second signpost of regional disparity. Less wealthy regions have higher unemployment rates.

There is more to the unemployment picture. People in regions with high unemployment rates tend to be without

| | |
|---|---|
| Atlantic region | 11.6% |
| Quebec | 8.8% |
| Ontario | 6.0% |
| Prairies | 3.4% |
| British Columbia | 8.3% |

Source: *Living Together*, 1977, p. 39.

**Fig. 2-2 Unemployment rate by region, 1975**

jobs longer. They also do not have the choice of jobs that people in rich regions do. We will see why this is true when we study the causes of regional disparity.

### Signpost 3: Educational differences

The figures in Fig. 2-3 may be of interest to you as students. The numbers show that people in less wealthy regions leave school early. People in richer regions stay in school longer. These figures on education are part of a large group of signposts called *social indicators.* They help to describe human life in a region. Other social indicators are housing and health care. These indicators show that, in general, the **standard of living** is highest in Ontario and Western Canada.

| | |
|---|---|
| Over 85% | Ontario |
| | British Columbia |
| | Alberta |
| 80-85% | Quebec |
| | Manitoba |
| | Saskatchewan |
| 70-80% | Newfoundland |
| | Nova Scotia |
| | New Brunswick |
| Under 70% | PEI |

Source: *Living Together*, 1977, p. 58.

**Fig. 2-3 Percentage of 16-year-olds in school, 1974-75**

Some other social indicators are crime rates and the number of suicides. It has been found that both these rates are high in wealthy regions. Therefore, before we decide where life is best, we must look at many social indicators.

Signpost 4: Migration

Migration is simply the movement of people from one place to another. People in less wealthy regions often migrate to richer ones. This movement is shown in Fig. 2-4. The numbers show the migration of people to and from regions in a twenty-year period. For example, 15% more people left the Atlantic region than moved in. About 28% more people moved into Ontario than moved out.

| | |
|---|---|
| Atlantic provinces | −15% |
| Quebec | +6% |
| Ontario | +28% |
| Prairies | −4% |
| British Columbia | +52% |

Source: *Living Together*, 1977, p. 175.

**Fig. 2-4 Migration rates across the country, 1951-1971**

These figures just give general trends for each region. The figures for individual provinces within a region may be quite different. For example, Fig. 2-4 shows that 4% more people moved out of the Prairies than moved in. This is just the general trend for the three Prairie provinces. In Saskatchewan, however, 25% more people moved out than moved in. And in Alberta, 20% more people moved in than moved out.

**QUICK QUIZ**

**Answer these questions true or false.**

1. Teenagers in less wealthy regions tend to remain in school a long time.
2. A part-time job is easier to find in a rich region than in a less wealthy one.
3. Income levels are an important signpost of regional disparity.
4. Unemployment is higher in the Atlantic provinces than on the Prairies.
5. Canadians tend to move from less wealthy regions to richer ones.
6. Education, health care, and housing are signposts called social indicators.
7. The suicide rate in the Atlantic provinces is higher than in more prosperous regions.

8. Ontario, Alberta, and British Columbia are generally thought of as rich provinces.
9. In the 1975 period, Quebec wages were the lowest in Canada.
10. Regional disparity means that some regions of Canada are richer than others.

**ORGANIZING BETTER**

1. Draw or obtain an outline map of the regions of Canada. Mark in the names of the regions. Under each of the regions, print important facts about wages, the unemployment rate, and the migration rate.
2. Here are a number of true or false questions about some of the tables in this section. Refer to the tables and then answer true or false.
   a) In 1975, the Prairies and Ontario had the lowest rates of unemployment. (Fig. 2-2)
   b) More than eight out of ten 16-year-olds in Manitoba were in school in 1975. (Fig. 2-3)
   c) Only two regions in Canada had an increase in migration during the 1951-71 period. (Fig. 2-4)

**USING YOUR KNOWLEDGE**

1. Is it true to say that Ontario, British Columbia, and Alberta are the most prosperous regions in Canada? Use figures to back up your answer.

**The causes of regional disparity**

We know that there are economic differences among the regions of Canada. The regions differ in income levels, job opportunities, and in many other ways. Why do these economic differences exist? We will attempt to answer the question in this section of the chapter.

There is no single reason for regional disparity. Economic differences are the result of *many* factors working together. We will look at these factors one by one. If we understand all the parts of the problem, we will be better able to solve it. However, keep in mind that all of these factors are working together to create economic disparity.

1. Physical features and climate

Landforms, soil, temperature, and precipitation will greatly affect the economy of an

**Farming in the Eastern Townships, Quebec. What causes of regional disparity can you see here?**

area. These factors bring both benefits and disadvantages to Canada's regions.

Physical features and climate can attract people to an area. Farm workers will be attracted to the St. Lawrence Lowlands or the Fraser Delta. In these areas, the soil is good and the climate is suitable for growing crops. Physical features and climate can also attract tourists. For example, tourists flock to the warm beaches of PEI. In winter, skiers are attracted to Quebec, with its Laurentian mountains and heavy snowfalls. In all these examples, physical features and climate boost a region's economy.

They can also bring disadvantages to an area. Because of the lack of good farmland, a region may have to import food. This drives up food prices. Also, floods, frost, and drought can destroy millions of dollars of crops. Heavy snowfalls in Quebec may draw tourists to the Laurentians. However, cities like Montreal spend millions of

dollars each year for snow removal. These examples show how physical features and climate can affect regional economies.

2. Location

The location of a region in relation to markets is important. Canada is a vast land. It costs money to move people and goods from one area to another. For example, the Atlantic region is far from manufacturing centres like Toronto and Montreal. It is therefore costly to move goods between these regions. In 1977, government funds paid 50% of Atlantic Canada's rail and truck costs.

Location may also prevent industrial growth in a region. Factory owners will not move to regions that are far from sources of skilled labour. Nor will they settle in areas far from sources of machinery parts.

The location of a region can help the economy. In Nova Scotia, for example, there is a provincial steel company, Sysco

67

**Regional disparity: developing natural resources in an open-pit iron mine, Atikokan, Ontario.**

Steel. In 1978 this company sold steel to Cuba and Venezuela. This sale was possible partly because of Nova Scotia's Atlantic location. There are many other examples of how location boosts economy. Hamilton, Ontario, is a major steel centre. It is located between US coal supplies and the iron ore reserves of Labrador. These examples show how location affects a region's economy.

### 3. Urbanization

Urbanization is the growth of cities. More and more Canadians are living in or close to cities. The Atlantic region is the least urbanized. British Columbia, on the other hand, is heavily urbanized. However the province has few mid-sized cities. Quebec and Ontario are also extremely urbanized. Fig. 2-5 gives you an idea of the distribution and size of Canadian cities.

The presence of cities and large towns can benefit a region. There are usually jobs in an urban area. Thus cities will attract a large labour force. These workers become buyers of products. Companies may see that there is a large number of buyers in a city. These companies may therefore set up plants in the area. This will create more jobs. The jobs attract more people. There is a "snowball effect", as population, jobs, and income grow together. Urbanization will therefore add to the wealth of a region.

There is a point, however, where the problems of urbanization outweigh the good points. It has been found that cities with a population of under 1.5 million benefit a region. But once the population grows larger than 1.5 million, the benefits decrease. Services tend to cost more. For example, it becomes costly to provide an adequate water supply. Also, problems like pollution and overcrowding seem to be more serious after this point. Development gets out of hand. The city is not as efficient as it once was.

Urbanization can therefore increase the wealth of a region. Many people however, think that it should be controlled, so that the problems do not outweigh the benefits.

### 4. Natural resources

A region rich in natural resources can produce income and jobs. Areas without resources may have little income and few jobs.

The reasons for this are not hard to understand. A region can sell its resources. Other parts of Canada, and the US always need natural resources. Also, many countries of the world need Canadian resources such as copper, iron, and aluminum. This demand creates jobs for workers in a region. For example, miners and forest workers are needed to make resources available to other regions.

Resource-based industries will also spring up in a region with resources. These industries bring wealth to a region. Jobs are also created. In British Columbia, for example, forestry is important. The province produces and sells all kinds of forest products. Then, forest-related industries create more jobs. For every forest worker there are hundreds of factory workers, office clerks, drivers, and dock workers. Thus, an economy with a resource base will be healthy.

### 5. Transportation

In Canada, regions are often separated from larger markets by great distances. Transportation systems help to bridge the distances. Regions can then gain access to large markets.

Regions with good transportation systems tend to be wealthy. Goods can be shipped easily and at a reasonable cost. Business is thus able to run smoothly. The Great Lakes-St. Lawrence Lowlands, for example, benefit greatly from the St. Lawrence Seaway. Ships are able to pass

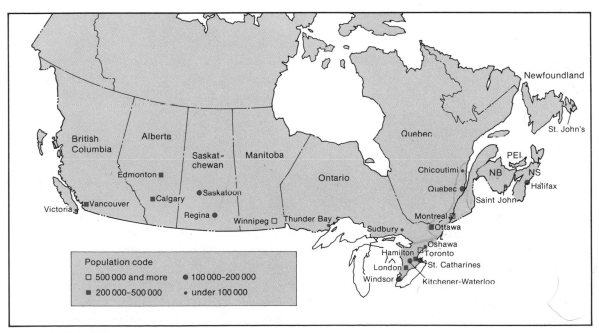

**Fig. 2-5 Urbanization**

from the Atlantic Ocean to ports along the Great Lakes.

Some areas have only a limited number of transportation systems. Because of location or physical features, systems may be hard to build. There may be no direct routes between a region and large urban centres. In such regions, transportation costs are high. The economy thus suffers. The federal government has helped the Atlantic region with its transport expenses. Without this help, the region would have trouble meeting costs. The Prairie provinces have been concerned about the cost of transporting processed goods from the Prairies. They feel that these costs should be lowered by government funds. Cheap transportation is important to the wealth of the Prairie region. Good transportation systems therefore affect the wealth of all Canada's regions.

## 6. Technology

A wheat farmer with a **combine** can do more work in a day than a hundred field hands. Fishing boats with radar can locate more fish than boats without this equipment can. Both the combine and the radar are examples of technology.

Technology is machinery or techniques designed to do certain things efficiently. In the industrial world, better methods of doing things are always being discovered. Regions that can use these discoveries tend to be wealthy. Technology makes business and industry work better. Areas that cannot adopt new methods are often not as well-off.

**Regional disparity: Technology. This Ontario Hydro control room permits the wise use of electricity.**

Some regions tend to use new methods more quickly than other regions do. Ontario, for example, ranks first in the use of computers. It is followed by the Prairies, Quebec, and BC. Shopping malls are a fairly new technique in **retail sales.** This technique is used most by Alberta, followed by BC.

Notice that in these examples, the richer regions use the new technology most often. Why is this? One reason is the cost of technology. Regions must be able to pay for computers or shopping malls. Second, a large population is needed. Shopping malls are worthwhile only if there are many buyers nearby.

### 7. Labour force

A skilled labour force can add to the wealth of a region. For example, a good manager can make a business more efficient. Skilled workers who use all their skills also increase production. Skilled workers tend to be out of a job less often than unskilled ones. They also have a better chance of finding a job quickly.

Why do some regions have a better work force than others? The main reason appears to be education opportunities. Some regions have a number of good high schools, universities, and colleges. People have the chance to get a good formal education. The regions also provide training programmes for specific jobs. These areas will thus turn out a skilled labour force.

**QUICK QUIZ**

**Answer these questions true or false.**
1. Income tends to be higher in regions with few cities.
2. Unemployment rates differ from region to region.
3. Climate has no effect on the wealth of a region.
4. If a region is close to large markets, it has a greater chance of being rich.
5. Natural resources do not affect the wealth of a region.
6. Natural resources tend to increase the number of jobs available in a region.
7. The St. Lawrence Seaway does not affect the prosperity of the Great Lakes-St. Lawrence region.
8. Technology refers to machines and devices designed to do things efficiently.
9. The high cost of technology restricts its use in some industries.
10. A skilled labour force increases the wealth of a region.

**READING BETTER**
1. Here are some statements about the effects of climate and natural resources on a region. Put these statements in your own words.
   a) "Climate can limit the range of farm products grown in a region. It may also raise the costs of construction in the area."
   b) "Much development can occur in a region that has large supplies of natural resources."
   c) "Climate can aid tourism, but it can hinder the economy in other ways."

**d)** "Resources can make regions richer. They do not always, however, improve the well-being of people in the region."

### How does regional disparity affect Canadians?

So far in the chapter we have seen that regional disparity exists. We have looked at some of the causes. This section shows how regional disparity affects Canadians. Below are interviews with people from three regions of Canada. The interviews should show that the economies of some regions are stronger than others. People's lives are affected by the economy in many basic ways. The lives of the following people reflect the differences in Canada's regions.

### Regional disparity affects people in many ways

| | |
|---|---|
| Standard of living | People in less wealthy regions do not enjoy the luxuries that many other Canadians have. Some people may be struggling for the necessities of life. |
| Job opportunities | People in less wealthy regions may have a harder time finding jobs. |
| Education | People in less wealthy regions may not get the training they need to earn high incomes. |
| Migration | Many people are tempted to move from less wealthy areas to richer ones. |
| Social and public services | Governments in less wealthy regions cannot provide services out of tax dollars. People have to do without parks and public projects. These services may be taken for granted in richer regions. |

### Interview 1: Margaret Yanish of Tuelon, Manitoba

John McQueen

My husband Tony and I live alone in our three-room house. All our children are grown-up. The region we live in is called the Interlake region. The government gave my boy Paul some training and he moved down to Winnipeg as a machinist. But my husband and I remain here.

Tony is a carpenter by trade. Years ago in the summer he used to earn extra money at an amusement park at Winnipeg Beach. Now that job is gone. He depends on his job as a carpenter. There's little work around here.

I tried to get part-time work but none is available here. Other women my age face the same problem. Our income is about $7 000 a year, so we do without a lot of things. We waited three weeks before we could afford to replace the picture tube in our TV. Most of my canned goods come from Winnipeg. A friend in the trucking business brings back discount canned goods for us. My husband Tony has four old trucks in our back yard. He takes parts from them whenever the truck he uses for work breaks down. Our life would be better if I could get a job.

### Interview 2: Malcolm Mitchell of Toronto

I'm in my last year of high school. My grades have been good all the way through school. I want to become a mechanical engineer. There are usually jobs available in the field. One of the universities in this province offers a great programme in that area. You take classes at the university, but at the same time you go out and do some work for companies. It's a good way to get education and work experience.

The university is in another city, but I can afford to go. I've never had much trouble getting a summer job. And I've been saving my money for university. I'm really looking forward to next year.

### Interview 3: Hazel Fenech of a small New Brunswick town

I was elected mayor in last November's election. The job of mayor in a small New Brunswick town is full of problems. I took the job, however, because I'm proud of this town. I want to see it improve, yet still keep the way of life we've had here for years.

Our problem is money. We have a large number of older people in the population. They can't pay high taxes for the park we want to restore on Seventh Street. Many of the sidewalks are in need of repair. We have to be careful about how we spend tax money. We often depend on service clubs such as the Lions and the Kinsmen to sponsor local improvements.

Government money is available for town improvement in the province. But I find that most of the money goes to bigger cities such as Moncton and Fredericton. The portion we get from the province doesn't meet our needs.

**USING YOUR KNOWLEDGE**

1. The interviews tell you quite a bit about the regions in which the three people live. Make a list of the benefits and disadvantages that each person experiences. Then decide whether each person lives in a wealthy, moderately wealthy, or poor region. Give reasons for your decisions.

2. Mrs. Yanish is typical of many people living in less wealthy regions. She and her husband have a hard time making ends meet. They have to stretch their budget even farther than the average Canadian does.

It is useful to draw up a budget of your expenses. You will know how much you are spending on various items. You will also know

73

whether or not you should cut back on your spending. How much do you spend on these items in a month: clothing, food, transportation, entertainment, and school supplies? Figure out your answer to the nearest dollar.

Now, turn to Fig. 2-1. Pick a province or region other than your own. Imagine that you were paid the average wage in that region. Compare it with the average wage for the region in which you live. If you moved to the new area, how would your budget be affected? Would you be able to spend more? Would you have to cut back? On which items would you increase or reduce your spending?

3. Suppose you have recently moved to a wealthier region of Canada. Write a letter home to tell your family about your new life. In your letter mention the following:
   a) Your present salary
   b) Your job
   c) Your housing
   d) How you travel to work and other places
   e) Friends you have made
   f) Your feelings about home

## Solutions to regional disparity

Some regions in Canada, such as the Great Lakes-St. Lawrence Lowlands, have many economic advantages. Other areas are less wealthy. Without outside help, these regions would not be able to survive. Wages would decline. Jobs would decrease as people and companies left for richer areas. Government help has always been needed by the less wealthy regions. In this section we look at how the federal government has dealt with regional disparity.

Since Confederation, the Canadian government has promised to reduce differences among regions. Progress has been slow. At times, parts of Canada have bitterly resented federal policies. For example, the Atlantic region and the Prairies have been angry. These areas have felt that government policy favoured central Canada.

In general, government programmes to reduce regional disparity fall into two groups. In the first group, the federal government helps businesses. It also gives funds to other levels of government. In the second group, funds go directly to the individual. Both groups of programmes have the same aim. This aim is to raise regional income and improve living standards. We will look at these government programmes in detail. Some suggestions for future action will also be proposed.

### Business and government programmes

*1. Department of Regional Economic Expansion (DREE)*

This federal department was set up to coordinate government aid programmes. For many years, the government had been helping less wealthy regions. Farm development programmes, for example, dated back to the **Depression.** These programmes did much to aid farmers. For instance, they helped farmers reclaim land, and improve livestock. In 1969, the farm aid programmes were brought together under one department, DREE.

In recent years, farming has played a minor role in the economy. Industry, on the other hand, is important. Therefore, since 1969, DREE has offered programmes for industrial development. The department subsidizes (gives money to) businesses to locate in less wealthy regions. This helps build up the economy of the region. This programme is often carried out with development departments of the different provinces. Other activities of DREE help industry indirectly to relocate. Here are some of DREE's activities:

1. Gives funds to industry to relocate
2. Gives funds to aid rural governments
3. Gives funds to aid small-town governments
4. Gives funds for **human resources** and research studies

Only about 30% of DREE money goes to industries already located in less wealthy regions. Money does go to industries in the Atlantic region, Quebec, eastern and northern Ontario, and parts of the Prairies.

How much success has DREE had? The department has helped farmers a good deal.

However, DREE's industrial programmes have been criticized. The criticism is that when industries move from wealthy to less wealthy regions, national production decreases. This seems to be the case. However, studies show that DREE programmes create jobs in less wealthy areas. About 25% more jobs have been created in these areas because of DREE.

### 2. Other government programmes

DREE is a small department, set up specifically to help regions prosper. But other government departments give aid, too. Their programmes assist industry, farmers, exporters, and the unemployed. Money is used for research, and for training people in new jobs. Funds are given to companies to help pay high fuel costs. These are just some of the ways in which government departments help regions. Fig. 2-6 shows the funds given by government departments to industries in various regions.

The programmes of the different government departments do help industry. However it is hard to know how much they do to reduce regional disparity. These government funds go to industries in rich regions as well as in less wealthy ones. This means that wealthy areas grow even richer. The gap between wealthy and less wealthy areas is thus not closed. DREE, on the other hand, gives aid mostly to less wealthy regions. It does this to permit less wealthy areas to catch up to rich ones. We can see that government funds sometimes work at cross-purposes.

### 3. Transport programmes

The government sponsors transport programmes. Their aim is to cut the cost of transporting goods. When the transport costs of goods are low, the goods themselves will cost less. For example, an Atlantic manufacturer who ships goods out of the region by truck or rail may receive a subsidy of 50%. This means that the government pays 50% of the shipping costs. Wood products and minerals are also shipped out of the region. There is a 30% subsidy on the shipping costs of these items. These subsidies, or money grants, help Atlantic producers cut costs. They can thus charge less for their products.

Transport programmes also exist on the Prairies. As early as 1897, the West was able to bargain for aid. This aid was used to reduce transport costs. The Prairies continue to push for these subsidies. The aid will encourage manufacturers to produce more. This in turn will raise incomes and provide jobs in the region.

### 4. Federal-provincial tax arrangements

Less wealthy provinces cannot offer their citizens as many services as wealthy ones can. Money is needed to pay for hospitals, teachers' salaries, and public projects. This money has to come from taxpayers. But taxpayers in less wealthy regions cannot

| Departments | Atlantic region | Quebec | Ontario | Prairies | British Columbia |
|---|---|---|---|---|---|
| Industry, Trade and Commerce programmes, Department of Agriculture programmes, Manpower and Immigration programmes | 20 | 27 | 22 | 37 | 17 |
| DREE programmes | 3 | 6 | 1 | 3 | 1 |

Source: *Living Together*, 1977, p. 170.

**Fig. 2-6 Number of government aid programmes (dollars per person in area)**

afford high taxes. Since the mid-1950s, federal and provincial governments have tried to solve the problem. They have come up with two answers. The first is equalization payments. The second is shared-cost programmes. In both programmes, tax money is transferred from government to government. Regional governments then spend the money to help their residents. Both programmes are examples of Canadians working together.

a) Equalization payments
In Canada, money from wealthy provinces goes to less wealthy ones. This has been going on for about twenty years. The amount of money given is worked out by a complex formula. The federal government adjusts these payments each year to meet changing conditions. Fig. 2-7 shows how money was allotted in 1977-78. As the map shows, wealthy provinces such as Ontario, Alberta, and BC do not receive equalization payments.

b) Shared-cost programmes
In the equalization payment programme, wealthy provinces receive no money. The "have" provinces help out the "have-not" ones. In shared-cost programmes, all provinces receive tax money from the federal government. Some of the money is given through DREE and other government programmes. The provinces then match federal money with their own. The money is used in a great number of ways. Here are a few:

Hospital insurance
Welfare programmes
Highway construction
Payments to doctors (Medicare)
Post-secondary education
Public transportation

What effect do these programmes have? In general, all provinces benefit from them. Wealthy provinces get a certain amount of financial aid. Less wealthy provinces, which need more aid than rich ones do, receive a great deal. In a year, for example, Newfoundland spends about $1 000 per person on services. These services include welfare, health, and education. Half of this money comes from the rich provinces through the federal government. A rich province,

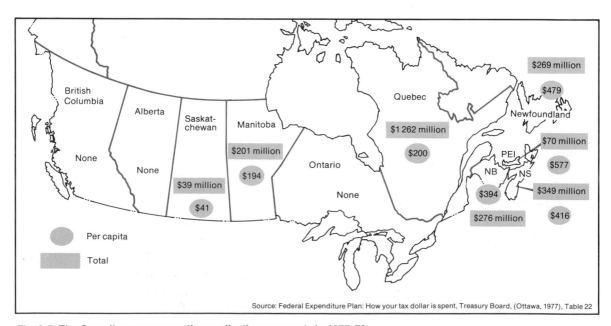

Fig. 2-7 The Canadian government's equalization payments in 1977-78

Alberta, spends about $1 200 per person on the same services. Of this amount, only $225 is transferred to the province from federal government funds. Alberta is wealthier than Newfoundland. It therefore pays more of the bill on its own.

### Programmes of direct aid to individuals

The federal government helps business and other levels of government. The government also gives aid directly to individuals. This is the second type of government programme designed to reduce regional disparity.

Direct aid comes to Canadians in many ways. Family allowance cheques are one form of aid. Unemployment insurance is another. In both of these programmes, money is sent directly to the individual. Old-age pensions are another example of direct government aid. Fig. 2-8 shows how much money each region receives on a *per capita* basis. (This is the amount given per person in the region.)

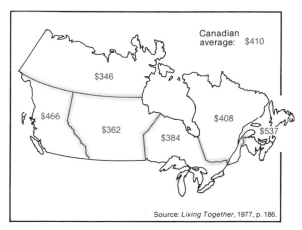

Source: *Living Together*, 1977, p. 186.

**Fig. 2-8 Federal transfer payments to individuals, 1974-75**

These government payments help narrow the gap between the rich and the less wealthy. Regions that are less prosperous receive more aid. This helps reduce disparity. The economic differences between wealthy and less wealthy regions still exist.

But these programmes have reduced differences in wealth by about 20%.

### Overall effect of solutions to regional disparity

The government has created many programmes aimed at solving the problem of regional disparity. What has been the overall effect of these programmes? Have regional disparities ceased because of government efforts? The answer is no. The Economic Council of Canada says that the results of the programmes are disappointing.

Regional disparities have been reduced slightly. However progress is slow. Unemployment is still high in many regions, and pockets of very low income still exist. Huge amounts of time and money have been spent to close the economic gap.

There is a brighter side to the picture. Government efforts have prevented matters from becoming worse. Living costs and unemployment would be higher without the government's programmes. The government is therefore meeting the challenge with some success. Regional disparity is a problem that will continue to demand attention in the future. New solutions will be needed.

### The future: Can we succeed?

What can we do in the future to reduce regional disparity? Here are some suggestions from the Economic Council.

1. Try to control government spending in all programmes. Each dollar used to fight regional disparity must be well spent.
2. Allow people in the different regions to have more of a say in government programmes. People living in an area know its needs and problems well. Informed citizens are more likely to make good decisions than are people in Ottawa.
3. Provide more help to keep young people in school. Create programmes that allow older people to upgrade their skills. Regions benefit from highly trained and skilled workers.

4. Try to keep city populations at the level of 1.5 million. Cities larger than this become less efficient, and money is wasted. Montreal and Toronto are huge cities in which the benefits from growth are decreasing. One solution to the problem is to encourage **satellite cities** near the larger ones.

5. Allow private business to have more say as to ways of increasing production. Ask trade associations and unions how they can increase output per person.

*In general, people in Canada complain about regional disparity. They think that standards should be the same all over the country. Not everyone feels this way, though. In the article below, a person from PEI expresses a different view.*

"What is good for North America is good for PEI."

This is the way a lot of Islanders (people from PEI) think today. We are told that life in this province should be more like life in the rest of Canada. We assume that PEI should bring itself in line with national standards. This means, for example, that our average wage should equal Canada's average wage. Our system of education should follow national trends.

Islanders should be careful. It is not wise to accept this point of view without thinking. Islanders should understand what it means to follow national standards.

Consider the issue of income. The average Islander makes less than the average Canadian living in Toronto, or even Halifax. Many Islanders thus believe that PEI is a poor "have-not" region. They want wages to increase, so that PEI meets the national standard. Islanders who want to meet these standards, however, cannot stop at wages. They will have to adopt national standards in other areas, too. Pollution is one example. Do Islanders want to meet national standards of pollution? Or think about traffic jams. It will be a long time before PEI can match the traffic snarls found in other regions.

Islanders may want to reach the national average wage. But, in general, higher wages are found in urban-industrial societies. Islanders will also have to accept the problems that come with this society. It would be nice to get national wages without the problems. But life does not work that way.

PEI is still, in general, a farming society. We are not yet industrialized. We must stop and think about whether or not we want to develop like the rest of the country. We must think about the problems that could result. We still have time to change our minds. There are still options open to us.

*Adapted from H. Bagole and D. Weale,* Cornelius Howatt: Superstar, *1973.*

**Rural PEI. How would this picture change if PEI becomes industrialize**

## Conclusion

Since Confederation, Canada has been faced with regional disparity. Even today, large numbers of Canadians live near or under the poverty line. Many other Canadians have most of their needs and wants met. Governments have done much to reduce economic differences among regions. However it is a difficult task, and progress is slow.

Many people have been questioning the fight against regional disparity. Governments encourage industry to locate in less wealthy regions. This creates jobs and raises income. But it also brings problems that are connected with industrial society. Are higher incomes worth the pollution, crowded conditions, and noise that industry can bring? Some people in less wealthy areas are asking themselves questions like this. What do you think?

**READING BETTER**

1. Reread the causes of regional disparity. Go over the main ideas in each paragraph. Then, make up four newspaper headlines that are based on some of these ideas. Here is an example: Food Prices in Shield Region High — Lack of Good Farm Land to Blame.

**ORGANIZING BETTER**

1. Diagrams are a good way of organizing information. Draw a circular diagram to show the various solutions to regional disparity. Use the model that is given here.

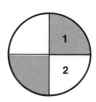

**USING YOUR KNOWLEDGE**

1. Imagine you are a reporter. You are to interview one of the three people who spoke about regional disparity. (Choose from the woman in Tuelon, the student, or the mayor.) You want to find out how regional disparity affects the person. Prepare the questions you will ask in the interview. Include such issues as the effect of government programmes.

**SOLVING PROBLEMS**

1. Go over the section on future solutions to regional disparities. Can you suggest two solutions that are not listed in the text?

**TAKING A STAND**

1. In this exercise you are asked to make some decisions in problem situations.
Problem 1: Regional versus national wealth
Jane A. owns a manufacturing plant in Ontario. Her profits are high. She employs about a hundred people. The plant is close to places where goods can be sold. Jane is thinking about moving her business to a less wealthy region. Through the DREE programme, she will receive help to make the move.

What are some things Jane should think about before moving? What do you think she should do?

Problem 2: Personal versus regional loyalty
Mike M. wants to move to a wealthier part of the country. He will be able to get a better job there. Hospital and other services are better. If Mike moves, he will be leaving the small town in which he grew up. His family has lived there for 175 years. Should Mike stay where he is, or move?

**RESEARCHING**

1. Find more information on one of the following topics and write a one or two page report on it.
   a) Transportation costs in the Atlantic
   b) DREE
   c) Equalization payments

## GLOSSARY

**Combine.** A piece of farm machinery that harvests grain.

**Depression.** A period of very poor economic conditions during the 1930s. Business activity slacked off, many people were jobless, and prices and wages fell.

**General trends.** Patterns of actions or events.

**Human resources.** The number and quality of people available for work in a certain area or nation.

**Retail sales.** Articles that are sold from a store.

**Satellite cities.** Small cities that are found near large cities. They are separate from the large cities, but still keep close ties with it. Governments may encourage people and businesses to move to these cities. They do this in order to help stop the growth of the large city.

**Standard of living.** A measurement of life style that looks at how many necessities and luxuries people have.

# UNIT TWO
# You and your government

In the first unit we learned that Canada is a land of diverse regions. It is increasingly an urban, highly industrialized nation. Yet there are huge, sparsely populated spaces; many of these areas will be sources of wealth in the future.

Across this huge land are spread twenty-three million Canadians. All of us are in need of certain services. Often these services can be best supplied by groups of people acting together. This is where government comes in. Our governments are groups of people who are acting together to fulfill common needs. Our type of government reflects the nature of our country and its people. Canadian government has evolved as a result of our diverse regions, cultural backgrounds, and experiences in history.

This unit explores several different aspects of government in Canada. The first chapter deals with the structure of the Canadian governmental system. In the second chapter we examine the Canadian economy. Governments at all levels play an active role in the economic lives of Canadians. They offer services that help Canadians meet economic problems. We will discover what services are offered, and how governments get the money to finance them.

The last chapter in the unit discusses Canada's legal system. We will look at the ways in which government protects Canadians, and keeps order in the land. The topic of human rights and responsibilities will also be studied.

Here are some questions that this unit attempts to answer.

**1** How does Canada's system of government work?

**2** What is Canada's economic system, and what role does government play in it?

**3** How does Canada's legal system work? What are the rights and responsibilities of Canadians?

**4** How large a role should governments play in the lives of Canadians?

# 1/Government structure, power, voters and politicians

## Contents

### Introduction

Government can be described as the political organization or system that influences people's actions and conduct. Can any Canadians say that government does not somehow affect their lives? Probably not. For this reason alone, then, it becomes important to know how government works. In Canada, people are also free to choose their government. Canadians elect individuals to represent them in government. Thus Canadians have a say in the policies and decisions that will affect them in the future. This is another reason for knowing about government.

This chapter will help you understand Canada's system of government. The following questions will be discussed:

1. **Why do we need government?**
2. **What kind of government does Canada have?**
3. **How is Canada's system of government set up?**
4. **How can individuals participate in and influence government in Canada?**

### The need for government and laws

To better understand the need for laws and government, let us look at men and women in a special situation. It is the distant future. A nuclear war has destroyed most of civilization. Deep beneath the surface of the earth a group of survivors live in a bomb shelter. They have set up a basic form of government and decided on the rules they will live by. They have also selected leaders.

Deadly nuclear radiation has poisoned the atmosphere of the world above. The survivors must stay below ground until the danger passes. In their underground shelter, they have the bare necessities of life. The survivors have limited food supplies, so food is strictly rationed. As the story begins, a guard in the shelter has caught a man stealing food.

---

### Bomb shelter

"You will stay here," said the guard, "until the judges come to pass sentence. Sit where you are. I want no trouble with you." The prisoner, whose name was Bill, was perspiring. He had stolen food and had been given a fair trial. He awaited sentencing from Irma, Janice, and George. Bill was afraid.

It had been three weeks since the explosion above ground. One hundred people had entered the bomb shelter just before the explosion. Contact with the outside world—or what remained of it—would be fatal. The people in the shelter were survivors and had to create their own society.

Just then the three judges came around the hallway to where Bill and the guard were stationed. Janice, the chief judge, looked at the prisoner. "Food is essential. By stealing it you endangered our lives, for the food must last us at least a year. You must pay the penalty for your crime, and the penalty is expulsion. That is one of the laws we decided on when we first moved down here. And everyone agreed to it—including you!"

"It's unfair," shouted Bill. "I've got a right to live. All of you, the majority, are ganging up on me. I said this at my trial and I'll say it again. It's unfair and it's undemocratic."

"You are a selfish man," replied George, the other judge. "Don't talk to us of your rights. You stole from the group. You agreed to live by our laws. You may have rights but so does society. You have shown yourself to be an enemy of our society, and now you must pay the penalty."

At this point, Janice motioned to the guard. "As chief judge," Janice said, "I hereby order you to leave our shelter. Mike will open the door. You will walk out of here. If you don't, the guards will force you out."

Bill turned to his left, as if looking for an escape. There was no escape. The shelter was small. At the end of the corridor was the steel door that led to the world above. Bill eyed the door as it was being opened for him. He hesitated a moment and then departed.

**Test your understanding of basic facts of the story "Bomb shelter". These questions require short answers.**

1. What was one of the first things that the survivors did when they moved into the shelter?
2. What was Bill's crime?
3. Why did Bill think his sentence was unfair?
4. How had Bill violated the rights of the majority in the shelter?
5. Why would expulsion from the shelter almost certainly lead to death?

**USING YOUR KNOWLEDGE**

1. Pretend that your class is cut off from the rest of the world. You have plenty of food and water, but no contact with anyone else. Imagine what problems your class would face and decide how these problems could be solved.

**TAKING A STAND**

1. A number of important issues about the need for government and law arise in "Bomb shelter". Where do you stand on the following issues?
   a) Should Bill have been punished for stealing food?
   b) Were the majority of the survivors really "ganging up" on Bill and depriving him of his individual rights? Or did they have a right to punish Bill?
   c) Should Bill have been given a second chance?

### The need for government

In moments of frustration people have often asked, "Why do we need a government?" Certainly many Canadians have come to feel that government plays too big a role in their lives. But the need for government seems to be basic. We could of course live in complete natural freedom—a world with no laws, no government. But what then would protect us from attack or help us to find a thief?

Canadian governments make laws to bring order to life. They make decisions about important issues, such as how scarce resources will be used. These decisions and laws are made peacefully. Government in Canada does not use bloodshed to operate.

Rather, it works with Canadians in a spirit of co-operation.

What governments do:

> Make decisions peacefully.
> Provide security from attack.
> Protect lives and property.
> Decide how to use scarce resources.
> Provide other services such as health care, education, etc.
> Establish and negotiate arrangements (e.g. trade, military) with other countries and governments.

### The powers of government

Governments in Canada have a great deal of power over citizens' lives. This means that they influence what Canadians do. Why does government have this power? In Canada, governments do not seize power and keep it by force. Rather, the people agree to give power to the government and obey its laws. In return, government offers safety and security. Governments therefore have power because Canadians have made a commitment to co-operation. If they are no longer satisfied with their governments, the people in Canada have the chance to change them peacefully.

In Canada the powers of government are usually divided into three parts, depending on the function of each part.

*Legislative powers:*

This is the power to make and approve laws. **Parliament** in Ottawa, your provincial legislature, and your town or city council are examples of groups that have legislative powers.

*Executive powers:*

This is the power to carry out the laws. The Cabinet is the name given to the group of politicians in Parliament who oversee the enforcing of laws.

*Judicial powers:*

Judicial power lies with the courts. They

**The Parliament Buildings, Ot**
**The round structure in the foreground is the Parliamentary Lib**

Reprinted by permission of the Hon. James Jerome, Speaker of the House of Con
W.J.L. C

decide who has broken laws and what penalties should be given.

## What kind of government do we have in Canada?

The governmental system in Canada is complex. Because of the way it is set up, and the way it functions, our government can be described in four ways. Government in Canada is
1. a constitutional monarchy
2. a federal system
3. a representative democracy
4. a party system

A look at these different aspects of the Canadian government will give us a better insight into its nature.

### 1. Constitutional monarchy

In theory, Canada is governed by a monarch (king or queen). Our monarch is also the monarch of the United Kingdom of Great Britain and Ireland; this is evidence of our British heritage. It has been a long time, however, since monarchs actually ruled by themselves in Canada. Today, Canadians are governed by Parliament and by provincial legislatures. Monarchs and Parliament have come to govern according to rules developed over the centuries. These rules limit the power of the monarch and describe how our Parliaments (federal and provincial) rule. Such a body of rules is called a constitution.

*The constitution and parliamentary government*

In Canada there are two kinds of constitution: written and unwritten. The written constitution is the British North America Act (BNA Act). It was passed by the British Parliament in 1867, legally creating the country Canada. The BNA Act describes the powers, parts and functions of our own Parliament and provincial legislatures.

There are other rules about the parts and functions of Parliament and provincial legislatures. These are found in laws and in traditions from the past. They are called the unwritten constitution.

Canadian governments must operate according to the rules of the BNA Act and the unwritten constitution. These rules set down the power of the **monarch** in Canada. Over the years this power has become largely symbolic. The monarch is the **head of state** in Canada, and all laws are passed in the monarch's name. Our monarch, as we know, is British.

**Queen Elizabeth II. The Queen is warmly welcomed whenever she visits Canada.**

The **Governor General** represents the monarch in Canada. The actual running of government, though, is not left to the Governor General. The people of Canada elect representatives to government, who then govern us. The Governor General takes the advice of these elected representatives.

*The Governor General*
According to the BNA Act, the Governor General is appointed by the King or Queen. Until 1952, British **aristocrats** were sent to Canada to represent the monarch. Since then, however, the Canadian government has recommended Canadians for the position. The Queen has then appointed the recommended persons.

What are the functions of the Governor General? Governors General open Parliament by reading the Speech from the Throne. This speech outlines the government's plans for that session of Parliament. Governors General also sign bills into law and appoint important officials, greet foreign leaders visiting Canada, and give out awards and medals. In general, the role of the Governor General is formal and symbolic.

Recent Governors General of Canada (*Canadian):

| | |
|---|---|
| 1940-1946 | Earl of Athlone |
| 1946-1952 | Viscount Alexander of Tunis |
| 1952-1959 | Vincent Massey* |
| 1959-1967 | General Georges Vanier* |
| 1967-1973 | Roland Michener* |
| 1973-1979 | Jules Leger* |
| 1979- | Edward Schreyer* |

2. Federal system of government

Canada is the second largest country in the world. Twenty-three million people are spread throughout the diverse regions of this huge area. The regions have different cultural and economic needs. For example, the Atlantic provinces are concerned about the sea. On the other hand, Saskatchewan, which has no sea coast, is much less concerned about the sea. The people in these regions are different, but yet they are the same in many ways. They need security from attack and protection of property and trade. They wish to co-operate to use natural resources and to improve trade and commerce.

**Queen Elizabeth II**

"By the Grace of God Queen of the United Kingdom, Canada, and Her other Realms and territories."

Eldest daughter of King George VI, Queen Elizabeth became monarch in 1952. As monarch of Canada she has opened Parliament, delivered speeches, visited towns, given out awards, and performed other duties.

The Queen's oldest son is Prince Charles, Prince of Wales. When the Queen dies, Charles will become King of the United Kingdom and Canada.

**OUR ROYAL HERITAGE**

Canada's royal heritage is evident in our society in several ways. Because the Queen is the official head of the country (head of state), her picture appears on stamps and currency (money). Military units in Canada show our royal heritage in their names. The Queen's Own Rifles of Canada and the Royal Regiment of Canada are two examples of this. The names of many other organizations and events also reflect our royal heritage: The Royal Canadian Mounted Police, the Queen's Plate.

## Issues in Canadian government:
## Is the role of the Governor General outdated in a modern democracy?

(A fictional case)

Retired general Julian Meister sat in his living room, listening to his wife and daughter discuss his future. Earlier that day the prime minister had suggested that Meister become Governor General. If Meister accepted the position, the PM would tell the Queen to announce the appointment. Meister was pleased by the offer, but did not know what to do. He went home and asked his family to present the pros and cons of accepting the offer.

Mrs. Meister said, "The job is really nothing. Governors General today have no real power. They can't make important decisions. If you take the job, the prime minister will tell you what to do. It is the PM's right to tell you what must be done. You would be better, Julian, to accept that job offer as President of Canadian Pacific Railway. Then you would be able to run the show. You would be in charge. Being Governor General is an honour, but it doesn't mean anything else. Actually, it must be very boring, giving out medals and reading speeches."

Young Carla did not agree. "Dad, as Governor General, you would be the highest official in Canada. You would be the head of state and Commander-in-Chief of the Armed Forces. Also, you would travel across Canada and act as official host to foreign **dignitaries** visiting Canada. And don't forget that your name would appear forever in Canadian history. But more important, the Governor General has the final say in government. Nothing would become law without your signature. I know you're expected to sign everything legally passed by Parliament. But if a special case or crisis came up, you would be the last safety valve. That's an important job. Making money as a company president is not as important."

What should General Meister do? Explain your answer.

## Federal: A word with two meanings

The term *federal* refers to a type of government where powers are divided between a central government and provincial governments. In Canada, we have a central government, which is located in Ottawa. There are also ten provincial governments. The word *federal* is also used in Canada to describe the *central government*, which has authority over all of Canada.

To provide for the needs of the whole country and for the needs of the different regions, a federal system was created in 1867. The central Parliament (also called the federal Parliament) answers the needs of the country. Ten provincial Parliaments (often called legislatures) look after re-gional needs. The BNA Act sets down the separate powers of each type of government.

The federal Parliament may make laws about certain issues for the whole of Canada. Among these issues are defence, money, postal service, and criminal law. The provinces may not make laws about these things. Each province passes its own laws in such areas as education or municipal government. The federal government may not pass laws on these matters. Shared federal and provincial powers lie in the area of agriculture, immigration, and certain taxes.

### The third level of government

We have just seen two levels of government, federal and provincial. There is also a third level. Provinces have created local, or municipal governments and boards of education. This third level of government is the one that has the most direct contact with citizens. The third level most often provides police protection, fire protection, water supplies, sewage treatment, garbage collection, schools, and other necessities of modern life.

3. Representative democracy

Canada is a democracy. This means government by the people. Thus, our constitution has combined rule by a monarch and rule by the people. The monarch is head of state and government is carried out in the monarch's name. The people choose the government that will act in the monarch's name.

**Terms associated with a representative democracy**

| | Name given to representative | Common term used for electoral district |
|---|---|---|
| Federal | Member of Parliament (MP) | Constituency or riding |
| Provincial | Member of Legislative Assembly (MLA) or Member of Provincial Parliament (MPP) In Quebec—Member of National Assembly (MNA) | Constituency or riding |
| Local | Councillor Alderperson Controller | Ward or district |

**The federal Parliament makes laws about issues such as postal service.**

**The House of Commons, Ottawa.**

Canada has representative democracy. In a true democracy, each citizen votes on every law that is proposed. Thus government by the people really exists. In "Bomb shelter", this true democracy was possible because there were so few people in the society. However, in a large country like Canada such direct democracy is generally impossible. How do you arrange to get millions of people to vote on every law? How would people with busy lives find time to keep informed about every issue? Because of such problems, we elect representatives to do the law-making for us. Our elected representatives to the federal Parliament meet in the **House of Commons.** They are called Members of Parliament (MPs).

Provincial representatives meet in the legislature or provincial Parliament. Their title is Member of the Legislative Assembly (MLA) or Member of Provincial Parliament (MPP). In Quebec the legislature is called the National Assembly. MNA stands for Member of the National Assembly.

Our elected representatives are responsible to the voters for what they decide to do. Thus, if voters are unhappy with their representatives, they can choose new ones at the next election.

Each representative is elected from a certain area. These areas are called constituencies (or ridings) in the federal and provincial government systems. For example, Prince Edward Island had 32 provincial constituencies in 1974. Ontario's legislature in 1974 had 125 constituencies. In local government, the electoral areas are often called wards.

### 4. Party system of government

In Canada today, we also have a party system of government. Most people elected to federal, provincial, and occasionally local governments are members of a political party. A political party is a group of people with common beliefs and plans for a country, province, or town. The party asks us to vote for its **candidate** in each riding or ward. If enough candidates from the party are elected, it may have control of the government and then be able to bring in its own ideas.

The beliefs of parties in Canada change from time to time. However, at each election, parties do try to present the people with some ideas of their beliefs and plans. This statement of plans and beliefs is called the *party platform.*

Our major federal political parties are the Liberal party, the New Democratic party, the Progressive Conservative party, and the Social Credit party. Each has a platform that it presents to the voters. In an election, each hopes to gain control of the government. This process will be described in more detail elsewhere in the chapter.

### Summary

We have described four aspects of government in Canada. One, we have a federal system of government. Canadians have several governments, each having power in different areas of our lives. Two, these governments are democratic, giving Canadians control over decisions made. Three, at the same time the governments are part of a constitutional monarchy. In it the Queen, represented by the Governor General, acts as head of state. The constitution, of which the BNA Act is part, provides rules that governments must obey. Four,

political parties ask voters to give them control of government machinery.

### The federal government of Canada

The federal Parliament has authority over all of Canada. Section 91 of the BNA Act gives the federal government the right to pass laws in the following areas:

Regulation of trade and commerce
Taxation
Postal service
The census and statistics
Defence
Salaries and allowances of federal employees
Navigation and shipping
Marine hospitals
Fisheries
Currency and coins
Banking
Weights and measures
Patents and copyrights
Indians and Indian reservation lands
Citizenship
Marriage and divorce
Criminal law
Penitentiaries

**ORGANIZING BETTER**

1. **Make up a chart in your notebook under the title "Kinds of government in Canada". Draw columns with the following headings:**
   **Constitutional monarchy**
   **Federal system of government**
   **Representative democracy**
   **Party system of government**
   a) **For each heading, write down the major facts that a student should know.**
   b) **Compare your chart with other students' charts. Be sure you compile as many separate points as possible.**
   c) **Ask questions about any points that you do not understand.**

**RESEARCHING**

1. **Find out more about one of Canada's Governors General. Write a brief biography, telling of the person's background, and of duties performed while Governor General.**

The federal Parliament consists of two branches:
1. *Executive*
   Governor General
   Prime minister
   Cabinet

2. *Legislature*
   House of Commons
   **Senate**

## The executive

In the BNA Act, executive power lies with the Governor General, who represents the Queen. In theory the Governor General, with a group of advisors and officials called the Cabinet, carries on the day-to-day government. In reality, however, this is not the case. It is the prime minister and the Cabinet who actually run the daily affairs of the federal government.

According to the rules of our unwritten constitution, the Governor General asks the leader of the largest party in the House of Commons to form a Cabinet. Cabinet members are chosen from the members of the prime minister's party who have been elected to the House of Commons. Senators may be chosen, but they are not elected representatives of the people. They are not responsible to voters and therefore are seldom chosen in our modern democracy. The cabinet members take responsibility for certain parts of government operation.

### The prime minister

The prime minister (PM) plays several important roles in our government system.
1. The prime minister is the head of government. This means that the PM does the following:
   —chooses and changes cabinet members
   —tells the Governor General when to summon Parliament
   —calls for an election whenever the PM wants one
   —names new senators
   —names new judges, including those in the Supreme Court of Canada
   —names senior **public** servants to government departments
   —leads the Cabinet and influences its decisions
   —decides what government business will go before the House of Commons and when it will be dealt with
   —speaks on behalf of the Cabinet in Parliament and in public
   —provides the Governor General with information about government operations, prepares the Speech from the Throne.

2. The prime minister is a national leader. Therefore, the PM
   —speaks on behalf of all Canadians at international meetings
   —speaks to Canadians and explains national concerns and goals
   —works with provincial prime ministers
   —represents Canada while on trips abroad
   —with the Governor General, greets foreign dignitaries visiting Canada
   —often opens new factories, schools, and hospitals.

3. The prime minister is a party leader. This means that the PM
   —tries to base government decisions on the party platform
   —supports party members seeking election
   —acts as a national spokesperson for the party
   —travels across Canada on behalf of the party, speaking and explaining party ideas
   —leads the party **caucus** in Parliament
   —gives out **patronage** (government jobs or favours to party members). The PM often rewards faithful party members by appointing them to vacant Senate seats.

The prime minister's job is complex and difficult. To help out, a special group of aides, the Prime Minister's Office (PMO), works directly for the prime minister.

94

### Checking the power of the prime minister

The prime minister is obviously very powerful. What is there to prevent a corrupt or sick person from abusing that power? There are several "checks" on the prime minister. The Cabinet, of course, may refuse to co-operate if the PM seems to be abusing power. The PM's party also may remove their leader. Parliament (including the PM's party) may also refuse to approve of abusive acts. It can do this by voting against the PM's proposals. Our free **media** let Canadians know what the prime minister is doing. This too is a check. The Governor General is perhaps the greatest check. In an emergency, the Governor General can refuse to do as the prime minister directs. The Governor General can even fire the PM. Thus, the prime minister is powerful, but this power is held in check.

### The Cabinet

The prime minister generally chooses the Cabinet from among those fellow party members already sitting in the House of Commons. The prime minister must try to choose people who are good leaders. The PM also tries to have representatives of all regions of Canada in the Cabinet. In addition, cabinet members should reflect some of the cultural groups in Canada. This task of choosing a Cabinet is obviously difficult, but worth the effort. The result should be a Cabinet that people will feel represents and understands all of Canada.

### The Cabinet as executive

After they are chosen, cabinet members are sworn into office by the Governor General. Each cabinet member is usually made responsible for a department of government. The minister is head of the department. The minister makes sure that the department does its job well. The minister does the following:
—presents the department budget to Parliament
—watches over the department budget
—asks for the advice of department members on problems before the Cabinet

**Organization of the Department of National Defence**

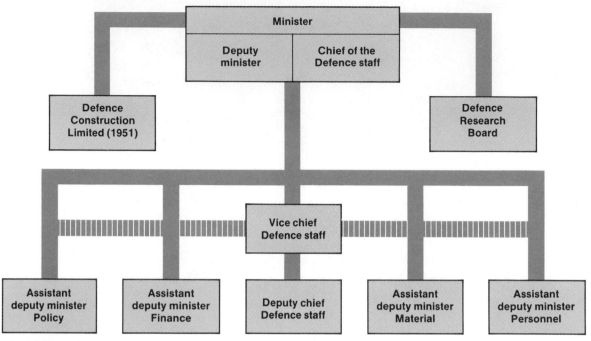

Fig. 1-1 Executive branch: The cabinet minister is the head of a government department

A cabinet meeting. Prime Minister Lester B. Pearson chairs a cabinet meeting in 1963.

—asks department members to draw up new laws to send to Parliament

—speaks for the department in Parliament and in public

—assumes responsibility for the actions of the department.

The cabinet members meet together under the leadership of the prime minister. They discuss all important decisions that the government must make. They decide what proposed laws (bills) to ask the legislative branch to approve. Cabinet members assume responsibility for the actions of the government. They support their leader, the prime minister. A cabinet member is expected to accept decisions made by the cabinet members as a whole. A minister who disagrees with a cabinet decision is expected to accept it silently, or resign. This is so because the Cabinet must always appear unified and capable to Parliament and to the country. This encourages confidence in the government.

## Issues in Canadian government
## The prime minister considers an election

(A fictional case)

Prime Minister Duval's government had been in office for nearly four years. During those years his Cabinet had managed government affairs well. Now Duval faced the problem of when to call an election. Should he call an election very soon, or wait a few months.

The public opinion polls showed that the voters' support for Duval was steady. However some of the cabinet members were not popular. Duval thought that perhaps he should wait a few months and replace the unpopular ministers. That could mean more votes.

However, it was now autumn and the winter was going to be hard. Unemployment was expected to rise. Expert civil servants had also predicted another rise in oil prices and a decline in the value of the dollar. The government would get a lot of criticism over those things. If an election was held now these problems would not have any effect on the voters. What should the prime minister do?

*Cabinet responsibility*

The Cabinet is responsible to the House of Commons for what it does. Sometimes a majority in the Commons votes a lack of confidence in the Cabinet. In such a case, the entire Cabinet is expected to resign. Then the prime minister will probably call an election. It is possible for the Governor General to invite someone else (often the leader of the next largest party) to form a Cabinet. However, this is unlikely in today's democracy.

The Cabinet is also responsible to the people. Cabinet ministers are MPs. Thus they must face the people in an election.

*Some cabinet jobs*

*Minister of Finance:*
This person prepares the federal budget, and assumes a big role in managing our economy. The Minister of Finance recommends tax cuts or raises to the Cabinet and Parliament.

*Minister of National Defence:*
This person supervises the armed forces and meets with other NATO leaders on defence issues. This minister also presents the budget money requests of the armed forces to Parliament.

*President of the Treasury Board:*
This person supervises government spending. All proposed bills must be cleared by the Treasury Board, to see if there is money to support them.

QUICK QUIZ
Answer these questions true or false.
1. Criminal law is a responsibility of the federal Parliament.
2. The Post Office is not the responsibility of the federal Parliament.
3. The prime minister chooses a Cabinet only from among senators.
4. The Cabinet is responsible to the House of Commons.
5. The prime minister has many jobs to do. Two

of them are calling elections and giving out party patronage.
6. The prime minister also acts as a provincial leader.
7. The prime minister is very powerful. That power is checked by Parliament and the Governor General.
8. Cabinet ministers are not responsible for what their departments do.

## The public service

This is a group of permanent employees of the executive branch of government. Public servants are not chosen for their political beliefs. Many have to pass hard exams to get their jobs. These people carry out the laws. Public servants who work for a department of government may also advise the minister on government problems or give information. Thus, public servants collect taxes, inspect food, gather **statistics,** write details for new laws, represent Canada abroad, sail ships, deliver mail, and do thousands of other jobs that keep our federal government going.

Senior public servants come to know a great deal about their departments. Cabinet ministers sometimes rely on these experts so much that the public servants have a large say in deciding government policy.

## Checking the power of the executive

The Cabinet, supported by its public service, is very powerful. How can it be controlled? How are the rights of Canadians protected against a Cabinet that abuses its power? Here is a summary of the checks on Cabinet power.

1. *Elections.* A general election must be held at least every five years. Cabinet members, who are generally MPs, must seek re-election. The people of their constituency may reject them. The voters of Canada may also reject their party.
2. *House of Commons.* The Cabinet must keep the cdifidence of a majority of the Commons. Sometimes, in a **vote of non-confidence**, the majority votes against the Cabinet. If this happens, the Cabinet must resign.
3. The *Opposition.* In the House of Commons this group acts as a watch-dog on cabinet actions.
4. The *party.* The members of a political party may withdraw support from a Cabinet. This can leave the Cabinet without the support of average Canadians.
5. *Governor General.* The Governor General is the head of state and legally holds all executive power. The Governor General may fire all or part of a Cabinet that abuses power. Because we live in a democracy, this power of one person would probably be used only in an emergency. The Governor General would most likely allow more democratic checks to operate first.
6. The *media.* News reports constantly inform Canadians of the Cabinet's actions.

**ORGANIZING BETTER**
1. A summary chart will help you to understand the executive branch better.
   a) List the powers and jobs of the following:
      the prime minister
      the Cabinet
      the public service
   b) Beside these, list the ways in which their powers are checked.

**USING YOUR KNOWLEDGE**
1. Imagine that you are trying to explain Canadian government to a visitor from France. Describe the differences between the Governor General, prime minister, Cabinet, and public service.
   In your explanation be sure to include how the different members of the executive get their jobs.

**RESEARCHING**
1. In a *Canada Yearbook* or vertical file, find out who the present members of the federal Cabinet are. Also, find out which part of Canada

each comes from. This will tell you whether or not the Cabinet represents many regions of Canada. What other factors does the PM seem to take into account when choosing a Cabinet?

2. Find out more about the constitutional crisis of 1925-1926. Governor General Byng and Prime Minister Mackenzie King disputed the powers of the Governor General and the PM. This incident, known as the King-Byng Affair, is famous in Canadian history.

3. Read about the career of one of Canada's prime ministers. In your reading, look for examples of some of the prime minister's jobs that were described in this section.

## The legislative branch

The House of Commons and the Senate make up the legislative branch of the federal government. The legislative branch may make, change, or **repeal** (remove) laws. A proposal that the House of Commons and Senate consider making law is called a *bill*.

Commons. All other bills may be introduced in either the Senate or the Commons.

### The House of Commons

Elections for the House of Commons must

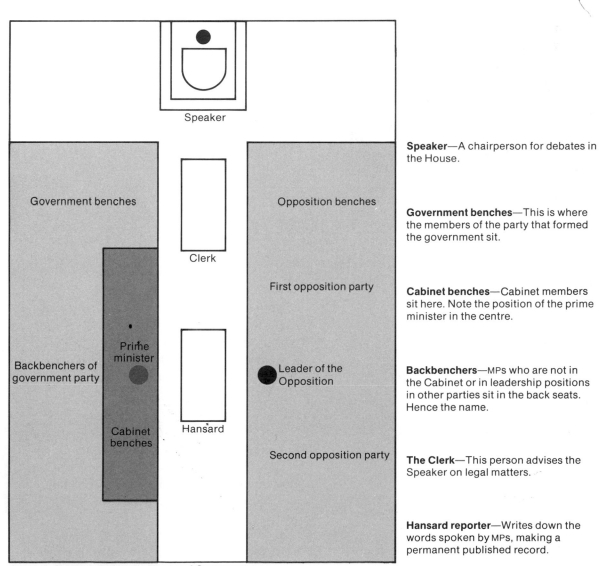

Speaker

Government benches

Clerk

Opposition benches

First opposition party

Prime minister

Leader of the Opposition

Backbenchers of government party

Cabinet benches

Hansard

Second opposition party

**Speaker**—A chairperson for debates in the House.

**Government benches**—This is where the members of the party that formed the government sit.

**Cabinet benches**—Cabinet members sit here. Note the position of the prime minister in the centre.

**Backbenchers**—MPs who are not in the Cabinet or in leadership positions in other parties sit in the back seats. Hence the name.

**The Clerk**—This person advises the Speaker on legal matters.

**Hansard reporter**—Writes down the words spoken by MPs, making a permanent published record.

**Fig. 1-2 Seating plan of the House of Commons**

The Speaker of the House of Commons. The pages and clerks in the picture help the Speaker run the affairs of the House of Commons.

occur every five years, unless the prime minister calls one sooner. Elected members of the House of Commons (MPs) each represent a constituency. Each MP is elected by that constituency. The total number of members in the Commons depends on the population of Canada. For example, in 1867 there were 181 members. In the late 1960s and until the first election after June 11, 1977, there were 264 members. For the first election following June 11, 1977, there were to be 282 members. This number will apply until the late 1980s.

Members of Parliament must be Canadian citizens. They have to be at least eighteen years old, and not otherwise disqualified by law. The House of Commons must meet at least once a year. Usually, however, there is enough business to require many months of hard work each year. Bills may be introduced into the House of Commons by any member. However, the business of governing Canada is very complex today. Therefore, the Cabinet usually controls most of the bills introduced.

*The Speaker*

The debates in the House of Commons are controlled by the Speaker. The Speaker is elected by all MPs. This person is in charge of the operation of the House, the bilingual translation services, House of Commons restaurants, and even the cleaning staff. The Speaker acts as both police and judge, keeping order and enforcing House of Commons rules.

The Senate

The Senate is the second part of the legislative branch. The Senate was originally created so that regions would be better represented in Parliament. It was also designed to provide a "sober (serious) second look" at bills passed by the House of Commons. The Senate can thus act as a check on the power of the House of

Commons. It does this by rejecting bills. However, the Senate may itself introduce bills, pass them, and send them to the Commons.

In theory, senators are appointed by the Governor General with the advice of the Cabinet. In reality, the prime minister chooses new senators whenever a vacancy occurs. Often the prime minister uses a Senate seat as a reward for faithful members of his own party. Senators must be Canadian citizens, at least thirty years old. They must live in the province for which they are appointed, and own at least $4 000 worth of property. Once they are appointed, senators may serve until age seventy-five.

There are a guaranteed number of senators for each region of Canada. Here is the breakdown:

| | |
|---|---|
| Ontario | 24 |
| Quebec | 24 |
| Atlantic provinces | 30 |
| Western provinces | 24 |
| Yukon | 1 |
| Northwest Territories | 1 |

The Senate is independent of the House of Commons. It appoints its own Speaker and runs its own affairs.

### The Senate under attack

We have seen that the Senate is not elected. Therefore it does not have to answer to the people for its actions. In our age of democracy this has sparked a lot of criticism. Also, the Senate tends to pass most bills exactly as they are sent by the Commons. It is thus criticized as being merely a **rubber stamp.** Ideas for reform of the Senate have emerged from time to time. Some critics have even suggested that it be eliminated because it plays no real role in modern government. These attacks have generally failed. Critics have not agreed on how to replace a body that represents regions and checks on the House of Commons power.

### How a bill becomes law

Where do ideas for bills come from? The following are possible sources:

The public service
The public
The Cabinet
A cabinet member or the prime minister
The media
A party platform
A senator
A member of Parliament

Most bills today come from the Cabinet. The ideas may come from the prime minister, a minister, or the public service. The following steps show how an idea becomes a bill, and how a bill becomes a law.

1. A cabinet minister has an idea on how to solve a problem.
2. This idea is explained at a cabinet meeting or to a cabinet committee. It is accepted or rejected.
3. If accepted, the idea is written up as a bill by lawyers and other experts in the public service.
4. A cabinet committee examines the bill in detail. The committee asks questions about the bill. Will it work? Will it be accepted in the House of Commons. How much money is needed? Is the money available?
5. The whole Cabinet accepts or rejects the bill.
6. The bill is explained to the government party caucus. Changes may be made, according to the caucus reaction. (Some bills are withdrawn because of a bad reaction from the caucus.)
7. Notice is given in the Commons that the bill will be introduced.
8. First reading. The cabinet member responsible for the bill explains its purpose. No debate.
9. Second reading. The cabinet minister responsible explains the bill in a major speech. The opposition asks questions,

**Fig. 1-3  How a bill becomes law**

debates, and criticizes. A vote is taken. The party caucus supports the minister's bill.

10. Committees of MPs then examine the bill in detail. The public may be able to give comments to the committees. Amendments (changes) may be made. A committee made up of the Whole House of Commons debates the bill again.
11. Third reading. Debate and vote. If passed, the bill goes to the Senate.
12. In the Senate, the bill goes through the same steps as it did in the Commons. Passage is usually much quicker. If an amendment is made, the bill returns to the Commons. If passed, the bill goes to the Governor General.
13. The bill is signed by the Governor General and thus given royal assent. The bill is now law.
14. The public service then puts the law into operation.

*The Opposition*

In the House of Commons, members sit according to which party they belong to. Opposite the government party (the largest party) sits Her Majesty's Loyal Opposition. The Opposition is made up of MPs from parties other than the one in power. The leader of the second-largest party in the House usually becomes the official Leader of the Opposition. Just as the prime minister speaks for the government, the Leader of the Opposition speaks for the largest opposition party. The whole Opposition plays the following roles:

1. Acts as a watch-dog over the government. The Opposition keeps an eye on what the government does. It speaks out when it thinks government actions are improper.
2. Checks the power of the government. Sometimes the Opposition feels that a bill is not good for the country. It can therefore try to slow down the passage of a government bill. The Opposition can use the delay time to alert voters and the news media.
3. Suggests amendments. The Opposition tries to improve bills or to change them so that they reflect Opposition ideas.
4. Offers a clear alternative for voters. By constantly criticizing government policy and suggesting new ideas, the Opposition offers voters an alternative for the next election.

Perhaps the Opposition best performs these roles during *Question Period*. This is a period of time set aside in the House of Commons so that MPs may ask the cabinet ministers questions. The ministers are required to answer (except when the answer is a state secret). During Question Period the Speaker gives the first questions to the Leader of the Opposition and the leaders of other smaller parties. This is the Opposition's chance to criticize the government and to demand answers. The news media attend and report the questions and answers to voters. In this way the Cabinet is held responsible for its actions.

The Opposition is, in effect, paid to criticize, but it does not unnecessarily hurt the functioning of government. Rather, this criticism is part of the governing process. Also, many bills are passed in Parliament with full Opposition agreement.

In sum, the House of Commons operates by majority rule, but the voice of the minority is free to speak, criticize, and offer alternatives.

**READING BETTER**
1. **How often must elections for the House of Commons be held?**
2. **What is a constituency?**
3. **Who can become a member of the House of Commons?**
4. **What does "MP" stand for, and who gets the title?**
5. **What is the job of the Speaker of the House?**
6. **How are senators chosen?**
7. **Why is the Senate often criticized?**

8. Where do ideas for bills come from?
9. What group controls the passage of a bill in the House of Commons?
10. What is the purpose of Question Period?

## RESEARCHING

1. Who is your MP? Write a profile of this person, and include the following information:
   Age
   Education
   Experience in government
   Party
   Support received in last election.
2. Which senators are from your province? A *Parliamentary Guide* or other library materials will contain this information. Write a profile on the senators.
3. If possible, watch a televised session of the House of Commons.

a) Identify the prime minister and Leader of the Opposition.
b) What sorts of issues are being debated or questioned?
c) Describe the atmosphere in the Commons. Is it relaxed? Formal? Serious?
d) How do MPs show their support for their party? How do they show that they are competing with MPs from other parties?
e) What does the Opposition ask about during Question Period?

## The judiciary

Trouble could arise if our executive branch were to interpret the laws it makes. In disputes between persons and the government, the executive might then rule most often in its own favour. For this reason we have courts that are independent of Parlia-

### Issues in Canadian government: The role of the MP

(A fictional case)

Burton Marsden faced the **deputy prime minister** and House Leader in her cluttered office. As a young MP, he realized that this woman was powerful in the party and in government. It was she who managed the flow of government business through the House of Commons. Burton was explaining why he opposed an important bill.

"This measure is supposed to protect our environment. But I can see that it leaves many loopholes for industrial polluters. Too many polluters will not be caught. I don't think the bill is tough enough. Neither do my constituents, who live in an industrial area. In fact I've received several thousand calls and letters against the bill. That's why I'm opposed to it."

"Burton, you know that in our position we need every vote," the House Leader rumbled. "The Cabinet has given the bill careful attention. The prime minister wants this bill passed quickly. The caucus has supported it. Your party needs, wants, and demands your vote. You know that when you accepted the party nomination you agreed to follow the party and its leadership. Now is the time to go along with the rest of the party."

Burton felt a terrible pressure on him. "But what can I do? If I follow the party I will be going against what my constituents want and what I want."

The House Leader interrupted. "And if you go against your party, you will risk losing its support in the next election. Think about that, Mr. Marsden, before you decide on your vote."

Burton Marsden was unsure. What should he do, follow the wishes of his constituents or the demands of his party?

## Issues in Canadian government:
## The role of the MP or MLA

(A fictional case)

Jeffrey had been an MP for nearly ten years. Today he sat in his office brooding over a problem that he would have to solve in a few minutes. A vote on abolishing the death penalty was about to take place in the House of Commons. MPs were, for this vote, free of party control. Jeffrey had thought that this freed him to vote as he pleased. But the fifteen thousand names on a petition in his office made him wonder. The petition was from Jeffrey's constituents. It asked him to vote for the death penalty. Yet Jeffrey himself was opposed to the death penalty. Now he wondered what to do. Should he act as the voice of the people and vote as they wished? Or should he follow his conscience and vote against capital punishment?

Some MPs claimed that they had been elected to do a job, as they saw fit. Constituents who did not like the job done could vote for someone else at the next election. Other MPs constantly consulted their voters, trying to represent their wishes. What should Jeffrey do?

ment. The courts can settle disputes fairly. It is illegal for politicians to try to influence judges' decisions. Judges are protected from Parliament; this helps to ensure a fair and honest court system.

The highest court in Canada is the Supreme Court. It interprets the meaning of laws, settles disputes between federal and provincial governments, and acts as a court of last appeal. Most courts that touch people's lives directly are operated by the provinces. More details on courts may be found in Chapter 3 of this unit.

### Summary

Canadians need governments. The federal government was created in 1867 to look after certain common needs of all Canadians. The three parts of the federal government each provide us with services. Each part of the system checks the powers of the other parts. Thus the democratic tradition in Canada is protected.

The majority rules in Parliament. However the constitution, the Opposition, and the judicial system ensure that minority rights are protected.

### Provincial and local governments
### Provincial government

The powers of provincial governments

When Canada was born in 1867 the provinces wished to keep certain powers and responsibilities. The provinces had by then developed different cultural backgrounds and different economies. The federal system recognizes these provincial differences. The BNA Act gives the provincial legislatures the right to pass laws in these areas:

Direct taxation (e.g., sales tax, income tax)
Hospitals
Marriage
Prisons
Courts
Local government
Education
Local public works (e.g., canals, roads)
All purely local matters

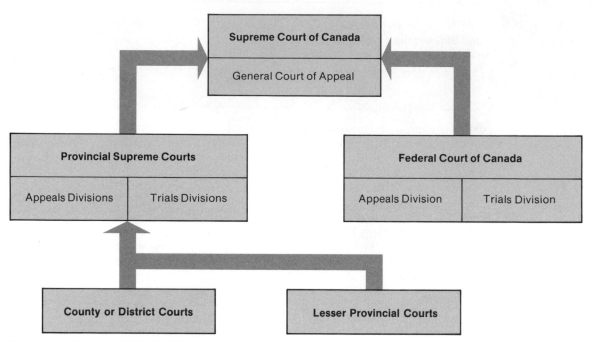

**Fig. 1-4 The Canadian judicial system**

Immigration, agriculture (shared with the federal Parliament).

In 1867, the Fathers of Confederation thought that the federal government would be more important than provincial governments. But times have changed. The provinces have assumed a new important place in our lives. Here are some examples of areas in which provincial governments are active today.

Transport: In 1867 people did not know how important cars and roads would become. The provinces have assumed power in this area. The provinces and the federal government must also co-operate on such things as airport locations, railway lines, and public transit.

Hospitals and welfare: Advances in medical science and medical care have made this area important. Provinces support our modern hospitals and help pay medical fees. Health and welfare is often the largest item in a provincial budget, as it is in federal budgets.

Local government: Cities spend money on housing, welfare, and many forms of recreation. These areas were not thought to be of government concern in 1867. Cities and towns also provide expensive essential services as sewage treatment, bus service, police, health inspection, fire fighting. The provinces are responsible for the overall structure of local government.

Education: Canadians today expect public education for all. Many people need and want special training and education beyond high school. Such expensive education was not provided in 1867!

Environment: Modern industries, unknown in 1867, may pollute and damage our environment. Along with the federal government, provinces have assumed a large role in protecting the environment. Regulations, inspections, and enforcement procedures cost a great deal of money.

The provinces have met the new challenges and have expanded their powers and importance in Canadian life.

Other changes since 1867

The Fathers of Confederation had intended the federal government to be stronger than the provincial governments. In fact, provincial laws could at one time be disallowed (rejected) by the federal Cabinet. Indeed between 1867 and 1887, 125 provincial acts were disallowed. This power still exists in the BNA Act. But today tradition requires that the provinces be left alone with their powers. Disputes between federal and provincial governments are now more likely to be resolved by negotiation.

In 1867 the federal government's control over the provinces was also reflected in the office of Lieutenant-Governor. This person plays the same role in provincial government as the Governor General plays in federal government. The Governor General appoints the Lieutenant-Governor, based on the advice of the prime minister. Thus the office of Lieutenant-Governor is a federal control on the provincial government. The Lieutenant-Governor can refuse to sign (reserve) provincial legislation until Ottawa is consulted. Today, however, the Lieutenant-Governor does not act as a federal agent of control. Again this shows how provincial power and independence

have grown since 1867. The federal powers of disallowance and control through the Lieutenant-Governor are generally unused. However they could, if necessary, act as a check on the power of the provincial governments.

### Finance

We have seen that provincial responsibilities have grown greatly since 1867. However, the provinces can pay for the programmes and services they offer only with direct taxes (e.g. sales tax, income tax). The federal government, which can pay its expenses with any kind of tax, is able to raise larger amounts of money. Thus the provinces and the federal government have to negotiate agreements for sharing tax money. The federal government today returns to the provinces much of the money it collects in taxes.

By co-operating, Canadians have created a system of sharing wealth. Canadians know that regional differences do exist. Yet they have also seen the need to provide a basic level of services all over Canada.

**A Federal-Provincial Conference. What topics are discussed at these meetings?**

Some provinces have been unable to provide basic services. They may have a small population or occasional economic problems. The federal government therefore uses tax money to redistribute wealth. Grants of money are given to certain provinces to ensure that government services are similar throughout Canada. In this way, Canadians have committed themselves to equality, sharing, and co-operation.

## The branches of provincial government

### The executive branch

Provincial governments are modelled on the federal government. The structure and function of the executive branch of both levels are similar. The following chart compares the names used in each level of government. Refer to the section on federal government for the function of each person or group.

| Provincial executive branch | Federal executive branch |
|---|---|
| Lieutenant-Governor | Governor General |
| Premier (Prime minister) | Prime minister |
| Cabinet | Cabinet |
| Civil service | Public service |

### The legislative branch

Today all provinces have just one chamber of legislature. There is no chamber that corresponds to the federal Senate. At one time most provinces did have such appointed chambers (usually called Legislative Councils), but they have been abolished.

All ten provincial legislatures (in Quebec called the National Assembly) are modelled on the House of Commons. They function in much the same way. Again, the premier and Cabinet are powerful, and political parties play an important role in government operation. Provincial bills become law in the same way that federal bills do. The only difference is that at the provincial level, no second legislative chamber exists. Once a bill is passed by a majority of the legislature and signed by the Lieutenant-Governor, it becomes law.

### The judiciary

Provincial courts exist to settle disputes and to try those charged with breaking laws. Each province has a Supreme Court.

The Legislature, Edmonton, Alberta.

However cases may be appealed even higher to the Supreme Court of Canada. All cases arising from the Criminal Code (federal law) are first tried in provincial courts. If necessary they then proceed through appeals to the Supreme Court of Canada.

As in the federal courts, provincial judges are independent of the other branches of government. They are protected from harassment by them. This helps to ensure a fair and honest court system.

*The Provincial court system:*
*Typical organization*

Supreme Court of Canada

Provincial Supreme Court

Court of Appeal

County Court

Lower courts
(Juvenile and Family Court, Magistrates' Court, Criminal Court, etc.)

## QUICK QUIZ

**Answer the following questions true or false.**
1. **Provincial governments have powers in the areas of education and local government.**
2. **The Fathers of Confederation wanted the provincial governments to be equal in importance to the federal government.**
3. **Provincial responsibilities have grown because our society has grown and new discoveries such as cars have been made.**
4. **Provincial legislative branches have a legislature and a council which is like the Senate.**
5. **The Lieutenant-Governor performs a job similar to that of the Governor General.**
6. **The provincial premier does the same job as the federal public service.**
7. **Bills are passed in the provincial legislature with only two readings.**
8. **Judges are independent of the executive and legislative branches of government.**

## ORGANIZING BETTER

1. **Be sure that you understand what each of the following does:**
   **Lieutenant-Governor**
   **Premier**
   **Cabinet**
   **Legislature**
   **Find the persons and groups in the federal system that correspond to the ones in the provincial system. Then use the federal government as a model and describe the duties of each of the above.**

## RESEARCHING

1. **Who is your representative in the provincial legislature? Write a profile of this person, giving the following information:**
   **Age**
   **Education**
   **Experience in government**
   **Party**
   **Support received in last election**
2. **Using a phone book, find the services offered by departments of your provincial government. Write down those which you or your family have used or been involved with in the last year. What do you discover?**
3. **Find the names and parties of Canada's ten provincial premiers.**

The crystal ball: Looking into the future of our federal system

No government system is perfect. This is true of the Canadian federal system. As society and people change, so too does the system of government and the rules by which it operates. The changes that have occurred since 1867 have put great strains on our system. Canadians have tried to revise the constitution on many occasions, so that the government may better solve new problems. However, the provinces and central government have seldom agreed upon a solution. The reform of the constitution has been slow and painful.

One problem has been when and how to bring the constitution to Canada. The BNA Act is a British law. Since 1931, Canadians have had the right to bring that law to Canada. We have been unable, however, to agree on a procedure for changing (amending) the constitution once it is home. In 1978, Pierre Elliott Trudeau promised to bring the BNA Act home, regardless of an agreement by the provinces. But this promise caused controversy. The following questions arose. Should any changes in the BNA Act affecting both federal and provincial governments need approval of all the concerned governments? Should we allow changes if seven of the eleven governments concerned approve? Should approval by three out of four regions (West, Ontario, Quebec, Atlantic provinces) be required?

### Regional demands

The provinces have grown very jealous of their power. They wish to strengthen it. Regional differences are used as the reasons for strengthening provincial powers. On the other hand, some Canadians believe that if the provinces are strengthened, they will be nearly independent of each other. Can we keep Canada together under such a system? The debate over such powers faces not just premiers and prime ministers, but all Canadians. The decisions that our national leaders make will affect how we live.

### Possible changes in powers

The provinces want and may get the following powers:

1. More say in immigration. It is now a shared power.
2. More say in economic issues such as tax cuts or increases, lending interest rates, trade, and tariffs. Provinces feel they should have this control because regional economies differ.
3. More control over resource development. (e.g., How much oil will be developed? What price will be charged? What exports will be made?) Provinces want more say in how their resources are used.
4. More say in appointments to the

Supreme Court of Canada. Provinces want to ensure that the court reflects provincial concerns. They want to be able to name new judges to the Supreme Court.
5. More say in the federal government. The role of the Senate could be changed so that it helps protect provincial concerns. Provinces suggest that perhaps each province could elect or appoint senators itself. Perhaps the Senate could have more say in what bills are made law. Or perhaps the Senate should be replaced by another body that better represents the provinces.

The future of our governmental system requires that these problems be solved. The solutions are not simply the concern of experts in law. In a democracy all citizens may influence how their country will be run. What would you do to change and improve the federal government system in Canada?

### TAKING A STAND
1. Should the provinces be given increased powers to govern, while the power of the federal government is weakened? Give reasons for your answer.

### RESEARCHING
1. Conduct a poll. Ask people in your area the following questions:
   a) Is the federal government too remote from your life?
   b) Should the provinces have more powers and the federal government less?
   c) Will increased local or provincial powers weaken Canadian unity?

## Municipal government

Municipal government and tensions in Canada

Have you been to a shopping mall? Have you ever gone up on an elevator or looked out from the balcony of an apartment? If you have done any of these things, you have shared an experience with millions of other Canadians. A process called *urbanization* (the growth of cities and their services) has

**What problems do shopping centres like this one pose for local governments?**

John McQueen

introduced these and other experiences to Canadians. And it has caused problems for Canada's city and town councillors and mayors.

Urbanization puts strains on the third level of government we are going to examine, local or municipal government. A look at urbanization will help us understand these strains.

### The challenge of urbanization

About a hundred years ago, only one out of every ten Canadians lived in a city of over

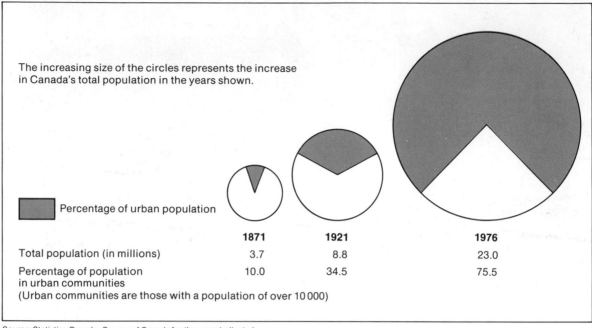

The increasing size of the circles represents the increase in Canada's total population in the years shown.

■ Percentage of urban population

| | 1871 | 1921 | 1976 |
|---|---|---|---|
| Total population (in millions) | 3.7 | 8.8 | 23.0 |
| Percentage of population in urban communities | 10.0 | 34.5 | 75.5 |

(Urban communities are those with a population of over 10 000)

Source: Statistics Canada, *Census of Canada* for the years indicated.

**Fig. 1-5  Canada: Growth of total population**

10 000 people. Canada was mainly a country of towns, villages, and farms. Local governments provided only a few services, such as road maintenance and fire and police protection. Today our country is a land of cities and growing towns. About 75% of Canadians live in towns of over 10 000 people.

*Urbanization: More than people living closely together*

We've seen that more and more Canadians are living in cities and large towns. But urbanization means more than this. It also involves a special city or town life style. Parks, shopping malls, stores, and movie houses create this life style in part. But a lot of our urban life style comes from local government.

Some of the things provided by a typical **municipality** today include:

Fire protection
Sewers
Police protection
Public libraries
Parks
Golf and tennis clubs
Public swimming pools
Electricity
Water service
Ambulance service
Public transit (buses and streetcars)
Bookmobiles
Ice hockey arenas
Senior citizens' homes
Animal and pet control
Snow removal

The structure and form of municipal government

The simplest form of local government is the town council, with councillors selected from wards. Over them is a mayor, who is responsible for the town government as a whole, and for the executive branch. A few officials such as the police chief and town clerk might be full-time or part-time employees of the town. As local government has grown, however, councils have expanded. In a larger municipality, other government officials may be executives in

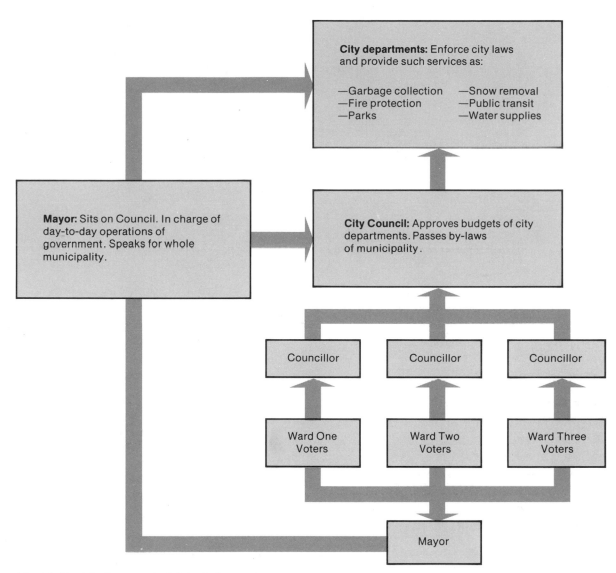

**Fig. 1-6 Municipal government: A typical example**

charge of such departments as planning boards and parks and recreation.

The municipal council proposes, debates, and passes local laws, called **by-laws.** Ideas for by-laws may come from councillors, the mayor, town officials, the media, or voters. Once they are passed by council, by-laws are carried out by the mayor and town officials. Offences against by-laws are tried by the lower courts of the provincial judicial system.

The town council also approves of a budget and sets local property tax rates.

Money raised from this source pays for government services and operations.

*Metropolitan government*

Small cities located near each other often have problems providing police, welfare, and housing services. However, by uniting they are able to offer cheaper, more efficient service over the whole area. Thus the idea of **metropolitan government** is born. This new government supplies certain common services. At the same time the member municipalities keep some control

113

**Some terms associated with local government**

| Head of municipal government's executive is often called | Municipal government's legislative branch members |
|---|---|
| Mayor | Councillor |
| Reeve | Alderperson |
| Overseer | Controller |
| Chairperson | |
| Warden | |

Which terms are used in your local government?

over local affairs. The earliest form of metropolitan government occurred in the Toronto area in the early 1950s. Others have since been set up in Halifax, Montreal, Quebec City, Winnipeg, and other Canadian cities.

### Regional government

Regional government brings the benefits of metropolitan government to small towns and rural areas. It operates in much the same way as metropolitan government does. Several towns, villages, and townships will be combined under one government. The members retain some local authority.

### Problems of the municipality

As cities have grown, so have the challenges facing them. One problem has been the problem of paying for services. Since the end of World War II, municipalities have sought a way of generating more tax dollars. Their main source of income has been a tax on local property. This tax does not bring in enough to pay for all services. Grants of money from the provincial government are also needed.

### Boards of education

These form another type of local government. Across Canada, local governments control education to a certain degree.

There is also central control by the provincial government. The province sets courses and approves books. This provincial control helps to keep the quality of education uniform across the province. At the same time, local boards of education provide for local needs and interests. For example, they decide when and where to build or close down schools.

Boards of education have been kept separate from municipal governments. In general, this is to ensure that money collected for education will be used only for this purpose.

### Present and future challenges

The responsibilities of local government have been growing. Local governments want more power in our government system.

The services that local governments provide are expensive. Urban life has created new problems in health, welfare, traffic, and recreation. If these problems are to be met, more money is needed. People are asking for more and more services from local governments.

Just as the provinces are seeking more power from the federal government, so cities are seeking more power from provinces. They wish a greater power to

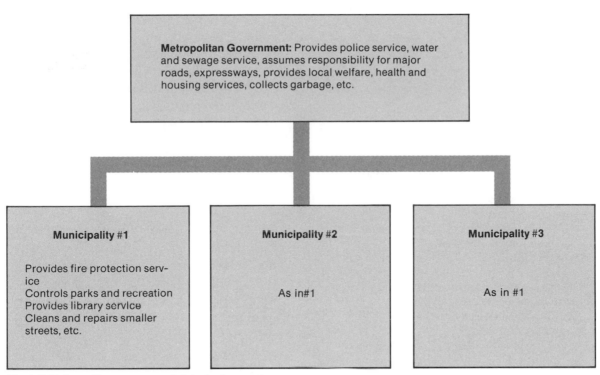

**Metropolitan Government:** Provides police service, water and sewage service, assumes responsibility for major roads, expressways, provides local welfare, health and housing services, collects garbage, etc.

**Municipality #1**

Provides fire protection service
Controls parks and recreation
Provides library service
Cleans and repairs smaller streets, etc.

**Municipality #2**

As in#1

**Municipality #3**

As in #1

**Fig. 1-7 Metropolitan government: A typical example**

## Issues in Canadian government:
## Board of education faces enrollment problem

(A fictional case)

The trustees of the Beaverland Board of Education met to make a final decision on the future of Louis St. Laurent Secondary School. This school was one of twelve under the Board's control. Built to provide education for 1 000 students, St. Laurent now had an enrollment of 350. Fewer students were expected next year. The Board's superintendents had studied the situation and recommended that St. Laurent be closed. Its students could be bused to nearby Memorial Collegiate, which was also under-enrolled. The superintendents said this would save the Board and taxpayers over one million dollars.

However parents and students from the St. Laurent area had petitioned to keep the school open. They argued that St. Laurent was their local school — it had educated tens of thousands of young people. Memorial was not theirs. Also they objected to the busing. Everybody had always walked to St. Laurent. Would students take part in Memorial's after-school activities when they had a bus to catch? The residents of the St. Laurent area threatened to campaign against trustees in the next election if they voted to close the school.

The trustees faced a decision. What would you do? Why?

tax. They want less control by the province. At the same time, cities and towns must co-operate with the provincial and federal governments to provide for the needs of Canadians.

READING BETTER
1. What role has urbanization played in creating problems for local government?
2. What role does the mayor play in local government?
3. How do local governments raise money to pay for their services?
4. Why have school boards been kept separate from municipal government?
5. What is the purpose of metropolitan government?
6. How is regional government similar to metropolitan government?

USING YOUR KNOWLEDGE
Here are a number of features of urbanization. Some or all of them may be found in your community. What challenges do you think they present to local government? For example, when cars were introduced to society, local governments had to consider rules on parking, traffic flow, road building, and other concerns.
Consider:
  Public transportation
  Shopping malls and plazas
  Apartment buildings
  Areas with very old, run-down homes
  Many people living in a small town area
  Desire by some to tear down homes and
    put up office buildings
  Recreational facilities

RESEARCHING
1. Find out the names of important people in your local government. Write profiles on the mayor and your councillor.
2. Use a phone book to find out what services are supplied by your local government. List those that you or your family have used in the past year. What do you discover?

## Conclusion: The structure and function of government in Canada

Canadians have created a federal system of government that has been meeting our needs for over a century. Yet in meeting our needs this system has undergone great strains. For the future we Canadians must consider how we want government structure and function to change. The changes that occur will affect the quality of our lives. The changes will reflect our values on democracy, regionalism, nationalism, and power. The changes cannot be left entirely to the experts, although we need their advice. Citizens of a democracy must decide for themselves the kind of government they want.

## Influencing your government

Canada is a democracy. Canadians choose their government and pay for its operation through taxes. They therefore have the right to try to change or influence government policy.

Citizens can influence government in several ways:
1. Voting in elections
2. Writing to MPs or to government departments
3. Joining interest or pressure groups
4. Supporting free information media
5. Joining a political party

Voting in elections is the basic way of influencing government in a democracy. With our votes we choose the people who represent us. We may vote for people who have made specific promises about what government should do. We may also refuse to return people to government if the promises they made have not been fulfilled.

Voting is basic to our democracy, yet elections do not take place very often. Most provincial elections are four years apart. Federal elections can be up to five years apart. Municipal elections tend to occur more frequently (as often as every year in some areas). Citizens often seek ways of influencing government between elections.

### To vote or not to vote

Many Canadians do not vote. In federal elections since 1950, an average of about 75% of eligible voters cast their ballots. In provincial elections the voter turnout varies from province to province, election to election. Often the provincial turnout is smaller than the federal one. Local elections often see very few voters at the polls. Sometimes less than 25% of eligible voters turn out.

Of course in our democracy citizens are as free not to vote as they are to vote. Some citizens even protest against government by not voting on purpose. However, governments spend much of our money and influence our lives greatly. Therefore, the concerned citizen will take voting seriously.

### Voting for the first time

Malcolm and Kimberley left school at 3:30 p.m. and headed for the polling station to vote. They had both turned eighteen just a while ago, so this was their first election. Both had studied the candidates, and knew for whom they wished to vote. But they did not know the actual process of voting, and so were a bit nervous.

At the polling place, Malcolm noted that there were no campaign signs or posters. This was to prevent keen campaigners from bothering voters. Only the candidates themselves were allowed to campaign on election day. And even they could not do so at the polling places.

Inside the polling place (in this case a church basement) there were signs to direct them to their polling station. Malcolm and Kimberley learned that each constituency is divided up into *polls*, or small subunits. In charge of each poll is a *deputy returning officer* (DRO) and a *poll clerk*. These two people work for the *returning officer* who is in charge of the overall voting procedures for the constituency. There are many polling places, DROs and poll clerks in a constituency.

Some weeks before election day the returning officer made a list of eligible voters. *Enumerators* had visited each home in the constituency to find the voters. Malcolm had been missed when the first list of voters was published. But Kim had told him he could get on the list by contacting the returning officer. Now the voters' list would be used to ensure that people voted only once. Kim and Malcolm identified themselves, and saw their names crossed off the voters' list. They then received their ballots. Behind a privacy screen they marked their ballots and folded them up. They handed their ballots to the DRO who placed them in the ballot box. Their voting was done.

"Nothing to it," said Malcolm.

"Yes, it is really easy. Now let's go home and watch the results on TV," said Kim.

When the polls closed, the DRO and the poll clerk counted the ballots. (Each candidate may appoint *scrutineers*, who watch the counting and witness its honesty.) A report from each poll was then sent to the returning officer, who kept a count for the whole constituency. Reporters used this information for their coverage of the election results.

*Election results: Federal*

After a general election, the party standings in the House of Commons will generally determine which party leader is called on by the Governor General to form a government. The following rules apply:

1. A party with a majority of members forms a government.
2. If no party has a majority, then the largest party may form the government. This would be called a *minority government*.
3. When there is no majority, two smaller parties may agree to combine. Such a **coalition** may then have a majority, or at least be the largest party. The Governor General may then call on the coalition to form a government.

**READING BETTER**

1. In your own words explain the roles of the following people in an election.
   a) Returning officer
   b) DRO
   c) Poll clerk
   d) Enumerator
   e) Scrutineer

**USING YOUR KNOWLEDGE**

1. Decide which party would likely form the government in the following federal general elections:

| 1957 | | 1958 | |
|---|---|---|---|
| Liberal | 105 | Liberal | 49 |
| PC[1] | 112 | PC | 208 |
| CCF[2] | 25 | CCF | 8 |
| Social Credit | 19 | Social Credit | 0 |
| Other | 4 | Other | 0 |
| | 265 | | 265 |

| 1963 | | 1974 | |
|---|---|---|---|
| Liberal | 129 | Liberal | 141 |
| PC | 95 | PC | 95 |
| NDP | 17 | NDP | 16 |
| Social Credit | 24 | Social Credit | 11 |
| Other | 0 | Other | 1 |
| | 265 | | 264 |

[1]PC = Progressive Conservative
[2]The Co-operative Commonwealth Federation (CCF) became the New Democratic Party (NDP) in 1961.

**TAKING A STAND**

1. Some places in Australia keep records of the people who have voted in elections. Those who do not vote are fined, unless they have a good reason (e.g. illness). Should such a system be started in Canada? Why or why not?

## A federal election

### Who can vote?

Canadian citizens who are at least eighteen years old and have lived in Canada for twelve months before the election.

### Who cannot vote?

— Officials in charge of the election itself
— The chief electoral officer, the assistant chief electoral officer, and the returning officer in each constituency
— Judges appointed by the federal government
— People in hospitals for the mentally ill
— People in jail
— People who have been found guilty of illegal election activities

**Discuss why those people listed above have been denied the right to vote in federal elections.**

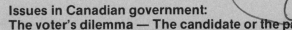

## Issues in Canadian government:
## The voter's dilemma — The candidate or the party?

Our electoral system and party politics pose a major problem to voters. The representative elected will of course be involved in the concerns of the constituency or ward. But the same representative must also be concerned with the affairs of an entire country, province, or city. What is good for a smaller area may be bad for the larger one.

Also, the voter knows that the party with a majority in the legislative branch will dominate that legislature. The voter may find that the local candidate for party X is not impressive. However party X's leader may be the best qualified to be prime minister or leader. What does the voter do? Vote for a poor candidate so that the party will win? Or elect the best candidate and leave the question of the next government open? There is no right answer to this dilemma. Voters themselves must decide.

### RESEARCHING

1. **Choose one person in your class to contact the clerk's office of your local government. This student is to find out what percentage of eligible voters actually voted in the last election. How do you account for the turnout?**

### Writing your MP; talking to public servants

Between elections Canadians can influence their government in many ways. They can write to their MPs with opinions, or they can request information or help. Canadians can also talk to public servants, who carry out the day-to-day business of government.

### Group action

Individual action is often slow. The voice of one may be lost among the voices of many. Canadians have thus often joined together to increase the strength of their voices. A collective voice can gain influence with government. Also, when groups support a free press and other media, their opinions, criticisms, and suggestions are given weight and importance.

### Pressure groups

Many groups have been formed by Canadians to put pressure on government. Canadians with similar needs, goals, or interests often form associations whose sole purpose is to influence government. Some groups raise money from their members. They hire experts to work for them, and open offices in Ottawa or provincial capitals. Other groups exist only for one goal. These groups disappear once the goal has been reached. Many local groups are run by interested volunteers. **Ratepayers associations,** for example, are run by volunteers who want to influence municipal government.

The highly organized, rich pressure groups spend money to be sure their messages are heard. Often they use the length of their membership list, or the importance of group members to impress government. Other groups organize letter-writing campaigns or petitions. Some hire lawyers and try to use the existing laws to start or stop government action. Groups like these have forced governments to control pollution, or move airports. Because of such groups, taxes for certain industries have been reduced, or parks have been created.

Pressure groups have been quite successful in influencing government. Some critics say, however, that their very success is dangerous to democracy. Does government listen too often to the well-organized minority interest group? Is the silent majority ignored amidst the demands of the interest groups? These questions face politicians and all citizens.

## USING YOUR KNOWLEDGE

1. Pressure groups are powerful and well-organized. They have great influence on government decisions. What should be done to ensure that their voices do not dominate the voices of the rest of the people? Consider the following solutions.
   a) Forbid pressure groups to give money to candidates in elections.
   b) Require all pressure groups to reveal their total membership.
   c) Give government tax money to all pressure groups. This will ensure that both rich and poor groups can operate.

## RESEARCHING

1. Find out about pressure groups in your area. What do they do? Whom do they represent? How much influence do they really have? The following are some national interest groups in Canada.
   National Farmers' Union
   Canadian Chamber of Commerce
   Canadian Labour Congress
   Canadian Medical Association
   Canadian Women's Clubs
   Canadian Catholic Conference
   Pollution Probe
   Canadian Civil Liberties Association

## Media

Newspapers, magazines, radio, and TV — these media inform us, as well as entertain us. They often act as "go-betweens", telling us what government is doing and telling government what people think. Our media are free to express criticism of the government. They are free to report on the mistakes and triumphs of government. Such freedom helps us to understand and influence our government. Indeed, in many cases the opinions or information given by reporters have caused government to change a plan or proposed law.

## TAKING A STAND

1. Governments often feel that certain information is secret or should be kept secret until a later date. For example, this may include the date of an election, the location of a new dam, or the amount of money to be spent on a new weapon. Sometimes the media discovers and reports these facts. Should the government have a right to stop such reports? Should there be government censorship? Why or why not?

## RESEARCHING

1. Examine your local newspaper and watch a news report on television.
   a) What news stories about government are being emphasized?
   b) Are the stories about the mistakes, failures, and problems of government, or about its successful plans or victories?
   c) Do the news reports express opinions about government? Do they provide opinions from more than one side of the issue? Do they make government leaders look foolish?
   (Note: In editorials news media do express opinions. News reports, however, are supposed to be factual and objective [neutral].)
   d) Is the media biased? Does it take sides or present only one point of view? Why or why not?

## Political parties

Political parties allow citizens to influence government. Political parties are open to all citizens who wish to join. Members may wish to become actively involved in election campaigns and fund-raising. Or they may simply wish to offer their support and thus add to the party's size. These members are not active in party activities.

*What the political party does*

1. Develops plans and goals that it wants government to follow.
2. Chooses candidates for elections. These candidates try to ensure that party goals are met.
3. Raises money for election campaigns. Individuals, groups, and businesses are asked for donations.

**A party leadership convention. What qualities do you think a political leader should have?**

4. Supports approved candidates with money, advertising, visiting politicians, and workers.
5. Conducts public opinion polls to find out what voters want and think.
6. Speaks to voters in all constituencies about party policies.
7. Chooses a party leader who could possibly become prime minister, premier, or mayor. (There are separate party organizations at each level of government.)
8. Provides services for voters: rides to polling places, information about voting and enumeration.

*The impact of parties on government*

Political parties are not mentioned in the BNA Act. However, they are now part of our political system. Laws about party finances and election behaviour have made them part of our "unwritten" constitution. The parties indeed are so powerful that they now control federal and provincial legislatures. Even in once **non-partisan** local government, parties are playing a bigger role. Parties use strong discipline, which keeps all elected members voting as a unit. Thus, a party with a majority of seats in a legislative branch controls that branch and the executive. The party's members are united in their party goals. They use their

A political campaign. What must candidates do to win votes?

majority to achieve those goals.

Parties are so powerful that few people without party support are elected to provincial or federal Parliament. "Independents" usually do not have enough money to pay for advertising, signs, and other aspects of modern election campaigns.

## The campaign

Election campaigns usually last about six weeks. There is no rule on their length. Some politicians in effect campaign all the time. They are trying to ensure victory at the next election. Once an official election date is announced, however, then the contest begins. Candidates try to inform voters of their qualifications and beliefs. Party platforms are explained. Through advertising, the policies of other parties are criticized. The media play a large role in the campaigns. They inform voters of debates, statements, rallies, and parades held by candidates and parties. The campaign becomes a massive attempt by candidates and parties to win votes. In the end it is the citizens, alone with a ballot and pencil, who decide the winner.

Campaign costs have become an issue of concern to many people. Some candidates have a lot of money to spend on their campaigns, while others do not. The following feature will explain the problem that arises.

### Election expenses

#### CANDIDATE A

This person received several donations from large corporations. Over $200 000 was received in total. This money was used to buy television time for catchy advertisements. Also, Candidate A used the money to send a full colour brochure to every voter in the constituency. In addition, large and expensive signs were purchased.

Candidate A was grateful to the corporations for their support. The candidate looked forward to their donations in future elections. However, Candidate A did not want the voters to know of this support. There was a chance that voters would misinterpret the support.

#### CANDIDATE B

This highly qualified person received no large donations from corporations. The candidate had no personal wealth. Candidate B relied on donations of a few dollars from supporters to buy signs and pay office expenses. Even then there was not enough money, so Candidate B arranged a loan from a bank. Even with the loan, TV advertisements were out of the question. Candidate B relied on visiting voters at home. Volunteers delivered one plain page of information to voters.

#### THE PROBLEM

Candidate B did have a chance of winning the election. However, experience has shown that Candidate A may have had a greater chance for victory. Expensive advertising often wins over many voters. This situation has been viewed by many critics as harmful in a democracy. They argue that money should not be what determines success in an election.

SOLUTIONS

Here are some solutions offered by these critics:
1. Limit campaign expenses to a certain amount of money per voter; for example, two dollars per voter.
2. Require a published list of all donations, including names of donors, before election day.
3. Forbid TV advertising.
4. Limit campaign donations to a certain figure. For example, a limit of $1 000 per donor could be set.
5. Forbid donations by corporations.
6. Use only government money for election expenses. For example, each candidate could be given an equal amount of money, say $10 000.

This type of control itself has been criticized. Why should voters not be free to donate their own money? Why should corporations be forbidden to spend their own money? Can privacy not be protected by keeping donors' names secret? Why should candidates be stopped from getting whatever donations they can?

What do you think?
1. How would each of the suggested controls on election expenses help keep elections fair and democratic?
2. Which would you approve of? Why?

THE FEDERAL ELECTION EXPENSES ACT

Some of the ideas mentioned above have in fact been used. The Federal Election Expenses Act was designed to provide open and fair elections. It says:
1. Spending is limited according to the number of eligible voters in a constituency.
2. All contributions over $100 must be publicly disclosed.
3. The government will pay part of the expenses of every candidate who gets more than 15% of the total votes.
4. The time allowed for advertising is controlled.

Do you agree with this act? Why or why not? Should it be changed in any way? How? Why?

Influencing your government: Conclusion

We live in a democracy. This means that Canadians are free to choose and influence government. Because governments are elected by us, they will listen. If we leave influencing government to others, we will have no say in our government. The challenge of the future for young citizens is to gain knowledge of government and confidence in being part of it. Will you play your part in influencing government?

## Conclusion

Government is our tool for making decisions about the needs of our country. The decisions and policies made by government affect the lives of all Canadians. Citizens who are concerned about their own future and the future of the country will try to influence government. Alert informed Canadians will also watch how government is changing, and ask questions about how it can be improved.

Here are some questions about our government. How would you answer them?

### The need for government action

Government, especially the Cabinet and public service, is doing and spending more than at any time in our history. Do you want government to keep doing more? Or should it leave more for individuals and private groups to do?

### Our lawmakers: The legislatures

Do you think our system of passing laws and debating policies takes too much time? How would you speed up the process and still give citizens the right to express their views?

### The judiciary

You have learned a little about our legal system. In another chapter you will examine the fairness and efficiency of our courts. Can Canadians devise a better court system — one that is faster, yet just?

### The role of media

How can the media present the news in an interesting, yet objective way? How can they reveal to us shortcomings in government that need correction? Is government becoming too complicated for most of us to understand? How can the media help fight this problem?

### Interest groups

Should we leave politics to the politicians? Or is there a vital role for interest groups to play in our democratic system? Has that role been played to its potential?

The two chapters that follow will give you more information on our government. They should help you with the answers to these different questions.

**READING BETTER**

1. Make a list of important terms associated with Canadian government that you have learned in this chapter. Test yourself and your fellow classmates on their meanings.

**ORGANIZING BETTER**

1. Make a summary chart of the people in government who represent you at each level. Give the name and party of each person.

**USING YOUR KNOWLEDGE**

1. Describe how each level of government in Canada affects your life.
2. Make up posters that explain the importance of voting or how to vote. Display these around your school.

**SOLVING PROBLEMS**

1. Review the structure of Canadian government. Then, decide on one thing you believe should be changed to produce better government. Explain the change and your reasons for it.

**TAKING A STAND**

1. Do you think that the governments of Canada as explained in this chapter meet the needs of people in Canada? Why or why not?

**RESEARCHING**

1. Make up a test about Canadian government that will help you find out what other people know about it. True or false questions are useful for this sort of test. Give the test to a few people. In general, how much do people know about the government? Write a short report on this question, discussing the results of your tests.

## GLOSSARY

**Aristocrat.** A person belonging to the nobility, usually with a title such as earl, lord, baron, dame, lady.

**By-laws.** Laws passed in a municipality.

**Candidate.** A person running in an election.

**Caucus.** The private meeting of members of Parliament from the same party.

**Censorship.** Official approval or rejection of books, news, films, etc.

**Coalition.** A temporary union of political parties.

**Deputy prime minister.** The person who fills in when the prime minister is not in Parliament.

**Dignitaries.** Officials holding an important government position.

**Editorials.** Newspaper articles expressing the opinions of the owners and managers of the newspaper.

**Head of State.** A person who symbolizes the whole country. In Canada the Governor General, representing the Queen, is head of state.

**House of Commons.** Part of the federal legislative branch of government.

**Media.** Television, radio, newspapers, and films.

**Metropolitan government.** A type of government where duties are divided between small, lower level governments and one large, upper level government.

**Monarch.** Ruler with the title of king or queen.

**Municipality.** A city or town with its own local government.

**Non-partisan.** Not involving political parties.

**Parliament.** In Ottawa, the meeting place of the House of Commons and Senate. May also refer to a provincial legislature.

**Patronage.** Favours done for members of a political party. These favours include jobs, contracts, and titles.

**Ratepayers association.** A group of taxpayers from a certain area that meet to discuss common municipal problems.

**Repeal.** To remove, to take away, especially laws.

**Rubber stamp.** Gives automatic approval, without first analyzing or thinking.

**Senate.** Part of the federal legislative branch of government.

**Statistics.** Numerical facts that give information about people or things.

**Vote of non-confidence.** A special vote in Parliament and provincial legislatures that shows the MPs disagree with what the ruling party is doing.

# 2/ The Canadian economy: Buyers and sellers

## Contents

### Introduction

The machine you see on page 128 is the Canadian economy. It is a huge noisy thing that makes people nervous. It can even frighten some Canadians.

The machine is less frightening if you understand it. This is not hard to do. The basic idea behind the machine is fairly simple. Canada's economy is, in general, a system of buyers and sellers. People need many products (clothes, books, etc.), and producers try to fill these needs. Producers buy materials and services to make their products. They then sell the products to people.

You may ask "Why is the machine so complicated?" Canadians have a huge number of needs. Not all of them can be filled. Therefore, a huge system has evolved to make decisions. Here are some of the issues the system must deal with:

What needs will be filled?
What should be produced?
How should these goods and services be produced?
Who will be able to buy them?

As we go through the chapter, we will get to know the machine well. The following questions will be answered:

1. **How does the economy work?**
2. **What are some major problems in our economy today?**
3. **How did the government get involved in our economy? Why?**

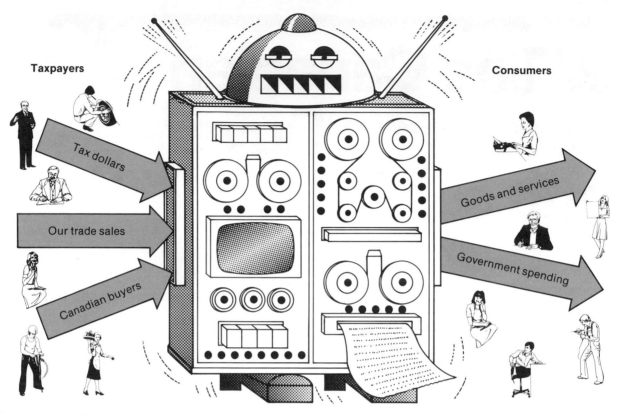

**Taxpayers**

Tax dollars

Our trade sales

Canadian buyers

**Consumers**

Goods and services

Government spending

Fig. 2-1  The Canadian economy

### 4. Is the government doing too much in the economy? Too little?

#### The economy: Where do you fit in?

We know that Canada's economy is like a big machine. We hear of issues such as inflation, taxes, and budgets. We may think that these issues concern mainly politicians and people in business. But the economy affects *all* people in many ways. A price increase in one part of the economy may affect prices in other areas. For example, farmers who raise cattle may have to meet high costs in a particular year. This may result in higher meat prices. Stores that sell the meat and consumers who buy it will thus be affected. This is why it is important to understand the system.

We will now look at the story of the Toomath family. Gerald Toomath loses his job as a furniture and appliance salesperson. Family income drops. The family must try to make ends meet when prices go up. We will see the many ways in which the economy touches the average Canadian family. The story will bring up the following ideas.

1. How rising prices and lack of jobs hurt Canadians.
2. How the three levels of government—federal, provincial, municipal—are involved in these problems.
3. Whether government should do more or less for the economy.

We will study these issues more closely in later sections of the book.

### The Toomath family and economic problems  (A fictional account)

INFLATION: THE GROCERY BILL

Gerald Toomath was alone in the apartment, waiting for his family to come home. His wife was a supervisor at a dry cleaning store. Their son, David, who was eighteen, worked at an auto supply store. They both would be home soon. Their daughter, Doreen, would also be home soon from high school. Doreen had a part-time job in a restaurant.

"It's a strange situation," Mr. Toomath thought to himself. "I've always said it is important to work, and now everyone works except me."

Gerald Toomath had been out of work now for three months. For years he had been a furniture and appliance salesperson. When sales fell he had been let go by his company. He had looked for another sales job in the furniture business. One person offered him a job moving furniture. He turned it down because he was a trained sales-person with years of experience. Selling was what he liked to do. He had tried **Canada Employment Centres** and several **employment agencies.** There was nothing in his line of work.

He started to unpack the groceries he had just bought. A year ago the same groceries had cost $53. They would last the family a week. Now they cost $58.

"It's crazy," he thought to himself. "But that's what inflation means. The price of a product goes up. Or you pay the same price for a product, but the package is smaller or the stuff is not as good. Everything is going up—gas, food, you name it. And it's happening when I'm not working. Since I'm not working, our family income is down. And we need money just to keep pace with inflation. I've only got my **unemployment insurance cheque** and what the wife and kids bring in. We have to cut back on our spending. But where?"

Mr. Toomath continued to unpack the groceries. He used to like shopping, but now he hated it. All he did these days was shop and look for a job. Lately, this pattern had been bothering him. He hated being without a job.

Just then his wife entered the apartment.

"Hello!" he called cheerfully as she came in the door.

"Hi," Rose Toomath said quietly. She sounded tired. She came into the kitchen and began to help her husband with the groceries.

"Here's the grocery bill, Rose," said Mr. Toomath. "I figure it's up ten percent from this time last year. We're getting hit from both ends. Prices are up and our income is down. What's more, I think the muffler on the car will have to be replaced. Where will we get the money to pay for all this?"

"I'm working now, Gerry," said Mrs. Toomath. "The store is going to be open two more nights a week. I can work extra hours. That will bring in $25 more a week for us. You know, all our money is going for things we need. We're not using it on luxuries. And we spend everything we make. In fact, we're using up what we had in the bank. We have to figure out other ways of saving money. It's getting hard, isn't it?" She tried to smile.

GOVERNMENT SPENDING: THE SWIMMING POOL

Mr. Toomath walked over to the window. He looked out at the school across the street from the apartment. There was a park around the school. The Regina Parks and Recreation Department had just finished building a hockey rink for the coming winter. Inside the school, Mr. Toomath recalled, was a $600 000 swimming pool. The money to build and run the school, rink, and pool came from the federal, provincial, and city governments. These governments got their money from the taxpayers.

**Consumers and inflation: During inflation, buyers often look for sales. Why?**

John McQueen

"I'm angry," Mr. Toomath said. "Here we are wondering where our next dollar is coming from. Over there is a swimming pool that I helped pay for. I'll bet there aren't ten people using it. We've had to cut back because our income has fallen. The government ought to cut back on its expenses, too. It spends too much and it taxes too much. If it spent less, it could tax us less."

"You don't want them to cut back on unemployment insurance, do you Gerry?" asked Mrs. Toomath. "Or take off rent controls? We've only had controls since 1976 in Saskatchewan."

"I still wish," said Mr. Toomath, "they hadn't put in that pool."

"That pool may seem like a great expense. But it gives jobs to lifeguards, instructors, the cleaning crew. A whole line of people are affected. They sell their services to their employers and get wages in return. The pool also provides a thing people want—recreation," answered Mrs. Toomath.

"Rose," said Mr. Toomath, "I don't like arguing about this. I'm just trying to see what has hit our family. It's something I want to understand. It seems to me the more the government keeps spending, the more prices go up. Higher prices mean inflation. With high prices, our **cost of living** goes up. Canadians have a right to be protected from this."

Rose Toomath understood her husband's anger. She felt it too. They both knew they had few answers. They did not understand what was happening to them or to the country. So many other people like Gerry did not understand. Few people knew how to solve the problem.

"At least the government is doing something for us," Mr. Toomath pointed out. "A lot of its money is spent to assist Canadians."

"Yes," added Mrs. Toomath. "You can get **unemployment insurance** until you find a job. David and Doreen work for more than the **minimum wage.** The government has rent controls on this apartment."

THE COST OF LIVING: DOREEN'S PROBLEM

At that moment a young girl came rushing into the apartment. It was Doreen, the Toomath's sixteen-year-old daughter. She was crying.

"What's wrong, Doreen?" asked Mr. Toomath.

"It's my friends at school. They've all decided to take up skiing this winter. They are going to form a ski club, and hold dances after skiing. Only members of the club can go. I can't afford to belong to the club. Ski equipment costs so much. It even costs too much to rent skis and buy ski clothes. I feel so left out! It's going to be a lonely winter."

Mr. Toomath looked at his daughter. He felt guilty. If he had been working, Doreen could have used her money for skis. She wouldn't be unhappy now. Doreen went into her room. Mr. and Mrs. Toomath started to make supper.

As the family's emotions cooled, the Toomath's son, David, came home from work. As soon as he saw his father he cried out, "Dad, have I got good news. You've got a job!"

"What!" exclaimed Mr. Toomath. "What do you mean, I've got a job?"

"You know my supervisor at work?" replied David. "Well, I asked him if they would be hiring anyone for November at the store. He said they will need two men for clerking. And that you could be one of them!" David was very excited.

"How much does it pay?" asked Mr. Toomath.

"Not very much," replied David. "Not much more than you get now on unemployment insurance."

"Maybe I should take this job until a better one comes along," said Mr. Toomath.

Mrs. Toomath studied her husband's face. She knew he had doubts about the job. It did not make use of his skills. It would lead him nowhere at his age. But it was a job and it would give him money.

Mr. Toomath looked around the table. His family wanted to see him back at work. And he himself wanted to hold a job again. "Well, son," he said slowly, "I'll have to think about it for a little while. I'll let you know what I decide tomorrow."

---

## QUICK QUIZ

These questions require short answers. This is *not* a test of memory. Look back at the story if you are unsure of an answer.

1. Why does Mr. Toomath consider his situation strange?
2. Where did Mr. Toomath go when he needed help finding work?
3. How does Mr. Toomath explain the term "inflation"?
4. Explain why the Toomaths need more money to keep pace with inflation.
5. Why does the swimming pool inside the school bother Mr. Toomath?
6. Where did the money to build the pool come from?
7. How has the pool been a help to the economy of the community?
8. Name at least four ways government helps the Toomaths.
9. What expenses can Doreen not afford?
10. What choice must Mr. Toomath make at the end of the story?

## READING BETTER

1. When you read, it is often important to look for details. To see how well you pick up details, read the statements below. Decide whether they are true or false.

Inflation: The grocery bill
a) The four members of the Toomath family are part of the Canadian work force.
b) Inflation is not a problem for the Toomath family.
c) Unemployment is not a problem for the Toomath family.
d) The Toomaths buy many luxury goods.

Government spending: The swimming pool
a) Swimming pools built inside schools are expensive.
b) The government spends money on many items in our economic system.
c) Canadians pay income taxes.
d) Married people do not have to pay income tax.

The cost of living: Doreen's problem
a) When people are unemployed for a while, their families often suffer.
b) Doreen is not affected by the cost of living.
c) Mr. Toomath does not feel guilty about what is happening to his daughter.

d) The Canadian government is deeply involved in our economy.

**The chance for a job**
a) Mr. Toomath has to make a choice. He can stay unemployed or take a job that is not in his field, and that does not pay well.
b) David helps his dad find a job.
c) Mr. Toomath does not consider working in an auto supply shop.
d) Mr. Toomath will continue to receive unemployment benefits if he works.

## ORGANIZING BETTER

1. The various levels of government help Canadians in many ways. Here is a list of some things that governments do. Which things appear in the story "The Toomath family and economic problems"?
   a) Build and maintain public buildings in the community.
   b) Prevent manufacturers from selling dangerous products.
   c) Check safety conditions in mines and other places of work.
   d) Fine companies for breaking the law.
   e) Help workers find jobs.
   f) Use money from taxes to support Canadians in need.

## USING YOUR KNOWLEDGE

1. Read through the story again. Find evidence to support this viewpoint: "Unemployment and inflation affect all members of the Toomath family." See what evidence you can find in the story to show how
   a) Mrs. Toomath has been affected.
   b) Doreen has suffered problems at school.
   c) David has taken steps to help his dad.

## TAKING A STAND

1. At the end of the story, Mr. Toomath is thinking about taking the job at the auto supply store. Pretend you are a friend of Mr. Toomath's. What advice would you give him? Should he take the job or wait until a better one comes along? Take time to think of good arguments to present to Mr. Toomath.

## How our economic system works

The Toomath story shows how the Canadian economy affects people. We saw how hard the family was hit by unemployment and inflation. How do these two problems come about? The problems, and others, arise when the economy is not working well. It is easier to understand the problems if we know how the system works. This is what we are going to look at in this section of the chapter.

### The Toomaths buy goods and services

Canada's economy is made up of buyers and sellers. Look at the Toomath family, for example. All members of the family need certain items. Therefore, they buy them. This means that they give producers money in exchange for items.

Some of these items, such as groceries and clothing, are *consumer goods*. They are physical objects that the family uses up (or consumes) over a period of time. Can you think of five consumer goods that *your* family buys?

The Toomaths do not buy consumer goods only. When they visit their doctor or when they take clothes to the dry cleaners, they purchase *consumer services*. These are actions done by persons for pay. Can you name two services you buy?

Both these types of purchases are important to consumers. Everything we buy is either a consumer good or service.

### The Toomaths sell their services

The Toomaths buy goods and services. But where do they get the money to exchange for these items? The answer is that they sell their services. The members of the Toomath family work; they give their services in return for a wage. By working, the Toomaths earn money to pay for the goods and services they buy.

The Toomaths earn money in other ways as well. For example, all the family members have bank accounts. They get *interest* on these accounts. Interest is the fee that a bank will pay people for letting it use their money. The Toomaths lend the government money when they buy bonds. Again, they receive interest. These are just a few ways in which the Toomaths earn money.

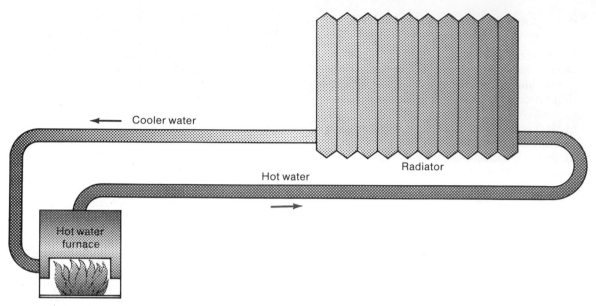

**Fig. 2-2 Hot water heating system**

The economic system: Two cycles

So far, we have seen that the Toomaths exchange money for goods and services. They get this money by giving services in exchange for wages. This is fairly easy to understand. At this point you may ask, "How does this buying and selling fit into a *system*? What *is* Canada's economic system?"

We can compare Canada's economic system to a hot water heating system. In hot water heating, water flows in a cycle. It flows through pipes from the furnace to the radiator. From the radiator, it flows back to the furnace. This cycle repeats itself without end.

Now we know that in Canada, a lot of buying and selling goes on. Thus there is a constant flow of money, goods, and services. Just as water flows between the radiator and the furnace, these items flow between people and Canadian business firms.

The economic system is more complex than the water heating system, though. Look at the water heating system diagram. You see that there is only one cycle in the system, the water cycle. In the economic system there are two cycles, the *money cycle* and the *goods and services cycle*.

We will discuss the money cycle first. Look at Fig. 2-3. The outer box shows the flow of money between the Toomaths and Regina business firms. When the Toomaths buy goods and services, they give money to the business firms. This is the first half of the cycle. The money they pay does come back to them. The family receives money from the firms in the form of wages. That is the second part of the cycle.

The inner box shows the goods and services cycle. The Toomath family sells its services to business firms. It does this when the family members work for wages. These services also come back to the family. This happens when the Toomaths buy goods and services.

Notice that the two cycles flow in different directions. Money payments move in one direction. Goods and services flow in another. This shows you the constant exchange that goes on. In Canada, goods and services are always being exchanged for money. This is our economic system.

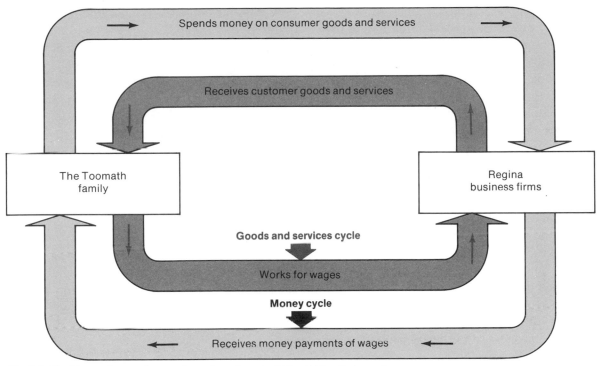

Fig. 2-3  The Toomaths pay for goods and services and are paid for their services

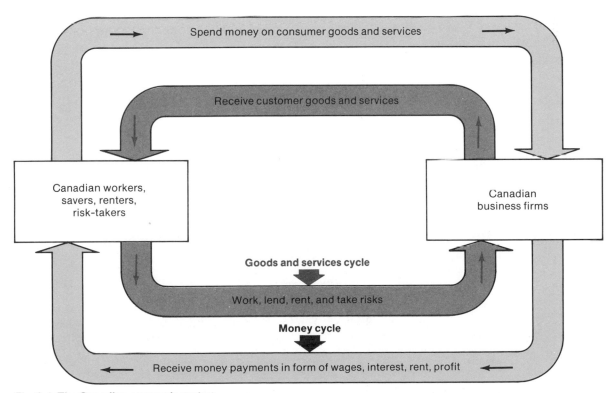

Fig. 2-4  The Canadian economic system

Fig. 2-3 shows you how money and services flow between the Toomaths and the Regina business firms. The economic system of Canada works in exactly the same way. Look at Fig. 2-4. The Regina business firms in Fig. 2-3 have been replaced by Canadian business firms. The Toomaths have been replaced by *Canadian workers, savers, renters, and risk-takers.* (The roles these people play are explained in Fig. 2-5.) These different groups represent Canadians as a whole.

Canadians spend money on consumer goods and services. This money comes back to them in wages, interest, profits, and rent. That is how the money cycle works.

In the goods and services cycle, Canadians perform services for business. They work at jobs, lend money, rent buildings, and take business risks to earn profits. Business uses these services. In return it offers Canadians many consumer goods and services. Therefore, services are returned to Canadians.

We now know that Canada's economy is made up of two cycles. Money flows in one direction, and goods and services flow in another. Canada's economy is healthy when the flow of money, goods, and services is steady.

## Economic illness: Unemployment and inflation

We said that Canada's economy is like a hot water heating system. Sometimes the water in the heating system does not flow well. The system breaks down. The same thing happens in Canada's economic system. Often money, goods, and services do not flow well. This creates economic problems. Our economic system breaks down even more easily than the heating system. Canada's economy is affected by factors outside of it. For example, it is affected by changes in the US economy. Trade decisions that are made by non-Canadians can also change it. So can war.

Two big problems in our economy are unemployment and inflation. We will look at them more closely.

### Unemployment comes from lack of spending

A hot water system often breaks down when the water does not move around. In a way, the same thing can happen to our economy. Let us say that only consumers spend money in our country. If consumers spend less money, then the flow of money from them to business will decrease. This means that the flow of products from business to consumers will also decrease.

| Canadians who sell services | What they sell | What they are paid |
| --- | --- | --- |
| Employees such as workers and managers | Their skills and abilities to perform a task | Wages, salaries, commissions, tips |
| Savers such as depositors at banks, buyers of bonds | They keep ownership of their property, but let others use it for a price | Fees, dividends, or interest |
| Renters such as landlords and rental companies | Like savers, they keep ownership but let others use their buildings, tools, machines, etc. | Rent, leasing fees |
| Risk-takers or entrepreneurs who start or invest in small businesses or big companies | Products or services that they themselves own | Business profits |

Fig. 2-5  Canadians who sell services

What will happen to the factories and stores that sell these goods? They, of course, will cut back or even close down. Workers and other income-earners will find that their situation has become tough. Their income will decrease. They will have even less money to spend. You can see that when the flow of money and goods slows down, economic problems arise.

### When the flow is too fast, inflation occurs

What happens to a heating system when the water is too hot? It boils over and races through the pipes. Thus the system will not work well.

The same kind of thing can happen in the economy. Sometimes the flow of money quickens. Money may flow faster than goods can be produced. When this happens, producers will charge more for their goods. Prices will rise.

This type of inflation occurred in Canada after both world wars. Consumers wanted new cars, home appliances, and other items they could not get in wartime. They now had the money to pay for these items. Prices soared.

Some prices rise because of increased costs. Businesses have to pay out money for wages, rent, raw materials, and transportation. These costs often rise more quickly than business firms can absorb them. The firms have to raise prices or they may go out of business. Few firms will choose to go **bankrupt.** They therefore raise prices.

QUICK QUIZ
**Place the correct word from the list in the blank spaces.**
> fall   lose   produce   spending   income
> rise   spends   rise

1. **If spending increases and the amount of goods made stays the same, prices will_____.**
2. **If spending decreases, workers will tend to _____ jobs.**
3. **Inflation occurs when prices _____ faster than business can _____ goods and services.**
4. **Inflation can be caused by an increase in costs. It can also be caused by an increase in _____.**
5. **The money that business _____ on wages is the _____ of workers.**
6. **Unemployment is mainly caused by a _____ in spending.**

Inflation hurts us all . . . especially those of us who cannot compete.

| | |
|---|---|
| People on pensions | These are usually older people. They no longer earn regular income through wages. |
| Older people | These people may or may not be on pensions. A person over fifty often has trouble finding a job. Society may look on that person as being "too old" to work. |
| Non-unionized workers | These people do not have a union to bargain for wages for them. |
| Single-income families | More and more families are living on only one income. Divorce and separation often mean that there is only one "breadwinner" in the family. |
| Young people, ages 18-26 | Many young people do not have skills to sell. These people are often the first to be laid off. Sometimes the rate of unemployment in this group is about 25%. |

Canada's most wanted economic criminals

Posters giving information about criminals wanted by the police are often displayed in public. Here are a number of "economic criminals". Their crime — blocking the smooth flow of money, goods, and services throughout Canada. You have already seen that inflation and unemployment are serious offenders. Others are "on the loose". Look them over. Select the five that you think are the worst offenders.

# WANTED

INFLATION

*Past record:* A tough customer after World War I. Prices after the war were 60% higher than pre-war figures. Also caused trouble after World War II. Behaved itself in the 1960s. Broke out again in the early 1970s. It reached highs of about 11% and 12% in 1974 and 1975.
*At present:* Named a public enemy by federal government's Anti-Inflation Board in 1975. Controls lifted. On parole now. Still dangerous.
*Victims:* All Canadians, especially pensioners, older people, non-unionized workers, single-income families, and young people.
*Prospects:* A bad customer for years to come. This is because of rising energy costs, heavy government spending, and heavy consumer spending. Can cause trouble throughout economy, if left unchecked. A definite chance to be named public enemy number one.

# WANTED

UNEMPLOYMENT

*Past record:* Since 1960s, has combined with inflation to hit the economy hard. One high point of crime career was the Depression of the 1930s. In 1978, hit 30% in some parts of Quebec and Maritimes. Some experts say it does not matter how wealthy Canada becomes. They say at least 6% of Canadian workers will always be without work.
*At present:* By the winter of 1977-78, 10 out of every 100 Canadian workers were without a job. This figure does not include those who had given up looking for a job. Actual unemployment crime figures may therefore be higher.
*Victims:* Attacks old and young, lower-income families and individuals. Causes family troubles and tensions. Robs merchants of possible sales.
*Prospects:* Could become public enemy number one.

**Poverty: This older person might put poverty at the top of his "most wanted" list of criminals.**

John McQueen

# WANTED

## POOR TRADE RECORD (A cat burglar)

*Past record:* Canada has always been a trading nation. This is because of its small population, many resources, and ties with Europe and the United States. Of all the goods we produce, 25% are exported. About 70% of the manufactured goods we use come from abroad. Our task has been to balance our imports and exports.

*At present:* In recent years, we have bought more from foreigners than we have sold. This situation cannot continue for too long. If it does, our money will be worth less and less. By 1978 our dollar was worth about 85¢ compared to the US dollar. Also, our imports will cost more. We will have trouble providing jobs for Canadians, and keeping prices low. If this criminal is not caught, consumers will suffer. They will find that goods cost more. Many industries will have to close for lack of a market. Jobs will continue to be lost. Canada's customers will turn to foreign companies for goods.

*Prospects:* Should be put in top five list. This criminal is sneaky. It acts behind the scenes where it is not noticed in daily living.

# WANTED

## POVERTY

*Past record:* Most people know what poverty means. Yet it is difficult to define this criminal precisely. Current definition: A family or person is poor if 70% or more of income is spent on clothing, food, and shelter. Since Confederation, poverty has been present in many Canadian homes.

*At present:* Still a serious threat, but record has improved since 1960s. About 13% of families still at or below poverty line. About 40% of individuals living alone are poor. Poverty is found in any province. However, it prefers to room outside of Ontario, British Columbia, and Alberta.

*Victims:* Strikes old, sick, children, single-parent families and others. Widespread in rural areas. Not as strong as it used to be. However still overcomes many Canadians.

*Prospects:* In the late 1970s there was talk of a "guaranteed income supplement". This means that no person in Canada would get less than the amount of money needed to stay above the poverty line.

# WANTED

## REGIONAL DISPARITY

*Past record:* Has been around since Confederation. Because of this criminal, some people are not as well-off as others. Canadians do not all have the same job opportunities, education levels, and income. The various regions in the country are at different levels of wealth.

*At present:* Each province has some depressed areas. Wealthy Ontario, for example, has areas in its northern and eastern parts that need aid. Is causing tensions across the country. Many regions feel that Confederation does not encourage flow of jobs, income, goods, and services into their region.

*Victims:* People in less wealthy regions hit hard. Incomes, for example, may be low because of lack of industry, or natural resources in area.

*Prospects:* Cannot be ignored any longer. Must be captured and taught to behave.

# WANTED

## INEFFICIENCY

*Past record:* Inefficiency is present when resources are wasted. Also when people do not find better ways of using them. In the 1960s Canada produced many goods and services. Risk-takers, workers, renters, and other "sellers of services" competed well with those in other nations. Canada's growth matched or surpassed growth in other nations. However, a lot of resources were wasted. Lately we have become less efficient. Our factories do not produce as much per worker as those in some foreign countries.

*At present:* Since 1975 our economic growth has not been above 5%. Inefficiency is robbing us of jobs, sales, and foreign customers.

*Victims:* All our goals have suffered because of this criminal. If we are efficient, we can produce jobs, goods, and services — a high quality of life.

*Prospects:* A real culprit since it persuades us to do our second best. May be in the top five list when most Canadians recognize its dangers.

**Match the entries in column A with those in column B.**

**Column A**

1. Main crime of all the "economic criminals".
2. Reached highs of 11% and 12% in 1974-75.
3. A cause of inflation.
4. Main crime of unemployment.
5. How unemployment robs merchants of sales.
6. If you spend 70% or more of your income on food, shelter, and clothing you are said to be . . . .
7. Means that some Canadians are not as well-off as others because of where they live in Canada.
8. Called a cat burglar because it does its work quietly.
9. If poor trade continues, this may happen.
10. What happens because of inefficiency.

**Column B**

a) Poor trade record.
b) Poor.
c) Rising cost of energy.
d) Leaves young and old without work.
e) Takes away income from potential buyers.
f) Inflation.
g) Regional disparity.
h) Exports may become more expensive.
i) Blocking the smooth flow of money, goods, and services.
j) Resources are wasted. Or people refuse to find ways to improve the use of resources.

USING YOUR KNOWLEDGE

1. Which of the economic criminals do you think is the worst? Inflation? Or is it unemployment? Here are some questions to ask yourself before making your choice:
   Which will most hurt our flow of goods and services?
   Which hurts more Canadians?
   Which is the hardest to get rid of?
(Can you think of some other questions to ask yourself before choosing?)

## Canada's mixed economy

We have seen that Canada's economic system is one of buyers and sellers. We rely on our abilities as buyers and sellers to make a living. Yet we may sometimes have trouble making ends meet. This is where the government comes in. The government has many rules and programmes that help us cope with our economic problems.

Because of all the help the government gives, many people are confused about our economic system. They wonder, "Is our system based on free choice? Or does the government control us and the economy?"

In the next sections we will find answers to these questions. We will find out exactly what kind of economy Canada has. Later on, we will see exactly what roles the government plays in our system.

**The Toomaths relied on their own talents and resources most of the time: Free enterprise**

We saw that the Toomath family, like most Canadians, were self-reliant. They used their own talents to earn income. They spent this income to meet their basic needs, such as food and clothing. In general, they were *free* to buy and sell as they chose. This kind of economic system is called *free enterprise*.

Free enterprise means that you as a consumer can get whatever you want. However you must be able to pay for it. If you want a car, you have to pay for it. A stereo? The care of a good doctor? A holiday? Again, the free enterprise theory says you must pay for these goods and services. If you cannot pay, you do not get them.

What about sellers in this system? In it, people or businesses are free to make a product or offer a service. Their main purpose is to make a profit. These sellers must follow certain rules if they are to succeed. They have to charge prices that people can afford. And they must sell safe products that are what they seem. If these rules are followed, sellers can expect to beat out their competitors. They can also expect to earn money and make a profit. Some sellers cannot (or refuse to) play by the rules. They either make little profit or go out of business.

Free enterprise is a tough "look-after-

**Big business: International Business Machines (IBM)**

**Small business**

yourself" system. Some buyers do not get what they want. Some sellers cannot sell their products. In the system there are many winners and losers.

**ORGANIZING BETTER**

1. **Here are some characteristics of the free enterprise system. (It is also called the** *free market system*.**) Match up each basic idea about the free enterprise system in column A with the description of the idea in column B.**

*Column A*
*Free enterprise theory*

1. **Competition**
2. **Private property**
3. **Private business**
4. **The desire for profits**
5. **Self-reliance and self-help**
6. **Freedom of contract**

*Column B*
*Description*

a) **Buyers and sellers are free to sell their services as they wish. No one tells them whom to work for or to whom they must sell.**
b) **Buyers and sellers fight among themselves. Buyers try to beat out other buyers. Sellers try to beat out other sellers. Buyers and sellers try to get the best of each other. It is "survival of the fittest".**
c) **People can run their own place of business. Government does not own or regulate business except to provide order and peace.**
d) **Sellers try to make as much money as they can from selling. Buyers, on the other hand, try to get the most for their money. This conflict decides prices and other basic economic decisions.**
e) **You do not ask for handouts. If you cannot pay your way, you do not go. You try your best. If you win, you win. If you lose, you lose.**
f) **Persons can own things — land, cars, houses — and use them as they want.**

But sometimes the Toomaths had to get help from the government: The government planned economy

Sometimes the Toomaths could not afford the things they needed. Take their apartment, for example. The Saskatchewan government helped them afford the rent by setting rent controls. The government helped them in many other ways. Look at the chart "Things that governments did for the Toomaths".

In free enterprise people get what they want if they pay for it. But not all people have the same buying power. Some people cannot afford the things they need. This raises some important questions. Should a child starve because its parents cannot buy proper food? Should it suffer illness because its parents cannot pay a doctor?

In some countries, governments have tried to solve this problem by taking full control of the economy. The government looks at the needs of the people and of the country. It then makes all the important economic decisions. It decides what goods and services will be offered. The government decides how goods will be made, and it sets prices. It also decides to whom goods and services will be offered.

This system is called the *planned economy*. It is much less competitive than the free enterprise system. There are fewer big winners and losers.

**ORGANIZING BETTER**

1. **Here are some characteristics of the planned economy. Again, you are to match up each basic idea about the system in column A with the description of the idea in column B.**

*Column A*
*The planned economy*

1. **Public ownership**
2. **Public control of production**
3. **Public control of income and career choice**
4. **Public control of distribution**
5. **Security and co-operation**

*Column B*
*Description*

a) **Rather than fight against other buyers and sellers (the survival of the fittest), citizens work together and share.**
b) **All property belongs to the state in the name of the people. This includes mines, factories, shops, and forests.**
c) **Government decides who gets what.**
d) **Managers of state factories decide how much of an item will be produced.**
e) **You are not free to decide what you will work at. Nor can you decide your level of wages.**

### Canada's mixed economy: A balancing act

Canada's economic system is like the free enterprise system in many ways. It also contains some features of the planned economy. We therefore say that today Canada has a *mixed economic system*. The economy is a "mix" of free enterprise and government planning.

How did this system come about? In the past, Canada's economy was always called a free enterprise system. It still contains many features of free enterprise. There is much private ownership. Buyers and sellers compete with each other. However, through the years, the system has changed. People have seen faults in the free enterprise system. They have asked, "Should Canadians go without food, shelter, and health care if they cannot pay?" Over the years Canada has decided that even people who cannot pay for these things should have them.

Today the government supplies Canadians with most "public" or "social" goods and services. These include parks, hospitals, bridges, schools, and railway service to remote areas. How many of these things would we have in a pure free enterprise system? Very few. Buyers do not have enough money. How many people, for example, can afford to build a national railway? It is clear, then, that the government plays a large role in our economy.

**QUICK QUIZ**
**Here are ten key ideas from the sections you have just read. Copy them in your notebook. Mark *F* beside the ideas that belong to the free**

---

### Things that governments did for the Toomaths

**Here are some things the various governments did for the family. These services are mentioned in the story.**

| *Federal government* | *Provincial government* | *City government* |
|---|---|---|
| Unemployment Insurance Commission paid Mr. Toomath a certain amount each month. | Enforced a minimum wage law. All provinces have one. Thus the wages of David and Doreen were higher than they may have been otherwise. | Paid the park workers and provided maintenance of parks and recreation. |
| Canada Employment Centres helped Mr. Toomath look for a job. | Enforced rent controls and provided a rent review board if a dispute arose between the landlord and the Toomaths. | |
| Helped pay for part of the costs of educating David and Doreen. | Provided schools for the Toomaths. About 1/3 of provincial spending is in the area of education. | |
| Together with the provincial and city governments helped build pool in high school. | | |

## Here are some other services offered by governments

| Federal government | Provincial government | City government |
|---|---|---|
| Provided family allowances for David and Doreen until the age of 18. | Operated Workmen's Compensation. It protects any member of the family who is injured while on the job. | Provided police protection around the clock for the apartment. |
| Maintained the RCMP. In Saskatchewan, they are the Provincial Police. | Operated a human rights commission to protect against discrimination. For example, Mr. Toomath could not be refused a job because he was too old. | Provided education for the Toomath family. It co-operated with the provincial government to do this. |
| Passed laws for the safety of the appliances Mr. Toomath sold. | Maintained health standards in the supermarket where Mr. Toomath bought groceries. | Issued business licences to many of the businesses the family dealt with. |
| Co-operated with the province to pay doctor and hospital bills. | Inspected the elevator in the apartment for safety. | Enforced noise and other privacy by-laws. |
| | Helped pay the doctor and hospital bills. | Passed zoning laws for the building of the apartment in which they live. |

**City government: Repairs to streets also provide jobs.**

144

enterprise system. Mark *G* beside the ideas associated with the government planned system.

1. Sellers try to make a lot of profit. Buyers try to get the most for their dollars.
2. You watch out for yourself.
3. The government controls or regulates prices.
4. Buyers and sellers regulate prices.
5. People pay for what they want. If they cannot pay, they do not get it.
6. All property belongs to the state.
7. People are not free to decide what they will work at. They cannot choose the levels of salary they want to aim at.
8. Instead of competing against each other, citizens work together and share.
9. There are many winners and losers.
10. The government controls levels of production.

### USING YOUR KNOWLEDGE

1. Below are some situations in the everyday lives of Canadians. Mark an *F* beside the situations related to the free enterprise system. Mark *G* beside the ones related to the government planned system.
   1. The family has to pay for a muffler out of its own pocket.
   2. Mr. Toomath is fired. He must leave his job and look elsewhere for work.
   3. David is hurt at work. The government pays the doctor bills.
   4. The school board and the city government decide to put a swimming pool in the local high school.
   5. Mr. Toomath gets angry at the federal government for not doing something about high prices.

## Confederation highway: the changing roles of government

We can see that today government in Canada plays a large role in the economy. This role has changed a lot since Confederation. In 1867 government's job was much simpler. The only role it played in the economy was "officer of the law", or "judge". It had little to do with the flow of goods and services across Canada.

Today all levels of government do much more. This confuses many people. They are not sure just what jobs government has.

This section of the chapter studies government's roles in the economy. As you read, ask yourself these questions: Is government playing too many roles? If so, on what roles should it cut back?

Roles of the government

1. Law officer/judge
2. Regulator
3. Servant
4. Business partner
5. Banker for the nation
6. Manager of the economy
7. Researcher
8. **Monopolist**

*1. Law officer/Judge*

Buyers and sellers in the market system need rules to play by. Most of the time, they follow the rules. But sometimes they clash. A law officer is needed to pull the players apart. Sometimes a judge is needed to decide who has lost and who has won. The judge must decide what the punishment or reward will be.

This was one of the first roles of government in Canada. It is still doing this job. There are always new problems to solve. Some players want to play by the old rules. Others want a new rule book altogether. Government must set up the new rules. It has to answer many questions about laws in the economy. Does Canada need laws to regulate weights and measures? How do you enforce laws to make sure cars do not rust through in one year? Should you have a law like that in the first place? What if only the buyers complain? What if the sellers think everything is fine? What do you do then?

There are many ways for government to play law officer and judge. As society gets more complex, so do the jobs we ask government to do.

*2. Regulator*

When a company has a *monopoly* on an item, it has complete control of the market.

**Why do you think governments regulate transit commissions?**

There are no competitors. The company can set prices as high as it wants. Monopolies can be a danger to consumers, who have to pay the high prices. This is where government steps in. Government regulates, or controls, monopolies. It tries to encourage competition in the market.

Sometimes government will allow monopolies. But it keeps a close watch on them. For example, telephone companies and cable TV companies are private enterprises. They have monopolies on the market. The government approves customer rates. This is to prevent high prices. The government also controls the profits made by the companies. It also makes sure that the service given by the companies is good.

Government regulates monopolies at the city level, too. For example, transit commissions are closely watched by the government. It also controls garbage collection companies and other service companies hired by cities.

Government sometimes refuses to allow monopolies in private business. It does this to lower prices and create free competition. As a regulator, government is allowing the basic laws of free enterprise to work.

*3. Servant*

In 1867, government provided few services. Today, they provide many services. In fact, some people call Canada a "welfare state" or a "service state". This means the government looks after the welfare of its citizens.

In general, people agree on a few of the services offered. We seem to agree that we need public schools, law courts, police forces, and good roads. But other services are harder to agree on. How high should the minimum wage be? Should rich people get family allowances? Should the government give oil companies money so they can explore for oil?

When governments are deciding whether or not to offer a service, they ask two questions. How much will it cost? Is it

146

worth the price? This second question is often hard to answer. People will often disagree with government's answer. Clearly, government's role as servant is not easy.

## 4. Business partner

Sometimes government will act as a partner with buyers and sellers. It will try to get them to work better together. For example, Canada Employment Centres attempt to bring workers and employers together. Also, city mayors and councils often deal with factory owners. They try to get these owners to locate in their area. In return, the city may offer lower taxes for a certain length of time.

Sometimes the government acts as a partner in railway building. It did this in the case of the CPR, for example. It participates in the building of canals and pipelines, and works with oil refineries. It helps chemical companies with research. The government is partner to many companies in our economy.

## 5. Banker for the nation

Canada's national bank is called the Bank of Canada. As banker for the federal government, it performs a number of important tasks. For example, the Bank of Canada distributes bank notes and coins. It sets the rate at which money is lent. In short, it takes care of all the money business for our national government. Its role is to keep the flow of money in our economic system running smoothly.

## 6. Manager of the economy

This is a fairly new role for government. The role grew after the Depression, and has kept on growing since World War II. The government slows rising prices (inflation) or stops falling prices (a recession or depression). It does this by adjusting the flow of money. It also changes the pace of its own taxing and spending. We will look at how the government deals with taxes later in the chapter.

## 7. Researcher

The market system needs information and new ideas in order to work. Much information (such as weather reports or crop conditions) is too hard for the average person to find alone. Also, many new questions (Can potatoes grow north of Sudbury?) would never be answered. Business will not often risk money to answer such questions . The government does all this research. It provides information on a huge number of subjects.

## 8. Monopolist

Governments do some jobs for the good of society. No one else wants to do them. Why not? Some of these jobs are real money-losers, or they will yield little profit. Companies therefore will not do them. Yet the jobs must be done. This is why the federal government runs our armed forces. Also, the Department of Transport constructs and runs our airports. Provinces run our school systems.

Government departments provide most of these services. In some cases, separate government companies are formed. Companies that governments form to do these jobs are called *Crown corporations*. Air Canada and the Canadian National Railways are examples of federal Crown corporations. Provinces also have Crown corporations. Cities run housing authorities and social service agencies. They also run health agencies and water works.

### Confederation Highway

Government in Canada plays many roles in the country's economy. A hundred years ago, though, its role was small. How did government acquire its present power? It did so very slowly.

In 1867, Canada was an agricultural nation with rich forest reserves. Most people still lived in small towns or on farms. Government's role was to act as officer of the law. That is, government kept law and order. It enforced the contracts that Canadians made with one another. It also protected private property.

Gradually, governments became more active.

—They regulated monopolies, although laws were not strict.

—They regulated certain business practices, such as loans and insurance.

—They began to pass the first "social" legislation and act as "public servant".

—They started to act as a business partner. They did this by helping companies develop, and by protecting the economies of different regions.

Government did more through the years. It affected the daily lives of more and more Canadians. Through World War I, the Depression of the 1930s, World War II, and the boom years of the 1950s and the 1960s, governments grew. Today they provide us with many services.

This is just a general outline of how the government has gained power. To get a better idea of how the service state developed, we will go down Confederation Highway. We will stop at important landmarks that show where the government took on more duties.

Confederation Highway landmarks

*National Policy, 1878*

Business partner. Federal government protected industries. It did this with high tariffs (taxes on imports). Promised to help private business build railway to the Pacific. Hoped to attract settlers to West. Tried to get people to use products made in central Canada.

*Canadian Pacific Railway, completed 1885*

Business partner. Federal government promoted idea of sea-to-sea nation. Project was backed by government of Canada with land grants and loans.

*Combines Investigation Act, 1889*

Regulator. Federal government started role as regulator. Made a law that today stops monopolies. Companies must use accurate advertising.

*Ontario Hydro, 1906*

Monopolist. Ontario was first province to own and operate electrical system for cheap hydroelectric power. All provinces finally came to run their hydro companies. They took them over from private enterprise.

*World War I, 1914*

Government created many boards to organize war effort. War had to be financed by government taxes.

*Canadian National Railways, 1923*

Monopolist. The Canadian government took over three railways. Today still operates them and other transport services as Canadian National.

*Old Age Pension Act, 1927*

Public servant. Up to this time, Canadians had to provide for their old age out of their own pockets. Many could not do this. Government set up old age pension plan. In Canada today, government pensions are available to the aged, the disabled, veterans, widows, and others.

*Canadian Broadcasting Act, 1932*

Monopolist. Canadians served by the public Canadian Broadcasting Corporation. As well, private radio and television stations transmit programmes.

*Bank of Canada, 1934*

Banker. The Bank of Canada founded to help stabilize the banking system of the country.

*Canadian Wheat Board, 1935*

Monopolist. In the middle of the Depression, grain growers in West needed help. Grain prices were low. Rail prices for their products were high. The Canadian Wheat

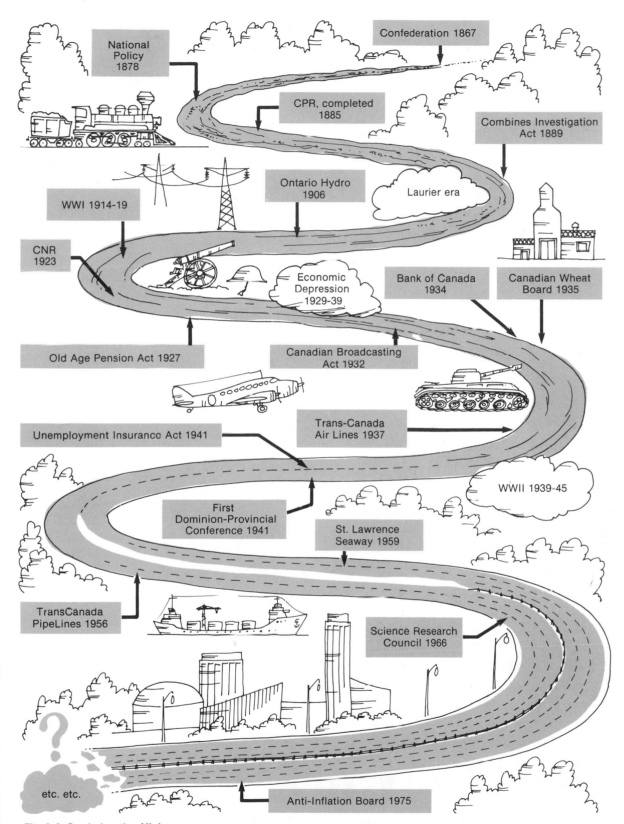

**Fig. 2-6 Confederation Highway**

Board was created to help growers sell wheat, barley, oats, and other grains. This role continues today. The idea of an agency to market and set prices for agricultural products has spread. **Marketing boards** today keep prices stable. They set production limits with farmers. Products such as eggs, butter, and some meats are examples of items covered.

*Trans-Canada Air Lines (later Air Canada), 1937*
Monopolist. Government provided regular air service across country. This was not yet provided by private airlines.

*First Dominion-Provincial Conference, 1941*
Manager. The Depression taught Canadian governments the need to consult and co-operate. Since 1941, provincial premiers have met with the prime minister. They discuss ways taxes can be shared to benefit all regions in Canada. Agreement is often difficult to reach.

*Unemployment Insurance Act, 1941*
Manager — social servant. Before the Unemployment Insurance Act was passed, jobless workers relied on their personal savings alone. Now most jobless workers have protection against unemployment. After a waiting period, they may receive payments while they seek a new job.

*TransCanada PipeLines, 1956*
Business partner. Government helped develop oil discoveries after World War II. Helped finance the first pipeline — natural gas — from Alberta to Quebec and Ontario.

*St. Lawrence Seaway, 1959*
Partner — monopolist. Ontario and Quebec, along with many American states and the US federal government built the St. Lawrence Seaway. Allowed sea-going vessels to enter the Great Lakes. Seaway is run by a government "authority". It sets tolls and manages the Seaway.

*Science Research Council, 1966*
Researcher. The Science Research Council is a Crown corporation. Its job is to make sure our country progresses in science and technology. It recommends projects the government may undertake. Many such research and advice bodies are part of government today.

*Anti-Inflation Board, 1975*
Manager. The government directly attempted to control wage and price changes. A first in peace-time Canada. Disbanded in 1978, but another agency replaced it. This new agency could *report* on inflation but could not *control* changes in prices.

## Why government became involved in our economy: A changing Canadian society

Today, governments at all levels are big, and they help a lot of people. They also spend a great deal of money. In 1972, government spent about 24 billion dollars. By 1977 that amount had more than doubled to about 49 billion dollars. Why are governments spending so much?

Is it because governments are "out of control?" Some people think this is partly true. In general, however, governments are a mirror of our society. If society changes, government must change to meet new needs. And if society demands that governments "do something", they usually will. The trouble is that this costs money.

Here are some recent trends in our society. See if you can understand why these trends make government spending grow.

| Issue | Its effect on government spending |
|---|---|
| **Population changes** | |
| Our population is more than twice as large as it was in 1941. Also in 1941, only 768 000 Canadians were over 65. By 1975, over 1 880 000 Canadians were in this age group. The number of young people in the population has grown, too. In 1941, 141 000 Canadian youths were between 10 to 14. Today the figure is near 2 600 000. | What strains do these changes have on schools? Housing and daycare centres? Parks? Hospitals and other health services? |
| **Urbanization** | |
| You have studied this topic in another chapter. More and more, Canada is becoming a nation of city-dwellers. | When cities grow, many things are needed. Cities need service roads and expressways. They need apartments and townhouses. Citizens want libraries and indoor shopping plazas. These services cost money. |
| **More concern for minority rights** | |
| Canada is a land of many ethnic groups. Since 1941, governments have done more for the country's minorities. More attention, for example, is being given to Native Peoples. Also, people are concerned about French-English relations. Today, governments are promoting the rights and interests of different groups. | In 1976 alone, the federal government spent $492 000 000 to help Canada's Native Peoples. It spent over $130 000 000 on programmes supporting the policy of two official languages. |
| **Consumerism** | |
| Since the early 1950s, consumers have started to make their voices heard. They want safer cars. They want better government services, and cheaper and better food. They want governments to "go to bat" for them. | The federal and provincial governments have answered the call of consumers for action. They have formed departments to act in consumers' interests. They have passed consumer protection laws. These laws protect Canadians from travel fraud and from poor products. How do you think this action affects government spending? People who work in government offices, for example, have to be paid. It also costs money to enforce the laws that protect consumers. |
| **Conservation and pollution controls** | |
| As industry grows, more of our natural wealth is used up. Pollution also becomes a problem. Citizens demand action; they want to make sure that the environment is protected. | Governments have been making and enforcing tougher conservation laws. This costs money, however. The money comes from our taxes. |

151

| Issue | Its effect on government spending |
|-------|-----------------------------------|

**Personal security**

In general, Canadians want security. Most want to know that their basic needs will be met. If Canadians cannot fill basic needs they expect the government to take action. They want governments to provide such services as health care, and aid to older people.

Governments provide Canadians with many basic services. There are, for example, health care programmes, unemployment insurance, and old-age pensions. These services help bring security to Canadians. However they are expensive.

**Our leisure society**

At the turn of the century, many people worked 72 hours a week. By the mid-1950s, the 40-hour work week had arrived. Today there is a move to cut the work week even more. This means that Canadians have more time to spend on leisure activities.

Governments do much in the area of leisure activities. They provide parks and recreation programmes, for example. Government pays for special sports events such as the Olympics. Much money is spent to help Canadians enjoy their leisure hours.

---

### Where does the government get its money?

All of the services and programmes provided by government cost money. Where does the money come from? Mostly from taxes.

Taxes are payments that Canadians have to make to the government. When government spends more money, taxes go up. This of course upsets many people. They ask "Why are governments spending so much? Is the spending out of control?" There are no easy answers to these questions.

The taxation system in Canada is complex. All levels of government have the power to tax Canadians. At each level, different types of taxes are collected. Fig. 2-7 shows you the various taxes collected by the federal government. Notice that all but seven cents of every dollar that the federal government has comes from taxes.

### Government budgets: How our tax money is spent

A budget is simply a plan for spending money. It shows how much was spent in a certain time period. It also shows what the money was spent on. Does your family have a budget? Perhaps it is not set down on paper. But most people plan how they will spend their money.

Governments have budgets too. They must have a clear idea of how much money they are spending each year. They also have to keep track of where the money goes.

In an earlier section we saw that society has been changing. Government spending has been changing with it. The more services people demand, the more money governments must pay. Government budgets become bigger. More money is

| | |
|---|---|
| Personal income taxes | 45¢ |
| Corporation taxes | 17¢ |
| Sales tax | 13¢ |
| Customs duties | 7¢ |
| Fees and payments to government agencies such as the CBC | 10¢ |
| Taxes on non-residents | 1¢ |
| Other sources of income | 7¢ |

**Fig. 2-7 Where the federal dollar comes from**

spent on a greater number of services.

We will get a good idea of how government spending has changed if we compare budgets. Look at the "menus" from the Confederation Restaurant. These menus are really budgets for two years, 1939 and 1975. They show you how much money all levels of government spent. They also list the services offered by governments in those two years.

**Fig. 2-8 Confederation Restaurant (All figures are approximate)**

CONFEDERATION RESTAURANT — 1939

*Our Motto:* Serving you from sea to sea
Average annual wage of production workers in manufacturing — $975

Established in 1867 and still going strong
*Owner:* The Canadian people
*Manager:* The federal, provincial, and municipal governments
*Your waiters:* The civil service

| FEDERAL DISHES | PRICES (1939) |
|---|---|
| —Basic welfare coverage: old age pensions, aid to veterans, municipal welfare payments, emergency health aid | |
| —Some co-operation with provinces in paying for costs of welfare | $404 million |
| —RCMP and armed forces | |
| —Basic safety regulations | |

| PROVINCIAL DISHES | PRICES (1939) |
|---|---|
| —Education | |
| —Health and welfare | |
| —Public works | |
| —Some regulation of business | $436 million |
| —Labour | |
| —Sanitation and waste removal | |
| —Parks | |

| MUNICIPAL DISHES | PRICES (1939) |
|---|---|
| —Education | |
| —Roads, sanitation | |
| —Some control of business | $365 million |
| —Sanitation and waste removal | |

$1 billion, 205 million

CONFEDERATION RESTAURANT — 1975

*Our Motto:* Serving you from sea to sea
Average annual wage of production workers in manufacturing — $10 209

Established in 1867 and still going strong
*Owner:* The Canadian people
*Manager:* The federal, provincial, and municipal governments
*Your waiters:* The civil service

| FEDERAL DISHES | PRICES (1975) |
|---|---|
| —Fancy welfare coverage: unemployment insurance, workers' compensation, family allowances, etc. | |
| —Basic health and medical costs | $28 billion |
| —Aid to provinces to help pay for education at all levels | |
| —Armed forces | |
| —Safety regulations | |
| —Protection of environment | |
| —Help to consumers | |
| —Thousands of crown corporations and agencies | |

| PROVINCIAL DISHES | PRICES (1975) |
|---|---|
| —Minimum wage laws, workers' compensation, etc. | |
| —Rent controls, housing help, etc. | |
| —University education | $20 billion |
| —Human rights commissions | |
| —Health and safety standards | |
| —Protection of environment | |
| —Help with doctor and health costs | |
| —Many public works | |

| MUNICIPAL DISHES | PRICES (1975) |
|---|---|
| —Parks and recreation | |
| —Police protection | |
| —Licences and fees | $14 billion |
| —Zoning laws | |
| —Public works such as roads and bridges | |
| —Education costs shared with provinces | |
| —Others | |

$62 billion

(Note to customer in Confederation Restaurant: A dollar in 1939 bought about four times as much as it did in 1975.)

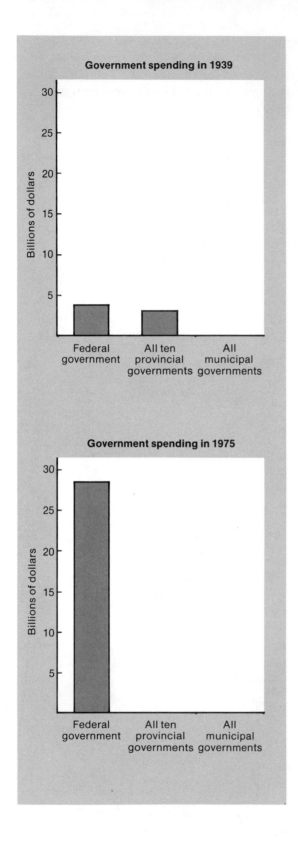

**Government spending in 1939**

Billions of dollars

Federal government · All ten provincial governments · All municipal governments

**Government spending in 1975**

Billions of dollars

Federal government · All ten provincial governments · All municipal governments

**READING BETTER**

1. These questions on the Confederation Restaurant require you to read for details.
   a) What was the average annual wage of production workers in Canada in 1939? In 1975?
   b) What are the three types of dishes served in the government restaurant? What do they stand for?
   c) Name two services given by the federal government in 1975 that are not found on the 1939 menu.
   d) What social changes have caused government to spend more money on parks and recreation? On zoning laws? On education? On airports?
   e) Which level of government in 1939 spent the least money? In 1975?
2. Draw a bar graph of government spending at three levels. Bar graphs can help us compare the amounts of money spent by governments in two different years. Here are two incomplete bar graphs. Copy them in your notebook and finish them. Then, answer these questions for each level of government.
   a) In what year did the government spend more money?
   b) How much more did it spend?

## Option cards: How big a role should government play in the economy?

The Confederation Restaurant "menu" gives a general picture of how government uses its money. Look again at the items on which government spends a lot of money. How do you feel about this type of government spending? Many Canadians think that government is spending too much. Other Canadians want government to spend more money in some areas, and less in others. Mr. Toomath, for example, wants government to spend money on unemployment benefits. But he does not want money spent on things that do not help him directly.

Below are three *option cards*. They present different viewpoints on government spending, and the role of government in the economy. The cards will help you decide how you feel about government and the economy. Write down in your notebook the option with which you agree. Give your reasons.

**Option card 1: William Johnson, individualist**

I'm against a lot of government spending. I think governments should always try to have **balanced budgets.** I don't like the idea of going into debt.

I'm what some people call an "old-time individualist". To me, the less the government is involved in the economy, the better. Government in Canada plays a large role in the economy. There are a lot of things about this that I object to.

First, government controls make it harder for business to operate. Governments seem to be regulating things more each year. Perhaps one day business will have no control at all.

Second, government spends money on things people should do themselves. Large parts of our governments' budgets go to "vital social services". We didn't have those services years ago and people got by. I say government should cut back in this area.

Lastly, I think that people should not go to university if they can't afford to. Governments should not have to give aid to keep universities running. If universities can't remain open without government support, they should close down.

**Option card 2: Josine Ranshek, *government interventionist***

My point of view is the opposite of Mr. Johnson's. I want government to get more involved in our economy, not less. As long as it can carry the debt, government should do more for the economy.

Without government control in the economy, the business world would be too fierce and brutal. Many Canadians would not accept such a world. They want government to set some of the rules.

Also, government tackles jobs that business cannot or will not handle. It can compete with private business. One keeps a check on the other. Canadians therefore get the best from both government and business.

A lot of people criticize the large number of services that the government provides. But I think we should be proud of our social services. Many Canadians need this help from the government to live. More should be done to give security to all people in the nation.

**Option card 3: Arlene Massik, moderate**

I am between Mr. Johnson and Ms. Ranshek in my views. I don't believe in an economy that is completely planned by the government. But I do feel that some government control is needed.

Governments should intervene in the economy in some ways. For example, they can encourage local producers. Governments should buy from local suppliers. This will help local industry.

As far as social services go, we should not cut off all help to needy persons. Many people depend on government aid to get by. But if we go too far the other way and give everyone something, then we create a welfare state. The desire to work and get ahead vanishes. A compromise is needed.

The last point I want to make concerns government spending. Sometimes government revenue (amount of money coming in) is lower than expected. Governments should therefore try to reduce their spending. A balance between the amount of money coming in and the amount going out must be found.

---

## Conclusion

Canada, as we have seen, has a mixed economy. It is a mixture of the government planned system and free enterprise. Each system has its own set of values. The government planned system is based on the belief that government should regulate prices and production. According to the free enterprise system, prices and production should be regulated by buyers and sellers. Each system has its strengths and weaknesses.

Because Canada's economy is based on two systems with different sets of values, conflicts often arise. Canadians are faced with many questions. When should the individual expect aid from government? How can Canadians mix self-reliance with government help so that human freedom and respect are retained? The future challenge for Canadians lies in finding answers to such questions.

**READING BETTER**

1. **Our economy is a huge buying and selling machine. Lately, government has been getting more and more involved in this machine. Look back over the chapter to find what government buys or sells in each of these cases.**
   **Air Canada**
   **Ontario Hydro**
   **St. Lawrence Seaway**
   **Canada Employment Centres**
   **Canadian National Railways**
   **Canadian Wheat Board**

**ORGANIZING BETTER**

1. **Mr. Toomath and his family found that government helps Canadians in many ways. They found, for example, that governments build schools, help workers find jobs, and provide vital services. Make a poster showing ways in which government helps Canadians in general. The following list of roles played by government will perhaps give you some ideas for your poster.**
   **Law officer/Judge**
   **Business partner**
   **Manager of the economy**
   **Regulator**
   **Researcher**
   **Monopolist**
   **Servant**
   **Banker for the nation**

**USING YOUR KNOWLEDGE**

1. **Suppose you had younger brothers or sisters who were to take this course next year. In simple language explain to them one or more of the following key ideas from the course. Use examples to make your explanation clear.**

   **Our economy is a system of buyers and sellers.**
   **Government at all levels is doing more and more for Canadians.**
   **Inflation is a major problem facing Canadians today.**
   **Some Canadians think governments do too much. Others think that they do not do enough.**

**SOLVING PROBLEMS**

1. **Here is a list of economic problems facing Canadians today. Below it is a list of the names of different economic problems. Show that you can identify problems; match up**

each problem with the correct label. Be ready to explain your answers.

Problem A. Some Canadians are paid more each year. Some find, however, that their wage increases do not match rising costs in fuel. They find that other items such as rent, clothing, and certain foods also cost more.

Problem B. Canada exports large amounts of raw materials. A great deal of investment money is brought into the country. Many radios, televisions, and other manufactured goods are imported.

Problem C. Jim Denkin and his wife have full-time jobs. Their wages, however, fall below the wage paid to the average Canadian family. They find that most of their money goes for food, clothing, and rent. They cannot save. They also have debts with credit card companies and at the bank.

Problem D. Sonya Jenkins graduated from high school three years ago. She has had trouble holding a job. She was fired from her last job because she was late so often. Like millions of Canadians she is no longer earning a wage.

Inflation
Our trade record
Unemployment
Inefficiency
Poverty
Regional disparity

2. People in Canada's regions have developed strong local opinions about economic nationalism. What could be done to allow the different regions to control foreign investment the way they want? Consider changes in the BNA Act or new laws or tax policies.

TAKING A STAND

1. You are writing a letter to an important official. You want to tell that person your opinion of an important economic issue facing you and your government. Start the letter with the phrase "I'm in favour of . . ." and complete the sentence. Then back up your opinion with some of the facts you have learned.

RESEARCHING

1. Choose one key idea from this chapter that interests you. In your library look up a magazine article or entry in *Canadian News Facts* related to the idea. Ask the librarian for help if you need it. Write up a short report on the article you have read.

2. Government, as we know, plays a large role in Canada's economy, and therefore in the lives of Canadians. To prevent government from acting in isolation, groups often try to influence its decisions. Big business often does this. So do unions. Unions are associations of workers that serve as a voice for workers.

   Find out more about unions and how they influence government. Refer to the card catalogue in your library under such headings as "unions", "trade unions", and "Canadian Labour Congress".

3. Find information on one of the following social services offered by government:
   Unemployment Insurance
   Family Allowance
   Old-Age Security
   Canada Pension Plan
   Any service offered by your provincial or municipal governments
   Write up a report on the service. Be sure that your report answers these questions:
   1. When was the service first offered?
   2. Why was it offered?
   3. What does the service offer?
   4. Who benefits from it?

## GLOSSARY

**Balanced budgets.** When governments spend only the amount of money that they have raised. They do not rely on credit.

**Bankrupt.** When people, companies or governments are unable to pay their debts.

**Canada Employment Centres.** Federal government bureaus that try to help people find jobs.

**Combines.** A combination of groups: a monopoly. They join together for business profit.

**Competition.** Rivalry or contest among people or groups.

**Cost of living.** A measure of the amount it costs to pay for all the things an average person buys.

**Employment agencies.** Privately-owned businesses that attempt to find jobs for people.

**Government interventionist.** A person who supports government involvement in all areas of society.

**Marketing board.** An agency appointed by the government. It sets prices and quotas for the production of eggs, poultry, and other farm products. Marketing boards are also found outside of the agricultural industry.

**Minimum wage.** All provinces and the federal government have minimum wage laws. They set the lowest wage that may legally be paid to a worker.

**Monopolist.** A person or company with control of a service or good.

**Private property.** The property that belongs to individuals and not to governments.

**Unemployment insurance.** Insurance given by the federal government to cover loss of work. Employees and employers pay into the fund.

**Unemployment insurance cheque.** A payment made by the federal government to unemployed persons who are able to work but cannot find a job.

# 3/The Canadian legal system: Human rights and responsibilities

## Contents

### Introduction

"The world would be easier to live in if there were no laws!" Have you ever heard anyone say this? Perhaps you feel this way when you receive a detention for breaking one of the rules at your school. When people are punished for breaking a law they often feel that they have lost part of their freedom. Freedom is important to most Canadians. Therefore, we become very upset when a set of rules seems to take away our right to act as we please. At times, we may even feel that we would be better off without rules or laws. But would we really be better off?

Throughout recorded time, all groups of people have lived by rules. In Canadian society, there are different sets of rules or laws created to keep order. Some of the rules about how we should behave are informal. For example, our families have rules that help to run the household. Our friendship groups have another set of informal rules that helps us to get along well together.

In Canada there are also formal rules. The laws of Canada exist to keep order, so that Canadians can lead productive and peaceful lives. In this chapter we will focus our attention on the formal laws of Canada. The chapter gives us an overview of the Canadian legal system. The following questions will be discussed:

1. **Do we need laws?**
2. **What are our human rights and responsibilities?**
3. **How can human rights be denied by Canadians?**

4. **What are the Criminal and Civil Courts, and how do they operate?**
5. **What is the role of the police in the Canadian legal system? The role of the Canadian prison system?**

### Life without laws

Before we examine the Canadian legal system we will take a look at what our life could be like without laws. The story "John's world" shows us a society where there are no laws.

---

### John's world

John got up at 7:45 a.m., ate breakfast, and left for school. At the corner, he had to wait for almost half an hour to cross the road. The cars were racing down the highway at high speeds. There were several accidents. Two of John's friends were hurt trying to get across the street.

John got to school at 9:30 a.m. All the doors were locked, so John walked around the building. He could see people inside some of the rooms. But there were a lot of students walking around outside. No one seemed to know what to do. Suddenly a window on the upper floor flew open and the principal stuck her head out.

"John! A three-week detention for not wearing red socks. Report to my office at 8:15 tonight," she yelled.

"I didn't know we had to wear red socks!" John cried.

"Ignorance is no excuse," the principal replied, slamming the window shut.

John finally found a lower-floor window open and climbed inside. He wandered around looking for his classes. At last he met one of his teachers.

"John, you failed history. I held the final exam at my home at 3 a.m. today. You weren't there, so you fail the course. I got together with all your teachers and we have decided to send you back to Grade 8. Turn in your books at the office." The teacher turned and walked away.

John went to his locker. The door was torn off the hinges. All his books and football equipment had been taken. He went to the office to report it. The principal told John that before he went back to elementary school he would have to pay for all the school property that had been taken. Since John had no money, the school took his ten-speed bike.

John felt dejected. Everything was in such a mess. There was no order, there were no rules. He decided to go home.

When John arrived home he found that his family had moved away. John was on his own. He was confused. He decided to phone the government to find out what had happened.

"Hello, is this the Solicitor General's office? It is? Well I want justice," John shouted into the receiver. "It's just not fair. There is no order; the whole world is nuts. You don't know what is going to happen to you."

"We eliminated the law," explained the voice at the other end of the line. "People said that it took away too much of their freedom, so we eliminated the laws, the courts, the police. From now on might is right. You do whatever you think you can get away with. You settle your own problems with your fellow citizens. You'll find that only the strongest people will get their way."

John was very upset as he hung up. "What am I going to do?" he cried out loud. There were no laws to help him find an answer. John would have to decide how to live for himself.

---

### QUICK QUIZ

These questions require short answers.

1. Why do some people object to laws and rules?
2. Why were two of John's friends hurt trying to cross the street?
3. Why was John sent back to elementary school?
4. According to the person in the Solicitor General's office, how were people to live in a world without laws?

### USING YOUR KNOWLEDGE

1. Explain in your own words the meaning of the phrase "might is right".
2. Who should be the leaders in our society?
   a) Those who are the most powerful because they control the guns.
   b) Those who are the most intelligent.
   c) Those who are the most popular.
   d) Your own opinion.
   Give reasons for your choice.
3. In general, when we do not have rules there is confusion. There is no order, and people are not sure what they should do. In a short essay predict what would happen if the referee were removed from a hockey, football, or basketball game.

### SOLVING PROBLEMS

1. All societies have laws. As you know, the purpose of the law is to provide order so that people can enjoy happy and productive lives. In the following situation you are given the chance to make a set of laws for a society.

### STAR TRAVELLERS

You and the four people in your group have been travelling in a spaceship. You have been visiting galaxies beyond your own. As you return to earth your spaceship develops engine trouble. The main engine explodes, damaging the fuel storage tanks and the oxygen tanks. You have only one small engine left. The computer feeds you the following facts:

a) It will take 50 days to reach earth.
b) You have a 30-day supply of food.
c) You have a 40-day supply of water.
d) You have a 50-day supply of fuel.
e) You have a 35-day supply of oxygen.

Your group must answer the following questions:

1. How will you make decisions?
2. What decisions must be made?
3. How will you divide the supplies?
4. What rules or laws will you want to make for the return voyage?
5. How will you enforce the rules?
6. How will you punish people who break the rules?
7. Do you think that you could make the return trip to earth without setting up laws?

### Rights and responsibilities

In the "Star travellers" problem, many students at one time or another think about killing one of the crew so that the remaining four can live. Most students reject this idea. Why? The answer is that we are human beings who recognize that people have certain rights. If you decide to kill someone to save yourself then you have taken away that person's right to life.

Another question that comes up in "Star travellers" is how to punish a person who breaks the rules. Perhaps the person has stolen extra food. This is a difficult problem. The person has shown a lack of responsibility. Each person on the spaceship is responsible for obeying the rules or laws that have been made. When people refuse to be responsible and they break the rules, they become criminals.

The situation in the spaceship is the same as the situation in Canadian society. Canadian citizens have certain rights. These rights, such as the right to life, should not be taken away. But Canadian citizens also have **responsibilities.** A person who refuses to live up to legal responsibilities becomes a criminal. In the rest of this chapter we examine the rights and responsibilities of the Canadian citizen. We also study how they affect the Canadian legal system.

### Human rights and responsibilities in the Canadian legal system

People are often more concerned with their rights than with their responsibilities. You will sometimes see people marching in the street and protesting that their rights have been taken away. Seldom, if ever, will you see people protesting because their responsibilities have been taken away.

If the Canadian legal system is to work properly, Canadians must stand up for both rights and responsibilities. Canada's legal system gives rights to Canadian citizens. It gives them responsibilities as well. We must agree to carry out our responsibilities as well as to receive our rights.

| *Rights* | *Responsibilities* |
|---|---|
| You have a right to the security of your person and property. Therefore, police are hired to protect you and your property. | But you also have certain responsibilities to meet. You should serve on a jury when you are asked. You also have a responsibility not to destroy other people's property. |

What are human rights?
Many people confuse the terms "rights", "liberties", and "freedom". Although each term has a slightly different meaning, for our purposes we will take them all to mean **human rights.** A human right is a power or privilege that belongs to a person by law. These rights are protected by law and cannot be taken away by another citizen or by the state. Canadians can expect the government to guarantee their human rights. If people in Canada do not receive their rights, the government must do something about it. For example, you have the right to own property, and you have security of that property. This means that if you buy a car, it is yours. Nobody can come and take it away from you. If, however, another person does take your car, the government must try to get your property back for you.

In Canada, most human rights are listed in the **Canadian Bill of Rights.** This bill was passed by Parliament in 1960. It is very important to understand what rights you have as a Canadian citizen. Therefore, we will examine the Canadian Bill of Rights in detail. It is also important to understand that you, as a citizen of Canada, must respect the rights of your fellow citizens.

Looking at Fig. 3-1, you will notice that the first column lists the rights. The second column gives you an example of what each right permits you to do. The next column outlines what you must not do. And the last column explains what you can do if someone tries to take the rights away.

**Fig. 3-1  What rights do Canadians possess?**

RIGHTS GUARANTEED BY CANADIAN BILL OF RIGHTS

| Right | What you can do | What you cannot do | How you can protect your rights |
|---|---|---|---|
| Security of person | Be free from attack or assault. | Attack, assault, or injure others. | Call the police. Call the Human Rights Commission. |
| Enjoyment of property and privacy | Have and enjoy property, homes, cars, furniture, etc. Be alone, unseen, quiet, without prying eyes or questions. | Invade the privacy of another with noise, etc. Destroy or trespass on the property of others. Expropriate property without fair payment. | Call the police. Call the Human Rights Commission. Call the Noise Control Bureau. |
| Freedom of religion | Worship as you please. | Deny someone a job, accommodation, or service because of religion. Deny freedom of religion to others. | Call the Human Rights Commission, etc. |
| Free speech | State opinions on public matters without fear of police or government. Speak inaccurately about a matter. Speak in a way that most people consider foolish. | Cause public mischief (e.g., you cannot call "Fire!"). Deny someone else the right to speak, while speaking yourself. Speak lies (slander) and hurt another's reputation. Speak obscenity. Encourage people to revolt against the government. Encourage people to kill racial, religious, or ethnic groups. | Call the Human Rights Commission or your local Civil Liberties Association. Hire a lawyer for expert advice (or seek free legal aid). Call a provincial **Ombudsman.** In the case of people being encouraged to kill members of racial, religious, or ethnic groups, call the police. |
| Right of dissent (Based on freedom of speech) | Disagree with and oppose the governments in Canada. Disagree with the law or rules. | Break the law without punishment. Encourage people to revolt. Deny others this right. | Call the Civil Liberties Association. Call the Ombudsman. |
| Freedom of assembly or association | Hold meetings. Form clubs, groups. Join a club or a political party. Hold a peaceful assembly or parade. | Hold a noisy parade at 4 o'clock in the morning. Riot. Organize to overthrow the government or to commit a crime. Prevent others from enjoying this right. | Call the Civil Liberties Association, Legal Aid Service, Human Rights Commission, or Ombudsman. Call the police. |

| Right | What you can do | What you cannot do | How you can protect your rights |
|---|---|---|---|
| Freedom of the press | Write and publish opinions on public matters without fear of police, or government censorship. Write and publish foolish statements. Write and publish inaccurate information. Distribute leaflets or books. | Publish lies that hurt someone's reputation. Publish obscenities or pornography. Encourage people to revolt or to kill racial, religious, or ethnic groups. | Call the Human Rights Commission or the Civil Liberties Association. Hire a lawyer (or seek free legal aid). Call a provincial Ombudsman. |
| Freedom of movement | Come and go as you please within Canada. Live where you wish. Leave or enter Canada. | Smuggle goods into Canada. Break existing laws. Trespass. Deprive others of this right. | Call the Civil Liberties Association or Human Rights Commission. |

RIGHTS GUARANTEED BY OTHER HUMAN RIGHTS LEGISLATION

| Right | What you can do | What you cannot do | How you can protect your rights |
|---|---|---|---|
| Equal opportunity | Get a job, buy or rent a home or apartment, or obtain service without regard to race, religion, colour, place of birth, ethnic origin, sex, or age. | Deny others equal opportunity. Advertise or post signs denying equal opportunity to others. | Call your provincial Human Rights Commission. |
| Right to an education | Get a free education up to or including university regardless of race, religion, colour, place of birth, ethnic origin, sex. | Leave school until age 16 (some exceptions in various provinces). Deprive others of this right. | Call the Human Rights Commission. Call a school board trustee. Obtain legal aid. |
| Right to health care | Obtain essential medical care regardless of income, race, religion, etc. | Deprive others of this right. | Call an ambulance. Call the Human Rights Commission. |
| Right to welfare | To receive money or aid when you are unemployed or unable to work or obtain an income, regardless of race, religion, colour, place of birth, ethnic origin, sex, age. | Obtain welfare as a result of cheating or lying. | Call City Hall, or the provincial government. Also, call the Human Rights Commission, or Ombudsman. |

**What three human rights are being exercised by the people in these photos?**

John McQueen

1. Make a chart in your notebook in which you list the rights given to Canadian citizens by the Canadian Bill of Rights. In your chart explain what each right allows you to do and what you have a responsibility not to do.

## USING YOUR KNOWLEDGE

1. Look at the following cases. For each one, explain what right has been taken away and which people have shown a lack of responsibility. Remember, people show a lack of responsibility when they do not do what they are required to do. Also remember that we must respect the rights of others.
   a) Judy Baker was refused a job by Stan Brown. Stan said that he did not want to hire Judy because she was a woman.
   b) Steve Kubeck moved to Canada with his parents. The whole Kubeck family became Canadian citizens. The local school in Steve's town refused to allow him to go to school because he was born in Poland.
   c) Dave Johnson punched Fred Stanoff in the nose at a town meeting. Dave said that he did it because "Fred was telling us a lot of socialist nonsense."
   d) Principal Renko would not allow Joan Doughtery and Art Nike to form a student rights club. Principal Renko said "These two students are radicals. They will use that group to fight for reforms or changes in school policy. Most of the students here are happy. I don't think we need a student rights group at our school."

## TAKING A STAND

1. Of all the rights that are listed in the chart, pick out the three that you feel are the most important. Be sure to have reasons for your choices. Be prepared to defend your point of view against the members of your class.

We know that each Canadian citizen has a responsibility to respect the rights of others. Unfortunately, in any society there are always a small number of misguided people who are taking away the human rights of their fellow citizens. Why do they do this? Is it because of greed, envy, ignorance, or **prejudice?**

In the next pages of the book we will try to discover why some Canadians are denying others their human rights. We will also find out what can be done to prevent this.

As you work through these pages always place yourself in the shoes of the people who have lost their rights. By doing this, you will realize how important human rights are to our way of life.

## Denying human rights

In Canada there is a federal government office called the Canadian Human Rights Commission. The Commission listens to Canadians whose human rights are being denied. Human rights commissions exist at the provincial government level, too.

When a complaint comes before the Commission, it sends out investigators to examine the case. The investigators may find that human rights are in fact being denied. They therefore talk to the people who are guilty of the offence, and try to settle the dispute. Most disputes that come before the Commission are resolved at this stage.

Sometimes, however, a problem cannot be solved in this way. The case therefore goes to a special Board of Inquiry. This board is usually chaired by a professor or dean of law. Witnesses are called and evidence is given before the chairperson. The chairperson considers the evidence and decides whether or not discrimination has taken place. If necessary, a penalty is given to the guilty party.

We will examine a real-life case that was brought before the Ontario Human Rights Commission. You will be asked for your opinion of the case.

## Sex discrimination charged

Gail Cummings, an 11-year-old goalie, was chosen by coach Barry Webb as a regular player for the Huntsville Atom All-Star Team. Gail filled out a Canadian Amateur Hockey Association Player Registration Certificate. She sent it to the Ontario Minor Hockey Association. Her registration card was refused because the OMHA docs not allow girls to play on its all-boy hockey teams. Gail had to stop playing for the Atom All-Stars. Gail's mother filed a complaint with the Ontario Human Rights Commission. She charged the OMHA with preventing Gail from using public services and buildings because of her sex.

The Ontario Human Rights Code states: No person shall deny to any person the use of services or facilities that are customarily used by the public because of race, creed, colour, age, sex, marital status, ancestry, or place of origin of the person.

The Ontario Human Rights Commission looked into the case. The Commission was not able to settle the case. A Board of Inquiry was held. Both sides presented their arguments to the chairperson of the board.

The OMHA defended its position by making the following points:

1. The OMHA is a private, voluntary association to promote hockey for boys in certain age groups. The OMHA is not a public service or a public facility. The Ontario Human Rights Code does not apply.
2. Many OMHA members would leave the Association if they were required to work with girls. There is no public demand to have girls and boys play hockey together. Therefore the Association should have the right to control its own membership.
3. The OMHA does not feel that it is socially or morally acceptable for boys and girls to play hockey together. Mixed competition may have bad effects on the players. For example, boys may be harmed by losing to girls in competition. Boys may also learn to roughhouse with girls, instead of treating them with respect.

Counsel for the Ontario Human Rights Commission stated the following points:

1. The OMHA was offering a number of services in a place to which the public is normally admitted, the Huntsville Arena. The action of the OMHA caused Gail Cummings to lose the right to these services solely because of her sex. This violates the Ontario Human Rights Code.
2. Coach Barry Webb reported that Gail was a good hockey player. She would have stayed with the team on the basis of her ability if the OMHA had not rejected her registration card.

**Gail Cummings**

The chairperson of the Board of Inquiry decided in favour of Gail Cummings. The chairperson ruled that by preventing Gail from playing on the Atom All-Star team, the OMHA was violating the Ontario Human Rights Code.

The chairperson ordered that
1. The OMHA apologize to Gail in writing.
2. The OMHA invite Gail to try out for the Huntsville team at her new age level.
3. The OMHA accept Gail Cummings as a player, if the coach felt she was good enough to make the team.
4. The OMHA accept any female player able to make an OMHA team.

## THE APPEAL

The OMHA appealed the Board of Inquiry decision. It took its appeal to the Supreme Court of Ontario. The Supreme Court rejected the Board of Inquiry decision. The Court said:
1. The OMHA is a private non-profit organization to promote hockey for boys. The Board of Inquiry was wrong in saying the facilities of the OMHA were open to the public.
2. The Human Rights Code does not intend to restrict the right of citizens to form athletic associations that are not public. The OMHA had every right to restrict its membership to boys. It is a private and not a public association.

Note: The Ontario Human Rights Commission has received permission to appeal the Ontario Supreme Court's decision.

---

**READING BETTER**
1. Why did the Supreme Court of Ontario overturn the Board of Inquiry decision on the Gail Cummings case?
2. What does this mean for Gail Cummings? For the OMHA?

**TAKING A STAND**
1. Do you agree with the Supreme Court's decision? Why or why not?

**RESEARCHING**
1. Research the Human Rights Commission in your own province. Have there been any similar cases to the Gail Cummings case? What was the decision? What were the reasons given?

### Let 'em play

Down in Nova Scotia, 11-year-old Tina Marie Forbes is getting ready to play hockey—real league games under the umbrella of the Yarmouth Minor Hockey Association. A judicial board of inquiry, set up by the Nova Scotia Human Rights Commission, has ruled that the YMHA does not have the right to exclude a player simply because she's a girl.

Source: *Edmonton Journal* 1978 11 1

In "The Allan Littlewood Story" we will take a close look at a person who denies the human rights of others. Allan Littlewood is a racial bigot. This means that he is prejudiced against certain groups of people because of their race or colour. In Canada today, there are many cases similar to the Littlewood case.

> In January 1975 two blacks were shot by a white on Toronto's Yonge Street. Police did not deny that they had been shot simply because they were black.

> In May 1975 a teenage boy was shot to death in a Toronto suburb by a white man. Witnesses said the gunman told them he was going to shoot the first black he saw.

> A Sikh temple in Vancouver has been repeatedly vandalized in the past few years. Doors have been broken, windows smashed and slogans painted on the walls.

Why are people like Allan Littlewood willing to deny the human rights of their fellow citizens? As you read the story and study the other materials in this section, you will discover the answer to this question. As you read the story, ask yourself these two questions.

1. Why is Allan denying these people their human rights?
2. How would I feel if Allan were denying me my human rights?

---

**The Allan Littlewood story (A fictional account)**

PART 1: ALLAN COMMITS A CRIME

Allan Littlewood was 17 years old. He stood about 1.5 m tall, and weighed 67 kg. Allan had hair the colour of wet sand, and liked wearing hunting boots with the laces undone. He dated girls, and loved pizza and cars. When Allan was in elementary school he played baseball, basketball, football, and hockey. However, he no longer played sports. These days Allan just hung around and worked on his car, a 1967 Mustang convertible.

Six months ago Allan lost his licence for drunken driving. Since then the Mustang had been sitting idle in the driveway. Allan's father refused to let Allan touch the car, not even to wash it. Mr. Littlewood has always been hard on Allan. When Allan made a mistake, Mr. Littlewood punished with a heavy hand. Once when Allan was nine years old he broke a neighbour's window by accident. Mr. Littlewood made Allan stay in his room Saturdays for three months. It was the same now. Allan had been grounded ever since the impaired driving charge. Life had turned sour for Allan.

*The neighbours' party*

It was a warm Saturday afternoon in June. Allan was sitting at the kitchen table trying to do his math homework. He ran his fingers through his hair nervously. Allan was frustrated. He hated the homework, and he hated not being able to see his friends.

"I'll never get this stupid stuff," he muttered. Allan did not understand how to do the math problems he was working on. He had not understood the work on Tuesday, the day of the important math test. Allan pulled a test paper from the back of his notebook. He stared at the big red 28/100 at the top of the page.

Suddenly Allan became very angry. He pounded his fist on the book. He wanted someone, something to blame for his failure on the test. He knew the real reason for the failure—he had skipped class, and had not done the homework. But that did not seem to matter now. Allan wanted to find another reason for his failure. His thoughts were disrupted by his father's shouting.

"Alice! Alice! Just listen to that racket! Those people don't give us a minute's peace with that huge family of theirs. And their food—they're smelling up the whole neighbourhood," shouted Mr. Littlewood. He was a tall man with a round face and a big belly. He stood at the window, glaring at the East Indian family who lived across the street. The family was having an outdoor party on its front lawn.

Mrs. Littlewood went over to the window and stood beside her husband. She was a small, tired-looking woman, with serious grey eyes. "Well Fred," she said quietly, "it seems to me that they have as much right to be outside as anyone else. Just last night your buddies were over for a barbecue. That barbecue lighter fluid you use gives off a strong odour. And you and your friends certainly made your share of noise."

"Rights! What rights have they got?" thundered Fred Littlewood. "We built this country by the sweat of our brow! And then these foreigners come in and expect to just take over. That guy's got five kids, no furniture, and a million relatives. If I had my way I'd send every one of them back to their own country."

"You know, Dad, I think you're right." Allan went into the living room where his parents were talking.

"Who asked you anyway?" shouted Mr. Littlewood, turning around from the window. "You get back in there and study. Do you think I need advice from somebody who gets 28 on a math exam? You just mind your business. Get in there and study and get that high school diploma. Otherwise those Pakistanis with their ten university degrees will get every job you go after."

"You're right, Dad. Those Pakistanis are to blame for all our troubles. At school all they do is study, every minute of the day. They don't watch hockey on TV or go driving around town with their friends. And because they do so well the teacher has to fail somebody. So Canadian guys like me get failed."

"You see Alice! I told you! Those people are ruining the country. It's just like that down at the taxi stand. Those people won't fight for higher wages. The dispatcher gives them the overtime work because they work cheap and never take breaks," cried Mr. Littlewood.

"Well, Fred, they have to make a living, don't they? You are always complaining that Allan doesn't work hard enough. The East Indians are hard workers. They're educated, and they want to get ahead. I don't see what's wrong with that. Besides, all this talk is going to make Allan prejudiced," said Mrs. Littlewood tiredly.

"Prejudiced? You don't have to worry about that, Mom! I already am prejudiced," said Allan, laughing at his mother. "I never told you this, Dad, but last fall I asked that Quirashi girl across the street if she wanted a ride to school. She looked kinda nervous at first, but then she started to get into the car. Before we could drive away her father comes flying out of the house yelling at her to get out of the car. He reaches the car and pulls her out. He's yelling away at her not to be so familiar with boys. He says he'll pick the boys she goes out with and stuff like that. Then he turns on me and tells me to get out. I tell him it's my street and I'll leave when I'm good and ready. Then he threatens to call the police, so I just laugh at him and peel out of there."

Mr. Littlewood's face was red with anger. "Did you hear that? Our son's not good enough for their daughter. Do you believe it? They come over here and they think they own the whole country!"

"That just isn't so, Fred." Mrs. Littlewood was annoyed. "I once talked to Mrs. Quirashi about boys and girls dating. She said that it was their custom for the parents to arrange the marriages of their children. They don't feel that it is proper for boys and girls to date much. They don't think young people should see each other without chaperones unless they are engaged. Quite frankly, I think she may have something. There are too many young people who are getting into trouble today."

"Oh sure," shouted Mr. Littlewood. "You go right ahead and stick up for them. They come in here by the millions, work cheap, and cause inflation. They thumb their nose at your own son and you stick up for them. Good lord, Alice, what's the matter with you?"

Alice Littlewood watched her husband and son go to the kitchen and get some beer. She turned to look once again out of the window. The East Indian family looked so happy and carefree. They didn't seem like bad people, she thought. They were just different, and that made them interesting. Her mind was made up. She would make friends with the Quirashis. Then Fred and Allan would see what nice people they really were.

*Trouble at school*

Things did not work out as Mrs. Littlewood had planned. In the months that followed, Allan became the leader of a small gang of **racist** bigots. Allan enjoyed the way the East Indian students at school feared him. It made him feel important. At first Allan and his friends simply shouted insults at the East Indians. After a while they began to push them around in the hall and knock the books out of their hands. Finally on June 3, Allan and two of his friends were suspended from school for a week. They had been caught in the washroom slapping a grade nine East Indian.

The school's examination results were posted on June 21. Allan learned that he had failed six of his seven subjects. Allan blamed his failure on the week-long suspension. He told his father, "If there were no Pakistanis in this country, I would never have been suspended and missed the review week. And if I hadn't missed the review week I would have passed every subject."

Allan was not pretending. He really believed that his failure was caused by East Indians. He thought it often and said it to others often. Eventually in his mind it became the truth.

*The fire bomb*

During the summer, Allan got his licence back, and took a job with his father at the taxi stand. Allan and Mr. Littlewood became better friends. Every day they would make up jokes about East Indians. On the weekend Allan and his friends drove around looking for East Indians to bother.

In September Allan did not return to school. He was unable to keep the job at the taxi stand, so he got a job in a car wash. The money was poor.

In the months that followed, the tires on the Mustang went bald, and the car needed a valve job. Allan could not pay for these repairs. Allan and his father had an argument about the money for the car. They no longer spoke to each other. Allan's life was a mess, and he knew why—the East Indians were to blame.

On November 11, Allan and his friends were arrested. They had thrown a fire bomb through the front window of a variety store owned by East Indians. The bomb hit the store owner's daughter on the side of the head. She died in the hospital the next day from first-degree burns to 80% of her body. Allan was convinced that this was yet another mess he had gotten into because of East Indians.

---

**QUICK QUIZ**

These questions require short answers.

1. Why did Allan lose his driver's licence?
2. Why did Allan fail his math test? (Two reasons)
3. When Mr. Littlewood criticized their neighbours' party, what did Mrs. Littlewood say?
4. Why did Mr. Quirashi not want his daughter to go in the car with Allan?
5. Why was Allan arrested?

**USING YOUR KNOWLEDGE**

1. a) Make a list of all the problems in Allan's life.
   b) Look up the meaning of the word "scapegoat" in a dictionary.
   c) How did Allan use the East Indians as scapegoats?

**SOLVING PROBLEMS**

1. Pretend that Allan is your friend. You want to help him and prevent him from ruining his life. Write him a letter in which you advise him on how to solve all the problems that he is having in his life. You should discuss all the problems that you listed in part a) of the "Using your knowledge" question.

What made Allan Littlewood a racial bigot? Fig. 3-2 outlines the characteristics of a racial bigot. Not all bigots have every one of these qualities. But some of these traits are present in all bigots. The story of Allan Littlewood clearly shows that both Allan and his father are bigots. The chart will give you further insights into why people like Allan and Mr. Littlewood deny their fellow citizens their human rights.

**ORGANIZING BETTER**

1. **Make a chart of two columns in your notebook. In one column list the qualities of a bigot. In the second give facts from the story that prove that Allan and his father have the qualities of bigots.**

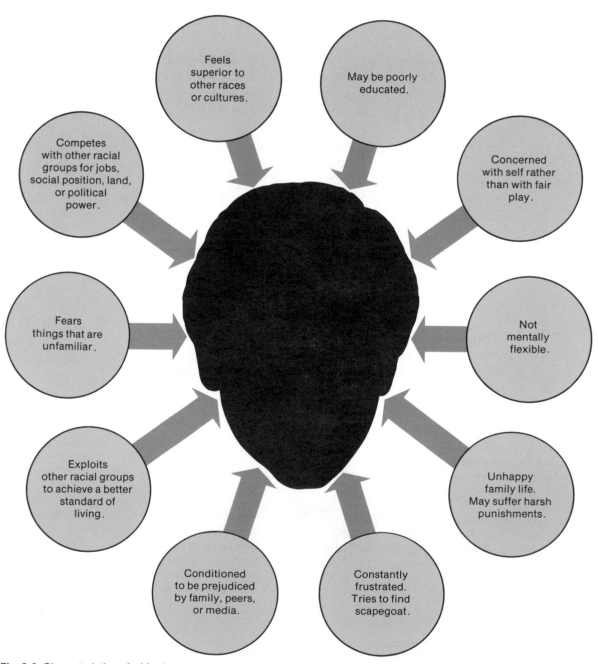

Feels superior to other races or cultures.

May be poorly educated.

Competes with other racial groups for jobs, social position, land, or political power.

Concerned with self rather than with fair play.

Fears things that are unfamiliar.

Not mentally flexible.

Exploits other racial groups to achieve a better standard of living.

Unhappy family life. May suffer harsh punishments.

Conditioned to be prejudiced by family, peers, or media.

Constantly frustrated. Tries to find scapegoat.

**Fig. 3-2 Characteristics of a bigot**

Characteristics of a tolerant person
Why is it that one person becomes a bigot and another person does not? In Fig. 3-2 we see that people's family lives, and the problems in their lives affect their attitudes towards others. But that does not answer the question completely. Mrs. Littlewood, for example, was exposed to her husband's prejudiced points of view. She suffered because of the country's inflation problems, just as her husband did. She also had a son who was in trouble with the law. Yet she did

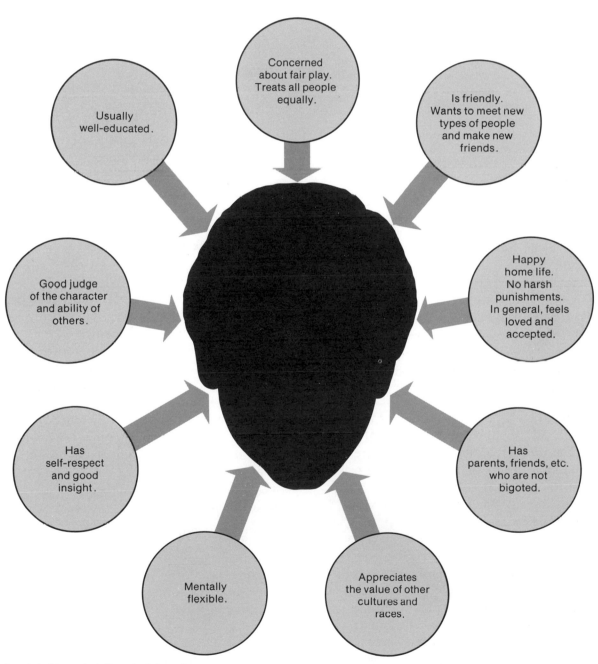

Fig. 3-3 **Characteristics of a tolerant person**

not use the East Indians as a scapegoat. Why?

Fig. 3-3 outlines the characteristics and background of a **tolerant** person. Of course most tolerant people do not have all the qualities listed in the chart. However, they usually have many of them. Read this chart carefully. Copy the characteristics of the tolerant person into your notebook.

**USING YOUR KNOWLEDGE**

1. **Reread the qualities that bigoted and tolerant people seem to possess.**
   a) **How would a tolerant person explain the following ideas to a less tolerant one?**
      i) **Canada's laws regarding human rights.**
      ii) **What prejudice did to Allan Littlewood.**
   b) **How would you feel if you were a victim of prejudice?**

## The Canadian legal system: Criminal and civil law

We need laws. Without them, there would be no order. Without laws, some people would deny us our human rights.

We have seen that there are different types of laws. Some are informal, such as the **social customs** in your family. Others are formal. These formal ones are the laws of the land. In Canada there are two main groups of laws: **criminal law** and **civil law.**

### Criminal law

Criminal law deals with wrongs for which people can be punished. It includes offences such as murder, arson, and theft. These crimes may be committed against individuals, but they are considered to be crimes against society. Thus, the federal government is responsible for bringing the offender to trial.

Criminal law is made by Parliament. The rules are set down in the **Criminal Code** of Canada. The Criminal Code also states how an offender will be punished. For example, Allan Littlewood is accused of committing two crimes, arson and murder. These crimes are listed in the Criminal Code. If he

is convicted Allan will serve a sentence laid down in the Criminal Code.

### Civil law

Civil law deals with property and civil rights. It is concerned with disputes between individuals or groups. These disputes may take place over contracts, personal relationships, or property. We saw that in criminal offences, the government takes the offender to trial. In civil cases, however, it is up to the injured party to take the case to court.

Suppose, for example, you lend your tennis racket to a classmate. The person loses it and refuses to pay for it. To get back the money you would sue the person for the cost of the racket in a civil court.

The provincial and federal governments share authority over civil law. Provinces have control over property and civil rights, for example, but the federal government controls such areas as banking.

## The five parts of the Canadian legal system

The Canadian legal system is more than just the laws of the land. The system is really made up of five parts: Canadian citizens, the government, the police, the courts, and the Canadian prison system. Look at Fig. 3-4. The chart describes the main parts of Canada's legal system. In the rest of this chapter, we will study the different parts of the system. In another chapter of the book we looked at the government and how it makes laws. Therefore we will examine the other parts of the system: the police, the courts, and the prisons.

### The police

The police are expected to enforce the laws of the country. In Canada there are three types of police forces: the Royal Canadian Mounted Police, provincial police forces, and municipal police.

The RCMP can enforce federal laws throughout the country. Usually, though,

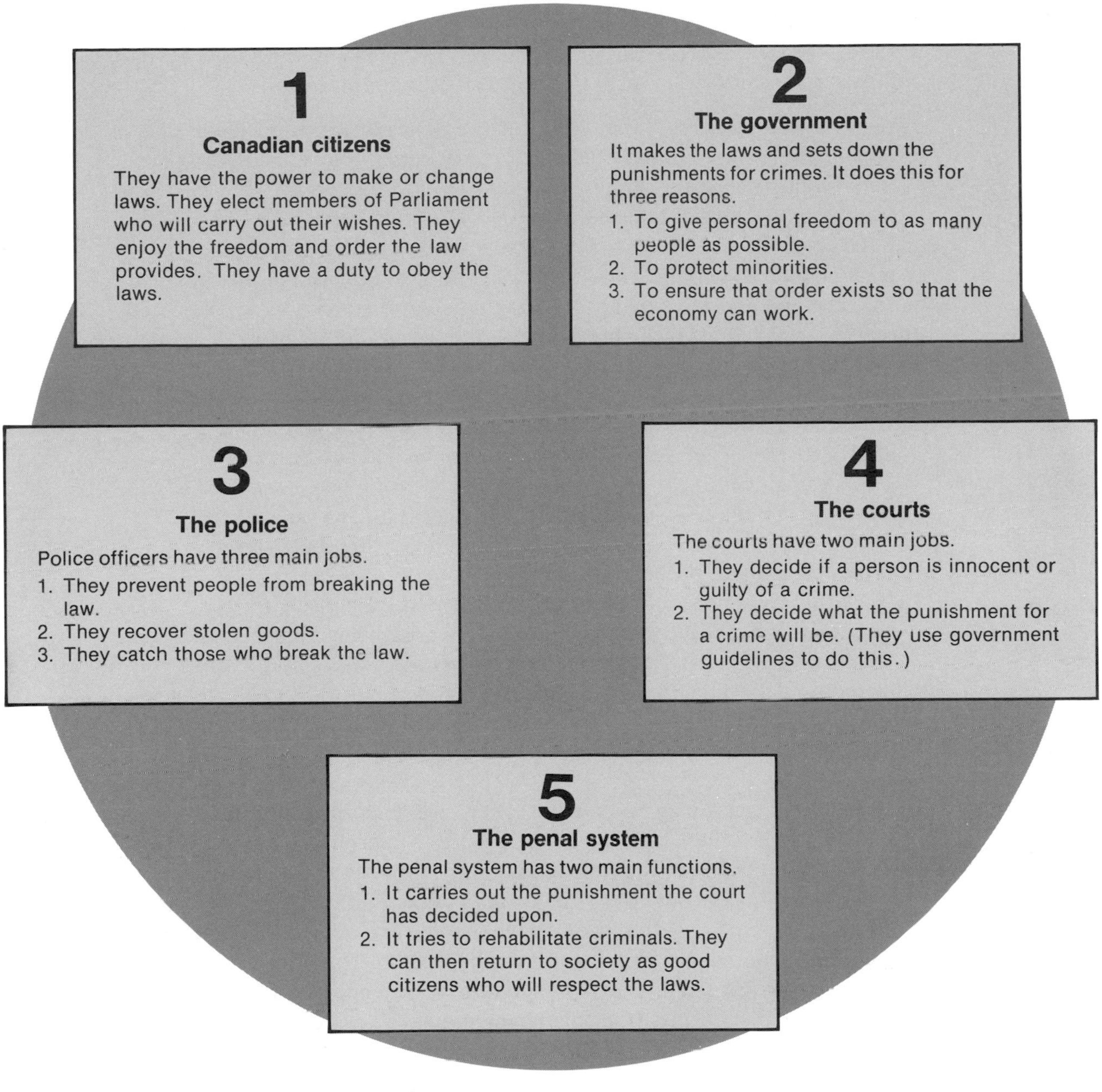

## 1
### Canadian citizens

They have the power to make or change laws. They elect members of Parliament who will carry out their wishes. They enjoy the freedom and order the law provides. They have a duty to obey the laws.

## 2
### The government

It makes the laws and sets down the punishments for crimes. It does this for three reasons.
1. To give personal freedom to as many people as possible.
2. To protect minorities.
3. To ensure that order exists so that the economy can work.

## 3
### The police

Police officers have three main jobs.
1. They prevent people from breaking the law.
2. They recover stolen goods.
3. They catch those who break the law.

## 4
### The courts

The courts have two main jobs.
1. They decide if a person is innocent or guilty of a crime.
2. They decide what the punishment for a crime will be. (They use government guidelines to do this.)

## 5
### The penal system

The penal system has two main functions.
1. It carries out the punishment the court has decided upon.
2. It tries to rehabilitate criminals. They can then return to society as good citizens who will respect the laws.

**Fig. 3-4 The five parts of the Canadian legal system**

RCMP officers enforce specific areas of law, such as the Narcotics Control Act. The RCMP also police eight of Canada's provinces and several municipalities across the country.

Ontario and Quebec have their own provincial police forces. They are responsible for law enforcement in their own provinces, except in areas served by local police. Local or municipal police include the forces found in counties, townships, and large cities. They enforce the Criminal Code, provincial laws, and municipal by-laws.

**What is it like to be a police officer?**

To discover the answer to this question, read the interview that follows. The interviewer is asking a police officer about the job.

**Interviewer:** Do you think that your job as a police officer is difficult?

**Police officer:** Yes, I think it is very difficult at times. You must have a lot of patience. For example, you have to investigate a lot of family fights between a husband and wife. It takes a great deal of patience to calm them down. You also have to know how to deal with people. Say you go walking in there acting really tough. Both the husband and wife will be attacking you before you know it.

**Interviewer:** What other qualities must you have as a police officer?

**Police officer:** Well, you have to be able to make split-second decisions at times. You also have to be intelligent and confident in yourself. We run into all types in this job. Some of the people we deal with are very clever. The police have to be just as clever or the offender will win.

**Interviewer:** So far we've talked about the qualities that a police officer as a person must have. What about skills? Are there special skills that a police officer must have?

**Police officer:** A police officer should be able to use a gun accurately. You also must be able to handle yourself in unarmed combat. You should be able to handle a car at high speeds. All of these skills will be required at some time or another in the job.

**Interviewer:** That brings up an interesting point. When do you use your gun? How do you decide when you should take out that pistol and use it?

**Police officer:** That's a good question. There are strict rules about using a gun. It's not like on TV where officers run around firing their guns all the time. There are only four situations in which you are allowed to take out your gun. You can take it out to defend your life or another person's life. You can take it out to make an arrest if you think that the person you are arresting is dangerous. You can take it out to kill a dangerous animal, or to kill an animal that is injured and is suffering. And finally you can take your gun out and fire it to give an alarm signal. Sometimes there is no other way to give an alarm.

Every officer knows the right time to take out a gun. If you stick by the rules you don't have any problems. If you use your gun for any reason you have to report it to your superior. The superior looks into your case to see if you were acting wisely.

**Interviewer:** I suppose your job varies from day to day. What are you expected to do on a typical day?

**Police officer:** Now that is a tough question! We have so many different types of jobs. I'm not sure I can tell you what a typical day is like. But I can tell you what types of jobs we do.

**What jobs do police officers do?**

As I said before, we have to deal with a lot of family problems. We deal with car accidents. Very often people are hurt in these accidents. We have to get them medical aid as quickly as possible. We have to collect evidence at the scene of all the accidents. We write out detailed reports on all our investigations. These reports are used in court. We have to be very careful to get the facts straight. The public doesn't know it, but we spend a lot of time writing out reports.

We also go to scenes of crimes, such as bank robberies. We have to gather the evidence and make reports on what we find. Then we search for the offender and the stolen goods.

**Interviewer:** Are there any jobs that you dislike?

**1**
Catch
criminals

**2**
Direct
traffic

**3**
Question people
suspected of
crimes

**4**
Testify
in court

**5**
Find
missing persons

**6**
Settle
family fights

**7**
Deal with
suicide cases

**8**
Hold stakeouts
and do undercover
work

**9**
Notify
relatives
of a death

**10**
Patrol
streets

**11**
Investigate
car accidents

**12**
Make reports
on accidents
and crimes

**Fig. 3-5 The jobs of a police officer**

180

**Police officer:** One of the worst jobs is telling parents that their child has been killed in a car accident. There is no easy way to do that. That is a terrible job.

Also we have to patrol the streets. Just driving around can be boring. A stakeout can be dull too. You just sit there and watch a building. You record who goes in and out. It's hard. You can't let your mind wander because you may miss something.

**Interviewer:** One last question. What can citizens do to help the police carry out their job?

**Police officer:** Well above all, citizens should obey the laws. They should also co-operate and give the police information when it is requested. If you see a crime being committed you should report it. You would be surprised how many people see crimes and never report them. If they did, it would really help us to solve crimes.

Another thing—police officers find it easier to do a better job when they feel that people support them. It's discouraging when somebody yells foul language at you. So people can help police officers by respecting them.

---

**READING BETTER**
1. What qualities must police officers possess?
2. What special skills must they have?
3. Why is a police officer's day varied?
4. Why must a police officer be able to deal with people?
5. When can police officers draw their guns?
6. List three ways in which citizens can help the police to enforce the law.

**TAKING A STAND**
1. Would you like to become a police officer? Give reasons for your answer.

**RESEARCHING**
1. A montage is a picture that is made up of many small pictures, articles, and story headlines. Make a montage that shows the ideas raised in the interview. You can look in newspapers and magazines for the pictures, stories, and headlines you need. The more ideas you show, the better your montage will be.

---

### The Allan Littlewood story

PART 2: THE POLICE ARREST ALLAN

At 8:05 p.m. a call came into the Central police station. Someone had thrown a fire bomb through a variety store window. Central police station contacted a police car in the area of the fire.

The two officers soon arrived at the scene. Flames were shooting out of the front window of the store. The officers raced from the car and began pushing bystanders away from the fire.

"Is everybody out of the store?" shouted Officer Smith.

Someone answered "yes". Officer Smith turned toward the voice. A man was kneeling on the sidewalk beside a little girl. She was wrapped in a blanket.

"Are you the store owner?" asked Officer Smith.

"Yes. My little girl is burned. I can't rouse her," shouted the man. His face showed panic.

"Has anybody called an ambulance?" shouted Officer Smith. The bystanders looked at one another and shook their heads. Smith stooped and swept the girl into his arms. "The kid is badly burned. I'll get her to the hospital," Smith yelled at his partner, Officer Jones.

"I'll stay and get statements from any witnesses. Go ahead," shouted Officer Jones.

With flashing lights and wailing siren, the police car disappeared down the street.

********

Officer Smith returned to the store an hour later.

"How is she?" asked Officer Jones, who was writing some notes on a pad.

"No chance. It will be a miracle if she gets through the night. What did you find out?" asked Smith.

Officer Jones told Smith what the witnesses had seen. At about 7:30 p.m. a 1967 or 1968 Mustang, licence number 638-803 or 808, pulled up in front of the store. Four boys got out. They went to the door and yelled racial slurs at the East Indian owner. The store owner came out and said he was going to call the police. The boys drove off. About twenty minutes later they returned. The driver of the car got out. He lit a match to a rag. One of the boys in the back seat shouted "Don't do it!" The driver ignored him. He ran toward the store, throwing the fire bomb through the front window.

"We know the car make and the licence number. I hope it isn't stolen. Did you get a description of any of the boys?" asked Smith.

Jones turned over several pages in his notebook. He answered, "Yes. A woman who lives across the street was sitting on her front veranda. She is the one who called the police. She said the driver was 18 or 19 years old. He had sandy blond hair. He wore a brown leather jacket and hunting boots. "

Officers Jones and Smith returned to police headquarters. They ran a check on the car. In less than an hour they had a name and address. They drove to the house of Frederick Littlewood.

Allan answered the door. The two officers identified themselves. Allan looked nervous. He told the officers that he had been driving the car. He said, however, that he didn't know anything about the fire.

"Allan, we want you to come to the police station. We need to ask you some more questions," said Officer Jones.

"Um...ah...can I get my coat?" asked Allan. Officer Jones nodded. Allan walked back down the hallway. He started to open the closet door. Suddenly, he broke into a run. He raced through the kitchen, out the back door, and across the lawn. Officer Smith was in hot pursuit. As Allan tried to climb over the back fence Officer Smith caught him. Smith grabbed him by the shirt and threw him to the ground. Allan jumped up, holding a small garden hoe.

"Drop that, son. You are going to get yourself hurt. Aren't you in enough trouble already?" asked Smith. The officer moved slowly toward Allan.

The boy lashed out. Smith blocked the attack and punched Littlewood. The boy fell backward. After a moment, he sat up. Allan yelled, "I'll have your job for that. You had no right to hit me. That's police brutality!"

**1**

Identify themselves as police officers.

**2**

Avoid using any more force than is necessary.

**3**

Tell people why they are being arrested.

**4**

Tell people that their statements can be used in court.

**5**

Tell people that they do not have to make a statement.

**6**

Give suspects the chance to call a lawyer. But sometimes a suspect will use the call to warn people. If officers think that this will happen, they do not have to let suspects make the phone call.

**Fig. 3-6 What police officers must do when making an arrest**

Officers Smith and Jones picked Allan up and dragged him to the police car.

At the police station, Smith told Allan that he was being arrested. The charges were arson and murder.

"You do not have to make a statement, Mr. Littlewood. If you do, it can be used in court against you," said Jones.

"Statement! I'll make my statement to the press. You guys beat me up. That's police brutality. I want to call the newspaper. I want to call my lawyer. I have a right to call my lawyer," shouted Allan.

Jones and Smith moved away so Allan would not hear them. "I don't think we should let him call a lawyer. Not yet. The other boys are still on the loose. He may call them and they may run. Let's see if we can round up the other boys. We can let him cool off overnight. He can call his lawyer in the morning."

Allan was led to a cell. The iron door closed. Allan Littlewood had been arrested.

## READING BETTER
1. What jobs did the police have to do as they looked into this crime?
2. Explain why Officer Smith hit Allan.

## ORGANIZING BETTER
1. Make a chart in your notebook. Draw a line down the middle of the page. At the top of the left column write "What police must do while making an arrest". At the top of the right column write "Actions by Smith and Jones in the Littlewood case". In the left column write down the six things that a police officer must do while making an arrest. In the right column write down facts from the story. These facts should show whether or not Smith and Jones did what they were supposed to do when they arrested Allan Littlewood.
2. Why must police officers follow rules when they make an arrest?

## USING YOUR KNOWLEDGE
1. Police officers often have to make quick decisions. Use facts from the story to prove that Officer Smith was able to make quick decisions.
2. Police officers spend a lot of time writing reports. Pretend that you are Officer Smith or Jones. Write up a report for the night of November 11. Remember that your report may be used as evidence at Allan's trial.

Therefore, be sure you include all the facts of the Littlewood case.

## TAKING A STAND
1. Take a stand on the issue, "Should Officer Smith have hit Allan?" Be sure that you have facts to back up your point of view.

The courts

When do courts take over cases? The power of the court begins when the police take an alleged offender into custody. The court also takes over after a citizen charges another citizen with damages.

Courts have two main jobs. First, they decide if the **defendant** is innocent or guilty. Second, they decide how the guilty people will be punished.

We know that Canada has two main types of law, criminal and civil law. Likewise, there are two types of courts, criminal and civil courts. To begin with, we will look at the criminal court system.

*The Canadian criminal court system*
The BNA Act gives the administration of justice to the provincial governments in

Canada. This means that the provincial courts must deal with criminal offences. In general, the Provincial Court: Criminal Division will handle minor criminal offences. The more serious criminal offences must go to the Supreme Court of the province. The Supreme Court of a province will also handle **appeals** from the other provincial courts.

We often hear people speak of higher and lower courts. In general, the higher provincial courts handle the more serious cases. The lower courts look after the less serious cases.

A moment ago, we said that the Supreme Court of a province handles appeals from lower courts. What does this mean? In all court cases a decision is made by a judge. This decision can be appealed. This means that the parties in the case can ask the court to think about the decision again. Perhaps then the decision will be changed.

Canada's criminal court system is not as complicated as it may seem. There are really only three main questions that must be answered in any court case.

1. What type of offence is it?
2. In what court will the case be tried?
3. In what court will the appeals be held?

To see how this system works we will follow a single case through the system. We will use the case of Shirley Stevens. Shirley has been charged with murder.

1. What type of offence is it?

First of all, Shirley Stevens appears before a judge. The judge decides what type of offence Shirley has committed. There are two types, *indictable offences* and *summary conviction offences*. Summary conviction offences are minor crimes. The penalty for them is a fine of up to $500 or six months in jail or both. Indictable offences are more serious crimes. Shirley's offence is indictable, because she killed someone.

2. In what court will the case be tried?

There are three kinds of courts to choose from. First, the Family Court handles family issues such as divorce, alimony, and juvenile (youth) problems. Second, the Provincial or Magistrates' Court handles fairly serious indictable offences. Finally, the Provincial Supreme Court looks after the most serious indictable offences. These are crimes such as murder, rape, and treason. Shirley Stevens murdered someone. Her case goes to the Provincial Supreme Court.

3. In what court will the appeals be held?

A sentence is passed by a certain court. If that sentence is appealed, the appeal usually goes to the next highest court. Shirley Stevens's case was tried in the Provincial Supreme Court. Her appeal goes first to the Appeals Division of that court. If Ms. Stevens and her lawyers are still not happy, they can bring their appeal to the Supreme Court of Canada.

Not all cases receive the right to an appeal. Appeals are granted for three main reasons. First, the judge may have made some error in conducting the trial. Second, the jury may have been shown to be prejudiced against the defendant. Third, new evidence may have been found.

The Supreme Court of Canada does not hear appeals of all kinds. It will hear the appeal if a case deals with a very difficult point of law. It also hears appeals if the case has aroused national interest and is of concern to the entire nation.

Examine Fig. 3-7. You will see that there are two types of offences, three main courts where trials take place, and three main appeal courts. The chart on the criminal court system will help you understand what you have just read. You will also understand the system better as you read Part 3 of the Allan Littlewood story. The story follows the exercises on the criminal court system. .

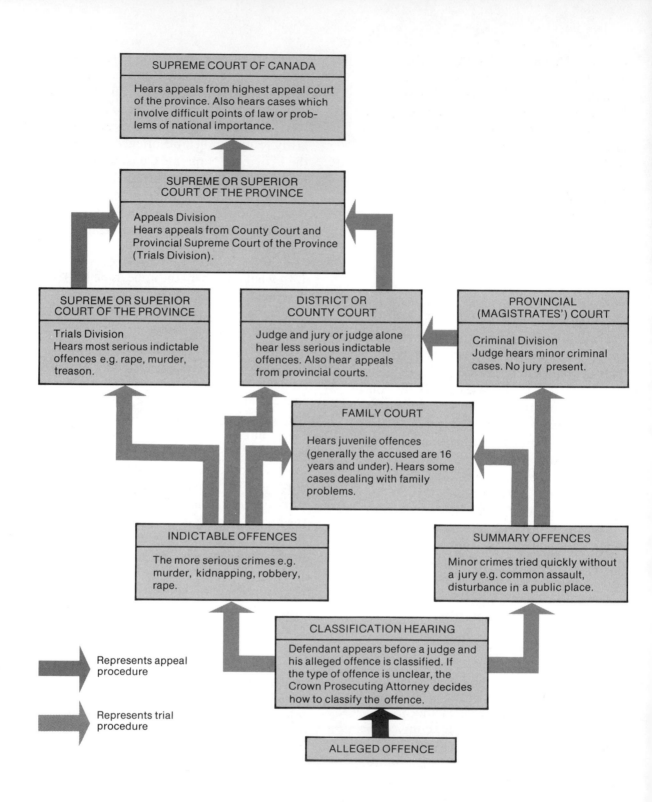

**SUPREME COURT OF CANADA**
Hears appeals from highest appeal court of the province. Also hears cases which involve difficult points of law or problems of national importance.

**SUPREME OR SUPERIOR COURT OF THE PROVINCE**
Appeals Division
Hears appeals from County Court and Provincial Supreme Court of the Province (Trials Division).

**SUPREME OR SUPERIOR COURT OF THE PROVINCE**
Trials Division
Hears most serious indictable offences e.g. rape, murder, treason.

**DISTRICT OR COUNTY COURT**
Judge and jury or judge alone hear less serious indictable offences. Also hear appeals from provincial courts.

**PROVINCIAL (MAGISTRATES') COURT**
Criminal Division
Judge hears minor criminal cases. No jury present.

**FAMILY COURT**
Hears juvenile offences (generally the accused are 16 years and under). Hears some cases dealing with family problems.

**INDICTABLE OFFENCES**
The more serious crimes e.g. murder, kidnapping, robbery, rape.

**SUMMARY OFFENCES**
Minor crimes tried quickly without a jury e.g. common assault, disturbance in a public place.

**CLASSIFICATION HEARING**
Defendant appears before a judge and his alleged offence is classified. If the type of offence is unclear, the Crown Prosecuting Attorney decides how to classify the offence.

**ALLEGED OFFENCE**

Represents appeal procedure

Represents trial procedure

**Fig. 3-7 The criminal court system and routes of appeal**

186

**ORGANIZING BETTER**

1. List the two types of offences.
2. List the three courts where trials are held.
3. List the three Appeal courts.

**USING YOUR KNOWLEDGE**

1. In each of the following cases, answer these three questions. What type of offence is involved? Where will the trial be held? Where will the appeals be held? Explain your answers.
   a) John Duntz is charged with assault.
   b) Mabel Jones is charged with shoplifting a book. The possible fine for the first offence is $100.
   c) Joe Grecco wants a divorce from his wife Louise.
   d) Peter Ostrinsky, age 12, is charged with breaking and entering.
   e) Amin Hajiani, age 24, is charged with car theft. The penalty could be two years in jail.

**RESEARCHING**

1. In your newspaper find stories on a number of criminal cases. In each case explain the nature of the offence, where the trial will be held, and where the appeal will be held.

---

### The Allan Littlewood story

PART 3: ALLAN LITTLEWOOD GOES TO COURT

Allan sat nervously on the bench in the defendant's waiting room of the courthouse. He could not get comfortable on the bench. He knew that the sheriff's deputy would be coming for him soon. He began going over what had happened in the last three-and-a-half months.

*Bail*

The day after his arrest he had appeared before a judge. The judge sternly charged him with an indictable offence.

"You are charged with the indictable offences of arson and murder," said the judge. "Do you wish to plead guilty or not guilty?"

Allan's father had hired the firm Thompson and Baldwin, Attorneys at Law, to defend Allan. Peter Baldwin stood and said, "We do not wish to plead at this time, Your Honour. The defendant's father has just hired our law firm to take this case. We will need more time to examine the evidence." The judge accepted the lawyer's request.

Then the judge turned to the police officer who had arrested Allan. The judge asked the officer whether or not Allan should be granted *bail*. Officer Smith said that he saw no reason why bail should not be granted. The judge set the bail at $20 000. Allan remembered how white his father's face went when he heard the figure.

In serious cases such as Allan's the court requires the defendant to put up a sum of money. When the money is paid, the defendant is released from jail. This money ensures that the defendant will show up for trial. This sum of money is called bail. Bail can be refused if the judge feels that the defendant may not show up for the trial.

After the bail was set, the judge *remanded* the case for three months. This meant that the case would not appear in court for three months. During this time the Crown Attorney and the Defence could prepare their evidence.

*Preparing for the trial*

In the next three months Allan met with his lawyers almost every day. They asked him questions about the night of the crime. They also brought in psychiatrists to test Allan. They all talked to him about his attitude toward East Indians.

The lawyers finally decided upon a defence. They would try and prove that Allan was temporarily insane. Allan had been drinking before the incident. The lawyers hoped to prove that Allan was intoxicated. They wanted to show that Allan did not know what he was doing.

---

**READING BETTER**
1. Why was Allan's offence not a summary conviction offence?
2. What does it mean when a person is denied bail?
3. What takes place in a criminal case between the time the case is remanded and the trial date?

---

*Plea bargaining*

Allan did not see his lawyers for several days. He wondered what was happening. His mother phoned to find out. She was told that Thompson and Baldwin were searching for character witnesses. These are people who would testify in court that Allan was a nice person. Allan's mother told him that his lawyers were having trouble finding people. Allan could not understand this.

Finally Thompson and Baldwin came over to the Littlewood house. They had a new plan. They wanted Allan to plead guilty to the lesser charge of manslaughter.

"I don't understand what you mean," said Allan. "Why should I plead guilty? Can't you get me off?"

"This is what we call *plea bargaining*, Allan," said Janice Thompson. "We are having trouble building a case. We are sure that one of your friends is going to become a **witness for the Crown.** There is a good chance that you will be found guilty. If you are found guilty on the murder charge the sentence will be life in prison. But if we make an agreement with the Crown to plead guilty to manslaughter the sentence will be eight to ten years or less."

"But why would the Crown agree to that?" asked Allan. His face had turned white. He finally saw that he might spend the rest of his life in prison.

"Plea bargaining is a common practice," said Baldwin. "It is good for both the accused person and the Crown. If the Crown's case isn't airtight the Crown will agree to make a bargain. This saves the court's time. That in turn saves the taxpayers a lot of money. In plea bargaining, the accused pleads guilty to a lesser charge. The Crown will accept this plea because it means that the accused will be punished. Plea bargaining may not result in the maximum punishment. But it does guarantee that the accused will not be set free.

Allan remembered that he felt shaken. If he agreed to the plea bargaining it meant that he would spend years in prison. At first he said no. Thompson and Baldwin argued. Allan finally agreed. Thompson contacted the Crown. She offered to plea bargain but the Crown refused. Allan felt sick and alone.

As he sat waiting for his trial to begin, Allan was more frightened than he had ever been before. He could spend most of his life locked away in prison. "How could this happen?" he thought. "How could this happen to me?"

---

**READING BETTER**
1. What is plea bargaining?
2. To what charge did Baldwin and Thompson suggest Allan plead guilty?
3. Why did they want Allan to plead guilty?
4. Why would the Crown accept a plea of guilty to a lesser charge?
5. Why do you think that the Crown refused Allan's plea?

---

*The trial*
As soon as the jury was chosen, Allan's trial began. Two sheriff's deputies brought Allan in, and seated him at the defence desk. One guard sat behind Allan. He had to make sure that Allan did not try to escape. Allan was afraid. He did not want to be punished.

*The opening statement*
The Crown Attorney got up and made the opening statement.

"We intend to prove that on the night of November 11, 1978, the defendant, Allan Littlewood, drove to the variety store. He got out of his car and lit a fire bomb. He threw the bomb into the window of the store. We intend to prove that Allan Littlewood hated East Indians. We want to show that he knew what he was doing when he threw the bomb. We will prove that Allan Littlewood intended to kill the members of the family."

After the Crown Attorney finished speaking, Peter Baldwin made the opening statement for the defence.

"Your Honour, ladies and gentlemen of the jury. I want you to be clear about what the Crown must prove in this case. It must prove that Allan, not one of his friends, threw the fire bomb. It must prove that the person who threw the bomb wanted to kill someone. The Crown will not be able to do this. You will see from our evidence that Allan did not intend to kill anyone. As a result, I am sure you will have mercy on this misguided boy. He is a product of his father's racial prejudice. This boy was not in his right mind on the night of November 11, 1978."

### Selecting the jury

A group of people are chosen from the list of voters. These people are called prospective jurors. They must be citizens of Canada and never have been sentenced to a twelve-month jail term. They come to the court where the Defence and Crown Attorneys ask them questions. The attorneys want to find out if the people will be suitable jurors.

Attorney Thompson asked the questions in the Allan Littlewood case. She asked the prospective jurors five questions.

Are you prejudiced against Allan Littlewood?

Do you have strong feelings about this type of case?

Do you have prior knowledge of this case?

Are you related to the victim or the accused?

Have you already decided if the accused is innocent or guilty?

**Lawyer Thompson**          **Prospective juror**

From these five questions the attorneys can see whether or not the people should be selected for the jury. The attorneys keep challenging prospective jurors until they finally agree on twelve people. These twelve jurors will hear the evidence in the case.

190

*Calling witnesses and cross-examination*

The trial went on for weeks. First the Crown presented its evidence, and called its witnesses. The Defence cross-examined each of the Crown witnesses. This means that Allan's lawyers questioned the witnesses about what they said. (Fig. 3-8 shows four reasons for cross-examining witnesses.)

After the Crown had completed its case the Defence presented its own case. Allan's lawyers presented their evidence and called their witnesses. After the Defence witnesses had given evidence they were cross-examined by the Crown.

Fig. 3-8 Four reasons for cross-examining witnesses

**USING YOUR KNOWLEDGE**

1. **Pick a person from your class to play Allan Littlewood. This student should know the Allan Littlewood story well. Pick three or four students to be the Attorneys for the Crown. They will cross-examine Allan and see if they can break down his story. The rest of the class will be the jury.**

*The final steps in a criminal trial*

After all the witnesses have been called and all the evidence has been given, there are still six more stages in a criminal trial.

1. Closing statement. After all the witnesses have been heard, each lawyer makes a short speech to the jury. First

the Crown Attorney speaks. Then the Defence lawyers make a speech. They sum up the facts that support their side of the story. They try hard to convince the jury to believe them.

2. Judge charges the jury. After the closing statements, the judge outlines how the law applies in the case. The judge tells the jury what facts it must base its decision on.

3. Jury deliberates. The jurors leave the courtroom. They are taken to a private room where they will make their decision. They must be unanimous. A jury whose members cannot agree is called a hung jury. This jury is discharged and a new one is chosen. The case must be tried over again.

4. Reading the verdict. The jury returns to the court. The jury foreman reads the verdict to the judge. The trial is then over.

5. Acquittal. If the jury finds the defendant not guilty it will bring in a verdict for *acquittal*. This means that the defendant is legally free to go.

6. Sentencing. If the defendant is found guilty, the judge will decide the punishment. This is called sentencing. The judge thinks about four factors before setting the sentence. These factors are shown in Fig. 3-9.

**USING YOUR KNOWLEDGE**
1. Why would the judge consider the four factors before passing sentence? Explain why each factor is considered.
2. Allan Littlewood was found guilty of arson and murder. What should his sentence be? Out of the punishments below, pick the one you think is right for Allan. Be sure to think about the four factors considered by the judge.
   a) Life in prison, eligible for parole after twenty years if behaviour is good.

**Fig. 3-9 Four factors that judges consider before passing sentence**

b) Removal from his family. Placed in mental hospital for treatment.
c) Freedom.

**TAKING A STAND**
1. Take a stand on the issue "Should Canada have the death penalty?".

**RESEARCHING**
1. In Canada today, public opinion polls show that more than 50% of the Canadian population supports the death penalty. Large numbers of experts in criminal behaviour feel that the death penalty is wrong. Using your library, newspapers, magazines, and other material your teacher will provide, answer the following questions.
   a) Is the prime minister in favour of the death penalty?
   b) What is the punishment for murder in Canada today?
   c) List five reasons for and against the death penalty.

---

### The Allan Littlewood story

PART 4: THE APPEAL

The day after the trial was over Thompson and Baldwin went to see Allan in jail. Allan was very depressed. He had been sentenced to ten years in prison.

"I...I can't go to jail," he said. "I can't stand to be kept in small places. Tell them I'm crazy. Tell them anything. You have to get the sentence changed!"

Allan buried his face in his hands and wept. The lawyers looked grim. They knew there was little chance. Only one hope remained.

"We can try for an appeal," said Thompson. "You have the right to one. We have thirty days to appeal your case if you want us to."

"Oh yes! Appeal and keep appealing. That way I can be kept out of prison forever," cried Allan.

"It doesn't work that way, Allan. There must be a good reason for an appeal. Ms. Thompson and I will have to go over the record of your trial carefully. We will look for some error. There are three main reasons for appeals. Maybe the judge has made some error in the way she conducted your trial. Perhaps the jury was not impartial to you. Or maybe we can come up with some new evidence for your case," said Baldwin.

Thompson and Baldwin searched. Finally they found what they were looking for. They learned that one of the jurors was married to an East Indian. The appeal was taken to the Appeals Division of the Provincial Supreme Court. The judges heard the appeal and upheld the original verdict. There was no evidence to show that the juror was prejudiced against Allan. The last bit of hope was gone. Allan Littlewood entered a **federal penitentiary** on January 10, 1979.

**1. List the three main reasons for appeals.**

*The civil court system in Canada*
You will remember that civil law is concerned with the claiming of **damages.** In this section we briefly look at Canada's civil court system. Then we examine a civil case and see how the civil court system would handle it.

*Civil courts and routes of appeal*
SMALL CLAIMS COURT    This court is for cases in which the damages sought are small. There are no lawyers involved. The judge listens to the evidence and decides what damages should be paid. In some provinces this court handles claims of up to $1 000. Find out what the limit is in your province.

COUNTY COURT    In most provinces, this court hears civil cases that involve sums of up to $7 500. It also hears appeals from cases in Small Claims Court. Find out the top amount of money that can be claimed in County Court in your province.

PROVINCIAL SUPREME COURT    In most provinces, this court hears cases where damages claimed are above $7 500. It also hears appeals from the County Court.

SUPREME COURT OF CANADA    This court hears only appeals. It does not try cases. It is composed of the Chief Justice of Canada and eight other judges. Each judge listens to appeal cases. Later the judges meet and discuss the cases. They then make a decision on the appeal. Before 1975, any case involving a claim of $10 000 could go to the Supreme Court for appeal. However, this took up too much time. Now the Court only hears appeals in cases that have a high public interest. It also accepts cases which involve difficult points of law.

---

**The David Robinson case (A fictional case based on real ones)**

David Robinson was a lawyer in a large law firm in Manitoba. He was well known around Winnipeg and in many parts of the province. He was a member of the Progressive Conservative party. Many people hoped that Robinson would one day be premier of the province. To most people, he seemed to be a fine lawyer. Some people, however, doubted his ability as a lawyer.

In 1971, Robinson lost an important law case. He was upset about this. He went to his handball club to work out and try to forget the courtroom defeat. When Robinson was in the shower he overheard Tom Johnson talking to someone. Johnson worked in the same firm as Robinson did. Johnson said, "Robinson is so stupid that he can't walk and chew gum at the same time. I wouldn't let him buy my dog licence let alone be my lawyer."

When Robinson heard this he was outraged. He decided to take civil action against Johnson. At the time, Robinson felt that Johnson's comment would not hurt his career. Therefore, he sued Johnson for only $500. Robinson merely wanted to teach Johnson a lesson and put him in his place. Robinson decided on $500 because he knew the sum would bring the case into Small Claims Court. Johnson was not going to argue the case. He was sorry for what he had said.

Before the case came up in court, however, Robinson learned something. The man Johnson was talking to in the locker room, Mr. Aaron Tyler, was important in the business world. This fact changed Robinson's point of view. Johnson's statement could affect Robinson's career. Tyler could repeat what Johnson had said to other people. These other people would perhaps not ask Robinson to be their lawyer.

With this in mind, Robinson decided to sue for $7 000. He hired a lawyer since he did not want to represent himself. The case of Robinson versus Johnson was scheduled to appear in County Court. At this point, Robinson learned another startling piece of information. Aaron Tyler was an important man in the Progressive Conservative party. Robinson now felt that his career as a lawyer and politician had been hurt by Johnson's remark. Robinson and his lawyer decided to sue for $200 000. The case came before the Supreme Court of Manitoba in October of 1973. The Court decided in favour of the *plaintiff* (Robinson, the person suing for the damages). It ordered the defendant, Johnson, to pay damages of $150 000.

Johnson was very upset. He felt he could prove that Robinson was a poor lawyer. He appealed the case. The appeal went before the Supreme Court of Canada in 1974. The Supreme Court agreed with the verdict of the Provincial Court. The Supreme Court gave the following ruling in the appeal.

Mr. Johnson is guilty of defamation of character. He made a statement to a Mr. Aaron Tyler about Mr. Robinson that is false. The statement suggested that Robinson was stupid and a poor lawyer. The statement did great harm to Mr. Robinson's reputation. His career as a lawyer and politician was put in danger. It may still be in danger. Therefore, we uphold the verdict and order the defendant to pay $150 000 to the plaintiff.

**Defamation**
You *defame* a person when you injure that person's good name. You make people in the community think less of the person. There are two main ways that you can defame a person, *libel* and *slander*. Libel means that your statements appear in print, on film, or on record. When you slander someone, you say damaging things about the person. Is Robinson charging Johnson with libel or slander?

**READING BETTER**
1. Which court handles a final appeal in a civil case?
2. Why did Robinson decide to sue Johnson?
3. Why did the court decide in favour of Robinson?

**ORGANIZING BETTER**
1. Make a chart in your book like this:

| Name of court | Type of case | Appeals |
| --- | --- | --- |
|  |  |  |

Use the chart to compare the four civil courts.

1. Explain why the Robinson case started out in Small Claims Court but ended up in the Supreme Court.

TAKING A STAND
1. One of the judges of the Supreme Court wrote a *minority opinion* on the Robinson case. This means that he did not agree with the opinions of the other eight judges. This is what he said:

> I do not feel that a clear-cut case of slander has taken place. I feel that Mr. Johnson was making a general comment on the one case that Mr. Robinson had just lost. There was evidence that Mr. Robinson did make an error in that case. He lost the case because of the error. To me this shows that Johnson's statement is founded in truth. Therefore the comment is not a slander.

Think about this minority opinion carefully. Then decide: was Johnson guilty of slander? Explain your answer.

The Canadian prison system

So far we have looked at the courts and the police in Canada's legal system. The last part of the system we will study is the prison system. The prisons have two main jobs to perform. First, by holding offenders they carry out the punishment that is given by the courts. Second, the prison system tries to reform offenders. It gives them the chance to accept responsibility for their actions and to return to society with a desire to obey the law.

*Canadian prisons*

In most provinces there are two levels of prisons. The provincial governments support a number of correctional institutions. The federal government supports the federal penitentiary system.

In some areas there are local jails or police lock-ups. Offenders are held in these

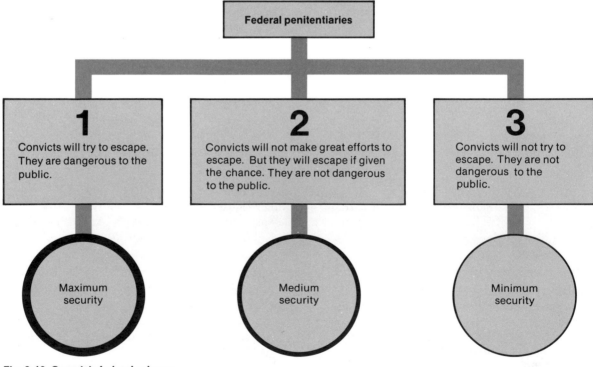

Canada's federal prisons are called penitentiaries. There are three main types. Which type do you think Allan Littlewood would be sent to?

**Federal penitentiaries**

**1** Convicts will try to escape. They are dangerous to the public.

Maximum security

**2** Convicts will not make great efforts to escape. But they will escape if given the chance. They are not dangerous to the public.

Medium security

**3** Convicts will not try to escape. They are not dangerous to the public.

Minimum security

Fig. 3-10  Canada's federal prisons

Courtyard, Old Chatham Jail. Regional Detention Centre, Toronto. **How are these jails similar?**

Ontario Ministry
of Correctional Services

jails overnight before being sent to a county or provincial jail. Provincial jails are holding jails. Offenders are held there while they are awaiting trial. Provincial jails are also used to hold offenders convicted of less serious crimes. Offenders serving a term of less than three months will go to a provincial jail. Sentences of three months to two years are served in provincial institutions. Sentences of over two years are usually served in federal penitentiaries.

### The prison system: Reception

Allan Littlewood would be sent to a federal maximum security prison. He would be considered dangerous to the public. As soon as Allan arrived at the prison he would go to "reception".

At reception, he would be given a uniform, his eating utensils, and toilet articles. The rules of the prison would be explained to him. A group of doctors and prison officials would talk to Allan during reception. This group is called the **Classification Board.** These people would interview Allan. They would also study his

case history from the court records. The Classification Board would want to discover what type of person Allan was. Would it be possible to reform him? What type of programme would help him? Would he cause trouble in the institution? These are the questions that the board would try to answer.

### The three main purposes of the prison system

To most Canadians the purpose of the prison system is to punish offenders. Some people are surprised to learn that the prison system tries to **rehabilitate** offenders. People within the prison system try to help offenders solve their emotional problems. For example, Allan Littlewood would spend time with prison psychologists. They would try to help Allan overcome his prejudice against East Indians. The prison would also try to provide Allan with more job skills. He would then be able to find a job when he left prison.

There are three main purposes for prisons in Canada. Fig. 3-11 outlines these purposes.

197

How will prison change an offender's point of view?

**Rehabilitation**

Some offenders are given psychiatric help. They are trained for jobs. They are helped to return to society. The offenders try to become law-abiding citizens.

**Retribution**

The offenders have hurt society. Therefore society now decides their punishment.

**Deterrence**

Punishing someone for a crime should prevent a person from committing another crime. The offender fears punishment.

**Fig. 3-11  The three purposes of the Canadian penal system**

**Eight ways to punish offenders**

| | |
|---|---|
| 1. Death penalty | The offender's life is taken. Abolished in Canada, July 1976. |
| 2. Whipping | The offender is placed in prison and whipped. Abolished in 1972. |
| 3. Imprisonment | After studying the Criminal Code, the judge decides on the length of the prison term to be served by the offender. The offender is then kept in prison for a certain period of time. |
| 4. Fines | The judge orders the person to pay a fine. The person who refuses to pay the fine is put in jail. |
| 5. Suspended sentence | Sometimes the judge feels that the offender will probably never commit another crime. In that case the court can *suspend* the sentence. This means that the offender is released without serving the sentence. |

| | |
|---|---|
| 6. Suspended sentence with probation | In some cases the judge may suspend the sentence but place the offender on **probation** for a period of time. If the offender breaks the conditions of the probation then the offender may have to serve the original sentence. |
| 7. Deportation | If offenders are not Canadian citizens they can be sent back to the country of their birth. |
| 8. Compensation | Offenders are expected to pay for loss or damage they have caused. This form of punishment is not used very often. |

### READING BETTER

1. What is the difference between a provincial jail and a federal penitentiary?
2. Where are serious offenders sent?
3. Who decides the type of prison to which an offender is sent?
4. Why did Allan Littlewood go to a federal penitentiary rather than to a provincial jail?
5. List five things that happen during the reception session when an offender arrives at prison.

### ORGANIZING BETTER

1. In your notebook list and explain eight ways of punishing offenders.

### TAKING A STAND

1. Below is a list of criminal cases. Which methods of handling offenders should be used in each case? Be sure that you have reasons to back up your point of view. Fig. 3-11 may help you think of reasons.
   a) A woman drives 120 km/h in an 80 km/h zone.
   b) A 22-year-old man steals an elderly lady's purse. During the robbery she tries to hold on to the purse. He beats her with his fist and then strangles her until she loses consciousness. Then he takes the purse.
   c) A convict in prison shoots and kills a prison guard.
   d) Dan steals a motorcycle. This is Dan's first offence.
   e) Karen throws rocks through all the windows of a commercial greenhouse. This is the third time she has been found guilty of vandalism.

   f) Arnold was born in Scotland. He has been in Canada six months. He is not a Canadian citizen. He has been found guilty of robbing a milk store.

### RESEARCHING

1. Recently there have been a number of riots and hostage-takings in Canadian prisons. Using magazines and newspapers, see if you can find some causes for the problems in the prisons of Canada today.

*Parole*

**Parole** is a system that allows prisoners to shorten their sentences. Prisoners become eligible for parole when they have served one third of their sentence, or seven years, whichever comes first. Parole is very important. It gives the prisoners some hope that they will be released early.

Parole is not automatic. There is a National Parole Board, and provincial parole boards. The members of these boards look at each application for parole. Before they release a prisoner on parole, they take into account certain factors. Some of these factors are shown in Fig. 3-13.

### USING YOUR KNOWLEDGE

1. Reread the five factors for deciding if a person should be paroled. Then decide which of the following prisoners most

**Fig. 3-12 Five factors parole boards consider before granting parole**

deserves a parole. Be sure to give reasons for your decision.

a) *John Brown* has served one third of his sentence. He has never been in prison before. As a teller in a bank he stole $10 000 of the bank's money. He has only been in trouble once while in prison. He got into a fight. John is very quiet. He seems to have suffered being away from his family. He has a wife and two children. The wife and children have moved. They are attending church regularly. They want John to return to them as soon as possible. John has a university education. While in prison he was trained to sell real estate. John's mother-in-law owns a real estate business. She is willing to give John a job.

b) *Reg Wheeler* has served one third of his sentence for armed robbery. Reg has been in trouble with the law since he was sixteen. He has been released on parole twice before. He swears this time that he has changed. He has attended all the rehabilitation sessions. Twice during his stay in prison he was involved in protests over food. He spent three days in solitary confinement for refusing to work in the machine shop. Reg has a grade ten education. He was trained as a plumber. He plans to start his own business when he gets out. Reg's wife has left him and never wants to see him again.

## Conclusion

This chapter has shown us that we need laws. Laws are meant to provide order.

Without informal rules and formal laws our lives would be chaotic. Laws also give us freedom. The Canadian legal system creates a set of human rights. These rights belong to all Canadians. They ensure that we will always be free to make choices about our lives.

We also learned that with freedom comes responsibility. We value our own rights. We must also respect the rights of others. Of course, not everybody does this. Some people, like Allan Littlewood, are willing to deny others their rights. This threatens the peace and order of our society.

The Canadian legal system, as we have seen, is ready to deal with this problem. The role of the police is to prevent crime and catch those who commit crimes. We learned that the courts take the offender from the police. They decide whether the suspect is innocent or guilty. If the person is guilty the courts decide what the punishment will be. The offender is then turned over to the Canadian prison system, which carries out the punishment. The police, the courts, the prisons: this is the machinery that the Canadian legal system uses to protect the rights of Canadians.

### READING BETTER
1. What is the difference between criminal and civil law?
2. Why is it important for Canadians to have a Canadian Bill of Rights?

### ORGANIZING BETTER
1. Explain the importance of the five parts of the Canadian legal system.

### USING YOUR KNOWLEDGE
1. Most people involved in the Canadian legal system believe that the system is always in need of reform. Look over the chapter and decide on one thing you would change about the Canadian legal system. Be sure to explain how your change would improve the system.

### SOLVING PROBLEMS
1. a) Look at the section of the chapter that outlines the jobs done by the police. Which job do you feel is most important?
   b) Develop a policy that will allow the police to do their most important job more effectively.

### TAKING A STAND
1. Take a stand on this issue: "Should there be capital punishment in Canada?"
2. Do you think Canada's prison system needs reforming? Give reasons for your point of view.

### RESEARCHING
1. Using your school library or books your teacher provides, find the following information:
   a) What are writs of assistance?
   b) Why were writs of assistance created?
   c) Why do some people feel that writs of assistance are not necessary?
2. Consumer law is an important part of the Canadian legal system. Special laws that enforce standards of fair play, care, and honesty protect consumers. There are government departments and many associations that have been set up to serve the interests of consumers. These agencies ensure that, for example, companies do not sell faulty products, or do not use false advertising. Find out more information about the following:
   a) Consumer and Corporate Affairs Department (federal government)
   b) The Canadian Association of Consumers
   c) The Canadian Consumer Council

## GLOSSARY

**Appeals.** Requests for a new trial in a higher court.

**Canadian Bill of Rights.** An act of Parliament that lists basic rights that all Canadians are entitled to.

**Civil law.** The area of law that deals with the private rights of citizens.

**Classification Board.** A group of doctors and wardens who interview people when they come into prison. The group tries to discover the best method of rehabilitating the prisoners.

**Criminal Code.** The body of laws that deals with criminal law.

**Criminal law.** The area of law that deals with crimes and punishments.

**Damages.** The sum of money claimed as compensation for injury or loss.

**Defendant.** The person charged with a crime. This person has not yet been proven innocent or guilty.

**Federal penitentiary.** A prison run by the federal government.

**Human rights.** Powers or privileges that belong to a person by law.

**Ombudsman.** A government official who examines and tries to solve citizens' problems with the government.

**Parole.** A programme in which criminals with good behaviour are released from prison before their sentence is over.

**Prejudice.** An unreasonable dislike or hatred for certain people or things.

**Probation.** A period of time during which a convicted person, who is not in jail, must fulfill certain requirements set by the court. This usually involves reporting regularly to a probation officer.

**Racist.** A person who discriminates against people because of their race.

**Rehabilitate.** To cure or bring back to a normal, healthy condition.

**Responsibilities.** Actions or behaviour that a person is morally obliged to account for.

**Scapegoat.** A person or thing blamed for the mistakes or problems of others.

**Social customs.** The traditional way of doing things in a community, country, or group.

**Tolerant.** Being able to accept other people and customs that may seem strange or different.

**Witness for the Crown.** A person who testifies for the Crown Attorney.

# PART TWO
## Yesterday, today, and tomorrow

# UNIT THREE:
# French-English relations in Canada

On November 15, 1976, the Parti Québecois won the provincial election in Quebec and became the new government of the province. One of the main goals of this party is to separate Quebec from the rest of Canada. Why do some French-speaking Canadians living in Quebec want to separate from the rest of Canada? Why is Canada having problems in French-English relations?

The answer to these questions is buried deep within our past. You will remember from your study of Canadian history in earlier years that both France and England established colonies in North America. For almost one hundred years the two nations fought with each other to gain control of North America.

Today, the French are the second-largest language group in Canada. Canadians of French ancestry form 28% of the Canadian population. French-speaking Canadians have a different language and a different culture, or way of life, from English-speaking Canadians. The two language groups have often clashed. Yet there have also been periods of happy co-operation. In 1713 and 1763 there were major wars between England and France. The treaties that were signed after these wars gave England control of most of North America. The French were forced to give up control of their colonies in New France, Acadia, Isle St. Jean (Prince Edward Island) and Isle Royale (Cape Breton). This did not end the problems between French-speaking and English-speaking people in North America. Over sixty thousand French-speaking colonists remained in North America under British rule. They feared and resented British control.

Today we are going through a crisis period in French-English relations. Canadians are trying to come to terms with the desire of some Quebeckers to break away from the rest of Canada. To find solutions to the problem, we must first understand it. We should know why some Quebeckers are unhappy in Canada, and why they think that separation is the answer.

In the next four chapters you will study French-English relations in Canada. As you work through the sections, keep in mind the four main questions listed below. When you finish this unit you will have a better understanding of Quebec's desire to separate. You may also come up with ways of putting an end to the crisis.

**1** What are the main problems in French-English relations?

**2** What caused the problems?

**3** How were problems solved in the past?

**4** Are there solutions to the problems today?

# 1/In the beginning: 1759-1867

## Contents

## Introduction

The problem of Canada's French-English relations is not simple. There are no easy solutions. This of course does not mean that there are no solutions at all. The first step in finding a solution is to discover the causes of the problem. To do this we will look at the early history of French-English relations. We will see where serious conflict between *francophones* (French-speaking people) and *anglophones* (English-speaking people) first occurred.

This chapter will deal with the questions listed below. As you read through the chapter, keep them in mind. When you have finished your reading, discuss the questions with your classmates.

1. **How did French-speaking people react to British control?**
2. **What problems arose between francophones and anglophones following the Conquest?**
3. **Why did the Loyalists dislike their situation in Quebec?**
4. **Why was Quebec divided into Upper and Lower Canada in 1791?**
5. **Did French-speaking people want to join in a confederation of British North American colonies in 1867?**

## A survey of French-English relations

All the members of your class should answer the questions in this survey. Your teacher will keep a record of the results.

After you have completed your study of French-English relations, take the survey again. In this way, you can see if the opinions of your class have changed as a result of your study.

Questionnaire on French-English relations
Answer each question "yes", "no", or "unsure", unless otherwise directed. Then hand in the answers to the teacher, who will tabulate the results.

1. Canada should be considered
   a) unilingual
   b) bilingual
   c) multilingual.
2. Every Canadian should be able to speak
   a) English
   b) French
   c) both.
3. The prime minister should be fluent in
   a) English
   b) French
   c) both.
4. Should anglophones and new immigrants in Quebec be forced to learn French?
5. Should a student who earns a secondary school diploma have to be fluent in both French and English?
6. Do you want to learn French?
7. Do you think that there should be bilingual signs in your section of Canada?
8. Do you think that everything printed in Canada should be in French and English?
9. Canada is basically
   a) an English country
   b) a country of two cultures, French and English
   c) a multicultural country.
10. Do you believe that the French should be forced to adopt an English way of life?
11. Do you think that French-speaking Canadians have any reason to be upset with their position in Canada?
12. Do you feel that Quebec is a special province that should be given rights and privileges that other provinces do not have?
13. Should the Canadian Armed Forces prevent Quebec from separating?
14. Have you ever been to Quebec?
15. Have you ever known both English-speaking Canadians and French-speaking Canadians on more than a casual basis?

**The British conquest and its results**
To discover why some French-speaking Canadians are upset in Canada today, we must look into the past. France and Britain began their struggle for the land of North America in the early 1600s. The English began settling in the area to be known as the **Thirteen Colonies** (roughly present-day New England). The French settled at Port Royale. Their influence grew along the St. Lawrence Valley and the areas of Acadia, Isle St. Jean, and Isle Royale (present-day Maritime provinces). Both the French and the English were interested in the Nova Scotia area. Thus the region of Acadia and Nova Scotia became a major area of conflict between France and Britain.

In 1713 there was a war between the two empires. France gave up control of part of Acadia (the area of present-day Nova Scotia) to the English. It was the first time that French-speaking settlers had come under the direct control of the English. The Acadians were permitted to leave Nova Scotia. Many moved to Isle St. Jean (Prince Edward Island) and Isle Royale (Cape Breton). The majority however, remained in Acadia under British control. These French-speaking people were a problem to the English during the years of war between France and Britain. The English governors feared the Acadians

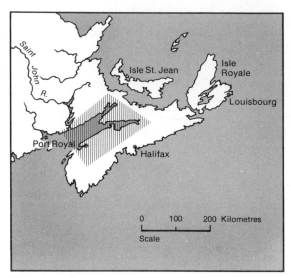

**Fig. 1-1 Acadia**

would be loyal to France during these wars. Therefore in 1755 Governor Charles Lawrence expelled more than 6000 French-speaking Acadians from Nova Scotia.

In 1759 Montcalm was defeated by Wolfe. This stopped the development of the French Empire in North America. The French colony of New France was captured and occupied by British troops. The Treaty of Paris, 1763, secured the British conquest of New France. A new era in French-English relations in North America was beginning. Now over 75 000 French-speaking people lived in North America under British rule.

What was it like to be a French-speaking person in a British colony in 1763? What was it like to be under the control of another people, a people who spoke a different language? Did the **Canadiens** feel like a defeated people? Did the English act like conquerors? To discover the answers to questions such as these, we will look at "The diary of Etienne Cartouche". Cartouche is a fictional character, but the diary reflects the feelings of the French-speaking people at the time. The diary covers the years 1762 to 1766.

**Expulsion of the Acadians. What might the man on the box and the soldier be thinking?**

### The diary of Etienne Cartouche

Etienne Cartouche was a **seigneur** living in the colony of New France. He owned a great deal of land northeast of Montreal. Cartouche decided to stay in Quebec; he hoped that the British conquerors would deal fairly with the French. Like all Canadiens, however, he feared what the future held for him. As you read passages from his diary, you will discover some reasons for the discontent that exists between French-speaking and English-speaking people in Canada today.

MARCH 22, 1762

Yesterday we had the first spring thaw. Here and there, on the tops of small hills, a gray-green grass is showing through the snow. It has been a hard winter. The snow drifts stand ten to fifteen feet high in some places. But with more days like yesterday, the snow will melt away. Spring will soon be here.

I marvel at the changing of the seasons—they are truly one of God's greatest works! Our priest is right—if people live in harmony with nature and the seasons they will be happy. That is why Canadiens are farmers. In the winter we are like the land—we rest. When nature comes alive in the spring, we also waken. We plough the fields and plant the crops. In the summer we profit from the warmth and sunshine, just as the rest of nature does. And in the fall we prepare the land and ourselves for the winter's rest. Crops are harvested and stored away for the long cold months. Yes, if people live this way they will not have to worry. They will lead long, happy lives.

If we French did not put our trust in God and live like this, we would go crazy. It is hard for us to realize that we have lost the war to the British. I feel ashamed that we are the defeated ones. It is sad to live as a beaten people.

But I have hope. I pray to my God. At least they have not taken away my religion, and they have not taken away my land. It could be much worse.

---

**USING YOUR KNOWLEDGE**

1. Etienne Cartouche is happy, and yet sad. What makes him happy? Why is he unhappy?
2. Explain in your own words what it means to live in harmony with the seasons. Do you agree with Cartouche's philosophy of life?

**TAKING A STAND**

1. Parents often give us a lot of orders and tell us what we can and cannot do.

a) How do you feel when your parents tell you what to do?
b) How are these feelings similar to Etienne Cartouche's feelings about being a Quebecker in a defeated Quebec? How are they different?

---

**A seigneur's home. Why might Cartouche not want to lose a home like this to the English?**

### Cartouche's fears

JULY 10, 1762

Last night it was very hot and muggy. Around three a.m. I woke up with a start. I was having the same nightmare that I have had almost every night for the last month. I dreamed that the soldiers in their red coats went to the door of the church and put up a bulletin. I can see the words on the notice so clearly.

1. All Roman Catholic churches will be closed.
2. All Roman Catholic, French-speaking people will give up their land. This land will be sold at a public auction to English-speaking members of the Protestant church.
3. No person will be allowed to speak French in a public place in His Majesty's Colony of Quebec.

*By order of His Majesty, George III*

Each person in the colony fears that this is what the future holds. Sixty thousand people stretched out along the banks of the St. Lawrence . . . all afraid their way of life will be swept away.

210

The Canadiens were afraid that the English would change their way of life completely. They feared that their land would be taken away, and their churches closed. They were afraid that they would be forced to speak English.

After the Conquest, General James Murray, who had taken part in the struggle for New France, became governor of the colony. He was to decide the fate of the Canadiens. The following letter will give you an idea of how Governor Murray treated them.

**Nathan Peters's letter to his brother in England**
*(A fictional account based on fact)*

Nathan Peters was the valet (personal manservant) to Governor Murray. As his valet, Peters spent a great deal of time in Murray's company. He often overheard conversations between Murray and his officers. Therefore, Peters had a good understanding of what Murray intended to do for the colony. As you read through the letter decide whether or not Cartouche had reason to fear English rule.

Dear Anthony,

The war with the French is over and we have won. The French troops have departed. My gentleman, Governor Murray, has been placed in charge of the entire colony. These are busy times for the governor, and so I am very busy, too! With all the official business of meeting with military leaders, French church officials, and seigneurs, the governor has to change his clothes several times a day.

I must tell you what it is like here. We have just come back from a tour of the colony. The town of Quebec is in ruins. The Canadiens are in a terrible situation. They have very few supplies because the war prevented them from cultivating and harvesting crops. They are very short of food. Also, our troops burned a great deal of food as they marched on their way to attack Quebec City.

Governor Murray is doing all he can to keep people from starving. Several officers have loaned large sums of money to the French leaders. Also, I heard that the English troops have decided to give up one day's supplies each month to help the Canadiens. This is rather sporting, don't you think? After all, up until several months ago the French were our enemies. I think that officers in the army—most of them are large landowners, you know—have great respect for the way of life in Quebec. It is an agricultural way of life. The love of the land gives the French and the English officers a common bond, I guess.

At any rate, Governor Murray has great respect for the Canadiens. He will do all in his power to see that they do not suffer. He feels that they have a tremendous desire to survive and preserve their French way of life. The governor is convinced of their value as a people. He said that he will not try to force them into an English way of life.

Yesterday I overheard him talking to a group of priests. He said he would do all he could to see that their religion is not outlawed and that their land is not taken away. I think the governor is being more than fair with these people.

There is one dark cloud on the horizon, however. There are great numbers of merchants flooding into the colony from the British colonies to the south. Most seem to come from the Boston area. These traders and merchants have no use for the army. I also fear that they would like to get rid of Governor Murray!

Just the other night the governor was outraged! A dispatch had just arrived from Montreal, the city where most of these new merchants have located. The dispatch was a list of the merchants' demands. They want an elected representative government, and a law preventing Catholics from holding government jobs. The governor said he would never turn the Canadiens over to that nest of vipers. But I fear that the merchants are working to get the general recalled to England.

If this merchant group has its way, perhaps I will be back in England much sooner than I thought.

*Your loving brother,*
*Nathan*

**Governor James Murray**

READING BETTER
1. What facts prove that the English did not want to crush the Canadien way of life after the Conquest?
2. Why did British army officers have sympathy for the defeated Canadiens?
3. What might prevent Governor Murray from helping the Canadiens as much as he wanted to?

USING YOUR KNOWLEDGE
1. Cartouche had three fears concerning the future. Do you think that his fears were justified? Base your opinion on the information in Peters's letter.

### The diary of Etienne Cartouche
### The "Bostonais" and the land claims

JULY 11, 1762

This afternoon while I was talking to Father Lamont in front of the house, two wagons came down the road. The men in the wagons had maps and they were marking out plots of land on them. Father Lamont spoke to them. His English is much better than mine. These men treated us with little respect. They laughed and made jokes about us. It made me angry to be treated this way, but I realized that there was no use getting upset over such a small matter. These are the "Bostonais", the men of Boston. More and more of them are coming into New France each week. I am told that they hope to make a lot of money here. It is tragic for us. They want Governor Murray to force all French Catholics off the land so that they can have it. Father Lamont has talked to the governor several times. He says that Governor Murray is a good man who detests these "Bostonais". They are greedy businessmen who think only about making money.

The men in the two wagons want land in our area. They said that they were marking off the sections they wanted. A large man with a black beard showed me his map. On it he had outlined the area he wanted with a red crayon. From what I saw on the map it seems that he wants almost all of my land. I told him that the area belonged to me. A smirk came from across his face and he said, "*Your* land, is it? Well, Mr. Frenchman, I think you have made a mistake. You people lost everything to us on the Plains of Abraham. The English own New France now."

The men in the wagons laughed and they rode away. Father put his arm around me. He said he was sure that Governor Murray would not allow these men to take away our land. I am not so sure. My heart is heavy and, like thousands of Canadiens, I fear dark days ahead.

213

## READING BETTER

1. According to Cartouche, what are the English-speaking people who came into New France after the Conquest interested in?

## USING YOUR KNOWLEDGE

1. a) Think of your home. Think of all the things that you own. If another person claimed to have the power to take away your home and all you owned, how would you feel? Answer in a paragraph of four or five sentences.

   b) Do you think that Cartouche feels the same way you do? Be sure to give reasons for your point of view.

2. If General Murray were removed as governor, which of the following would probably happen? Give reasons to back up your point of view.
   a) The Bostonais would try to get a new governor who would be willing to give them the Canadiens' land.
   b) The Bostonais would apologize to Cartouche for wanting his land.
   c) The Bostonais would be upset and demand that Murray be given his job back.
   d) Cartouche would be very upset. He would feel that there was now more chance of losing his land.

### Cartouche and the English merchant

OCTOBER 25, 1763

All the crops are in the barns. The Lord has been good to us. It was a good harvest. My land yielded more crops than needed, so I sold all the extra to a Mr. Johnson. He has just opened a flour mill. Father Lamont encouraged me to do this to establish good relations with these new English-speaking businessmen. I suppose it is a good idea, but I'm not sure it will work. I don't think I will ever be able to be on good terms with these Protestant English people. I don't understand them at all. All Mr. Johnson thinks about is making more money. He tried to convince me that I must clear more land to put in wheat. I told him the land that has already been cleared provides enough for the needs of my family and tenants. If my tenants clear more land, it will take up all their time. They will not be able to enjoy themselves and their families. He looked at me as if I were crazy. He said, "You've got to expand, Cartouche! You can't just sit still. We must have progress. We have to build this area up, make it into a city. Bring in new industry, new shops and trades."

He was quite enthused about this. He called it progress. To me, it seemed like foolishness. Why should we want to build our peaceful village into a dirty, crowded city?

I think Mr. Johnson's problem is that he doesn't have time to think about what is really important in life. I'm sure that Mr. Johnson feels I am too lazy to get ahead. It seems to me that we are two different types of people. It will be hard for the Canadiens and the English to get along because their ideas about life are so different.

### Reaction to the Proclamation of 1763

NOVEMBER 7, 1764

There are great rumblings in the colony. I have just returned from Montreal. The English-speaking merchants are in an ugly mood. Over a year ago the government of England passed the Proclamation of 1763. This law outlined how the colony of New France was to be governed. There was to be a governor, who would be helped by a council. The Proclamation also promised that a representative

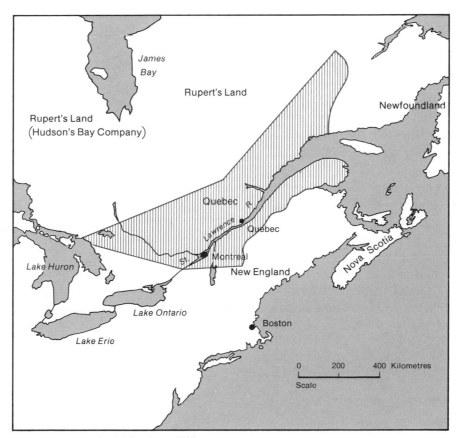

**Fig. 1-2  Boundaries of Quebec, 1763**

government would be set up in the future. As I understand it, in the Thirteen Colonies, each area has the right to elect a representative to the government. The merchants are outraged that there is still no elected assembly in this colony.

When I was in Montreal there was talk of this matter in all the stores and taverns. A large group of merchants held a torchlight parade in the centre of the city. The air was filled with shouts of "The rights of Englishmen", "English law for an English colony", and other such things. The merchants gave speeches in which they denounced the Proclamation and Governor Murray. They were especially mad at Murray. It seems that they feel he is too friendly with us. After the speeches, they **burned Murray in effigy.** They sent around a petition calling for Murray to be fired as governor. If they take Murray away, I fear that the Canadiens in New France will be worse off than ever.

### Dirty English tricks

NOVEMBER 15, 1764

The first snows of winter came today. A new season is upon us, the season of rest. Father Lamont came by for supper. He told me that the English-speaking people in the colony are waging a great campaign for self-government. They also want all English laws applied to our colony immediately. This would be a disaster for the Canadiens. According to English law a Roman Catholic cannot hold office. This would mean that all the people elected would be English-speaking Protestants. Their main aim is to have all the English laws applied to the colony. We would surely lose our language and religion.

Most of the **habitants** can neither read nor write. If all the English laws were put into effect I fear that the Canadiens could easily be cheated by some of these English-speaking merchants. Some of these men are true villains, and not to be trusted. That huge man with the black beard who was out here trying to take my land is just such a person. His name is Amos Durfee. He has swindled seven Canadiens out of their land. Apparently, there are some laws that they did not know about. They didn't understand what was happening. Before they knew it, the court had ordered them out of their homes. Father Lamont has gone to see the governor. It may be the law but there is no justice in it. What a black Christmas it will be for those families. I don't know whether or not we Canadiens will be able to survive.

### Unexpected benefits for the habitants

OCTOBER 27, 1766

God has given us another good harvest. The barns are filled for the winter and the corn cribs are overflowing. But the habitants are not satisfied. Greed is an evil thing. It spreads quickly and quietly, taking victims where you least expect it. I never thought I would see the tenants on my seigneury fail to pay their dues.

They refuse to bring their wheat to my mill to be ground. Instead, they are going to Mr. Johnson's. And they will not give me my share of the crop. What is worse, Father Lamont tells me that everywhere in the colony the habitants are refusing to pay the **tithes** to the Church. The English law is to blame for all this trouble. It does not require the people to pay tithes or honour seigneurial obligations. Unless **Governor Carleton** listens to us, French society will fall apart.

I went down to Pierre Lebeau's cottage to see what the problem was. It was such an uncomfortable situation! Pierre is one of my best tenants, a very friendly fellow. But yesterday he would not even invite me inside. You could tell by his eyes that he felt guilty about not paying his dues. I did not beat around the bush. I asked him straight out why he was not bringing his wheat to my mill to be ground into flour. He said that the times have changed. The old laws of New France no longer exist. The habitants no longer have to pay tithes or seigneurial dues. He said that even though he didn't like the situation, the colony was now English. Seigneurial dues are not part of English law.

The man's a fool. He says that he is going to take his wheat into town and sell it to Mr. Johnson. I asked him what he would do over the winter if he sold his wheat. He said that he would live on the profits from the sale of his wheat. But I know that when the February snow falls he will be broke and his family will starve. Once again, he will be at my door for help. Then we will see what he thinks of the English laws.

**Sir Guy Carleton**

READING BETTER

1. How did Amos Durfee take advantage of the Canadiens?
2. Why were the English-speaking merchants upset with the Proclamation of 1763?

SOLVING PROBLEMS

1. Your teacher will place you in a group with other students in your class. One student will be the chairperson. The chairperson's job is to see that you complete the work in the time period your teacher gives you. Another student will be the recorder. This student's job is to make notes.
   a) Make a list of all the events in Quebec that upset Etienne Cartouche.
   b) Pretend that you are a member of the British government. You must develop a policy that will solve Cartouche's problems. Each group will present its policy to the class. Decide which policy is the best.

## The Quebec Act, 1774

We discovered from our study of the diary of Etienne Cartouche that the people of Quebec were not very happy. They were afraid that the English would take away their land and religion. They were also upset because a very ambitious group of merchants and traders from Boston had arrived in the colony. These merchants took advantage of their powerful position. They tricked uneducated Canadiens out of their money and land. The governor of the colony, General Murray, tried to protect the Canadiens. However, the English-speaking merchants made a fuss about the Proclamation of 1763. As a result Murray was sent back to England. A new governor, Sir Guy Carleton, was sent to the colony.

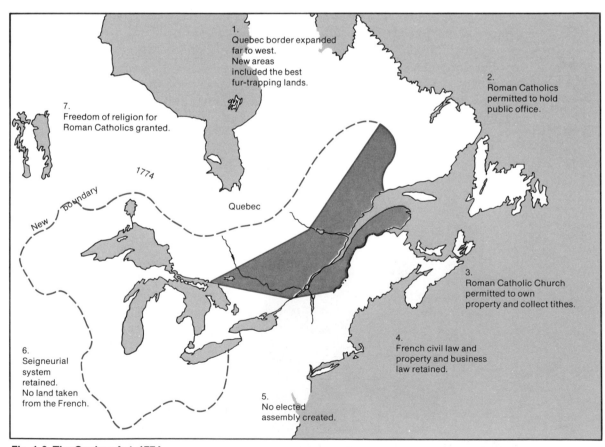

1. Quebec border expanded far to west. New areas included the best fur-trapping lands.
2. Roman Catholics permitted to hold public office.
3. Roman Catholic Church permitted to own property and collect tithes.
4. French civil law and property and business law retained.
5. No elected assembly created.
6. Seigneurial system retained. No land taken from the French.
7. Freedom of religion for Roman Catholics granted.

1774 New boundary

Quebec

Fig. 1-3 The Quebec Act, 1774

Would he side with the Canadiens or with the small number of English-speaking merchants? No one was sure.

In 1770, Carleton returned to England to get a law passed. This law would determine how the colony of Quebec was to be run. In 1774, he returned with the Quebec Act. Fig. 1-3 outlines the main points of the Quebec Act. Do you think that Carleton sided with the English-speaking merchants or with the Canadiens?

Reaction to the Quebec Act: On-the-street interviews

The Quebec Act was controversial. People reacted to it in many different ways. The following interviews show a few of the various reactions. In "People react to the Quebec Act" a reporter goes up to people in the streets of Quebec and asks them what they think about the newly-passed Act. The interviews are fictional, but they reflect actual opinion about the Act at the time. The first person interviewed is the governor of the colony, Sir Guy Carleton.

**People react to the Quebec Act**

**Sir Guy Carleton:** I certainly think the Quebec Act is good. It pleases many French-speaking people, which is important. I spent four years in England trying to convince King George III that the Thirteen Colonies are going to rebel against England. If they do, it is important that the Canadiens in this colony are satisfied with life under British rule. If they are not satisfied, they may join the rebellion. Or they may try to defeat the small British army here in the colony and once again join with France. The Quebec Act gives a great deal to the Roman Catholic Church and to the seigneurs. The clergy and the seigneurs will therefore persuade the people to be loyal to England. I would not be surprised if the Canadiens volunteered to fight on England's side!

Some of the English-speaking businessmen from Montreal are upset. But they are a very small minority. There are 70 000 or more Canadiens and only 5 000 English-speaking people in the colony. You have to be realistic and try to please the majority. If we are to govern Quebec, we must keep the Canadiens happy. The Quebec Act makes them happy. I think it is good strategy on England's part.

**Interviewer:** Thank you Governor Carleton. Excuse me, sir. I'm out here asking people what they think of the Quebec Act. What is your name, and what do you do?

**Nathan Squibs:** My name is Nathan Squibs and I'm in pots and pans. You've probably heard of my company—Squibs and Sons, Pots, Pans, and Kitchen Wares. I have warehouses in Boston, Halifax, and Montreal. You want my opinion of the Quebec Act? I'll be glad to give it to you. I think the Act is terrible. First of all, it will make Quebec a French colony rather than an English one. In the Act, Carleton gives the French their religion, their language, and their laws. It is my humble opinion that this colony should be made into an English one. I don't see why the English-speaking people in this colony should lose their rights. We don't have the right to vote. We don't have the right to elect representatives to an assembly. We are being ruled by a King three thousand miles away across the Atlantic Ocean. There's no doubt in my mind—the Quebec Act is a mistake.

**Interviewer:** Thank you, Mr. Squibs. Hello, Father. Can I have a moment of your time? Would you tell us what the Church thinks about the Quebec Act?

**Father Lamont:** Well, my son, I can't speak for the entire Church. I can tell you, though, that I think the Quebec Act is a wonderful thing. The act guarantees freedom of religion. It states that the Church can own property and collect tithes. It permits Roman Catholics to hold office. This means that members of the Church can sit on the council and have a say in the way the colony is run. I think that the British government has been fair to Catholics. The Act does not protect the French language, but it does protect the Church and the seigneurs. They will make sure that the French culture and language survive. All Canadiens should be happy about the Act.

**Interviewer:** Thank you for your time, Father. Excuse me, madame. I'd like to know what you think of the Quebec Act. What is your name and occupation?

**Madame Lebeau:** I am a habitant, Madame Lebeau. I think the Act is terrible. I have nothing against the Church or the seigneurs, but I liked not having to pay the tithes to the Church, or dues to the seigneurs. The Quebec Act will force me to pay them again. And I'll tell you something else. I've heard rumours that the English gave us the act just to get us on their side. They think that we will fight if trouble starts with the Thirteen Colonies. Well, I won't. If the English want to fight, let them fight. I'm not getting killed over some argument a bunch of English-speaking people are having!

**Interviewer:** Thank you for stopping to answer the question, Madame Lebeau. Sir, I want to know how people feel about the Quebec Act. What is your name, and what do you do?

**Etienne Cartouche:** My name is Etienne Cartouche. I am a seigneur, and I own a large area of land northeast of Montreal. There are over fifty tenants on my land. Madame Lebeau, whom you were just talking to—she is one of them. I'm sure she feels just as I do. The Quebec Act is the best thing that could possibly happen to the colony.

The Act restores the Church, and the power of the seigneur. It allows us to keep our own language and laws. Some people will grumble over the taxes for a while, but they will come to see that this is the French way of life. We have survived much hardship in the past. By living as our ancestors did, we will continue to preserve the French identity in the colony.

It is too bad that the anglophones are against the Act. They are upset because they didn't get elections and representative government. They don't realize that this would be impossible in our colony. Take the Lebeaus. They can neither read nor write. They need the Church and their seigneur to direct them. The Quebec Act is the means by which God has saved the French. Our future is secure.

---

**READING BETTER**

1. From what you have read in this interview, do you think that the seigneur understands how his tenants feel about the Quebec Act?

**ORGANIZING BETTER**

1. In your notebook, draw three columns. In the first column, write the name of each person interviewed about the Quebec Act. In the second, write whether the person is for or against the Quebec Act. In the third column, write out the reasons the person gives for being for or against the Act.

**USING YOUR KNOWLEDGE**

1. You are to write a short essay of one page. To prepare for this essay, you should read over the material from Cartouche's diary and the Quebec Act. In your essay explain how the Canadiens and English-speaking people began to dislike and distrust each other in the period from 1760 to 1774.

**TAKING A STAND**

1. Take a stand on this issue: "Should the British government have passed the Quebec Act?" Write down the reasons for your point of view and be prepared to defend it in class.

## Loyalists in Quebec

Shortly after the Quebec Act was passed, a revolution did break out in the Thirteen Colonies. The Canadiens did not join with the rebels, but remained neutral. Some Canadiens fought for the British cause. However, as Madame Lebeau suggested, most of them would not fight on the English side against the rebels. By 1779, the American colonies had defeated the British armies and the Thirteen Colonies became the United States of America.

During the revolution in the Thirteen Colonies there were large groups of people who did not want to rebel. These people were called "Loyalists". They were called this because they were loyal to Britain and refused to fight against the British army. When the rebels won, the Loyalists had to leave the United States. Many returned to England, but 35 000 went to live in Nova Scotia, and 10 000 went to Quebec. They hoped to be rewarded by the British government for their loyalty. The following letters give you an idea of how the Loyalists suffered while living in the Thirteen Colonies. The letters also show how the Loyalists reacted to their new home in Quebec, and how the French felt about the newcomers.

---

**A Loyalist's reaction to Quebec—A bitter disappointment
(A fictional account)**

Elizabeth Sinclair is the wife of Robert Sinclair. Mr. Sinclair owned a great deal of land near Boston. When the rebellion broke out in the Thirteen Colonies, Mr. Sinclair refused to join the rebels. Because of this, he was tarred and feathered by a group of angry rebels. The

**Loyalists moving to Quebec. List three things these Loyalists might be thinking about.**

Sinclairs then left everything they owned and moved to Quebec.

The Sinclairs felt they had suffered a great deal because of their loyalty to England. They hoped that the British government would reward them for their loyalty. Unfortunately, when they arrived in Quebec, they discovered a new type of home. Quebec was not at all like the English colony they had left. Because of the Quebec Act, the Canadiens still owned all the best cleared land. The Roman Catholic religion was practised, and there were no elected Assemblies. The Sinclairs were bitterly disappointed.

In the letter that follows, Elizabeth Sinclair is writing to her sister, Margaret. Margaret is also a Loyalist. She and her family have moved to Shelburne, Nova Scotia.

### A night of terror

The Sinclair Tract, Ottawa Valley
July 10, 1784

Dear Margaret,
I wish so often that our families could be together again. When I think of what the war has cost us, I wonder if we were wise to remain loyal to England. When I think of our great home in Boston, and of all we have left behind—my silver and china, my closets full of fine gowns, our friends, our happiness—I cannot but cry. I am sure that you feel the same way. We have paid a bitter price for our loyalty.

Margaret, I must tell you what happened to Robert just after the British surrendered to the rebels. I have not told anyone about it, because the memories were too painful. But now I feel as though I simply must share the horror of that night with someone.

It was in the fall of 1775. The British had just been defeated in the Boston area. We Loyalists lived in constant fear. We tried to keep guard over our homes and possessions. Sometimes in the middle of the night a wagon would pass. We would hear drunken men's voices yelling insults at Robert and the Tory cause. And then finally it happened.

We could see them coming down the road holding their torches in the night. From a distance it looked as though a fiery snake was winding its way around the hill and down our lane. They were drinking all the while. We hoped they would just yell and throw things at the house and then go away. But they started to build a bonfire right in front of the house. I thought I would go crazy when I realized what they were doing. In the firelight, we could see that they were plucking the feathers off our geese. I had heard of tar and feathering parties, but I never dreamed that it would one day happen to us.

Robert took down his hunting rifle, and led me and the boys to a room at the back of the house. We all sat there, waiting. There was silence for a long time. The crackling of the firewood and the bubbling of the tar were the only sounds breaking that uneasy stillness. Suddenly, I was aware of a strange pink glow in the room. They were burning our barn! Robert picked up his rifle, warned us to stay where we were, and ran out the door.

From the window I watched him run into the middle of the group. Like a wildman he started clubbing the villains with his rifle. But he was only one man against a large group. They overpowered him and dragged him off to the front of the house. I knew they were taking him to the tar.

I couldn't help myself, Margaret—I raced out the door toward Robert. Before I could reach him, two men grabbed me. "You just stay right here and watch what the men of Boston can do to a Tory traitor," they said mockingly.

They held me and made me watch. The sight has burned itself in my mind. Toward the end of the thing, I could take it no longer. I suppose I passed out for a while. I'm not sure how much later it was, but when I awoke Robert was straddled on a rail taken from our fence. He looked like a giant bird with white feathers and black shiny skin. His face was a mask of agony. The torches began to move off down the lane and I realized that they were carrying him off.

I turned to the house and saw that some of the men had stayed behind. A few of them were carrying our possessions out of the house and loading the pieces they wanted in a wagon. Others in the gang were taking chairs and tables and throwing them on the fire.

Margaret, I'm not sure to this day how we all did not lose our minds. Robert still hasn't fully recovered from the incident. The horror of that night will be with me to my grave. We have suffered bitterly for our King and country. Yet we have not been rewarded for our loyalty. I have decided to tell everyone the story of that night. These people who run Quebec must be made to see how much we have suffered. Perhaps then we will receive the kind of treatment we deserve.

*Your loving sister,*
*Elizabeth*

---

**READING BETTER**
1. **Who are the Loyalists?**
2. **Why did the Loyalists come to Quebec?**
3. **"The Loyalists suffered because they refused to join the rebels in their fight against England." In your notebook, make a list of facts that prove this statement to be true.**

### Discontent breeds hatred

As we saw in Elizabeth Sinclair's first letter, the Loyalists suffered terribly for their loyalty to England. When they came to Quebec, they expected to be repaid for this loyalty. Elizabeth Sinclair wanted everyone to know how much she and her family had suffered. She hoped for great rewards in Quebec. They did receive some rewards. They were given land, but they had to go into the woods and clear it. This was a terrible hardship. To many Loyalists, life in Quebec seemed more like a punishment than a reward.

The Loyalists looked at the Canadiens in Quebec. They were angry at how well these French-speaking people were treated. The French had been defeated. They were the former enemies of England. Most of the Canadiens had refused to fight in the revolutionary wars. Why then were they given so much in the Quebec Act, and the Loyalists given so little? Slowly, the Loyalists grew unhappy over their own situation. This resulted in bad feelings between the French-speaking and English-speaking people in Quebec.

Below is a second letter from Elizabeth Sinclair to her sister in Shelburne. It clearly shows why the Loyalists disliked the Canadiens in Quebec.

---

The Sinclair Tract, Ottawa Valley
January 24, 1789

Dear Margaret,
Oh, these Quebec winters, they go on and on! The first snow fell on October 18 and since then we have had snow every week. I wish I were in Boston again—the winters there were never as severe as this. What's more, in Boston you had some human society. Here on our tract, we are so far away from our nearest neighbours, the Wilkes family. They are fine people—true Loyalists who lost everything in New York.

The Wilkes are just as unhappy in this godforsaken place as we are. The land we were given is far to the west of Montreal. The soil is often boggy, and the dampness breeds fever in the spring. We had to carve our homestead out of the bush. In eight years, we have cleared only a small part of our land. It is backbreaking labour, and I am afraid that Robert is not up to it. He has never fully regained his strength since that horrible night years ago.

**What hardships did the Loyalists in Quebec have to face?**

Is this hard life the reward we get for being loyal to England? It seems to me that we should have been given the good land along the shores of the St. Lawrence River. The Canadiens who live there should have been sent away to work in this bushland. After all, they are the conquered people! Mr. Wilkes says that the Canadiens get all the favours because of the prying hand of the Roman Catholic Church.

Margaret, you have no idea how lucky you are not to have to deal with the Canadiens. They are farmers to the bone. They have no sense of culture! The only people of quality in Quebec are the merchants in Montreal. Of course, they are all English-speaking people. Most of the Canadiens want nothing to do with business. They act as if it were a sin to go out and make money.

On a trip to Montreal last year, I overheard a Canadien seigneur talking in an inn to one of the governor's councillors. He was telling the councillor that English-speaking people are always in too much of a rush. He said that we race around trying to build up a great fortune. When we finally do get all the money and possessions we want, we are too old to enjoy them! He went on to say that to have a happy life, one should live close to the land, slowly, and in harmony with nature. Can you imagine! And that councillor just sat there nodding his head

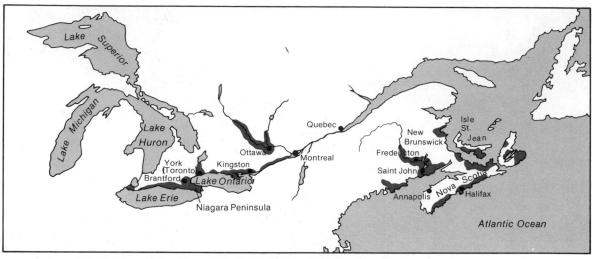

**Fig. 1-4 Loyalist settlements in the Maritimes and Upper Canada**

like a fool. I felt like going over to their table and asking the Frenchman how he expected stores and ships to be built if everyone stayed home and cultivated a patch of land. We cannot have progress unless we are constantly building and bringing in new businesses.

The thing that bothers me most is that the Canadiens have great influence over the governor. He does what they want. That Carleton is a fool for bringing in the Quebec Act. He allowed the use of French civil law in Quebec. That means that all business must be conducted using French rules. It is impossible!

Here is another example of how the Canadiens control things here. The seigneurs and the Church feel it would not be wise to have an elected Assembly. They go to speak to the governor, and he takes away rights that English people have had for years.

I know that you may find this hard to believe Margaret, but you can go anywhere in Quebec, outside of Montreal, and you will not be able to find people who speak English. Can you believe that? We live in a British colony, and most people don't speak English. I tell you, the French may have lost the colony on the battlefield, but somehow they retained control over it.

The only hope for us is to split the colony in two. The Canadiens can farm in their section. In the other section we shall have English laws, an elected Assembly, and as much progress and prosperity as possible. Some people are seriously considering this as a solution to our problems. For our sake, I hope that this idea will become reality.

*I remain, your loving sister,*
*Elizabeth*

1. Why is Elizabeth Sinclair unhappy with her new home on the Upper Ottawa River?
2. Elizabeth Sinclair is not pleased with the Quebec Act. Which points in the act does she object to?
3. Reread "People react to the Quebec Act". Which person's ideas are similar to Elizabeth Sinclair's? What are these ideas?
4. What solution to the problem in Quebec does Elizabeth Sinclair propose?

## USING YOUR KNOWLEDGE

1. When people are having a great number of problems in life, they often look for a scapegoat. A scapegoat is usually someone or something that troubled people blame for these problems. Recall that in the Allan Littlewood story Allan and his father used the East Indians as a scapegoat. Do you think that Elizabeth Sinclair is using the Canadiens as a scapegoat? Be sure that you have facts to back up your point of view.
3. Work with a group of students, and write a short play. Show what would happen if Elizabeth Sinclair and Etienne Cartouche met at a party. You should have parts for each member of your group. Your play should point out the differences in their philosophies of life. You can put your play on in front of the class, or tape it with sound effects, or even make a videotape of it.

## French-English relations: The first one hundred years (1760-1860)

In the one hundred years following the Conquest, there were a number of situations that caused friction between the French-speaking and English-speaking peoples in Canada. The discontent of the Loyalists, the dirty tricks played by men like Durfee, the different points of view about farming and commerce—all of these added to the gulf that existed between the two groups. But even with these problems, the francophones and anglophones were still able to cooperate. Whenever trouble between the French-speaking and English-speaking peoples arose, the government tried to find a solution that would keep both groups happy. Look at the following time line. You will see how often the government was able to find solutions to difficulties.

### French-English relations: A time line of the first 100 years

| | |
|---|---|
| 1760-63 | The Canadiens are worried. They are not sure how they will be treated by the English. Will they be able to keep their land, their religion, their language? |
| 1763-70 | With *the Proclamation of 1763*, General Murray is named governor. He is sympathetic to the Canadiens. Large numbers of English-speaking merchants, mostly from Boston, begin to settle in Quebec. They want to make the French colony into a typically English one. They want to eliminate the French influence. This, of course, makes the Canadiens fearful about their future. |
| 1770-80 | *Sir Guy Carleton* is the new governor of Quebec. He is very sympathetic to the Canadiens. The *Quebec Act* is passed. It protects the Canadiens' religion, land, and laws. The Canadiens are very happy. |
| 1780-90 | The American colonies win the revolutionary war against England. Large numbers of Loyalists flood into Quebec. They are upset because the Canadiens have the good land and many other benefits. The Loyalists grow to dislike the Canadiens because they seem to have more influence with the government than the Loyalists themselves do. |

| | |
|---|---|
| 1791-1837 | The discontent of the English-speaking people in Quebec results in the *Constitutional Act of 1791*. The English get their own colony, Upper Canada, which corresponds more or less to present-day southern Ontario. The Canadiens get their own colony, Lower Canada, which corresponds to present-day southern Quebec. For the most part, there is less conflict between the Canadiens and the English-speaking people after Quebec is divided into two colonies. |
| 1837-40 | There are *rebellions* in both Upper and Lower Canada. These rebellions have little to do with friction between francophones and anglophones. In both cases, the rebels want a more democratic system of government. The rebellions are important in the history of French-English relations because the British government sends Lord Durham to study the problems. The government follows the advice given in the *Durham Report* and joins Upper and Lower Canada into one colony. This new colony is called the *United Canadas*. Both Upper Canada (now called *Canada West*) and Lower Canada (now called *Canada East*) are given an equal number of seats in Canada's Parliament. |
| 1841-60 | For the most part the French-speaking and English-speaking peoples work well together in the new colony. They try to develop canals and railways. Many more French-speaking Canadians take an interest in business. The two Canadian political parties, the *Liberals* and the *Conservatives*, emerge in this period. There are both French-speaking and English-speaking members in these political parties. |
| 1860-67 | By 1860, there are serious problems in the United Canadas. It becomes difficult for either the Conservatives or Liberals to get a majority in the government. As a result, there are numerous elections and the government gets little work done. Many politicians feel that by making the English colonies in North America (Canada, Nova Scotia, New Brunswick) into one big country, the problems will be solved. This plan of union is called *Confederation*. |

## ORGANIZING BETTER

1. Copy the time line into your notebook.
2. Make a list of all the problems in French-English relations that occurred from 1760 to 1860. What solutions did the government find for each of these problems?

## RESEARCHING

1. Some historians say that the rebellion in Lower Canada was partly caused by problems between the Canadiens and the English-speaking people. See if you can discover whether or not the rebellion in Lower Canada was in fact caused by friction between the two groups. Use your school library or books that your teacher will provide.
2. Write a *short* biography (an account of a person's life) of Lord Durham. Outline the main ideas that he gave in his report on problems in Canada in 1837.
3. You are to make a short report to your class. Half of the class members will pretend that they are Canadiens and the other half will be English-speaking people. In your report explain which period in the time line you would like to have lived in and why. You will have to do library research for this report.
4. Research and write a report on one of the following topics:
   Proclamation of 1763
   Constitutional Act of 1791
   Rebellions in Upper and Lower Canada
   Formation of the Liberal and Conservative parties

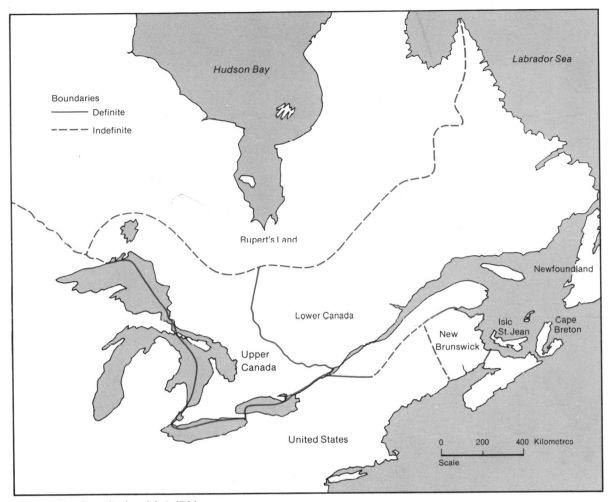

**Fig. 1-5 The Constitutional Act, 1791**

## The battle over Confederation

The task of uniting the British colonies into one large country was difficult. The colonies were Canada (Canada East and Canada West), Nova Scotia, and New Brunswick. In each of the colonies there were people who felt that Confederation was a bad idea. In this section of the book we are not concerned with the fight for Confederation. We do, however, want to discover the ways in which Confederation affected French-English relations. To do this we must learn whether or not Canada East (later Quebec) wanted Confederation.

In Canada East the battle over

Confederation was fought between two great champions of French-speaking Canadians. On the one side was the leader of the Conservative party in Quebec, and a former prime minister, George Etienne Cartier. On the other side was the leader of the Liberal party in Canada East, A.A. Dorion. One of these men wanted the colony to join Confederation and the other did not.

We will look at the arguments each of these Canadians gave to defend his stand. Afterward, you can decide which of the men was most convincing.

> I am George Etienne Cartier.
> I believe that Confederation
> is good for Canada East.
> These are my reasons.

Public Archives of Canada

**1** There is political deadlock in the United Canadas. We have had four new governments in the last three years. There have been too many expensive elections. Because of the deadlock, the government cannot function properly and no work is being done. Confederation is a way out of deadlock.

**2** There is a real danger that the United States will invade Canada. The northern states have just defeated the South in the Civil War. Britain supported the South. The victorious North is angry about this and may invade Canada to get even with Britain. Canada also faces invasion by the **Fenians.** If our colonies are united, we will be able to defend ourselves more easily.

**3** Canada East cannot remain in isolation. To have **commercial prosperity** we must expand and join with the other British colonies of North America. We can build a railway to the eastern colonies (Maritimes). This will give Canada East access to an ice-free port in the winter. Commercial growth will mean more jobs and more money for everyone.

**4** There are **tariffs** between Canada and the eastern colonies. This means that our goods are expensive in the east. Confederation will get rid of these tariffs. Our goods will cost less and we will sell more in the eastern regions. We will all make more money.

**5** Confederation is a **federal union.** This means that the provinces will have complete control over local affairs. We will be able to protect our language, religion, and way of life. The federal government will only look after things that concern the whole country, such as trade rules and defence. The federal government will not interfere in local affairs.

**6** I believe that Dorion is opposed to Confederation because he wants Canada East to join up with the United States.

**7** The great leaders of Canada East want Confederation. The Church has said that it is a good idea. Confederation will guarantee, in writing, freedom of religion and the right to use the French language in Canada.

**8** I believe that in the future the French-speaking and English-speaking Canadians will work together in harmony. They will have a common interest. They will both want to build a strong Canada.

**9** Dorion says that the English-speaking majority will take advantage of the French-speaking minority. I say that the English spirit of fair play would never allow these people to do anything that went against the wishes of French-speaking Canadians.

I am Antoine Aimé Dorion.
I believe that Confederation will hurt
Canada East. These are my reasons.

Public Archives of Canada

**1** Cartier seems to feel that we are in danger from the United States. I say that we are in no danger at all. The best thing that Canada can do is to keep quiet. We should keep out of any arguments that the United States has with England. If we do not provide a reason for war with the United States, then there will be no war. If there is no war, then we can save all the money that Cartier wants to spend on railways, soldiers, and ships.

**2** Cartier and all his friends in the Conservative party want Confederation mainly so they can use the money from all the colonies to build a railway to the Maritimes. Cartier is a part-owner of the Grand Trunk Railway. For years he has been getting the government to help pay for Grand Trunk projects. Now he and the Grand Trunk want to build a railway to the east coast. They don't have enough money, so they want the two Maritime colonies to help them out. If you ask Cartier why we need the railway, he will say it is for defence. But I tell you the real reason is so that Cartier and his friends can make more money.

**3** The federal system that Cartier thinks is so wonderful will not benefit Canada East. Powers that we now have in Canada East—control over business, taxation, marriage and divorce, and all criminal law—these would all be taken over by the new federal government. As far as I am concerned, when you give away power you are weaker, not stronger. To protect the French way of life, we must be strong. We cannot give power away to the English-speaking majority and still expect to be able to protect ourselves.

**4** Cartier talks about federal union. He says that we will have control over local affairs. That is not strictly true. We will have control over local affairs only as long as the federal government permits us to have the power. The federal government has the power to veto (disallow) any law passed in a province. This means that it can reject any law that we pass in Canada East.

**5** Cartier thinks that in the future there will be harmony between francophones and anglophones. That will not be so. In the future, some English-speaking Canadians will come up with the idea that Canada should have only one language and one way of life. And you can be sure that that one language and way of life won't be French.

**6** The people of Canada East do not understand this idea of union. They do not want a change. I have petitions with the names of over 20 000 people who oppose Confederation. The leaders of Canada East may want Confederation, but the people do not.

**7** We in Canada East are different from the people in the rest of the English colonies in North America. We have a distinct language and culture. If we join with the other colonies, we will always be arguing and fighting. In the end, we will come to hate each other.

**8** We must not join Confederation because we will be a minority group in a land of English-speaking people. When the English-speaking majority wants to do something, they will do it whether the French-speaking people want to or not. French Canadian rights may not be respected. What if English Canada wants to go to war but French Canada does not? There is no guarantee that French Canada will not be forced to go.

---

**READING BETTER**
1. Why does Dorion feel that Canada has nothing to fear from the United States?
2. What self-interest does Dorion accuse Cartier of having?
3. What factual information does Dorion use to prove that the people of Canada East are opposed to Confederation?

**ORGANIZING BETTER**
1. List three faults that Dorion finds with the federal system of union.

**USING YOUR KNOWLEDGE**
1. In a short essay of one or two paragraphs, prove that A.A. Dorion does not trust the English. Be sure to use facts to back up your point of view.

2. Make a chart in your notebook. Draw a line down your page to make two columns. At the top of one column write "Cartier", and at the top of the other, "Dorion". Now compare the views of Cartier and Dorion under these four headings:
   a) The danger from the United States.
   b) Protection of French rights.
   c) The nature of English-speaking Canadians.
   d) The future of French-English relations resulting from Confederation.
3. Imagine that you are a francophone (or anglophone) living in Canada East in 1866. You are part of a group that is making posters to convince people to be for (or against) Confederation. Make a poster that reflects your point of view. Your poster should show why you think your viewpoint is correct, and why opposing views are wrong.

TAKING A STAND

1. Take a stand on this issue: "Should French-speaking Canadians have accepted Confederation?" Be sure that you use facts to back up your point of view. You may want to go to the library for more information to use in your argument. Note: In this debate, you are to take the point of view of a French-speaking Canadian living in Canada East.

## French-speaking Canadians join Confederation

George Etienne Cartier was a powerful politician. He was able to convince French-speaking people in Canada East that Confederation was a good idea. However, in the battle to bring Canada East into Confederation, Cartier lost a great deal of support in the area. He won the election by a slim majority. This meant that there were almost as many people against the idea of Confederation as there were in favour of it. The arguments of A.A. Dorion made many French-speaking Canadians in Canada East feel uneasy. They faced their first years in Confederation with much uncertainty.

## Conclusion

In this chapter we discovered that French-speaking Canadians have a great desire to survive as a distinct group. When the francophones in New France were forced to live under British control their strength of will allowed them to preserve their way of life. With the help of sympathetic English governors, such as Carlton and Murray, they were able to retain their language, religion, and land.

We also saw that the French Canadian way of life often irritated English-speaking people. This was especially true when the Canadien way of life seemed to prevent the anglophones from accomplishing their goals. We saw how the Loyalists became angry when they were not allowed to have elections. They became more upset when they realized that the French Canadian view of business and commerce was different from their own. Eventually, this discontent resulted in bad feelings between the French-speaking and English-speaking people.

Despite this conflict, many of the early leaders of our country refused to give up the idea that the two groups could live together in harmony. They often succeeded in convincing the people of their belief. Therefore, when it became beneficial for the francophones and anglophones to join together, the two groups did so. We learned that in 1840, Upper Canada and Lower Canada united; in 1867, Canada East agreed to join Confederation.

From the years 1760 to 1867, solutions were found to many of the problems between French-speaking and English-speaking people. But what about the future? The next chapter discusses how the two groups got along in the first fifty years after Confederation.

READING BETTER

1. What aspects of Etienne Cartouche's philosophy would Elizabeth Sinclair disagree with?

ORGANIZING BETTER

1. Make a list of all the major historical figures

discussed in this chapter. For each, write a short paragraph explaining how the person affected French-English relations in Canada.

USING YOUR KNOWLEDGE

1. Which of the following characters would most logically have made the following statement? Give reasons for your answers.
   Characters: Elizabeth Sinclair, Dorion, Cartier, Cartouche, Carlton.
   Statement: "Quebec is the home of French-speaking Canadians. The French Canadian way of life should be protected within its borders. The anglophones should accept the fact that they are the minority. They should not expect special privileges."

SOLVING PROBLEMS

1. Pretend that you are Cartier or Dorion. You want to convince the people of Canada East that your view of Confederation is the correct one. Plan an advertising campaign that will appear in local papers.

TAKING A STAND

1. In 1780, should the British government have taken the land away from the Canadiens and given it to the Loyalists? Be sure to give reasons for your point of view.

RESEARCHING

1. Cartier and Dorion are important politicians. Using books in your library, see if you can discover three beliefs held by each man that would affect French-English relations.

## GLOSSARY

**Burn in effigy.** An effigy is a model or representation of a person. Often when people were upset with someone, they would make a cloth dummy of the person. They would put the person's name on the dummy, hoist it on a pole, and set it on fire.

**Canadiens.** French-speaking inhabitants of New France.

**Commercial prosperity.** This means that all businesses are flourishing and everyone is becoming richer. There is much economic growth.

**Federal union.** This occurs when two or more nations join to form one nation that is ruled by two levels of government.

**Fenians.** A secret society of Irish people formed in New York in 1858. Their purpose was to free Ireland from English rule. They began their fight by attacking the British colonies in North America.

**Governor Carleton.** A representative of the British government who replaced Governor Murray after the Proclamation of 1763.

**Habitants.** People who rented and worked farms owned by seigneurs. In return for the seigneurs' land and protection, the habitants would pay rent and bring their wheat to the seigneurs' mill to be ground.

**Seigneurs.** People of influence who received grants of land from the monarch. The seigneurs would then rent parcels of this land to the habitants in return for certain services.

**Tariffs.** A tax placed on imports.

**Thirteen Colonies.** The English colonies located along the Atlantic coast of America.

**Tithes.** Payments made to the Church to keep it operating.

# 2/The first fifty years after Confederation: 1867-1917

## Contents

### Introduction

After Confederation, Canadians hoped that there would no longer be problems between the French-speaking and the English-speaking peoples. The power to make laws was divided between the provincial and the federal governments. People thought that this would keep the provinces happy, and put an end to the francophones' fear of English control.

Unfortunately, Confederation offered no simple solution to French-English conflict. In the first fifty years after Confederation, the two groups disagreed over three serious issues. They were:

1. The Riel Rebellions and the execution of Riel;
2. The elimination of French schools in Manitoba;
3. The Conscription Crisis of 1917.

Each of these issues increased the bad feelings between French-speaking and English-speaking Canadians. The tension created over these issues is still present in French-English relations. In this chapter we study these important issues and their effect on the two language groups. The chapter attempts to answer the following questions:

1. **Why did the French-speaking people begin to doubt Confederation?**
2. **Who was Louis Riel and how did he affect French-English relations?**
3. **Why did the government of Manitoba eliminate French schools and what effect did this situation have on French-English relations?**
4. **What was the Conscription Crisis of 1917 and how did it affect French-English relations?**

**John A. Macdonald, Prime Minister of Canada during both Riel Rebellions. The Riel question eventually destroyed French Canadians' trust in Macdonald.**

## The French begin to doubt Confederation: The power of disallowance

Not long after 1867 some French-speaking Canadians began to think that perhaps A.A. Dorion had been correct. Dorion had predicted that the English-speaking majority in Confederation would force its will on French Canada.

During the discussions about Confederation, Macdonald had demanded that the federal government in Ottawa have the *power of disallowance* over provincial laws. This means that the federal government had the power to reject any law passed by the provincial governments if it felt that the law was not good for the whole country. Macdonald believed that if the provinces had the power to do just as they wished it would be hard to keep the country united. George Cartier told Macdonald that he did not like this power of disallowance. Cartier was afraid that the federal government would use this power to overrule the wishes of the francophones in Quebec.

In the early years after Confederation, Prime Minister Macdonald was forced to reject many provincial laws. The followers of Dorion began to suggest that the federal power of disallowance would make it impossible to protect the French language, religion, and way of life. More and more French-speaking Canadians were becoming upset. Cartier told Quebec that Macdonald and the federal government could be trusted to protect the French way of life. Dorion and his followers said they could not be trusted. Who was correct—Cartier or Dorion? To find the answer to this question we will examine the Riel Rebellions.

### READING BETTER

1. What is the federal power of disallowance? Why did this power make the followers of A.A. Dorion fearful?

### USING YOUR KNOWLEDGE

1. If you were the prime minister of Canada,

which of the following provincial laws would you disallow? Be sure to give reasons to back up your point of view. Remember that the purpose of the power of disallowance was to prevent provinces from passing laws that would hurt Canada as a whole.

a) A law that says that citizens of the province do not have to serve in the army
b) A law that requires all high school students in the province to take five courses in French before receiving a diploma
c) A law that forbids persons twenty-five years of age and younger to consume alcohol
d) A law that says citizens of the province do not have to pay federal income tax
e) A law that raises the speed limit in the province from 60 km/h to 65 km/h
f) A law that gives tax benefits to companies that move to this province

## The Riel Rebellions

### Louis Riel and the Red River Rebellion

The settlement of Red River was located roughly where the city of Winnipeg stands today. By the 1840s it was occupied mostly by Métis, who were people of European and Indian ancestry. The Métis had little interest in farming or establishing a permanent settlement at Red River. They were a hunting people forced to follow the buffalo herds, and so life was nomadic. The settlement was little more than a cluster of Métis tents around the Fort Garry trading post.

In the 1850s and 1860s, however, large numbers of English-speaking settlers began to move into Red River. They established a growing and prosperous settlement. In the late 1860s, the Canadian government began to worry about the number of settlers coming into the colony from the United States. Consequently, the government arranged to buy the Northwest from the Hudson's Bay Company.

There was one major problem, however. The Métis had not taken part in the negotiations for the sale of the land, nor had their interests been safe-guarded. Thus,

Public Archives of Canada

**Louis Riel and his councillors after the first Riel Rebellion, 1869-70.**

when the Canadian government sent out a team of people to survey the Métis lands, trouble erupted.

At this point, a young Métis leader, Louis Riel, decided to take action. Riel felt that Métis land rights had to be guaranteed before Canada took over the settlement. He also stressed that the Métis wanted to choose the governor for the area. The Métis disliked the man, McDougall, whom the prime minister had appointed to the position. Riel also believed that there should be no mass immigration from Ontario. He felt that the educated English-speaking people would take advantage of the uneducated Métis.

Riel disregarded the objections of some of the English-speaking settlers of Red River. He organized a band of Métis who forced the surveying team to pack up their equipment and leave. He then sent another group of Métis to prevent the new governor, McDougall, from entering the colony.

Riel was concerned that some of the English-speaking settlers were gathering an armed force to take over the colony. He felt that the only way to secure Métis control over the settlement was to capture Fort Garry. The Métis did this late in November, 1869. Later they arrested several English-speaking agitators in the colony. Shortly after the take-over, there was an election. Riel was elected president.

But Riel's prisoners did not give up. Several escaped from prison. About six weeks later one of them, Thomas Scott, led a revolt against Riel's government. Riel arrested Scott and several other English-speaking settlers. Scott was eventually placed on trial for treason, and found guilty. He was taken outside the walls of Fort Garry and shot.

Meanwhile, the government of Canada was carrying on negotiations with Riel's government. Prime Minister Macdonald hoped to settle the Métis grievances. He

**Thomas Scott. What caused friction between Scott and Riel?**

wanted to bring the Red River colony into Confederation peacefully. With the execution of Scott, however, these hopes vanished. The citizens of Ontario were outraged that an English-speaking Protestant had been killed by a French-speaking Catholic.

The longer Macdonald delayed action in the Red River situation the more complex the problem became. English Canada demanded that a military force be sent to crush the Riel Rebellion. French Canada demanded that the rights of the Métis be protected. The Red River situation was quickly becoming a national crisis in French-English relations. Finally, Macdonald acted. His government passed a bill that established the Province of Manitoba. A new governor, whom the Métis agreed upon, was to be sent to take over the colony. Each Métis was to receive a land grant of 240 acres. The Métis were given the right to vote and the Red River colony was given a representative in Parliament.

These actions satisfied French Canada. The rights of the Métis were being protected. And to satisfy the English Canadians, Macdonald sent a military force to Red River. The force was to help keep order in the colony. When the military force arrived at Fort Garry, Riel fled south to the United States. The government force quickly took control of the fort and the first Riel Rebellion was over.

It appeared that Macdonald had avoided a crisis in French-English relations. Confederation seemed to be working; French-speaking and English-speaking Canadians had solved a national crisis without tearing each other apart. In 1870, the future of French-English relations seemed promising.

### The second Riel Rebellion: The Northwest Rebellion, 1885

For almost 15 years, relations between francophones and anglophones were generally good. By 1885, however, trouble was brewing in the Northwest Territories. After the first rebellion many of the Métis decided that they would not stay at Red River. Large settlements did not suit the Métis hunter lifestyle. They travelled farther west to present-day Saskatchewan. Unfortunately, by 1885, the buffalo herds had almost disappeared. Also, English settlers were beginning to move into the area, and the government of Canada had built a railway to the very doorstep of the Métis camps. Once again surveyors appeared, and the Métis feared that they might lose their land. They sent for Riel.

Riel agreed to come to Saskatchewan and help the Métis solve their problems. He drew up a Bill of Rights for the Métis and sent it to Ottawa. Macdonald, who was still prime minister, had a number of other problems on his mind. He therefore seemed to ignore the Métis demands. After waiting four months, Riel concluded that the government had no intention of meeting the Métis demands. He immediately appointed a Métis hunter, Gabriel Dumont, as his military commander. Riel set up a rebel · government and formed an alliance with discontented Indian groups in the area.

Macdonald had reacted to the rumblings in the Northwest by ordering General Middleton, the commander of the Canadian militia, to Winnipeg. Under Middleton, the Winnipeg militia had already begun to move west. But before they arrived, open rebellion had erupted.

The only representatives of the Canadian government in the Northwest Territories were the North West Mounted Police. They, too, had heard about the revolt. A force from Regina had begun to move north to try to stop it. But at Duck Lake, Dumont and his Métis forces successfully ambushed them. Shortly after this rebel victory, Riel's Indian allies attacked a settlement at Frog Lake and killed nine settlers.

People in eastern Canada were in a frenzy after news of these events reached them. Militia in many Canadian centres quickly prepared to go west. Using the newly constructed Canadian Pacific Railway, troops were rushed to the scene of the

**Gabriel Dumont, the leader of the Métis forces against General Middleton 1885.**

rebellion. Riel's commander, Dumont, was an excellent leader. Though greatly outnumbered, he and his group managed to defeat Middleton's force at Fish Creek. Riel's Indian allies, led by Poundmaker and Big Bear, also defeated the government forces in early battles. For a time it appeared as if Middleton might be defeated by the rebels.

The government forces, however, had superior military equipment and they greatly outnumbered the rebels. Eventually, the rebel stronghold of Batoche was surrounded. Government forces shelled the rebels into submission on May 12, 1885. Riel surrendered on May 15, Gabriel Dumont escaped to the United States, and

Big Bear surrendered later in the summer. Riel's second rebellion was over. More people had died, and Indians had been encouraged to rebel. This time, however, Riel was behind bars. Would French-English relations be able to weather the storm of the second Riel Rebellion?

### What is to be done with Louis Riel?

On August 1, 1885, in the courthouse in Regina, Judge Richardson was ready to read the verdict in the trial of Louis David Riel. All the evidence had been heard, and all the witnesses called. Riel had made his final, emotional speech to the jury. The courtroom was hushed as the judge began to read the verdict.

**The militia troops under General Middleton, 1885.**

Public Archives of Canada

"Louis Riel, you are charged with treason. Here is the sentence of this court upon you. You will be taken to the guard room of the Mounted Police station in Regina. You will be kept there until September 18, at which time you will be taken to the place of execution to be hanged by the neck until you are dead. May God have mercy on your soul."

Was Louis Riel really going to die for his part in the Northwest Rebellion? As soon as the verdict was announced the province of Quebec was up in arms. It felt that Riel was not totally to blame for the rebellions in the west. Many Canadians agreed with this point of view. They felt that the rebellions were caused by ignorance, mismanagement, and delay on the part of John A. Macdonald and the Conservative government in Ottawa. If Macdonald was partly to blame for the violence in the west, then why should Riel be executed for treason?

Many Canadians demanded that Macdonald change Riel's death penalty to a prison term. Prime Minister Macdonald was not sure what to do.

The following is a fictional account of what might have happened if John A. Macdonald had asked the advice of some members of his government. Two of the MPs in the story are from Ontario; they want to see Riel hang. The other two are French-speaking Canadians who feel that Riel should be pardoned.

1. Why did Riel decide to take over Fort Garry?
2. Who was the first elected president of Red River?
3. Who was the prime minister of Canada at the time of the first rebellion?
4. Who was the prime minister at the time of the second rebellion?
5. Name an English settler who led a revolt against Riel's government at Fort Garry.
6. Which province in particular got upset when Scott was executed?
7. Which province demanded that the Métis rights be respected?
8. In which province is the Red River area located?
9. After the Red River Rebellion, where did the Métis move to?
10. Where did Riel's rebel group attack a small group of Mounted Police?

### John A. Macdonald's decision: Should Riel hang?

Sir John A. Macdonald stood looking out the window of his office. A man was walking across the ice-covered Ottawa River toward the town of Hull. As Macdonald watched the man, he wondered, "Is that man a French Canadian? If he is, what will he do if I have Riel executed? Will he vote for me in the next election?"

Before Macdonald could decide, the door of his office opened and four men entered.

"Come in gentlemen," said Macdonald. "I have a decision to make and I want your opinions before I make it." Macdonald directed his four guests to places around a large table in the centre of the office.

On the prime minister's right was Archibald Thompson, member of Parliament from a riding in Ontario. Thompson was a Conservative party member; he also belonged to the **Orange Lodge.** He liked neither Catholics nor French-speaking Canadians. He wanted to see Canada become a country of one language, one culture, and one religion. Thompson wanted Riel to hang.

Sitting on Thompson's right was Henry Hopkins, member from a Nova Scotia riding. Hopkins was very pro-British. He felt that if Riel was not executed, the francophones in Quebec would think that they could rebel and not be punished. Hopkins detested those who were not loyal to the British monarch. Because he saw Riel as a traitor, he felt that the rebel should hang.

Sitting on the prime minister's left was Pierre Robichaud, the member of Parliament from a riding in New Brunswick. Robichaud was a Roman Catholic and a French-speaking Canadian. He felt that Riel was a hero of the French Canadian people. He believed that outside Quebec, French-speaking Canadians had no way of defending their rights. Therefore, if the government of Canada did not protect the rights of French-speaking Canadians outside Quebec, Robichaud believed that there would be many more French Canadian rebellions.

Next to Robichaud sat Louis Lanctôt. Lanctôt was a man of great learning and a fine speaker. He was a staunch defender of French Quebec. Lanctôt had supported Confederation along with Cartier. In 1885, however, he was beginning to think that perhaps A. A. Dorion had been right to oppose Confederation.

Sir John A. Macdonald looked slowly around the table at each of the men. Then he spoke. "Gentlemen, we must decide whether or not Louis Riel is to be executed. As I see it, there are three issues involved in the Riel case. First, did Riel commit treason? Second, did he commit murder? And third, is he insane?"

Lanctôt spoke first. "Mr. Prime Minister, francophones in Quebec are saying that you delayed making a decision about what should have been done in the Red River and Northwest Rebellions. They think that

Public Archives of Canada

**What problems did the Riel issue create for Macdonald?**

**Battle of Batoche, 1885. How does this picture show Dumont's military skill?**

your delay made the situation worse. In a sense, the delays were the cause of much of the trouble. The government should have taken swift action to defend the Métis land claims. It should have protected the honest but uneducated Métis from greedy people who were at Red River to take over Métis land. If this had been done there might not have been a rebellion. People are saying that the government's delays caused the Métis to get more upset. They felt that nothing was going to be done to help them. Eventually, they got so upset that they were willing to fight. Some people are also saying that the government mismanaged both rebellions. Sir John, you must admit that you were not familiar with the problems at Red River. And you did delay making a decision about both rebellions, in the hope that the problems would solve themselves."

"Well, Louis, I will admit that I did delay taking action. But this stuff about mismanagement is ridiculous! I think you have been having dinner with too many Liberals," said Macdonald.

"Mr. Prime Minister, I would say that Lanctôt has been having dinner with too many disloyal French-speaking Catholics," declared Thompson. "I speak for a large number of people in Ontario. They feel that Riel is guilty of treason. We have facts to back up our point of view. For example, Riel sent a telegram from Batoche on May 6, 1885, to the President of the United States. In the telegram he asked the US to invade the West to save the Métis people."

"Yes, and there is more," added Hopkins. "Riel also stopped official government surveyors from doing their job at Red River. He prevented the governor from entering the Red River colony and taking over his duties. He led one hundred Métis in an attack on Fort Garry, which was official government property. Any one of these acts makes him guilty of treason. The penalty for treason is death."

"Listen, those facts are true but they only tell half the story," said Robichaud. He leafed hurriedly through the papers he had in front of him. "Here it is," he said, taking a paper from the pile. "Before you decide whether or not Riel's actions were treasonous, you must consider these facts. Riel was the only educated Métis at Red River. Someone had to protect the uneducated Métis. Also, when Riel stopped the surveyors, he was merely defending the Métis right to the land. The Métis thought the surveyors were going to take their land. If Riel hadn't acted, those surveyors would have been shot down. In a sense, Riel saved their lives. And the point you make about keeping Governor McDougall out of the colony is very weak. McDougall was a poor choice to send as governor to Red River. The Métis hated him because he had insulted their beloved Bishop Taché. Also, they believed that McDougall had stolen Indian lands when he drew up the **Treaty of Manitoulin Island.** The Métis felt that McDougall was anti-French and anti-Indian. How would you react if you were a Métis?"

---

QUICK QUIZ
1. Which one of the MPs is an Orangeman?
2. Which MP feels that there may be more rebellions unless Riel is hanged?
3. Which of the MPs is the most anti-French?
4. Why did the Métis dislike Governor McDougall? (Two reasons)
5. According to Robichaud, what might have

happened to the surveyors if Riel had not forced them to leave?

ORGANIZING BETTER
1. List all the facts that suggest Riel was guilty of treason.
2. List all the facts that suggest Riel was not guilty of treason.

---

THE GOVERNMENT REPORT

Sir John A. Macdonald waited until all the MPs had finished speaking. Then he said, "Well gentlemen, I see that you all have strong opinions on the matter. I have something here that will surely interest you. A while ago, I asked a member of the North West Mounted Police to investigate the Riel affair. This is the report he submitted to me. I'll read it to you, and then I'd like to hear your comments." He began to read.

**Report on the activities of Louis Riel**

**Riel's activities**

There is some evidence to support the following statements.
1. In the spring of 1870, Louis Riel contacted the governor of the state of Minnesota. He asked if it would be possible for the Red River colony to join with the United States.

2. In the Métis demands of 1870, Riel asked that a railway be built south from Red River to the US border.
3. When Riel took over Fort Garry, he became president, rather than prime minister, of the settlement.
4. Riel broke the law on several occasions. During the first rebellion, Riel stole money from the Hudson's Bay Company offices. Also, while Riel lived in the United States, he was arrested for trying to rig an election.

### Interpretation of above information

The activities described in points 1 to 3 suggest that Riel was a traitor to his country. He asked the governor of Minnesota if the Red River settlement could join with the US. Some people believe that he wanted a railway to the US so that American troops could be rushed into Red River before Canadian troops could reach the settlement. Also, by becoming president of the colony, Riel seemed to be preparing the Métis for an American system of government.

The last point suggests that Riel was treacherous and irresponsible. He appears to have no respect for the laws of any country.

In sum, the findings of this study indicate that Riel is a danger to Canada.

As Macdonald finished reading, Lanctôt stood up angrily. "This report is ridiculous, Sir John!" he said. "There are a number of errors in the information. Riel did ask for a railway to the US border. He thought it would increase trade and help the Métis with more jobs. In those same lists of demands, he asked for a seat in the Canadian House of Commons. Does that show that he is a traitor? The report also says he stole money. In fact, he asked for the money as a loan. When the Hudson's Bay Company refused, he took it so he could get supplies for the people at Red River. The point about his talking to the governor of Minnesota is true. However, you must remember that John Schultz, one of Riel's great enemies at Red River, had escaped. Riel thought he was going to raise an army of Orangemen in Ontario who would come to Red River and slaughter the Métis. Riel contacted the governor so he could get some protection for the innocent Métis people."

"Listen here, Lanctôt!" shouted Thompson, getting to his feet. "You talk a lot about Orangemen killing people. The fact is that Riel is the one who did all the killing. All the Orangemen did was to try to stop the murdering."

---

**ORGANIZING BETTER**

1. Make a chart of two columns in your notebook. At the top of one column write "Riel is a traitor". At the top of the other write "Riel is not a traitor". In the first column list all the facts given in the report that show Riel to be a dangerous traitor. In the second, list the arguments given by Lanctôt to defend Riel's actions.

"Gentlemen, calm down. Let's forget about the report for a moment. I want to discuss the issue of whether or not Riel is a murderer and whether or not he is insane. I suggest that we start with the issue of whether or not he is a murderer," said the prime minister.

"I think it is clear that Riel is responsible for numerous deaths. He is a murderer. He killed Thomas Scott," said Hopkins.

"That is not the exact truth," said Lanctôt. "Scott was captured by Riel and placed in jail with his friends. Riel did this to protect these Ontario Orangemen from the Métis. But Scott and his friends escaped from the jail and they attacked Fort Garry. Scott was recaptured. He was put on trial for treason against the new government of Red River, found guilty, and executed. Riel was only the leader of the government. He didn't find Scott guilty of treason. He didn't shoot Scott himself. It was all done legally."

"The trial of Thomas Scott was a mockery," shouted Thompson. "They had decided that Scott was guilty before they heard the first witness. Also, how can Riel have a man tried for treason against an illegal government? If you believe what you are saying, Lanctôt, then you believe that Riel had the right to set up his own government. This is a British country, Lanctôt. If you go against the government, you are a traitor. And traitors die."

"Riel's government could be considered legal, since Red River was not part of Canada at that point," said Lanctôt. "Also, Riel visited Scott and Scott mocked Riel. Scott said that he would never follow a government led by an inferior race of people. Remember that Riel was **paranoid.** He could not stand this type of treatment. His mind snapped. He went insane and allowed the killing to be carried out."

**The execution of Thomas Scott. If you lived in Ontario in 1870 how might you have reacted to this picture?**

"Riel was not insane!" objected Thompson. "You want to trick the prime minister into believing that he was insane. You think that Sir John will use it as an excuse to let Riel off. Well, it's just not true, Lanctôt, and you know it."

"You have all read reports on Riel's mental health, haven't you?" asked the prime minister. "What do you think of them? Hopkins?"

"Well, Sir John, the reports seem to stress the fact that Riel is a **religious fanatic.** He feels that he talks to God. He feels it is his duty to save the world. Many religious people have had the same characteristics and we don't consider them insane. For me, the reports do not prove that Riel was insane," concluded Hopkins.

"And besides," interrupted Thompson, "the commissioners appointed to investigate Riel's sanity felt that Riel was sane. Some people who were involved in the rebellions said that Riel was using all that religious talk to impress the uneducated Métis. He did this to get the Métis to follow him in the rebellions. Riel is clearly not insane."

"Well, there doesn't seem to be a way of telling for sure whether Riel is sane or insane," said Macdonald. "Perhaps we had better get back to the issue of whether or not he is a murderer."

"I agree with the prime minister," said Thompson. "It is clear that Riel caused a number of deaths, and was out for blood. I have read some reports about the massacre at Duck Lake. They tell of Riel standing up in the saddle screaming for the Métis to kill in the name of the Father, the Son, and the Holy Ghost."

"That report goes on to tell how Riel prevented the Métis from butchering the survivors of the Duck Lake battle," replied Robichaud angrily. "He is not a blood-thirsty killer. He is a man fighting for his people's rights. The only way he could defend their rights was to take up arms. And when you take up arms, people get killed. Even you can see that, can't you, Thompson?"

"I can see things very clearly, Robichaud," answered Thompson. "I can see that Riel stirred up the Indians. He gave them guns, and set them loose to kill. He told the Indians to go out and destroy the white enemy. What about the rights of the people at Frog Lake who were slaughtered by Wandering Spirit? How can you defend this man? He is clearly a killer."

Louis Lanctôt stood up and began to walk around the table. He was deep in thought. "I want you to understand our point of view, Mr. Prime Minister," he finally said. "We see Riel as a defender of the rights of a minority group. Riel was defending the French-speaking Métis. When Riel fled from Fort Garry in 1870 and the British troops arrived, the soldiers hurt innocent Métis. Riel had to take up arms to prevent this type of thing from happening. To French Canada, Riel is a hero because he defended the French-speaking minority. In Canada, we francophones are a minority. We look up to people who defend our rights.

"If you decide to execute Riel, the people in Quebec will see this as

**Wandering Spirit, leader of the Frog Lake attack, 1885.**

the killing of a man who defended French Canadian rights. I feel that you will lose the support of French Canada, Sir John. Come Robichaud, I don't think we can say any more than that."

The two French Canadians got up and walked out of the room. The door closed quietly behind them.

"Mr. Prime Minister, the decision is in your hands," said Hopkins as he got up to go. "I feel that it is beyond dispute that Riel committed acts of treason and caused the deaths of numerous people. He should die for these crimes." Hopkins then left.

"Sir John, I won't beat around the bush," said Thompson. "You have to execute him. It is simple politics. Ontario is more powerful than Quebec, and Ontario wants Riel to die. He must die, Mr. Prime Minister. He is guilty."

Then Thompson was gone. Macdonald was left alone with conflicting opinions and facts, and a terrible decision to make. He sat for a long time staring out the window across the river at the French Canadian town of Hull.

**TAKING A STAND**

1. When Sir John A. Macdonald was making his decision about Riel, he had three issues to consider:
   a) Whether or not Riel committed treason and murder.
   b) Whether or not Riel was insane.
   c) Whether or not a decision to hang Riel would alienate a certain section of the country and keep it from voting for the Conservative party.

Consider all the issues, facts, and political considerations. Then take a stand on this issue: "Should Riel have been hanged?" Write out your point of view in an essay. Your essay should be approximately six hundred words long.

**READING BETTER**

1. What arguments do Thompson and Hopkins give to show that Riel is a murderer?
2. What arguments do they give to suggest that Riel is not insane?
3. What arguments do Lanctôt and Robichaud give for not hanging Riel?

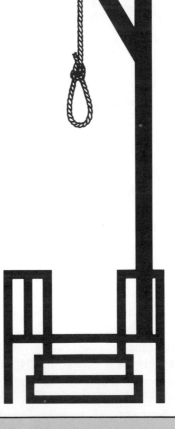

The English population is satisfied. The Orangemen in Ontario feel that justice has triumphed. They have won a great victory over French-speaking Canadians.

The francophones of Quebec begin to suspect that A.A. Dorion may have been right about Confederation. The English-speaking majority is forcing its wishes on the French-speaking minority.

Confederation survives its first major crisis. By switching political parties French-speaking Canadians feel that they still can get a fair deal in Confederation.

Honoré Mercier, a Quebec politician, begins to organize those who are upset about Riel's execution. In the election of 1887, he defeats the Conservatives in the Quebec provincial election.

French Canada begins to reject John A. Macdonald as its leader. It begins to leave the Conservative party, and joins Laurier and the Liberal party.

Mercier begins to pass pro-French laws in Quebec such as the Jesuit Estates Act. This upsets the English-speaking majority in the rest of Canada.

Wilfrid Laurier attacks Macdonald and the Conservatives for executing Riel. He begins to emerge as a national leader of French Canada, and a strong force in the national Liberal party.

Note: Remember that there are national Conservative and Liberal parties and also provincial Conservative and Liberal parties.

**Fig. 2-1 The results of the Riel execution**

### The effect of the Riel Rebellions on French-English relations

The Riel Rebellions and the execution of Riel greatly affected French-English relations. New generations of Canadians were suddenly forced to realize that Canada was a bicultural nation. Francophones from Quebec and anglophones from Ontario were distinct groups who had different points of view concerning the Riel situation. To the francophones, Riel was a hero. To the anglophones, he was a murderer and traitor. The story about Macdonald's decision to hang Riel showed that both groups were angry over the Riel issue. Anger can breed distrust and distrust can often breed hatred. Such was the case with the Riel situation.

French-speaking Canadians began to switch their loyalty from the Conservative party of John A. Macdonald. They turned to the Liberal party and politicians like Wilfrid Laurier and Honoré Mercier. An attitude that "these francophones must be put in their place" began to emerge in many sections of English Canada. The co-operation and good feelings built up during the years of George Cartier's alliance with Macdonald were quickly vanishing. They were being replaced by distrust.

The decade after the Riel crisis was a crucial time in French-English relations. If francophone and anglophone leaders tried to co-operate, the wall of distrust between the two groups would be broken down. If, however, they chose not to co-operate, the distrust would increase. What would they do? To discover the answer to this question we will examine the Manitoba School Crisis.

### The Manitoba School Crisis

As you will recall from Fig. 2-1, the francophones in Quebec were upset. Therefore they elected Honoré Mercier as premier of Quebec. Mercier was similar to A.A. Dorion in his thinking. He believed that the English-speaking majority could not be trusted to defend the French-speaking minority's rights. Mercier thought that the only way to protect French rights was to have a strong pro-French provincial government in Quebec. As soon as he became premier, Mercier passed several laws that greatly angered large sections of the English-speaking population. An Ontario politician, Dalton McCarthy, became extremely upset with Mercier's actions. He decided to devote his political career to destroying the French influence in Canada.

One of McCarthy's most important actions was his support of groups in Manitoba that wished to eliminate French schools in that province. Because of McCarthy's activities in Manitoba there was another major crisis in French-English relations after Confederation. To help us understand Dalton McCarthy and the Manitoba school problem we will first examine the career of this politician.

---

### Dalton McCarthy (1836-1898): A biographical sketch

Dalton McCarthy was one of the most outspoken of all Canadian political leaders. He felt that Canada should be completely English. McCarthy thought that it would be best for Canada if the French-speaking Canadians gave up their language, religion, and way of life, and imitated the English. McCarthy's views caused him a great deal of trouble during his life. There were large numbers of Canadians who, at different times, agreed with him. However, McCarthy was

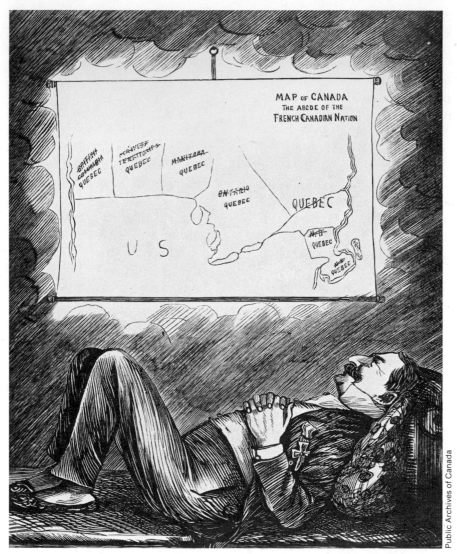

Map of Canada text within image:

MAP OF CANADA
THE ABODE OF THE
FRENCH CANADIAN NATION

**This cartoon was called "Mercier's Dream". Why?**

never able to convince the majority of Canadians to follow his ideas.

McCarthy was born near Dublin in Ireland. Like many of the Irish, he came to Canada in 1847 to escape the starvation and poverty in Ireland. The McCarthy family settled in Barrie, Ontario. Dalton grew up there and became a lawyer like his father. In 1869, he married Emma Lally. Over the next five years he concentrated on raising his family and looking after the family law business. In 1876, however, he was persuaded by the Conservative party to run in the election of that year. He did, and he won.

In 1879, McCarthy moved his business and his family to Toronto. He set up his own law firm in Toronto. He was well respected by John A. Macdonald and the members of the Conservative party. McCarthy did so well in politics that some members of the Conservative party felt that he would take over the leadership of the party when Macdonald retired. In 1889, however, Dalton McCarthy fell out of favour with Macdonald and the Conservative party. Against Macdonald's wishes he began a campaign to crush French Canadian influence in Canada.

To understand McCarthy's attitude, you must rememer that he came from Ireland. Over the years in Ireland there had been a lot of trouble between Protestants and Catholics. McCarthy was an Irish Protestant and he did not trust Catholics. Since most French-speaking Canadians were Catholics, McCarthy feared their influence. McCarthy was closely associated with the Orange Lodge, which was very anti-Catholic and anti-French.

During the Riel crisis, McCarthy saw how the French-speaking members of Macdonald's government fought for mercy for Riel. McCarthy did not feel that Riel deserved mercy. He argued for the death penalty. When Riel was executed, McCarthy felt that justice had been done. However when French-speaking Canadians protested Riel's execution, McCarthy felt that the francophones were becoming a danger to a strong, united Canada. Therefore, he began his campaign to crush French Canadian influence.

In Quebec at this time, Honoré Mercier was organizing protests against the hanging of Riel. Mercier attacked the French-speaking Canadians in Macdonald's government who supported the decision to hang Riel. He then gathered together all the francophone politicians in Quebec who distrusted the anglophones. With this group, Mercier won the Quebec election of 1887, defeating the provincial Conservative party.

The first thing that Mercier's government did was to bring out a *Jesuit Estates Act*. This act paid the Roman Catholic Church $400 000. This money was a payment for land that the British government had taken away from the Roman Catholic Church after the Conquest in 1759-60.

Dalton McCarthy felt that Honoré Mercier was a danger to Canada. He felt that this Jesuit Estates Act was not fair to the anglophones in Quebec. Why should their tax money be given to the Roman Catholic Church? He also felt that the Jesuits should not be paid for the lost land.

McCarthy felt that the French were becoming too pushy and too demanding. He thought that they must not be allowed to disagree with the decisions of the government in Ottawa. According to McCarthy, the French must not be allowed to pass acts such as the Jesuit Estates Act in the province of Quebec. The English-speaking majority in Canada did not agree with this bill. In other words, McCarthy did not agree with the idea of a federal union. He did not want francophones to have control over their own affairs in Quebec. With this in mind, McCarthy founded a group called *The Equal Rights Association*. This group wanted to eliminate all the rights that French-speaking people had been given in Confederation.

It was not long before McCarthy found an opportunity to carry on his battle against the francophones. In 1889, he heard that there were people in Manitoba who supported his idea of crushing the French influence. The *Manitoba Act* of 1870 gave francophones the right to their own schools. It also made French one of the official languages of the province. The anti-French group in Manitoba wanted to get rid of these rights. In an effort to help the group, McCarthy went to Manitoba in the summer of 1889.

---

READING BETTER
1. Why do you think that McCarthy was never able to convince most Canadians that the francophones should be assimilated (absorbed) into the British culture of Canada?
2. Why was McCarthy anti-French?
3. Who was Honoré Mercier?
4. What was the Jesuit Estates Act?
5. Why did the Jesuit Estates Act cause problems between the francophones and the anglophones in Canada?
6. What was the name of the group that McCarthy formed? What was the purpose of this group?
7. Why did McCarthy go to Manitoba in 1889?

Dalton McCarthy and Joseph Martin attack French schools

On August 5, 1889, Dalton McCarthy went before a large group of people in the town of Portage La Prairie, Manitoba. He explained why there should be only one school system in Manitoba. After McCarthy finished speaking, the Attorney General of Manitoba, Joseph Martin, spoke to the crowd. The speeches given below are adapted from those given by McCarthy and Martin that day. As you read through them, list the reasons that each man gives for not allowing French Catholic schools in Manitoba. Also, list the reasons they give for eliminating the French language in Manitoba.

---

### Dalton McCarthy attacks French schools

Ladies and gentlemen, I am angry that our great English country is being ruined by a small group of people who want both French and English school systems. I am angry that this small group wants to make our English country a bilingual one, a country where people speak two languages. This is *not* a French country. We speak English in this country and we should have only English schools.

I want to tell you what happened in the state of Louisiana several years ago. There were a lot of French-speaking people in that state. They wanted to have their own language. They wanted their own schools and they wanted to be able to use French in the courts of the state government. They had rallies and marches. They waved flags and said that it was their right to speak and teach French. And what did the government of the United States do? Was it weak like that pro-French group in Ottawa? No it was not. It told the francophones in Louisiana that they must speak English. And that was the end of the matter. The United States is a strong country with one language. And it is so strong partly because the government forced the French to speak English.

I was proud and happy to learn that your provincial government is going to try to eliminate the French schools in this province. The whole nation must see to it that Canada is British in the schools, in the courts, and in the homes. Each of you can help make our country completely British. Before you vote for a candidate, Liberal or Conservative, make sure that person is in favour of an English Canada.

We have a hard fight ahead of us. The francophones feel that they have a right to the French language and to French schools. The longer we delay the more they will believe in these rights. We must start today! We must start here in Manitoba to eliminate the rights of the French! I say "No more French language, no more French schools"! I say "One people, one language, one school system"!

*Based on reports in the* Manitoba Free Press *1889 8 7.*


## Joseph Martin attacks French schools

I want to thank Mr. McCarthy for coming to speak to us today. He has brought us words of wisdom. I'd like at this time to give you my views on the issue.

In the province of Quebec they can have French schools and the French language. They have had these rights since 1763. The rights are deeply rooted in the minds of the francophones of Quebec. Here in Manitoba it is a different story. This is a new area of the country. French-speaking people have not been here for centuries, as they were in Quebec. Therefore, there is no need to give them rights to their language and schools. If we delay, French rights in the West will become deeply rooted, just as they are in Quebec. My government wants to act at once to eliminate the French language and the French school system.

I am angry when I have to read bills that come to me to be signed and they are written in French. I am angry when a person comes to my office and wants to speak to me in French. And it makes me angry to see that the anglophones in this province have to pay their hard-earned money in taxes to keep French schools open. This is not right. My government wants to correct this situation. We intend to close the French schools, and eliminate the use of the French language in this province.

*Based on reports in the* Manitoba Free Press, *1889 8 7.*

1. McCarthy and Martin feel that the French schools in Manitoba should be closed. They also feel that French should be eliminated as one of the official languages of Manitoba. List all the arguments they give to convince people of their beliefs.

## USING YOUR KNOWLEDGE

1. Both Cartier and Dorion made predictions about what would happen if Quebec joined Confederation. After reading the speeches given by McCarthy and Martin, decide which man was correct, Cartier or Dorion. Give reasons for your answer.

## SOLVING PROBLEMS

1. To find solutions to a problem, you must be able to break it down and understand the various parts or factors in it. There was a serious problem developing in Manitoba in 1889. Answer the following questions on the Manitoba problem. This will help you to identify and understand the different parts of the problem.
   a) What issue does the problem deal with?
   b) Who are the people involved in the problem?
   c) What are the points of view of the people involved in the problem situation?
   d) Does this problem affect only Manitoba, or could it affect the entire nation?
   e) Which of the following values has prompted McCarthy to develop his particular point of view? Give reasons to explain your choice.
      i) Love of country, the desire for a strong country
      ii) The desire for equal rights for all Canadians
      iii) Belief in majority rule
      iv) Self-interest
      v) Desire for money
      vi) Belief in minority rights

The Manitoba School Crisis: The sequence of events, Part 1

The government of Manitoba put the suggestions given by McCarthy and Martin into effect quickly. In 1890, the government of Premier Greenway passed laws that eliminated French schools. These laws also abolished French as an official language of the province.

In 1870, when Manitoba joined Canada and the Manitoba Act was passed, the population of Manitoba was half franco-phone and half anglophone. But by the late 1880s, because of increased English immigration, the anglophones were a large majority. Because of costs, the English-speaking majority no longer wished to support two school systems or French as an official language. The anglophones sup-ported Dalton McCarthy when he suggested that the French schools be eliminated.

It is important to remember that, in general, French-speaking people were Catholic, and that the French schools were also Catholic. Catholics were angry that French Catholic schools in Manitoba had been closed. It was not long before the Catholics of Manitoba, both French and English, found a champion to fight for their lost rights. He was a Catholic priest by the name of Alexandre Antonin Taché. To discover the French and Catholic point of view in the Manitoba crisis we will examine the career of Taché.

**Alexandre Antonin Taché (1823-1894): A biographical sketch**

Archbishop Taché was a great leader of French-speaking Canadians. He tried whenever he could to defend the French. At the same time he tried to promote good relations and understanding between the French-speaking and English-speaking peoples in Canada.

**Bishop Taché. Explain why he has been called a "great Canadian".**

Taché was born at Rivière-du-Loup in Quebec on July 23, 1823. He went to school in Montreal and in 1844 he decided to become a priest in the Roman Catholic Church. The following year, the Church sent him to the Red River territory as a missionary among the Métis.

Taché worked hard to help the Métis have a good life. He was well appreciated by these western French-speaking Canadians. Because of this, the Church put him in charge of this entire area of Manitoba. In 1851 Taché was made bishop of the Red River area.

In 1869, when the Métis uprising broke out, Taché was in Rome visiting the head of the Roman Catholic Church, the Pope. As soon as he learned of the rebellion he returned to Manitoba. Taché wanted to help settle the problems between the Métis and the English-speaking Canadians. On the way back from Rome, he stopped in Ottawa to discuss the Red River problem with Macdonald and

Cartier. Taché was appointed a representative of the Canadian government. He was to try to make peace with Riel and the rebels. Taché felt sure that he could restore peace to the settlement if Macdonald and Cartier would agree to pardon all the rebels. Macdonald and Cartier agreed, and Taché headed west to bring peace to troubled Red River.

Taché worked tirelessly to quiet the fears of the Métis. Eventually, he succeeded. The rebels agreed to release all the English-speaking prisoners held at Fort Garry. They also agreed to send a delegation to Ottawa to discuss a settlement. During the negotiations Bishop Taché suggested that French be made an official language in Manitoba. He also felt that the French should have their own Catholic schools. His ideas were accepted. The Red River area became the first to enter Canada after Confederation.

In 1885, Riel and the Métis population of Saskatchewan rose in rebellion. Taché, who had been made an archbishop in 1871, was unable to prevent bloodshed even though he did try. Riel no longer saw himself as the political leader of the Métis. Now he thought he was a religious prophet engaged in a holy war. Taché opposed everything Riel stood for in this second Métis rebellion. As a result, there was little hope of peaceful settlement.

Taché failed to prevent the bloodshed of the Northwest Rebellion. Despite this, he continued his work in western Canada after the uprising. He kept trying to promote peace and understanding between French-speaking and English-speaking groups in western Canada. Taché was greatly saddened when he saw how the execution of Riel was splitting the country into warring camps. When Dalton McCarthy went to Manitoba to deliver his anti-French speeches, Taché knew that the tension between the francophones and the anglophones would grow.

As soon as the Greenway government outlawed French schools, Taché became the leader of a group that was trying to have the law changed. In 1893, Taché wrote a short booklet. In it he tried to convince the government of Manitoba to reverse its decision to close all the French schools. The following document is adapted from the arguments used by Taché in his book.

### TACHÉ ATTACKS THE ONE-SCHOOL SYSTEM

The two-school system was created by law. It was a fair system. Both the anglophones and the francophones paid tax money to run the schools. Francophones and anglophones, Catholics and Protestants were treated equally. The English Protestant schools passed on the English language, culture, and religion to the English-speaking children. The French schools passed on the French language, culture, and religion to the French-speaking children. Parents were free to choose the schools that their children were to attend.

For 19 years the system worked well. Both the francophones and the anglophones were happy. The francophones did not try to force their ideas on the anglophones and the anglophones did not try to force their ideas on the francophones. The two groups lived together in peace and harmony.

But in May 1890, the government of Manitoba passed a law that closed the French schools. Even though the French Catholic schools were gone, the francophones and the Catholics still had to pay to support the English Protestant schools. The French-speaking Canadians of Manitoba felt that the law was unfair. Why should they be forced to support schools that do not teach their children their own language? Schools that do not teach French culture and history? Schools that do not permit francophones to learn about their own religion?

The English schools use English books and employ English-speaking teachers. They teach about the British way of life and about the Protestant religion. Why should a Roman Catholic, French child be forced to read English books, be taught by English-speaking teachers, and learn about the Protestant religion?

The law that has ended the two-school system is bad. The people who made the law hoped that it would force the French to adopt the English way of life. All the law did, however, was make happy French people into angry ones. The law has upset the peaceful relations between the francophones and the anglophones in Manitoba.

Some people say that we are traitors to Canada, we francophones who will not follow this law. They are wrong. For six generations my ancestors lived along the St. Lawrence River. Canada is my home. I never had, and I never will have another home. Manitoba and western Canada have been my life for fifty years. I love it here. I work hard to make it a fine place for all Canadians to live in. I will work for this goal until the day I die. I am a Canadian now and forever.

All that I want for the francophones of Manitoba are the rights that all anglophones have. I want freedom for the French-speaking Canadians of Manitoba—freedom of religion and freedom of language.

*Adapted from "Are the Public Schools of Manitoba the Continuation of the Protestant Schools of the same Province?", A.A. Taché, April 20, 1893.*

---

**READING BETTER**

1. List the arguments that Taché uses to prove that Manitoba should be allowed to have French schools.

**USING YOUR KNOWLEDGE**

1. a) Make a list of five qualities that a great person should have.
   b) Make two lists, one for McCarthy and one

for Taché. In each list write the qualities and achievements that prove that the men were above average.

## TAKING A STAND

1. In your opinion, who is the greater Canadian, Taché or McCarthy? Be sure to use facts to back up your point of view. Be prepared to defend your viewpoint.
2. Go back over your notes and read the arguments in favour of and against French schools in Manitoba. After you have reread the arguments take a stand on the issue: "Should the government of Manitoba have outlawed French schools?" Be sure that you have facts to back up your viewpoint. Be prepared to defend your point of view.

The Manitoba School Crisis: The sequence of events, Part 2

In 1890, Manitoba passed laws eliminating French schools and removing French as an official language. Taché and his supporters asked the federal government to disallow these laws. The federal government tried to delay its decision on the issue. The government realized that if it sided with French-speaking Canadians, then it would lose the support of English-speaking Canadians. If it sided with Manitoba, however, and refused to disallow the laws, it would lose French Canadian support.

Because the federal government was not acting, Taché and his followers took their case to court. It took several years before all the appeals in the case were heard. Finally, in 1895, the court ordered the federal government to take action in the Manitoba case. The Conservative government prepared a remedial bill. This bill would give back the rights of the francophones in Manitoba. Before the government could bring the bill before Parliament, however, its term of office ran out. An election had to be called.

The main issue of the 1896 election was the remedial bill. The Conservatives defended their remedial bill. They felt that the federal government must force

Manitoba to give back the French schools. The Liberals, led by Wilfrid Laurier, attacked the remedial bill. Laurier argued that the remedial bill interfered with provincial rights. He also disliked the idea of Ottawa forcing Manitoba to change its laws. Laurier wanted Manitoba and the federal government to negotiate a settlement. This way, the French-speaking Catholics had a better chance of obtaining their rights.

In the election, the Conservatives were defeated and Wilfrid Laurier was the new prime minister of Canada. Laurier wasted little time in carrying out his ideas on the Manitoba problem. He quickly organized meetings with Premier Greenway of Manitoba. After several discussions they agreed on a compromise.

The *Laurier-Greenway Compromise* had three main points.

1. The taxpayers of Manitoba would not have to support Catholic or French schools.
2. Public schools with a sufficient number of Catholic students could hire priests to teach religious education. There had to be at least forty Catholic pupils in town schools and ten in rural schools.
3. In any public school where ten or more students spoke French, instruction had to be given in French if the parents asked for it.

## READING BETTER

1. When Taché asked the federal government to disallow the Manitoba law that eliminated French schools, the government delayed taking action. Why?
2. What was the remedial bill?
3. What was Wilfrid Laurier's position on the remedial bill?

## USING YOUR KNOWLEDGE

1. Predict how each of the following people would react to the Laurier-Greenway Compromise:

260

**Wilfrid Laurier, Prime Minister, 1896-1911.**

**Thomas Greenway, Premier of Manitoba.**

a) Archbishop Taché
b) Dalton McCarthy
c) the relatives of Thomas Scott
d) the relatives of Louis Riel

2. According to the Laurier-Greenway Compromise, what would happen in each of the following cases:
   a) A French member of the Board of Education in a small Manitoba town wants to use 20% of the tax money set aside for schools in the area to build an all-French school.
   b) In Winnipeg, the Greenway High School has 93 French Catholic students. The principal says that it is too expensive to hire a priest to teach religious education. He will, however, permit 93 students to have one period a day in French.
   c) In a small Manitoba town, there are sixteen French families. Only half want their children educated in English. The other half apply to the school board to have their children educated in French.

The effects of the Manitoba School Crisis

Once the Laurier-Greenway compromise had been put into effect, many people thought the French language school crisis was over. However, they were mistaken. The French-speaking minority remembered Dorion's prediction that the English-speaking majority would take away French rights. They saw that Dorion could be right. They also realized that the Confederation agreement, the *British North America Act*, was not clear on the rights of francophones outside of Quebec. Once again French-speaking Canadians began to fear for their way of life. They decided to switch their allegiance from the Conservative to the Liberal party. In 1896, French-speaking Canadians placed their hopes for survival in the hands of a fellow French-speaking Canadian. They elected Wilfrid Laurier prime minister.

The fears of the French-speaking Canadians were well founded. English Canada had listened to the arguments of Dalton McCarthy. Many of the anglophones thought that perhaps Canada would

261

be stronger with only one language and one way of life.

At the turn of the century, thousands of immigrants poured into Canada. Canadians asked, "Should these immigrant groups be allowed to keep their own language and way of life?" The English-speaking majority, remembering McCarthy's words, answered "No". If Canada was to be strong, there must be one Canada—English Canada. Many anglophones felt that all minorities—including the French-speaking Canadians—should be "Canadianized".

In the years that followed the Manitoba School Crisis, other crises arose over French language education. In each and every case the English-speaking majority decided to deny the French minority their rights. In Ontario, Saskatchewan, and Alberta the right to French schools was denied. Finally, in 1916, in the middle of World War I, Manitoba repealed (cancelled) the law that permitted French language education. Once more the question of French language rights erupted.

## World War I and the Conscription Crisis

In the years after the Manitoba School Crisis, Canada as a whole was enjoying great prosperity. Railways were being built, mines opened, and new industries set up. Jobs were plentiful. All this helped to ease the tension between English-speaking and French-speaking Canadians. These tensions never completely disappeared though. They were kept alive by English Canada's desire to eliminate French language education outside Quebec.

During the early years of the nineteenth century, Europe was also full of tension. England, France, Germany, Austria, and Russia were continually bickering. Eventually, national pride and disputes over colonies brought these nations to the brink of war. In August, 1914, Germany invaded

Belgium. This forced England to declare war on Germany. As part of the **British Empire,** Canada was automatically at war when England declared its intentions.

In the early years of the war, Canadians did an excellent job supporting England and her allies with men and supplies. Initially, Canadians served in the war on a voluntary basis. For several years there were enough volunteers to meet the war needs. By 1916, however, the number of casualties had become high. The number of men volunteering to serve was not large enough to meet the war needs. As a result, recruiting efforts were increased. One method used to increase recruiting was to have young women give a white feather to men in civilian clothes. The white feather symbolized cowardice. It was hoped that those who received the white feather would be shamed into joining the army.

The death tolls in Europe were staggering. With each battle, hundreds of thousands of men were killed. In the Battles of the Somme alone, over 24 000 Canadians were killed or wounded. No matter how hard the recruiters tried, they simply could not reach their required totals. Slowly the nation realized that the voluntary service system was failing. At the same time, the nation also became aware of the fact that Quebec was providing few volunteers. The population of Quebec and Ontario were similar in size. The number of volunteers, however, was drastically different, as Fig. 2-2 clearly shows.

When the voluntary system could not supply enough men, the government was forced to consider other methods of getting men to serve in the army. The most obvious method was a conscription or draft system in which men would be forced to serve in the armed forces. There was one nagging question however, that made the government unable to decide on conscription. If it did decide to use conscription, what would the effect be on French-English relations in Canada? Most French-speaking Canadians in Quebec refused to volunteer for the army. How would they react if they were forced to join?

The conscription issue caused a crisis in French-English relations. To gain insights into the crisis, we will first read about the careers of Robert Borden and Henri Bourassa.

---

*Population (Last census)*

| Ontario | Quebec |
|---------|--------|
| 2 523 274 | 2 003 232 |

Enlistments to March 15th, 1917

| | | | | |
|--|--|--|--|--|
| London | ............ 32 770 | | Montreal | ............ 39 986 |
| Toronto | ............ 89 422 | | Quebec | ............. 8 064 |
| Kingston | ............ 45 265 | | Total | ............ 48 050 |
| Total | ............ 167 457 | | | |

*Quotas under militia scheme*

| 19 038 | 7 014 |
|--------|-------|

The quotas called for under this scheme are distributed as follows:

| *London:* | | *Montreal:* | |
|-----------|------|-------------|------|
| 7th Fusiliers | 1 002 | 1st Regt. | 1 002 |
| Windsor, 21st | 1 002 | 3rd and 58th | 1 002 |
| Woodstock, 22nd | 1 002 | 5th Highlanders | 1 002 |
| St. Thomas, 25th | 1 002 | 65th Regiment | 1 002 |
| | | Sherbrooke, 53rd | 1 002 |
| *Toronto:* | | Quebec 8th | 1 002 |
| 2nd Queen's Own | 1 002 | Quebec 9th | 1 002 |
| 10th Grenadiers | 1 002 | | 7 014 |
| 48th Highlanders | 1 002 | | |
| 109th Regt. | 1 002 | | |
| 110th Irish | 1 002 | | |
| | | | |
| *Hamilton:* | | | |
| 14th Regt. | 1 002 | | |
| 91st Highlanders | 1 002 | | |
| St. Catharines, 19th | 1 002 | | |
| Brantford, 38th | 1 002 | | |
| Sault Ste. Marie, 51st | 1 002 | | |
| Kingston, 14th | 1 002 | | |
| Belleville, 15th | 1 002 | | |
| Brockville, 41st | 1 002 | | |
| Ottawa, 43rd and GGFG | 1 002 | | |
| Peterboro, 57th | 1 002 | | |
| | 19 038 | | |

**Fig. 2-2 Voluntary enlistment, 1914-1917**

### Robert Borden, defender of the British Empire

Robert Borden was born in the small village of Grand Pré, Nova Scotia. A clever young man, Borden became a brilliant lawyer. He did so well as a lawyer that the Conservative party of Canada thought he would be a good member of Parliament. The Conservatives asked him to run in the election of 1896. Borden won easily in the riding of Halifax, but the Conservative party suffered a terrible defeat at the hands of Laurier and the Liberal party.

Laurier was a hard-working prime minister and a strong party leader. Many Conservatives felt that their party needed a new leader if they were ever going to defeat Laurier. They decided that Robert Borden had the best chance of beating Laurier. Thus, in 1901 they chose Borden as the new leader of the Conservative party.

Borden made a great effort to get the Conservatives organized. Laurier, however, was a brilliant politician. The Conservatives lost both the 1904 and 1908 elections.

After the 1908 defeat, Borden began to criticize Laurier by saying that the prime minister was making Canada weaker. Borden accused the Liberals of refusing to have close ties with England. According to Borden, the Liberals were becoming friendlier with the United States. With the danger of war between England and Germany growing stronger, Borden suggested closer ties with Britain. Borden wanted Canada to do more to help Britain remain strong.

In 1911, Canadians listened to Robert Borden's call for closer ties with England. In the election of that year, Laurier was finally defeated. After almost ten years of hard work, defeats, and recoveries, Robert Borden became Canada's prime minister. His years in office were to mark a low point in French-English relations.

### ROBERT BORDEN AND THE CONSCRIPTION ISSUE

Three years after Borden was elected prime minister, war broke out in Europe. Borden was a hard-working wartime prime minister. He did two important things. First, he inspired Canadians to join in the war effort. Secondly, he organized and directed the great Canadian contribution to the war.

Borden recognized that World War I was a new type of war. It was a world war. To win, England would need all the help Canada could give. Canada must supply arms, ships, food, and above all, soldiers. For several years, Canada supplied what was needed. Then, in 1917, Borden went to England to attend the Imperial War Cabinet. This was a meeting of the allied nations who were fighting on England's side against the Germans. At this conference, Borden became convinced that Canada had to increase the number of soldiers it was sending to Europe. Borden knew that he could not get enough soldiers if he waited for men to volunteer. Therefore he decided to force men to join the army.

**Robert Borden. "We must support Britain."**

When Borden's government passed the Military Service Act, which made conscription legal, he found that he had a real crisis on his hands. A large number of Canadians—mostly French-speaking—refused to join the army and fight in Europe. In the next section we look at a leader who defended the anti-conscription stand.

1. Why did the Conservative party of Canada ask Borden to run as a Conservative?
2. Borden had a great deal of trouble defeating Sir Wilfrid Laurier, but he finally succeeded in the election of 1911. What strategy did Borden use to defeat Laurier and the Liberals?
3. Why do Canadians refer to Borden as a great wartime prime minister? (Two reasons)

USING YOUR KNOWLEDGE
1. Imagine that you are Robert Borden. Write an entry in your diary that outlines the "blackest day" in your life, and how you feel about it. Your diary entry should be about two paragraphs of four or five sentences each.

RESEARCHING
1. Some people have said that Robert Borden had great determination and would never quit. From library books, find out more about Borden and his career. Then use facts from the biographical sketch in the text and from your own research to prove this statement true or false.

### Henri Bourassa: Champion of French Canadian rights

Henri Bourassa was born in Montreal in 1868. He worked as a newspaper reporter for years. Finally he founded the great French Canadian daily paper, *Le Devoir*. Between 1910 and 1932 he was the head of this newspaper. He used it to get his ideas across to the people of Quebec. Before he founded *Le Devoir*, Bourassa ran for Parliament. He won a seat in 1896 as a follower of Laurier. Shortly after his election, Bourassa had a fight with Laurier about whether or not Canada should send troops to fight in the **Boer War.** England was involved in this war. Laurier thought that Canada should send troops, but Bourassa did not. As a result, Bourassa resigned his seat in Parliament in 1899.

From 1899 until his death in 1952, Bourassa fought to have Canada break all ties with England. Bourassa felt that Canada should not think of itself as a colony of England. He thought that Canada should consider itself an independent nation. It is not hard to see why Bourassa and his followers would not want to send Canadian soldiers to fight in World War I. Bourassa felt that England and France were fighting against Germany to see who could build up the greatest empire. As far as Bourassa was concerned, this war had nothing at all to do with Canada. The following is an adapted version of a speech in which Bourassa explains his point of view.

BOURASSA REJECTS THE BRITISH EMPIRE AND IMPERIALISM

**British imperialism** is a bad thing. Some people say that it is good because it helps spread British democracy and British traditions such as fair play and freedom of speech. I say that this is not so. British imperialism is simply a desire on the part of the British government to get more land. Britain wants to become richer and more powerful.

British imperialism began because England had a great navy, and brave explorers. It took over large areas of the world. Now England is full of pride. It does not want to give up any land that it holds. It does

**Henri Bourassa in 1910: "It is not our war."**

not want any other country to have as many colonics as it has. So it must fight to defend what it has. To defend its Empire, England needs soldiers. It has used up almost all the able-bodied men in England and therefore it looks to Canada for help. No one would volunteer if England said, "We want you to send your young men to fight a war for us so that we can stay rich and powerful." Instead the English yell patriotic slogans such as "Britain has always ruled the waves", or "Britons never shall be slaves", or "If England is rich all the Empire is rich". But this is not true. Canada does not become rich by fighting in England's war. We become poor because we lose our young men on battlefields on the other side of the world. We lose them in wars we know little or nothing about.

267

French-speaking Canadians were greatly influenced by Bourassa's ideas. They also had many other reasons for refusing to get involved in World War I. As we read the diary of Emile Cartouche, these reasons will become clear.

READING BETTER
1. Why did Bourassa have such a great influence over French Canadians?
2. Why did Bourassa resign from the Laurier government?
3. Why was Bourassa opposed to sending Canadian troops to fight in World War I?

USING YOUR KNOWLEDGE
1. Who would be most likely to express the following opinions, Bourassa or Borden? Be sure to give reasons for your point of view.
   a) The British are emptying the Canadian pocketbook.
   b) Canada is for Canadians. I am a Canadian first and last. I never think of England at all.
   c) French-speaking Canadians are Canadians. They must do their share. They benefit from being Canadian and now they must pay for that privilege.
   d) The war has cost too many lives. It must be ended at once. We can end the war with a great victory. But for victory we need men.

RESEARCHING
1. Bourassa stopped supporting Laurier in 1899 because Laurier wanted to send troops to fight in the Boer War. Using your school library or books provided by your teacher find the answers to these questions:
   a) What caused the Boer War?
   b) What were the results of the Boer War?
   c) What reasons did Laurier give for sending troops to fight in this war?
   d) What effect did the Boer War have on French-English relations in Canada?

A French-speaking Canadian reacts to the conscription issue

Emile Cartouche was able to trace his ancestry back to the founders of New France. One of his ancestors was Etienne Cartouche. We examined Etienne's diary when we were studying the Canadiens' reaction to the conquest of New France in 1759. Emile, like his ancestor Etienne, always kept a diary. We will examine a section of this diary to learn how French-speaking Canadians reacted to the conscription issue of 1917.

Emile Cartouche's family is prosperous. His uncle, Benoît Cartouche, operates the huge family farm. Emile's other uncle, Danton Cartouche, operates a large wood-products factory in Cabano, a small town in eastern Quebec. Emile's father is a lawyer who heads his own firm. This firm is one of the largest in Quebec City.

In June 1916, Emile was enjoying a well-deserved summer vacation. He had successfully completed his second year of university in Quebec City. He and his friends Jacques Modi and Henri Trudeau went to Montreal for a week. The first entry in the diary is written while the boys are still in Montreal.

JUNE 11, 1916

Montreal is wonderful in June. We spent a fine day walking about in the old part of the city. There was, however, one unpleasant incident that almost spoiled the day.

We almost got into a fight with a group of English-speaking boys from McGill University. They had all just enlisted in the army and they were celebrating. They asked us if we were afraid to go and fight in the great war. Modi was ready to fight them—he has such a bad temper. But we got him away before anything happened.

We cannot seem to forget about the war. Everywhere you go there are recruiting stations. Some French Canadians have joined, but not many. Like Modi says, "Why should I join to save the British Empire? The English in Canada won't allow French-speaking Canadians to have their own schools outside of Quebec!"

I also heard that the British are forcing the French to go into English units. I don't see why the French can't have their own units. I want no part of this war.

SEPTEMBER 29, 1916

It is good to be back in school and see old friends. But this year there seems to be a new tension in the air. Everyone here is uneasy about the war. The school is filled with rumours that Borden will force us to join the army. They call the policy "conscription".

Already in September 10 000 Canadians have died. Modi says that the British generals are incompetent. He says that if we go to fight in the war we will simply be food for the guns. To go seems like sure death.

NOVEMBER 11, 1916

A group of government officials and several leaders of the Church came to speak to the student body. They were trying to convince us all to enlist. They hardly had a chance to speak though. Every time they tried to give their arguments, Modi started up a chant of "Bourassa, Bourassa". They eventually gave up. I learned that Sam Hughes, the government minister in charge of recruitment, is an Orangeman. He distrusts French-speaking Canadians and refuses to promote French-speaking Canadian officers. Right then and there I decided that I would never join voluntarily! Never!

MAY 14, 1917

Exams are over. I have passed all my courses. But my happiness today was spoiled by an incident that took place at the railway station. Some soldiers who were travelling through Quebec were at the station. When they saw us lounging around the station, they started to insult us. I can understand how they felt. Ontario has supplied 184 000 volunteers, and Quebec has given only 47 000. If I were in their shoes, I'd yell insults too.

I was upset when Modi and some others opened the garbage cans and threw rotten vegetables at them. When they see their friends shot down they will remember that we threw garbage at them. They will hate French-speaking Canadians because of that incident. And yet, I still agree with Modi when he says "They are free to choose. If they want to go and fight to save England, let them." There is no reason for us to go. We are Canadians and as Bourassa says, "It is not Canada's war."

### JUNE 1, 1917

Ever since Borden announced on May 18 that he was going to seek conscription of 100 000 men, it has been wild around our house. Father is working with the Liberals to try and force the government to have a referendum. Laurier feels that all Canadians should make their feelings known. Modi and other students are organizing rallies. The papers are full of conscription. Everyone is waiting to hear what Bourassa will say.

### AUGUST 8, 1917

Bourassa has finally made his position clear. In a series of articles in *Le Devoir* he says that conscription is a bad idea. Borden is determined, however, to push a conscription law through Parliament. Almost every MP from Quebec is opposed to the bill.

### NOVEMBER 3, 1917

Borden has called an election. The only real issue in it is conscription. We are all working for Laurier.

### DECEMBER 20, 1917

There is no Christmas spirit in our home these days. Ever since we learned the election results, my father has been in a violent temper. "We are isolated," he keeps saying to my mother. "The French-speaking people in this country are alone!"

He is right, of course. Borden won 153 seats and Laurier won only 73. Almost all Laurier's seats are in Quebec. French Canada is directly opposed to the rest of Canada over the issue of conscription. We are truly isolated.

### MARCH 3, 1918

The Church and most of the newspapers in Quebec are urging us to accept the conscription law. They tell us to enter the army when we receive our notice. I am not sure what I will do. I wait for the mail each day with fear. Modi received his notice, but he refused to report. Many other students are doing the same thing. Recently, the police have been going to the university looking for those people who were conscripted but refused to go. Modi says that he would rather die fighting for his rights in Quebec and Canada than die in Europe fighting for the British Empire.

### MARCH 31, 1918

I still cannot believe it. For three days I have not eaten. Quebec City is in chaos. Two days ago a student was stopped by the police for evading conscription and arrested. Word quickly spread around the school and throughout the city. Modi made a speech and a large group of students went down to the police station. The police refused

**Anti-Conscription demonstration, 1917. Is the Latour Company for or against Borden?**

to give the man up. Before we knew what had happened someone yelled fire. The police station was soon engulfed in flames.

We began to march down the street and sing. I lost sight of Modi but I knew that he was near the front of the march. We stopped at the offices of the *Chronicle*, a pro-conscription English paper. Someone broke in and the offices were wrecked.

The next day Modi took me to a meeting in an old warehouse in the lower city. We made plans to attack the offices of the Conscription Department and destroy all the conscription records. As soon as it was dark, people began to gather. We all marched on the conscription offices. The police did nothing to stop us. Then suddenly the doors of the building opened and soldiers raced out at us. They were all English-speaking Canadians. We later learned that they were members of the Toronto Batallion.

I can still see their faces. They were just like the boys on the train. They hated us. Their bayonets were fixed and they just ran at us. Some of the group stayed to fight the soldiers. Most of us turned to run and it was chaos. We fell over one another like bowling pins. Henri had his hand crushed. Modi was beaten to the ground. I tore my clothes and suffered a cut over the eye. So many people were injured. I just can't believe it.

1. Why did Cartouche and his friends almost get into a fight with the boys from McGill?
2. Why did Cartouche decide he would never join the army on a voluntary basis?
3. By May 1917, how many soldiers from Ontario and Quebec had volunteered?
4. When Borden announced conscription on May 18, 1917, how many men did he want to conscript?
5. What political leader wanted a referendum in which all Canadians would be given a chance to vote on the conscription issue?

USING YOUR KNOWLEDGE
1. The wartime diary of Emile Cartouche shows how groups of people can come to hate one another. Write an essay of at least one page. Use information from the diary to explain how the Conscription Crisis produced hatred between francophones and anglophones in Canada.

TAKING A STAND
1. At times your government will do something

that you do not agree with. In the Cartouche diary we see that the Canadian government passed a conscription law that most French-speaking Canadians disagreed with. People protest over government policies in a number of ways. Which of the following protest actions do you think are most effective?
a) Write a letter to your MP protesting the government action
b) Take up a petition against the action
c) Refuse to work until the government changes its mind
d) Burn down government buildings
e) Kidnap government officials and hold them until the government changes its mind
f) Hold a march and picket government offices
g) Get a group together and drive a number of cars onto the highways at rush hour. Stop the cars and leave them there.

### The great debate

In the following debate, students discuss whether or not Canada should have adopted conscription during World War I.

**Teacher:** The issue that we are going to debate is this: Should Canada have adopted conscription in 1917? The students participating in the discussion have researched the issue and are prepared to argue their points. Arguing in favour of conscription are Christie, John, Jayar, and Sue. Arguing against conscription are Verena, Kim, Bob, and Nigel.

**Christie:** As part of the British Empire, Canada was at war as soon as Britain was at war. If you are at war you must send troops. Besides, the Allies were protecting both the British and the French Empire against the Germans. The Germans were trying to take over the British and French colonies. Since the French Empire was being protected, the francophones in Canada should also have sent troops.

**Nigel:** French-speaking Canadians had very few relations with France. And besides, the English had complete control of the army. They made all the decisions. Canadians had no say. The English generals were doing a terrible job, too. They were depending on old military tactics in a war that was being fought with new military machines such as the machine gun. As a result, thousands of men were being killed. If you went you were sure to die. I can see why the French-speaking Canadians didn't want to go. Also, almost all French-speaking Canadians opposed conscription. It was not right to force so large a group of Canadians to follow a law they disagreed with. The voluntary method was best.

**Bob:** Besides, if you read what Bourassa said you can see that imperialism just brings money to the mother country. Why did Canadians have to go and fight in a European war? Why did Canadians have to help Britain or France when those countries and not Canada were the ones who benefited from imperialism?

**John:** We owed Britain our help. British money helped to develop Canada. If it weren't for the English who started up the lumber industry and the railways, we would not have as many industries as we have today. Many of our ancestors came from England. They helped build a country for us. In World War I it was our turn to help England by sending soldiers to fight.

**Kim:** Maybe English-speaking Canadians did owe a debt to England. But the francophones didn't. The English conquered the French. English-speaking Canadians killed Riel. The English refused to allow French schools outside of Quebec. There were no French Canadian regiments in the army. Consequently, the French-speaking Canadians in the army felt isolated. How would you like to be put into a regiment and shipped off to Europe with a bunch of guys who can't speak your language? If the anglophones wanted to fight for England they were free to. But the francophones should not have been forced to.

**Jayar:** That's not fair! The French-speaking Canadians benefited from the jobs that were provided by the lumber industry in Quebec. They benefited from the growth in the Canadian economy that England helped create. Then they refused to fight! It's true that the English conquered the French. But England was very fair with the French-speaking Canadians. They were given their language, religion, and land. In World War I it was the francophones' turn to be fair to England. There were tremendous numbers of casualties. Unless the army received new reinforcements there would have been even greater losses. Unless the Canadians supplied large numbers of troops, the troops that were already there would have been slaughtered. We had to have conscription to save the lives of Canadians who were already fighting.

**Sue:** Also, if Canada sent large numbers of troops and we helped to win the war, then Canada would become a more important country. Canada had to prove that it was more than just a child that had to be protected by the mother country, England. Canada wanted to help to defend the mother country and perhaps even save the mother country. This would show that Canada was ready to be independent. Conscription was a hard decision for Borden but it was essential. If Canada was ever to take its place as a great power in the world, it would have to help defeat Germany.

**Christie:** I want to challenge the point Kim made. She said that there were no French Canadian regiments. Another point that the French Canadians complained about in 1917 was the fact that the officers all spoke English. Well, what did they expect? Most of the people in Canada spoke English. You couldn't have a two-language army. No one would know what was going on. If the officers shouted out an order in French all the English soldiers would not understand. It would be chaos.

**Kim:** That's fine for you to say, but I bet if the shoe were on the other foot you would change your mind. What if we put you in a Polish army? You can't speak Polish. How would you feel?

**Verena:** I want to raise a point. If the French-speaking Canadians fought in this war, large numbers could be killed. Then the francophones could disappear as a large minority of the Canadian population. The francophones were already a minority. There was no more immigration from France. But more and more people kept coming to Canada from England. As more English came in, the percentage of the population that was French-speaking grew smaller and smaller. The French-speaking Canadians tried to prevent this by having large families. Now, if a whole generation of young French-speaking Canadians went over to Europe and got killed, there would be very few French Canadian babies born. Consequently the French-speaking Canadians would be a smaller percentage of the population.

**Sue:** That may be so. But it does not change the fact that the law said that Canada was at war when England was at war. If Canada was at war then all Canadians had to fight. It would not be fair to the rest of the country if French Canada was allowed to decide that it didn't want to fight. Why should English-speaking Canadians fight to protect Canada when French-speaking Canadians do not have to fight. If the Germans won the war they might try to take over Canada. We were fighting to protect ourselves.

**Nigel:** That's not true. The Atlantic Ocean and the United States would protect us. Canada was in no real danger in 1917.

---

**RESEARCHING**

1. Use the text and books from the library to answer the following questions:
   a) Why was a strong navy important to a government that had colonies?
   b) Why did Germany want a navy that could rival the British navy?
   c) Outline one dispute that England, Germany, and France had over colonies.
   d) What are the benefits of having colonies?
   e) How do the colonies benefit from being part of an empire?

**USING YOUR KNOWLEDGE**

1. During the debate the students make the following statements:
   a) The Germans were trying to take over the British and the French colonies.
   b) Imperialism just brings money to the mother country. Canada did not benefit

from being part of the British Empire. Using the facts that you have found for the research question above, decide whether or not these are true statements.

TAKING A STAND

1. Make a pro/con chart in your notebook on the issue: "Should Canada have adopted conscription?" Divide your page into two columns. In one column, list all the reasons for which Canada should have adopted conscription. In the other, list the reasons for which it should not have done so. After you have completed the chart read it over carefully. Decide where you stand on the issue. Be prepared to defend your point of view.

## Conclusion

In this chapter we discovered that in the first fifty years after Confederation there were three main crises in French-English relations. In the first crisis, Louis Riel, a French Métis leader, organized two rebellions in western Canada. Riel hoped to establish the rights of the Métis. When he was captured, however, he was regarded as a traitor by the Canadian government and executed. It appeared to French-speaking Canadians that neither John A. Macdonald nor the federal government could be trusted to protect French rights. Consequently, francophones began to listen to Wilfrid Laurier and the Liberal Party. In Quebec they elected Honoré Mercier as premier. Mercier was committed to building a strong Quebec government that would have the power to defend French rights.

We also saw a second crisis in French-English relations after Confederation, the Manitoba School Crisis. We learned that Dalton McCarthy, an anti-French Ontario Orangeman, travelled to Manitoba to advocate the elimination of French rights. The government of Premier Greenway adopted McCarthy's ideas and eliminated French schools in the province. Archbishop Taché quickly organized opposition to this

infringement on French rights. Eventually, the Conservative federal government was forced to disallow the Manitoba law. It brought in a remedial bill. Before the bill could be passed, however, an election was called. French-speaking Canadians realized that Confederation did not seem to protect French rights outside Quebec. In choosing a new prime minister, they decided to put their faith in a fellow French Canadian. The result was the election of Wilfrid Laurier and his Liberal party. Following this, the Laurier-Greenway Compromise was passed. The compromise re-established French language education in Manitoba.

The third and most significant crisis after Confederation was the Conscription Crisis in 1917. In this crisis, the English-speaking majority forced French-speaking Canadians to join the war effort. The francophones, however, were opposed to the war. It was clear to francophones that English Canada did not regard the French as one of the nation's founding peoples. They regarded the French as just another minority that had to be "Canadianized". Consequently, francophones realized that their survival was in danger. The English-speaking majority could crush a French-speaking candidate for prime minister, and they could take away French rights. If French-speaking Canadians were to survive they had to find a way to protect themselves.

After the first fifty years of Confederation the future of French Canada was in question. The second fifty years could see the elimination of the French as a distinctive cultural group in North America. Many francophones felt that their only hope was to isolate themselves in Quebec. They wanted to develop a provincial government strong enough to confront the English-speaking majority. The second fifty years after Confederation would decide—could French Canada and its distinctive way of life survive?

## READING BETTER

1. For each of the people below, write a short paragraph describing the person's role in the various crises in French-English relations.
   a) John A. Macdonald (Riel Rebellions)
   b) Dalton McCarthy (Manitoba School Crisis)
   c) Alexandre Antonin Taché (Manitoba School Crisis)
   d) Robert Borden (Conscription Crisis)
   e) Henri Bourassa (Conscription Crisis)

## ORGANIZING BETTER

1. Write a short paragraph explaining the causes of the three crises in French-English relations between 1867 and 1917.

## USING YOUR KNOWLEDGE

1. Why would a francophone living in Canada from 1867 to 1917 be upset with the English-speaking majority? Give five reasons and explain them.

## SOLVING PROBLEMS

1. We know that before we can solve a problem, we must understand it completely. In one of the exercises in this chapter, you were asked to explain the Manitoba School problem. In this exercise, you will be asked to do the same for either the Riel or Conscription problem. Choose one of the two problems. Try to explain the problem clearly. These questions will help you identify different parts of the problem.
   a) What issue does the problem deal with?
   b) Who are the people involved in the problem situation?
   c) What are their points of view? Why do they hold these views?
   d) How is Canada being affected by the problem?

## TAKING A STAND

1. Which of the three crises caused the most serious friction between francophones and anglophones in Canada? Be sure you back up your answer with facts.

## RESEARCHING

1. Using your library, find twenty new facts about the three crises in French-English relations from 1867 to 1917.
2. Try to find out why the remedial bill, passed in 1896 to overcome the Manitoba School Crisis, was repealed in 1916.

## GLOSSARY

**British Empire.** The United Kingdom and all its dominions and colonies.

**British imperialism.** Britain's practice of trying to obtain and control as many colonies as possible.

**Boer War.** A war from 1889 to 1902 in which Britain fought the Boers in South Africa. The Boers were South African settlers of Dutch ancestry.

**Orange Lodge.** A society originally organized in Ireland, dedicated to the support of Protestantism.

**Paranoid.** People who are paranoid suffer from a mental disorder. It causes them to believe that they are almost superhuman, or that other people are always plotting against them.

**Religious fanatic.** A person with extreme and unreasonable religious enthusiasm.

**Treaty of Manitoulin Island.** An agreement made in 1860 in which the government purchased Manitoulin Island from the Ottawa Indians.

# 3/The growing discontent: 1917-1967

## Contents

### Introduction

The three main crises that took place in the fifty years following Confederation hurt French-English relations. French-speaking Canadians were deeply concerned about their survival as a distinct group. How would they be able to survive the second fifty years after Confederation?

This chapter examines three francophone leaders who tried to answer this question. The leaders were Lionel Groulx, Maurice Duplessis, and Jean Lesage. Each had his own solutions to the problem of preserving the French language and culture in Quebec.

We shall see that during the period from 1917 to 1967, Quebec changed in many ways. Until World War I, Quebeckers generally had a rural life style. Gradually, however, industry was introduced in the province. Quebeckers moved from the farms to the cities. Many tried to build Quebec up into a strong, thriving province. Quebeckers took more steps to protect their language and culture. This often led to clashes.

You will learn more about these topics as you work through the chapter. The following questions will be discussed:

1. **Who were Lionel Groulx, Maurice Duplessis, and Jean Lesage? How did their ideas affect Quebec and French-English relations in Canada?**
2. **How and why did the French Canadian way of life change between 1917 and 1967?**
3. **What is the Quiet Revolution, and how did it affect French-English relations?**
4. **Why did the Quiet Revolution become violent?**

Public Archives of Canada

**Lionel Groulx holding his famous study of Dollard. What two events made Groulx so pro-francophone in his thinking?**

## After World War I: Healing the scars from the Conscription Crisis

By the end of World War I, French-speaking Canadians were afraid that their way of life would not survive. The English-speaking majority was continuing to try to "Canadianize" minority groups. The Conscription Crisis had marked a low point in French-English relations. It appeared that there would be an open clash between the two groups. This clash, however, did not take place.

The conscription riots in Quebec shocked Canadians. At first, English Canada was angry with Quebec. But with victory in the war, and a post-war boom in industry, Canadians had a chance to reflect on the Conscription Crisis. Many leaders in English Canada realized that conscription had left a deep scar on French-English relations. Therefore the anglophone prime ministers who took office after the war did everything in their power to make Quebec feel at home in Canada. For the most part they were successful.

In the years after the war, French Canadian leaders worked hard to make sure Quebec rights were protected. Henri Bourassa kept trying to get Canadians to think of themselves as Canadians, rather than as members of the British Empire. The premiers of Quebec began to develop Quebec's vast natural resources, such as timber and minerals. The premiers encouraged industries to move to Quebec.

During the 1920s Quebec prospered. Shoe, clothing, steel, tobacco, and sugar industries were built in the province. More and more people moved from farms to cities. They got jobs in the new factories. They made more money in the factories than they had been making on the farms. The French-speaking Canadians in Quebec were able to buy more and own more.

The leaders of Quebec wanted the province to be strong and rich, with many factories and mines. They felt that Quebec would then be powerful enough to protect itself. The leaders also encouraged people to have a large number of children. If Quebec had a high birth rate then French-speaking Canadians would make up a larger percentage of the Canadian population. Quebec's leaders felt that if the French were a larger group, then the English-speaking majority would not dare take away their rights.

Not all French-speaking Canadians, however, were convinced that their way of life could be protected by factories, mines, and large families. Although many of the leaders of English Canada were trying to please the French, a small group of French-speaking Canadians was still very bitter. The Riel execution, the Manitoba school problems, and the conscription issue still caused pain. One man in particular, Lionel Groulx, never forgot the problems of the French in the first fifty years after Confederation. Groulx was determined that during the second fifty years of Canada's history, the English-speaking majority would not dominate French Canada.

The next section of the chapter deals with Groulx's career. As you read through it, carefully examine the ways in which Groulx tried to promote the survival of French Canada.

### Lionel Groulx and the discontented minority

Lionel Groulx was born in Vaudreuil, Quebec in 1878. As a young boy on his father's farm, he heard people talking about the Riel execution. In his teenage years, he heard stories of the Manitoba School Crisis. These two events had a deep and lasting effect on the young Groulx. He could not understand why francophones allowed anglophones to treat them badly. Were francophones inferior? Were the anglophones better and wiser people? These questions bothered young Lionel.

Lionel Groulx's father was a farmer in the summer and a lumberjack in the winter.

Young Lionel had no desire to follow in his father's footsteps. He did well in school and was a fine debater. In high school he became a student rebel. He protested about anything that suggested that French-speaking Canadians were inferior to English-speaking Canadians.

Groulx eventually decided to become a priest. When he graduated he was sent to Valleyfield, a small town outside Montreal, to teach religion. He was a great success with his students. He inspired them to have pride in their French Canadian way of life. In 1906, however, he decided to leave the Valleyfield school. He travelled to Europe for more study.

In France, Groulx examined the art, music, novels, and history of the French people. He also went to Switzerland to study. Slowly, he became convinced that the French way of life was as good as, if not better than, the English way of life. He decided to convince his fellow French-speaking Canadians that they should stand up for their rights. He wanted to teach them to stop being dominated by the English-speaking majority.

With this goal in mind, Groulx returned to Quebec in 1909. He was given a church to look after. At once, he organized the people of that church in support of Henri Bourassa. Groulx became deeply involved in Bourassa's **nationalist movement.** He decided to write materials that would make French-speaking Canadians proud of their past.

Groulx gave up his church work to do research. By 1914, he was ready to rewrite the history of Canada. His works would show how French-speaking Canadians had been abused. They would tell French-speaking Canadians to stand up for their rights. Groulx returned to Montreal and accepted a job as a history teacher at the University of Montreal.

Groulx was a clever man and an excellent speaker. He had a flare for the dramatic.

His lectures on French Canada's past excited his students. In a short time his fame had spread throughout Quebec.

Henri Bourassa sent reporters from his paper, *Le Devoir*, to the university. They sat in on Groulx's classes and praised him in their reports. From all over Quebec students came to hear Groulx speak. When they heard him, they loved him. His words filled them with pride. No longer did they have to feel less than perfect because they had not been born in an English-speaking home.

What was it that Lionel Groulx told the vast crowds that flocked to hear him speak? He told them that the French-speaking people had suffered greatly during the years after the conquest of New France. Groulx made the colonial period of New France appear to have been a **Golden Age.** The leaders of New France were shown as great heroes, who performed deeds beyond normal human ability.

Groulx also praised the Quebec farmer who lived in harmony with the seasons. At the same time, he attacked the anglophones who wanted to develop the commerce and industry of Quebec. In almost every lecture the francophones were the heroes and the anglophones were the villains. Many other Canadian historians were upset by Groulx's history lectures and writings. They claimed that he was distorting the facts and giving a biased viewpoint. Groulx paid little attention to their criticisms. He was willing to slant his history so that everyone would see the French-speaking Canadians as great people.

Groulx realized that French people had to unite if they were ever going to be strong enough to resist the English majority. He travelled to France to promote closer ties between Quebec and France. As well, he visited French-speaking communities all over Canada and the United States. In some of his speeches Groulx argued for a union of all people of the French race.

The people listened to Groulx's ideas but they did not want to take any action. The majority of Quebeckers were enjoying the prosperity of the "Roaring Twenties". New industries had opened in Quebec. This meant new jobs, more money, and better homes. The people of Quebec were happy. They listened to Groulx because he gave them pride in themselves. But when he told them to stay on the farm and not to work in the new factories that were owned by anglophones, they refused to follow his advice. As a result, Lionel Groulx and his band of followers remained a discontented minority. They were among the people who refused to forget Riel, the Manitoba school problem, and conscription.

## READING BETTER

1. Why did Lionel Groulx not become a farmer like his father?
2. How did Groulx become convinced that the French way of life was just as good as the English way of life?
3. How did Groulx interpret Canadian history?
4. What was Lionel Groulx's goal in life?
5. Look up the word "nationalist" in a dictionary. Put the definition in your notebook. Was Groulx a French Canadian nationalist? Give facts from the text to support your answer.
6. List five ideas that Groulx presented in his writings and lectures.
7. Why didn't all French-speaking Canadians become followers of Lionel Groulx?

## USING YOUR KNOWLEDGE

1. In a short paragraph for each person, explain how the following people would react to Lionel Groulx and his ideas. You should base your predictions on what you know about Groulx and about the people in the list. Be sure that you give reasons for your predictions.
   a) Henri Bourassa
   b) Archbishop Taché
   c) Dalton McCarthy
   d) George Cartier
   e) A.A. Dorion
   f) Louis Riel
   g) John A. Macdonald
2. What effect do you think Lionel Groulx had on French-English relations in Canada? Did

he make them better or worse? Give facts to back up your point of view.

1. Groulx was willing to slant his history so that French-speaking Canadians would have pride in themselves. This means that Groulx considered the French-speaking people's pride in themselves to be more important than the accuracy of historical facts. He valued his people's pride more than historical accuracy. Many Canadian historians feel that Groulx should not have distorted the truth. They question Groulx's values.

a) Examine each of the situations given below. Decide in each case whether or not you think that the truth should have been distorted. You must question the values involved, and decide which are more important.

i) Lucy had just played in the second game of the bantam hockey semi-final. Her team lost 7 to 2. Lucy was the goalie. Her coach, Miss McKay, felt that Lucy played a poor game. She knew that Lucy could play much better. After the game Lucy asked her coach "Do you think it's my fault that we lost, Miss McKay?" She replied, "No, Lucy, the whole team had a bad night. We will beat them next game. You never let us down, Lucy. You are the core of our team."

*Issue*: Should the coach have distorted the truth?

ii) There were many problems in Germany after World War I. Inflation made German money of little value. During the Depression many people were out of work. People were starving. Because Germany had lost the war, the German people lost pride in themselves. Also, because Germany had lost the war, it had to pay great sums of money to the victorious Allies. There were so many problems that Germans were beginning to give up hope. If the people gave up hope, then there was little chance that Germany would ever recover. Hitler began telling the German people that Jews, Communists, and others were to blame for all Germany's problems. Some Germans knew that these people were not to blame, yet they went along with Hitler. They thought that if the Germans believed that certain groups had caused all their country's problems, then they would no longer blame themselves. They could have pride in themselves once again. With self-pride, perhaps the Germans would begin to work again. The nation could thus be saved.

*Issue*: Should the Germans who knew the truth have allowed Hitler to openly blame certain people for Germany's problems?

b) Take a stand on this issue: Should Lionel Groulx have slanted his history lectures and books so that the French-speaking Canadians would have pride in themselves? Back up your point of view with facts from the text. You may also want to use information from the case studies in part a) to help support your point of view.

## Defending the farm life

In the 1920s and 1930s Lionel Groulx and other leading French-speaking Canadians glorified farm life. They wanted Quebec's farmers to feel proud of their way of life. They knew, however, that sooner or later the farmers would come into contact with the richer life style of industrial society. Lionel Groulx and others like him did not want farmers to feel inferior just because they had less money. They were convinced that money could not bring true happiness. Groulx and his followers believed that happiness came only to those who worked hard, loved God, were kind to their neighbours, and stayed away from the evils of the city. With this in mind, they wrote stories and gave speeches that praised the life of the farmer. The following is an example of this type of writing. How do you react to it?

### The nobility of the plough

In the past, people gained honour with their swords. In battle, people stained their swords with blood in defence of king and country. The ancestors of the people of Quebec did not gain their nobility with the sword. They gained their nobility with the sweat of their brows. They gained their nobility by clearing the land and preparing the soil for the seeds.

Your ancestors have left you a great inheritance. No, it is not money. What good is money? Money only buys things that rust or fade away. No, the inheritance that they left you is land—land that they cultivated into the paradise you enjoy today. Your ancestors were great people. From a wilderness of trees they built this province of rolling fields and peaceful meadows. I say to you, be proud that you come from a race of farmers. Be proud that you are farmers.

I am sad to say that there are people who will tell you not to be proud to be farmers. Just the other day a very rich woman from Montreal drove through our area. She had her driver stop the car. She opened her window and said to me, "You French Canadians are a hundred years behind the times. You have not progressed one bit

**The beauty of small farms of Quebec. Why would Etienne Cartouche appreciate this picture?**

since the Conquest. You still stay on your farms in your run-down little houses. Your people are dead to progress. History has left you behind. Nobody runs a small farm in the twentieth century. There is no money in it." The car drove off, leaving the fresh country air tainted with gasoline fumes. This woman really believes she is happy. But I know she is wrong. This woman is rich, but she is not content. Her life breeds discontent, but our life breeds contentment.

Look at your small home. The carpentry is rough, but the faces of those within it are happy. Each day you get up and have a great breakfast and go out into the field. With satisfaction you walk behind your horses, directing the plough. When you look up from your work, you can see your wife and children. They can see you. You sow the seeds and bring forth food as God intended. You come home tired. You enjoy your family. You pray. You sleep in peace because you live an honest life. Be assured that your life is blessed by God.

Stand up for your life. Never feel that you are second-class because you are a farmer. Instead, look on the English as if they are second-class because they toil in industry. Feel sorry for your brothers and sisters who have moved to the cities. They never know the joy of hard labour in the fields. They never experience the nobility of the plough.

---

**READING BETTER**
1. Look up the word "nobility", and write the definition in your notebook. Then explain in your own words what is meant by "nobility of the plough".
2. According to the author, why should the French-speaking Canadian farmer be happy to stay on the farm? Give three reasons.
3. Why does the author have so little respect for money and jobs in industry?

**USING YOUR KNOWLEDGE**
1. Imagine that you are a French-speaking Canadian farmer. You have just heard the speech on "The nobility of the plough". Write a short letter to a friend in which you explain how you feel as a result of the speech.
2. Why did the rich woman from Montreal say that the French-speaking Canadians had been left behind by history? Do you agree or disagree with her?

**TAKING A STAND**
1. Take a stand on the issue: "Should French-speaking Canadian farmers stay on the farm, or should they move to the cities where they can earn more money?" Back up your point of view with facts. Be prepared to defend your point of view in front of the class.

## Duplessis: Provincial rights and a strong Quebec

In the 1920s most French-speaking Canadians in Quebec made more money than they had in the past. Therefore many paid little attention to the complaints of Lionel Groulx and his followers. In the 1930s, however, French Canadians were no longer so confident about their future. The **Great Depression** crushed Quebec's hopes. Companies closed their doors, great numbers of workers were laid off, and unemployment was widespread. People lost their cars, their homes, and their savings.

During these dark days, French-speaking Canadians began to listen to a new voice, the voice of Maurice Duplessis. Duplessis was the premier of Quebec. He held this office from the mid-1930s to the late 1950s, except for the years during World War II. During the whole period, Duplessis was one of the most influential people in Quebec.

Duplessis was a skilled politician. Throughout his career he was a supporter of provincial rights. Duplessis reasoned that if the provinces were strong, then Quebec would also be strong. A strong Quebec could easily prevent Ottawa and the English-speaking majority from tampering with the French Canadian way of life.

There is another side to Duplessis, however. Some historians have suggested that Duplessis was more like a dictator than a premier of a province in a democratic country. The following two stories deal with the career of Duplessis. As you read through them, keep these questions in mind. Was Duplessis a great Canadian leader or a dictator? What effect did the career of Maurice Duplessis have on French-English relations?

The first story takes place in an old farmhouse located several miles east of Rivière-du-Loup. René Charpentier, 82 years old, talks to his granddaughter about Duplessis. The year is 1959.

---

### Maurice Duplessis, saviour of French Canada: What grandfathers tell grandchildren

"Grandpère! Why do you look so sad? Is something wrong?" Eleven-year-old Louisette Charpentier had been standing near the fire in the big kitchen of her grandfather's farmhouse. Now she quickly crossed the room to where the old man was seated.

The old man ran his hand through the girl's dark hair and sighed. "An old friend of mine has died. Perhaps you have heard of him. It is Maurice Duplessis, the premier of the province of Quebec. Do you know about him?" asked the old man. The girl shook her head.

"No, how could you?" said the old man, smiling down at the upturned face. "You are too young to know of Mighty Maurice."

"Why do you call him Mighty Maurice?" asked Louisette.

"Well, my child, it is because he was the mightiest politician and the greatest leader French Canada has ever known."

As he began to tell the child about Duplessis, the old man's spirits seemed to rise. He went over to the mantle, took down his pipe, and filled it. As he lit it he sat down in the great leather chair opposite the girl.

"Back in the 1930s, during the Great Depression, things were very bad here in these parts. Nobody had money. Mortgages were coming due. Some people were losing their land. Everybody was ready to give up hope. There was no help coming from the prime minister of Canada. There was no help coming from the premier of Quebec. It seemed as if we were a forgotten people. And then Mighty Maurice arrived to save the day."

The old man looked off into space, and into the past.

"I can see it just as if it were yesterday. Duplessis started up a new political party, the Union Nationale. I can see him standing on a platform just outside the town hall. He was talking about foreign ownership."

"What's foreign ownership, Grandpère?" asked the young girl. She had moved over and was sitting on the floor by her grandfather.

"Foreign ownership is when people from outside Canada own the industries and mines and lumber mills. People from England and the United States had invested their money in businesses in Quebec. During the Depression when nobody was making money these people wanted to get their money back. They closed down businesses or fired most of the workers. Duplessis explained to us how these foreign owners were to blame for all our problems in the Depression.

"Maurice promised that he would break the control that anglophones had on business in Quebec. He said that when he broke their control he would transfer more businesses to French-speaking Canadians. When he did that the Depression would be over for us. You see, if we controlled the businesses then we would keep them open. That way, French-speaking Canadians would be able to keep their jobs.

"Duplessis also explained to us that the federal government in Ottawa cannot be trusted. Mighty Maurice, he fought with the federal government all his life. He wanted Quebec and all the provinces to have more powers. He wanted those powers so that he could help the people of Quebec. He wanted to smash the grasp that the anglophones have on business in Quebec."

The old man bent down toward the girl who was looking up, wide-eyed, at her grandfather. It was as if the old man were going to pass on a great secret to his grandchild. "The federal government," he whispered, "is in the pocket of the anglophones. They control it. Even a French-speaking prime minister like Laurier or St. Laurent can do nothing to stop the English-speaking majority. Listen child, and listen well. Mighty Maurice knew this and he told this to me, just as I am telling it to you. The only way that French Canada can protect itself is by having a strong leader in a strong Quebec. The strong leader must fight against Ottawa. This leader must use every muscle and every bit of his brain to protect Quebec from English Canada. And that is what Mighty Maurice did, until the day he died."

The grandfather settled back in his chair and continued his story. "They set out to get Duplessis. Those federal politicians had to get him because he was causing them too much trouble. Maurice was after more tax money for Quebec. He would have got it, but all the politicians ganged up on him in 1939. Maurice lost the election.

"The prime minister, Mackenzie King, thought he had seen the last of Mighty Maurice. But he didn't know what kind of a man he was dealing with. Maurice reorganized the Union Nationale party and just waited for his chance. He didn't have to wait long.

"You see, around the time that Duplessis was defeated, war broke out in Europe. Canada was in the fighting right from the start. Duplessis knew it and so did everybody else in Quebec. We all knew that it wouldn't be long until the second Conscription Crisis. You see, conscription is when people are forced to take part in the war. Borden passed a conscription law in 1917. I had to go and fight. I was shot in

**Maurice Duplessis: Dictator or saviour?**

Public Archives of Canada

the leg. Maurice knew that the English-speaking Canadians would try again to bring in conscription. Prime Minister King said there would never be conscription. But before the end of the war he passed a conscription law. Duplessis fought against this second attempt to force French-speaking Canadians to fight. But the English-speaking majority forced conscription on us.

"Toward the end of the war, Duplessis waged a tremendous campaign to be re-elected. He promised that Quebec would get a full share of the **post-war prosperity.** He also gave out the old cry that Quebec had to be strong if we were to be protected from Ottawa and the anglophones.

"In the 1944 election I worked my heart out for Maurice Duplessis and the Union Nationale party. Everybody in the area worked for Mighty Maurice. We worked because Duplessis was our only hope. Maurice explained to us that most of the people in Ottawa could not be trusted. If we were to protect ourselves and our religion we had to have a strong leader like Maurice Duplessis."

The girl now understood her grandfather's sadness. Quebec had lost a truly great man.

1. Why did Charpentier call Maurice Duplessis the greatest leader French Canada has ever known? Give five reasons.
2. What problems did people have during the Depression?
3. Why did Duplessis fight against the federal government?
4. Give one reason why the people in Quebec would vote for Duplessis in 1936 and in 1944.
5. Are Maurice Duplessis' ideas about Quebec and Canada like those of George Etienne Cartier or of A.A. Dorion? Be sure to give facts to back up your point of view.
6. Old Charpentier accepted the idea that anglophones could not be trusted. What experiences in his life made him distrust anglophones?

RESEARCHING
1. The Depression of the 1930s was a major event in Canadian history. Do some research on the Depression. Use your school library or books that your teacher will provide. See if you can find the answers to the following questions:
   a) What caused the Depression?
   b) How did the Depression affect Canadians?
   c) How did Canada get out of the Depression?
   d) In 1936, what solutions did Maurice Duplessis offer for the Depression problems in Quebec?
   e) From what you have learned of the Depression, do you think that Duplessis' solutions would work? Be sure to give facts to back up your point of view.

### Maurice Duplessis, dictator of Quebec: What fathers tell their children

The steady clicking of the rails and the gentle rocking of the train almost lulled Louisette to sleep. This morning her father had come to Rivière-du-Loup to pick her up. Louisette had been staying with her grandfather all summer. Now they were heading back to Montreal.

The girl shifted in her seat and glanced at the magazine her father was reading. To her surprise she saw the name "Duplessis" in one of the headlines.

"Hey, Papa, are you reading about Mighty Maurice?"

"I see that your grandfather has been telling you stories," replied her father.

"Yes, Grandpère told me all about Mighty Maurice and how great he was. You voted for him in all the elections, didn't you?" asked the girl, looking up expectantly at her father.

Pierre Charpentier said nothing for a moment. He was thinking about what he would say. He did not want the child to lose respect for her grandfather. And yet, he did not want her to think of Duplessis as a great hero.

"Well Louisette, people have different opinions about Maurice Duplessis. Some people, like your grandfather, think that Duplessis was a great leader. Others, however, do not agree."

"I don't understand, Papa. How can they think that Mighty Maurice was not a hero after all the great things he did?" asked the girl.

"You see this magazine?" asked the father, showing his daughter the cover. Louisette read the title, *Cité Libre*. "The people who write this magazine—people like Pierre Trudeau, Gérard Pelletier, and

Jean Marchand—they all feel that Duplessis did a poor job of running Quebec."

"What about the things he did during the Depression to help all the poor people? What about the way he stood up to Ottawa? What about the way he protected us from the English?" asked the girl excitedly. She was getting angry. Who were these people, this Trudeau and his friends? How dare they attack her grandfather's great hero, Mighty Maurice!

"Well dear, it is just not that simple. You see, Duplessis was a clever politician. He used the anglophones as a scapegoat."

The girl looked puzzled. Her father continued.

"A scapegoat is someone or something that you blame for your problems. You get rid of your anger by getting mad at the scapegoat. Duplessis made the people of Quebec think that the anglophones were to blame for all the problems of the Depression. By blaming the anglophones he became popular with many people in Quebec. But the English-speaking people were not to blame. The Depression was caused by a stock market crash in the United States.

"Duplessis didn't solve all the problems of the Depression, either. He really couldn't because the Depression was world-wide. The Depression was not over until World War II. When the war started many factories reopened. Everybody got jobs again."

The father looked down at his daughter. He could see that the child was confused. He thought for a moment and then went on.

"Maurice Duplessis carried on a war with Ottawa to get more power for the province. But other English-speaking premiers, like Hepburn of Ontario, did that too. Duplessis tried to make the people of Quebec believe that he was the only one willing to fight with Ottawa. He wanted to look like a hero so that everybody would vote for him."

"Grandpère says that he fought with Ottawa to try to help the people of Quebec," protested Louisette. "Grandpère says that Ottawa had all the tax money and Quebec had all the problems. Ottawa refused to give Quebec money to help its poor people."

"That is only partly true, Louisette. Since the time of Confederation Canada has changed. The provinces were given more responsibilities. They had to look after **social welfare programmes.** This includes taking care of old-age pensions, hospitals, health care, welfare, and payments to workers who have lost their jobs! The provinces had all these jobs to do. During the Depression so many people were out of work that there was very little tax money. The provinces didn't have enough money to handle these new jobs. So premiers like Duplessis and Hepburn fought with Ottawa to get more money from the federal government. Before the matter was decided, World War II came along. People were no longer out of work. The people of Quebec got their jobs back. Duplessis could no longer use the anglophones as a scapegoat. The result was that he lost the election in 1939.

"Here's something I'll bet your grandfather didn't tell you. When Duplessis didn't agree with people, or when he felt threatened by them, he took away their freedom. He had what he called a 'padlock law'. This gave the police the power to close any building in which **subversive activities** were going on. The law was originally passed to give the government power to crush Communists. Duplessis used this law to crush his personal enemies. He shut down newspapers that criticized him. He outlawed student groups that criticized him. Does that sound like a hero?

"What Duplessis did was to allow foreign companies to come into Quebec. These companies developed the natural resources of the province. They grew rich. The companies would give Duplessis large amounts of money at election time. With this money he paid for advertising. With all the advertising he easily defeated his opponents. The result was that he was in power from 1945 to 1959."

"But what is wrong with that?" asked the girl. "Grandpère says that Duplessis was just protecting us from people who wanted to change everything in Quebec."

"Your grandfather was probably talking about the trade unions. The unions just wanted to get higher wages for their workers. But Duplessis made a deal with the owners of the big companies. Duplessis agreed to crush the unions, so that the owners would not have to pay the workers higher wages. To repay Duplessis, the owners gave him great sums of money so that he could win the elections.

"It wasn't fair because Duplessis and his friends became rich while the workers remained poor. They barely had enough to live on. That is why I am working for the Liberal party. The Liberal party of Quebec feels that it is time for a change in Quebec. Grandpère's Mighty Maurice was in office far too long. It is time for Quebec to change, to get up-to-date. There are new voices in Quebec, people like Pierre Trudeau, René Lévesque, and Jean Lesage. They all have new plans for the province."

"But grandpère says. . . ." The girl could not remember what her grandfather said. She sat looking at her father. She was no longer sure about Mighty Maurice. Was he a good or bad leader? The girl could not decide. The train rolled on, clicking tirelessly over the rails toward Montreal.

---

**READING BETTER**
1. Why does Pierre Charpentier not believe Maurice Duplessis was a great leader? Give five reasons.
2. Why did Duplessis have a "padlock law?"
3. Why was Duplessis against unions?

**TAKING A STAND**
1. If you were a French-speaking Canadian would you vote for or against Maurice Duplessis in an election? Make sure that you have reasons to back up your point of view, and be prepared to defend it.

## Jean Lesage and the Quiet Revolution

The Depression of the 1930s had made the people of Quebec aware that their relationship with the federal government in Ottawa was important. Ottawa controlled the money. Without money the province was weak. A weak Quebec was unable to defend the French Canadian way of life. Through the 1940s and 1950s French-speaking Canadians continued to question the relationship that Quebec had with the rest of Canada. Government research seemed to show that Quebec was not receiving its fair share of Canada's wealth.

In the past, Quebec had been mostly a rural, agricultural province. It did not seem concerned about sharing in Canada's industrial wealth. By the late 1950s, however, this attitude no longer prevailed. A drastic change had taken place in Quebec in the years since World War I. Most Quebeckers had moved from the farms into the cities. The slow rural life had been replaced by the rapid pace of an industrial economy. As Quebec changed so did the average Quebecker. The traditional French-speaking Canadians were gone forever. Demanding and vocal French-speaking Canadians had taken their place.

**ORGANIZING BETTER**

1. Make a chart in your notebook. You are to compare a traditional French-speaking Canadian with a new French-speaking Canadian. Compare the two using the following headings:
   a) Type of work
   b) Education
   c) Religious practices
   d) Source of advice
   e) Attitude toward life

---

### The traditional French-speaking Canadians in Quebec

1. Most spoke only French.
2. Most had little or no formal education. They were generally farmers. Men who were educated tended to become lawyers, doctors, teachers, or priests.
3. Most women were homemakers.
4. Most Quebeckers tended to be attached to the Church and to their priests.
5. Most knew little about the government. They voted as their priests advised.

### The new French-speaking Canadians in Quebec

1. In general they speak French, but many understand English as well.
2. Most have a high school education and live in cities. Many are industrial labourers. Those with higher education go into business, or become engineers, doctors, lawyers, and teachers. Fewer become priests.
3. Many more women are educated and have chosen careers outside the home.
5. In general they know more about government. They are concerned about how it affects their lives. Many consider separatism as a possible way of improving their lives.

1. **A revolution is a complete and radical change. Between the years 1917 and 1967 there was a complete and radical change in French Canada. Imagine that you are a French Canadian who had been frozen in 1917 and unfrozen in 1967. Which of the changes that had taken place in Quebec would you feel to be the greatest?**

In the fifty years following World War I, a revolution took place in Quebec. In most revolutions there are battles, riots, and killings. In the Quebec revolution, however, not a shot was fired. It was a quiet revolution. As we have seen, the average French-speaking Canadian had changed completely. Maurice Duplessis and the Union Nationale party were not prepared to change with the times. As a result, shortly after the death of Duplessis, the new French-speaking Canadian rejected the Union Nationale party. Jean Lesage was elected premier of Quebec.

When Lesage was elected premier in 1960, the province had six serious problems. Unless these problems could be

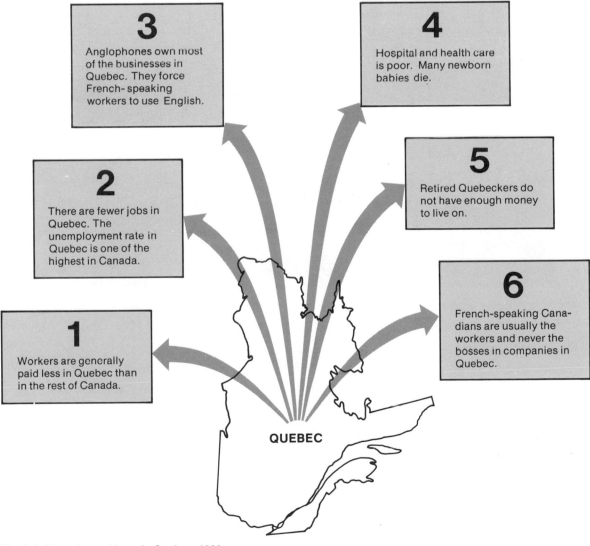

**Fig. 3-1 Six major problems in Quebec, 1960**

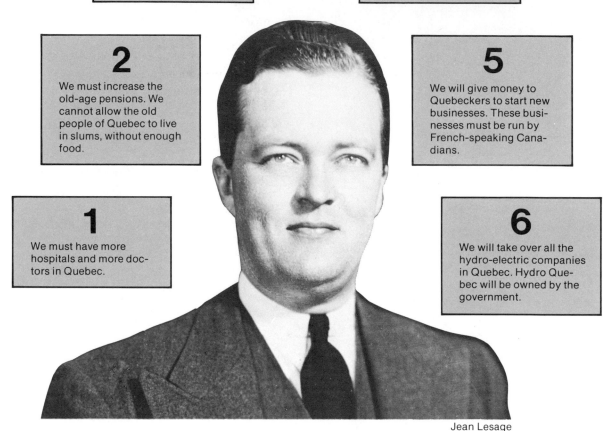

**3** We must have new laws that increase the wages paid to workers. Workers in Quebec must earn as much money as workers doing the same job elsewhere in Canada.

**4** We must provide jobs. To do this we will develop Quebec's vast natural resources. We will open new paper mills and new mines.

**2** We must increase the old-age pensions. We cannot allow the old people of Quebec to live in slums, without enough food.

**5** We will give money to Quebeckers to start new businesses. These businesses must be run by French-speaking Canadians.

**1** We must have more hospitals and more doctors in Quebec.

**6** We will take over all the hydro-electric companies in Quebec. Hydro Quebec will be owned by the government.

Jean Lesage

**Quebec is full of problems. I think that these ideas will help solve the problems.**

**Fig. 3-2 Jean Lesage: Solutions to the problems**

solved, French-speaking Canadians would be unable to achieve a higher standard of living. Realizing this fact, Lesage set out to solve the six problems. Examine Fig. 3-1 and Fig. 3-2. You will discover the six problems and the solutions suggested by Lesage.

Reaction to Lesage's policies

Lesage's government was aware of the problems and the goals of French-speaking Canadians in Quebec. The government began to pass laws based on Lesage's

solutions to Quebec's problems. Lesage's government passed laws to build new hospitals, and increase wages and old-age pensions. The government passed laws to provide funds for Quebeckers who wanted to start their own businesses. Lesage also made plans to force private hydro companies to sell out to the government so that Hydro Quebec could be set up. Many Canadians became upset. They felt that the government should not interfere in private business.

Most Canadians were uninformed about

affairs in Quebec. Most Canadians were unaware that French-speaking Canadians had changed. They assumed that French Canada was satisfied with its relationship to the rest of Canada. It had been almost half a century since the violence of the Conscription Crisis. On the surface, French-English relations appeared to be excellent.

During the Depression, the provinces had gained tremendous power. Now, in the 1960s, under Jean Lesage, Quebec would use this power to reshape society in Quebec. As this reshaping process began, few Canadians understood it. With ignorance came fear. Before long, a full-scale crisis in French-English relations was in the making.

Jean Lesage wanted to change Quebec and bring it into the mainstream of twentieth-century industrial life. He wanted French-speaking Canadians to have a full share in this new industrialized Quebec. To bring about these changes Lesage had to change the nature of the partnership that Quebec had with both Ottawa and the English-speaking minority in Quebec.

Resistance and conflict did not stop Premier Lesage. To make sure that he had the support of the people of Quebec, he called an election in 1962. Lesage and the Liberals campaigned under the slogan "Maîtres chez nous" or "Masters in our own house". Lesage was victorious. Immediately, he set to work to build a new Quebec.

English Canada, however, did not understand Quebec's desire for a new type of partnership with the rest of Canada. It felt that Quebec did not have a right to make these changes. Consequently, English Canada resisted. The result has been unceasing conflict between French-speaking and English-speaking Canadians.

### ORGANIZING BETTER

1. Draw two columns in your notebook. Head the first one, "The problems in Quebec in 1960", and the second one "Solutions to the problems". In the first column list Quebec's problems. In the second column, list wherever possible Lesage's solutions. Refer to Figs. 3-1 and 3-2 for help.

### USING YOUR KNOWLEDGE

1. If you were living in Quebec in 1960, which would you consider to be the worst problem? Be sure to give reasons to back up your point of view.
2. You know that there were six main problems in Quebec in 1960. Predict which problem each of the following people would consider to be the most serious.
   a) John Baker is a retired security guard from the railway.
   b) Madeleine Lessing is an expectant mother.
   c) Jeanne Lebois is just finishing university. She hopes to become an executive in one of Montreal's big insurance companies.
   d) Art Degais, age 17, has just dropped out of school.
   e) Pierre Artois is the father of seven. He works in a lumber mill.
3. The premiers of the provinces are supposed to run the provinces so that the people in them are happy. If problems exist, the premiers are supposed to solve them. If people are unhappy, the premiers must find out why, and then pass laws to correct the situation. Using this description of a premier's job, decide whether or not Jean Lesage was a good premier. Give reasons for your viewpoint.

### Results of the Quiet Revolution

The Quebec of the 1960s was far different from the Quebec of 1917. Many people in Quebec felt that the changes that had taken place produced some bad side effects. First, the traditional French Canadian way of life seemed to be disappearing. Second, the French language seemed to be in danger of disappearing. Third, French-speaking Canadians seemed to have only the lowest-paying jobs. After his second electoral victory in 1962, Jean Lesage was determined to change these three things. To do this, however, he felt that he had to control the following three aspects of Quebec life.

The first thing I must do is to give a job to each Quebecker. To do this I must have complete control of all tax money so that it can be used to create jobs in Quebec.

Second, I must be allowed to give more of the top jobs to French-speaking Canadians. The anglophones will no longer be allowed to control all the high-paying jobs.

Third, I must have complete control of how the French language is used in Quebec.

These three demands brought Lesage into conflict with Ottawa, and with the other provinces of Canada. To them, it seemed as if Quebec wanted special privileges. The other provinces did not control all the tax money. Thus they asked, "Why should Quebec be treated differently from any other provinces in Canada?" The federal government and most Canadians could not see why the province of Quebec had to be given special privileges. Quebeckers felt that they should be given special privileges. They argued that Quebec was the homeland of one of Canada's two founding peoples, and of Canada's largest minority. Twenty-nine percent of the Canadian population was French-speaking. Also, French Canadians had their own language and way of life. They felt different from the rest of Canada. As well, they felt that Quebec had to have **special status** if it was to preserve its unique way of life.

During the early 1960s Canada was divided into two groups. On the one side were the French-speaking Canadians who demanded special status. On the other side was the rest of Canada, which felt that Quebec should not be given special rights and privileges. All across the country people were upset by what was happening. Very few Canadians understood what was bothering Quebec. Most Canadians knew, however, that they did not like what Quebec was doing. To get a clearer picture of why so many people were upset by Jean Lesage and his government we will look at "The Diary of Bobby Jones".

Bobby Jones is an English-speaking Canadian who lives in Dorval, a suburb of Montreal. He started a diary in 1960 when he was ten, and kept it until 1967. These excerpts from his diary clearly show how the actions of the Lesage government affected people in Quebec.

**English-speaking Quebeckers and the Quiet Revolution:
The diary of Bobby Jones**

JUNE 23, 1960

Mom and Dad had some friends over to our house last night. I was supposed to be in bed, but I sneaked down and listened to what they were talking about.

They were talking about the election that was held last week. My mom said that she was afraid that this man Jean Lesage would mean trouble for English Canada. Lesage will bring in changes, my dad said. Another man said that if Lesage made too many changes he would move his family over to Cornwall, which is in Ontario. My friend Andy Baxter said his parents would consider moving if the francophones started to cause trouble.

AUGUST 22, 1961

Wow! You should see what is happening up at our cottage. There are about a million earthmovers and tractors coming in. My dad is really upset because all that heavy equipment has wrecked the road. We got a flat tire. Dad says that he is going to write a letter to Premier Lesage and make him pay for the tire.

Mr. Dubois, who lives at the lake all year round, says that the tractors are part of the government's new policy. The Lesage government is going to build a big lumber camp and open some mines in the northern area beyond our lake. I asked Mr. Dubois why Lesage wanted to do that. Mr. Dubois said it was to provide jobs for people like his sons.

His oldest son is lazy. He just sits around on the dock all day. He said something to my mom that made her real mad. She yelled at him. "Why don't you go out and get a job instead of sitting around here bothering people with your rude remarks?" she shouted.

He jumped up and said, "There are no jobs. You English-speaking people get all the good jobs. We French are the first to lose our jobs."

I wish I was older. I would have hit him for talking to Mom like that.

I guess these mines will be good for that Dubois guy. But the two other Dubois boys are still in school. I guess maybe Mr. Dubois is going to make them go out to work. I guess maybe they need money. Their house is real dumpy. The Dubois kid who is my age always wears old shoes with holes in them.

---

**READING BETTER**

1. **How did Mr. and Mrs. Jones and their friends react to the victory of Jean Lesage and the Liberal party in June, 1960?**
2. **In what two ways did their friends intend to defend themselves against the Lesage government?**
3. **What changes did Bobby see in Quebec as a result of the Lesage victory?**
4. **Why do you think that Jean Lesage brought about these changes?**
5. **What evidence is there in the diary to show that French-English relations in Quebec in 1960 were not good?**

---

SEPTEMBER 15, 1961

Andy Baxter may have to move. His dad is all upset about that guy Lesage. Reg Prévost, the guy who sits beside me in school, doesn't understand it. Reg says that his dad thinks Lesage is a great leader. Reg's dad says that Lesage is going to make sure that French-speaking Canadians get a fair deal. Reg says that they have been cheated by Canada. I asked him how they have been cheated. He said that he didn't know, but he would ask.

DECEMBER 21, 1961

I had a great day. I went over to Reg's house. We watched the hockey game on TV.

Mr. Prévost came down to the recreation room where Reg and I were watching the game. He said, "Reg tells me that you don't understand why French-speaking Canadians feel cheated."

"That's right," I answered. He told me that the anglophones have all the best jobs. They make more money. They own all the businesses. They refuse to learn to speak French, but they expect the francophones to learn English. Mr. Prévost said it's not fair. So Jean Lesage is going to make sure that French-speaking Canadians have a better chance at getting more jobs, jobs that pay more money. Mr. Prévost said that Lesage is giving French-speaking Canadians a chance to enjoy a good life.

I asked him why francophones didn't get good jobs in the past. He said that the anglophones had the best jobs sewn up. I'm not sure, but it seems to me that the best jobs would go to the people who could do the best work. If the francophones were the best then they would get the best jobs. It still doesn't make sense to me.

---

**READING BETTER**
1. Why does Mr. Prévost like Jean Lesage?

**USING YOUR KNOWLEDGE**
1. From what you know about French-English relations so far, try to explain why the francophones did not have the best jobs in the province of Quebec.

---

MAY 6, 1962

Mr. Baxter came over to our house last night. He was really angry. Mom made me go upstairs, but I sat on the stairs and listened.

Andy's dad says he is going to take the Lesage government to court and sue them. It seems that the government passed some new labour laws. They are forcing Mr. Baxter to spend a lot of money at his clothing factory. He said he has to build some new washrooms and lunchrooms. Also he has to give the workers more holidays and more time off for breaks. And what bothers him the most is that he is going to have to pay them more money. He said that he will be **bankrupt** if he spends all that money.

Dad said that the new labour laws will help the French-speaking workers. Dad said that they were poor, and needed more money. When Dad said this, Mr. Baxter really blew his stack. He started saying that Dad probably voted for Lesage. Dad said that he didn't vote for Lesage. Mr. Baxter didn't listen. He walked out and slammed the door. Boy, would I ever be in trouble if I did that!

MAY 9, 1962

Mr. Baxter came up to us after church and apologized. As we walked back home he told us that the Lesage government was up to more dirty tricks. Lesage is giving money to francophones so they can start up French businesses. Mr. Baxter says that isn't fair. There is a French guy who is getting money from Lesage to start a clothing factory. This factory is going to make it harder for Mr. Baxter to sell his products. What really bugs Mr. Baxter is that Lesage is using Baxter's own tax money to start up the factory that will drive him out of business. Mr. Baxter says he is going to move to Ontario. He says that there the government doesn't use your own money to put you out of business.

MAY 12, 1962

I was over at Reg's house today. I was telling him how the Baxters were going to move. I don't want Andy to move. I was pretty upset and said that Lesage was stupid. Mrs. Prévost heard me and asked me why I said that. I told her and she said that Lesage passed the labour laws and was giving money to French businesses because the French in Quebec are so much worse off than other people. She said that people in Quebec make only two thirds of what the people in the rest of Canada make. Also, there are more people out of work in Quebec than in the rest of Canada. Mrs. Prévost really thinks Lesage is the greatest, too. I guess Lesage is doing good things for French-speaking people but bad things for English-speaking people. It's too bad he can't do something good for everybody.

---

**READING BETTER**

1. Why does Mr. Baxter feel that Lesage's labour laws are going to bankrupt him?
2. Why is Lesage giving money out to French-speaking people who want to start a business?
3. Explain in your own words what Mr. Baxter meant when he said that Lesage was using Baxter's own money to put him out of business.

**SOLVING PROBLEMS**

1. a) Look over Bobby's diary for May 6, 9, and 12. From Bobby's point of view, what problem is the Lesage government causing?
   b) Name three groups in Quebec who are involved in this problem.
   c) What would be the attitude of each of the groups to this problem?

**TAKING A STAND**

1. One of the policies of the Lesage government was to give tax money to French Canadian businesses. Do you think Lesage should have given this money? Be prepared to defend your point of view.
2. Under which of the following circumstances do you think that the government should give out money?
   a) To a local hockey team so that it can play in a hockey tournament in Europe.
   b) To a 16-year-old who has left home and has no job. He has dropped out of school.
   c) To a 17-year-old girl who leaves home to have a baby. The father of the baby refuses to marry her.
   d) To a local high school band to provide equipment.

**A typical Quebec scene in 1900—making maple sugar.**

JULY 17, 1962

I went over to Andy's place this morning. The moving van was there.
It was very sad. Andy and I didn't know what to say to each other.
We just stood there and looked at one another. I sure hated to see him
go. Mr. Baxter said that he had to leave because of Lesage's policies.
He told my dad that it was going to get worse. He said that the FLQ
terrorists will kill all the anglophones if they don't move out of
Quebec. My parents are really scared. In the paper yesterday there
was a story about another explosion in a mailbox. An old man was
killed. I could hear Mom and Dad talking about it in their room.
They stopped when I came around.

JULY 20, 1964

We just got back from our holidays. We went to visit my cousins who
live in Lethbridge, Alberta. I liked it there.

Every night my aunt and uncle and mom and dad talked about
what was happening in Quebec. My aunt would get really worked up.
She doesn't understand what the francophones in Quebec want. She

**A typical industrial scene in Quebec today. What changes have taken place?**

said that the French lost Quebec in the Conquest of 1759. They were defeated, so now they don't have any rights. My aunt shouted that they should not have gotten their language rights after the Conquest. Then we wouldn't have these problems today. It would be like it is in the United States. The US is like a big melting pot. All the groups go in—Italians, French, Germans, Spanish—and they all come out American. My aunt said that if we had it like that in Canada we would have no problem with the francophones.

My dad tried to explain the situation to her, but she just didn't seem to want to listen. Dad said that the French-speaking Canadians were not immigrants. But my aunt said that didn't matter. She yelled that Canada is an English country and that francophones have to learn that fact. Lesage wants the prime minister to give Quebec special rights. Quebec also wants more money. My aunt said that francophones in Quebec have no right to these special privileges.

Boy, my aunt was mad! I guess people in other parts of Canada don't like what Lesage is doing either. Dad says that people in western Canada are really upset. I thought to myself that Mr. or Mrs. Prévost should have been there to talk to my aunt. Maybe they could have made her understand. My aunt thinks that French-speaking Canadians are really greedy. But they aren't. They are just like us, as far as I can see.

NOVEMBER 7, 1965

We had an assembly at school today. One of Jean Lesage's cabinet ministers came to the school to speak to us. Some of the kids skipped out but I stayed to listen.

He said that Quebec is in a battle with Ottawa. He says that Quebec must win the war if the French Canadian way of life is to survive. I guess he is French, but he spoke English really well. Some young guys in suits and ties who came with the cabinet minister gave us a copy of his speech. They told us to take it home. I'm going to paste it in the diary. Maybe it will be worth something some day. Our history teacher says that stuff like this is a historical document. She says that historical documents should be kept for future generations.

### Quebec's war with Ottawa

I want you students to understand that the federal government in Ottawa is causing problems for Quebec. Mr. Lesage and I know that we have a large number of problems in Quebec. We want to solve these problems.

In Quebec we have high unemployment, lower incomes than in English Canada, and few French-speaking Canadians in high-paying executive jobs.

Most of you are English-speaking students. Think how you would feel if your father or mother were out of work. Or if they got paid less than somebody else for doing the same job. Or if they had no chance to get a promotion just because they were anglophones. That is how it is for French-speaking Canadians. If this situation does not change, more and more people in Quebec will become angry. These angry people will listen to the revolutionaries and the terrorists. The result will be more bombings and acts of violence. Is that what you English-speaking people want?

Of course you don't want that. You don't want it and your parents don't want it. And we certainly don't want that situation. We in the Liberal party of Jean Lesage merely want a change. We want to change Quebec so that each Quebecker has a fair chance to make a good living.

For these changes to come about, Premier Lesage's Four Point Policy must be adopted by Ottawa. These are the four points.

1. Quebec must set up a ministry of education. We want to change the education system in Quebec so that we can train Quebeckers to fill the top jobs in industry. We want to produce engineers and scientists who will help Quebec to develop its vast natural resources. We want to set up community colleges that will train the young people of Quebec to take jobs in industry and commerce.

2. Ottawa must allow Quebec complete control in developing the natural resources of the province. Ottawa is worried about too many US companies owning our mining and lumber industries. We in Quebec want to accept US money so that we can develop these resources now. These resources mean jobs for Quebeckers. Ottawa must stay out of our affairs and allow us to develop these resources now.

3. We want Ottawa to take a smaller share of the taxes collected in Quebec. We want Ottawa to give Quebec grants of money. We need this money. We have to provide more and better health care. We have to build hospitals. We have to increase the pensions for our old people. We have to build community colleges. We have to open up new departments in government so that we can protect the French language and way of life.

   In the past we have not received our fair share of Canada's wealth. Now Ottawa must give us great amounts of money so that we can make these changes in Quebec. Ottawa gets too great a share of the income tax money collected in Quebec. This must stop.

4. Finally we want the federal government to meet with the provinces on a regular basis. The federal government must meet with us to discuss our problems. Too often in the past the federal government has made decisions without understanding what Quebec feels should be done. Very often what has been good for Ottawa has been bad for Quebec.

   Remember this! Remember that Quebec is not getting a fair deal in Confederation. There are more jobs and money in English Canada than in Quebec. Jean Lesage and the Liberal party want to change this. To make these changes we need money. Ottawa must give us that money. If it refuses, then it does not want to give a fair deal to Quebec.

When this guy stopped talking we all stood up and cheered. I'm not sure why, but we just cheered like crazy. I wonder why the prime minister doesn't give the French in Quebec what they want? It seems to me that everybody should get a fair deal.

---

**READING BETTER**
1. **Why do the Baxters leave Montreal?**
2. **How do Bobby's relatives react to the situation in Quebec? Include five points they made.**
3. **According to the cabinet minister's speech, why does Quebec want a ministry of education? List three reasons.**
4. **Why is Ottawa unwilling to give Quebec control of the natural resources located in Quebec?**
5. **Why does Quebec want control of these natural resources?**
6. **Why does Quebec want more tax money? Give four reasons.**
7. **What are the three main problems in Quebec mentioned by the cabinet minister in his speech?**

The Quiet Revolution becomes violent: Crisis at St. Leonard
During the Quiet Revolution in Quebec, French Canada began an intense period of self-examination. French-speaking Canadians looked at their language, their religion, and every other aspect of their way of life. The results of this examination greatly upset them. For example, they discovered

## Lesage's war with Ottawa: Three demands

When Lesage tried to bring Quebec into the mainstream of twentieth-century industrial life he discovered that he was being stopped. The federal government in Ottawa held powers that Quebec needed to achieve its goal. When Lesage tried to get these powers from the federal government, it refused. As a result, a struggle developed between Ottawa and Quebec. These are the three key powers that Lesage wanted for Quebec.

**1**

**Ottawa must take a smaller share of the taxes collected in Quebec.**

**2**

**Ottawa must meet with Quebec on a regular basis. Before Ottawa makes decisions, it must consult with Quebec and the other provinces.**

**3**

**Ottawa must allow Quebec to have complete control over the natural resources in Quebec.**

In general, the people of Canada were not willing to allow Quebec to have these special powers. The federal government heeded the wishes of Canadians and refused to give Quebec these powers. Also, the federal government wanted to guard its own powers. If the federal government loses powers, it has difficulty running the country.

As a result of the struggle with Ottawa, French-speaking Canadians in Quebec began to feel as if English-speaking Canadians were preventing them from realizing their potential.

that the French language spoken in Quebec had become a **patois.** They also discovered that more and more people in Quebec were learning English so they could get better jobs in the English-controlled business world. There was a very real danger that the French language would disappear in Quebec.

Concerned French-speaking Canadians began to grope for a solution to this problem. One solution that they tried was to force everyone in Quebec to learn French. Many people in Quebec, however, did not want to be forced to learn French.

In 1968, in the suburb of St. Leonard, a group of French Canadian nationalists led by Raymond Lemieux tried to force English and Italian children to learn French. The result was the "Crisis at St. Leonard". In an effort to understand this crisis we will look at "The Joe Rizzo story". This story is fictional, but it is based on events that actually took place in St. Leonard.

## The Joe Rizzo story

PART 1: A BAD DAY FOR JOE RIZZO

Joseph Rizzo was born in Italy. In 1960 he immigrated to Canada in the hope of building a good life for himself in a new land. Soon after he arrived, Joe took a job in construction.

In the summer of 1969 Joe was working on a construction site in Dorval, which is a suburb in the western section of Montreal. By this time he had married and had two sons. On August 26 he was unloading bricks when his boss called to him.

"Hey, Joe, when you finish unloading those bricks will you come in here for a minute? I want to talk to you," yelled Mr. Johnson, the boss on the construction site.

Walking over to the shed, Joe felt uneasy. He felt as if something bad were going to happen. Mr. Johnson did not talk to the labourers very often. When he did it usually meant trouble. This time was no exception.

"Well, Joe," said Mr. Johnson, "You know how it is. Business is pretty slack. We just can't keep a lot of you guys on. Call me in about a month. We may get the contract for that new grocery store in St. Leonard."

Joe was disappointed, but he did not like to let people know when he was upset. Smiling he said, "I'll call in a month, then. If we get that job in St. Leonard, I can save money by not having to drive to work. I live in St. Leonard."

"So you live in St. Leonard, do you Joe?" asked Johnson. "I heard on the news at lunchtime that the 'League for the French Language' in St. Leonard wants to stop teaching English to kids in grades one and two."

"I thought the government was going to force the schools to teach English this year," said Joe. He could feel himself getting angry. "Last year they stopped teaching English in grade one. A bunch of the parents had to start schools in their basements to teach the kids English. Last year there were over two hundred of our kids learning English in basements. That's not good enough! My son Bobby starts school this year. He is going to go to a regular school and be taught by regular teachers. And he is going to be taught in English!" Joe turned and walked away.

Later that night Joe Rizzo pushed himself through the crowd of parents in the local elementary school auditorium. The meeting had been called to discuss English language education. Joe took a seat in the second row from the front. Mrs. Burgess, the leader of the Parents' Association, walked quickly across the auditorium stage to the microphone.

"Ladies and gentlemen, if you all take your seats we will get right down to business," said Mrs. Burgess.

"We better get right down to education in English or somebody's head is going to roll!" shouted somebody in the audience. Joe Rizzo shouted, "Right on!" The audience broke into nervous laughter.

"Yes," answered Mrs. Burgess, "that is our business here tonight. We want education in English for our children and we are going to get it. I have been in contact with the **Minister of Education.** He has a compromise that I think may work. He has suggested that we start regular private schools to teach our children English. This means that we would have complete control of the schools!"

"Who is going to pay for these private schools?" shouted a man from the back of the auditorium.

"The provincial government will pay for 80% of the school costs. We will have to come up with the remaining 20%," said Mrs. Burgess.

Joe was on his feet like a shot. "I already pay taxes for schools," he said angrily. "Why should we pay for both public and private schools? Look, I lost my job today and I haven't got money to pay for private schools. That guy Lemieux and his League for the French Language are looking for real trouble. I think that we should blow up a few schools. Then the government would know that we mean business. Or maybe we should take over a school and refuse to allow it to stop teaching English."

Joe's suggestions were greeted by cheers from some people and boos from others.

"Joe, I think that we have to steer clear of violence," said Mrs. Burgess. "If we turn to violence some innocent people will get hurt. We don't want violence in St. Leonard. I don't want my children having to fight their way into a school. I think our best bet is to contact our MP in Ottawa. I'm sure that the prime minister is upset by what is happening in St. Leonard."

After some discussion Mrs. Burgess's suggestion was accepted.

---

**READING BETTER**
1. What two things caused the "bad day" for Joe Rizzo?
2. What is the problem in St. Leonard?
3. Who are the participants in the problem?
4. What was the compromise developed by the government of Quebec to solve the problem in St. Leonard?
5. Why did the Parents' Association reject the compromise solution?

6. The St. Leonard Board of Education developed a policy that would force new immigrants to Quebec to learn French rather than English. Outline this policy.

**USING YOUR KNOWLEDGE**
1. How do you think people in other parts of Canada would react to the problem in St. Leonard? Be sure to give reasons for your point of view.

---

PART 2: THE WOMAN FROM OTTAWA

The long black Cadillac pulled silently up to the residence of the premier of Quebec. The driver jumped out and quickly opened the back door of the car. A woman carrying a thin attaché case got out and moved quickly into the house.

The woman was ushered into a small study where five people had already gathered. They were the premier of Quebec, the Minister of Education, and three other powerful people in the Quebec government.

"I'm glad to see you have arrived without the press spotting you," said the premier.

The woman from Ottawa stood silently for a moment, looking at the premier. Then she spoke. "What do you people think you are doing in St. Leonard? I thought you had more brains than this."

The five Quebec officials stiffened. The woman from Ottawa placed her attaché case on the table and spoke again.

"Canada is a bilingual country. We are spending millions of dollars to convince English Canada to give the French language an equal chance. And what do you people do? You let Lemieux turn St. Leonard into a unilingual area. Parents can't choose if their children will learn English or French. Don't you see what St. Leonard is doing? It is turning the rest of Canada against French-speaking Canadians."

"English Canada doesn't care about what happens in French Canada," said the Minister of Education. "It never has. And I want to remind you that education is a provincial matter. Ottawa has no business interfering in the affairs of Quebec. Go back to Ottawa and tell the prime minister to mind his own business. We don't want the advice of Ottawa on this matter."

"We are trying to keep this country from splitting apart," answered the woman from Ottawa coldly. "If we can't convince Canadians to have a bilingual Canada then the problems between francophones and anglophones will get worse. The result will be either more FLQ terrorism or a growth in the support for separation. Maybe that is what you want. Maybe you are a separatist?"

The Minister of Education jumped from his seat. "You know very well that we are not separatists. We are French-speaking Canadians. We believe that the government of Quebec has the power to protect French-speaking Canadians. Ottawa can't protect francophones. There are too many anglophones in the Parliament at Ottawa. The anglophone will never understand the francophone. Therefore, it is up to Quebec to make sure that French Canada survives. The prime minister understands that, doesn't he?"

"The prime minister understands that your policy concerning St. Leonard is ruining the chances of building a bilingual Canada. You have to be reasonable. The premier of Ontario is willing to build French schools. A lot of the voters in Ontario think that French schools are a waste of money. If you eliminate English schools in Quebec the people of Ontario will eliminate French schools in Ontario. If you eliminate English schools in Quebec, English Canada will become angry. It will refuse to solve the problems between anglophones and francophones. Then the terrorists and separatists will emerge. They will say that there is no hope for Quebec unless it separates from Canada. Is that what you want?"

"I'm not sure what to say to you," said the premier of Quebec. "We know how the prime minister feels, but we have a problem. If we allow English education, we lose the support of the Quebec nationalists. The nationalists fear that if all the immigrants learn English, there will one day no longer be a strong French-speaking majority in Quebec. When there is no longer a strong French Quebec, then who will protect French rights? Also, if we lose the support of these Quebec nationalists we will lose the next election. On the other hand, if we don't allow English education the anglophones may move their businesses out of Quebec. Then we will have higher unemployment. There is no easy answer to this problem. We have compromised. The public schools will be French and we will pay for 80% of the private English schools. We can do no more, and we will not change our minds. This meeting is over."

The premier turned quickly and went out the door. All the other Quebec officials got up and followed. The woman from Ottawa was left alone. She had failed. The prime minister would not be happy.

1. Why did the woman from Ottawa come to talk with the premier of Quebec?
2. Why was the prime minister upset with what was happening in St. Leonard?
3. What did the woman from Ottawa predict would happen if Quebec refused to allow English education in St. Leonard?
4. Why could Ottawa not force Quebec to allow English education in St. Leonard?
5. Why was the premier of Quebec unable to do what the woman from Ottawa asked?

**SOLVING PROBLEMS**

1. The woman from Ottawa failed. Pretend that the prime minister has sent you on a second mission to talk to the premier of Quebec. Compose two arguments that you would use to try and convince the premier that he should allow English education in St. Leonard. Be prepared to defend your arguments.

PART 3: VIOLENCE IN ST. LEONARD

Raymond Lemieux, the leader of the League for the French Language was also upset by the compromise of the Quebec government. To Lemieux and his followers, St. Leonard symbolized a battle in the war to preserve the French language and culture. They felt that unless action was taken the francophones would become a minority in Quebec within 25 years. The birthrate had dropped in Quebec. French-speaking Canadians were no longer having large families. There was very little immigration from France. Most of the new immigrants to Quebec wanted their children to learn English. Lemieux and his followers felt that French-speaking Canadians must ensure that the French language did not disappear in Quebec. To do this, they were willing to fight.

Lemieux called a large public meeting at Jérôme Le Royer School in St. Leonard.

As the time of the meeting approached, Joe Rizzo and his friends entered the school gymnasium. There were a lot of Italians in the crowd. There were also many French-speaking Canadians. The Italians sat in the chairs on the left side of the gymnasium and the francophones sat on the right side. The two groups glared at each other across the aisle. St. Leonard was becoming a bitter place in which to live.

Suddenly a hush fell over the crowd. A man, accompanied by several burly bodyguards, was moving up onto a platform at one end of the gymnasium. It was Lemieux.

As soon as Lemieux began to speak Joe jumped to his feet and began to boo. All Joe's buddies did the same. Soon the entire Italian section was on its feet. The booing was loud and long.

"You are babies!" shouted Lemieux into the microphone.

"We want English schools!" cried Joe. The French began to boo.

Lemieux came down off the stage and walked to the back of the gymnasium. He began to talk to the news reporters there. Suddenly a chair flew through the air. It hit Lemieux on the head. In a matter of seconds the gymnasium was transformed into a scene of chaos. People were shoving and punching each other. The air was filled with venomous curses in French, English, and Italian. Finally, police in riot gear poured in through every door.

They pushed the Italians to the front of the gymnasium and the French to the back.

All was calm for a moment.

"You're nothing but a bunch of separatist fools!" shouted Joe Rizzo.

"Quebec for Quebeckers!" came the reply. "Italians go home!"

The two groups surged toward one another again and the battle resumed. This time the police forced the Italians out the side exits into the school yard. The doors were slammed shut and bolted. Peace was restored.

Raymond Lemieux mounted the platform and went to the microphone. Wiping a trickle of blood from his face he began to speak.

"If the province of Quebec allows English private schools then French Canada is doomed. Unless we fight to save our language and way of life, Quebec will cease to exist. This has been only one of many battles we will have to fight. But we French-speaking Canadians will not give up. We will not be driven out of our land."

---

## READING BETTER

1. How did Joe Rizzo and his friends disrupt the meeting?
2. Why did Joe and his friends disrupt the meeting?
3. Why is Lemieux against the idea of English private schools?

## USING YOUR KNOWLEDGE

1. What effect do you think the crisis at St. Leonard had on French-English relations? Be sure to give facts to back up your point of view.

## TAKING A STAND

1. a) Give one reason why each of the following could be considered responsible for the violence that broke out in the school gymnasium.
     i) the police
     ii) the provincial government
     iii) the Italians involved in the fight
     iv) the francophones involved in the fight
     v) the principal of the school
     vi) Raymond Lemieux
     vii) Joe Rizzo
   b) Which of the above do you think is *most*

responsible for the violence at the school? Be prepared to back up your point of view with facts.

2. Assume that you are a French-speaking Canadian. Which of the following methods would you use to convince Mr. Rizzo that his children should learn French? Be prepared to defend your answer.
   a) I would punch him in the nose.
   b) I would send the police around to his house to collect his children and take them to the French school.
   c) I would give him some money if he would send his children to French schools.
   d) I would leave him alone and force all the businesses to use French.
   e) I would try to make him understand how the French-speaking Quebeckers feel about the issue.

3. Read over the Joe Rizzo story again. At the top of a new page in your notebook, write this issue: "Should the premier of Quebec allow the St. Leonard School Board to outlaw English education?" Divide the page down the middle. On one side list the reasons for which English education should be outlawed. On the other side list the reasons for which it

should not be outlawed. **Each time you come to a fact in your reading that deals with the issue put it in the proper column. After you have completed this pro and con chart, read it over and decide where you stand on the issue. Be prepared to defend your point of view.**

## Conclusion

After the first Conscription Crisis, French-speaking Canadians had a major problem. How could they make sure that the French Canadian way of life survived? In this chapter we discovered that one answer to this question came from Lionel Groulx and his followers. Groulx suggested that French-speaking Canadians have pride in themselves and in their rural life style. He suggested that French-speaking Canadians isolate themselves in Quebec and ignore the industrialized world.

This answer did not satisfy French Canada. Promises of wealth made young people run from the farms to factories and mines. Unfortunately, no sooner did many of them take jobs in factories than the Great Depression hit. Large numbers of French-speaking Canadians were thus out of work.

At this time, a second solution to the question of French Canada's survival was offered. This solution came from Maurice Duplessis. He suggested that the province of Quebec should take over some of the powers held by the federal government. Duplessis wanted the English-dominated federal government to become weaker. He also wanted the government of the province of Quebec to become stronger. In this way, then, Quebec would be able to protect the French way of life.

Duplessis wished to retain a rural life style for Quebec. Many French-speaking Canadians, however, wished to play a greater role in Canada's industrial development. The hopes, dreams, and ambitions of this group were represented by Jean Lesage and the Quiet Revolution which swept Quebec in the 1960s.

Jean Lesage wanted to help French-speaking Canadians raise their standards of living and live happy and productive lives. To do this, Lesage had to demand a change in the partnership that Quebec had with the federal government. He wanted special status for Quebec. English Canada could not understand why Quebec required special privileges. Therefore, the government refused Lesage's requests. Consequently, many French-speaking Canadians became convinced that English Canada was preventing them from reaching their full potential.

In this chapter we also discovered that during the Quiet Revolution, French Canada began to examine its way of life. It discovered that the quality and use of the French language were deteriorating. To solve this problem it tried to force more people to learn French. These efforts often resulted in violent clashes, such as the one between Italians and French in St. Leonard.

In sum, francophones feared that the French way of life might not survive. In 1967, French Canada was still fighting for survival. The politicians of Quebec were warring with Ottawa, demanding special status. Ottawa was refusing to grant special status. Tension between French-speaking and English-speaking Canadians was increasing. Both francophones and anglophones were becoming frustrated and bitter. What would be the result of this seemingly increasing conflict? In the next chapter we will look at the main results of the Quiet Revolution in Quebec.

**READING BETTER**
1. **Name the three French-speaking Canadian leaders who greatly affected French-English relations between 1917-1967.**

**ORGANIZING BETTER**
1. **In one or two paragraphs for each of these leaders, outline how they affected French-English relations.**

## USING YOUR KNOWLEDGE

1. Explain which of the three leaders would most likely have made the following statements. Be sure to give reasons for your choices.
   a) Quebec must have complete control in developing its natural resources. It is acceptable for Quebec to use US money to develop the resources.
   b) The English cannot be trusted.
   c) Quebec should remain a rural province in which the Roman Catholic Church guides the people in all aspects of their lives.
   d) I believe that the French way of life is superior in many aspects to the English way of life. Why, therefore, should we take a back seat to the anglophones?

## SOLVING PROBLEMS

1. We have examined about 200 years of the history of French-English relations in Canada. It is clear that relations between Canada's two founding peoples have not been good at all times.
   a) List four main types of problems that have caused friction between the two language groups.
   b) You have been named a member of a special task force to solve the problems that exist between francophones and anglophones in Canada. Try to develop some policies that will eliminate the four problem areas you mentioned in part a) of this question.

## TAKING A STAND

1. Which of the three leaders dealt with in this chapter was most responsible for bad feelings between French-speaking and English-speaking people in Canada? You must have reasons for your point of view. Be prepared to defend your view in a class debate.

## RESEARCHING

1. The Union Nationale party was defeated in 1960 by the Liberal party of Jean Lesage. Using books in your library discover which political parties and leaders have controlled Quebec since Lesage's Liberals were defeated.

## GLOSSARY

**Bankrupt.** The state of being unable to pay debts and carry on business.

**Golden Age.** A time when everything seems to be perfect. A happy, prosperous period.

**Great Depression.** The period of very poor economic conditions during the 1930s.

**Minister of Education.** The cabinet member at the head of the Ministry of Education.

**Nationalist movement.** A movement directed at achieving independence for one's country. Its supporters have a great devotion to their nation.

**Patois.** A dialect or a local version of a language that differs from the accepted standard. By the 1960s the language in Quebec was said to be a patois—a mixture of French and English.

**Postwar prosperity.** A period of growth and excellent economic conditions following World War II.

**Social welfare programmes.** Government programmes such as pensions and welfare, that help individuals with certain problems.

**Special status.** A position that sets someone or something apart from others. It usually brings with it special treatment or powers.

**Subversive activities.** Actions that try to destroy or overthrow.

# 4/An angry Quebec: Terrorism, separatism, or biculturalism?

## Contents

### Introduction

In the last chapter, we saw that throughout much of the twentieth century Quebec went through a Quiet Revolution. During this time the province became more and more unhappy with its relationship to the rest of Canada. Because of the continual friction between anglophones and francophones, both groups were angry and frustrated.

This chapter examines three ways in which Canadians reacted to this conflict between Quebec and English Canada. We will look at the terrorist movement, the separatist movement, and the federal government's policy of bilingualism and biculturalism. The following questions will be explored:

1. **What is the FLQ and how has it affected French-English relations?**
2. **How did the separatist party, the Parti Québecois, become so powerful in Quebec?**
3. **What is the Canadian government doing to prevent the separation of Quebec?**

### Why is Quebec angry?

Examine Fig. 4-1 and you will see what Quebec discovered when it examined its position as compared to the rest of Canada. Captain Quebec sums up Quebeckers' feelings when he says "I'm angry and I'm not going to take it any more!" French-speaking Canadians in Quebec felt that there were serious problems in the partnership that Quebec had made with the rest of Canada at the time of Confederation. In Fig. 4-1, the Captain Quebec illustration, you will see some of their main complaints.

English-speaking Canadians felt that

The French-speaking Canadians are the workers and the English-speaking Canadians are the bosses. The French-speaking Canadians receive fewer promotions than the English-speaking Canadians do.

Infant mortality rates are 50% higher in Quebec than in the rest of Canada. This is due partly to poor health care.

French-speaking Canadians are paid less than English-speaking Canadians for doing the same job. The francophones have the same education and experience as the anglophones.

French-speaking Canadians make up 28% of Canada's population. The francophones are the largest minority group in Canada, but they are given no special status.

Decisions about Quebec's economy are made by the anglophones who own the companies.

Ninety percent of the people immigrating to Quebec are English-speaking.

I'm angry and I'm not going to take it any more!

Most companies owned by anglophones force employees to speak English.

Only 18% of federal government jobs are held by French-speaking Canadians. They should have 28% of the jobs because they make up 28% of the population. If French-speaking Canadians held 28% of the federal government jobs, there would be less unemployment in Quebec.

The unemployment rate is higher in Quebec than in the rest of Canada.

| 1971 | |
|---|---|
| Quebec — | 8.2% |
| Canada — | 5.8% |

The average income is lower in Quebec than in the rest of Canada.

| 1970 | |
|---|---|
| Quebec — | $2 794 |
| Canada — | $3 091 |

Fig. 4-1 Why Quebec is angry

Quebec's problems were not caused by faults in the province's partnership with Canada. Rather, they suggested that Quebec's traditionally rural way of life was to blame. Most French-speaking Canadians were trained to be farmers, doctors, or lawyers. They were not trained for jobs in business or in industry. Yet, Quebeckers had been warned about the dangers of staying with a strictly rural way of life. As early as the 1840s George Cartier had said that the people of French Canada must become involved in business. Most people did not listen, however.

We can see that francophone and anglophone Canadians did not agree about what was causing Quebec's problems. For example, studies showed that few French-speaking Canadians held top positions in Canada's business world. French-speaking Canadians were angry. Many concluded that this situation existed because the anglophones were refusing to promote the francophones. The anglophone business community saw the situation differently. Examine the Doug Wright cartoon and you will discover the English point of view on this problem.

A reaction to government action

IT SEEMS TO ME THAT, FOR YEARS AND YEARS, MANAGEMENT IN THIS COUNTRY HAS BEEN VERY AWARE OF CANADA'S FRENCH-SPEAKING POPULATION

A YOUNG FRENCH-CANADIAN WITH PROPER QUALIFICATIONS WAS ALWAYS WELCOMED WITH OPEN ARMS BY ANY ORGANIZATION DOING BUSINESS NATIONALLY

THE REASON THERE WERE SO FEW OF THEM WAS - THEY DIDN'T HAVE THE EDUCATION AND SO LACKED THE KNOW-HOW AND EXPERIENCE OF THE BETTER JOBS

BUT QUEBEC IS, AT LAST, UP-DATING ITS SCHOOLS AND SOON THERE WILL BE PLENTY OF YOUNG QUEBECERS WITH TECHNICAL EDUCATIONS

BUT POLITICIANS WON'T WAIT, THEY WANT THE VOTES **NOW**, AND POLITICAL PRESSURE CAN STAMPEDE PRIVATE INDUSTRY, CROWN CORPORATIONS AND GOVERNMENT DEPARTMENTS

I HATE TO SEE INDIVIDUALS PROMOTED BECAUSE OF THEIR LANGUAGE OR ETHNIC ORIGIN OR FOR ANY REASON EXCEPT PURE ABILITY! DOES THAT MAKE ME A BIGOT? —NO

DOUG WRIGHT

The Spectator-HAMILTON

Reprinted with permission of Doug Wright, *Spectator*, Hamilton

**READING BETTER**

1. **According to the cartoonist, is anglophone-owned business to blame for the problems some French Canadians had in getting jobs in anglophone-run businesses? Prove your point of view by quoting some lines from the cartoon.**
2. **According to the cartoon, why did many French-speaking Canadians fail to become bosses in companies owned by anglophones?**
3. **The cartoonist speaks of political pressure stampeding private industry. What does he mean by political pressure? What is it that the politicians want business to do?**
4. **Would the cartoonist agree with a policy that forced businesses to hire French-speaking Canadians as managers? Be sure to give information from the cartoon to back up your point of view.**

We see that the anglophones felt the francophones in Canada were to blame for their own problems. We should realize, however, that the anglophones tended to overlook certain facts. For example, French-speaking Canadians with the same education and experience were paid less than English-speaking Canadians. The francophones, on the other hand, seemed to ignore the part that their history played in producing a lower standard of living in Quebec. They blamed Quebec's partnership with English Canada for their problems.

It was difficult to decide who or what was to blame for the situation in Quebec. It was clear, however, that Quebec no longer wanted to accept what it felt was an inferior position. Lesage and other Quebec premiers such as Daniel Johnson and Jean Bertrand demanded special privileges. They wanted to raise Quebec's standard of living. English Canada refused to grant Quebec these special privileges. When this happened, some French-speaking Canadians became so frustrated that they wanted to separate from the rest of Canada and set up an independent nation. A small group of these separatists became so bitter that they were willing to kill to achieve their goal. These French-speaking Canadians are known as the FLQ (Front de Libération du Québec) **terrorists.**

The next section of the chapter, the story of Louis Penchon, will help you understand

313

the terrorists. The story also explains some of the reasons for which French-speaking Canadians have become separatists. As you read through the story keep these two questions in mind: Why did Penchon become a separatist? Why was he willing to kill to get what he wanted?

---

**Louis Penchon: The story of a terrorist**

PART I: UNEMPLOYED AND ANGRY

In January 1965, two men were standing beside large piles of boxes on the shipping dock of the Regis Paper Box Company in Montreal.

"Well Louis, I hate to tell you this but you didn't get the supervisor position. Stanley got it." Art Daniels was nervous. He could not look the younger man in the eyes.

The younger man was Louis Penchon. Louis was a tall, athletic young man. He had worked in the box factory since he was sixteen. Art Daniels, the night-shift supervisor, had taught him how to repair and set up the gluing machines. Two years ago, Louis had been placed in charge of the night-shift crew on the small gluing machine. A year ago he was placed in charge of the larger gluer on the day shift. The future looked bright for Louis Penchon. When an important position, supervisor of the day shift, became available, Louis applied for the job.

Now Louis looked down at his feet. They were covered with fine, pale yellow box dust and bits of broken cardboard.

"I don't understand it. Why didn't I get the job? That creep Stanley, he doesn't know the machines like I do. I know more about this factory, I know more about every part of the box-making operation. Why him and not me?"

"Well kid, it's like I told you before you applied. Mr. Stevenson likes the person in charge to speak English. He doesn't know French and you don't speak English well. The supervisor has to be able to speak French to the workers and English to the bosses," explained Daniels. He shifted nervously from one foot to the other.

Louis pushed past Daniels and ran up to the main offices on the second floor. He didn't wait to be admitted. Rather, he raced past the president's secretary and burst into Mr. Stevenson's office. Mr. Stevenson, a dignified-looking man with grey hair, was talking to a dark-haired woman. When Penchon rushed in, Mr. Stevenson looked up. In an irritated voice he asked, "What is the problem Penchon? Can't you see we're having a conference?"

Penchon stood silent. He could not think of the English words he wanted to say. He could feel his courage slipping away. Suddenly, he felt ashamed as he stood there in his old, soiled work clothes.

"Look, Penchon," said Mr. Stevenson, getting up and coming over to Louis, "I suppose you are upset because you didn't get the supervisor's job. I can understand that, but you have to see it from my point of view. Stanley is an anglophone. All the instructions that come into the factory are written in English. Your English is not as good as his. You may not understand the instructions that I give. Something could go wrong, and that costs money. I'm in business to make money, not to lose it."

Mr. Stevenson tried to usher Louis out of the office, but the young man pulled his arm away.

"I could learn English. I know more English than Stanley knows French," said Penchon in French.

"What did he say?" asked Stevenson. The dark-haired woman **translated** what Louis had said. The woman was now completely involved. She quickly translated back and forth for the entire conversation between Penchon and Stevenson.

"Maybe you could learn English, Penchon. But the job you applied for is open now, not in five years when you know English," said Stevenson.

"But it is not fair," protested Penchon. "I've worked here longer. I do a better job than Stanley and you gave him the job."

"That may be so, Penchon, but I don't want to have to bring a translator in here, like we are doing now, every time I want to talk to my supervisor. We have to do things quickly around here. We are here to make money. And time is money. I have not got the time to waste translating my instructions to you," said Mr. Stevenson, who was beginning to get angry.

"You don't need a translator, Mr. Stevenson. You need to learn the language of the majority of the people in this province. If you are clever enough to run this company, why can't you learn French? You've lived in Quebec all your life and you've never learned French. You expect the French to learn English if they want to talk to you. What makes you think that your language is more important than mine?" demanded Penchon.

Mr. Stevenson's eyes narrowed. He was very angry now and his words showed his anger. "Listen here, Penchon. Don't forget whom you are talking to. You French should be glad that there are English people around who have enough business sense to run a factory. Without us there would be no factories and you wouldn't have a job. It is my money that built this factory. My brains are keeping it going. No French labourer is going to tell me that I should learn French. Penchon, if you don't get out of here right now you are fired!"

Louis could not control himself. Before he realized what he was doing he punched Mr. Stevenson in the face.

1. Place the following list of events in the proper order as they would have happened in the life of Louis Penchon.
   a) He decides to leave school
   b) He punches Mr. Stevenson in the face
   c) He applies for a job at Regis Box Company
   d) He is told by Art Daniels that he did not get the job as supervisor
   e) He meets Stanley
2. Outline the reasons for which Mr. Stevenson did not give the job to Louis, and the reasons for which Louis felt he should get the job.

1. Give one reason why Louis Penchon would go to each of the following people and places on the day that he was fired.
   a) a lawyer   b) an employment agency
   c) his parents

1. Take a stand on the issue: "Should Louis Penchon have been given the job of supervisor in the box factory?" Be prepared to defend your point of view.

PART 2: LOUIS MAKES NEW FRIENDS

After Louis was fired, he walked around the city for hours. He was not aware of where he was going. He suddenly found himself near the university. The loud music and laughter of the students lured him into a nearby tavern. Finding a table in the corner, he tried to forget about his problems.

After a while, Louis realized that someone was watching him. Turning, he saw a young man sitting at the table next to him. He smiled at Louis and said, "You don't look too happy."

Louis gave a shrug. The young man, whose name was Marc Lefèbre, gave a sympathetic smile. He got up and went over to Louis's table.

Louis did not usually make friends easily. Somehow it seemed different with Marc. He seemed to have a way of gaining a person's confidence. Louis trusted him. Before long he had told Marc all about his problems at the factory.

"Quebeckers are a sad people. We are servants in our own home. We are the slaves of the anglophones. Wherever there is power it is in the hands of the anglophones," said Marc.

"You know, it's funny," replied Louis. "I've always felt that French-speaking Canadians as a group were getting a raw deal. But I never heard it expressed as well as you say it."

"Thank you," said Marc. "But Louis, you are not a French-speaking Canadian. You are a *Québecois*, a person of Quebec. Canada is for the English. Quebec is for the French. In Canada, there will always be Mr. Stevensons. But in a free Quebec, good Québecois like yourself will run the factories. Quebec has been in bondage to English Canada but the day is coming when we will be free. And I tell you, Louis, Jean Lesage does not have the answer. If we follow the politicians it will take a hundred years. I want Quebec to be free in my lifetime."

Louis nodded his agreement. "To freedom!" he shouted, raising his glass above his head. After talking a little more, Marc gave Louis a pamphlet. Louis gave Marc his address and they parted.

When Louis arrived home it was late. His father was asleep. Louis had no mother. She had left shortly after Louis was born. Louis took the pamphlet Marc had given him out of his pocket. It was entitled "French Canada has been cheated". Flopping down on his bed, Louis began to read. The first part of the pamphlet told how the English had cheated and abused French-speaking Canadians throughout history. The pamphlet ended with the following advice:

Be proud, French people of Quebec. We link the east to the west in Canada. We control the St. Lawrence. This waterway brings goods from the world to the centre of Canada and the United States. Quebec has a vast supply of natural resources. We have riches. We have money to buy the world's products. We have strong people who are willing to work. What more do we need? We should be free. We should have our own country.

Why should we give all this away to Canada? We should take power from Ottawa. We should have an independent Quebec, where the wealth will be shared by all Québecois. And if the English don't like it, they will die.

After he had finished reading, Louis sat thinking for a long time. He imagined kicking Mr. Stevenson out of the box factory and taking his place as president of the company. He imagined himself shooting Stevenson. He would be important if he killed Stevenson. He would be a hero. He would be like a mysterious spy in a movie. These thoughts made Louis feel good. He picked up the pamphlet and reread the article. He reread it until he knew almost every word by heart.

---

**READING BETTER**
1. How did Louis end up talking to Marc?
2. What is the pamphlet that Marc gave Louis about?
3. After reading the pamphlet, what does Louis want to do to Mr. Stevenson?

**USING YOUR KNOWLEDGE**
1. Would the author of the pamphlet "French Canada has been cheated" agree with the ideas of the following people? Be sure to give facts to back up your answers.
   a) Archbishop Taché
   b) Louis Riel
   c) Thomas Scott
   d) Henri Bourassa
   e) Robert Borden
   f) A.A. Dorion
2. Why was Louis influenced by Marc and the pamphlet?

---

PART 3: LOUIS JOINS THE FLQ

His hands pushed deeply into his jacket pockets, Louis Penchon walked briskly down the shabby street that ran along the river. At the bottom of a little hill was a dock and a house. He went to the house and knocked on the door. The door opened and a bright light blinded him.

317

"What do you want?" demanded a gruff voice. There was fear in the voice.

"Marc Lefèbre told me to meet him here about a job," Louis said. Louis could not see inside. The blinding light came from a flashlight the man was holding. In a moment Marc was at the door pulling him inside and introducing him to people.

"Sarah, this is Louis Penchon. He lost his job because he couldn't speak enough English. Pierre, this is Louis. He has been looking for work for three months." Marc conducted him around the room and introduced him to the twenty or so people that were there.

When his eyes became accustomed to the light Louis seated himself on a large cushion in the corner of the room. Meeting people was not something that Louis liked. He liked it even less tonight with Marc telling them all about his failure to find work. "They will all think I'm a real loser," he thought.

Oddly, though, these people did not seem to consider him a loser. It was as if his hard luck made him important in the eyes of this group. They all smiled at him. They shook his hand and clapped him on the back. Louis felt important. He liked that feeling.

"Because there are some new people here tonight, I want Jacques to tell his story," said Marc. "I think his story is really what our movement is all about. What Jacques has to say of himself and his family is what Quebec has to say of itself."

Jacques was a tall, slender man with a thin, pale face. He seemed nervous as he began to speak.

"Well, my story is like this. My father was a painter here in Montreal. Sometimes he would be out of work for a couple of months but he always got a job again sooner or later. We never had it easy, but we didn't starve either. There were four kids in our family. Three other kids died before they got to be a year old.

"When my father was in his mid-fifties he got laid off. He couldn't get any more work. I was the only one in the house who was working. I made $80 a week and I gave $55 to my parents so that the family could keep going."

"Didn't you get welfare or anything?" asked a girl.

"Sure," said Jacques. "My father got $145 from the welfare people each month. He went four years without a job. And he looked. He went out every day and looked but they wouldn't hire him. They said he was too old. After two years of this, my brother, who was only fourteen, left school. He got a job in the bakery with me, doing odd jobs."

Jacques stopped speaking. He looked as if he did not know what to say next.

"Tell them about the place where you lived," urged Marc.

"We had to move to this crummy apartment building. There were holes in the walls and cockroaches all over the place. I remember there were big chunks of plaster peeling off the walls. That place cost

318

us $58 a month. We couldn't afford to go anywhere else. The landlord, an anglophone, wouldn't fix anything. The place was a dump—broken windows and garbage in the halls.

"The apartment was heated by a wood stove. The pipes were rotten and the place was always filled with smoke. My mother had asthma. The smoke would fill up and she would wheeze. She coughed up this yellow mucus all the time. My father watched my mother slowly dying of the asthma. It was driving him crazy.

"We came home from work one night, my brother and I. They were all sitting in the living room. They were all crying. My father had borrowed a gun from the old guy down the hall. He just stuck the barrel in his mouth and pulled the trigger. I went into the room where he did it. The police and everybody were there. It was awful. I see that room all the time. I dream about it at night." Jacques stopped talking and covered his face with his hands. Nobody said anything. Louis felt panicky. He had a strong urge to jump up and run out of the place.

They all sat for a long time. No one said anything. Louis wondered what he was getting into with these people. Why were they here? Was he supposed to give money to Jacques, or what?

Finally Marc got up and passed out some sheets of paper that he had taken out of his briefcase. As he was doing this he said, "We have some new people with us here tonight. They don't know why they are here. They came in the hope of getting a job. But they are really here because they want justice for the Québecois.

Guy Bonnard, a short stocky man who had been leaning against the wall, began to speak. He paced back and forth, up and down the room. The more he talked, the louder he got. Louis liked him. He had power. He was respected by the group.

"That's right. We all are here because we want justice and freedom for Quebec. We are an oppressed people. The statistics tell the story. In Quebec in 1961 the English were the highest paid people in the province. On the average an English person's salary was $5 000 per year. Scandinavians made a few dollars less and then came the Dutch, the Jews and Germans, Poles and Asians. Down the line, third from the bottom, just ahead of the Italians and the Canadian Indians, came the French Canadians.

"We are servants in our own province. We are out of work like this man Penchon. Or we work at the worst jobs with the least pay. We make 38% less than the English. Why is that? Are we 38% inferior to the English? Is this not a lack of freedom we have in Quebec? Do we not have to struggle for our freedom?"

"Listen," said Louis who was getting excited, "what you say makes sense. But I don't see what we are supposed to do."

"Look at the sheet that Marc gave you," Guy answered. "Read it! Read it and you will see what you are here for."

Louis read the sheet, that was entitled "Notice to the population of the state of Quebec".

**Notice to the population of the state of Quebec**

The Front de Libération du Québec, the FLQ, is a revolutionary movement of volunteers who are ready to die for the independence of Quebec.

The suicide-commandos of the FLQ have as their mission the complete destruction by **sabotage** of:

a) All buildings and operations of the federal government, the RCMP, and the Canadian Armed Forces.
b) All the English-language newspapers in Quebec.
c) All businesses that discriminate against French-speaking workers; all businesses that do not use French as the main language of daily operation; all businesses that advertise in English.
d) Anyone who works with or helps the anglophones in Quebec.

All members of the FLQ have Republic of Quebec identification cards which they carry when they are committing acts of sabotage. They are engaged in a war, so the wounded should be treated as prisoners of war. Treat the members as soldiers according to the Geneva Convention on the rules of war.

"Have you finished reading, Penchon?" asked Bonnard. "Will you join in our fight for the liberation of Quebec? Or will you just sit back like Quebeckers have done for years and take it?"

Louis's eyes were wide with excitement. He felt important. These revolutionaries had picked him. But should he join? He could end up in jail or dead. Louis was confused.

**READING BETTER**
1. Why do you think that Marc held the meeting in an isolated place?
2. Explain in your own words why the father of Jacques killed himself.
3. Why would Marc want Jacques to tell this story of his family?

**ORGANIZING BETTER**
1. Make a list of the people and businesses that the FLQ are going to sabotage.

**USING YOUR KNOWLEDGE**
1. If you had been invited to this meeting what three questions would you have asked of the FLQ before joining the group? Your questions should lead you to a better understanding of what the FLQ was after, and what it intended to do.
2. Try to predict whether or not Louis will join the FLQ. Look carefully at his character and background, and also at the type of people at the meeting before you make your prediction. Explain the reasons for your prediction.

PART 4: THE LIFE OF A TERRORIST

In the weeks and months that followed the first meeting, Louis got together with Marc many times. They talked for hours about the problems of Quebec. Marc gave Louis books and articles to read. Slowly, Louis became convinced that he had to become a member of the FLQ. Marc told him that the FLQ was divided up into cells, or small groups. Each group was given a special job to do. Some groups or cells collected information. Some cells wrote and distributed **propaganda.** Marc told Louis that the leaders of the movement felt that Louis was best suited to an **activist cell.** Louis liked that idea. The activist cells were the most glamorous. He would be carrying out acts of sabotage. It was like being a movie star. Louis began to think of himself as a man of action. He felt very important.

Louis started to attend the meetings of cell 21, "Bluebird" cell. In a short time, he learned how the cell operated. Bluebird was an activist cell that carried out raids and bombings. Every member had a code name. Louis's code name was "Box". The members of Bluebird never contacted other cells. Therefore if Bluebird members were captured by police they would know very little about the entire FLQ operation.

Throughout the winter of 1965, Bluebird planned a bank robbery. The cell needed money to run its terrorist operations. The easiest way to get money was to steal it. When Louis learned what they were planning he felt excited. He felt daring, brave. "People will learn to fear the Box," he thought to himself.

In the spring of 1966, Bluebird carried out its plans. First the members broke into an army warehouse and stole several machine guns. They raided a construction site and stole two cases of dynamite. Then they pulled up to the main branch of the Bank of Montreal in Drummondville. Louis was the first one out of the car. He wore a stocking over his face. Firing a round with his machine gun, he yelled that the people must clear the streets. He strutted up and down in front of the bank. If anyone tried to approach he fired off a round in the air. The other members of Bluebird entered the bank and stole $23 000. Louis yelled out, "Beware the wrath of the Box!"

When he was not working with Bluebird, Louis would stay in his room. In front of the mirror he practised telling people what to do. He liked to pretend he was gunning down Stevenson, his former boss. He went over the words he would say to Stevenson. He would spit in his face and slap him around. He acted it all out in front of the mirror. It made him feel powerful. He was a man to be feared.

In the summer of 1966, there was a strike at a Montreal shoe factory. Marc called Bluebird cell into action. They were to set a bomb off at the factory. Marc hoped this action would draw the company's attention to the workers' demands. Marc and other cell leaders believed that if the FLQ helped the workers, then the workers would support the FLQ.

Marc sent Louis to the factory to see how Bluebird could get the bomb into the factory. When Louis arrived there were a large number of strikers marching around in front of the building. He stood across the street from the factory for several hours watching everything that went on. He watched every person who went in and out of the factory.

One man in particular interested Louis. The man went into the factory carrying a number of shoe boxes and came out empty-handed

**FLQ bomb explodes. How would the people in this picture feel?**

several minutes later. Louis went across the street and struck up a conversation with one of the strikers. After talking for a while Louis found out that the man with the shoe boxes was returning rejects from local stores in Montreal. That was it! He could put the bomb in one of the shoe boxes. Then, dressed like the man making the deliveries, he could take it into the factory.

Louis returned to Bluebird headquarters. He explained the plan to the members of his cell. Most of them liked it, but Marc had one concern.

"Where do you put the boxes when you take them into the office?" he asked.

"The delivery man just took the boxes in and set them on the floor against the wall," answered Louis.

"Well, what about the secretary? She will be in the room. She could be killed," said Marc.

Louis looked at him for a moment. Then he looked around at the other members of the cell. "Sounds like you are getting soft," he said. "What do we care about the secretary? She can be sacrificed for the good of Quebec, can't she? If she were any good she wouldn't work for that English company!" He looked around at the others. They didn't say anything. They looked at Marc.

"What are you looking at him for?" shouted Louis. "The Box is the only one with guts. In every revolution people have to die. That lady will die in the war to free Quebec. Are we terrorists or babies? Are you afraid of a little blood?"

Marc said nothing and the plan was accepted.

On August 18, 1966, Louis Penchon arrived in front of the shoe factory in a blue pickup truck. He was wearing a uniform identical to the one worn by the other man delivering boxes. Carrying an armful of shoe boxes he got out of the truck and went into the front office of the factory.

"Oh, you must be new. Just put them over here by my desk," said the secretary with a smile. Louis said nothing. He placed the boxes on the floor. A tiny wire jiggled as the boxes hit the floor. The wire snapped. Eight sticks of dynamite exploded. The blast caught Louis Penchon in the chest.

The day after Louis's remains were buried, Marc went looking for a replacement.

---

**READING BETTER**

1. List the three types of terrorist cells in the FLQ. What was the purpose of each type of cell?
2. To what type of cell did Louis Penchon belong?
3. What was the name of Louis's cell and what was his code name?
4. Why did the Bluebird members have code names?
5. How did Louis die?

**USING YOUR KNOWLEDGE**

1. You are a police investigator. You have captured Louis Penchon before he is killed. You want to ask Louis questions about his activities. You also want to uncover information that will lead to the destruction of the FLQ. Write a short dialogue (one page) of the conversation that would take place.

**TAKING A STAND**

1. Which of the following explanations do you feel is closest to the truth? Be sure that you have facts to back up your point of view.
   a) Louis Penchon is a poor young man who suffered because he was a French-speaking Canadian. He has been treated very badly. Everything that he has done is justified. French-speaking Canadians have been ill-treated for a long time. The only way that they can protect themselves against the Stevensons of this world is to become terrorists.
   b) Louis Penchon is a fool. He is insecure. He has had a few rough breaks but so have a lot of other people. He just likes feeling important. He really likes pushing people around. He doesn't care about anybody except himself.
   c) Louis Penchon is a victim of a terrorist named Marc. Marc talked him into becoming a terrorist. He taught Louis to be evil. Louis was a very nice person. He just started to hang around with the wrong kind of people. They convinced him that you have to be tough to survive. This turned Louis into a mean person.

History of the Front de Libération du Québec— FLQ

Louis Penchon is a fictional character but the terrorists of the FLQ were very real people. They operated actively in Quebec from 1960 until 1970. During these years the FLQ plotted a violent revolution to take over the government of Quebec. The terrorists bombed and kidnapped. In the end they failed. The following time line gives you a brief history of the group.

## Ten years of terror—A time line

|  |  |  |
|---|---|---|
| | 1960 | The FLQ movement is founded by George Shoeters, a 33-year-old student at the University of Montreal. The group wants Quebec to separate from the rest of Canada. At first, it hopes to achieve separation peacefully by forming a separatist party and winning an election. |
| March | 1963 | The FLQ feels that it will take too long to achieve its goals if it waits for an election. The group decides to adopt terrorist tactics. It begins to bomb armories, RCMP stations, CNR stations, and federal government buildings. It tries to show the rest of Canada that it wants the federal government to abandon its control of Quebec. |
| April | 1963 | Wilfred Owen, a 65-year-old watchman, is killed when a bomb goes off in an alley behind an army recruiting centre. Owen was emptying the garbage when the bomb went off in the trash cans. All Quebec's leaders condemn the FLQ and its terrorist tactics. |
| May | 1963 | The FLQ begins to plant bombs in mailboxes in the rich English suburb of Westmount, in Montreal. The provincial government offers a $50 000 reward to anyone catching members of the FLQ. |
| June | 1963 | Police get information that leads to arrests of FLQ members. Many of the leaders are captured. The police discover large amounts of ammunition, guns, and explosives at a cottage north of Montreal. Canada begins to fear a Quebec revolution. |
| Late early | 1963- 1964 | The FLQ recovers. It recruits new members from discontented young people in Quebec. It puts out an underground paper called *The Hatchet.* The movement is greatly influenced by Communists. The leaders of the FLQ visit Cuba to learn effective guerrilla warfare tactics. Such tactics were used by Fidel Castro when he carried out his Communist revolution on the island of Cuba in 1959. |
| | 1965-1966 | The Communist cell system of organization is set up and operating. The FLQ robs banks to get money. It raids armories to get guns. It bombs private companies that are having labour problems with their workers in order to gain the support of the workers. |
| Summer | 1966- 1967 | Pierre Vallières, an FLQ leader, is arrested while conducting a hunger strike in front of the United Nations building in New York City. He is charged, along with other FLQ members, with the murder of Thérèse Morin. This woman died when a bomb exploded at the shoe company in which she worked. FLQ leaders are tried and jailed. |
| | 1967-1969 | The FLQ needs time to recover from the loss of its leaders who were put in prison. The group reorganizes. By 1969 it is again active. It sets off bombs in the Montreal Stock Exchange. |

6

**October Crisis, 1970. The government calls out the army.**

| | | |
|---|---|---|
| June | 1970 | In the provincial election the Parti Québecois of René Lévesque wins 23% of the vote. The FLQ is not satisfied. It develops a new tactic which it hopes will force Canada to allow Quebec to set up a separate country. It decides to kidnap leading politicians. |
| October | 1970 | With great swiftness the FLQ strikes. Terrorists kidnap James Cross, the British Trade Commissioner, and later, Pierre Laporte, the Quebec Labour Minister. They kill Laporte, and release James Cross. Kidnappers of Cross are allowed to fly to Cuba for protection. Some people are arrested in connection with the Laporte case. |
| December | 1978 | Some of the kidnappers of James Cross decide to return to Canada from European exile. This means they must stand trial for kidnapping and extortion. |
| The future | | We cannot be sure that the FLQ is dead. If René Lévesque and the Parti Québecois fail to separate Quebec from the rest of Canada, the bombings and kidnappings may begin again. |

## READING BETTER

1. In some years the FLQ seemed very active, but in others it did very little. Two years in particular were active ones for the FLQ. What years were these? Why do you think the FLQ was so active during these periods?

## ORGANIZING BETTER

1. Take a page in your notebook and write "Ten years of terror" at the top of the page. Down the left-hand side of the page draw a straight line. This will be your time line. At intervals of about 5 cm (three or four lines in your notebook) put in the following dates: 1960, 1963, 1964, 1965-66, 1966-67, 1967-69, and 1970. Opposite each one of these dates write in the main events concerning the FLQ that happened in that time period. When you have finished you will have a history of the FLQ movement in your notebook.

## USING YOUR KNOWLEDGE

1. An editorial in a newspaper is the editor's point of view on some topic that is in the news. Different papers express different points of view on the same events. For example, a paper in Alberta, a province rich in oil, may suggest in an editorial that Canada raise the price of oil. On the other hand a newspaper in Nova Scotia, a province that must import all its oil, may say that it is unwise to increase the price of oil. In editorials, the writers give arguments to show why their points of view are correct. They give facts to back up their points of view.

On May 5, 1966, the FLQ left a bomb in a shoe box at La Grenade shoe factory. The FLQ phoned the factory and warned them that a bomb would go off. The manager of the company ignored the call because he had received similar calls before and nothing had happened. The bomb went off and Thérèse Morin, a secretary in the office, was killed.

You will write two editorials of one paragraph each. The first editorial will be from *The Hatchet*, the FLQ newspaper. The second will be from an English-language newspaper in Montreal. The editorials should show that these two papers have different points of view on this incident.

## What are terrorists really like?

What are terrorists really like? What do they think of themselves? Why are they willing to kill? What type of backgrounds do they have? When doctors talked to terrorists who were captured in Quebec, they discovered that most terrorists have similar characteristics. Fig. 4-2 outlines the characteristics of a typical terrorist. Do you know anyone who is like the terrorist described in this diagram?

## ORGANIZING BETTER

1. In Fig. 4-2, three of the characteristics of a typical terrorist deal with what the person's background is like. One deals with an ability, and six characteristics are related to the terrorist's personality. Make a chart in your notebook. Put down these three headings: background, ability, and personality. Enter each of the characteristics of a terrorist in the proper column.

## USING YOUR KNOWLEDGE

1. Read over the six characteristics of the terrorist's personality. In a short letter to a friend explain why you like or dislike a person who has a terrorist's personality.

## René Lévesque and the separatist movement

In the early 1960s, there were several small separatist political parties in Quebec. They were unable to gain any support in provincial elections. In the late 1960s, René Lévesque left the Liberal party of Jean Lesage. He joined all the separatist parties together to form the Parti Québecois. As leader, Lévesque began to organize the party throughout Quebec. In its first election in 1970, Lévesque's party won 23% of the vote. In 1973 the percentage of the vote increased to 30%. In November 1976, the Parti Québecois won the election in Quebec and René Lévesque became premier of the province.

The members of the Parti Québecois believe in an independent Quebec. These separatists do not want to use violence to obtain independence. They want to gain power and support in Quebec. Then they

**Fig. 4-2 What are terrorists really like?**

intend to negotiate Quebec's independence with the federal government of Canada.

Why the separatists won the 1976 election
There has always been separatist sentiment in Quebec. At the time of Confederation, A.A. Dorion and his followers did not want Canada East to join with the other colonies to form Canada. They were, in effect, separatists. After the Riel execution in 1885, Premier Mercier of Quebec began to question whether union with the rest of Canada was a good idea for French Canada. After the Conscription Crisis in

327

**1** Are we masters in our own house when Ottawa controls all the laws dealing with newspapers, radio, and television?

**2** Are we masters in our own house when Ottawa controls immigration? Should Ottawa be free to allow as many English-speaking people into Quebec as it wants?

**3** Are we masters in our own house when Ottawa appoints the judges who decide on laws made in Quebec?

**4** Are we masters in our own house when Ottawa makes laws that affect business and the whole economy of Quebec?

**I say that we are not masters in our own house until Quebec has separated from the rest of Canada. That is why I am a separatist.**

**Fig. 4-3 René Lévesque: Why I am a separatist**

1917, many French-speaking Canadians felt they would be better off on their own.

In the 1960s it became clear that French Canada wanted a greater share of Canada's wealth. It wanted to be sure that the French Canadian way of life would be preserved. Jean Lesage and the Liberal party tried to achieve these goals by negotiating with Ottawa. However, English Canada rejected Quebec's demands for "special status". Many French-speaking Canadians began to look for other ways of achieving their goals.

One of the most popular suggestions was the idea that Quebec should separate from the rest of Canada. In 1968, Lévesque brought the people who supported the idea of separatism together and formed the Parti Québecois. In the party's first two elections its strength was increased. The party did not, however, come close to victory. Then

in 1976, three factors combined to produce a Parti Québecois victory.

The first factor was René Lévesque himself. Lévesque is a clever man. He is a brilliant politician and a hard worker. He is very determined. To a large extent, his ability as party leader and his personal popularity accounted for the 1976 election success. The second factor in the Parti Québecois victory was the lack of popularity of Robert Bourassa's Liberal government. The vast majority of Quebeckers, both French-speaking and English-speaking, felt that Bourassa and his government had done a poor job of running the province. The third and final factor was the Parti Québecois strategy of downplaying the separatism issue. During the campaign Lévesque and the other Parti Québecois candidates seldom mentioned

# FRENCH DISAPPEARS

| **1** | **2** | **3** |
|---|---|---|
| About 90% of the people immigrating to Quebec have not been French-speaking. Therefore, as time goes on, more and more people in Quebec will be English-speaking. | The birthrate in Quebec is the lowest of any province in Canada. Therefore, in the future few children will be raised in French. | Most businesses in Quebec demand that the workers use English. Many French-speaking Canadians want their children to learn English so they can get good jobs. |

**Fig. 4-4 Why Quebeckers feared that the French language was disappearing**

separatism. They stressed the need for more efficient, honest government. They suggested that the separatism issue would be dealt with at a later time in a provincial **referendum.** As a result, the voters of Quebec elected a Parti Québecois government on November 16, 1976.

The separatists in power
This section of the chapter will help us understand an important policy of the Parti Québecois government. We will examine the following questions:
1. Why are the separatists so concerned about the French language?
2. What is the Charter of the French Language? Why was it created?

*Bill 101, the Charter of the French Language*
You will remember from the Captain Quebec diagram (Fig. 4-1) that Quebeckers feared that the French language was disappearing. There were three reasons for this fear. These reasons are shown in Fig. 4-4.

READING BETTER
1. Why is it possible that in the future there may be very few people in Quebec who speak French?

USING YOUR KNOWLEDGE
1. **You are a French-speaking Canadian, and you want to be sure that French does not disappear as the main language spoken in Quebec. What policy would you ask the government to adopt?**

The Parti Québecois government shared this concern. If the French language disappeared then the entire French way of life could soon disappear. What could the government do?

The government's answer to the problem was Bill 101. This bill was passed in August 1977. It is called "The Charter of the French Language". Bill 101 has four main points.
1. French is the official language of the province of Quebec.
2. All business of the Quebec government and courts will be carried on in French.
3. The people of Quebec have a right to:
   a) speak French at work

b) be waited on in French in stores

c) be taught in French at school

4. All children must be taught in French. To help the English-speaking minority who live in Quebec, Bill 101 made the following exceptions.

A child may be educated in English:

a) If one parent was educated at an English school in Quebec.

b) If one parent went to an English school anywhere, and the parent was living in Quebec before August, 1977.

c) If the child's older brothers or sisters went to English schools.

## ORGANIZING BETTER

1. Put the heading "Bill 101: The Charter of the French Language" in your notebook.
2. List the four main points of the charter.
3. List the three exceptions to the last point.

## USING YOUR KNOWLEDGE

1. According to Bill 101 which of the following would not be allowed to happen?
   a) Mr. Stevenson of the Regis Paper Box Company demands that all supervisors speak English.
   b) Mr. Stevenson is forced to learn French.
   c) Mr. Stevenson attended Dorval High School, which is an English school. He wants to send his son to Dorval High School, but the government says he has to send his child to a French school.
   d) Joe Rizzo's youngest son is ready to go to school. His brother has attended a St. Leonard English school. The government tells Mr. Rizzo that his son must go to a French school because Mr. Rizzo was not educated in an English school.
   e) Joe Rizzo goes to the corner store to buy milk. He asks for milk in English and the clerk refuses to serve him. The clerk says that he must speak French.
   f) Pierre LeBlanc goes to Mrs. Jones's insurance company in Montreal. Mrs. Jones invites him into her office. When she starts to tell him about insurance, he demands that she speak French. The government informs Mrs. Jones that she must learn French or hire a French-speaking salesperson.

2. The Parti Québecois passed Bill 101 because it felt that French must become the common language of all Quebeckers. The party did, however, want to respect the language rights of minorities in Quebec. How does Bill 101 show the party's interest in preserving the rights of the English-speaking minority?

Reprinted with permission of Blaine, *Spectator*, Hamilton

**The champions: Trudeau and Lévesque**

## READING BETTER

1. Who is the man on the motorcycle?
2. Who is the man in the sidecar?
3. Why does the man in the sidecar have such a sly look on his face?
4. This is a political cartoon. Political cartoons attack or defend people or points of view. They do this with symbols. Each object in the cartoon represents something in real life. Match up the following real-life political situations with the symbols in the cartoons.
   a) The nation of Canada
   b) The prime minister running the country
   c) The province of Quebec
   d) The desire of the Parti Québecois to separate from the rest of Canada
   e) The referendum in Quebec

Symbols
   a) The wrench
   b) Trudeau riding the motorcycle

c) **The sidecar**
d) **The motorcycle**
e) **The sidecar going off on its own**

5. **What is the main idea that the cartoonist is trying to present?**

We know that Quebeckers felt that they were not getting a fair deal in Confederation. They were also afraid that their language and culture were disappearing. René Lévesque and the Parti Québecois had ideas on how to solve the problems. Once in power, the party passed Bill 101. This was, as we learned, designed to preserve the French language. The Parti Québecois also supported the idea of separatism. It felt that many of Quebec's problems could perhaps be solved if the province were independent.

Many Canadians disagreed with this policy. They wanted to see Quebec remain a part of Canada. One such person was Pierre Trudeau. He did not feel that separatism was the answer to the problems between Quebec and the rest of Canada. Rather, Trudeau suggested a national policy of bilingualism and biculturalism as a possible solution.

Trudeau and the Liberals won the federal election of 1968. In the years that followed, they had a chance to put their policy into effect. The following sections examine Trudeau's policy of bilingualism and biculturalism.

### Trudeau and a bilingual, bicultural Canada

As soon as Trudeau became prime minister, he and his liberal government tried to improve French-English relations. The best way to do this, thought Trudeau, was to follow the suggestions of the Royal Commission on Bilingualism and Biculturalism.

The "Bi and Bi" Commission was set up by the government of Lester B. Pearson in July, 1963. Its purpose was to study problems in French-English relations. The commission reported that Canadian unity was in serious danger. If Canada were to survive, francophones and anglophones would have to learn to co-operate. To promote this co-operation, the commission made a number of suggestions about what Canadians should do.

Trudeau made Canadians aware of the two main suggestions of the commission. These suggestions are shown in Fig. 4-5.

---

**Suggestion 1**

The English-speaking people of Canada must accept the French-speaking people as their equals. They must accept the fact that Canada is a bilingual and a bicultural country. The Canadian people must accept the fact that Canada has two founding peoples, the French and the English.

**Suggestion 2**

The francophones of Quebec must forget about past injustices. They must stop blaming English Canada for all Quebec's problems. French-speaking Canadians have to start thinking about what is best for all of Canada. They can no longer think only of what is best for Quebec.

---

**Fig. 4-5  Suggestions of the Bi & Bi Commission**

1. In what ways have English-speaking people not accepted French Canadians as true equals?
2. In what ways have the French-speaking Canadians blamed English Canada for the problems of Quebec?
3. What past injustices do the French Canadians have to forget?
4. Which of the people below would make the following statements about Trudeau's ideas on bilingualism and biculturalism?

   People
   1. A member of the FLQ
   2. Jean Lesage
   3. Bobby Jones's aunt in Manitoba

   Statements
   1. I can't see why he says that we are bilingual. There are more than two language groups in Canada. I think English is the main language and all the rest are not important.
   2. Forget the past? That is impossible! I will not forget what the English have done to us. I will seek justice for French Canadians, even if it means destroying the English completely.
   3. This is a good start. But Trudeau must go farther. He must give more power to Quebec. Quebeckers must have more control of what happens in Quebec.

*Trudeau and the Official Languages Act*
Trudeau was convinced that Canadians must accept the idea that Canada is a bilingual, bicultural country. To make sure that Canadians did accept this idea, his government passed the Official Languages Act, 1969. The act has four main points.

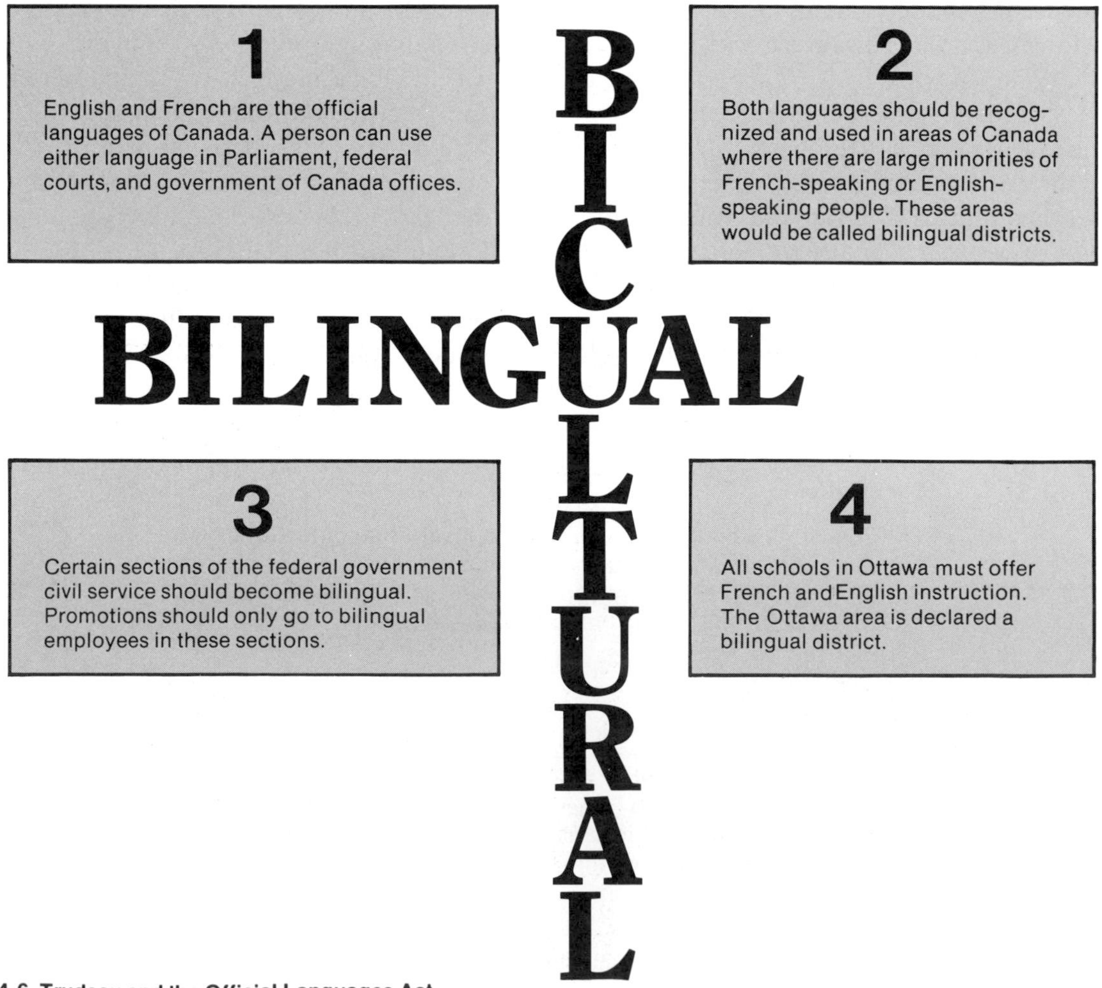

**1**
English and French are the official languages of Canada. A person can use either language in Parliament, federal courts, and government of Canada offices.

**2**
Both languages should be recognized and used in areas of Canada where there are large minorities of French-speaking or English-speaking people. These areas would be called bilingual districts.

**3**
Certain sections of the federal government civil service should become bilingual. Promotions should only go to bilingual employees in these sections.

**4**
All schools in Ottawa must offer French and English instruction. The Ottawa area is declared a bilingual district.

BICULTURAL BILINGUAL

Fig. 4-6 Trudeau and the Official Languages Act

332

1. Which of the following will result from the Official Languages Act?
   a) Chinese people will no longer be able to speak Chinese in Canada.
   b) A French-speaking Canadian will be able to get an income tax form in French.
   c) English-speaking Canadians will have to use tax forms that are written in French.
   d) French-speaking Canadians living in Ottawa will not have the right to send their children to a French school.
   e) A brilliant military leader who is working for the Department of Defence (civil service) will not get a promotion unless he or she can speak French and English.
   f) Bilingual traffic signs will appear in sections of Canada where there are large French-speaking minorities.
2. The governments of various provinces in Canada have complained that Trudeau's bilingualism policies cost a great deal of money. List five ways that the Trudeau policy would force the provinces to spend money.
3. Try to find out how many French-speaking people live in your area.

TAKING A STAND

1. Do you think that Canada should be considered a bilingual-bicultural country?

Trudeau and more bilingualism

Many Canadians refused to accept the idea that Canada was a bilingual and bicultural country. Trudeau did not give up. He faced heavy opposition, but he was willing to work hard to convince Canadians of his bilingualism policy. The government is still trying to persuade Canadians that the ideas shown in Fig. 4-7 must also be accepted.

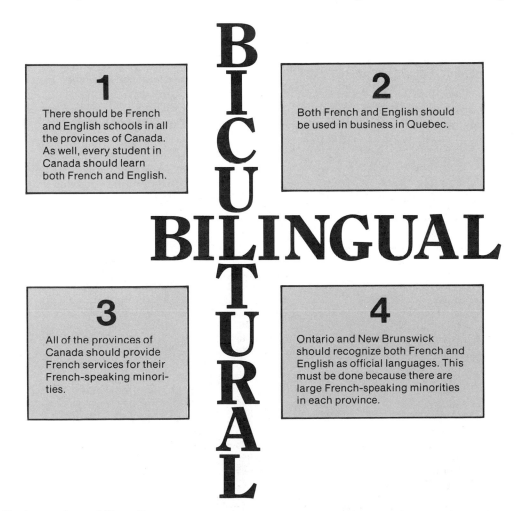

**BICULTURAL / BILINGUAL**

**1** There should be French and English schools in all the provinces of Canada. As well, every student in Canada should learn both French and English.

**2** Both French and English should be used in business in Quebec.

**3** All of the provinces of Canada should provide French services for their French-speaking minorities.

**4** Ontario and New Brunswick should recognize both French and English as official languages. This must be done because there are large French-speaking minorities in each province.

Fig. 4-7 Trudeau and more bilingualism

It is still not clear whether or not Canadians will accept the idea of a bilingual and bicultural Canada. The government's bilingualism programme has cost a great deal of money. Some experts estimate the cost to be over $700 million. Many Canadians support the policy. Others feel that the policy is too pro-French and that French is being forced on them. Will most Canadians come to accept the policy of bilingualism and biculturalism? What does the future hold?

**The future: Will Canada accept bilingualism?**

Will French-English relations get better or worse? No one can tell what the future holds. One thing is certain, however. If Canadians from all over the country do not believe that Canada is a bilingual and bicultural country, then French-speaking Canadians will be discontented.

What do you predict will happen? Will the government's bilingualism policies succeed in making Canada a truly bilingual and bicultural country? Read the following material and see if you are better able to answer this question.

French-speaking Canadians outside Quebec
There are over 5 800 000 French-speaking people living in Canada. Of these people, more than 4 800 000 live in Quebec. This means that there are another million French-speaking Canadians spread out across the other provinces. The separatists of Quebec must realize that if they separate from Canada, there will still be a large number of French-speaking people left in the country. If separation does take place, Canadians may be upset at the French. Canadians may not be willing to put money and effort into bilingual programmes for the remaining French-speaking people in the country.

Examine Fig. 4-8. It shows the numbers of people from English, French, and other language groups living in each province.

**READING BETTER**

1. Besides Quebec, which province has the greatest number of French-speaking Canadians?
2. Are there more French-speaking Canadians in Canada than there are members of other minority groups?
3. Which province has the least number of French-speaking Canadians?

**USING YOUR KNOWLEDGE**

1. Using these figures can you explain why the federal government suggested that Ontario and New Brunswick should recognize two official languages?

| Canada and province | Population | English Number | French Number | Other Number | Not stated Number |
|---|---|---|---|---|---|
| CANADA | 22 992 600 | 14 122 170 | 5 887 205 | 2 537 615 | 445 020 |
| Newfoundland | 557 725 | 545 340 | 2 760 | 3 965 | 5 665 |
| Prince Edward Island | 118 230 | 109 745 | 6 545 | 935 | 1 005 |
| Nova Scotia | 828 570 | 768 070 | 36 870 | 13 625 | 10 010 |
| New Brunswick | 677 250 | 435 975 | 223 780 | 6 925 | 10 565 |
| Quebec | 6 234 445 | 800 680 | 4 989 245 | 334 055 | 110 470 |
| Ontario | 8 264 465 | 6 457 645 | 462 070 | 1 178 670 | 166 080 |
| Manitoba | 1 021 510 | 727 240 | 54 745 | 218 875 | 20 645 |
| Saskatchewan | 921 325 | 715 685 | 26 710 | 163 935 | 14 995 |
| Alberta | 1 838 040 | 1 482 725 | 44 440 | 272 395 | 38 480 |
| British Columbia | 2 466 610 | 2 037 645 | 38 430 | 325 610 | 64 930 |
| Yukon | 21 840 | 18 940 | 525 | 1 630 | 745 |
| Northwest Territories | 42 610 | 23 085 | 1 095 | 16 995 | 1 435 |

Note: Calculations based on rounded data.
Source: *1976 Canada Census*. Reproduced with permission of the Minister of Supply and Services Canada
**Fig. 4-8 Distribution of language groups in Canada**

Canada is made up of a large number of ethnic groups. The government's policy of bilingualism assumes that Canadians will accept the idea that Canada has two founding peoples. Study the following statistics and decide whether or not you think that Canadians will accept the policy.

| Ethnic group | 1921 | 1941 | 1961 | 1971 |
|---|---|---|---|---|
| Black | 18 291 | 22 174 | 32 127 | 34 445 |
| British Isles | 4 868 738 | 5 715 904 | 7 996 669 | 9 624 115 |
| English | 2 545 358 | 2 968 402 | 4 195 175 | |
| Irish | 1 107 803 | 1 267 702 | 1 753 351 | |
| Scottish | 1 173 625 | 1 403 974 | 1 902 302 | |
| Other | 41 952 | 75 826 | 145 841 | |
| French | 2 452 743 | 3 483 038 | 5 540 346 | 6 180 120 |
| Austrian, n.o.s. | 107 671 | 37 715 | 106 535 | 42 120 |
| Belgian | 20 234 | 29 711 | 61 382 | 51 135 |
| Chinese | 39 587 | 34 627 | 58 197 | 118 815 |
| Czech and Slovak | 8 840 | 42 912 | 73 061 | 81 870 |
| Finnish* | 21 494 | 41 683 | 59 436 | 59 215 |
| German | 294 635 | 464 682 | 1 049 599 | 1 317 200 |
| Greek | 5 740 | 11 692 | 56 475 | 124 475 |
| Hungarian | 13 181 | 54 582 | 126 220 | 131 890 |
| Indian and Inuit | 113 724 | 125 521** | 220 121 | 312 760 |
| Italian | 66 769 | 112 625 | 450 351 | 730 820 |
| Japanese | 15 868 | 23 149 | 29 157 | 37 260 |
| Jewish | 126 196 | 170 241 | 173 344 | 296 945 |
| Lithuanian | 1 970 | 7 789 | 27 629 | 24 535 |
| Netherlander | 117 505 | 212 863 | 429 679 | 425 945 |
| Polish | 53 403 | 167 485 | 323 517 | 316 430 |
| Romanian | 13 470 | 24 689 | 43 805 | 27 375 |
| Russian | 100 064 | 83 708 | 119 168 | 64 475 |
| Scandinavian | 167 359 | 244 603 | 386 534 | 384 795 |
| Danish | 21 124 | 37 439 | 85 473 | 75 725 |
| Icelandic | 15 876 | 21 050 | 30 623 | 27 905 |
| Norwegian | 68 856 | 100 718 | 148 681 | 179 290 |
| Swedish | 61 503 | 85 396 | 121 757 | 101 870 |
| Ukrainian | 106 721 | 305 929 | 473 337 | 580 660 |
| Yugoslav | 3 906 | 21 214 | 68 587 | 104 955 |
| Other European | 17 945 | 9 787 | 88 190 | 194 850 |
| Other Asian | 10 459 | 16 288 | 34 399 | 129 460 |
| Other and unknown | 21 436 | 42 028 | 210 382 | 171 645 |
| Total*** | 8 787 949 | 11 506 655 | 18 238 247 | 21 568 310 |

*Includes Estonian prior to 1951
**Excludes persons of mixed Indian and other parentage
***Excludes Newfoundland prior to 1951
n.o.s. Not otherwise specified

Source: Censuses of Canada

**Fig. 4-9    Population by ethnic group, Canada 1921-1971**

**READING BETTER**
1. **Which were the five largest ethnic groups in Canada in 1971?**
2. **Since 1921 has Canada become more British or more French?**
3. **Which ethnic group has increased the most numerically since 1921?**
4. **Which ethnic group has the greatest percentage increase in its population?**

**TAKING A STAND**
1. **Do you think Canadians will accept the bilingual, bicultural policy as expressed in the Official Languages Act (1969)? What evidence can you use to support your view?**

Reprinted with permission of M.R. Tingley

## USING YOUR KNOWLEDGE

1. **A cartoon is often a very good way to criticize a government policy. It is also a good way to support a policy. Is the cartoonist in favour of or against the policy of bilingualism?**

### Areas of large French-speaking Canadian population in the Maritimes

Since the time of the first settlements in the Maritimes, people of French origin have lived in the Atlantic provinces. Today, the descendants of the early French-speaking settlers live mostly in the northern and eastern parts of New Brunswick, on the western tip of Prince Edward Island, and in the northern and southern parts of Nova Scotia. A small number live in Newfoundland. French-speaking Canadians are a minority in all four provinces. They make up almost 33% of New Brunswick's population, but only 5% of PEI's population, 4% of Nova Scotia's, and .5% of Newfoundland's. In the past, as the French moved from the rural areas into the cities, they often gave up their French language and way of life. In recent years, however, the French-speaking community in the Maritimes has made an effort to assert itself. The city of Moncton, in New Brunswick, has become the cultural centre of the French-speaking Maritimers. How do people of French origin living in Moncton feel about French-English relations? Would they like to move to Quebec so that they could take part in Lévesque's separatist movement? Or are they happy where they are? The following fictionalized interview will give us some answers to these questions.

### The woman from Moncton

**Interviewer:** Mrs. Béland, I am here today to find out how French people living outside Quebec feel about French-English relations. What is it like for a French-speaking Canadian living outside Quebec?

**Mrs. Béland:** First, I want to tell you that I am an Acadian. My ancestors settled in New Brunswick over three hundred years ago. I am proud of my roots. I feel that the Acadians are very special. Because our people have been here for three centuries, we have a right to expect that our language and culture will be respected. And in New Brunswick these rights are respected. This province has two official languages, French and English. That's the way it should be.

But you know, even though the government recognizes two official languages it is still difficult to preserve our language and way of life. I moved to Moncton in 1966. Before that I lived in Restigouche County up near the Quebec border. Up in Restigouche nearly everybody works in the wood products industry. Most people still live on farms or in small villages. Over 70% of our county was Roman Catholic and nearly 30% spoke no English at all. Even if you did learn English you still spoke French in your own home. It was easy for us to protect our language and way of life. We were isolated from the English influence.

But down here in Moncton it is entirely different. When I came here the first thing that I noticed was that people speak English everywhere. A while ago my daughter got a job in a department store. The first thing she mentioned when she came home was that nobody spoke French at work. My son works in a factory and it is the same thing. English is the language of business. Nobody says you have to speak English, but we all do because it is the accepted thing.

So what I am saying is that we have many of the same concerns as the people in Quebec. We are worried that our language will disappear.

**Interviewer:** Would you move to Quebec if it separated?

**Mrs. Béland:** Why would I do that? I am Acadian. I am not a Quebecker. If Quebec separates, though, I think we will be much worse off. I think that English Canada won't do a thing for the French-speaking Canadians left in Canada.

**Interviewer:** Is it not true that a Parti Acadien has been formed in the Maritimes? This party is said to advocate a separate Acadian province.

**Mrs. Béland:** Yes that is true, but the party is just a small group of radicals. Most Acadians are very conservative. We don't want any drastic changes. We have French radio and television and newspapers. The province of New Brunswick is officially bilingual. Our culture is protected.

1. Which of the three Maritime provinces has the largest French population?
2. Is there a danger that even with bilingualism the Acadian way of life in New Brunswick could disappear?

USING YOUR KNOWLEDGE
1. Which of the following statements might Mrs. Béland have made?
   a) I think René Lévesque is the saviour of French Canada.
   b) I would vote for the Parti Acadien.
   c) I don't see why PEI should not have more French media services. In comparison to Nova Scotia it is not doing well at all.
   d) I am very upset to see that in the bilingual high school in Moncton students all speak English outside the classroom.

## Conclusion

In this unit we have examined in detail the history of French-English relations. It is important to understand the background to Canada's current problems. By looking at our country's past, we may find clues to the future. Does Canada's history suggest that the nation can continue to overcome problems between anglophones and francophones? Or are the ties between the two language groups too weak to hold the nation together?

Our study shows that we have reason to be confident. In the past, solutions have been found to problems in French-English relations. With hard work, Canadians can continue to find solutions.

The government is trying to put the policy of a bilingual-bicultural Canada into effect. Some people feel that this policy is dividing Canada. According to public opinion polls, however, more and more Canadians seem to agree that the federal government should provide services in both official languages. Many Canadians also agree that they should be free to choose the language in which their children will be educated.

This does not mean that every Canadian supports the idea of a bilingual, bicultural Canada. Certain groups feel that bilingualism is being forced on them. Other groups are not willing to pay the money needed for French-language education in their areas. The Parti Québecois is not satisfied with the bilingual-bicultural policy, either. It believes that Quebec should be a unilingual, French-speaking province. At present, Canada is in danger of splitting apart. Many Canadians and their elected representatives are therefore taking a second look at their beliefs. They are starting to look for compromises.

One way of approaching the problem in French-English relations is to examine the situation carefully. Solutions can perhaps be found if Canadians are willing to see the problem from the other group's point of view. If both anglophones and francophones agree to compromise, all Canadians will have a chance to lead happy and productive lives.

READING BETTER
1. List three possible solutions to problems between French-speaking and English-speaking Canadians that have been suggested in this chapter.

ORGANIZING BETTER
1. Put these three headings across the top of a page in your notebook: a) Terrorism and separation; b) René Lévesque and negotiated separatism; c) Bilingualism. Draw a column for each heading. In each column give reasons that explain why the solution to the French-English problem should be adopted.

USING YOUR KNOWLEDGE
1. Imagine that you are writing a letter to the editor of a local newspaper. In your letter, state whether or not all the people in your area should speak both French and English. Explain your viewpoint, using facts from the text.

SOLVING PROBLEMS
1. Which of the three movements discussed in

this chapter—terrorism, separatism, biculturalism—offers the best solution to the French-English problem? Be sure to analyze the problem, and look carefully at each of the movements.

TAKING A STAND
1. Do you think that the policy of bilingualism and biculturalism alone is enough to solve the problems in French-English relations? Should more be done? If so, what?

RESEARCHING
1. Using newspapers and your library, find out the names of all the political parties in Quebec today. Also find the names of the party leaders, and the parties' solutions to French-English problems in Canada today.

## GLOSSARY

**Activist cell.** Part of an organization that takes direct action to achieve an end. It does things instead of just talking or planning.

**Injustices.** Actions or situations that are wrong or unfair.

**Propaganda.** Information that is designed to support a particular point of view.

**Referendum.** A vote in which the people of a country approve or reject a proposed government law.

**Sabotage.** Deliberate destruction or damage.

**Terrorists.** Persons who use violence to achieve their goals.

**Translated.** Changed from one language to another.

# UNIT FOUR
# Canadian-American relations

The two families had lived next door to each other for generations. Throughout the years, the family members had argued about fences, stray dogs, loud music. But they had also shared weddings and birthday parties, and worked together to mend fences and put up sheds. Through all the generations the two families came to know and understand each other.

In many ways this story describes relations between Canada and the United States of America. Throughout history the two countries have often disagreed and exchanged challenges, threats, and even a few shots. However the record of relations between Canada and the United States is generally one of peace, co-operation, and friendliness. Canada and the US have been at peace for over 150 years. The two countries are separated by the world's longest undefended border. The two federal governments have worked together on great projects such as the St. Lawrence Seaway.

Perhaps the comment that people make most often about Canada's relations with the United States is that we are each other's best customers. In fact, the amount of trade across the Canada-US border is the world's largest. Certainly the physical features of North America — the Rocky Mountains, the Great Plains, the Great Lakes–St. Lawrence River system, and the Atlantic Coast — have tied us together. But our two countries are joined by more than trade and geography. The way our peoples live is the same in many ways. We share similar values on democracy, human rights, and world peace.

We recognize that the US is our closest neighbour, friend, and partner. But we must not forget that the United States is older, richer, and more powerful than Canada. It has influenced us greatly. Through the years, Canadians have spent much time debating the pros and cons of this influence.

This unit of *Canada Today* discusses Canada-US relations. We will try to find answers to three major questions.

**1** What role does the US play in Canada's economy?

**2** How does the US influence Canadian culture?

**3** How does US influence affect Canada as a nation?

# 1/ Economic relations

## Contents

### Introduction

Here are some basic facts about economic relations between Canada and the US:

—The value of the trade between Canada and the US is the greatest in the world. It is worth over $60 billion a year.

—Non-Canadians own nearly 60% of Canada's industries. Most of this foreign ownership is **American.**

—Canadians and Americans have joined together to build some of the world's greatest engineering projects. In the past they have built the St. Lawrence Seaway and the Columbia River Project. The Alaska-Yukon Pipeline, to be started in the early 1980s, will be the world's most expensive project.

These facts show that the economic relations between Canada and the United States are important. For over two hundred years Canadians have been examining and debating these relations. Of special concern is the issue of US ownership. Many Canadians complain that American ownership of industries in Canada is bad for Canada. Others respond by pointing out the great benefits received from American ownership of factories, mines, stores, and other businesses.

At the end of this chapter you will be asked to take a stand on the US ownership and **investment** issues. To help you form your opinion, this chapter will give you some information about US economic activity in Canada. The following central questions will be studied:

1. **How did Americans come to control so much of our economy?**
2. **What are the good and bad results of American investment?**

342

3. How have Canada and the United States co-operated economically in the past? Has that co-operation helped or hurt Canada?
4. What, if anything, should be done about American influence in the Canadian economy?

**Foreign investment: Defining the situation**

The following tables show that non-Canadians own well over half of the largest businesses in Canada. Indeed, statistics on foreign ownership help us learn many facts.

1. Look at Fig. 1-1. It gives information about the owners of businesses in Canada for the year 1975. In each category figure out the percentage of businesses that are foreign-owned.
2. Look at Fig. 1-2. What percentage of all foreign investment was American in 1967? How much has US investment increased since 1945? (Note: To invest in a company you do not have to own it.

Investing involves using your money in one way or another. For example, you may own shares in a company, or lend money to a company.)
3. Look at Fig. 1-3. It shows public opinion about US investment in Canada between 1964 and 1978. By what percentage did public opinion increase or decrease in each section from 1964 to 1978?

| 25 largest businesses in Canada | 13 are Canadian-owned 12 are foreign-owned |
| --- | --- |
| 50 largest businesses in Canada | 27 are Canadian-owned 23 are foreign-owned |
| 100 largest businesses in Canada | 40 are Canadian-owned 60 are foreign-owned |
| 500 largest businesses in Canada | 220 are Canadian-owned 280 are foreign-owned |

Source: *Fortune Magazine* ©1976, Time Inc.

**Fig. 1-1 Foreign ownership and Canada's largest businesses**

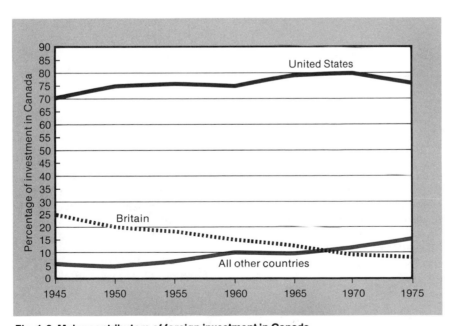

**Fig. 1-2 Major contributors of foreign investment in Canada**

In a 1978 Gallup Poll, the following question was asked:
"Do you think there is enough now or would you like to see more US capital invested in Canada?" The table below shows the national trend since 1964.

| | Enough now | Like to see more | Don't know |
|---|---|---|---|
| 1964 | 46% | 33% | 21% |
| 1967 | 60 | 24 | 16 |
| 1970 | 62 | 25 | 13 |
| 1972 | 67 | 22 | 11 |
| 1975 | 71 | 16 | 13 |
| 1977 | 69 | 20 | 12 |
| 1978 | 69 | 23 | 9 |

Note: Percentages may not add to exactly 100 because of rounding.

Source: *The Gallup Poll Report*, 1978 8 12

**Fig. 1-3 Public opinion poll about US investment in Canada**

ORGANIZING BETTER

1. **You will have to refer to Fig. 1-2 to do this question. Copy the chart below in your notebook. For the USA, Britain, and the other countries, state the percentage that each contributed to foreign investment in Canada in the years stated. Compare your charts with other students' charts.**

| Country | 1945 | 1950 | 1955 | 1960 | 1965 | 1970 | 1975 |
|---|---|---|---|---|---|---|---|
| USA | | | | | | | |
| Britain | | | | | | | |
| Other countries | | | | | | | |

RESEARCHING

1. a) **Ask this question of people you know. Compile the results for your whole class.**
   "**Do you think there is enough US investment in Canada now or would you like to see more?**"
   b) **How do your results compare with the results in Fig. 1-3? How do you account for this?**

## Canada-US relations: A brief historical overview

When we are studying the ties between two countries, it is often helpful for us to know about the history of these ties. This section discusses the way Canada grew to be friendly with the US. We will also look at Canada's earliest foreign investors, and the importance of foreign investment.

In the beginning

Money from France helped develop early Canada. French trading companies sent explorers to Canada to look for gold, silver, and furs. The **Company of New France** used its money to buy blankets, guns, axes, pots, and brandy. These items were traded to Canada's Native Peoples for furs. French investment in Canada paid off. When furs were sold in France, trading company owners made a profit. Fig. 1-4 gives you a fictional example of trading companies' costs and profits.

The early French people in business built docks and warehouses in New France. The government of France built forts and homes. The Roman Catholic Church gave money for hospitals, schools, and churches.

After the Conquest of 1759-60, the British replaced the French as a source of money for investment. This British money was used to build canals and railroads. In many cases, profits went to the British owners or to banks in Britain.

READING BETTER

1. **Why did French business people and merchants risk investing their money in New France?**

USING YOUR KNOWLEDGE

1. **What could the owner of the Pierre Chauvin Fur Company (Fig. 1-4) do to get a bigger profit?**

To the south of New France were the Thirteen Colonies, which later joined together to form the United States of America. The Thirteen Colonies were under British rule. They competed with New France (which after 1763 was called Quebec) for furs and land. In the Quebec Act of 1774, Britain gave Quebec control

```
Pierre Chauvin Fur Company (costs in French
pounds)

Costs:       200 guns
             500 blankets
             1 000 jugs of brandy        1 000
             Ships rented                2 000
                   Total costs           3 000

Income:      500 fine beaver skins
             100 fox furs
             30 bear skins
             800 ordinary beaver pelts
             30 wild mink
             300 deer skins              4 000
                   Profit for owners     1 000
```

**Fig. 1-4 Budget of a fictional fur trading company, 1688**

over large parts of land south of the Great
Lakes. Because of this, the American colonists were angry at Britain. This anger over
the Quebec Act became one of the factors
leading to the American Revolution,
1776-1783.

During their revolution against Britain,
the Americans invaded Quebec. They tried
to get the Canadiens (people living in
Quebec at the time) to join them. The
Canadiens stayed neutral. By not joining
with the Thirteen Colonies, Quebec and the
Atlantic colonies (New Brunswick, Nova
Scotia, Prince Edward Island, and Newfoundland) expressed the wish to remain
independent of the United States.

The influence of the United States slowly
crept into **British North America.** Americans loyal to Britain began to leave the
United States. They were welcomed to
British North America and given land.
Although these settlers were loyal to Britain
and King George III, their way of life was
"American". They brought to Canada some
very American ideas on government and
business. They also brought American
expressions of speech. In short, they introduced an American way of life.

Other Americans also came later to
places like southern Ontario. These settlers
were simply looking for good farmland.

The War of 1812 was a war between

Britain and the United States of America.
The United States invaded British North
America. Some Loyalists were ready to
fight back but other colonists often were
not. Some helped the Americans. In the
Atlantic colonies there is even historical
evidence to show that some trade with the
US did not stop. Many colonists and
Americans wanted to make money with
friends, not fight.

The Treaty of Ghent in 1814 ended the
war. Over the next few decades British
North America grew in population and
wealth. Trade with the United States
continued. Indeed, canals were built along
the St. Lawrence River to attract American
trade. However trade with the US was still
not as important as trade with Britain.
Britain gave special trade privileges to
products of its colonies.

In 1845, the trade privileges ended.
Britain began **free trade** with the world.
British North America suddenly faced
economic problems. The colonists had to
compete with the world's countries to sell
grain, lumber, and fish to Britain. As a
result of these problems, business leaders in
Montreal took drastic action. They
announced an **annexation manifesto;** this
was a demand to join the United States.
This demand was rejected by most colonists. But other ways to solve economic
problems were needed.

Then came the Americans

In 1854, the USA and British North America
began reciprocity. This meant that natural
products could pass freely across the border
between the USA and British North
America. There would be no protective
tariffs to make American products more
expensive than domestic (home) products.

The results were good. Trade between the
USA and British North America tripled.
Trade with the US became an important
part of life for British North America.

**Settlers thrashing grain in a barn. How have farming methods changed since then?**

The end of reciprocity and new hope in Confederation

During the American Civil War (1861-1865) the British showed support for the South. The northern states were angry, and cancelled the Reciprocity Treaty. This hurt business in British North America. As a result more people in the separate British colonies of **Canada,** New Brunswick, Newfoundland, Nova Scotia, and Prince Edward Island were ready to consider creating a new country. The colonists hoped that trade between the colonies of British North America would improve if they united as one country.

There were other reasons for Confederation. One was the fear of an American invasion. There had been incidents to show that some Americans were ready to fight to take over British North America. In 1838 the Hunter's Lodges had organized an invasion. They were defeated by British soldiers and Canadian **militia.** During the Civil War some people in the northern states were angry with British support for the South. Their anger not only ended reciprocity but led to plans for an invasion of Canada.

In 1867 Confederation was achieved. Canada, Nova Scotia, and New Brunswick united to form a single nation. In 1869, the **Northwest** was purchased from the Hudson's Bay Company. Manitoba entered Confederation in 1870, and British Columbia entered in 1871. Prince Edward Island entered in 1873. Canada now stretched from the Atlantic to the Pacific. The united provinces were better able to resist threats from the United States.

Around this time, negotiations about east coast and Great Lakes fishing were carried on with the United States. The United States recognized Canada's rights in those areas. In recognizing these rights, the United States also recognized that Canada existed as a nation.

The next task was to build and populate this new but empty country. The US was not interested in reciprocity again, so another method of stimulating the economy was needed. In 1878 John A. Macdonald convinced the country that his National Policy would help the economy. The policy had three main points.

### The National Policy

1. Complete the Canadian Pacific Railway (CPR). This would unite Canada. The railway would carry settlers to the West. It would return wheat to the East. The government of Canada loaned money to the CPR to ensure that it would be finished. The CPR also borrowed money in New York and London. This money was used to pay wages, and buy rails and trains.

2. Attract settlers to the West. The federal government offered packages of 160 acres (64 ha) of free land in the West. People from eastern Canada, central Canada, Europe, and the United States would go west seeking land, wealth, and adventure.

3. Establish a protective tariff. American **manufactured goods** would be taxed at the border. This would make Canadian-made goods cheaper than imports. Canadian people would buy Canadian goods and Canadian industry would grow.

### The tariff

The National Policy was controversial. The tariff would cause debates for years. Compare the following points of view. Which do you agree with?

---

### 1. Ned Snodgrass: A farmer

The tariff is a cheat! It protects those rich factory owners in Ontario. I'm forced to buy my rakes, stoves, and shoes from Ontario or Montreal because even if they are expensive, American goods cost more. But I have to sell my crops on the world market. When I get a good price, I can afford the Canadian-made stuff. But sometimes I don't get much at all. Then what am I supposed to do? I say get rid of the tariff. Let us buy whatever goods are cheapest, even if they aren't Canadian. I sell to the world, I want to buy from the world.

### 2. Jacob Bounder: A Toronto stove factory owner

I worked hard to build this factory. I worked hard to produce this Canadian-made stove. Without the tariff, those Americans would beat my business down in a few years. They're so much bigger that they can make stoves for less money than I can. People would then buy American stoves, not mine. I believe that most of us in Toronto who have worked hard to develop Canadian businesses would be ruined without the tariff. If we're ruined, then Canada will be too. Keep the Yankees out!

### 3. Ebenezer Tweed: Manufacturer from Cleveland, Ohio, USA

The tariff doesn't mean much to me. I just bought a small plant in a place called Hamilton, in Ontario. We're going to make our Tweed Arrow plough there. We'll sell them all over Canada to the new settlers. By opening a plant in Canada, I can get around the tariff. I'm also pretty sure I can lick the Canadian competition too. That fellow in Toronto, Massey, has been protected by the tariff. He's grown lazy. Now he'll get some real competition. You watch.

---

**ORGANIZING BETTER**
1. Make a list of the ways in which reciprocity hurt Canada and another list of the ways in which it helped Canada.
2. Make a list of the ways in which the National Policy helped Canada. Make another list of the ways in which it hurt Canada.

**TAKING A STAND**
1. Whom do you agree with — Ned Snodgrass, Jacob Bounder, or Ebenezer Tweed? Why?

The CPR was completed in 1885, but the National Policy seemed to be a failure. Settlers did not flock to the West. Industries did not grow rapidly. In fact, Canada suffered an economic **depression**. In the late 1880s another group of annexationists appeared in Canada. This group demanded union with the United States as a solution to these problems. Again, annexation was rejected. In the election of 1891, Macdonald and the National Policy won. Ontario and Quebec gave the greatest support to the National Policy. The West was strongly opposed to the tariff and would remain opposed to it.

Suddenly in the mid-1890s the economy began to improve. There was little free land left in the United States, so more settlers moved to Canada. The CPR carried people and manufactured goods west. It brought grain east to be sold around the world. The boom was so great that another transcontinental railroad was started.

By 1911 the great immigration boom was in full swing. But then an economic **recession** hit the nation. The world price of wheat was down. Farmers' incomes were therefore lower. The Canadian economy sagged. The Liberal government of Wilfrid Laurier was under great pressure from the West and the Atlantic provinces to end the tariff. Laurier agreed and chose to seek reciprocity with the United States. Again Canadians faced the issue, "Should we adopt reciprocity with the United States?"

The question was answered in the 1911 election. Laurier and the Liberals were defeated. Canadians had rejected the idea of reciprocity with the US.

**Sir Wilfrid Laurier**

| Election results of 1911 | |
| --- | --- |
| Conservative seats | 134 |
| Liberal seats | 87 |

The Liberals won in Alberta, Saskatchewan, and the Maritimes. The Conservatives won in Ontario, British Columbia, and Manitoba. They also won 27 of 65 seats in Quebec.

USING YOUR KNOWLEDGE

1. Look at the election results. How do they show regional differences?

TAKING A STAND

1. How would you have voted In 1911? Why? (Note: Who was not allowed to vote in 1911?)

The growth of American ownership

Even though Canadians rejected free trade with the US, American influence in Canada's economy grew steadily between 1911 and 1945. The Americans had money; Canada needed investment to build industry and mines. Still, until 1945, most foreign money and ownership in Canada was British. Britain was the "mother country", so Canadians did not mind its investment.

After World War II (1939-45), however, the British were exhausted economically. They had no money to spare for investment in Canada. Yet Canada was going through the biggest boom period in its history. Europe was in ruins, and it would buy whatever Canada could make or grow. The American economy also boomed. The US needed more raw materials for its factories. Canadians in business turned to the USA for investment money. Americans in business came to Canada to buy mines and industries that would give them a good profit. From 1946 to 1953, American firms built 307 branches in Canada.

How did Canadians react? In general, they welcomed US investment. The American-owned firms provided good jobs. New industries made Canada richer. There was little unemployment. The governments collected new tax dollars to provide pensions, baby bonuses, and education. People agreed with Clarence Decatur Howe who said:

> Let us face facts. Had it not been for the United States, our development would have been slower and some of our great projects would still be far in the future.

*C. D. Howe at the Hamilton Chamber of Commerce, April, 1956. Quoted in E. McInnis, Canada: A Political and Social History, (New York: Holt, Rinehart and Winston, 1967), p. 525.*

**Clarence Decatur Howe: A great Canadian**

Clarence Decatur (C.D.) Howe was born in Massachusetts, USA in 1886. He became a Canadian citizen in 1913. C.D. Howe was a major figure in Canada's economic growth. In the 1930s he was Minister of Transport in Mackenzie King's Liberal government. Howe was responsible for setting up the Canadian Broadcasting Corporation (CBC) and Trans-Canada Air Lines (later Air Canada). During the Second World War, this "hard-nosed" engineer was in charge of Canada's economic war effort. Young, rich people in business went to Ottawa to work for C.D. These volunteers often took a salary of only one dollar. Among the "dollar-a-year men" were such future multi-millionaires as E.P. Taylor. People in business greatly admired C.D.'s drive and determination. He understood business and business understood him. Howe can rightly be given a great deal of credit for building the wartime factories which became the basis of Canada's modern industry.

After the war, Howe was probably the most important figure in the government, next to the prime minister. He was a great organizer. He could get other people to work hard. He believed in private business and he encouraged it. He was a man of enterprise.

In the 1950s when Canada's economy boomed, it was again partly because of Howe. C.D. had put wartime weapons factories up for sale at 65% below their original price. People in private business bought them and the boom of the 1950s started. Until 1957 Howe, as Minister of Trade and Commerce in the St. Laurent Cabinet, was in charge of government policy on business. During that period Canada's economy boomed. During that time almost three million dollars a day came to Canada from the United States.

C.D. Howe died in Montreal in 1960.

---

**READING BETTER**
1. **Why was foreign investment needed in Canada in the 1950s?**
2. **Why might C.D. Howe have been willing to encourage American investment?**

**USING YOUR KNOWLEDGE**
1. **C.D. Howe did not believe in reciprocity. He did not propose free trade with the US. What did C.D. Howe believe in? Reread the biography of Howe and think about what he gained for Canada before answering.**
2. **In Canada in the late 1970s there was a great deal of unemployment among Canadians aged 16-25. If these unemployed young Canadians had lived in the early 1950s instead, what would their job prospects have been? Why?**

**RESEARCHING**
1. **In your library find out about the big projects that Howe referred to in the quotation. Make a report to your class. Use the card catalogue and encyclopaedias in the library. Ask the librarian for help if you do not know how to use these.**

The 1950s: The reaction

While the great boom of the 1950s was on, a few Canadians began to worry about the country's independence. Was all that US

investment good for Canada? Should the government try to stop it?

One of the first conflicts in opinion came in 1956, with a debate on a new gas pipeline. The questions about American ownership came to national attention. The Liberal government of Louis St. Laurent was defeated over the pipeline issue and John Diefenbaker formed a Conservative government. After 21 years, the Conservatives were again in power in Ottawa.

*The pipeline debate of 1956: Crisis in Ottawa*
The member of Parliament stood in the aisle and shook his fist at the Speaker of the Commons. The Speaker called "Order, order." His cries were lost in the noise in Canada's Parliament on that day in 1956. M.J. Coldwell of the CCF party ran up to the desk of the Clerk of the House. He shouted, "You can't do this!" Usually quiet and serious, Coldwell was now furious. He was not the only one to lose his temper. Donald Fleming, a Conservative MP, was told to leave the Commons. He had resisted the rulings of the Speaker and refused to sit down.

What caused this uproar?

**John Diefenbaker**

**Louis St. Laurent**

The Liberal government of Louis St. Laurent had introduced a bill that would provide a loan to the TransCanada PipeLines company. This firm wanted to build a pipeline from Alberta to Montreal. Natural gas would then be sold to Ontario, Quebec, and the United States. TransCanada PipeLines had been unable to raise the money to get started. It turned to the government for a loan.

C.D. Howe, then Minister of Trade and Commerce, had proposed a plan. His plan would provide a loan to the company. It would also have the government build the part of the pipeline that crossed northern Ontario. This would cost $118 million. The government would then rent the pipeline to TransCanada. Thus the rented pipeline would help the company. TransCanada would not have to spend $118 million for the northern Ontario line.

Why did this plan cause problems? The following points help explain.

1. TransCanada PipeLines was 83% American-owned.
2. Much of the natural gas passing through the pipeline would be sold to the US.
3. Canadian banks and insurance companies were afraid to lend TransCanada

PipeLines the money it needed.

The pipeline affair caused great public concern. American ownership was becoming a public issue. Should the Canadian government loan money to TransCanada PipeLines? The press and Canadians all over the country debated this question.

In Parliament, the opposition wanted to debate the issue as well. C.D. Howe was impatient and unwilling to debate. The government forced the bill through using *closure*. This is a special rule limiting the amount of time a bill is discussed. It is rarely used. Because the government used closure, and because the Speaker always sided with the government, Coldwell, Fleming, and others raised the storm of protest. But closure cut opposition speaking time in the Commons. Eventually the bill was passed and the pipeline was built.

The pipeline debate caused as much concern over the rights of Parliament as it did over American ownership. However this second issue became one of increasing concern. Top leaders in government as well as average citizens became worried. One such leader who worried about American influence in our economy was Walter Gordon.

**Walter Gordon: A great Canadian**

In 1963 Walter Gordon was Liberal Minister of Finance in Ottawa. His job included making up the budget for Canada. Gordon suggested that action be taken to stop American control of our economy. He wanted a 30% tax on **shares** in Canadian companies that were sold to foreigners. This would discourage sales to Americans. Canadians in business were outraged. They wanted to be free to sell to anybody. They also did not want to have their supplies of American money cut off. The money was needed for economic growth. Political pressure forced Gordon to withdraw his tax proposal.

Despite this defeat, Gordon did not give up. In 1970 he became founder of the Committee for an Independent Canada. This group of economic nationalists attracted many other important Canadians. They agitated publicly for controls on foreign ownership. Despite their activity, however, over $20 000 000 in American money and control continued to pour into Canada every week. Walter Gordon and the Committee for an Independent Canada have not, however, given up their struggle.

---

**ORGANIZING BETTER**
1. Which of Howe's ideas would nationalists object to? Why?
2. List the ways in which Canada would gain from the TransCanada pipeline. How would Canada lose?

**USING YOUR KNOWLEDGE**
1. Why would people in business favour a protective tariff, yet oppose controls on foreign ownership?
2. Make up a definition for "economic nationalist".

**TAKING A STAND**
1. Debate the following statements:
   a) The National Policy hurt farmers and fishers but it made Canada a great nation.
   b) Canada is dependent on the United States. It always has been, and probably always will be.
   c) Wealth and jobs are more important than some idea about true independence. You can starve on independence.

Although Walter Gordon's 1963 plans to control American ownership were shelved, the issue still existed. The federal government began several inquiries into foreign ownership. Two major studies were the *Watkins Report* and the *Gray Report*, named after the chairpersons of the inquiry teams. The studies revealed to Canadians many facts about foreign ownership. Foreign ownership in general, and American ownership in particular, became front-page news stories across Canada. The debate continued throughout the 1970s.

Canada and the United States have fought and competed for wealth in North America. We have seen how, through the years, these two countries have been closely tied economically. The next section asks whether or not these ties are good for Canada.

**The debate over foreign ownership**

Foreign ownership of our industries has become a major public issue. In Ontario and Quebec, where most manufacturing is done, the debate is hottest. Other regions find themselves involved, too. Indeed, the government of Saskatchewan has actually bought up American-owned potash mines. In Alberta, publisher Mel Hurtig has become a leading national critic of foreign ownership.

But in each region there are also those who want more foreign ownership. The foreign owners are willing to risk their money; they create jobs and pay taxes.

Many provinces try hard to attract foreign industry for these reasons. They are even willing to provide loans.

Thus with one group opposed to foreign ownership and another group happy with it, the scene for a national debate is set. The following sections will help you to take a stand in the debate.

---

**The economic nationalists state their case: A dialogue between students**

**Mary:** I'm an economic nationalist. I don't think that Canada can be truly independent until we control our own economy.

**Gord:** But we control it now don't we? I mean, the government does run things. It taxes. It passes laws. Nobody tells the government what to do, except the people when they vote.

**Mary:** The government does run the country. But the businesses of Canada are supposed to be free. They can make their own decisions about what to make. They decide when to hire. They decide what prices to charge. They decide when to close down. The governments of Canada have some control over these issues, but the businesses are still very free.

**Gord:** That's true. But I still don't understand how this makes Canada less independent.

**Mary:** It's because Americans run the companies that we are less independent. We have no real say in a lot of important decisions. It's like when your folks go away for a weekend and leave you to look after the house. You're running the house for a couple of days, but you know you had better not do anything your parents wouldn't like. If you have to do something big like decide on whether or not to call a plumber to fix a leak, you'd want to call your parents. It's their money that pays the bills, so you'd want to have their permission.

**Gord:** I see your point there. You mean that Canada's like the teenager and the parents are the American owners.

**Mary:** That's it. All major decisions and lots of money come from the States. Even the people who run the Canadian branch plants are often Americans. They're sent up here to keep an eye on things. They've also got the ideas on how to run the company.

**Gord:** That's right. Just like when your parents try to guide you and make big decisions for you. You can be independent only when you grow up and have full control over your life. Then you make your own money, decide how to spend it, and come up with your own ideas about living.

**Mary:** And that's why I'm an economic nationalist. Our country has to grow up and stand on its own. Only when we own and run our own businesses will we be truly independent. Until then the Americans will always have some control over us.

---

ORGANIZING BETTER
1. **In point form, list the reasons for which Mary is an economic nationalist.**
2. **Make a comparison chart showing on one side how a teenager is not fully independent, and on the other side, how Canada may not be.**

The economic nationalists want Canada to have an economy run by and for Canadians. They believe that this is essential for true independence. One of the major areas of Canada-US economic relations in which the nationalists see a lack of independence is the branch plant.

The branch plant economy

Have you ever noticed that companies often have "of Canada" as part of their names? Look around you as you drive in a city.

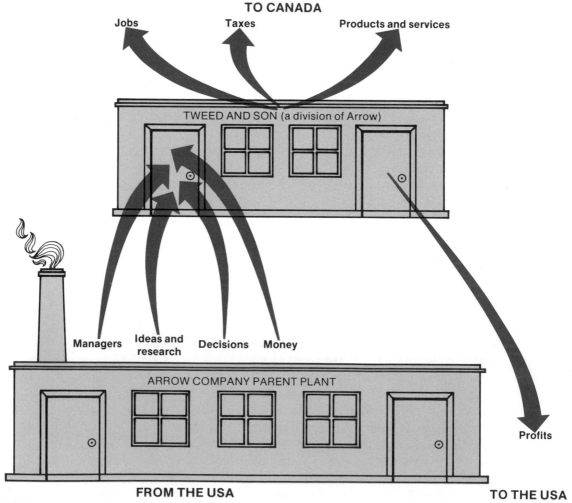

Fig. 1-5  The branch plant

354

Check the Yellow Pages. Wherever companies operate or advertise, you will see "of Canada". This usually means that the company is a branch plant. Many other branch plants do not include "of Canada" in their names. Have you seen these?

Sara Lee
General Electric
Michelin
Shell Oil
Ford
Texaco
Black and Decker
Alka-Seltzer

These are names of some common branch plants. The parent plants (and ownership) are in foreign countries. For most branch plants in Canada, the parent branch is in the United States.

Branch plants are created when a foreign company opens a factory in Canada. It may build its own plant or buy up a Canadian industry. The new branch plant then makes the same product as the parent plant. This product is marked "Made in Canada". Often it is exactly the same as another product marked "Made in the USA". By building a branch plant in Canada, a foreign company jumps the **tariff barrier.** The company can sell its product in Canada at competitive prices. Profits from operations go to the American owners. New jobs, a new product, and taxes paid by foreign companies go to Canadians. Read "The Acme Tire and Bathing Cap Company story" to see how this happens.

---

**The Acme Tire and Bathing Cap Company story — Part 1**

Once upon a time, the Acme Tire and Bathing Cap Company of New York made a unique ladies' garment. It was advertised on TV and was very popular. Along the US border, many Canadians saw the advertisements and looked for Acme bathing caps in the stores. There were none.

Because so many Canadians wrote letters asking where they could buy the bathing cap, Thurlock Freepish, owner of Acme, made a visit to Canada. He saw that there was nothing like the Acme bathing cap in Canada. He saw that he could sell lots of Acmes there and make big profits. At first Freepish tried shipping US-made Acmes across the border. The tariff, however, made the Acme caps so expensive that few were sold. Finally, Freepish found a small Canadian factory in Quebec that was just right. He offered so much money for it that the owner sold out. Soon Acme Tire and Bathing Cap Company of Canada was producing 10 000 caps a week. The plant was made larger, and more workers were hired. By the end of the first year, Freepish was $500 000 richer — after taxes.

---

What is wrong with branch plants?

In this story everything seems to end well. Freepish is richer. The Canadian who sells Freepish the factory makes money on the deal. Acme of Canada expands and hires more Canadian workers. Freepish pays income tax in Canada. What could be nicer?

Today, 60% of our industries are foreign-owned or foreign-controlled. In most cases "foreign" means "American". These US owners run the businesses for their own benefit. They obey Canadian laws and hire Canadian workers. Economic nationalists, however, are not pleased with the branch plants. They have three major complaints.

1. Major decisions on what to make and where are made by the parent plant in the United States. These decisions may be good for the American owners but bad for Canada. Lay-offs or slowdowns occur in Canada first. The parent plant is protected at the expense of the branch plant.

2. The managers running the branch plants are often Americans sent up from the parent plant. Canadians often cannot get the top jobs. Canadians then do not get the experience and training needed to run the business. Therefore, they have to rely on Americans.

3. Ideas and inventions come to Canada from the United States. The parent plant spends money in the United States to find new ideas. New ideas will, of course, help the parent. The Canadians are not given money to work on new ideas. Thus they do not get a chance to develop many new products.

In short, economic nationalists believe that branch plants hurt Canada more than they help. Let's continue the Acme story to show what their arguments mean.

**Which of these companies are American-owned?**

### The Acme Tire and Bathing Cap Company story — Part 2

When Acme Tire and Bathing Cap of Canada opened, Thurlock Freepish sent his brother Morton to run the plant. Eight other specialists from New York were also sent to make sure the new Canadian caps met Acme's standards. Morton moved to Montreal. His family loved the safe streets, restaurants, schools, and cultural life.

The mayor of Montreal was happy too. Acme was a well-known name. As the company grew, more Montrealers got jobs. After two years, Thurlock Freepish began to send promising young executives to Montreal to work under Morton and gain experience.

In 1977, Thurlock invented a new bias-ply cap that became a big success. He opened a new wing at the New York plant and trained new managers. The bias-ply cap sold very well, increasing Acme's profits. When it came time to start production in Canada in 1978, the best young managers from the New York plant were sent to Montreal. They showed the Canadians what to do. Special parts were imported from the parent plant.

Because of its famous name and expensive advertisements, Acme soon outsold all Canadian bathing caps. A small New Brunswick company that made bias-ply caps could not compete. The owner of that plant went out of business.

In 1979, there was a sudden change in fashion. Sales went down as the market declined. Freepish saw his profits go down. What should he do? It was getting expensive to keep the whole Canadian plant open. Freepish decided to transfer the entire bias-ply section of his business to New York. He ordered Morton to stop production and lay off workers in the bias-ply section. From then on, all Acme bias-ply bathing caps sold in Canada would be labelled "Made in the USA". In this way the New York plant was kept going at full speed. Freepish's total profits went up again.

In Canada, a few more workers collected unemployment.

---

**QUICK QUIZ**

Test your knowledge of the material in this chapter. Complete these sentences in your notebook.

1. A person who wants to have Canada's businesses run by and for Canadians is called . . . .
2. When a foreign company opens a plant in Canada it is called a . . . .
3. Most foreign ownership in Canada is . . . .
4. Two benefits of foreign ownership are . . . .
5. Economic nationalists believe that Canadians do not get executive jobs in branch plants because . . . .

**READING BETTER**

1. Why are branch plants built in Canada?

2. What is the purpose of a tariff barrier? How did the Acme Company "jump" the tariff barrier?
3. What benefits does Canada receive from branch plants?
4. Explain why the Acme Tire and Bathing Cap Company of Canada is a good example of a branch plant.
5. Which of the following are basic beliefs of economic nationalists? Mark them with an "X". Justify your choices with facts from the text.

| | |
|---|---|
| Competition | Jobs for Canadians |
| Independence | Increasing taxes |
| Sharing | Resenting Americans |
| Wealth for Canada | Freedom for all |

1. Make a chart. Compare each of the economic nationalist's three complaints about branch plants with what happened at the Acme Tire and Bathing Cap Company.

USING YOUR KNOWLEDGE

1. a) Check your local phonebook and list the branch plants that are operating in your community.
   b) How may these branch plants affect the economy of your community?

TAKING A STAND

1. Do you think the Acme Tire and Bathing Cap Company was good or bad for Canada? Give reasons for your answer.
2. Are you an economic nationalist? Why or why not? Discuss this with your classmates.

The other side of the coin: A defence of American investment

Some people in Canada are just as loyal to their country as the economic nationalists are. However these Canadians do not object to foreign ownership. In fact, they believe that it is important to Canada's future. In this section we look at the arguments of this group of people.

---

**Dialogue: Students from western Canada and the Atlantic provinces discuss foreign investment**

**Lois:** I think we need more American investment in Canada. The Americans are willing to bring their money up here to start businesses. Allowing them to earn profits in return is fair.

**Rita:** I agree with you. It seems to me that only people in Ontario are upset about American control of the economy. Most people in the Atlantic provinces feel that the more American investment we get, the better off we'll be.

**Lois:** Do you mean that people in the Atlantic area think that foreign ownership will make them richer, and that it's good?

**Rita:** That's right. In New Brunswick, an American company wants to build a liquified natural gas project. This plant would supply its product to the United States only. It would be built on a good harbour near the border. Many Maritimers are delighted to get this project.

**Lois:** I can understand why. It provides construction jobs. Some of the materials used are sure to be purchased in the Atlantic provinces. This will help fight unemployment and boost the economy.

**Rita:** That's what most people hope. And who really cares if it's American-owned? Besides, you don't see any big companies from Ontario coming down here to operate.

**Lois:** We feel the same in the West. I come from Calgary and we've really benefited from foreign investment. The big foreign-owned oil companies risk their own money to explore for oil and gas. The oil economy means a lot to Saskatchewan and Alberta. The provincial governments earn a lot of money from oil and gas. It means very low income taxes in Alberta and a high standard of living. I, for one, am very grateful.

**Rita:** It seems that some provinces have already used foreign money to build industry. Now they want to stop that foreign control — for everybody. They don't see that the West and the East desperately need foreign investment to develop industries and jobs. I think the Ontario nationalists are thinking only of themselves.

**Lois:** That's what many people in the West think, too. Some are more upset about Ontario's economic power than they are about Quebec separation. My Uncle Norris gets really furious every time he sees a food box with "Toronto" or "Ontario" on it. He says our wheat is grown out west, shipped to Ontario, made into frozen cakes, and then sent back to Calgary. Why can't we have a factory in the West that makes frozen cakes? Why can't we make cars? We'd save money on transporting them from Ontario!

**Rita:** Right! Why, the people in Toronto and all southern Ontario seem to think that what's good for them is good for all Canadians. I think it's time to have them listen to the rest of us.

**Lois:** What the government needs is a new policy that encourages foreign investment to go to areas where industry is needed. You know — a tax break or something to make the West and the East look like better places to build factories. Ontario's government could then pass laws to discourage foreign control. Each region of Canada has different needs.

**Rita:** That sounds good to me. Let's write a letter to Ottawa about this. You write to your MP and I'll write to mine.

---

**ORGANIZING BETTER**

1. Make a list of the ways in which Rita and Lois differ from economic nationalists.
2. Which basic beliefs do Rita and Lois seem to hold strongest in the dialogue?
   Freedom of choice
   Wealth
   Equality
   Motherhood
   Conservation
   Central control
   Regional control
   Free speech

**TAKING A STAND**

1. Do you agree with the point of view expressed by Rita and Lois? Discuss this with your classmates.

---

**A hard look at reality** *by Darlene Stahl*
*A fictionalized account based on fact*

The economic nationalists argue that American branch plants hurt Canada. What they forget is that if branch plants were not here, then Canada would have much less industry. Or at best another branch plant owned by citizens of a country other than the USA would be there.

I feel that American investment is good for Canada. I'll try to prove my point in two ways. First I'll review some basic facts. Then I'll tell you the story of the Henry Brothers Foods company.

Canada is rich in resources. Among the most important are fish, lumber, and minerals. All these resources must be developed before they can be put to use. For example, mines must be built before minerals can be extracted. Also, these minerals have to be shipped to the different factories that will use them. All this costs money.

Where does the money come from? History shows that at first it came from France and Britain. Since 1945, most foreign money has come from the United States. Canada has accepted US investment for two reasons. First, our country needed money to build industries, and the US had lots of it. Second, the United States is close by, and it gets along well with Canada.

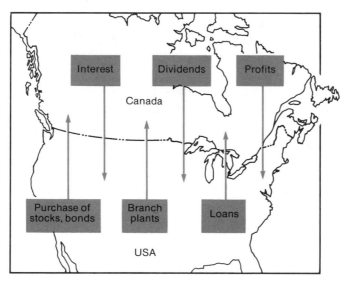

Fig. 1-6 **American investment in Canada and the return on that investment**

You already know these facts. Let me introduce some points not mentioned before. From 1946 to 1957 Canada's economy boomed. Foreign investment caused about 20% of the income growth during that period. It caused about the same increase in income again between 1962 and 1968. We of course know that most of the foreign investment was American.

Most of the new US-owned industries make a profit for their owners. Canada also benefits from these industries. Taxes on the profits have to be paid to Canada. Loans to Canadians in business help them start Canadian-owned industries. Government bonds purchased by Americans help build dams, highways, hospitals, and sewage-disposal plants in Canada.

Branch plants also help Canada. They often bring new products and ideas with them. Many of these may never otherwise come to Canada. Also, branch plants can afford to take risks because they are part of a larger company. If the venture fails, the main company can support the branch plant.

All these facts show that foreign investment is beneficial to

Canada. There is one more good reason for continuing to allow foreign investment in the country. Many large parts of Canada do not have much industry. These areas want to grow economically the way Ontario has. In the East and West the resources and workers are ready. They need American investment. Central Canada does not seem to have the money or desire to provide what is needed in these regions.

---

## ORGANIZING BETTER

1. Why does Darlene Stahl believe that Canada needs foreign investment? Make a list. Try to find five or six different reasons.

2. Return to the dialogue between Rita and Lois. Make a list of the arguments that appear both in their dialogue and in Stahl's explanation.

---

### The story of Henry Brothers Foods *by Darlene Stahl*
*A fictional account*
*This story will help you to understand the arguments that I've just made. D.S.*

Walter Henry sat brooding in his office in downtown Winnipeg. It was the main office of Henry Brothers Foods. The company's symbol — a sheaf of wheat — and its motto, "All the food that's good to eat," were known to most Canadians.

Today Walter sat brooding because the profits were down again. He knew that in a few minutes his niece Joan would again suggest selling the business to the giant General Company of Iowa, USA. Walter had heard about General's offer before.

Walter Henry was tired. The fight to keep the business going was getting harder and harder. The banks did not want to make loans to someone who had trouble making a profit.

Just then young Joan Henry entered the office and spoke gently to her uncle.

"Well Uncle Walt, have you considered the General offer? It's very good, you know. You'll end up a rich man."

Her uncle turned to her. "I've got two questions. First, why does General, a big American company, still want us?"

Joan had long ago grown used to her uncle's blunt, loud voice. "The General people say they're looking for new investments. They think that as a branch plant, Henry Brothers Foods will help them make more profit."

Walter had a glint in his eyes. "Yes, I can see that. What about you and everybody else around here? Will you lose your jobs?"

"Well Uncle, you and I would each get some stock in General. I've been offered a job as international vice-president of General. As for everybody else, they will keep their present jobs."

"It sounds good and yet I hate to sell. . . . Oh blast! What am I blathering on about? I'm old and tired. The company is in trouble. If I don't sell out now we'll all go broke. Okay Joan, let's start serious negotiations with General."

A few months later the deal was completed. Several experts from the General head office arrived to plan the changeover. For the next year Henry Brothers Foods still did not make a profit. In fact it lost money. But within five years it was a success. The Winnipeg factory doubled in size.

Walter Henry retired to a farm near Brandon and raised champion Holstein cattle. Joan Henry was a success as vice-president of the General Company.

*That is the end of the story. As far as I, Darlene Stahl, am concerned, it is a story of happiness and success. Americans in business have proven to be good neighbours and partners. Let's not allow economic nationalists to end it all!*

---

**READING BETTER**

1. **Find an example from the story for each of the reasons for supporting foreign ownership.**
2. **What benefits did Canada receive from the General Company's take-over of Henry Brothers Foods?**

**USING YOUR KNOWLEDGE**

1. **How would an economic nationalist argue that the take-over of Henry Brothers was bad for Canada? Be sure to review the section on economic nationalism before writing your answer.**
2. **How would Darlene Stahl defend what the Acme Tire and Bathing Cap Company did in Canada? Review that story before you answer.**

**TAKING A STAND**

1. **If you were Walter Henry, would you have agreed to sell your company? Why or why not?**

## Continentalism and free trade

So far you have studied the history of Canada-USA economic relations. You have also explored the debate over branch plants and foreign investment. There is another important issue in Canada-US relations that

should be examined. At one time in our history it was called reciprocity. Today it is more likely to be called *free trade* or even *continentalism*.

Free trade means that trade barriers between Canada and the United States are removed. Goods travel freely back and forth across the border without being taxed. Continentalists believe in free trade. But they go even further, and ask that Canada and the United States share the riches of North America with each other. "The waters, the air, the mountains, and the plains — all of these we now share. Perhaps we should also share minerals, wood, and energy," the continentalist suggests. "We North Americans would be richer if we shared. We cannot ignore our neighbours. We should help each other."

The basic questions of free trade and continentalism today will be examined through the following case studies.

1. The Columbia River Treaty, 1961
2. The Alaska-Yukon Pipeline Agreement, 1977
3. Free trade today

---

**Case 1: The Columbia River Treaty — 1961**

*Issue:* Should Canada and the United States co-operate to develop the Columbia River? The Columbia River is the fourth-largest in North America. It begins in Canada, but ends at the Pacific Ocean in Washington State. The Americans have built some of the world's

**Mica Dam, Columbia River Treaty project. How would it change life in this area?**

largest dams on the Columbia. Still, in the 1950s they needed more electricity than their large dams could provide. They turned to the northern section of the river and to their northern neighbour for help. Here is part of the debate.

**W.A.C. Bennett** — Then premier of British Columbia and leader of the Social Credit Party.

I wanted very much to make a deal with the Americans. We could build dams here in British Columbia that would help our neighbours. These dams would store water. The electricity would be made in the US. We would sell them our share of that electricity for 25 to 60 years. In other words, I wanted to let them have all of the power for 25 years. In return we would get a certain amount of cash.

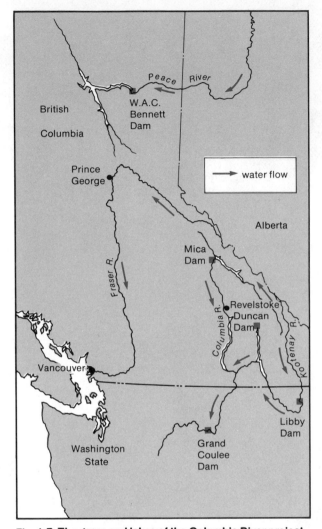

**Fig. 1-7 The dams and lakes of the Columbia River project**

I wanted to use this money to build a power project on the Peace River. The Columbia wasn't as good for us as for the Americans. I put my big project on the Peace River where more of my own people would be helped.

Mind you, it took a lot of persuasion to get this. Diefenbaker, the prime minister, was against this. His idea was for the Americans to give us half of the electricity they would get. There was a big fight about it. Davie Fulton, one of Dief's boys, even said it would be like selling New York for a few beads. Well, I won in the end. I got a better deal for British Columbia. We created jobs, we helped start new industries on the Peace River. I'm proud of the Columbia development.

I made sure that certain conditions were set down when the first part of the agreement was completed. We would either get the power generated by the United States at no cost to us. Or we could be paid in cash at the current market value for our share of the power. The choice would be the option of the government of British Columbia. We could not lose!

*With permission of W.A.C. Bennett*

**General Andrew McNaughton** — Canadian representative of the **International Joint Commission.** He was also Commander of the First Canadian Army in 1943-44 and Minister of National Defence in 1944.

I believed that a shared use of our resources would make us less independent.I tried to protect Canada's water resources from the demands of the water and power hungry Americans. I think that the best way to help our neighbours would have been to build the dams ourselves. We would have sold electricity to the Americans at the going rate. We should have done this only for a year or two at a time. This would be necessary if we ever wanted to use it ourselves.

For example, if we sold them power for 15 years, they would build factories to use it. They would get used to that power. If after 15 years we decided to cut off the power — well, imagine the protest they would raise. Once you sell power for a long time, it's like giving the power away for good. So you can see that I wanted to protect our water and electricity for our own use.

*Adapted from comments by General A.G.L. McNaughton. See R.E. Richardson,* Developing Water Resources, *(Toronto: McGraw-Hill Ryerson, 1970), pp. 55-79.*

THE DECISION — 1961

The government of John Diefenbaker had to choose between the plans put forward by McNaughton and Bennett. Diefenbaker

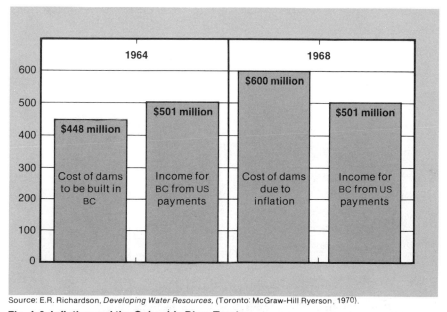

Source: E.R. Richardson, *Developing Water Resources,* (Toronto: McGraw-Hill Ryerson, 1970).

**Fig. 1-8 Inflation and the Columbia River Treaty**

accepted Bennett's plan and his provincial demands, allowing power to be sold over a long period. Bennett was to use the cash for his Peace River project.

### THE RESULTS

By the late 1970s, the dams were in place. British Columbia received cash for its part of the deal. However, the amount of money agreed upon was no longer enough to pay for the new power projects. BC had sold power at 1964 prices. The cost of dams had gone up and had to be paid for at 1970 prices. Did BC lose?

### THE COLUMBIA RIVER PROJECT — GAINS AND LOSSES

John Diefenbaker thought that the Columbia River Treaty was another good example of Canadian-US co-operation. He placed any problems that came up at W.A.C. Bennett's door.

| *Gains* | *Losses* |
|---|---|
| —New lakes | —Flooded valleys, farms, towns |
| —More construction jobs | —Due to inflation, BC's income from treaty buys less. Dams cost over $600 million. |
| —Cash money — $501 million — for BC to use for building dams and producing electricity. | |

---

**READING BETTER**

1. Why was General McNaughton opposed to the Columbia River Treaty?
2. Why was W.A.C. Bennett in favour of the treaty?
3. Why did Premier Bennett insist on getting a cash payment from the Americans?
4. Show how the Columbia River Treaty is an example of continentalism.
5. How did inflation affect the cost of the dams?

---

BC Hydro

**The W.A.C. Bennett Dam. Why was this dam built on the Peace River?**

## Case 2: The Foothills Pipeline—1977

*Issue:* Should Canada have made an agreement with the United States to allow a natural gas pipeline to be built from Alaska to the southern States?

### THE PROBLEM — THE US VIEW

Alaska has natural gas. The rest of the United States is short of gas for heat and industry. President Jimmy Carter rejected a plan to bring liquid gas from Alaska to the lower states by ship. He said it would be too dangerous to the environment, and too expensive. An accident at sea could cause a major disaster.

Another way to transport the gas would be through a pipeline. Such a pipeline would have to pass through Canada. It would be safer to use a pipeline than to put gas in ships. It would also cost much less. This would mean cheaper fuel. Would Canadians agree?

### THE SITUATION — THE CANADIAN VIEW

Prime Minister Trudeau had said, "At some point we have to be reasonable with them (the States)." Trudeau did not want to hurt the US. He knew that the States needed fuel desperately. The problem facing the government was the route of the pipeline. What route would be the safest? The cheapest? What kind of deal would be best for Canada?

To help the government decide, two special commissions were appointed. These were to investigate the problems and report back to Ottawa.

### THE COMMISSIONS

The Berger Commission
Head: Mr. Justice Thomas Berger
Route considered: Mackenzie River Valley
Recommendations:
1. There should be no pipeline across the northern Yukon from Alaska to the Mackenzie River. Such a pipeline would endanger the environment. Wildlife would be disturbed. Natural wilderness would be destroyed by construction.
2. No pipeline should be built down the Mackenzie Valley until 1987. If built sooner it could destroy the way of life of the Indians and Inuit. They need to protect their traditional culture.
3. Indians and Inuit in the north need time to settle **land claims.** Their future prosperity could depend on court decisions as to who owns the land.
4. We do not know how much gas there is in the Mackenzie River Delta. It would be better to delay building until we know for sure how much gas there is.

367

5. Indians and Inuit may not benefit. Many of them do not have the training for many construction jobs. When the pipeline is finished and the jobs end, they will have gained little.

The Lysyk Commission
Head: Dean Kenneth Lysyk
Route considered: Alaska Highway
Recommendations:
1. Building a pipeline beside the Alaska Highway would not do much more damage to the Yukon or its people. The highway has already had any bad effects.
2. The Indians have land claims. They believe some of their land was taken away illegally. These land claims are more important to people in the Yukon than is any pipeline.
3. No pipeline should be built before 1981. This will allow land claims to be settled.
4. A special government agency must be established to protect Yukoners and their land.
5. At least $200 million should be paid into a special fund. This Yukon Heritage Fund will help improve life for Yukoners.

THE DECISION

The Mackenzie Valley route was proposed by a group of Canadian and American oil companies.

The Alaska Highway route was proposed by Bob Blair, an Alberta businessman and head of Foothills Pipe Line (Yukon) Ltd.

In 1977, the government chose the Alaska Highway route. Blair was allowed to build the pipeline from Alaska to the lower states. His

**The Alaska-Yukon pipeline**

These facts will help you decide about the pipeline and continentalism.
Length: 8 000 km in total, 2 700 km in Canada.
Cost: Estimated at $10 billion. This is twenty times more than the cost of the St. Lawrence Seaway.
Planned start of construction: Early 1980s.
Planned end of construction: Mid 1980s.
Estimated amount of money to be spent in Canada during construction: $3 billion.
Total estimated benefit from all sources to Canada during life of the pipeline: $13.6 billion.
Size of pipe: 142 cm in diameter.
Estimated number of jobs created in Canada: 2 000 in construction and others on manufacturing pipe, etc. Total 68 000 man years. (One man year = one person working for one year.)
Source: *Toronto Star* 1978 4 5

company would then allow the Americans to use the pipeline. Because Blair was Canadian, this large project seemed more Canadian. An agreement for building the pipeline was made between the United States and Canada. It included the following points:

1. The Foothills company must lend $200 million to the federal government. This money will be used to help the Yukon. The government will repay the loan by reducing property taxes that the company will pay in the Yukon.
2. The pipeline will pass through Whitehorse. A **spur line** may be built to Dawson. This may later be connected to the Mackenzie Delta where there is Canadian gas.
3. Neither the Canadian nor US governments will guarantee any loans. Foothills is on its own.
4. Construction will start in the early 1980s. The project will cost around $10 billion.

**Fig. 1-9  The two proposed pipeline routes**

SUMMARY: WAS THIS A GOOD DEAL FOR CANADA?

*Pros*

1. The pipeline company will pay $250 million in taxes to the Yukon. This will help Yukoners.

2. Foothills Pipe Line (Yukon) Ltd. is Canadian-owned.

3. The company will lend $200 million to the federal government. This money will be used to help people in the Yukon.

4. Canada will later be able to share the pipeline. A spur line may be built from Whitehorse to Dawson. Gas for Canadians will travel in the same large pipe.

5. Jobs in the building of the pipeline will go to Canadians. Many Canadians are unemployed.

6. Canada's total gain from the deal is expected to be $530 million and the creation of jobs.

*Cons*

1. The US will gain most from the pipeline. When Canadian gas in the Arctic is ready, an expensive spur line will be needed.

2. The Foothills company will have to borrow money from US banks and insurance companies. There is not enough money in Canada.

3. Some experts want the Canadian government to guarantee any loans to Blair's company. This would commit all Canadians to support a pipeline for American gas.

4. Native Peoples in the north have claimed some of the land that is to be used for the pipeline. These claims must be settled first.

5. A gas explosion could hurt the environment.

6. Some Canadian money will be invested in a pipeline that helps the Americans. This money could be used to help Canadians.

---

**READING BETTER**

1. **Explain in your own words why Prime Minister Trudeau felt that Canada has to be reasonable with the US.**
2. **How much money will Canada gain from this pipeline?**

**ORGANIZING BETTER**

1. **Compare the Berger and Lysyk Commissions. How are they similar and how do they differ?**
2. **Does the government agreement with the US take care of the recommendations made by** Dean Lysyk? Make a chart of Lysyk's recommendations. Match these with the government decision and the pros and cons of the deal.
3. **Review the pipeline debate of 1956 that is discussed earlier in the chapter. Make up a chart showing ways in which the two pipeline issues are the same, and a chart showing how they are different. What do you conclude?**

**TAKING A STAND**

1. **Should Canada have agreed to a pipeline going across its territory to the USA?**

---

### Case 3 — Free trade today

In our look at the history of Canada-US relations, we briefly studied some of the history of reciprocity. In the late 1970s reciprocity, or free trade, again became a national issue. When Canada was suffering from high unemployment and a sagging economy, some experts suggested that free trade with the United States could be a cure. The issue was again a regional one. The West and East were generally in favour of free trade, while central Canada, the industrial area, opposed it. In addition, there was a move for freer trade around the world. The GATT (General Agreement on Tariffs and Trade) was being worked out among 94 nations, including Canada. Freer trade was an issue at GATT meetings. Once again, Canada had to make decisions on the question of reciprocity.

ISSUE: SHOULD CANADA ADOPT FREE TRADE?

*The debate is explored through the records of the* Puslinch Times. *(These are fictional newspaper accounts based on real situations.)*
1. *Interview. This week Lamar Lafont of our Business Department interviews Fred Freetrader, Research Assistant with the Economic Council of Canada.*

**Lafont:** The Economic Council has again recommended free trade for Canada. What would this mean?

**Freetrader:** It means that there would be fewer restrictions on what could be imported and sold in Canada. All protective tariffs would be removed. No Canadian industry would be protected from the competition of cheaper foreign goods.

**Lafont:** Can you give us a concrete example of what all this means?

**Freetrader:** Well, for example, there's a small lamp company in your township — Peabody Lamp Company. They make table lamps that sell for about fifty dollars. There's a tariff on similar imported lamps. The tariff raises the price of the foreign-made lamps to about sixty dollars. With free trade, there would be no restrictions on imported lamps. We would have free competition.

**Lafont:** That could create problems for Puslinch, couldn't it? Inexpensive lamps from Japan would sell better than ours, and force our plant out of business. Surely the Economic Council sees this. Is that what you want?

**Freetrader:** You've raised a good point. First, we're mostly interested in free trade with the US. That nation is our biggest customer now. And we're its biggest customer. So it makes sense to have free trade with the States.

Secondly, yes, we want to have some Canadian plants close. Right now they are protected by tariffs and **import quotas.** Therefore, they don't have to worry much about competition. The result is high-priced Canadian goods. Free trade would mean that Canadians could buy cheaper goods.

**Lafont:** All these theories sound fine. But don't forget that the Peabody Lamp Company employs 75 people. What happens to them? Do they starve so that someone in Vancouver can have a less expensive lamp?

**Freetrader:** You're making the picture sound blacker than it is. If Peabody can make good lamps at a reasonable price, they'll be OK. Peabody may be able to compete. If Peabody can't compete — well the country will be better off without it. The company is just not efficient. You see, with free trade, we'll sell many of our own products to the US. We'll sell products that we make better than they do. At the same time, we'll get cheaper products ourselves. Badly run, protected Canadian businesses will disappear. We truly believe that Canada will be better off.

**Lafont:** I know that the Economic Council has recommended free trade for years. In the old days the Liberal Party believed in it. But why should voters in Puslinch vote for free trade today? Why should they take a chance on losing their jobs? Wouldn't they rather pay higher prices for Canadian-made goods than risk losing their jobs?

**Freetrader:** It is a gamble. But we economic experts think that Canada will be better off. New jobs will be created in competitive industries like mobile housing, small aircraft, asbestos, and so on. People will be able to shift jobs. Besides, plants won't close overnight all over the country. Good heavens, no! Over ten or twenty years new jobs will be created.

**Lafont:** Well, thank you for your time Mr. Freetrader. I hope the people back home will learn as much from this interview as I have.

**Freetrader:** My pleasure.

2. *The following are letters to the editor of the* Puslinch Times.

*Farmer for free trade*

I agree completely with Fred Freetrader's ideas. As a farmer, I've always been in a dilemma. I sell my barley and oats according to world prices. Some years they're high and I do well. Other years the prices are low and I hardly break even. But whatever those grain prices are like, I've still got to buy high-priced Canadian cars, stoves, radios, and tractors.

So I'm all for free trade. We can use less expensive televisions and cars! It's time to make the factory owners in Ontario work a little harder for their dollars.

*Seymour Perkins*

*Economy hurt by free trade*

Has it ever occurred to people like Fred Freetrader that Canada has a branch plant economy? If we have free trade with the US, the need for branch plants disappears. Companies can make all the products at their main plants in the US and ship what they need to Canada. We will lose jobs and tariff money paid by US companies. Canada's economy will be seriously hurt if we go to free trade.

*Maria Louise Pellicci*

1. A person in favour of sharing the resources of North America is called a . . . .
2. It was once called reciprocity. Today it is more often called . . . .
3. Whom did Premier W.A.C. Bennett disagree sharply with over the Columbia River Treaty?
4. The decision to build the Alaska-Yukon pipeline may be called continentalist because:
   a) The pipeline goes from the Atlantic to the Pacific
   b) Canada is helping the United States and will share benefits
   c) Canada is dictating terms of agreement to the United States
   d) All of these
5. Match item in column A with the correct name in column B.
   Column A
   a) Columbia River Treaty
   b) Mackenzie Valley pipeline route
   c) Alaska-Yukon pipeline route
   Column B
   Berger
   Bennett
   Lysyk

READING BETTER

1. What worries Ms. Pellicci most about free trade?
2. What pleases Mr. Perkins most about free trade?

ORGANIZING BETTER

1. For each of the three case studies, state how Canada gains and loses in wealth and independence. Make a neat chart, and put your information in point form.
2. Make up a large chart with the following columns:
   a) What free trade is
   b) How free trade is defended
   c) How free trade is attacked
   Fill in the chart with points made in the text. Which items on the chart do you agree with? Mark each with an "X". Which column has the most marks?

USING YOUR KNOWLEDGE

1. Who do you think gets more out of continentalism, Canada or the US?

TAKING A STAND

1. Should Canada have free trade with the United States? Refer to facts you have studied in this chapter to defend your position.
2. Are you a continentalist, or an economic nationalist, or do you stand between the two positions? What facts, arguments, or ideas have most influenced your opinion?

## Solving the problem of American influence in the Canadian economy

In reading through this chapter you have learned about branch plants, economic nationalism, free trade, continentalism, and many other aspects of Canada-United States economic relations. You have also taken a stand on several of these issues. The last part of the chapter looks at solutions to the problems created by American influence in our economy. The section attempts to answer these questions:

1. What steps have already been taken to control foreign ownership?
2. What further steps should be taken to control foreign ownership?

After you study this material, you will be better able to decide on the best solutions to the problem.

What has the federal government already done to control American influence in the Canadian economy?

*1. FIRA — The Foreign Investment Review Agency*

This agency was created in 1974 to screen foreign investment coming into Canada. FIRA can reject any project or take-over that it believes will not benefit Canada. Between 1974 and 1978 the agency approved 778 bids by foreigners to take over Canadian companies. Only 224 applications were turned down.

Here are some typical FIRA approvals:
—Gold Fields American Corporation of New York received permission to take over Darius Gold Mines, Fervat Gold Mines, and Alpha Gold Mines (all of Toronto).

—Hatalpa Company of West Germany received permission to buy the Oxford Foundry and Machine Company of Truro, Nova Scotia. Hatalpa plans to expand the factory to make hydraulic and marine products.

### 2. CDC — The Canada Development Corporation

Launched in 1972, the CDC was created by the federal government. Its purpose is to invest money in Canadian business or even to buy shares in foreign businesses that are operating in Canada. CDC began with $250 million, which was given to it by the government. The corporation raised another $100 million by selling shares to the Canadian people. CDC bought stocks in other companies, and even bought whole companies. By 1977 it was the 36th largest corporation in Canada. The CDC has helped to build strong Canadian-controlled businesses. This adds to Canada's independence.

Here are some typical CDC investments:
—Complete ownership of Polysar Ltd. This Sarnia, Ontario plant makes plastics, latex, and synthetic rubber. Value: $400 million.
—30% ownership of Texasgulf Inc., a huge mining company with operations in Canada. Texasgulf is one of the 500 largest firms in the US.
—Ownership of CDC Oil and Gas Ltd., which explores for and produces oil and natural gas in western Canada. Value: $125 million.
—Ownership of Connlab Holdings. This company makes drugs and does medical research. It is one of the few companies in the world to make insulin, which helps diabetics. Value: $100 million.

### 3. Specific laws

i) By law, Canadians must be owners of the following types of companies operating in Canada.
 a) Banks — 25% foreign ownership allowed.
 b) Trust and loan companies (federal) — 25% foreign ownership allowed.
 c) TV and radio broadcasting — 20% foreign ownership allowed.
ii) Bus, train, and airline companies are controlled by the Canadian Transport Commission. This government agency makes sure that foreign-owned transport companies work to help Canadians.
iii) Energy — oil, coal, gas, electricity — is controlled by the National Energy Board. It controls construction, shipment, and even prices. Foreign ownership in uranium mines or industries is limited to 33%.

### 4. Tax incentives

i) Canadians may make a tax deduction for income earned from investing money in Canadian-owned companies. This is done when income tax returns are made out each spring.

For example, Georgina has invested $100 000 in the Canada Development Corporation. She earned $1 000 last year from this investment. She may claim an income deduction of this amount. If Georgina had invested in MGM Pictures of Hollywood, USA, she would not have been allowed to deduct the interest.

ii) The cost of advertisements placed in Canadian newspapers or magazines may be used as an income tax deduction. If the paper or magazine is more than 25% foreign-owned, then no deduction is allowed. This encourages Canadian companies to advertise in Canadian-owned papers. This also stops foreign take-overs of Canadian papers and magazines because foreign owners may not make any money from advertising.

**USING YOUR KNOWLEDGE**
**1. Examine carefully each solution that has**

already been tried. Decide why it may or may not work well to stop foreign control of our economy.
2. **Decide which of the solutions are fair to both Canadian and American investors and tell why.**
3. **Which of the attempted solutions do you think is best?**

Should more be done?
Many nationalists believe that more should be done to stop foreign investment and control in our economy.

1. **Eric Kierans** — Former head of the Montreal Stock Exchange and former Liberal MP and Postmaster General.
   I believe that we should get rid of tariffs. We can eliminate them gradually, over a period of ten years. The owners of branch plants will then want to sell out. There is no point in having a branch plant if there is no tariff.

   Another part of my plan is to have a lower tax on Canadian-owned corporations. This will mean that they will have more money to buy branch plants from US companies who want to sell. A higher tax on foreign-controlled companies will encourage them to sell out to Canadians.

   Of course, some weak Canadian firms will disappear. But my plan will make it possible for Canadians to buy up foreign-owned businesses.
   *Adapted from* Canadian Forum *1972 1-2, pp. 52-53.*

2. **Walter Gordon** — Former Liberal MP and Minister of Finance in Ottawa. A founder of the Committee for an Independent Canada.
   I don't think the government has to take over all foreign-controlled business. This is not what Canadians in business want. I think we need only start with the 32 largest foreign-owned companies. They should be given 10 years to sell out to Canadians. We should allow no more than 25% foreign-ownership in them.

These 32 foreign-owned companies are the ones most important to Canadian independence. If Canadians controlled them it would mean we had independent control over most of our economy. I believe we could do this for about $15 billion. Spread over ten years, this amount of money is something Canadians can afford.
*Adapted from Walter Gordon,* Toronto Star *1977 11 22.*

Other solutions
*1. Buy "Canadian"*
Have the governments of Canada buy only Canadian products. The federal government spends billions every year. If each province also joined in a "Buy Canadian only" project, profits would go to Canadian industry instead of to foreign-owned industry. Governments buy items such as these:

| | |
|---|---|
| Aircraft | Ferry boats |
| Snowmobiles | Typewriters |
| Shoes | Paper clips |

*2. Nationalize*
The government itself could take over ownership of industries. A fair price could be paid to the branch plant owners. The federal government already owns *Air Canada, Canadian National Railways*, and hundreds of other businesses.
Example: The government of Saskatchewan is buying back the province's foreign-owned potash industry. Saskatchewan has one of the world's largest deposits of potash, which is used in fertilizer.

In 1976 the government-owned Potash Corporation of Saskatchewan (PCS) bought the Duval Mine near Saskatoon for $128 million. Two other mines were bought for $221 million.

In 1978 the PCS negotiated to buy the Amax Mine for $85 million. This gave PCS ownership of 34% of the potash industry in Saskatchewan. All the mines had been American-owned.

### 3. Special taxes

Products made in foreign-owned branch plants would get an extra tax. Profits made by branch plants could also be taxed more. It is hoped that Canadians would not buy the more expensive products. Perhaps then, branch plant owners would sell out to Canadians.

### TAKING A STAND

1. Which of the suggested solutions do you think would work? Why?
2. Which suggested solutions do you think would be unfair to Canadians or Americans? Why?
3. Which of these solutions do you think should be tried? (Note: If you answer "none", defend your position with facts from this chapter.)

## Conclusion

The fact that Canada's closest neighbour is a rich and powerful nation cannot be ignored. Nor can we forget the huge role that Americans play in our economy. We cannot stay out of the public debate about American economic influence. Decisions that are made about US investment will affect the size of our paycheques and the number of jobs open to us. As citizens we can influence those decisions with our votes. We can write letters or join with others who believe as we do. But it is essential to weigh both sides of the issue carefully and take a reasoned stand. What did you decide?

### READING BETTER

1. Here are some terms that were used in the chapter. Write one or two sentences that define or explain each term.
   Protective tariff
   National policy
   Foreign investment
   Continentalism
   Profit
   CDC

### ORGANIZING BETTER

1. Review your work on this chapter by rereading your notes. Skim through the text again.

You can also work with a partner and make up ten basic fact questions that you should now be able to answer about Canadian-US economic relations. Test other people in the class.

### USING YOUR KNOWLEDGE

1. Turn back to the chapter introduction. Write a short paragraph answering each question listed in the introduction.

### SOLVING PROBLEMS

1. This chapter has shown that people from different parts of Canada have different opinions about American influence in our economy. These conflicting opinions can be a problem. Your goal is to solve the disputes among Canada's regions over what to do about foreign ownership. To do this, follow the steps of the problem-solving model carefully.

### TAKING A STAND

1. Show other people in your class your opinion of US influence in Canada's economy. Make up a poster on one of the following topics that clearly advertises your point of view.
   Branch plants
   Free trade
   Continentalism
   The Alaska-Yukon pipeline
   Solutions to the problem of American influence
   The Columbia River Treaty

### RESEARCHING

1. Find out more about economic nationalism. Write a report about what economic nationalists believe and what they want to do.
2. Find out more about the history of Canadian-American relations. Write a report about one of the following topics:
   Quebec and the American Revolution
   The War of 1812
   The United Empire Loyalists
   The American role in the Rebellions of 1837
   The Reciprocity Treaty of 1854
   Canada and the American Civil War
   The Underground Railroad
   The Canadian West and the American West
   The Aroostook War
   The Alaska Boundary Dispute

## GLOSSARY

**American.** Citizen of or anything belonging to the United States of America.

**Annexation Manifesto.** Declaration made in 1849 recommending that Canada join the USA. People who supported this idea were called annexationists.

**British North America.** The area of North America that is now Canada.

**Canada.** Created in 1840 when Upper Canada (Ontario) and Lower Canada (Quebec) were united by Britain.

**Company of New France.** One hundred French people in business invested money in this fur trading company, hoping to earn a profit.

**Depression.** An economic slump. There is usually high unemployment, low wages, few goods being made, and little or no investment.

**Free trade.** No barriers to buying or selling goods between nations.

**Import quota.** A limit placed on the amount of a certain item that may be brought into Canada. For example, the number of pairs of Russian hockey skates brought into the country may be restricted to 1 000.

**International Joint Commission.** An agency created by Canada and the United States to supervise control of boundaries and international waterways.

**Investment.** Money used to make a profit. You make an investment when you give loans, buy stocks, or own property. There is always an element of risk, because profits may not be earned. Sometimes you can lose the money you invest.

**Land claims.** Canada's Native Peoples have sometimes had their land taken away from them illegally. They have been claiming payment for this property. They either ask for a return of the land, or for money. Huge amounts of land and money are involved.

**Manufactured goods.** Items that are made by hand or by machine, especially by machine. Examples: iron pots, tractors, buttons, cloth.

**Militia.** Part-time soldiers. In the nineteenth century, most able-bodied men were required to serve in the militia.

**Northwest.** The area that consists of the provinces of Manitoba, Saskatchewan, Alberta, and the Northwest Territories.

**Recession.** A mild economic slump. Not as bad as a depression.

**Shares.** Any of the portions into which the ownership of a company or piece of property is divided. Also called "stock". Shares in a company may be bought at a stock exchange.

**Spur line.** A side line connected to the main pipe.

**Tariff barrier.** A tariff is a tax on goods or materials brought into a country. A high tariff can be used to keep foreign goods out. Thus it acts as a barrier.

# 2/Canada and the US: A question of culture

---

**Contents**

---

**Introduction**

Canada and the United States have much in common. They share the geography of a continent, and the world's greatest trade. Canada and the US share a multicultural heritage, because both nations have become home for people born in different nations around the world. The two countries share people as well. Millions of Canadians and **Americans** have crossed the border to find homes and jobs in the neighbouring country. Many people feel that Canada and the United States share one other important aspect—culture.

What is culture? The culture of a people is basically its way of life. This way of life is made up of many features such as language, dress, music, literature, games, foods, and religions. Through the years, the US has developed a distinct American culture.

Canada shares in this culture. Canadians enjoy sports, foods, and entertainments that are American in origin.

Many Canadians fear that Canada is becoming too *Americanized*. This means that our culture is growing more and more American. They say that because of the US influence on our culture, we do not have a strong Canadian identity. Even in Quebec, people are worried about being Americanized. (In Quebec, however, this worry is part of an overall fear about the influence of the *anglophone* culture).

This chapter examines the American influence on Canadian culture. The material you read will help you form an opinion about whether or not Canada's culture is becoming too Americanized. The chapter deals with these basic questions:

1. **What is the Canadian identity?**
2. **How has American culture influenced Canadians?**
3. **What should be done to stop the US influence and create a strong Canadian culture?**

**Setting the scene: Similarities and differences between Canada and the US**

The following story introduces you to some similarities and differences between Canada and the US. It also shows how some people react to the US influence in Canadian life.

---

### Journey into a strange land

Mary-Lou Richards cried herself to sleep every night for a month. Her father's announcement that he was being transferred had come without warning. He was to start work in another city one month later. She was sure that she would miss her social life—the tennis, the swimming, the camping trips, the dances. Would she be able to enjoy these activities in a new country? What would she do for fun in a strange land with strange new people? Mary-Lou Richards, age 15, was frightened. She knew very little about Newtown, Canada, which was to be her new home.

Don Richards explained the move to his family in this way: "This move won't be the last we'll make. If I can succeed as chief engineer, the next step up will be vice-president. That would mean I'd be working in the Caltron head office in Atlanta again. We'll be back in the States before you know it. In the meantime, we get a chance to see a foreign country. Anyway, it's not as far from home or as different from here as you think."

THREE MONTHS LATER

Eric Weiskopf had also been transferred to Newtown by the same company. Eric was originally from Kitchener, Ontario and he had worked for Caltron in Montreal and Kingston. In Newtown, Eric soon found himself working closely with Don Richards. As both were new in the city and without friends, Eric invited Don and his wife Rhoda over one Saturday night. They were exchanging views on Newtown.

"We drove up from Atlanta," explained Rhoda in her quiet American drawl. "I don't mind telling you that the kids were pretty miserable about moving to Canada. After we crossed the border, they were looking out the car windows to see what this country was like. I guess they expected it to be completely different from the US. But nothing was really strange. Then when we got off the **turnpike** at Newtown, they saw the most amazing thing. There was a *McDonald's*, just like at home! Mary-Lou was so happy to see that familiar sign. We were all laughing because the kids had been so worried about coming to a foreign country. The *McDonald's* was so homey."

"Still there must have been some things that took getting used to," said Eric.

"Not really," answered Don. "We find the Canadian life style about the same as the American one. Clothes, cars, appliances—just about everything we were used to back home in the US is here. I've found it easier to feel at home in Newtown than I did in Atlanta when we moved there from Boston."

Eric was surprised to hear this. He had always believed that the US was different from Canada.

"And the kids are really very happy now," said Rhoda. "Our son can still watch his favourite TV programmes. Mary-Lou hears her favourite rock bands on the radio. Don can still see baseball and football on television. We're really enjoying ourselves up here."

Later, after the Richardses had left, Eric asked his wife, "Helen, did you ever think that we weren't different from Americans?"

Helen was tired but she could see that Eric was a bit upset. "No. Some of them talk with a different accent, but that's about it." She paused, trying to say something that might calm Eric. "No, I guess we're not really different people. We live about the same kind of lives."

Eric was troubled. Helen seemed to look on the differences between Americans and Canadians in the same way that the Richardses did. To Eric, this was astonishing. He had never thought of himself as an American, or like an American. Yet that list of things that made the Richardses feel at home—music, television, products—upset him. "What is a Canadian," he asked others at work, "if there is no difference between us and Americans?"

Eric's soul-searching about being Canadian did not stop. Caltron's Newtown plant had many Americans working in top management jobs. Eric's new sense of being Canadian made him look for American influences. He noticed that Don Richards always hired American engineers to work in his office. Most of them had gone to the same American university as Richards. Eric also noticed that Caltron advertisements used what he called "American" spelling. Helen told him to stop worrying about such little things or else he would go crazy. Eric agreed and threw himself into his job. He too hoped to become a vice-president.

It was at a management meeting the next month that Eric lost his chance for promotion. All of the managers were sitting around a table in the vice-president's office. Eric was giving a report on successful sales. He included a paragraph about a new electronic door lock being designed by one of Caltron's Canadian customers.

"I think that this lock would be a useful item for us. There's nothing like it available in North America right now," said Eric.

"Well", replied Don, the chief engineer, "it sure sounds interesting. But frankly, Eric, we'll just have to put it aside for now. Head Office has already decided on a locking system and we'll have to stick with it."

Eric smiled and finished his sales report. The advertising manager, recently promoted from Atlanta, then outlined the latest campaign to sell Caltron products. Eric's eye caught something that made him interrupt her.

"I think there are some changes that you'll have to make for our market. You've used the letters E-Z to stand for 'easy'. In Canada many people pronounce that letter as 'zed'. The ad makes no sense if you read it as 'E-Zed way to wash your car'. And again the spelling of 'neighbor' should be changed. Canadians still tend to use o-u-r at the end of such words."

The advertising manager defended her ideas, saying that the US spelling and pronunciation were already common all over Canada.

"Well, they weren't always," snapped Eric. "If we're selling in Canada then we should produce ads that are truly Canadian. Anything else is a cheap trick that may insult Canadian customers. Don't forget that's who we're selling to."

The vice-president intervened. "We'll look into the changes, Eric. Thanks for your observations." She seemed confused and upset about Eric's outburst.

Eric Weiskopf found out two weeks later that Don Richards had been promoted to vice-president. Three months after that, Eric quit his job to become sales manager for the small Canadian-owned company that made electronic door locks.

## READING BETTER

1. In what ways did the Richards family find Canada to be the same as the United States?
2. Why did Eric Weiskopf become upset after the Richards's visit?
3. Why did Eric quit his job with Caltron?

## USING YOUR KNOWLEDGE

1. What aspects of life in Canada would you expect an American to find strange or unfamiliar? Why?
2. Make a list of ways in which Caltron may have helped spread American culture in Canada.

## TAKING A STAND

1. Do you agree with Don Richards that Canada is not different from the States? Why or why not?
2. "Having the same foods, music, sports, TV shows, and life styles as the Americans is not really important. Canada can be independent despite these similarities." Do you agree? Why or why not?
   Note: You will be asked similar questions later, after you have finished this chapter.
3. Was Eric Weiskopf right to quit his job? Why or why not?

## RESEARCHING

1. Conduct a survey among people you know. Ask: Is Canada different from the United States? How?
2. Use Chapter 4 of Unit 3 and materials in a library to find out how Quebeckers have tried to protect their language. What kinds of problems was the French language facing in Quebec? Compare the French language problem with the one of the Americanization of English-speaking Canada.

The short story presents some of the issues about American cultural influences in Canada. It shows that there are great similarities in language and life style. The story also points out that these similarities cause debate among Canadians. This debate will be presented in greater detail later in the chapter. Before that, however, we will take a brief look at the history of American influence on Canadian culture. This overview will show how the cultures of Canada and the United States came to be similar.

## Historical overview of US influence on Canadian culture

*In the beginning*

Before Europeans arrived on this continent there were several distinct North American cultures. Different groups of Indians and Inuit had their own languages, customs, and traditions.

The European colonists brought their own cultures to North America. They brought their laws, religions, styles of dress, and language. Over time, the Native Peoples adopted many European cultural traits or were forced to accept them. At the same time, life in the North American wilderness changed the Europeans. Many foods, words, and customs of the Native Peoples became part of the colonists' culture. Thus, the colonists slowly became different from their European cousins.

Even though their culture was changing, the colonists were still tied to their European homelands. These homelands continued to be a source of culture and identity. When ties with the mother country were cut, however, distinct cultures grew. For example, after the English Conquest of 1759, the French in North America were cut off from France. Thus a distinct French Canadian culture grew.

To the south, a distinct American culture also developed for similar reasons. Although it was based on a British heritage, it was unique. After the American Revolution this development quickened. Although British and French styles of clothing or literature were admired and copied, a distinct US culture emerged. Language, politics, literature, and foods were among the aspects of culture that developed in the US. By the twentieth century American culture began to influence the world.

British settlers in the Atlantic colonies and Quebec imported aspects of British culture, such as sports, dress, and government. This pattern would continue for as long as British people settled in Canada.

When the British became a majority in British North America, they reinforced British law and administration with their religion, customs, and culture.

## American culture arrives

The Loyalists brought a different cultural influence to British North America after 1783. Although these people were loyal to Britain, they were also American. They brought to the British colonies American styles of speech, government, and business. Other American settlers who flooded into the area that is present-day Ontario around 1800 and again after 1814 also brought American culture. For example, most of the first Methodist, Presbyterian, and Baptist ministers in Ontario were Americans. American ideas on education also strongly influenced schools in Upper Canada and in the Atlantic colonies. The idea of free schools, run by local trustees and paid for by property taxes, was adopted from US ideas. American political ideas were also imported. Canada boiled with debate over ideas of American democracy and popular control of government.

The distinctive culture of Lower Canada (Quebec) was defended from both British and American influences. Cultural leaders like **François-Xavier Garneau** and **Octave Crémazie** helped preserve it in the early 1800s as did the influence of the Roman Catholic Church.

After the end of the Civil War in 1865, American influences on Canadian culture continued to grow. American "dime novels" became very popular in Canada. Heroes of the American "Wild West" were as popular in Kingston and Halifax as in Chicago and Boston. The American humorist Mark Twain charmed the United States, Canada, and the whole world with his works.

Even though British and US influences were strong, Canadian culture did grow in the late 1800s and early 1900s. Poets Archibald Lampman, Bliss Carman, and Duncan Scott wrote about the anglophone Canadian experience. Novelists Gilbert Parker, Charles G.D. Roberts, and William Kirby turned out romantic novels about old Quebec and Acadia. Stephen Leacock wrote humorous pieces about life in small Canadian towns. His stories have become world-famous. Canadian writers in general, though, had a hard time gaining recognition at home. The most popular books were still British or American.

## The twentieth century

In the twentieth century, American cultural influences in countries all over the world grew stronger. The impact that US culture had on Canada was immense.

In the first decades of the century, Canadians eagerly received US films, novels, radio, records, jazz music, and much more. Canadian cultural leaders did exist, but they had to struggle to be recognized. Some, such as the Canadian painters of the **Group of Seven**, were criticized or rejected for many years. Other cultural leaders had to achieve success in the US before Canadians would recognize them.

The Canadian government saw how great the US influence was in radio and films. It decided to do something to protect Canadian talent. The Canadian Radio Commission was formed in 1932. It controlled broadcasting and made sure that Canadian programmes were aired. In 1936 the Canadian Broadcasting Corporation (CBC) was created. This corporation was owned by the people of Canada and was supported by tax dollars. It gave Canadian performers a chance to be seen and recognized. In 1939 the National Film Board was formed to boost the Canadian film industry.

Throughout the century, much Canadian talent has appeared. The Royal Winnipeg Ballet and the National Ballet of Canada

**Veronica Tennant and James Kudelka of the National Ballet of Canada**

have achieved international fame. The Montreal Symphony and Toronto Symphony orchestras have grown in talent and reputation. The Stratford Festival Theatre in Ontario has received much praise. The theatre attracts stars from Britain and the United States.

In spite of these successes, Canada in the twentieth century has been flooded with American culture. Radio, films, books, magazines—all have swamped struggling Canadian counterparts.

### Television and sports

The 1950s saw the influence of American culture increase. The coming of television was one cause. Hundreds of thousands of Canadian homes sprouted TV antennae to receive not only the CBC but also American stations near the border. Canadians produced some memorable shows—*The Plouffe Family, Wayne and Shuster, Juliette, Cross Canada Hit Parade*, and others. Still, apart from NHL hockey broadcasts, the most popular programmes in Canada were American. The people demanded that public and private networks carry their favourite American programmes.

The 1950s, 1960s, and 1970s also saw American influence in sports increase. The NHL, ruled by American owners, expanded heavily in the US. The Canadian Football League (CFL) was dominated more and more by imported American talent. However, it demanded limits on the number of Americans playing on each team. It therefore continued to produce

The Toronto Symphony

**The Toronto Symphony Orchestra with Music Director Andrew Davis. Cultural events in Canada attract bigger audiences than sporting events do.**

Robert C. Ragsdale

**The Stratford Festival Theatre, Ontario. This theatre is world-famous for the plays it produces.**

Canadian stars. Baseball, popular for decades in the US, increased its appeal in Canada when Montreal got a franchise in the National League. Toronto later joined the American League. Indeed, Canadian professional sports were continental in scope.

### The Massey Report

The *Massey Report,* 1951, sprang from Canada's concern about Americanization. It clearly identified the need for truly Canadian cultural growth. It pointed out the strong American influences that hurt this growth. As a result of the *Massey Report*, the *Canada Council* was created. Its purpose was to help develop Canadian culture. The Canada Council provides money to support artists, scholars, musicians, and writers.

### Education

Concern about Americanization also existed in schools. Canadian universities often had many American teachers on staff. Many of them were hired on merit alone, or because there were no qualified Canadians available. Critics feared that the US teachers would pass on American views and **cultural values** to Canadian students. They were also afraid that the American professors would hire fellow Americans. This would leave qualified Canadian teachers without jobs.

In high schools and elementary schools there was concern about the use of American texts. These texts used American examples and referred to American achievements. This could leave Canadian students with a better knowledge of the US than of their own country. Because of this concern the *Canada Studies Foundation* was created in 1970. It was designed to promote Canadian studies in schools and help produce Canadian learning materials.

### Multiculturalism

Immigration from France, Britain, and the United States has strongly affected Canada's culture. Once the National Policy took effect in the 1890s, large numbers of immigrants from other countries began coming to Canada. Immigration increased greatly again after 1945. In general these people were absorbed into either the English or French language groups of Canada. However, the immigrants did retain aspects of their own original cultures. This helped create a multicultural atmosphere that has become an increasingly important part of Canada's culture. It has helped to give Canada a unique identity. The governments of the 1960s and 1970s officially encouraged a multicultural identity for Canada. Even so, critics of US influence in Canada claimed that all segments of Canada's culture were being Americanized.

### Conclusion

This section on the history of Canada's culture shows that Canada has had to struggle to create a cultural identity of its own. Many people fear that the country is becoming more and more Americanized. The questions you must deal with are these: Does Canada have a distinct culture and identity? Is it more realistic to speak of a North American culture? The next section of the chapter deals with Canadian identity. It explores those aspects of our culture that are truly Canadian.

**QUICK QUIZ**
**Test your understanding of this section. These questions require short answers.**
1. **When Europeans first came to North America they found distinct cultures already established by _____.**
2. **Why did Quebec develop a distinct culture?**
3. **What influenced the cultures of the colonists in North America?**
4. **Who brought the first American cultural influences to Canada?**

Stephen Leacock

Lucy Maud Montgomery

Louis Hémon

5. What are three inventions in the technological field that helped to Americanize Canadian culture in the twentieth century?
6. What have Canadian artists often had to do before gaining recognition at home?
7. Name three national agencies created to support culture in Canada.
8. Immigration from non-English or non-French countries produced _____ in Canada.

ORGANIZING BETTER

1. Make a list of ways in which American culture has been brought to Canada.
2. Make a list of ways in which Canadians have defended their own cultural growth.
3. Write down three important ideas that you have learned from this history. Compare your list with other students' lists and make up a master list of important ideas. Do you agree with everybody else on what the important

ideas are? Discuss the ideas on the list with your teacher and classmates.

RESEARCHING

1. Here is a list of some important Canadians in the field of literature. Find out if your school library has any of their works. Look up one of these writers in a Canadian encyclopaedia or dictionary of biography. Report to your class.

| | |
|---|---|
| François-Xavier Garneau | Gabrielle Roy |
| Octave Crémazie | Roger Lemelin |
| Archibald Lampman | Yves Thériault |
| Lucy Maud Montgomery | Robertson Davies |
| Sara Jeannette Duncan | Margaret Laurence |
| Stephen Leacock | Irving Layton |
| Ralph Connor | Anne Hébert |
| Mazo de la Roche | Marie-Claire Blais |
| Hugh MacLennan | Margaret Atwood |
| Morley Callaghan | James Reaney |

Hugh McLennan

Margaret Laurence

Anne Hébert

Gisèle Freund

387

### The Canadian identity

What is a Canadian? What makes Canadians a distinct group of people? What is it that makes us a nation? Many Canadians have answered these questions in different ways. At the end of this section you will be asked for your own answers.

Identity is based partly on where you live—geographical location. Canadians share a land that is vast, and made up of many different regions. Many Canadians take pride in the diversity of their land. Another part of identity is common goals and shared history. Canadians of course have a common past and share certain values that have developed from their experiences. There are symbols of this identity. The flag is an obvious example. Can you think of other symbols of identity? Try making a collection of these in your class.

Sometimes it is difficult to show others that we are Canadian. When Canadians travel in Europe, they often wear some kind of maple leaf emblem. This tells Europeans "I am a Canadian". Without the symbol Europeans often find it difficult to tell a Canadian from an American.

The custom of wearing a maple leaf while travelling points out a weakness in our identity that worries a lot of Canadians. Americans and English-speaking Canadians are very much alike. Do you remember what Rhoda and Don Richards said in the story, "Journey into a strange land"? Many Canadians, including most

Julian Cleva

**Travelling Canadians often state their national identity.**

**economic nationalists,** find the need for a Canadian identity very important. They believe that a country cannot be independent without a distinct identity. These nationalists say that culture is the essential ingredient in that separate identity.

Some Canadians, however, find the issue of Canadian identity unimportant. "Why keep asking what a Canadian is?" they ask. "We should just relax and be what we are!" Canadian humorist Gary Lautens has tried to define "being Canadian" for his readers.

---

### You feel Canadian in a snowstorm     by Gary Lautens

Some critics claim Canadians have no identity, but that's ridiculous. Here are just a few simple ways you can tell us from the rest of the world.

A Canadian has a white salt stain halfway up his trouser leg.

A Canadian wants a storm door for his birthday.

A Canadian considers it one of the great thrills of life when snow doesn't stick to his shovel.

A Canadian cries when he sees the snowplough heading for the driveway he just shovelled out.

A Canadian woman burns her bra only if she's out of wood.

When a Canadian thinks of Hell, he wonders what the heating bill must be.

A Canadian gets mad at anyone who breathes in her car because it frosts the windshield.

A Canadian knows it's morning when the sky in the east turns from black to dark grey.

A Canadian wonders if the car behind is going to stop.

A Canadian gets a wild look in his eye and sucks on his mitts every time he passes a travel agency advertising a special to Nassau.

*Reprinted with permission of the* Toronto Star

## Canadian culture quiz

Test yourself on Canadian culture. Answers are found at the back of the book.

1. Which of the following people are Canadian?

| | |
|---|---|
| Liona Boyd | Judy LaMarsh |
| Lise Payette | Smoky Smith |
| Karen Kain | Alice Munro |
| Maggie Smith | Abby Hoffman |
| Frank Shuster | Marie Osmond |
| René Simard | Bob Dylan |
| Isaac Asimov | Frederick Banting |
| Anne Murray | Patsy Gallant |
| John Denver | Maurice Richard |
| William Shatner | Oscar Peterson |

2. Which of the following were invented in Canada?

| | |
|---|---|
| Corn flakes | Acrylic plastic |
| Paint rollers | Nylon |
| Computers | Zippers |
| Newsprint | "Slingshot" football goalposts |
| Kerosene | |
| Combine harvesters | Baseball |
| Snowblowers | Five-pin bowling |
| Colour TV | Snowmobiles |
| Hydrofoils | Insulin |
| Telephones | Airplanes |

3. Which of the following people are Canadian authors?

| | |
|---|---|
| Germaine Guèvremont | George Lucas |
| Margaret Atwood | Gabrielle Roy |
| Ernest Hemingway | Virginia Woolf |
| Mazo de la Roche | Ayn Rand |
| Farley Mowat | Adele Wiseman |
| Isaac Asimov | Mordecai Richler |
| William Shakespeare | Jane Austen |

**READING BETTER**

1. What parts of our common identity is Gary Lautens writing about?
2. If Lautens didn't use the word "Canadian" so much, what other parts of the world could he be talking about?

**TAKING A STAND**

1. Write a short essay on the topic "What is a Canadian?" Rely on your own knowledge and what you have learned in this chapter so far. Be as creative as you can!
2. Do you think that the Canadian identity is important? Give reasons for your answer.

**RESEARCHING**

1. Find out more about some of the famous Canadians mentioned in the Canadian culture quiz. Use sources found in your school library.
2. Make up your own test to find out whether or not people you know are Americanized.

## The American influence on Canadian culture: Television

Coming to grips with the Canadian identity is difficult indeed. Must Canadians have a distinct culture to be truly independent? Has the Americanization of Canada's culture been harmful or good?

One of the cultural areas in which American influence has been hotly debated is television. Indeed, there are government rules about Canadian content on TV and radio. These rules limit American influences. In the following case study you will be presented with facts and opinions about the influence of US television on Canada's culture. You must decide whether or not American television stops the growth of a unique Canadian culture. If it does, what should be done about the problem?

### Case study: Television

A SUMMARY OF FACTS ABOUT TV VIEWING

The average Canadian watches 3.5 hours of television each day. Only sleeping and working take up more of Canadians' time than watching TV.

About 50% of Canadians can receive American TV stations.

About 40% of programming on Canadian stations may be American. Canadians living in border areas watch more American TV than Canadian TV.

American TV programmes are made by Americans and generally for Americans. They are part of the American culture.

About 86% of American TV programmes contain some form of violence.

Television influences people even if they do not realize it.

Attitudes formed by children carry over until the late teen years.

These facts are based on research by social scientists. They show that television-viewing plays a big part in our lives. They also show that watching American-made programmes is popular in Canada. What effect does this have on us? The following point of view suggests that we do not admire Canadian talent because of the influences of American TV. Read it and then decide for yourself.

THE VICIOUS CIRCLE: A POINT OF VIEW
We watch so much American TV that many of us think American performers are better than Canadian ones. We listen to so much American and British music that we often think Canadian musicians and singers are inferior. Many of us read so many American books and magazines that we will not buy a book by a Canadian. ("Who ever heard of them anyway?" we ask.) This kind of attitude creates a vicious circle.

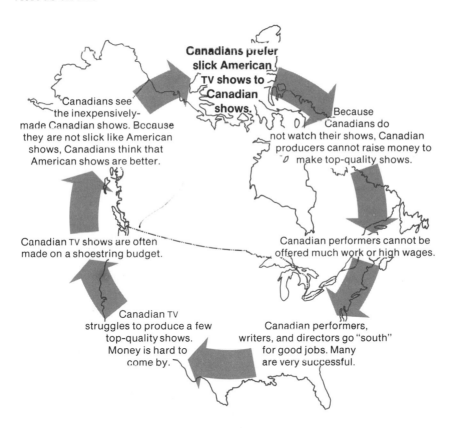

Canadians prefer slick American TV shows to Canadian shows.

Because Canadians do not watch their shows, Canadian producers cannot raise money to make top-quality shows.

Canadian performers cannot be offered much work or high wages.

Canadian performers, writers, and directors go "south" for good jobs. Many are very successful.

Canadian TV struggles to produce a few top-quality shows. Money is hard to come by.

Canadian TV shows are often made on a shoestring budget.

Canadians see the inexpensively-made Canadian shows. Because they are not slick like American shows, Canadians think that American shows are better.

This vicious circle that affects Canadian attitudes has another aspect. By watching and coming to prefer American programmes, Canadians are changed. For example, TV teaches Canadians a lot about the United States and US culture. Are they missing a chance to learn about their own history and culture by not watching Canadian shows?

What can be done to break the vicious circle? The CBC often tries to get a well-known foreign star to play a part in a Canadian show. It hopes that the star will attract many more viewers. This in turn means that people will want to put up more money for productions. When shows are popular, advertisers will pay more for commercial time. The CBC will then use this money to make more Canadian shows. This helps preserve the Canadian culture.

UNION SAYS NO

The Association of Canadian Television and Radio Artists (ACTRA) has, in the past, refused to give work permits to non-Canadian

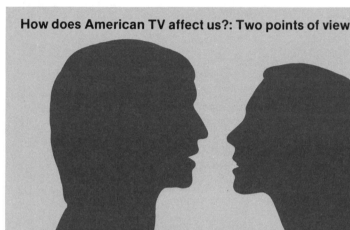

**How does American TV affect us?: Two points of view**

*Al Feldman*

Personally, I enjoy watching American shows. They're well made, they have good actors and actresses, and there's a great deal of variety. They are good entertainment. The action shows are my favourites. They show "good" people against "bad" ones, and the good ones usually win.

As far as I can see, these shows are no danger to Canadians. They show basic funny situations or experiences that all human beings have. Many Canadians have also had the chance to become big stars on American TV. They get their breaks on US programmes.

*Mona Sadowski*

American TV teaches the American way of life. This is not good for Canadians. We are quickly becoming Americans because we constantly see and hear about the American way of life. Some surveys show that Canadian children can name famous Americans, but no Canadians. These same kids think that the White House is Canadian. They think that our courts and police are just like the ones they see on American TV. Well, it's not like that. We're practically strangers in our own country.

If we watched nothing but Canadian shows, we'd learn about life in Canada and have a stronger identity. Also, fine Canadian actors and actresses could then find good jobs in Canada.

performers. The permission of this union is necessary for a non-Canadian actor or actress to work in Canada. ACTRA argues that its Canadian members are as good as imported ones. Canadian performers must be allowed to work in their own country. ACTRA's attitude toward non-Canadian performers is different from the CBC's. Even though both are trying to help Canadian culture, they often disagree.

For example, in September 1977, ACTRA refused a work permit to American singer Joan Morris. The CBC had imported Miss Morris to star in a programme about the old days in the Northwest. ACTRA was angry because there were five Canadian singers who had had up to eleven years experience in such shows. They were good singers but they did not have the "reputation" of the American Miss Morris.

As a result of the union action, the show was delayed. The Canadian dancers, singers, and camera operators had to wait for ACTRA and the CBC to solve their dispute.

Both ACTRA and the CBC are trying to promote Canadian talent and Canadian culture. The two organizations go about it in different ways. Which approach do you think is best? Why?

---

**ORGANIZING BETTER**
1. In your own words, write down the central idea of "The vicious circle".
2. Also in your own words, write down a secondary idea that "The vicious circle" is trying to express.
3. List in point form the arguments made by both Mona and Al.

**USING YOUR KNOWLEDGE**
1. Name some Canadian TV shows that you think prove "The vicious circle" wrong. Explain your choices and compare them with the choices made by your classmates.

**TAKING A STAND**
1. Do you think that by watching American-made TV programmes Canadians prevent the growth of Canadian culture? Why or why not?

**RESEARCHING**
1. a) List your favourite TV shows. Where is each of them made?
   b) Compare your list with those of your classmates. What do you find about the viewing habits of your class?
2. Conduct a poll among your fellow students and family.
   Ask these questions:
   a) Do you enjoy watching American-made TV shows?
   b) Which is your favourite?
   c) Do you enjoy watching Canadian-made TV shows?
   d) Which is your favourite?
   e) Would you be in favour of barring all American programmes from Canadian stations? Why or why not?
   f) Add some questions of your own here.

---

SOLVING THE PROBLEM
The influence of American TV has caused a great deal of discussion in Canada. Because of this talk, Canadians have already put controls on television and radio. Other suggestions have been made, but they have not yet been put into action.

**Dinah Christie**

**Al Waxman**

**Anne Murray**

In this section you will find the following:
1. Information on what has been done already to stop the Americanization of Canadians through television.
2. Suggestions on what more can be done.
3. A discussion about what to do.

This will help you to decide what, if anything, should be done about the influence of American TV on Canadian culture.

1. What has been done?

a) *The Canadian Radio-Television and Telecommunications Commission*

Better known as the CRTC, this government agency was created in 1968. Its job is to supervise radio and TV broadcasting in Canada. Among its duties are the following:

i) To issue broadcasting licences to Canadian-owned companies only.

ii) To set rules about the number of commercials allowed on TV. In 1978 the limit was twelve minutes per hour.

iii) To refuse to renew the licences of TV or radio stations that do not show local programmes. Stations that do not follow other rules may also lose their licences.

iv) To make rules about Canadian content on TV and radio.

| *1968* | *1971* | *1972* |
|---|---|---|
| 40% of **prime time** TV had to be Canadian. | 50% of prime time TV had to be Canadian. | 60% of prime time TV had to be Canadian. |

v) To require **cable TV** companies to substitute Canadian commercials for American ones on US channels.

vi) To require cable TV companies to carry Canadian channels in preference over American channels. Channels must be carried in the following order of importance:
1) CBC (English and French)
2) Private Canadian networks (e.g., CTV)
3) Independent Canadian stations
4) Local and educational stations
5) Non-Canadian stations

**TAKING A STAND**
1. Are the CRTC rules on Canadian content fair? Give reasons for your answer.
2. Should the number of minutes of commercials be increased or reduced? How would your decision affect private TV stations owned by people in business?

**RESEARCHING**
1. Look in local TV programme listings. What percentage of programmes carried on Canadian stations are in fact Canadian? (Look at shows in the 6 p.m. to midnight time period.)
2. Watch television. Count the number of minutes of commercials in one hour on Canadian TV. If possible, compare this to the number of commercial minutes on a US channel during the same period of time.

b) *The Canadian Broadcasting Corporation (CBC)*

Created in 1936, the CBC is owned by the Canadian people, through the federal government. The CBC first began regular TV broadcasts in 1952. The **Broadcasting Act** requires that CBC programmes be mostly Canadian in content. The CBC is not a money-making enterprise. Canadian programmes— plays, new shows, or series—are broadcast even if there are no sponsors. The CBC also broadcasts to all parts of Canada. This is expensive, so the CBC loses money. The losses are covered by tax money.

The CBC also carries some US shows because they are very popular. Advertisers will pay good money to show their products during US shows. This permits the CBC to make some money.

The CBC is the main employer of Canadian performers in Canada. Therefore, it helps keep these artists, and Canadian culture, alive.

**TAKING A STAND**
1. Should the CBC care about commercials? It is losing money each year already, so should it try to sell more commercials by showing popular US programmes? Or should it rely only on tax money to pay its expenses?
2. Is the CBC doing a good job of strengthening Canadian culture? Why or why not?

**RESEARCHING**
1. Check the TV listings. What Canadian TV programmes does CBC carry?

2. What more should be done?

a) *Cut all American shows on Canadian TV*

"Through TV, Canadians are losing their identity. They talk like Americans and they come to believe what Americans believe. In fact, Canadians will one day be Americans." This argument leads some supporters of Canadian culture to suggest a ban on imported TV programmes. All TV shows on CBC and CTV would then be written and made by Canadians, for Canadians. This would give Canadians a chance to learn about their own culture.

b) *Jam all TV broadcasts from the US or put all TV sets on cable and then ban US channels*

Both of these ideas would have the same result—Canadians would not receive US channels. In the jamming process, electronic devices are used to block US broadcasts into Canada. The Americans may object if we interfere with their signals. Many Canadians may also object.

If all TV sets were hooked up to cable systems, no jamming would be needed. The cable system would simply not supply US channels to Canadian homes. Because 50% of Canadians can receive US stations, it would be an expensive operation. However, in cities like Toronto, Hamilton, Montreal, Vancouver, and Halifax, most homes are now on cable systems.

With this solution Canadians would be able to receive only Canadian stations. If we used this solution together with solution a), a great change in our viewing habits could be made.

---

**ORGANIZING BETTER**

1. How does each solution propose to help Canadian culture and end Americanization? Make a chart to help you organize the facts.

**TAKING A STAND**

1. a) Which of the proposed solutions would do the most to end the Americanization of our TV culture?

   b) Which solution would you prefer?

---

**3. I want my favourite programme**

A scene in Mr. Brown's classroom, Thompson Secondary School. Students are discussing solutions to the problem of the influence of American TV on Canadian culture.

**Doris:** I prefer the total ban on US programmes and US channels. As Canadians, we have to develop our own culture.

**Boris:** I sure don't agree with that. Who wants to watch all those Canadian shows—they're boring.

**Doris:** They are not!

**Boris:** Maybe you don't think so, but everybody in my family prefers American shows. They're really entertaining. We'd miss them if they disappeared.

**Doris:** I'm willing to give up those US shows. The facts reveal that our culture is becoming more and more American. Aren't you concerned about your country?

**Boris:** You bet I am—but I'm also concerned about freedom of choice in Canada. Let's not have the government telling us we can't watch TV shows from the States. Pretty soon they may be telling us which Canadian shows to watch.

**Horace:** Well you two seem to be arguing over what's more important—preserving a Canadian culture or preserving freedom of choice. Isn't it possible to reach a compromise? Couldn't we reduce the number of American shows on Canadian networks and still allow people to switch to US channels?

**Boris:** I suppose that would be all right. But the networks should also carry some shows that the people want, not just what the government says they should carry.

**Doris:** Just a minute, Boris. There's no great attack on your freedom. It's just that more people like me want to stop the Americanization of Canada! If enough of us want that, then we'll be a majority—a democratic majority!

---

**ORGANIZING BETTER**

1. Summarize the three students' points of view.

**TAKING A STAND**

1. Which of the students do you agree with? Give reasons for your answer.

## How else can Canadian culture become Americanized?

So far we have studied the American influence on Canadian television. There are many other areas of our culture that are in danger of Americanization.

### Popular music

American stars receive a great deal of publicity on Canadian radio, TV, and in magazines from the States. Canadians are caught up in the publicity and they often prefer US performers to Canadians.

In addition, Canadian performers are seldom happy with their careers until they have "made it" in the US. They generally cannot make as much money in Canada as in the US. Also, Canadian performers do not get the recognition in Canada they deserve. In fact, many Canadians have had to achieve success in the USA before being recognized at home.

The CRTC rules on Canadian content have meant that Canadian musicians are heard more often on radio. But some critics believe that the smaller Canadian population means that Canadian records will have smaller sales. They say that this makes musicians' salaries in Canada lower than in the US. Therefore, Canadians will probably always be drawn to the United States. Also, the US continues to dominate pop music in the world. It therefore will always be a magnet that draws Canadians.

### Books

An American magazine, *Time*, once pointed out that Canada has a large number of high-calibre writers for the size of its population. There are many excellent Canadian authors, such as Morley Callaghan and Margaret Laurence, who have achieved international recognition. Yet Canadians still prefer to buy foreign, usually American, books.

**Canadian magazines face stiff competition from US publications. What Canadian magazines do you read?**

### Magazines

*Time, Popular Mechanics, Better Homes and Gardens*, and many other popular magazines in Canada are American. *Maclean's, Chatelaine*, and *Miss Chatelaine* are Canada's largest-selling Canadian magazines, next to the giants—*Readers' Digest* and *TV Guide.* These last two were originally American-owned. They still have some American content.

Since the 1920s, Canadian magazines have been struggling to gain the popularity of US magazines. Yet, in Canada today, the American magazine, *National Geographic*, outsells *Canadian Geographic*.

### Other cultural art forms

Symphony orchestras, ballet, opera, theatre—all of these are popular in Canada. In 1978, for example, Canadians showed great interest in symphony orchestras. They helped support some of the world's finest symphonies. The Toronto Symphony won great international acclaim as a result of its tour of China in 1978.

Very often the policy of these different groups is to hire the best musician or dancer, regardless of national origin. Should Canadians always be hired before foreigners?

### Education

Are you acquiring a good knowledge of Canada in school? Who has written your textbooks? Does your English course cover works by Canadian authors? Critics have claimed that Canadian schools do not teach enough about Canada and Canadian culture. Are schools doing a better job today?

Many university professors are American. They often get their jobs because they are experts in their field. Sometimes they get their jobs because American teachers are the ones who hire new teachers. Should Canadians be hired before foreigners?

### RESEARCHING

1. Read about the Toronto Blue Jays and the Montreal Expos in major league baseball.
   a) How many Canadians play for these teams?
   b) How many Canadians play major league baseball?
   c) These teams play a sport that is the US national pastime. Does this fact support the idea that Canada is, to a certain extent, Americanized?
2. What are the Canadian Football League's rules about American players? Why does the CFL accept American players? Form a hypothesis (educated guess). If the American Football League wants to establish a team in your province, should the federal government stop it?

### Conclusion

The United States has influenced Canadian culture for a long time. It has affected what Canadians read, watch on television, or dance to. If the trend of Americanization continues, what will happen to the Canadian identity? The answer is often debated. Some people are not worried about the issue. They believe that anglophone Canada is part of a North American culture. They feel that American cultural influences are natural, and cannot be stopped.

Other people are concerned about the Canadian identity. They raise many questions about the problems of US influence. Has enough been done to stop the Americanization of Canada? What else can be done? Is the Americanization of Canadian culture inevitable? The answers to these questions must be made by the citizens of Canada. What have you decided?

### READING BETTER

1. Write one or two sentences explaining each of the following:
   Canada Council
   Massey Report
   Multiculturalism
   ACTRA
   CRTC
   CBC

## ORGANIZING BETTER

1. a) Make a list of the major benefits Canada has received from American cultural influences. Base your answer on the material in the chapter.
   b) Make a second list of the major problems that American culture poses to Canadian culture.
   c) Compare your list with a classmate's. Discuss any points on which you disagree.

## USING YOUR KNOWLEDGE

1. Mexico is also a close neighbour of the United States. Using knowledge you have gained in this chapter, describe how Mexico may possibly have been influenced by American culture. Be sure to cover both the problems and benefits of Americanization. Also, be sure to consider how Mexico may be similar to or different from Canada.
2. If you were suddenly in a position to do something about cultural relations between Canada and the United States of America, what would you do? (Remember, you can choose to do nothing!) Explain your action to your class.

## SOLVING PROBLEMS

1. Work out a solution to the problem of US influence on Canadian culture. Follow the problem-solving model given in Countdown Canada. You may use this as your goal: Helping Canadian culture, reducing American cultural influence.

## TAKING A STAND

1. Earlier in this chapter you were asked the following question: "Having the same foods, music, sports, TV shows, and life styles as the Americans is not really important. Canada can be independent despite these similarities." Do you agree? Why or why not? Now that you have finished the whole chapter, has your answer changed? What further information can you give to back up your opinion?
2. What is a Canadian? Answer this question again.

## RESEARCHING

1. Find more information on the Canada Council and write up a short report. Be sure your report answers the following questions:
   a) How does the Council operate?
   b) To whom does it give money?
   c) What people have already received money from it?

## GLOSSARY

**Americans.** People from the United States of America.

**Broadcasting Act.** An act of Parliament that regulates broadcasting in Canada. It includes rules on Canadian content.

**Cable TV.** A system of broadcasting in which television signals are sent through underground cables instead of through the air. Private companies supply this service to people.

**Cultural values.** Principles or standards accepted by a group of people.

**Economic nationalists.** People who believe that the interests of their own country should always come first in any economic question.

**François-Xavier Garneau.** A Quebec historian and author born in 1809. His most famous work was a four-volume history of Canada.

**Group of Seven.** An informal organization of Canadian painters that existed from 1920-1933.

**Octave Crémazie.** A poet born in Quebec City in 1827. His poems were, in general, patriotic. He has been called Canada's first national poet.

**Prime time.** The period of time when the largest number of people watch television. This is usually between 6:30 p.m. and 11:00 p.m.

**Turnpike.** A freeway or super-highway.

**How has the US influenced the NHL and the CFL?**

CBC Photo

# UNIT FIVE
# Canada and the world

At times in the past many Canadians have felt isolated from the cares of the rest of the world. As one man said, "We live in a fireproof house, far from any flames." There is some debate as to whether or not this statement was ever true. It is certainly not true today.

Canada is one of 150 countries in this world. We live in a modern age of jet travel and intercontinental missiles. No nation is too far away to be unaffected by the problems of the world. Our country's area makes up one half of North America. This gives us Atlantic, Pacific, and Arctic links to the world. We have vast resources such as iron, coal, hydroelectric power, wood, and food. Because of these resources and our industries, we are important to the wealth and progress of other countries. Our huge trade with the USA ties us closely to this superpower that plays a leading role in the world. For all these reasons, Canada is directly involved in world concerns.

Canada's people are also involved with the world's countries. Canada has encouraged immigration for many years. As a result, Canada now has citizens who can trace their backgrounds to every continent. Canadians have memories of and links to the lands of their ancestors. Thus, triumphs or problems in every part of the world are important to many Canadians. This unit will help us to realize that we are not only Canadian citizens but global citizens. We will attempt to find answers to the following questions.

**1** What role has Canada played in war? Should Canada get involved in war in the future?

**2** What has Canada done to keep world peace? Should Canada help keep world peace in the future?

**3** What are some world concerns facing Canadians?

# 1/Canada and war

---

## Contents

---

### Introduction

November 11. For many students it is just a holiday. But for many Canadians it is a day of remembrance. In a minute of silence the sacrifice of 100 000 Canadian lives is remembered. That is the number of men and women killed during the two world wars. It is hoped that never again will Canadians be asked to sacrifice their lives for their country. Yet in a tense and war-torn world, Canadians must face questions about security. Each generation must decide for itself when, if ever, Canada should go to war.

Canadians have fought around the world. They have fought in the name of the British Empire, of Canada, and of the **United Nations.** They have fought to protect the independence of Canada and of many other countries. They have performed great feats of heroism in combat.

Canadians have turned their whole society toward war efforts. In Canada today, we maintain expensive armed forces. They are prepared to defend Canada and to co-operate in defending friends of Canada in Europe or in other parts of the world.

War and defence are controversial. The wars, the sacrifices, the disputes on how to conduct wars—these have affected the lives and attitudes of millions. The effects of war have changed the ways Canadians think about fellow Canadians. War has also changed attitudes about Canada's role in the world. Thus war has played a large role in the lives of millions of Canadians.

This chapter begins with a fictional story placed sometime in the future. The story is about a critical situation facing Canada. Even though the situation is made-up, it is based on well-known facts and theories about world events. You will be challenged to decide what to do and why. Following the story are studies of the world wars, the Cold War, and a discussion of defence today. By the end of the chapter you will be able to answer the following central questions:

1. **Why has Canada gone to war in the past?**

2. **What have Canadians done in wartime?**
3. **What effects have these wars had on Canada?**
4. **When should Canada go to war?**
5. **Should Canadians prepare for a future war?**

---

### War decision

Lightning was flickering at the windows as the prime minister of Canada, Michael Gagnon, called the caucus meeting to order.

"Ladies and gentlemen, I have spent the morning in conference with Minister of Foreign Affairs Judith Simmons and Defence Minister Jack McCluskey. We have been discussing the latest events in Europe. As a result of messages from **NATO**, I have ordered Defence Minister McCluskey to put all our armed forces on full alert. We will scrap the set agenda and decide now on our public position. I call on Mrs. Simmons to explain further."

The room was silent, the MPs surprised and attentive.

"Thank you, Mr. Prime Minister. Ladies and gentlemen, I am sure that you have been following the rise in tension between the East and the West. You all know that relations between the Soviet Union and the United States have been poor. That new American long-range missile has scared the Russians. They don't want to make any more agreements to control weapons. Also, they've been complaining about the treatment their fishing fleet has been getting off our coast and off the American coast. **Communists** in France and Italy have suddenly become close to their Russian friends again. They're complaining about anti-Soviet propaganda. Also, the Soviet ambassador has stormed out of the UN. Americans in Moscow are being arrested on phony spy charges. The Soviet navy has been putting more ships into the Mediterranean. More Soviet planes have tested our radar in the Arctic. Of course, the Europeans have been getting very worried about this. These are just the usual signs of trouble. But here are some facts you may not know. A few new Russian leaders have been appearing lately. We know nothing about these people. Also, the Soviet space programme has put six new satellites into orbit. We haven't been able to figure out exactly what the Soviet Union is up to.

"Last night the Soviets made their big move. They surprised us by informing NATO that twelve Soviet tank divisions will cross into Turkey at 6:00 p.m., our time, today. They say they will occupy Turkey for six weeks and then leave. Their purpose is to protect

Turkey from what they call 'bandit, warmongering leaders' who are a threat to world peace. They also plan to free 23 000 Turkish Communists from prison. These people were arrested for staging anti-government riots. The Russians say they will not use nuclear weapons. They stress that this is a temporary measure. They only want to be sure that their neighbour is friendly toward them. I have advised Prime Minister Gagnon that . . ."

"This means war!" Heads turned. Young Paul Roper, MP from Nova Scotia, was on his feet. "Turkey is a member of NATO and so are we. It is our duty to defend free countries!"

Gagnon, too, stood up. "Mr. Roper, your strong beliefs on freedom are well-known. But you must not try to stampede us. We will hear the facts. We will debate the alternatives. Then the government will take action. As a lawyer, Mr. Roper, I'm sure you'll agree that this is the proper course."

"Mr. Prime Minister, I'm also sure that Canada will do its duty as a NATO member and go to the aid of Turkey. As I see it, there's very little debate needed. Our duty is clear."

"Oh, sit down," said Joe Minardi, an Ontario MP. "You'll have us in the middle of a nuclear war." He paused and turned to the prime minister. "Mr. Prime Minister, certainly this sounds serious. But I for one see no reason to overreact. The Turkish government has made some serious mistakes this past year. Maybe the Soviets have good reason to do this. Besides, they've promised to leave after six weeks. I think we should go slowly and easily with this."

"Nonsense! Pardon me, Joe, but that's nonsense." Vera Leschak of Alberta stood across the room from Minardi. "Joe, you've forgotten some history and some politics. One, the Russians have done this sort of thing before. Remember how they occupied Czechoslovakia in the 1940s? Remember the Russian tanks in Hungary, Poland, Czechoslovakia, and so on in the 1950s and 1960s? The Russians have been building up their army and getting ready for this Turkish invasion for years. History shows that the Soviets can't be trusted, Joe. Now, a second thing—the Canadian people. They've always stood for democracy and against communism . . ."

Minardi interrupted. "Surely you can't call that new Turkish government a full democracy. It's run by the generals and they haven't been too happy in NATO lately!"

"Turkey's democracy may not meet our standards now but it could," replied Leschak. "Under the Russians, the Turks will never have any choices. We've fought for freedom and democracy before. We'll do it again if we have to."

"That's right," added Jack McCluskey. "I fought to defeat Hitler and preserve freedom. I'm proud of our record. As NATO members, we owe it to ourselves to give the Turks our full support."

Monique Lamarre, the oldest Quebec MP, caught the PM's eye and spoke next.

"Monsieur McCluskey, let us not exaggerate our history. Most Canadians went to war in 1939 out of loyalty to Britain. The European troubles made no sense to many Canadians, just as they made no sense to many Americans. Now to me, this present case is similar. Turkey is far away. The Russian threat is not that great. Because Russia is a big power it can probably be trusted. Any country as powerful and rich as Russia won't risk a world war. At least, we can afford to wait before we go to war."

"That's ridiculous," muttered Leschak.

Lamarre exploded, "What do you mean, 'ridiculous'? We in Quebec have always stood for what we believed was best for Canada. Now you want us to follow the Americans into war? They control NATO. Their new missiles have fed Russian fears. Let's keep a cool head and try to save the world. Let's think for ourselves. We must never go to war automatically. There are other solutions, even in this case."

Judith Simmons was at the microphone, trying to calm people down. "Please, we'll arrive at a solution, but let's all remember that we're on the same side. Now I agree that we shouldn't just go to war automatically. But we must also remember that the Soviets are dedicated to spreading communism. They say that they'll remain only a short time in Turkey. Can we afford to let them have their way? Will they not try it again and again? Will we be so afraid of nuclear war that we never stop them from this type of aggression? I say NATO must take a firm stand now. That means we prepare for war."

"But what can Canada do?" asked a voice from the back.

"Well, we've got our forces in Europe on alert," explained Jack McCluskey. "Our fifty combat aircraft could be ready for action in Turkey tomorrow. Another hundred aircraft could be ready to fight in Europe in five days. Our airportable brigade of 4 000 soldiers is ready to move on 12 hours' notice. With our own NATO forces in Germany, we could have 10 000 troops ready to fight by next week. Of course, the US, Britain, Germany, and other NATO members would provide most of the troops.

"Our forces are not big in size but they're well equipped and tough. The Americans, British, and West Germans are the backbone of NATO. Our troops will show Turkey and NATO that we stand behind them."

Joe Minardi was furious. "Have you taken leave of your senses? Why waste precious lives? This will lead to a nuclear war. We must insist that NATO act with caution. If the other members won't, then we must. What good will 10 000 soldiers and 150 aircraft do? I say this is lunacy! The people of Canada won't stand for it!"

"Won't stand for it!" The caucus was in an uproar. Leschak paced up and down the room. "The Canadian people won't stand for it if we welch on our agreements. They won't stand for it if Canada is embarrassed by cowards like you. You heard Judy. You know what the government wants to do. It's time you developed a little party discipline."

"This has gone far enough!" Gagnon was at the microphone. All heads turned to him. "Thank you for outlining both sides of the issue. I think it's time we made a plan. The Cabinet will consider your ideas in a meeting in one hour. We have got to face the Commons this evening. The news about the Russians is leaking out. Now here's the way I see it."

---

**READING BETTER**

1. The story points out that trouble was arising between the Soviets and NATO. Pretend you are a Canadian spy reporting to your government. Write a short message like a telegram to warn that trouble is coming. Be as brief and accurate as you can.
2. Explain in your own words why the Soviets wanted to invade Turkey. In your answer, be sure to mention the following:
   a) How far Turkey is from Canada
   b) At least two things Russia wanted from Turkey
3. a) What threats, if any, were the Soviets making indirectly to Canada?
   b) Why did some MPs think Canada should be ready to fight?
   c) Why were some MPs opposed to Canadian military action?

**ORGANIZING BETTER**

1. Make up two columns in your notebook. Select five facts from the story. Write some questions about these facts in the first column. In the second column, write down your answers. See if two of your classmates can answer all five questions correctly.

**TAKING A STAND**

1. It is difficult to decide when Canada should go to war. Here are some suggestions.
   i) When Canada is invaded or attacked.
   ii) When Canadians somewhere in the world are attacked or killed.
   iii) When countries located close to Canada are attacked or invaded (e.g., USA).
   iv) When countries that are allies of Canada are attacked or invaded. Allies are countries that have agreed to help one another. Members of NATO are Canada's allies, for example. Canada has trade and cultural ties with them.
   v) When small or weak countries are invaded by powerful neighbours (e.g., China invades South Korea).
   vi) When members of the Commonwealth are attacked or invaded (e.g., Jamaica, Pakistan). Again, Canada has trade and cultural ties with these countries.
   vii) To stop a country that refuses to recognize the rights of other countries to trade freely or develop economically.
   viii) To help Canada's "mother" countries, Britain and France.

   a) Suggest other occasions when Canada may go to war.
   b) Which of these may be the cause of war in "War decision"?
   c) Discuss whether or not each reason for going to war that is presented in the list is, in your opinion, valid. This will help you clarify your position.
2. What would you do in the story if you had to make the decision? Why?

## World War I, 1914–1918

It was called the Great War. In it over 25 million people died. Of these, 60 000 were Canadians. In addition, over 178 000 Canadians were wounded between 1914 and 1918.

World War I had a tremendous impact on Canada. Deaths and injuries touched people in nearly every town. Almost every family knew people who had lost someone, or had seen someone return home wounded.

There was more than just personal impact. Some historians claim that Canada as a nation was truly created in World War I. They believe that the victories and brave deeds of Canadians at war developed national pride. People in this country began to think of themselves less as British subjects and more as Canadians. In the war the world began to recognize Canada as an independent country.

In this section we will examine the many ways—good and bad—in which the war affected Canada. Our purpose is not to study all aspects of World War I in detail. Rather, we will look at examples that help us understand why the war is an important part of Canadian history.

### How it began: 1914

World War I began in Europe. For many years there had been disputes among European nations. They disagreed over colonies in Africa, borders in Europe, and the freedom of various groups of people inside Austria-Hungary. These disputes will not be covered here. They may, however, be easily researched in any good library.

By 1914 Europe was essentially divided into two camps. They were:

| *The Triple Alliance* | *The Triple Entente* |
| --- | --- |
| Germany | France |
| Austria-Hungary | Russia |
| Italy (joined the Entente in 1915) | Great Britain |

In June 1914, Archduke Ferdinand of Austria-Hungary was assassinated. The murderer was from the small state of Serbia (now part of Yugoslavia). Throughout June and July of 1914 tensions in Europe rose. Austria-Hungary threatened Serbia. The Russians promised to help Serbia. Germany then promised to help Austria-Hungary. A chain of events involved each of the major European powers in the dispute. On August 1, the French army prepared for war. On August 3, the German army invaded Belgium. This attack brought in the British, who had promised to defend Belgium. World War I had begun.

### How Canada became involved

At the time, Canada was a member of the British Empire. Therefore, Canada was legally at war as soon as Britain was. The Canadian government was not consulted about the war. The Canadian Parliament did not vote on going to war.

The Canadian Parliament could, however, decide what to do in the war. It could decide to send soldiers, or to send only food and clothing. It could also decide to do nothing about the war. This was not likely, since most Canadians felt loyal to Britain. They wanted to help the mother country.

A large group of Canadians did, however, speak out against the war. According to this group, the war seemed to have nothing to do with Canada's interests.

The following readings show the conflicting points of view over Canada's role in the war.

---

**Three points of view**

ROBERT BORDEN, prime minister

We are part of the British Empire, so of course we are at war. That is the law. We will now decide on the form of aid that we should send to Britain. I believe that we should send soldiers to fight in France beside the British army. Canadians will be proud to fight for their King and country.

*Adapted from comments made by Borden in the House of Commons, August 18, 1914.*

WILFRID LAURIER, Leader of the Opposition

We are at war. That is the law. It is now our job to decide what to do about this sad fact. My hope is that the war will soon be over and our aid will not be needed. We should offer money and food to France and Britain.

*Adapted from comments made by Laurier in the House of Commons, August 18, 1914.*

HENRI BOURASSA, nationalist and publisher of *Le Devoir*, Montreal

Some people have claimed that it is Canada's duty to fight in this war. That is false. Britain got into this war by itself, without even asking Canada for an opinion. Therefore, Canadians do not have any duty or responsibility to fight in it.

If in fact Canadians are in danger, it is because we are connected to Britain. If the British government got us into this position of danger, then they should defend us! We should not have to fight in this European war.

*Adapted from "The Duty of Canada at the Present Hour," Henri Bourassa. In* Changing Perspectives in Canadian History, *eds. K. MacKindy et al. (Don Mills: Dent, 1971), pp.288-289.*

---

**READING BETTER**
1. In point form, summarize what each of the politicians wanted to do.

**USING YOUR KNOWLEDGE**
1. Which groups of people in Canada would most likely be in favour of the war? Which would most likely be opposed?
2. Review the list of reasons for Canada to go to war given in this chapter's first "Taking a stand" exercise. Which of the reasons applies to Canada's situation in 1914?
3. Which countries involved in the war were important to Canada? Explain your choices.

**RESEARCHING**
1. Find out more about the causes of World War I. There are many books that cover this topic in most libraries.
   The following are topics that could be reported on:
   a) The immediate causes of the war
   b) The long-range causes of the war
   c) Germany's role in starting the war
   d) The roles of France and Russia in starting the war
   e) How Britain and the British Empire became involved

   f) Why the United States did not join the war in 1914

   Your teacher may suggest other topics or actual books to use. The table of contents and index in specific books will help you find the pages you want. In the library, use the card catalogue. Encyclopaedias are also a good source of information. Check under the headings for each country and also under World War I.

The decision

The government decided to send Canadian soldiers and economic aid to Britain. In September 1914, the First Canadian Division assembled and left for Britain. Volunteers flocked to join the Canadian army. In a country of just 8 million people, an average of 10 000 men volunteered each month. Following the near defeat of France in 1914, Canada became fully committed to the war.

In the following section, some Canadians explain their reasons for joining the war effort.

### 1914–1918: Why did they join up?

The following people are fictional. They do, however, express ideas that were common at the time.

KEN McCAIN—Manitoba

When the war started I wanted to go, but I was too young, only fifteen. By the time I was seventeen, I couldn't wait any longer. I guess I was afraid the war would end before I got a chance to participate. Anyway, I lied about my age and joined the cavalry. I was a good rider and being a farm boy, I knew horses.

We got some training here and in France. We were really good. Every one of us was good with horses and tough—boy, were we tough! We didn't do much fighting until 1917 at Cambrai. I was with the Fort Garry Horse Regiment. We rode across a canal and charged some guns. The Germans scattered. They were scared to death. Just a few weeks later, I had my foot shot off.

We went, I guess, because of patriotism and adventure. War seemed like fun at first, although it wasn't later on. I don't regret fighting in it.

**Happy Canadians return from the victory at Vimy Ridge.**

Public Archives of Canada

ROY PEARSOLL—Ontario

I had several reasons for going to war. I went out of patriotism, although the loyalty I felt was more to Britain than to Canada. I suppose I also thought that the cause was just. Most of all, though, I went for the adventure. War seemed to be exciting and romantic. A lot of other people were getting involved in the excitement, and I didn't want to be left out.

ALF BARKER—Nova Scotia

Canada was at war. England was at war. I felt it was my duty to join up. We had to stop the Germans before they took over everything. You know, they didn't have democracy or our kind of freedom. Any man would join up to protect his people. The cowards stayed home.

---

**READING BETTER**
1. What is meant by the term "patriotism"?
2. To what or to whom were these men being patriotic?
3. List the things that these men believed were important to life.

**TAKING A STAND**
1. a) Review the reasons for which you felt Canada should go to war in "War decision".
   b) Review the reasons for which Canada went to war in 1914.
   c) Review the causes of World War I.
   d) Outside of Quebec in 1914, Canadians felt close ties with Britain. Many Canadians thought of themselves as being as much British as Canadian. These people supported Borden's views. French-speaking Canadians, however, generally supported the positions of Laurier or Bourassa. Thus, there was a split in Canada over what to do in 1914.
   Do you think Borden did the right thing in deciding to send volunteer soldiers? Discuss this question in class.

The Canadian role in World War I

The Canadian army entered combat in the spring of 1915. Five thousand Canadians were killed or wounded in the first week. Canadians at home read about the poison gas attacks at Ypres and the hand-to-hand fighting between Canadians and Germans. As the war dragged on the Canadian army would be in many bitter battles. Thousands died in the trench war. Yet the struggle aroused pride in Canadians. Canada's army soon gained a reputation for bravery and good organization. General Currie, Commander of the Canadian Corps, was rated among the best generals on the Allied side. Canadian victories in battle included Ypres, Vimy, Passchendaele, Hill 70, Sanctuary Wood, Amiens, and Cambrai.

Canadians also fought in British Empire forces. Many thousands served in the Royal Navy and the Royal Flying Corps. Indeed, Billy Bishop, a Canadian in the Royal Flying Corps, was an outstanding pilot.

---

### The Victoria Cross: For valour

The "VC" is the British Empire's highest award for bravery. Very few people ever win it. Those who do are real war heroes. The following were among the 62 Canadians awarded the VC in World War I.

MAJOR O.M. LEARMOUTH of Quebec City

Major Learmouth was only 23, but he was a tough soldier. During the battle of Hill 70, Learmouth led his men against the German trenches. Even after he was wounded he stood with his men. When German hand grenades were thrown at him, Learmouth caught them and threw them back. He was wounded a second time, but still he fought on. His leg was broken, but Major Learmouth refused to leave his men. After the battle, he insisted on stopping at headquarters to report. He was near death as he did so. Learmouth was awarded the Victoria Cross after he died.

### SECOND LIEUTENANT A.A. McLEOD of Winnipeg

Eighteen-year-old McLeod was a pilot of an observer aircraft. While on a mission in March 1918, McLeod's slow plane was attacked by eight German Fokker triplanes. Young McLeod twisted his plane through the sky so that his observer was able to shoot down three of the German triplanes. The other German planes did not give up, however. When his own plane burst into flames, McLeod climbed onto the wing, leaning over into the cockpit to control his machine. Both McLeod and the observer were wounded but they kept fighting back until their plane crashed. On the ground, German soldiers fired at the burning plane. Despite six wounds, McLeod dragged the observer to a safe place. The observer lost a leg, but lived. McLeod was awarded the Victoria Cross, but he died later in Winnipeg from his wounds.

Public Archives of Canada

r Arthur Currie, Commander of the Canadian
orps.

Canada's Billy Bishop, one of the great aces of World War I.

413

This Quebec factory was one of many which opened up to meet Canada's war needs.

READING BETTER
1. Did these men show patriotism? Why?
2. What other values did these heroes stand for?

TAKING A STAND
1. Why do you think that these, and other heroes of war, behaved as they did? Write a paragraph explaining your thoughts.
2. Why would some people criticize the actions of VC winners and say that they were foolish?
3. Some people feel that when persons who take part in a war are made into heroes, then war is being glorified. This may encourage people to want war. What do you think about this? Write a short paragraph explaining your opinions.

The war at home

In Canada, the war was responsible for the growth of many new industries. Women played a large role in the war effort. They took over the jobs left vacant by men who had enlisted. Women drove streetcars, delivered mail, made bullets, airplanes, and rifles. Canadian women also served overseas as nurses. At home Canadians helped pay for the war effort by buying war bonds. The fact sheet on Canada in World War I helps summarize some of Canada's contributions to the war.

Women contributed to the war effort in many ways. This nurse helped the Canadian forces overseas.

**Fact sheet: Canada in World War I**

*Population:* 8 000 000

*Size of army* 1918: 600 000
*Size of navy* 1918: 8 000

*Casualties* Dead: 60 000
Wounded: 178 000

*Total cost of the war to Canada:* $3 billion
(Annual federal budget before 1914, about $130 million)

*Canadian production:*
Number of people working in war factories, 1918: 350 000
Value of shells produced: $60 milion
Total value of war production: $1 billion

*Agricultural growth during war:*
—Cheese exports up 300%
—Pork exports up 535%
—Beef exports up 6 755%
—Wheat exports up 2 183%

## Conscription

The crisis over conscription created a split between anglophone and francophone Canadians. Part of this conflict has already been covered in Unit 3, Chapter 3. Review that section again. Now that you have looked at the causes of World War I and at Canada's contribution, you may have a different opinion about the conscription issue.

Many Canadians other than the francophones objected to conscription. In Ontario and Manitoba, farmers opposed the conscription of their sons. They argued that without young men to help with the harvests, the war effort would suffer. Many of these farmers came from families that had been in Canada for generations. They were often not ready to fight over European troubles.

There were also people whose religious beliefs prevented them from fighting. It was legal to ask for permission to stay out of the army. But these **conscientious objectors** were insulted by other citizens when they legally tried to avoid conscription.

Thus the conflict over conscription did not occur only between anglophones and francophones. There were strongly opposing views inside each province. These bitter feelings would last for decades.

### What did Canada gain from World War I?

What did Canada gain from a war that had started far from its shores? What did Canada lose in a war that had not involved the nation at all when it began? A **balance sheet** may be drawn up. It is up to you to decide, in general, whether Canada gained or lost in World War I.

---

### World War I: The balance sheet

*What we lost*

—60 000 Canadians dead—mostly young men.

—178 000 Canadians wounded—mostly young men.

—The government spent over $3 billion during the war. (Before the war, the government spent about $130 million each year.)

—The war debt cost Canadian taxpayers about $150 million per year until World War II.

—Many Canadians made huge amounts of money from the war, often through dishonest methods. Most workers got few raises. Prices of food and other goods were sky-high.

—The Conscription Crisis caused bad feelings in the country.

*What we gained*

—New factories—more than 1 000 of them.

—Increased farm production. New lands were used for growing wheat. Farmers' income went up.

—Pride and identity. Canadian victories in battle brought recognition from the world. Canadian identity grew with pride in soldiers.

—Recognition. The world recognized Canada as an independent nation. Canada had its own seat at the peace conference. Later, Canada had its own seat in the League of Nations. Ties with Great Britain were loosened.

—Canada helped assure freedom for the conquered countries of Europe.

## ORGANIZING BETTER

1. Make a list summarizing the ways in which Canada contributed to World War I. Decide how important this contribution was. Keep in mind such things as:
   a) How Canada entered the war
   b) Size of Canada's population
   c) Sacrifices made

## RESEARCHING

1. Find out more about Canadian battles in World War I. Most libraries have many books on this subject. Check the card catalogue, encyclopaedias, and general histories of Canada.
   Some battles to report on are:
   Ypres, April 1915
   Festubert
   St. Eloi
   Sanctuary Wood
   Courcelette
   Vimy Ridge
   Hill 70
   Passchendaele
   Amiens
   Hindenburg Line
   Canal du Nord
   Cambrai
   Other topics to report on are:
   1. Life in the trenches
   2. The Peace Conference, 1919
   3. Women and the war
   4. The war at sea
   5. The growth of Canadian industries
   6. Songs and entertainment in World War I

## TAKING A STAND

1. Did Canada gain or lose in World War I? Review the causes of the war and the events briefly described before you explain your answer.

Horses still played a big role in warfare in World War I. However, machine guns and tanks made them obsolete.

## World War II, 1939-1945

When World War I was over, Europe was tired and weak. National leaders were determined to prevent another such disaster. President Woodrow Wilson of the USA was responsible for creating the League of Nations. This organization would try to keep peace and prevent another world war. For the next thirty years the League attempted to keep peace. As we know from history, it failed.

Despite the League's ultimate failure, it did succeed in giving recognition to Canada as an independent nation. Canada was considered an equal to the other nations. It was therefore given a seat at the League's Assembly of Nations. But Canadians did not want to play a large role in world affairs. The split over conscription convinced many that Canada must be careful in foreign affairs. Further conflict over what to do in relations with the world would be dangerous to the country.

However, events in Europe again led Canada to war. In this section we look at Canada's role in World War II.

### How did World War II start?

World War II started in September 1939 when Nazi Germany invaded Poland. The events leading up to the war are complex. You will be able to learn much about them through your own research. This section of the chapter concentrates on how Canada became involved in the war.

When Adolf Hitler gained power in Germany in 1933, the country was in a state of economic depression. So, too, was the rest of the world. Hitler and his Nazi party offered the people some reasons for their problems. Hitler blamed Germany's problems on the terms of the Treaty of Versailles. He also blamed Communists and Jews. Hitler said he would get rid of the Jews and any others who, he claimed, had hurt Germany. His goal was to regain the country's lost lands and power.

Once in power, the Nazis built up the German armed forces. They began to threaten neighbouring countries. Laws were created to restrict Jews and other "enemies" of Nazi Germany. Many Jews, Communists, and anti-Nazi Germans were jailed and beaten. Some were killed. Through such actions, the Nazis wanted to show they were attacking the causes of Germany's problems.

Hitler and the Nazis did manage to restore some national pride through their policies. They also reduced unemployment in the country. But the price paid was a loss of civil and human rights.

In 1938, the Nazis began to take over neighbouring countries. In March 1938, they invaded Austria. In June, Hitler began to move against Czechoslovakia. In September 1938, at the **Munich Conference** Hitler promised to take only part of Czechoslovakia. He said it would be his "last demand". But in March 1939, the Nazis took over the rest of Czechoslovakia. Poland would be next.

At first many people in the world felt that a number of Hitler's demands were acceptable. Despite Hitler's actions in 1938, many people tried to appease him. They were willing to give him what he wanted because they feared another world war. By the summer of 1939, however, Hitler had proved to many that he could not be trusted.

### How did Canada enter World War II?

In September 1939, Canada did not have to go to war automatically, as it did in 1914. The **Statute of Westminster** of 1931 had made Canada independent from Britain. However, in Canada, support for Britain was still strong. So, too, was disgust with the Nazis. Thus, Prime Minister Mackenzie King called Parliament to meet on September 10. A declaration of war was debated and passed in Parliament. Mackenzie King let it be known that the government planned to send only a few soldiers. Most Canadian help would take the form of food and manufactured goods. Conscription was not to be used.

Canada was again at war.

How did World War II start?
The following fictional reports are based on real newspaper articles of the time.

---

**The headlines tell the story:** *The Puslinch Times*

*January 30, 1933* **MR. HITLER FORMS A GOVERNMENT**

Mr. Adolf Hitler of the Nazi Party was accepted today by President Hindenburg as the leader of a new government. Mr. Hitler has promised to avenge the German defeat of 1918. He has also promised to stop the spread of communism and restore German pride.

*March 23, 1933* **GERMAN EMERGENCY**

The German Parliament has given Mr. Adolf Hitler special powers to deal with a national emergency. Some observers believe that the Nazi party caused the trouble so that Mr. Hitler could ask for an end to legal protection of rights.

*July 31, 1935* **HITLER A SUCCESS**

The Nazi government, under its leader Adolf Hitler, has announced that unemployment has dropped. The number of unemployed dropped from 6 000 000 in January 1933 to 2 000 000 this month. A spokesman for Mr. Hitler said that more jobs were being created each day.

*August, 1935* **GERMAN AIR FORCE GROWING**

Since Mr. Hitler rebuilt the German Air Force, many new pilots have been trained. New machines are purchased each week. Foreign experts believe that soon the *Luftwaffe* will be among the largest air forces in Europe.

*March 13, 1938* **GERMANS INVADE AUSTRIA**

The Premier of Austria, Mr. Schuschnigg, has failed to stop a German take-over of Austria. The German army yesterday crossed the border with no opposition. Tomorrow Adolf Hitler is expected to arrive in Vienna. Austrian Nazis who helped bring about this affair are preparing a huge welcome. Austria will now be part of Germany.

*March 18, 1938* **BRITAIN TAKES NO ACTION**

Prime Minister Neville Chamberlain has announced in London that Britain will not try to stop Hitler's take-over of Austria. Mr. Chamberlain will seek other ways of dealing with Hitler's demands. It is known that Mr. Chamberlain desires peace. He believes that many German demands are justified.

*June 12, 1938* **DOES HITLER WANT CZECHOSLOVAKIA TOO?**

It is more and more obvious that Adolf Hitler means to take over as much of Czechoslovakia as he can. German radio and newspapers

419

announce new demands every day. Czech government officials are trying to find help against German demands. The question is: What will the British and French do about Hitler's latest moves? Will Chamberlain give up his desire to keep peace?

*October 2, 1938*  **PEACE SAVED AT MUNICH**

Today Germany agreed to take only the part of Czechoslovakia in which German-speaking people live. Mr. Neville Chamberlain believes he has stopped a war by letting Hitler have some of his demands. Mr. Hitler has also announced that he wants no more territory in Europe. Peace has been preserved.

*November 10, 1938*  **NAZIS KILL JEWS**

Three days ago a young Jewish student shot and killed a German diplomat in Paris. Last night Jewish shops, homes, and synagogues all over Germany were attacked by Nazis. Many German Jews were killed. Over $23 million in damage was done.

*March 15, 1939*  **NAZIS INVADE CZECHOSLOVAKIA**

The German army today seized what remained of Czechoslovakia. Only last fall Hitler promised that he would take no more land. Experts in London and Paris now believe that Poland will be next on the Nazis' list.

*September 1, 1939*  **GERMANY INVADES POLAND**

Charging that the Poles had attacked first, the Nazis today began to invade Poland. The Polish government has denied the charges. It claims that there has been a German plot to seize Poland.

*September 4, 1939*  **BRITAIN AT WAR!**

The Germans have not answered British demands to pull out of Poland. War has been declared. France, too, is at war.

*September 10, 1939*  **CANADA AT WAR!**

His Majesty King George VI today declared a state of war between Canada and Germany. Earlier in Ottawa, Parliament had voted to declare war. It then asked the King to make the official announcement.

Part of the government plan is to provide only a few combat troops. Most of Canada's effort is expected to be put into industry and farming. Prime Minister Mackenzie King has also announced that there will be no conscription.

---

Canada at war

As Europe was drawn nearer to war again in the mid-1930s, Canadians were more concerned about jobs than about Hitler. The Great Depression had put millions out of work. Canadians struggled to make ends meet. Slowly, however, world events in the late 1930s drew Canadian attention. The actions of Hitler and Mussolini aroused concern. By September 1939, Canadians

Hitler used parades, pageants, and huge assemblies to excite the imaginations of his supporters.

knew that war was possible. Canada's armed forces, however, were in poor shape. There were only a handful of trained people, and few ships, tanks, and airplanes. It would take several years for the armed forces to reach effective fighting levels.

In 1914, Canadians had been enthusiastic about joining in the war. They did not feel the same way in 1939. They had learned some lessons from the Great War. Mackenzie King made careful plans and showed great concern for national unity. Only after the defeat of France in 1940 did Canada make a full-scale war effort. By then the struggle was more desperate.

France, Belgium, the Netherlands, Norway, and other countries had fallen to the Nazis. Britain stood alone and was in danger. In 1941, Japan declared war against Britain and the USA. In the same year, Canada declared war on Japan.

The drive for victory required the efforts of the whole country. Volunteers flocked to the armed forces. Many of them went to help Britain. Many went to defend freedom. Many went because they needed work after the Depression. By 1942 Canada was ready to make major contributions to the fighting.

1. a) Review the causes of World War I. Make a list of the causes of both world wars. Find similarities and differences and write them in your notebook.
   b) How did Canada enter World War I? What was the difference in 1939?
2. a) Was Canada threatened by Germany in 1939?
   b) Why did Canada decide to enter the war in 1939? Explore all the possible reasons for the decision.

**TAKING A STAND**

1. Should Canada have entered World War II? Why or why not?

**RESEARCHING**

1. Find out more about the causes of World War II. Libraries have much information on this subject. Check the card catalogue and encyclopaedias.
   Some topics are:
   The Nazi party
   Adolf Hitler
   The Munich Crisis
   The role of the Treaty of Versailles, 1919
   The League of Nations
   German rearmament
   Neville Chamberlain and appeasement
   The German-Soviet Pact of 1939
   Benito Mussolini
   Japan-United States relations
   Canada declares war, 1939
2. Find out why Canada went to war with Japan in 1941.

What did Canadians do in World War II? It would take an entire book to answer this question fully. A few readings, however, will show you the scope of Canadian actions and contributions. Study them and complete the exercises that follow. These readings will provide statistics, stories of bravery, and a brief look at the role of women in the war. You can learn more about Canada's contribution to World War II if you do some research on your own.

---

### The Victoria Cross: For valour

PRIVATE "SMOKY" SMITH

While fighting in northern Italy, Smith led his anti-tank team to attack some Germans on a road. Suddenly a Mark V tank rumbled toward them, firing its machine gun. Only ten metres away, Smith fired his anti-tank gun, stopping the enemy. However, ten Germans with machine guns leaped from the back of the tank and charged Smith. Standing in the middle of the road, Smith coolly shot four of the Germans. The others ran off. "Smoky" Smith was awarded the Victoria Cross.

COMPANY SERGEANT-MAJOR J. R. OSBORN

When the Japanese attacked Hong Kong in December 1941, there were 1 975 Canadian soldiers helping to defend the colony. The Japanese were too strong for the Canadian, Indian, and British soldiers. Osborn led a small group of Canadians in a desperate fight to hold a hilltop. As the Japanese threw hand grenades, Osborn caught them like baseballs and threw them back. When one fell where he couldn't pick it up, Osborn took desperate action. He shouted a warning to the others and then jumped onto the grenade as it exploded. He saved at least six other soldiers who later became prisoners. Osborn was awarded a Victoria Cross posthumously.

### Fact Sheet: Canada and World War II

*Population of Canada:* 11 000 000

*A vast system of factories:*
In World War II, Canada became a truly industrial nation. The Canadian government spent about $12 000 000 per day buying war materials. Many supplies were sent to Russia, Britain, China, and India.

*Canadian production:*

| | |
|---|---|
| The record: | 14 000 planes |
| | 700 000 trucks |
| | 50 000 armoured vehicles |
| | (6 000 tanks from Montreal alone) |
| | 1 500 000 machine guns |
| | 100 000 artillery guns |
| | 900 ships |

*The Armed Forces:*

| | |
|---|---|
| The Royal Canadian Navy: | 373 ships |
| | 90 000 men and women |
| The Royal Canadian Air Force: | 45 squadrons overseas |
| | 250 000 men and women |
| The Canadian Army: | 5⅔ divisions overseas |
| | 730 000 men and women |

Total: 1 000 000 people served in the armed forces
Casualties: 41 700 dead or missing

*Other statistics:*
Value of all war goods produced: $10 billion
Cost of war: $20 billion
Government investment in factories: $1 500 000 000
Commonwealth Air Training Plan: 130 000 flyers from the British Commonwealth and British Empire were trained in Canada
Agriculture: 40% increase in agricultural production

**In World War II, women played a bigger role in the armed forces. Should women today be in combat units?**

Women worked in industries during the World Wars. How would this fact change their role in Canadian society?

ORGANIZING BETTER
1. Summarize in your own words the ways in which Canadians contributed to the war effort.

TAKING A STAND
1. What is your evaluation of Canada's contributions to World War II? Write a paragraph on the question.

RESEARCHING
1. Canadians fought in many battles during World War II. Most libraries have many books on the subject. Check the card catalogue, encyclopaedias, and general histories of Canada.
   Some topics to report on:
   The Battle of Britain, 1940
   The Dieppe Raid, 1942
   The Battle of the Atlantic
   The invasion of Sicily, 1943
   The Italian campaign, 1943-44
   Hong Kong, 1941
   D-Day, June 6, 1944
   General Crerar
   The Battle of the Falaise Gap, 1944
   Battles in Normandy, 1944
   The Battle of the Scheldt, 1944

   The Rhineland Battle, 1945
   The liberation of the Netherlands
   Bomber command
   Convoys to Russia
   The Commonwealth Air Training Plan
2. Draw a map of Europe, locating major battlefields on it.

Conscription Crisis—Again
During the battles in Normandy in 1944, the Second and Third Canadian Divisions suffered more losses than any other British or Canadian divisions. They were in the hottest part of the battle. The army needed more men, but there were not enough volunteers available. Were conscripted soldiers to be sent to France? Would there be another crisis?

Prime Minister Mackenzie King had done his best to avoid another Conscription Crisis. When Canada declared war in 1939, King promised never to introduce conscription. The country would stress sending "things", not soldiers, in this war. Only volunteers were to be sent.

The disaster of the summer of 1940 changed this. France was defeated. Britain and the Commonwealth faced Germany alone. While Britain stood alone, Canada made plans to increase its armed forces. These plans included conscription. The National Resources Mobilization Act (NRMA) would require men to serve in the army, but only for home defence. King promised that they would not be sent overseas.

In December 1941, the war became even more serious as a result of Japan's attack on Pearl Harbor. Canada was shocked when 300 Canadian soldiers were killed in fighting and 1700 were taken as prisoners at Hong Kong. Furthermore, Canada's west coast was open to Japanese attack.

The demands to send conscripts overseas were very strong. Mackenzie King decided to hold a referendum. All Canadian citizens would be asked, "Should the government be released from its promise of not sending conscripts overseas to fight?"

*Referendum results, April, 1942*
English Canadians voted to release the government from its promise. With the exception of Quebec, the average was 80% in favour of conscription for overseas service. In Quebec only 27% were in favour of it. Quebec insisted that the government's promise be kept.

Mackenzie King had decided not to use conscripts until he was forced to. The Canadian army had been stationed in Britain but had not yet been in combat. Reinforcements were still not needed. The picture had changed by October 1944. Losses were high. The army asked for conscripts. Eventually, the Minister of Defence, Colonel Ralston, also asked the prime minister to send the conscripts.

Steps in the Conscription Crisis, 1944

1. October, 1944. Colonel Ralston decides that conscripts must be sent.

2. November 1, 1944. Mackenzie King disagrees and fires Ralston.
3. November. Mackenzie King chooses General Andy McNaughton to replace Ralston.
4. November. General McNaughton cannot persuade conscripts to volunteer to fight in Europe.
5. November. Mackenzie King seeks and gets support of Louis St. Laurent on the conscription issue.
6. November 27, 1944. Mackenzie King announces his decision to send 13 000 conscripts to Europe.

*Results of the decision on conscription*
The results of the conscription decision were mixed. However, the crisis was not as severe as the one in 1917. Many French-speaking Canadian leaders recognized Mackenzie King's efforts and supported him on this issue. Prime Minister Mackenzie King had worked hard to keep Canada united. C.G. "Chubby" Power, Minister of National Defence for Air and an MP from Quebec, resigned. Power had promised voters in Quebec that conscripts would not be sent overseas. However, Louis St. Laurent, Minister of Justice and a Quebec MP, did not resign. St. Laurent opposed conscription but decided to support Mackenzie King. St. Laurent apparently believed that if he did not, then Mackenzie King might be forced to resign. A new prime minister might bring in very strong policies on conscription. This would split Canada badly. St. Laurent therefore decided to back Mackenzie King. This key support from St. Laurent permitted Mackenzie King to order conscripts overseas. (Only 2 463 of the conscripts finally did serve in combat.) There was some outrage and shock in Quebec, but the crisis was under Mackenzie King's control. Politically, he did not suffer much. However, national unity was again strained.

A protest meeting against conscription in Quebec, 1944. Why were many French Canadians against conscription?

## QUICK QUIZ

These questions require short answers.

1. What did Prime Minister Mackenzie King promise about conscription in 1939?
2. Why did Mackenzie King introduce conscription for home defence in 1940?
3. What is the name given to a vote by all people on a question?
4. Why did Defence Minister Ralston recommend conscription in 1944?
5. What important French Canadian cabinet minister supported Mackenzie King on conscription?

## USING YOUR KNOWLEDGE

1. Imagine that you are a conscript who refuses to volunteer for overseas service. Write a letter to General McNaughton explaining your stand. These letters can be distributed around the class for comparison.

## TAKING A STAND

1. Do you think that Prime Minister Mackenzie King was right to delay sending conscripts to Europe? Why or why not?

The balance sheet

Did Canadians gain or lose from World War II? Again a balance sheet may help you decide.

## World War II: The balance sheet

*What we lost*

—40 000 Canadians died. Thousands more were injured or crippled.

—Once again, the conscription issue caused bad feelings in the country.

—The war cost Canada $12 000 000 per day.

*What we gained*

—A part in the successful battle for freedom and human dignity.

—Further recognition as an independent nation.

—A vast system of factories that made Canada one of the world's richest nations.

—Pride in Canadian victories in battle, and in farm and factory production.

—Self-confidence as a nation.

---

### USING YOUR KNOWLEDGE

1. Make up the front page of a newspaper that could have come out the day Canada went to war in 1939 or on the last day of the war in 1945. Include headlines, a cartoon, news reports on causes, plans, public opinions, leaders, etc. You may want to do some research in a library to find information for your newspaper.

### TAKING A STAND

1. Should Canada have entered World War II? Review the balance sheet for World War II before you answer.

### RESEARCHING

1. Find out about the *Holocaust*. This term refers to the Nazi murder of 6 000 000 people, mostly Jews.
   What effect might knowledge of the concentration camps have had on people who argued about Canada being in the war?

## The Cold War

After World War II, people again hoped for a lasting world peace. Many nations decided to work actively to build a better, more peaceful world. Thus, in 1945, the United Nations was created. The 51 founding members of the organization promised to try to prevent wars and protect human rights. The UN's aim was to promote co-operation among the world's nations. Many armies, including Canada's, were greatly reduced in size following World War II and the founding of the UN. This was done partly to show faith in the newly created UN. (The UN and Canada's role in the organization will be discussed at length in the next chapters.)

Despite these efforts toward peace, serious conflicts began to develop. A new type of war, the Cold War, came into existence. The Cold War involved a struggle between the United States and its allies, and the Soviet Union and its allies. This struggle is referred to as the "Cold War" because no war was openly declared. Few shots were fired. It was a war of "nerves" rather than of shooting. Hostility between the two opposing blocks of countries was often expressed in spoken arguments or threats. Each camp used spies and propaganda to strengthen its position. Each side also tried to build up its arms in case open fighting broke out. This is referred to as the *arms race*.

How did the Cold War come about? To answer this, we must return to the end of

World War II. By the end of the war, the armies of the US, Britain, France, Canada, and the other allies had driven German forces out of western Europe. The Allies occupied the western part of Europe. The Soviet army occupied several eastern European countries. By 1947, there were communist governments in Bulgaria, Hungary, Romania, and Poland. In 1948, Czechoslovakia, too, fell under communist control. Winston Churchill spoke of an **Iron Curtain** that separated these countries from the West.

The Soviet Union claimed that it needed the eastern European countries as protection against future German aggression. The western countries did not agree with this. They feared that the Soviet Union would try to spread its control all over Europe. Indeed, a gap was opening up between the World War II allies.

There were many other points of conflict between the West and the Soviet Union. For example, the two could not agree over what to do with European countries freed in the war. Also, the West, which valued individual freedom and democracy, was opposed to many of the ideas of communism. Western countries were concerned about the communist threat to Greece and Turkey. For these and other reasons, friction and distrust grew between the West and the USSR.

One of the first important conflicts between the two parties occurred in 1948. The Soviet Union **blockaded** Berlin. It hoped to force the western powers to give up their rights to the city. The attempt failed. It did, however, increase the tension between the West and the USSR.

Western countries were worried about the spread of communism to western Europe and to the rest of the world. Therefore, in 1949, several countries joined to form the North Atlantic Treaty Organization (NATO). The purpose of NATO was to check the spread of communism.

Here is a list of the NATO members:

*Founding members 1949*

| | |
|---|---|
| Belgium | Italy |
| Britain | Luxembourg |
| Canada | The Netherlands |
| Denmark | Norway |
| France | Portugal |
| Iceland | United States |

*Other members*

Turkey (1952)
Greece (1952)
West Germany (1955)

In 1955, the Soviet Union organized the eastern European countries into a rival military alliance. This alliance was called the *Warsaw Pact*. The following are members of the Pact:

| | |
|---|---|
| Albania | Hungary |
| Bulgaria | Poland |
| Czechoslovakia | Romania |
| East Germany | USSR |

Yugoslavia—was a founding member, but no longer a part of the Pact.

Throughout the 1950s, 1960s, and 1970s, relations between the western and communist countries have been sometimes relaxed and sometimes strained. A few times, the Cold War has threatened to become "hot". The Cuban Missile Crisis is one important example. In the early 1960s, the USSR appeared to be installing missile bases in Cuba. The US feared that these bases would be used for a Soviet attack on the US. In protest, the US effected a naval blockade of Cuba. The two countries were on the brink of war. The USSR backed down, however, and dismantled its bases.

In the 1960s, Canada's role in NATO was questioned. Some Canadians felt that the Cold War had ended. Others feared that Canada would lose its independence because NATO was dominated by the US. Indeed, relations between the US and the

The *Aurora*, an anti-submarine patrol plane. Why does Canada need such aircraft?

USSR seemed to be improving. (This relaxation of strained relations between countries is called *detente*.) Detente seemed to show that Canada's role in NATO needed reviewing. The whole question of Canada's defence spending and role in NATO was, therefore, re-examined in the 1970s.

### In defence of Canada: Today and tomorrow

The most visible and costly aspect of our security is the regular armed forces. One of their main jobs is to protect Canada. They may also be used to help Canada's friends. Canadians do not have a tradition of keeping large standing forces. In World Wars I and II, Canada's army was built up almost from scratch. Until then the **militia** had been Canada's main defence. World events since 1945 have led to a change. Our armed forces today are not large in comparison to those of the United States, Britain, or France. However, they are large compared to the size of Canada's forces in peacetime before 1939. Canada today is also a member of NATO. Its members have pledged to defend each other. To belong to NATO, a nation must have a certain level of armed forces. As members of NATO, both Canada and the United States have soldiers stationed in Europe to help defend Europe from Warsaw Pact aggression.

In the late 1970s, defence policy was concerned with the size and usefulness of armed forces. What size should Canada's forces be? What weapons should they have? Should Canadians be stationed in Europe? NATO is very concerned with the actions of the Soviet Union. In 1978, the Soviet Union had two and a half times the number of tanks and aircraft that the NATO allies had. Why did the Soviets build up their armed forces? Were they afraid of an attack by the United States? Hadn't the USA and NATO promised never to be the first attacker? British experts believed that the Russians had more arms than they needed to defend themselves. It was a very confusing situation and it raised these questions for Canadians:

1. Should we increase the size of our armed forces?
2. Should we spend more money on new weapons?

3. Should we remain a member of NATO? Look at the statistics in Figs. 1-1 and 1-2 and decide for yourself.

**ORGANIZING BETTER**

1. **Look at Fig. 1-1. In which areas is NATO stronger?**
2. **Look at Fig. 1-2.**
   a) **Which countries spent less than Canada?**
   b) **Where did Canada rank in total spending?**
   c) **Which countries spent less on defence per person than Canada did?**
   d) **Where did Canada rank in spending per person of the population?**

|  | NATO | Canada's share | Warsaw Pact | USSR's share |
|---|---|---|---|---|
| Army divisions | 64 | 1/3 | 103 | 58 |
| Battle tanks | 11 300 | 50 | 27 900 | 16 050 |
| Ground support aircraft (provide close air support to land forces) | 2 028 | 50 | 1 725 | 1 050 |
| Interceptors (provide air-to-air defence against other aircraft) | 655 | 0 | 3 025 | 1 325 |

Source: *The Military Balance 1978-79*, International Institute for Strategic Studies, London, 1978
**Fig. 1-1 Strength in NATO versus Warsaw Pact**

|  | Total in millions of dollars | Dollars per person of population |
|---|---|---|
| Belgium | 2 476 | 253 |
| Britain | 13 579 | 239 |
| Canada | 3 635 | 153 |
| Denmark | 1 320 | 259 |
| France | 17 518 | 325 |
| Germany | 21 355 | 337 |
| Greece | 1 523 | 164 |
| Italy | 5 610 | 98 |
| Luxembourg | 37 | 100 |
| The Netherlands | 4 208 | 301 |
| Norway | 1 291 | 316 |
| Portugal | 568 | 62 |
| Turkey | 2 286 | 54 |
| United States | 113 000 | 517 |
| Soviet Union (included for comparison) | 133 000 | 508 |

Source: *The Military Balance 1977-78*, International Institute of Strategic Studies, London
**Fig. 1-2 NATO—Membership spending on defence, 1978**

### The debate: Should Canada stay in NATO?

**NO!**

When NATO was formed in 1948, most of Europe was in ruins. World War II had hurt the Europeans so badly that they needed our help. Today France, West Germany, and Britain have recovered. The smaller nations have also recovered. In fact, some are richer than we are! I think it's time they looked after themselves.

Another reason for getting out of NATO is the amount of power the United States has in it. The Americans really run NATO. They control most of the nuclear weapons NATO could use. The result is that NATO does what the USA wants. In my opinion, the US uses NATO to scare the Russians into having a large army. That's a danger to peace.

We should, therefore, get out of NATO. The Europeans don't need us, and it's run by the Americans.

If we don't quit it altogether, we should at least pull our troops out of Europe. We've got 5 000 soldiers and their families there. They cost a fortune to keep and there aren't enough of them to do any good in war.

**YES!**

The Russians are still a threat to world peace. They keep a huge army in Europe "for defence". This seems to mean that they have some plans for attack. We need to be in NATO to show the Russians that the countries of the free western world stand together.

In addition, as long as we're a part of NATO, we have a lot of allies. The Russians won't start anything with us because they know we have NATO members on our side.

Another thing is that Europe is an important market for our manufactured goods and raw materials. If we pulled out of NATO, it would break faith with Europe. In return, the European countries might not buy what we have for sale. This would really hurt the economy.

Anybody who wants to quit NATO and pull our troops out of Europe is foolish. The cost of keeping troops there is low compared to the losses our economy might face if we insult the rest of the NATO members.

In my opinion, we should send more soldiers to Europe. That would show the Russians that Canadians are willing to take a stand.

Defence spending—enough?

The Canadian armed forces do other jobs that are not related to NATO. Among their jobs are:

1. Air-sea rescue—helping people in trouble.
2. Patrol of Canada's coastal waters—searching for ships or submarines that are in Canada's waters illegally. Patrolling fishing areas.
3. Air defence—protecting against attacks from the air. As a partner with the United States, Canada is part of the *North American Air Defence Command* (NORAD).
4. Helping civilian authorities.
   Examples—Olympic Games security, 1976.
   —Prison duty during riots or strikes.
   —National disasters (floods, storms, forest fires, etc.)
5. Patrol and defence of the Arctic.
6. Peacekeeping—in Cyprus and the Middle East.

By the late 1970s it was clear that all of these duties placed a great strain on the armed forces. Their equipment was getting old and the forces did not have enough people. The federal government had frozen defence spending in the early 1970s. However, in 1975, it again decided to spend money on military equipment.

New defence purchases, 1976-78

128 *Leopard* tanks for Canada's NATO forces.

18 *Aurora* long-range patrol aircraft for defence of Canada's coasts.

350 *Cougar* armoured cars for use in NATO and home defence.

An estimated 150 new fighter aircraft.

These items are very expensive. However, our NATO allies are pleased to see that we have better equipent. Much of the new equipment will be made in Canada. Thus, jobs will be provided. Is this enough? Should Canada spend more on defence? Look at the comparison between Canada and the Netherlands in Fig. 1-3.

**ORGANIZING FACTS**
1. **Which of the two countries is bigger? Check an atlas to find the area of each country.**
2. **Which country spends most per person on defence?**
3. **Why may it be argued that the Netherlands needs to spend more? Use an atlas to help you form an answer.**

**TAKING A STAND**
1. **Should Canada spend more on defence now and in the future?**

**RESEARCHING**
1. **Conduct a poll. Ask other students, your teachers, parents, and friends the following questions.**
   **Be sure that they have answered the questions in this poll only once. Results will**

|  | Canada | The Netherlands |
|---|---|---|
| Population | 23 700 000 | 13 000 000 |
| Defence spending | $3 635 000 000 | $4 208 000 000 |
| Total number of people in armed forces | 80 000 | 109 700 |
| Tanks | 144 | 800 |
| Armoured personnel carriers | 1 112 | 2 000 |
| Self-propelled artillery | 50 | 180 |
| Combat aircraft | 214 | 162 |
| Combat ships | 26 | 72 |

Source: *The Military Balance 1978-79*, International Institute for Strategic Studies, London, 1978.
**Fig. 1-3 Defence equipment and spending, Canada and the Netherlands**

The *Leopard* tank, purchased in the late 1970s for Canada's NATO forces.

Canadian Forces Photo

not be accurate if they have answered more than one time.
   a) **Do you know what NATO is?**
   b) **Do you think that there is any kind of Warsaw Pact threat to Canada or NATO?**
   c) **Do you think Canada spends enough on defence?**
   d) **Should Canada be a member of NATO?**
2. **Use the library to find out more about the Warsaw Pact. How does it compare with NATO?**

## Conclusion

At times in the past, Canadians have committed themselves to war. They have fought in Europe and Asia. They have fought for freedom, democracy, independence, and the rule of law.

The decisions to fight were controversial. While many volunteered to join the war effort, many others objected to Canada's role in the wars. Today, looking at history, we may find it hard to judge those decisions to go to war. The values of Canadians in 1914 and 1939 were different from the values we hold today. Still, we can use those decisions to help us understand our world today.

Today we must weigh our own values and make our own decisions about defence and war. We must judge for ourselves the level of defence preparation we want in Canada. It is important to balance the need for defence with the demands for medical care, pollution control, energy development, and industrial growth. Above all, we should consider defence needs in terms of the world and our relations to other countries. The decisions we make may not be easy, but they are ours because we are citizens of a democracy. The decisions we make will affect our taxes, our security, and our peace. What have you decided about these issues?

## READING BETTER

1. Write a sentence or two explaining each of the following:

   | | |
   |---|---|
   | NATO | national security |
   | conscription | defence spending |
   | referendum | Warsaw Pact |

## ORGANIZING BETTER

1. Make up a time chart that will place events in this chapter in *chronological order*. Begin with the date 1914 and end with this year. Fill in all other dates and events covered in "Canada and war" in the order in which they occurred.

## USING YOUR KNOWLEDGE

1. Could Canada have stayed out of World War I? Why or why not?
2. In your own words, explain the term "national pride". How did World War I help Canada's national pride to grow?
3. "Hitler was a criminal. He refused to obey world laws." What facts can be used to prove this statement? Are there facts to disprove this?
4. How are the events of the late 1930s different from those described in "War decision"? How are they the same?

## SOLVING PROBLEMS

1. What would you do to reduce tensions in the world, especially between the communist and non-communist worlds? Use the problem-solving model to help you decide.

## TAKING A STAND

1. Examine the following situations and decide for each of them whether or not citizens should be *forced* to serve their country. Give reasons for your decision in each case. Discuss this question in class.
   a) To fight an invader
   b) To fight a huge forest fire in the Yukon
   c) To defend a neighbour (e.g., the USA) from an invader
   d) To defend freedom and democracy in Greece
   e) To defend Germany from a Soviet invasion
   f) To help Canadian soldiers already in battle
   g) To help after a flood in your town
2. Should Canada have conscription today? Should all Canadians 18 to 20 years of age be required to serve two years in the armed forces?
3. Now that you have a better knowledge of Canada and war, decide again what you think Prime Minister Gagnon should do in the story "War decision". Write your new position down. How does it compare with your original decision? Explain to the class.

## RESEARCHING

1. Conduct a poll. Find out the opinions of other groups of people on some of the issues discussed in this chapter. If you can, interview all kinds of people—veterans, university students, immigrants, and other groups.

## GLOSSARY

**Balance sheet.** A list that shows how opposite things compare with each other.

**Blockaded.** Closed off by some sort of barrier.

**Communists.** Persons who support an economic theory based on community ownership of property. The USSR and China are two countries that follow this theory.

**Conscientious objectors.** Persons who refuse to take part in war because they believe it is wrong.

**Iron Curtain.** A barrier against communication or contact between communist Eastern Europe and countries with different beliefs. The Iron Curtain is not a *physical* barrier. A barrier is said to exist because information and ideas from other countries are not allowed into Soviet-controlled ones.

**Militia.** Part-time soldiers. Citizens who join the militia often spend one evening a week in training.

**Munich Conference.** A meeting in 1938 of Britain, France, and Germany. Britain and France agreed to allow Nazi Germany to take over part of Czechoslovakia.

**NATO.** The North Atlantic Treaty Organization. An international group of nations pledged to defend each other from attack.

**Statute of Westminster.** An act of the British Parliament which, in effect, made Canada's Parliament independent from Britain.

**United Nations.** An international organization of nations devoted to world peace and security.

# 2/Canada and peace

## Contents

## Introduction

Every day in the news we are confronted with the lack of peace in the world. Quite often conflict is open and violent—nations are at war with each other, or citizens of a country riot in protest against the government. Around the world terrible new weapons are built and sold as nations prepare for a possible clash. In our nuclear age of computers, guided missiles, and satellites, no nation is remote from these dangers.

There is also much unrest of a quieter nature. Millions of people die each day from starvation and disease. We hear stories of poverty and unhappiness.

Humankind is aware of the unrest and conflict in the world. Great efforts are made to establish and keep peace. World leaders praise peace, and try to end conflicts among nations, or among the citizens of a single nation. Organizations like the United Nations have been created to help keep peace, and to ease people's suffering and misery.

In this chapter you will first examine the concept of peace. You will learn about ways to develop peace in your own life. The chapter then focuses on the United Nations and peacekeeping. Canada's role in these different areas will be studied. You, as a citizen, will be asked to judge how well Canada is doing in helping to keep peace. Thus, the central questions of this chapter are:

1. **What is peace?**
2. **How can you create peace in your own life?**

3. **How can peace be created in the world?**
4. **How should Canada help keep world peace?**

### Peace begins with you

It is difficult to define peace. Peace is more than freedom from war. It is freedom from conflict or unrest of any kind. It is good will and order. This order does not necessarily have to be physical—it can be mental as well. For example, peace is people living and working together with respect and co-operation.

We may live in a country that is at peace, and yet we may not be at peace with our family or classmates. There is no peace when people constantly argue, steal, or insult. There is no peace when human beings worry about where tomorrow's meals will come from. There is no peace when one person is angry and unable to improve life.

The opposite of peace is conflict. There are many forms of conflict, from war between nations, to hatred between neighbours, to an argument over whose turn it is to put out the garbage.

| Qualities of peace | Qualities of conflict |
| --- | --- |
| Happiness for all | Anger |
| Good health | Hatred |
| Friendliness | Stress |
| Co-operation | Fear |
| Self-respect | Violence |
| Long life | Sickness |
| Help | Destruction |

### Does peace mean a life without excitement?

Some people feel that if everybody were to smile and be respectful all the time, then life would not be exciting. This is not necessarily true. A peaceful life may still contain competition, struggle, success and failure, and excitement. People in a peaceful world may still play hockey, football, or soccer. They may still have businesses that compete for a market. A peaceful world may still have all of this and more—but within a framework of respect, caring, and help. A peaceful world tries to eliminate unnecessary violence to people—violence to the body or mind.

### How do we achieve peace?

In a peaceful country, people are friendly and they respect each other. They work hard at keeping the peace, for its existence is not accidental. People are different, so conflicts and disagreements will naturally arise. Perhaps there is simple conflict over which movie to go to, or at what time to come home from a party. In a place of peace, these conflicts are settled in a way that does not hurt anyone in body or mind. This takes work—all the time.

In order to understand peacekeeping, it is useful to know how peace is broken. If we know what causes conflicts among people, we may be able to keep peace. Here are some examples of conflicts. In each case, how is the peace broken? Who is to blame? Why?

*Case 1: Anger 2, Peace 0*
Ralph: Mom, after the dance tonight, I'm going over to Nancy's place. She's having a party.
Mom: Doesn't the dance end at 11:30?
Ralph: Yes.
Mom: Well, you're due home as soon as it's over. There will be no party for you.
Ralph: Why not? The rest of the kids will be there.
Mom: I don't care what the rest of the kids are doing. You'll come home right after the dance or else. At least I care where my kids are and what time they stay out to.
Ralph: That's not fair!
Mom: Don't talk to me like that. Maybe you shouldn't even go to the dance!

*Case 2: Insults 4, Peace 0*
Doreen: Miss Warwick wants us to type

this in letter style. Then we must organize the pages.

Carole: That's not what she said. You never get things straight.

Doreen: What do you mean by that? I'm just repeating what she said. I've got it straight!

Carole: It's supposed to be manuscript style. Can't you see that!

Doreen: Why don't you leave me alone?

Miss Warwick: Is that job done yet?

In both of the sample cases, people are making life hard for themselves or others. Of course, these are only sample situations of peace breaking down. Think of a few cases of your own. Share them with the class. Try to list the reasons for which peace breaks down in people's lives.

### Some general causes of conflict

There are some basic causes of conflict. The following are among the most usual causes:

| | |
|---|---|
| Greed | Poor communication |
| Lack of respect for others | Lack of knowledge |
| Frustration | Selfishness |

Think of examples that illustrate these causes of conflict. Share them with the members of your class.

### How do we keep peace?

A conflict may appear to end if one of the parties gives up. But is that really peace? Probably not. One party may feel jealous, bitter, or resentful. When seeking peace, we must try to create a true, lasting peace. All

This is not peace.

Public Archives of Canada

sides in a conflict must be content. All sides must also want peace. All sides must be willing to *compromise*. Compromise is the key to creating peace. Look at the example below. How is a compromise reached?

Owen: There's no way I'm going to that detention. I was only two minutes late.

Mr. Sidchuck: If you keep that up I'll have to send you to the office. I'm just trying to do my job. Do you want to make a big deal out of this?

Owen: I've got nothing against you, sir. But I worked hard to get into the band. If I miss that rehearsal tonight, I may lose my spot. Can I serve it tomorrow, sir?

Mr. Sidchuck: All right, Owen, you're in a spot. Come tomorrow at three o'clock.

Turning conflict into peace

Here are some suggestions about what to do when conflict arises.

1. If you feel that a conflict is starting, stop and ask yourself, "What is this all about?"
2. Show respect for others. Be careful about what you say.
3. With tact, tell others what you think and feel. They need to know.
4. Listen carefully to others and ask them questions. Find out what they really want.
5. Remember that you have rights and so do others.
6. Suggest compromises that may please everybody concerned.
7. Ask for a break. Take a cooling-off period to think things over. During the break, write down what you want and what others want.
8. Do not get upset needlessly. Keep calm.
9. Get somebody else to listen to both sides of the argument and offer solutions.

USING YOUR KNOWLEDGE

1. Return to the two short dialogues in the section "How do we achieve peace?" Re-write them so that they end in peace.
2. Write a dialogue for each of the following situations. Use the steps for turning conflict into peace, so that the situation is resolved peacefully.

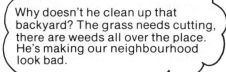

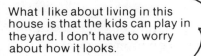

## The art of negotiating

We have already looked at a list of ways of keeping peace. There are many systems of making or keeping peace. One common method is *negotiating*. In *negotiation,* people try to reach an agreement. Winning is not the goal. Negotiators try to arrive at a peaceful solution to a conflict, a solution that all sides are happy with. In the fictional interview below, an experienced negotiator talks about her business.

**Interviewer:** Mrs. Thomas, you've taken part in many negotiations. What is the most important thing to remember?

**Mrs. Thomas:** I guess you have to remember that the negotiation process is a competition. However, for negotiation to work, the parties must be willing to reach an agreement that they're all happy with. If you're out to destroy the opposition, then negotiation won't work.

**Interviewer:** It seems to be a pleasant process. Where does the competition come in?

**Mrs. Thomas:** All the parties in a dispute may want to have a peaceful solution, but they still compete. Each party tries to get as much as it can. For example, unions and employers may have decided not to get violent. But that doesn't mean that they won't each try to get as much as possible.

**Interviewer:** How do negotiations begin? Do the parties ask for a lot at first and then reduce their demands as they go along?

**Mrs. Thomas:** Yes, give-and-take is part of it. All parties must be ready to give a little. If you start high and refuse to budge, you're in trouble. The other parties may give up on you, and that's not what you want.

**Interviewer:** How do you know when you've reached that magic point of agreement where everybody's happy?

**Mrs. Thomas:** There are no rules about it. At a certain point each party has won some of its demands and accepts compromises in other areas. Then there's agreement. Negotiating is hard and rules about when to stop don't work. Only through experience can a negotiator learn to judge when the parties have reached agreement.

---

**ORGANIZING BETTER**

1. What are three important things that negotiators must remember?
2. Which of the peacekeeping steps listed in the section "Turning conflict into peace" are used by Mrs. Thomas in her negotiations?

**USING YOUR KNOWLEDGE**

1. Act out the following meeting, using the rules of peacekeeping and negotiating. This enactment can be done in groups or by a panel in front of the whole class.

**SITUATION:**
Tenants in a high-rise apartment building are upset. Their rent is to be raised $150 per month. They are presently paying anywhere between $200 and $350 per month. The tenants have met and elected two people to represent them. These people will meet with the owner and the building superintendent to discuss the problem.

**FACTS:**

*The owner*
—The cost of fuel is going up rapidly. It has doubled in the past two years.
—The owner is used to making a profit of $40 000 per year. Last year it dropped to just $6 000.
—The cost of repairs is going up. Plumbers, painters, and other workers get very high wages.
—There are other buildings in the area in which rents have gone up.

*The tenants*
—The building is fifteen years old.
—Most of the tenants have been there for at least ten years.
—The building has not been painted for at least two years.
—Rents in some other buildings have gone up only $50 to $75.

**Is poverty peace?**

**Is neglect of the aged peace?**

—The elevators often do not work.
—There are other newer apartments available in town.

## Heroes of peace

Sports and war heroes receive great public attention. They are given medals, money, and often, important jobs. But what about those people who help make peace? Since 1901, a special Nobel Peace Prize has been awarded to individuals or groups who make the world a more peaceful place in which to live.

The Nobel Prize was created by Alfred Nobel, inventor of dynamite and a Swedish millionaire. In his will, Nobel directed that the interest earned on his fortune was to be used for prizes each year. Committees of experts decide who should receive awards in physics, chemistry, medicine, literature, and peace-making. Nobel believed that great achievements in these areas improved the world. The prizes are not awarded if the experts can find no deserving persons.

The Peace Prize winner is chosen by the Norwegian parliament (*Storthing*), just as Nobel directed. The prize consists of a gold medal and a cash award of about $175 000. Prizes were not awarded between 1914 and 1917 and again from 1939 to 1943 because of the wars. Between 1901 and 1977, there have been 19 years altogether in which no Peace Prize was awarded.

Here are two brief biographies of Nobel Peace Prize winners. Their lives prove that human beings can do much to make peace in this world. Their biographies also show that people can contribute to world peace in many ways.

### 1957: Lester B. Pearson

Pearson was born in Toronto in 1897. He served in the Royal Flying Corps in 1917 and later attended the University of Toronto and Oxford University in Britain. Pearson taught history at the University of Toronto for several years. Afterward, he joined the **Department of External Affairs.** There he quickly became one of Canada's greatest diplomats.

Pearson was very much involved in the creation of the United Nations in 1945 and 1946. He was nominated by Britain and the US for the job of first secretary-general of the United Nations. Soviet opposition prevented him from getting the job. While Pearson was serving as President of the UN General Assembly in 1953, he was again nominated for the job. Once again, he did not receive the appointment because of Soviet opposition.

In 1948, Pearson entered Canadian federal politics as a Liberal. He became the Minister of External Affairs.

When war broke out between Israel and Egypt in 1956, world peace was once again threatened. The conflict began in 1956, when the government of Egypt nationalized the Suez Canal. (This means it took over ownership and control of the canal.) France and Britain wanted to protect their interests in the canal. France therefore persuaded Israel to start a war with Egypt. France and Britain

**Lester B. Pearson receives the Nobel Peace Prize from the Nobel Committee President.**

then took advantage of the war and sent troops to occupy the Suez Canal.

At first the UN seemed unable to act. France and Britain were important members of the Security Council, and allies of the United States. The Soviet Union feared that these countries would come to control the UN. A war scare hit the world.

At this point, Pearson was leading Canada's delegation at the UN. He suggested creating a special police force to stop the fighting and prevent a new war. Israel agreed to withdraw from Egypt and have this UN peacekeeping force patrol border areas. Thus, Pearson was responsible for creating the UN peacekeeping forces. Since then, they have been used many times in the Middle East and in Cyprus, Vietnam, and Africa.

Pearson believed that ignorance created fear and that fear was an enemy of peace. He believed that hunger and poverty were also a danger to peace. He once said that human beings make great efforts to prepare for war, yet they prepare for peace very poorly.

Lester B. Pearson was prime minister of Canada from 1963 to 1968. He was awarded the Nobel Peace Prize in 1957.

### 1970: Dr. Norman Borlaug

The Nobel Peace Prize to Dr. Borlaug stated: "More than any other single person of his age, he has helped provide bread for a hungry world." Born in Iowa in the United States, Dr. Borlaug is an expert in **plant genetics.** In 1944, he began working on a special project in Mexico. His goal was to develop a new type of wheat that would produce more grain than the older types. Borlaug finally produced a new dwarf wheat. As a result, farmers could get twice as much wheat out of a one-acre [0.4 ha] field as before.

For Mexico the results were important. Mexico had needed to buy American wheat in the 1940s. However, by 1956 Mexico was growing more wheat than it needed.

Borlaug then took his new wheat to Pakistan. The **"Green Revolution"** spread rapidly to India, Turkey, Iran, and other countries. The changes in farm production were tremendous. In 1968 India produced a record wheat crop. If its population growth could be controlled, India would be able to feed itself. Borlaug's "Green Revolution" had similar effects all over the world.

Dr. Borlaug believes that population growth is the world's greatest problem. If food production cannot keep up with it, then millions, perhaps billions, of people will starve. He was awarded the Nobel Peace Prize in 1970.

The Canadian Press

**Dr. Norman Borlaug's discoveries started a _Green Revolution_.**

1. Briefly state in your own words what both Nobel Peace Prize winners did to deserve the awards.
2. Values are things that are important to people. For example, honesty, justice, and wealth are values. People's values may be discovered by examining what the people say and do. What values did the Nobel Peace Prize winners have?
3. Turn back to the chapter "Canada and war" and review the sections on Victoria Cross winners. Do you think being a hero of peace is as hard as being a war hero? Why or why not?

RESEARCHING

1. Find out more about other Nobel Peace Prize winners. Here are some other famous winners:

| | |
|---|---|
| Albert Schweitzer | Albert Luthuli |
| Menachem Begin | Betty Williams |
| Anwar Sadat | Mairead Corrigan |
| Sato Eisaku | UNICEF |
| Emily Greene Balch | International |
| Leon Jouhaux | Red Cross |
| Jane Addams | |

## Canada and the United Nations

World peace and Canada's role

We have seen that people can create peace in their own lives. Nations, too, try to keep peace, both within their boundaries and with other countries.

In other chapters of this book we examined problems that have disturbed Canada's peace. We know that Canadians have solved many of these problems. It is possible for Canada to help solve problems in the world as well. In this section we look at Canada's role in the United Nations, an organization devoted to peacekeeping.

The United Nations and peace

How many people died in the two world wars? Fifty million? There are no accurate figures—only guesses. But one thing is certain—the waste of life and materials was staggering. The countries that had joined together to defeat Nazi Germany and its allies were determined to make sure that such waste never occurred again. They promised to join a new, world organization called the United Nations.

The UN was founded on October 24, 1945. Canada was one of the fifty original members. By 1978 membership in the UN had grown to 149 countries. All but a few of the countries on this planet are now UN members.

The purpose of the UN is expressed in its charter (constitution).

*Charter: Important goals of the UN*
(This is a simplified version of the UN Charter.)
—To keep peace in the world. To save future generations from the horrors of war.
—To develop friendly relations among nations.
—To defend human rights. To advance the dignity and value of all persons. To advance the equal rights of men and women.
—To advance justice and respect for the law.

*How can these goals be reached?*
—By being tolerant of others. By living in peace as good neighbours.
—By promising never to use war to settle disputes with neighbours.
—By promising to stop nations that use war or disobey laws.
—By using UN agencies to help improve the lives of people all over the world. These UN agencies include the World Health Organization (WHO) and the United Nations Children's Fund (UNICEF).

READING BETTER

1. In a dictionary, find a meaning for the word "tolerant".
2. Make up a short story of a few sentences for each point in the charter to show that you understand the various points. Compare stories with other students and check to see that you have all understood the charter.

**United Nations headquarters in New York City, USA.**

How does the UN work?

From its headquarters in New York City, the UN operates over thirty agencies around the world. These agencies try to promote peace and a better life (See Fig. 2-1).

*1. The General Assembly*

The General Assembly is the principal body of the United Nations. Here, the world's problems are discussed. In the General Assembly, each member nation has a delegate who votes on UN plans and requests. These plans are called resolutions. Each nation has one vote on any resolutions discussed. The president of the Assembly is elected by the member countries each year. The members of the Assembly pay for UN operations.

*2. The Security Council*

The Security Council has the important job of keeping world peace. For example, sometimes warring nations will let a neutral army stand between them and keep peace. The Security Council has the power to create these special peacekeeping forces.

The Council consists of the world's five **Great Powers.** These are Britain, China, France, the USA, and the USSR. In addition to these five permanent members, there are ten other nations that serve for two-year terms. Canada has served on the Council in 1948-49, 1958-59, 1966-68, and 1977-78.

The Great Powers control what the Security Council can do. They have the right of veto. This means that if one of the powers votes against a certain proposal, that proposal is defeated. For example, the Security Council may

447

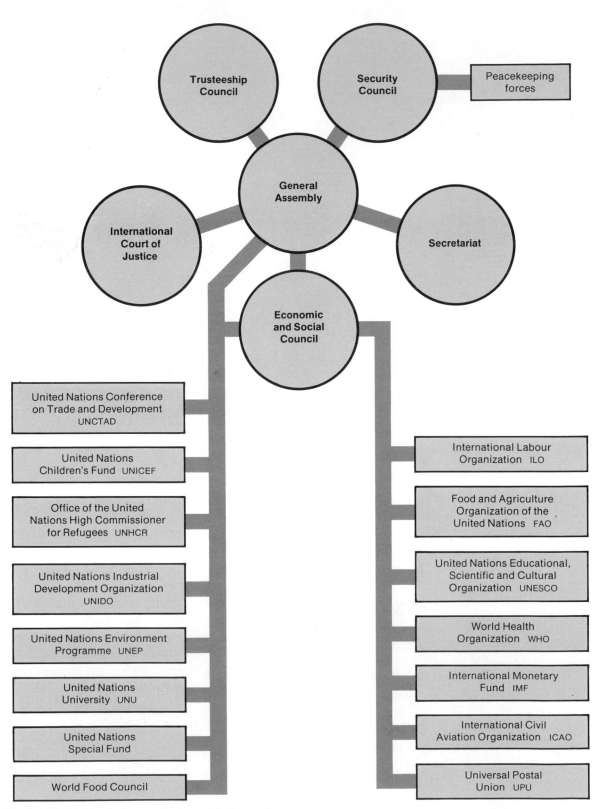

**Fig. 2-1 The United Nations and some related agencies**

consider a suggestion to stop trade with South Africa. If only Britain votes against it, then the proposal is still defeated. This veto power ensures that all the Great Powers agree on any action taken.

3. *The Secretariat*

This is a group of over 10 000 people who work for the UN. It is made up of people from all countries. The Secretariat carries on the everyday operations of the UN. The secretary-general is in charge of this working operation. This person is considered a world leader because of the importance of the UN.

UN secretaries-general

| | |
|---|---|
| Trygve Lie | 1945-1952 |
| Dag Hammarskjöld | 1953-1961 |
| U Thant | 1961-1972 |
| Kurt Waldheim | 1972- |

The secretary-general must work hard, travel a lot, and be respected by the **superpowers.** Dag Hammarskjöld had the greatest reputation of the four secretaries-general for his clear, active leadership. He was a strong personality, brave in the face of threats, and a good organizer. The world mourned when he died in a mysterious plane crash in Africa in 1961.

**ORGANIZING BETTER**

1. **In your notebook, briefly describe each of the main parts of the United Nations under these headings: Name, Members, Job.**
2. **The Security Council has been described as the most important part of the UN. What facts prove this to be true?**

The UN in action

How does the United Nations help create peace? Here is a case in which UN action has helped make the world more peaceful. Following the case study is a profile of Dr. Brock Chisholm, head of the World Health Organization from 1948 to 1953.

---

**Case study: The war on smallpox**

Do you have a small circular white scar on one of your arms? If you do, you are just one of hundreds of millions or perhaps billions of people who do. That scar is the mark of a smallpox vaccination. This vaccination protects you from one of the world's most deadly diseases. For centuries smallpox has been killing millions of people. Those who survive the disease are scarred by the pox marks left on their faces and bodies. The scar on your arm is typical of the kinds of scars that cover survivors. When accurate counts were first taken, over 2.5 million people around the world were sick with smallpox in one year.

The World Health Organization (WHO) is a part of the UN. In 1967 the WHO declared a ten-year campaign to wipe out smallpox. In that year, there were 10 to 15 million cases of the disease spread out over 44 of the world's countries. In the WHO's campaign, millions of people were vaccinated. By 1970, smallpox cases were found in only 17 countries. By 1973, smallpox was found in 10 countries. The WHO declared that if no cases were found in 1979 smallpox would be completely beaten. Canada contributed nearly $2 million to the war against this disease.

The campaign against smallpox was so encouraging that by 1978 some Canadian doctors no longer used the vaccination. Still, caution must be used. If people are unprotected, the disease may flare up again. Millions of people—Canadians included—could be killed or scarred.

### Dr. Brock Chisholm: Profile of a leader

From 1948 to 1953 the head of the World Health Organization was Dr. Brock Chisholm of Canada. Before taking over at the WHO, Dr. Chisholm was a famous Canadian doctor.

In World War I, Chisholm joined the army at age 18. He fought in France. After 1918, he attended medical schools in Toronto and England. Dr. Chisholm became a **psychiatrist,** treating patients in Toronto throughout the 1930s.

In World War II, Dr. Chisholm again served in the army. He rose to the rank of major general. In 1944, he was invited by Prime Minister Mackenzie King to become Deputy Minister of National Health. In that post, Dr. Chisholm had a great influence on the health of Canadians.

Dr. Chisholm was never afraid to speak his mind. In the 1940s, for example, he said that the Santa Claus myth had bad effects on children. This criticism created a great public upset. Dr. Chisholm was able to work hard and concentrate, and he expressed his ideas well. These qualities led to his appointment as head of the WHO.

Peace was one of Dr. Chisholm's major concerns. He believed it could be created if children were taught to care for people and to respect the rights of others. He believed that children should be taught to be citizens of the world.

Dr. Brock Chisholm died in 1971, at the age of 75.

---

**READING BETTER**
1. Review the Charter of the UN. Which point of the charter is shown by the case study "The war on smallpox"?
2. Examine Fig. 2-1.
   a) Which branch of the UN would students who are worried about pollution write to?
   b) Which branch of the UN would Canada and Poland appeal to about a dispute over art treasures?

**RESEARCHING**
1. Find out more about how the UN works. Use encyclopaedias and other library materials.
2. a) In an encyclopaedia, find out about smallpox. Write a report on its history, causes, and effects.
   b) Find out how many people in your class have smallpox vaccinations. What dangers exist if they are not vaccinated?

### The UN, peacekeeping, and Canada

Keeping peace is the major role of the United Nations. But this is a difficult and dangerous job. The League of Nations tried to do the job between 1919 and 1939 and it failed. The United Nations has had to create new ways of stopping small wars and preventing them from becoming big ones.

This section examines the UN's job of peacekeeping and Canada's role in it. We already know that Lester Pearson helped create peacekeeping forces. We will find out more about Canada's role as we answer the following questions:

1. What is peacekeeping and how has Canada contributed to it?
2. Should Canada continue to contribute to UN peacekeeping?

**Canada's contributions to the United Nations, 1945-1976**

| | |
|---|---|
| Total | $873 774 000 |
| *Selected examples* | |
| Peacekeeping on Cyprus | $27 000 000 |
| Peacekeeping on Golan Heights (Syria) and Sinai (Egypt) | 8 377 000 |
| UNICEF | 33 875 000 |
| WHO | 32 976 000 |
| Fund for drug abuse control | 950 000 |
| World Food Programme | 241 749 000 |
| United Nations Development Programme | 161 071 000 |

Source: "Canada's Contribution to the UN", Reference Paper 93, Minister of Supply and Services, 1977 8.

**Middle East crisis (A fictional scene)**

The five people gathered around the table looked grim. They had been meeting in a conference room of the UN building for three days. Their goal was to work out a cease-fire agreement. Four were UN delegates from Arab countries—Syria, Lebanon, Egypt, and Jordan. The fifth person in the room was the secretary-general of the United Nations.

In the same building, but on a different floor, was the delegation from Israel. The Arabs would not meet directly with the Israelis, so the secretary-general acted as a go-between.

A cease-fire agreement was needed because fighting had again broken out in the Middle East. It was not a full war. The conflict was serious enough, however, for the Security Council to pass a resolution asking both sides to stop fighting. Another UN peace-keeping force was proposed to stand between the warring parties.

The secretary-general was pleased because an agreement had nearly been reached. The last job was to select the peacekeepers.

"The Brazilians, Irish, and Indians are ready to send troops. Will you agree to let them send peacekeeping forces?" asked the secretary-general.

Canadian soldiers on patrol for the UN in Cyprus. How do trained fighters help keep peace?

"Yes, of course," said the delegate from Syria. "They are neutral and capable. I think I can speak for all of us in accepting them." There were no objections from the other delegates.

"I would also like to propose the Canadians," said the secretary-general. This suggestion was greeted with definite scowls of disapproval. The secretary-general hurried to explain her choice. "They are the most experienced peacekeepers in the world. Canadian military forces have been part of every major peace force that we've ever had."

Again, the Syrian delegate spoke for the rest. "The Canadians do indeed have a good reputation. I know that you're also going to point out how well-equipped they are, and how honest their officials are. But from a political point of view, I'm not so sure they are a good choice."

"Yes, especially from a political view," said the delegate from Egypt. "Our people cannot see any difference between the Canadians and the Americans. Both give strong support to Israel. They are both partners in NATO. Canada is just a puppet of the United States. We want peacekeepers to be truly neutral."

"Please remember, Canada has not sold weapons to Israel. I know that it stands for peace. It is ready to send soldiers to help keep the peace and that is important," answered the secretary-general, trying again to have Canada be part of the new force.

"Our embassy in Ottawa keeps us well-informed of Canadian public opinion," said the Lebanese delegate. "Most Canadians support Israel. They send millions of dollars in aid to Israel each year. In my opinion, the Canadians may want peace, but they are on Israel's side. I suggest that they be kept off this peacekeeping force."

The secretary-general was not about to lose a chance for a cease-fire agreement just to get Canada on the peace force. "Well, since you object, I will not persist. Who would you suggest as a fourth?"

After further discussion and several phone calls, Sweden was selected as the fourth peacekeeper. The meeting broke up and the secretary-general went to see the Israeli delegation. On her way, she passed the Canadian ambassador in the hall. A shake of the head was the only message needed. For the first time, Canada would not be part of a major peacekeeping force. (This fictional scene presents a real problem facing Canada in its peacekeeping efforts.)

Canadian Forces Photo

**The Canadian Armed Forces provide technical services for UN forces, Lebanon, 1978.**

1. In this scene, what is the job of the secretary-general?
2. Why did the delegates in this scene welcome the Brazilians, Irish, and Indians in the peacekeeping force?
3. a) Why did the delegates object to Canada?
   b) Why were the Canadians suggested in the first place?
4. What part of the UN Charter is being put into action in this scene? (You may want to refer to the UN Charter to answer this question.)
5. What does this scene show about Canada's commitment to the UN?
6. How are other actions by Canadians hurting Canada's commitment to the UN?
7. From this story what can you conclude about the problems facing a country that wants to be a peacekeeper?

Canada and peacekeeping—The record

The United Nations has tried to keep peace in the world. It has improved the lives of millions. It has helped stop several wars.

Canada is committed to the UN and to the job of peacekeeping. Canadian soldiers have served around the world in the name of the UN. Hundreds have been killed over the years. The record of this service and the UN's role in peacekeeping is outlined below. Exercises and a debate about peacekeeping follow the record.

*Korea, 1950*

In 1950, North Korea attacked South Korea. Following a US proposal, the UN agreed to protect South Korea. This was done according to the UN Charter. One section of the charter permits the UN to use war methods to stop countries that do not respect the rights of others. The United States and South Korea provided most of the soldiers used in this war for peace. Other soldiers were sent by many nations. Among them were Britain, Turkey, Australia, and Canada. Four hundred and

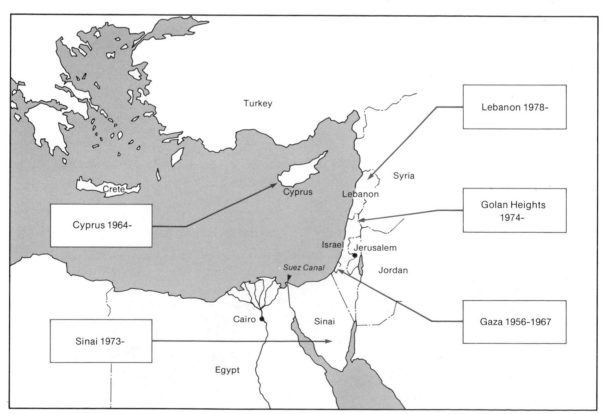

Fig. 2-2 Canada's peacekeeping role: The Eastern Mediterranean Sea

six Canadians were killed during the Korean War. Over one thousand were wounded.

The UN action was **controversial.** Many Canadians were pleased that Canada had a role in stopping communist **aggression** in South Korea. Other Canadians were pleased to have the UN working to save small countries from aggressive neighbours. Some Canadians, however, believed that the USA was using the UN. They said that the US used the UN to justify American actions in Korea. This was believed to be dishonest. The same controversy was discussed around the world.

Eventually, a **truce** was negotiated between North and South Korea. The invading North Koreans had been forced out of South Korea. Since then, no permanent peace has been arranged. As a result, UN observers are still present in Korea.

### Suez, 1956

Israel attacked Egypt in 1956, taking the Sinai area and one bank of the Suez Canal. Britain and France also invaded Egypt. These two countries announced publicly that they were protecting the Suez Canal from the Egyptian-Israeli conflict. In reality they had co-operated with Israel.

People around the world were shocked at the British and French action. It was not considered correct to use force to solve the Canal problems. Both the United States and the Soviet Union were upset. The Soviets even threatened to step in themselves. There was a threat to world peace.

At the United Nations, efforts were made to stop the fighting. Lester Pearson, Canada's Minister of External Affairs, was able to arrange a truce and a peacekeeping force. The British and French withdrew. The Israelis pulled back to their border.

The United Nations Emergency Force (UNEF) patrolled the border between Israel and Egypt. About 1 100 Canadian soldiers were part of UNEF.

In 1967, Egypt asked the UN to leave. The Canadians were asked to leave first, because of pro-Israel public opinion in Canada. In a war that started soon after the UNEF left, Israel again captured the Sinai area. The cost to Canada of helping keep the peace from 1956 to 1967 was $6 million.

### Cyprus, 1964

This island in the Mediterranean Sea is occupied by two groups of people, the Turkish Cypriots and the Greek Cypriots. These two groups have been fighting each other since 1571. In 1878 Cyprus became a **protectorate** of Great Britain. It was granted independence in 1960.

In 1964, the UN agreed to provide a peacekeeping force to prevent further fighting. Canada was then invited to send troops. Between 1964 and 1970, there were about 1 000 Canadian soldiers on the island. From 1971 to 1978, the number was reduced to 500. These Canadians patrolled the **Green Line** between the two groups of Cypriots. In emergencies, the Canadian force was increased to over 1 100 soldiers.

The Cyprus peacekeeping force has been very expensive. Between 1964 and 1976, the cost to Canadian taxpayers was $27 million.

### The Congo, 1960

When the Congo, (now Zaire), became independent of Belgium in 1960, fighting broke out among rival political groups. The Security Council took steps to restore peace. The Congolese government agreed to this help.

The UN operation in the Congo was the biggest of all peacekeeping operations up to 1979. Over 20 000 soldiers from 19 countries served in the Congo. The total cost was $400 million. The UN force stopped the civil war and restored peace by 1964.

The Canadian Armed Forces supplied a modern signalling unit of 280 persons and some aircraft. The cost to Canadian taxpayers was $5 910 000.

*The Middle East, 1973-1974*
On October 6, 1973, war broke out again between Israel and its neighbours. A ceasefire was negotiated on October 22, and two UN peacekeeping forces were sent in. One force, made up of troops from Austria and Iran, patrolled between Israel and Syria on the Golan Heights. The other force, made up of troops from Denmark, Finland, Ghana, and Sweden, patrolled between Israel and Egypt in the Sinai.

At first, Canadian forces were not invited to be part of the peacekeeping forces. Arab leaders felt that Canadians were on Israel's side. However, Canadian forces were highly experienced in peacekeeping and had the most modern equipment. The UN was able to have the Canadians act as a support force, along with the Poles. They provided supplies, transportation, and communication to the two main peacekeeping forces. Over 1 000 Canadians were on duty at any given time between 1973 and 1978. The cost to the Canadian taxpayers was $8 377 000 for the first three years.

*Lebanon, 1978*
For years southern Lebanon, next to Israel, had been a base for Palestinian terrorists. They made attacks on Israel which they had sworn to destroy. After a terrorist attack in early 1978, Israel invaded southern Lebanon. Lebanon itself was in the middle of a civil war to stop the terrorists. The United Nations feared that Arab nations might help Lebanon by attacking Israel. This would further endanger peace in the area. A Security Council resolution called on Israel to withdraw. The Council also suggested sending another peacekeeping force. It would patrol southern Lebanon and try to keep peace. France, Ghana, Norway, and other nations agreed to provide troops for the new UN force. Expert Canadian soldiers would take part supplying communications. The UN again prevented another major war in the Middle East.

**READING BETTER**
1. **Why was "peacekeeping" created by the UN?**
2. **How did Canada participate in peacekeeping?**
3. **How long have some of the wars mentioned been going on?**

**Debate: Should Canada continue its role in UN peacekeeping?**

YES
By being a part of UN peacekeeping forces, Canada is doing a lot for world peace. What better way is there for Canadians to show their commitment to peace?

Another important point is that Canadians have become skilled in peacekeeping. Our armed forces are ranked among the best peacekeepers. The skill of Canada's peacekeeping forces is recognized around the world. Canada thus has a reputation for peace.

This good reputation as a peacekeeper helps the Canadian identity. Too many people in the world see Canada as a part of the USA. By helping to keep peace, Canada shows its independence. Our country shows that it is not controlled by the US, a nuclear superpower.

NO
Our troops may be good at what they do, but history shows that peacekeeping forces do not produce lasting peace. For example, the UNEF was taken out of Egypt in 1967. This was ten years after it went in. After it left, another war started. The UN force went back in 1973 and is still there. The situation is the same in Cyprus. Peacekeeping forces have been there for years, but there is still

Canadian Forces Photo

**Should Canada contribute to peacekeeping forces?**

no lasting peace. In fact, in recent years the situation has grown worse. The country is badly divided, so conflict is inevitable.

Peacekeeping is also expensive. The Cyprus force has cost us $37 million. This cost would be acceptable if lasting peace were achieved. However, the force is still needed to prevent fighting.

Canada has done its share of peacekeeping. Our country should pull its troops out of the UN peacekeeping forces. Other countries can take up their share of the responsibility.

**USING YOUR KNOWLEDGE**

1. Write a letter to your MP or to the Minister of External Affairs. Give your opinion on whether or not Canada should continue its role in peacekeeping.

**TAKING A STAND**

1. Which opinion do you agree with more? Why?
2. Find other facts from this chapter to back up your own opinion. Write down your position in your notebook.

## Conclusion

Peace does not come easily. It is the product of hard work. People all over the world suffer because of hunger, disease, and war. Concerned "global citizens" have made great efforts to overcome these troubles and to achieve peace.

The United Nations was created to help keep peace on this planet. It has tried to prevent wars and has sent peacekeeping forces to stop wars that did start. The UN has also tried to fight disease, hunger, and other threats to peace.

Canadians in the past have proudly committed their country to the UN. Today, however, Canada's role in the organization is being questioned. Canadians today are faced with a challenge. They must decide what they want to do to achieve peace in the world, with the UN and on their own. What are you ready to do to create peace?

**READING BETTER**

1. In a sentence for each, explain why the following people are important:

   Lester B. Pearson        Dag Hammarskjöld
   Norman Borlaug           Kurt Waldheim

**ORGANIZING BETTER**

1. What are four main ideas that this chapter tries to emphasize? Write one sentence describing each idea. Compile one big list containing what your class thinks the central ideas of the chapter are.
2. Work with several students to make up a Quick quiz on the facts of this chapter. Test yourselves and other groups.

**USING YOUR KNOWLEDGE**

1. Make up a poster or radio commercial that shows the people in your school what the United Nations has done to keep world peace.

## SOLVING PROBLEMS

1. How can we create more peace at home and in this world? Using the problem-solving model, suggest how this question may be answered. Explain your solution to your class. Be prepared to answer questions about your solution.

## TAKING A STAND

1. There are many wars around the world each year. Should the UN be declared a failure because of this?

## RESEARCHING

1. Do research in a library on some of the following topics. Remember to use the card catalogue and encyclopaedias.

Nobel Peace Prize winners
The UN and the Korean War, 1950
The UN and the Suez Crisis, 1956
The Canadian Armed Forces and peacekeeping
How the United Nations works
The life of Dag Hammarskjöld (or another UN secretary-general)
The life of Lester B. Pearson
The art of negotiating

## GLOSSARY

**Aggression.** Hostile behaviour, attacks.

**Controversial.** Causing much discussion and argument.

**Department of External Affairs.** A federal government department in charge of Canada's relations with other countries.

**Great Powers.** In 1945, this name was given to the most powerful nations at the time. They were the US, the USSR, Britain, France, and China.

**Green Line.** The line that divides the opposing forces.

**Green Revolution.** The development of new plants and farming techniques which resulted in larger crop yields.

**Plant genetics.** The study of breeding new types of plants.

**Protectorate.** A nation that is controlled and protected by a stronger nation.

**Psychiatrist.** A medical doctor who treats psychological disorders of the mind.

**Superpowers.** Nations with huge armed forces, wealth, and large populations. Examples are the USA, the USSR, and perhaps China.

**Truce.** An agreement to stop fighting.

# 3/World issues for today

## Contents

### Introduction

So far in this unit, we have discussed major issues such as war and peace. These subjects are of concern to people all over the world. There are many other issues of world concern. Because Canadians are, after all, also global citizens, they should be familiar with these concerns. Canada is a democratic country, so its citizens have a say in the way the country responds to world issues. Informed Canadians can suggest changes or propose solutions to problems. In other words, they can play a role in forming Canada's **foreign policy.**

This chapter presents studies of some world concerns. There are three in-depth studies: the first deals with the world food crisis; the second with Canada and the sea; the last with nuclear energy and nuclear weapons.

Once you have worked through the chapter you will have a better knowledge of these world concerns. You will be able to answer the following questions.

1. **Why is there a world food crisis? What can Canada do to help?**
2. **Who owns the seas and seabeds? How can Canada protect its interests in the sea?**
3. **Should Canada sell nuclear reactors to other countries? What controls should be put on nuclear technology?**

### Case study 1: Canada and the food crisis

The world's population is growing and so is the demand for food. Whenever bad weather kills crops in Canada or in India, world food supplies are smaller. Thus, millions of people around the world do not have enough to eat. Hundreds of thousands die of starvation each year.

Most Canadians are far from the cries of starving babies, and the rage of people fighting over food. We are among the best-fed people on earth. Stories of starvation often seem strange and unreal to us. The problem is real, though. The United

Nations is trying to fight starvation. However the number of deaths continues to mount and the danger of greater famine is growing. Some experts believe that the food crisis is the greatest threat to peace in world history.

The first section of this chapter examines the world food problem. The section is organized around four basic questions. You will be better able to answer them by the end of the chapter.

1. What is the problem?
2. How did the problem come about?
3. What has Canada done to help?
4. What can Canada do in the future?

## The problem

The following article will help give you a clearer picture of the food crisis.

Children seem to die first in food shortages. Why?

### A grim ride on the death truck in Bangladesh—1974
*by Jack Cahill*

Mr. Haq drives a truck around the city of Dacca in Bangladesh. His job is picking up dead bodies from the streets. So far today he has found five men, three women and four children. In the last five months, over 100 000 people have starved to death in Bangladesh.

Floods and crop failures have forced thousands of starving farm people to Dacca. Mr. Haq is kept very busy because even in Dacca there is not enough food.

Despite the grim nature of his work, Mr. Haq likes his job. "I feel I'm doing good," he says. "I can't feed them. I can't even feed myself. But I can help give the dead ones a decent *Moslem* burial.

"It is true that the children upset me. They don't weigh anything at all. They are just bones. They are no trouble to pick up. But it is because they have seen nothing at all of life except starvation. That is what worries and upsets me."

Mr. Haq works for a Moslem charity called the Essential Society of Islam. This group does not have enough money to stop starvation. Instead, it tries to give the victims the decent religious burial that starving families cannot afford.

The truck wanders around the city, past crying, dying, naked little children. Their skin hangs loosely from their bones. The streets are crowded with people sleeping on the sidewalks. They have no homes, and many are just waiting to die.

Most of the country people have sold their land at ridiculously low prices so that they could get money to buy food. When they have nothing left they leave for Dacca.

Each day Mr. Haq visits the railway station where the poor farmers arrive. Today he finds an abandoned, sick and starving baby. But the baby is not yet dead and he leaves it behind. Nearby, a baby has just died and its mother is crying with grief. She will not yet give it up for the truck. A few miles further on, a man of 50 lies dead by the road. He was the father of a family and his bones are pushing through his skin.

The government is trying hard to move the hungry and homeless to special camps. Street kitchens are also used to try to get food to those who need it. But it is not enough. The daily ration given out is one four-ounce wafer of bread per adult. The United Nations says that people need about twelve ounces per day to stay alive.

People line up for hours waiting for a chance to get one wafer. When the kitchens run out, there are riots.

After riding all day with Mr. Haq, I returned to my expensive hotel for dinner. I ordered pepper steak, but I couldn't eat it. It made me feel sick.

*Source:* Toronto Star, *1974 11 26.*

---

**READING BETTER**

1. What caused the deaths in Dacca?
2. What was Mr. Haq's job?
3. Besides hunger, what other problems did people in Dacca have?
4. What did the people of Dacca need most?
5. Using an atlas, find out where Bangladesh is. What is the distance between your home and Dacca?

Where is the food crisis?: The geography of hunger

Although poor people in many countries, including Canada, are often hungry, the crisis is confined to certain areas. Figs. 3-1, 3-2, and 3-3 help to show where the crisis is.

**READING BETTER**

1. How many years did it take the world population to reach the following numbers?
   a) 1.5 billion
   b)  3 billion
   c)  6 billion
2. a) According to Fig. 3-2, which country has the lowest average number of kilojoules of food consumed per person per day? What is that country's projected population for the year 2000?
   b) Find that country on the map in Fig. 3-3. What are its neighbours? Find their rate of population growth and food intake. (Note: a high growth rate means that the population doubles sooner.)
3. What is the difference in kilojoules consumed in Canada and in the crisis areas?
4. Do areas with low kilojoule levels have high growth rates?

**USING YOUR KNOWLEDGE**

1. Using the figures in Fig. 3-1, predict the types of problems that the world will face in the year 2000, if the estimates of growth are correct.
2. Canadians eat more kilojoules of food per day than people in the crisis areas. How would this help us remain a rich, healthy nation?

*What is the problem?*

The very poorest countries in the world (such as those in Fig. 3-2, excluding Canada) have a total population of 650 million people. These people do not have enough to eat. They wear rags, they own nothing, they can neither read nor write, they live in hovels. They spend each day just trying to stay alive.

461

| Year | Estimated world population |
|------|---------------------------|
| 1750 | 800 million |
| 1800 | 1.0 billion |
| 1900 | 1.6 billion |
| 1964 | 3.2 billion |
| 2000 | 6.3 billion |

Source: UN

**Fig. 3-1 Estimated world population**

| | Average number of kilojoules consumed per person per day | Number of years to double population | Projected population to year 2000 (in millions) |
|---|---|---|---|
| Bangladesh | 7728 | 21 | 188.1 |
| Bolivia | 7980 | 29 | 12.0 |
| Central African Republic | 9240 | 32 | 3.3 |
| Chad | 8862 | 29 | 8.4 |
| Ecuador | 8442 | 21 | 18.3 |
| Ethiopia | 9072 | 33 | 53.1 |
| Haiti | 7266 | 28 | 11.6 |
| India | 8694 | 27 | 1249.2 |
| Mali | 8652 | 29 | 11.5 |
| Mauritania | 8274 | 32 | 2.6 |
| Niger | 8736 | 24 | 11.1 |
| Senegal | 9954 | 29 | 9.2 |
| Sri Lanka | 9114 | 29 | 26.5 |
| Sudan | 9072 | 22 | 45.3 |
| Upper Volta | 7182 | 33 | 11.2 |
| Canada* | 13856 | 41 | 29.4 |

*Note: Industrial workers in Canada need over 12600 kilojoules of food each day to do an effective job.
Source: UN

**Fig. 3-2  Food intake compared to population growth**

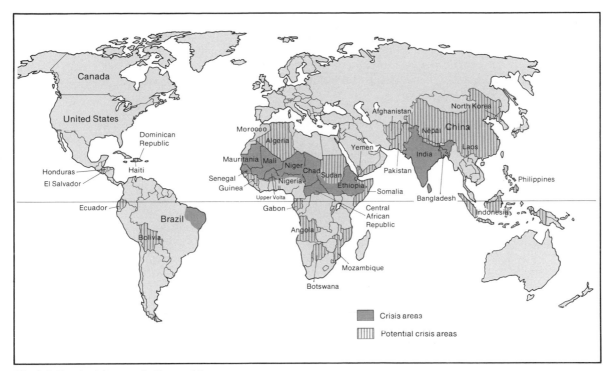

**Fig. 3-3  Food crisis areas in the world**

**What is the cartoonist's message?**

463

**Fact sheet**

1. The average income of people living in the very poor countries is less than $350 per year. In Canada the figure is over $7 000.
2. The average *daily* food intake of people in the poor countries is:
   2 ounces of rice
   1 small potato
   1 small piece of onion
   1 cup of plain tea
3. World population growth is tremendous. By the year 2000, China and India will each have more than 1 billion citizens.
4. Many countries cannot produce enough food to feed all of their citizens.
5. People get sick easily when not properly fed. Here are some common diseases:
   a) Rickets: Caused by a lack of Vitamin D. Produces soft, deformed bones in children.
   b) Beriberi: Caused by too little **thiamin** (found in vegetables, eggs, and whole grain). Produces heart trouble, liver diseases, and brain damage.
   c) Pellagra: Caused by a lack of **niacin** (found in brown rice, fish, and meat). Produces skin disease, diarrhea, and insanity.
   d) Kwashiorkor: Caused by a lack of **protein** (found in milk, meat, fish, beans, and nuts). Produces swollen stomachs, especially in children. Protein hunger also causes brain damage in children. Hair turns red.
6. Future generations suffer because of present-day starvation. Children who live to become adults usually never fully recover from the effects of starvation. They may spend the rest of their lives with brain damage, deformed arms and legs, or constant illness. Because starvation affects mothers, babies are often born damaged.
7. Leaders in poor countries see that people in Canada and other nations are wealthy and healthy. They become angry and frustrated at the differences of wealth in the world.
8. Even in Canada, many people are not well fed. In any area where there is poverty, there are people who do not obtain the right foods. Also, many wealthy Canadians suffer from **malnutrition** because they eat foods that have no value. Are you one of them? List what you have eaten each day for the last week and compare your list to *Canada's Food Guide* (Fig. 3-4).
9. North Americans spend over $3 billion a year on prepared pet food. This is enough money to feed the hungry people of the world for a year.
10. In 1977 the **World Bank** stated that if $15 billion a year were invested in the poor countries of the world, the people in those nations would begin to have a decent life.
11. Each year the world's countries spend $375 billion on weapons.

## Eat a variety of foods from each group every day

(Canada's Food Guide)

Energy needs vary with age, sex and activity. Foods selected according to the guide can supply 1000-1400 calories. For additional energy, increase the number and size of servings from the various food groups or add other foods.

### milk and milk products

| | |
|---|---|
| Children up to 11 years | 2-3 servings |
| Adolescents | 3-4 servings |
| Pregnant and nursing women | 3-4 servings |
| Adults | 2 servings |

Skim, 2%, whole, buttermilk, reconstituted dry or evaporated milk may be used as a beverage or as the main ingredient in other foods. Cheese may also be chosen.

**Examples of one serving**
250 ml (1 cup) milk, yoghurt or cottage cheese
45 g (1½ ounces) cheddar or process cheese

In addition, a supplement of vitamin D is recommended when milk is consumed which does not contain added vitamin D

### meat and alternates
### 2 servings

**Examples of one serving**
60 to 90 g (2-3 ounces) cooked lean meat, poultry, liver or fish
60 ml (4 tablespoons) peanut butter
250 ml (1 cup) cooked dried peas, beans or lentils
80 to 250 ml (⅓-1 cup) nuts or seeds
60 g (2 ounces) cheddar, process or cottage cheese
2 eggs

### bread and cereals
### 3-5 servings

whole grain or enriched. Whole grain products are recommended.

**Examples of one serving**
1 slice bread
125 to 250 ml (½-1 cup) cooked or ready-to-eat cereal
1 roll or muffin
125 to 200 ml (½-¾ cup) cooked rice, macaroni, spaghetti

### fruits and vegetables
### 4-5 servings

Include at least two vegetables.

Choose a variety of both vegetables and fruits — cooked, raw or their juices. Include yellow or green or green leafy vegetables.

**Examples of one serving**
125 ml (½ cup) vegetables or fruits
125 ml (½ cup) juice
1 medium potato, carrot, tomato, peach, apple, orange or banana

**Fig. 3-4  Canada's Food Guide**

Source: *Shopping for Food and Nutrition.* Reproduced by permission of the Minister of Supply and Services Canada.

**READING BETTER**
**Prove or disprove each of the following statements, using facts from the Fact sheet. Write your answers in your notebook.**
a) **People in poor countries are angry because they are so poor.**
b) **If you have suffered from starvation, then working hard is more difficult than if you were healthy all your life.**
c) **There is not enough money in the world to help the poor.**

What is the cause of the problem?
Here is an interview with Mrs. Shanta Chittagong of the United Nations. The interview is fictional, but it accurately presents the basic causes of the food crisis.

**Interviewer:** The food crisis has been with us for some time and it looks like it will remain with us for a long time. What caused it?

**Mrs. Chittagong:** That question is not easy to answer. There are many different reasons, and they are different from country to country. But I suppose that an unfavourable climate is one of the main causes.

**Interviewer:** You mean that floods or droughts ruin crops?

**Mrs. Chittagong:** Yes. You see, many countries in the world are able to produce just enough food to feed the population. When bad weather destroys crops, then there is not enough. India is such a country.

**Interviewer:** I thought that the Green Revolution made India able to feed itself.

**Mrs. Chittagong:** It's true that for a few years, in the 1960s and 1970s, the Green Revolution introduced new types of grain. These grew so well that India and other poor countries could feed themselves for a few years. But this situation did not last. These countries have complex problems. First, there is population growth.

**Interviewer:** You mean that countries like India grew more food but the population grew so fast that soon they were short of food again?

**Mrs. Chittagong:** Yes, that's it. India's population, for example, will double by the year 2000. There will be about one billion people by then. That's a tremendous number to feed.

**Interviewer:** Why is something not done to slow population growth?

**Mrs. Chittagong:** That's a most difficult problem. How do you tell a poor couple that they should have fewer children? They know that if they limit their family to just two children both may die. Then who will look after that couple when they get old? We have to fight disease, tradition, ignorance, and poverty to bring down population growth.

**Interviewer:** But India is a big country with good land. Why can't Indians keep on feeding themselves in spite of the population problem?

**Mrs. Chittagong:** Well, India and many poor countries have other problems as well. I've already mentioned the climate. Many of these countries are hit by cyclones or floods that destroy crops. The people of Chad have another type of climate problem to cope with. The Sahara Desert is moving in on them—at the rate of 8 km a year!

Countries like India may have enough farm land and rain to support their populations. The problems are organization, transportation, education, and equipment.

**Interviewer:** You mean roads, trucks, good farming methods, and tractors?

**Mrs. Chittagong:** Yes. Farmers must be taught to use new farming techniques and equipment. What is needed is money, and experts

**This picture shows some effects of drought in Colombia, Latin America.**

to teach the people. Many countries don't have enough experts.

Also, it is expensive to build good roads and to buy trucks to transport food. In the rainy season, most country roads are flooded. Trucks cannot move.

**Interviewer:** I see your point. In Canada we have good paved or gravel roads and lots of trucks. There's no trouble getting food into the big cities. What else makes it difficult to feed the population?

**Mrs. Chittagong:** There is usually a shortage of fertilizer. Fertilizer has to be imported from countries that have the chemicals to make it. In the last few years the cost of fertilizer has tripled.

**Interviewer:** Many Canadians know that Canada has been helping underdeveloped countries for years. But it looks like no progress is being made in the fight against hunger. Where does our aid go? Why hasn't it helped?

**Mrs. Chittagong:** One good reason is that the Canadian food aid just helps the starving keep alive. It doesn't solve the other problems. Money that is given is appreciated but it's nowhere near enough.

I also have to admit that many countries do not use the money where it's needed. There are even cases where wheat donated by Canada, Australia, and the United States has been sold, not given away, to those who need it. That is criminal.

**Interviewer:** A few years ago Canada gave Bangladesh a satellite communication station worth $8 million. It gave Bangladesh better connections with the rest of the world. What do you think of that?

**Mrs. Chittagong:** It was most generous of Canada. But in Bangladesh there are 80 million people and less than 100 000 telephones. I wish the money had been spent on better sewage systems to fight disease.

**Interviewer:** I see your point. Thank you very much for your comments.

*Summary: The causes of the food crisis*
Overpopulation
Lack of good transportation
Natural disasters
Lack of education
Lack of governmental organization
High cost of fertilizer
Traditions
Crime

**ORGANIZING BETTER**

1. **Copy down the above list in your notebook. Reread the interview and then, in your own words, explain each item on the list more fully.**

What has Canada done?
Since 1945, Canada has played a major role in helping poor countries. Our help comes from two sources: the government and private charities.

*The government's role*
The federal government, which acts for all Canadians, has become a strong world leader in foreign aid. In 1950, Canada helped start the **Colombo Plan.** This aid programme was at first limited to the **Commonwealth.** It later grew to include most of South Asia as well as Africa.

Canada's first gift to the Colombo Plan was $10 million for food aid to India. By 1957 Canada had given $37 million to the Colombo Plan. This money helped build a cement plant in Pakistan, a nuclear reactor in India, and electricity and water projects in other countries in Asia.

In 1970, the *Canadian International Development Agency* (CIDA) was created to manage Canada's foreign aid. Its budget in 1971 was $334 million. By 1978, CIDA's budget was over $1 billion. CIDA gets its money from the taxes paid by Canadians.

**What is meant by the "three worlds"—first world, second world, third world?**

Quite often, when people talk about the world's countries in general terms, they group the countries into three broad categories. These categories are the "three worlds".

**The first world:** Consists of countries such as France, Britain, Sweden, the United States, Canada, Belgium, and Japan. The first world is wealthy, and usually democratic.

**The second world:** Consists of the communist countries such as the USSR, Hungary, and East Germany. The second world is wealthy, but generally not as rich as the first world.

**The third world:** Consists of former colonies of first world countries, plus a few other poor nations. The third world includes such countries as India, Bolivia, Bangladesh, Senegal, Ghana, and Brazil. They are trying to get the same rights and wealth as the first and second worlds.

(Some experts believe that the poorest nations should be called the fourth world.)

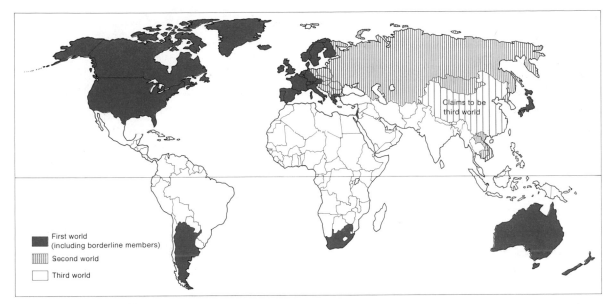

**Fig. 3-5 The three worlds**

| | |
|---|---|
| World Food Programme | 84.0 |
| India | 81.5 |
| Pakistan | 63.2 |
| Bangladesh | 37.3 |
| Indonesia | 22.4 |
| Tunisia | 14.4 |
| Tanzania | 14.0 |
| Niger | 10.0 |
| Kenya | 9.3 |
| Rwanda | 7.4 |
| Senegal | 7.0 |
| Ivory Coast | 7.0 |
| Algeria | 6.5 |
| Haiti | 4.3 |
| Cuba | 4.3 |
| International Rice Research Institute | 1.1 |

Source: CIDA

**Fig. 3-6. Some examples of where CIDA's aid money goes (in millions of dollars), 1978**

**ORGANIZING BETTER**

1. Look at Figs. 3-3 and 3-6. Which of the countries getting CIDA aid are having a food crisis?
2. How many countries in the world give more of their wealth to help others than Canada does (Fig. 3-7)?

**TAKING A STAND**

1. Is Canada's foreign aid going to the right places? Explain your answer.
2. Should Canada give more aid to the underdeveloped nations? Why?

*The role of private charities*

Around the world, concerned people have formed groups that try to help the millions of starving poor. These private charities ask for donations. They then buy food and medicine. The charities also send volunteers and experts to help the poor. In Canada some of their donations come from people like you and from CIDA.

| Nation (1975) | Percentage of total national wealth spent on foreign aid |
|---|---|
| Sweden | .82 |
| Netherlands | .75 |
| Norway | .66 |
| France | .62 |
| Australia | .61 |
| Belgium | .59 |
| Canada | .58 |
| Denmark | .58 |
| New Zealand | .52 |
| Germany | .40 |
| United Kingdom | .37 |
| USA | .26 |

Source: Organization for Economic Co-operation and Development (OECD), Paris, 1976.

**Fig. 3-7 How does our record of aid compare with other nations' records?**

Canadian Hunger Foundation, 323 Chapel St., Ottawa.

Canadian Red Cross Society, various offices in Canada.

Canadian Save the Children Fund, 70 Hayter St., Toronto and other locations.

Canadian University Service Overseas, 151 Slater St., Ottawa.

CARE Canada, 1312 Bank St., Ottawa.

The Overseas Book Centre, 896 Queen St. West, Toronto.

Oxfam Canada, 175 Carlton St., Toronto.

The Unitarian Service Committee of Canada, 56 Sparks St., Ottawa.

The World Development and Relief Fund. This group is run by the Protestant and Catholic Churches.

World Vision of Canada, 410 Consumers Rd., Willowdale, Ontario.

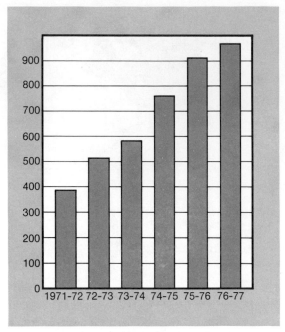

**Fig. 3-8  Growth of total Canadian official development assistance**

### Portrait of a person who cares: Dr. Lotta Hitschmanova

In 33 years of helping the needy overseas, Dr. Lotta Hitschmanova has travelled around the world many times. Between 1945 and 1978, Dr. Hitschmanova helped raise almost $18 million in cash and just over $15 million in clothing, food, and medical supplies.

Dr. Hitschmanova was born in Czechoslovakia. She came to Canada in 1942, escaping the war in Europe. Because she had seen so much destruction and hunger, she vowed to spend her life helping others in need.

In 1945 Dr. Hitschmanova founded the Unitarian Service Committee of Canada (USC). She has been executive director of this organization ever since. This non-religious organization operates relief and education projects around the world. Its 39 branches in Canada appeal to Canadians for donations.

In 1978 the USC raised $3.5 million in cash and supplies. Milk, clothing, and medicine were sent to USC projects around the world. The USC also contributes to the education of poor students. In Lesotho, Africa, students from isolated areas are given USC scholarships. This money pays for their high school education.

One of Dr. Hitschmanova's main concerns is that the items sent by the USC actually reach the people who need them. She proudly states that "None of our shipments are stolen or sold."

Dr. Hitschmanova has received many awards for her services to the

470

needy. She is an officer of the Order of Canada, and in 1975 was selected Woman of the Year by the Rideau Kiwanis Club. The French government made her a Chevalier of Public Health and awarded her the French Medal of Gratitude. The president of Korea has awarded her the Public Service Medal of Korea. The prime minister of India and several Indian cities have also honoured Dr. Hitschmanova. In 1967 she was the first woman to be awarded the Athena Messolova Gold Medal in Athens, Greece. Other honours from nations, cities, and service organizations have been awarded to Dr. Hitschmanova.

Dr. Lotta Hitschmanova is just one of many dedicated and concerned Canadians who help the world's poor.

---

**USING YOUR KNOWLEDGE**
1. **How is the USC different from CIDA?**
2. **How does Dr. Hitschmanova's career show the meaning of the word "humanitarian"?**

Should Canada spend more on aid to poor countries?

In 1975 a national poll showed that 53% of Canadians answered *yes* to this question. Do you think public opinion is the same today?

Here are some opinions on the question, presented in the form of letters to the editor. The people writing the letters are fictional, but the opinions expressed are often heard today.

Dr. Lotta Hitschmanova

Unitarian Service Committee of Canada

---

To the editor:

For some years I have donated money to CARE and purchased UNICEF cards. I do believe in aiding our sisters and brothers in the world. But my idea of the type of help we should give is changing. We should not give away money or food. We should help others to help themselves. Our money would be better spent if we helped the poor nations learn more about population control, agriculture, and medicine.

Florence Bongard
Oshawa, Ontario

To the editor:

I have before me a clipping taken from a newspaper of the year 1900. The heading is "Famine to hit India soon". A warning was sent to England telling of the food shortage that was expected to occur in India after a drought. The article also states that the people were living a hand-to-mouth existence. This clipping shows that India's problem has existed for a long time. We haven't been able to help much so far and there is probably nothing we can do in the future either. We would be better to save our aid money and spend it on Canada's poor and jobless.

Mrs. Hilda MacTavish
Sussex, NB

To the editor:

"No man is an island." Let us not forget this old line. We do not live alone and isolated. Anything that hurts or kills people 10 000 miles away also hurts us. Those who die are human beings like us. We just happen to be lucky enough to live in a wealthy part of the world. Next time you complain about tax dollars going to help a starving child in Africa, remember that he or she may someday find a cure for cancer and save your life!

Anna Petrillo
Mississauga, Ontario

To the editor:

I see that some of our aid money is going to nations that do not respect human rights. Surely we can find worthier countries to help.

Arnold Swierczynski
Red Deer, Alberta

To the editor:

I fear that if we do not help the poor nations now, they will grow to hate us. We are fat, rich, and well fed compared to the people in those countries. I am afraid to think of what will happen to us if the poor nations ever rise up in anger against us. What will they do to those who had so much and shared so little? History shows that they will destroy us. Let us share now, before it is too late.

Kimberley Robin
Hull, PQ

---

**READING BETTER**
1. **Decide which letters are for foreign aid and which are against it.**

**ORGANIZING BETTER**
1. **In your notebook briefly summarize, in your own words, the point of view expressed in each letter.**

**TAKING A STAND**
1. **Write your own letter to the editor expressing your opinions on Canada's aid to poor countries.**

What can you do?
If you believe that Canadians have a duty to help the poor of the world, consider the following possible actions.
1. Include CARE or some such agency on your Christmas gift list each year.
2. Sponsor a child in the *Foster Parents Plan.* This can be done by individuals, classes, or schools.
3. Raise funds in school by having a "starvation lunch" to illustrate the problem of the poor.
4. Write a letter to your MP urging that the government do more to help people around the world. Include ideas on how to persuade Canadians to help out more.
5. Start a "small change" collection at home or school to raise money.
6. Collect old clothing to send to international charity agencies as well as for use in Canada.
If you believe Canada is doing too much,

**A typical CIDA project. How will the skills learned by these students help them improve their country?**

you can try to change government policy. One way to do this is to write to your MP expressing your opinions. Your letter should be written so that it gains the MP's attention and respect.

The food crisis: Summary
Millions of people are starving. While they starve there can be no true peace in the world.

Canada has played a role in fighting hunger. Our money and help have been given to the United Nations and directly to needy countries. There are many people alive in this world because of Canadian aid. Our money and help have also been used to train and equip countries to help themselves.

Whether or not this foreign aid policy will be continued is a matter for Canadians to decide. As global citizens we should be ready to examine and discuss these important matters.

**USING YOUR KNOWLEDGE**
1. **Explain why the food crisis is a threat to world peace.**

**Case study 2: Canada and the sea**
Canada's relations with many of the world's countries have been formed because of an interest in the sea. Canada has the world's longest sea coast. The greatest fishing grounds in the world lie off our country's east coast—the Grand Banks. Fishers from other lands have been using the Grand

473

Banks for over five hundred years. In fact, Canada's fishing grounds supply many countries with much of their food. Canadian seafoods—BC salmon, cod, lobster, and others—are world-famous.

As the world's population grows, the seas are becoming more and more important as a source of food. If too many fish are caught, however, a problem is created. The supplies of fish in the sea will be reduced. If overfishing continues, fish may no longer be available in large amounts. Such an event could hurt not only Canada, but the world as well.

The sea is important for other reasons, too. The world is searching for more sources of energy and raw materials for industry. The seabeds off Canada's coasts seem to be a source of these resources. Thus, the interests of Canada and the world are centred, to a large extent, on Canadian coastal waters.

The basic questions to be explored in this section are:
1. Who owns the seas and the seabeds?
2. What problems does Canada face in its surrounding seas?
3. What should Canada do to control its surrounding seas?

---

### The problem: A fisher's story

*The PUSLINCH TIMES presents a story on the problems faced by independent east coast fishers. James Haskin, 52, of Dark Cove, Newfoundland, tells of his life as a fisher and explains his latest frustrations. The story is fictional, but it presents an accurate view of real situations.*

In the old days, we used to go out nearly every day and catch a full load of fish. That was true of almost every boat in the **outports.** And it was true all over the Atlantic provinces. Life was hard too. The weather can be very cruel and cold. Many a good man has been lost in the winter storms. We have rescue helicopters now, but they are often too far away to help in time.

I used to catch cod mostly—it was the most important fish. In the late 1960s it got harder and harder to get a full load. I'd go out and there, just beyond the **12-mile limit** (22 km), would be the big foreign **trawlers.** They moved along in lines sweeping up everything in the water.

You should see those foreign boats up close. They've got radar, sonar, and all kinds of fancy equipment. I've seen three trawlers pull up to a factory ship, unload, and race off to catch more fish. From what I've heard, the factory ships clean and freeze thousands of tonnes of fish. They don't need factories on shore.

A lot of the foreign boats are trying to catch fish that we're not interested in—argentines, capelin, and the like. They grind them up into fish meal. What worries me is that they probably grind up everything in their nets, regardless of the size or type of fish.

To sum up the situation, there's a lot of fishing going on. Yet there's less fish to catch all the time. If we independent fishers can't catch more, we'll probably join the other people on unemployment.

You can starve trying to fish.

1. a) **List things that make life hard for James Haskin.**
   b) **Which of those things on your list could Haskins control himself? Was the fact that he was having trouble making a living his own fault?**

Solutions: The sea and the law
Traditionally, a country owned all the sea within three nautical miles (5.6 km) of its coast. This was about the range of a seventeenth-century cannon. The seas within this limit were called territorial waters. The rest of the seas—the high seas—were free for the use of all people. This idea was respected in international law.

But the old laws often did not meet modern needs. Therefore, the United Nations began special Law of the Seas Conferences in 1958. (Others have been held in 1960, 1974, 1975, and 1976.) In these conferences, the nations of the world tried to develop new laws. However, agreement over laws of the sea did not come easily. Concerned Canadians saw the sea threatened by pollution and overfishing. Yet no new laws were established.

*Canada acts*
The government of Canada decided not to wait until the UN conferences produced new laws. Canada would act to protect its own coastal waters and fishers.

In 1964 Canada added a 9-mile (16.7 km) fishing zone to its three miles of territorial waters. In 1970 the territorial limit was also extended to 12 nautical miles (22 km). This meant that Canada had full legal control over fishing within the limit. It could also legally control ships, pollution, and travel inside the 12-mile area.

The Arctic Ocean and its coastline seem to be more easily damaged by pollution than other areas. In 1970, therefore, another law extended Canada's control of the seas to a zone 100 nautical miles (185 km) from the Arctic coast. This gave Canada more control over pollution problems in the area.

*The 200-mile zone*
In 1976 the government of Canada again took action to protect coastal waters and fisheries. It announced that 200-mile (370 km) economic zones were being set up (see Fig. 3-9). No foreigners would be allowed to fish in these zones without a licence. All oil exploration and sea mining would also require Canadian licences. The 200-mile economic zones went into effect on January 1, 1977.

The new zones had several purposes:

1. To help protect the fish stock. Without protection the fish supply might be entirely used up.
2. To protect Canadian fishers from foreign competition. Many Canadians could no longer make a living at fishing because foreign boats got most of the fish.
3. To stop overfishing by Canadians and foreigners.

The law worked this way:

1. **Quotas** on catches were set. Foreigners could not catch cod or haddock on the Nova Scotia shelf. Canadians, too, had to obey quotas.
2. Licences were granted only to foreign ships agreeing to provide information on catches and to obey quotas.
3. Net sizes were limited. It was hoped that young fish would escape and live to be caught when fully grown.
4. A penalty for violating the regulations was set:

   —A ship captain could be fined up to $25 000 and/or two years in jail. The ship, its catch, and its licence could also be taken.
   —If there was a good reason, all ships from a certain country could be denied licences.

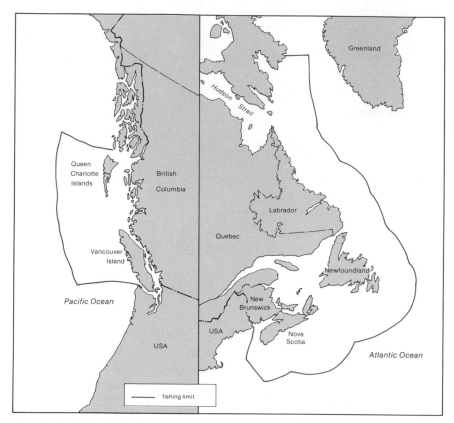

**Fig. 3-9  The 200-mile fishing zone**

A fisheries inspector at work. What sorts of things might he be checking for?

Fisheries and Oceans

*International recognition*

The Canadian government had taken a chance in declaring the 200-mile limit. No new laws of the sea had been agreed upon at the UN. Therefore, Canada's action might not be legal. It was feared that other nations would not respect Canada's so-called law. However, Russian, Portuguese, West German, and other fishing captains have applied for fishing licences. Ship captains arrested by Canadian patrols have paid fines. Negotiations between the Soviet Union and Canada over fishing in the zones have been carried out. Thus, Canada's economic zones appear to have been accepted by other nations.

Other countries have also declared 200-mile zones. These zones require new boundaries between nations where none have existed before. Drawing the new boundaries has been difficult. In 1978 Canada and the USA were unable to reach agreement on the new borders. Each country forbade fishers from the other country to cross the disputed border. Yet despite these arguments, peaceful negotiations continued over the new borders.

Thus while waiting for new international laws of the sea, Canada has moved to protect coastal waters. However, these moves have sparked controversy within Canada.

**ORGANIZING BETTER**

1. **Review the problems that fishers have according to James Haskin. Make a list of these problems. Mark "200" beside those problems that are supposed to be solved by the 200-mile limit.**

*Patrolling Canada's fishing zones*

Special patrols by Canadian ships and aircraft are used to enforce the rules of the economic zones. But the area that must be

---

**Fact sheet: The fishing industry in Canada**

—There are 40 000 Canadian fishing boats—95% are under 22.68 tonnes (25 tons).
—The average Canadian eats 6 kg of fish each year. (The average Japanese eats 54 kg of fish a year.)
—Most fish caught by Canadians on the Grand Banks are sold to the USA or to Europe.
—The British are the biggest foreign buyers of canned BC salmon.
—The fishing industry was worth about $600 million each year in the 1970s. This was about the value of the nickel mining industry.
—Newfoundland fish-processing plants alone can handle about 450 million kg of fish each year. However, the plants were running at 40% of their capacity in the late 1970s. Fish-processing plants in Nova Scotia and BC were also running below capacity. Because of overfishing and competition, fewer fish were caught.
—75% of the people living along the east coast have some connection with fishing.
—250 000 people on the east coast make their living entirely from fishing.
—The fish catch was declining rapidly before the 200-mile limit was set.
—In 1978, the federal government took steps to stop other countries from taking over Canadian fish-processing plants. German and Dutch companies wanted to buy up Canadian factories. They would probably then hire Dutch and German ships to catch fish for them. The government wanted to keep Canadian fishers employed.

covered is huge. In 1978 the Department of Fisheries had just eleven ships to patrol both coasts. These patrols cost $12 million. Naval ships could be used for fisheries patrol, but this would take them away from their defence jobs. Thus the new economic zones are posing problems of law enforcement and economy.

The patrols and the zoning rules, however, do seem to work. Overcoming huge waves and severe cold, Canadian inspectors board foreign fishing vessels at sea. They check licences and the catches. In 1977, one Russian captain was arrested for catching fifty tonnes of capelin without a licence. He was fined $15 000. Other arrests and convictions have been made.

The number of foreign vessels operating in the zones has declined. In 1977 only 500 foreign vessels fished the Grand Banks.

Before the new rules were enforced, there were about 1 500 foreign ships. Improved catches for Canadian fishers in 1978 also show that the zoning system may be working.

The debate: Is the 200-mile zone good for Canada?
In this section, a variety of opinions on the 200-mile limit are expressed in letters to the editor. As you read, make a summary of each letter. Make a brief note of each writer's opinion on the following:
    the 200-mile limit
    the need for more or fewer rules
    facts used to back up the opinions
    other solutions to the problems
When you have finished, divide the letters into those *for* and those *against* the 200-mile limit.

---

### STOP ALL FOREIGN FISHING

The government took a big step in declaring the 200-mile limit. However, the limit is not as good as many people have been led to think. For example, the Soviets are still given licences and they still take out big catches. As far as I can see there's no real change in the number of foreign ships fishing the Banks.

Also, the patrolling is not good enough. There aren't enough ships. Often the people on patrol can't board the foreign vessels because of bad weather. In the meantime, who knows what the foreign ships are catching? I've seen a few patrol planes. But what can a plane flying by tell about the fishing?

With my own eyes, I've seen the foreign trawlers at work inside the 200-mile zone. I've seen Canadian catches go down in weight. I've seen plenty of good Canadian fishers give up their work. The 200-mile limit was supposed to help us out, but it hasn't.

The government should close the fishing zone to foreigners. Let the Atlantic fishers catch the food that those other countries want. That way we'll create jobs for Canadians and food for others. We could have the best fishing industry in the world.

James Haskin
Dark Cove, Newfoundland

### OTHERS HAVE A RIGHT TO FISH

What a narrow point of view some people have about the world. All of a sudden they're ready to tell dozens of countries that they can't fish on the Grand Banks and other coastal fishing areas. Many of these countries have been relying on the fish caught in Canada's waters for centuries. They have been fishing these waters longer than Canada has existed as a nation!

It's time we remembered that we don't own the sea. We just cannot take it all for ourselves.

The government policy of 1977 is fair. Save the fish, save some for us, and allow other countries to have a share through licences. But we should not keep out all foreign fishers.

Professor L.T. Pinelli
Victoria, BC

## BUILD MORE CANADIAN TRAWLERS

The government in Ottawa has tried to protect our fishing industry. But I think it should go one step further. It's obvious from reading James Haskin's fishing story that fishers need better trawlers and more modern equipment. We can't afford them because we're not making enough money. We're not making enough money because of foreign competition!

The government has to make loans available to people in the fishing industry. Then we can get better trawlers and more of them. We don't need factory ships because our boats won't be far from home. But we do need a government that is willing to do as much for fishers as it does for miners and farmers!

James Bain
Montague, PEI

## GO SLOW: AVOID A FISH WAR

The problem of the 200-mile limit is not as easy to solve as some believe. International laws are good only if other nations agree to obey them. Canada declared the 200-mile economic zone on its own. That means that not every country in the world recognizes the zone.

It is true that the government has reached agreement on the zone with the USSR, East Germany, Romania, and others. However, if we said that nobody but Canadians could fish, then we'd really have trouble. Don't forget the *Cod War* between Iceland and Britain. The British refused to recognize the Iceland fishing limit and, as a result, there were naval confrontations! Gunboats from the two countries even took to charging each other.

Canada can't go too quickly with the 200-mile economic zone. Other countries have to get used to the idea.

Christine Garneau
Pointe Claire, PQ

## TAKING A STAND

1. **What do you think about the problems of the east coast fisheries? Discuss these questions in class:**
   a) **Is the 200-mile economic zone a good idea?**
   b) **Should foreign ships be allowed to fish inside the zone?**
   c) **Should the federal government do more to protect our fisheries? Should it give cheap loans so that fishers can buy better boats? Should it spend more on patrol boats?**

Problem solving—Diplomats in action

Canada faces other problems, besides fishing, that are related to the sea. As yet these problems are unsolved. The 200-mile economic zone, for instance, does not solve the problem of pollution. The United Nations is trying to solve these other problems.

Your class should be divided into five committees of roughly equal size. Each committee will be given a problem described below and asked to solve it. At the end of the time period set by your teacher, each committee should make a report to the class.

Committees must:
1. Use the problem-solving model found in Countdown Canada.
2. Make a written record of what is done at each step.
3. Use the library to find extra information.
4. Explain their problem, the steps used to solve it, and the final decision.
5. Defend their solution in front of the whole class.

*The goals:*

In this exercise the goals you aim for as you try to solve your problems are the same as the goals set out by the federal government in the 1970s. In other words, you will be trying to do the same job as diplomats. They too must think of Canada's goals when trying to solve international problems.

GOALS FOR THE 1970s, FOR CANADIANS AND THE WORLD

1. Economic growth—includes providing jobs.
2. Independence—includes ownership, control of Canadian territory.
3. Peace—non-violence and peaceful change.
4. Security—safety for Canada.
5. Justice—equality and equal rights.
6. A better quality of life—includes happiness, good health, a comfortable standard of living.
7. Agreeable environment—includes conservation, anti-pollution tactics, controlled population.

Adapted from *Fourth Report Respecting Foreign Policy for Canadians,* Canada, House of Commons, 1971 6, p. 48.

*Problem 1: Fish do not know about borders or zones*

Setting a 200-mile economic zone may affect people, but the fish have not heard about it. They insist on swimming wherever they please. Often they swim outside the zone and are caught by waiting fishing boats from other countries. On the high seas, beyond the 200-mile zone, the Canadian patrols cannot enforce Canadian quotas. Foreign fishers are free to catch as much fish on the high seas as they want. Thus, there are fewer fish in the economic zone. Canada has suggested having the same quotas beyond the zone as within it. Other nations have rejected this idea. What should be done about high-seas fishing?

*Problem 2: "There's gold in them thar waters"*

The sea is rich in minerals. The world needs minerals to use in manufacturing. There is also oil under the continental shelf.

Minerals can be found in the water and on the floor of the sea. The deposits on the sea floor are often found in nodules (round lumps). It is estimated that there are enough copper nodules to last the world for 1 100

How do deep-sea oil-drilling rigs pose a danger to the environment?

years at present consumption rates.

Much of this mineral wealth lies on the sea floor off Canada's coast. At present there are few clear rules about who owns the minerals or who has a right to mine them. In addition, the nations of the world cannot agree on what should be done with nodules in the deep seas, far from any nation's shores. Should they go to any nation that can get them? What should be done about the minerals in the seas?

*Problem 3: The poor want a share*
Canada's natural resources and access to fishing have helped make the nation wealthy. Many countries, however, lack resources. Many countries are landlocked and have no seacoast at all. These nations are therefore claiming a fair share of all the riches of the sea. They argue that the seas belong to everybody on earth. They also say

that if they are ever to overcome poverty, then they must have a fair share of the wealth of the seas. This includes the wealth lying off Canada's coast.

Some Canadians say that the riches of the sea belong to the country nearest them, or to the countries that can get them.

What should be done about sharing the sea's wealth?

*Problem 4: Pollution*
If pollution of the sea is not controlled, some of its riches will be lost forever. If pollution becomes bad enough, life on earth may be in danger, for the sea supplies us with oxygen.

Oil spills are one of the biggest dangers. Most oil spills occur when tankers carrying oil from one country to another collide or run aground.

Often the country that is responsible for

481

the oil tanker will not do its duty and clean up the mess. This job then falls to the countries whose territory has been damaged by the oil.

In 1970 the tanker *Arrow* ran aground in Chedabucto Bay, Nova Scotia. The *Arrow* was registered under the flag of Liberia. It dumped millions of litres of oil into the sea, killed 4 800 birds, and coated beaches up to 160 km away with oil. It cost Canada $3 100 000 to clean up the mess. By modern standards, the *Arrow* spill was small.

Other problems are created when chemical pollution caused in one country affects seas all over the world. Drilling for oil from the seabed may also cause pollution.

What should be done about pollution of the seas?

*Problem 5: The icy Arctic*
The Arctic Ocean is shared by Canada, Iceland, Norway, Greenland, the United States, and the Soviet Union. Over 3 000 000 km² of this ocean never melts. The Arctic environment is very special and fragile. Seas in warmer parts of the world can repair damage caused by people. The Arctic environment cannot easily repair itself.

The Arctic Ocean is in danger of being damaged. People have discovered that this ocean is a frontier of untold wealth. Already oil, gas, and minerals have been found in it. Today, American and Soviet submarines travel under the Arctic to explore the area.

What should be done to protect this special ocean?

Canada and the sea: Summary
The world's population is growing. Many countries of the world, including Canada, need more food, more energy, more resources. The seas surrounding Canada are a rich source of these necessities. Thus, the interests of Canada and the world have converged on our coastal waters.

What can Canada do to protect its interests in these areas?

**Case study 3: Canada and nuclear energy**
When most people come across the word "nuclear", they often think of powerful bombs—atomic bombs. Indeed, these weapons are both powerful and deadly.

However, there are more peaceful uses for nuclear energy. Electricity may be produced cheaply by nuclear reactors. At present, electricity made by nuclear reactors costs about half as much as electricity made by oil-burning or natural-gas-burning plants. The waste products of these reactors, however, may be used to make atomic bombs.

Canada has designed and built excellent nuclear reactors. The nation has sold some of these reactors to other countries. The decision to sell reactors is part of the Canadian government's foreign policy.

In a democracy, citizens often change their minds about their country's policies. They may learn more about an issue and want to change government policies on it. This is what happened with Canada's policy of selling nuclear reactors. In the late 1970s, this policy was being challenged.

Canadians have thought twice about selling reactors because the problems surrounding nuclear energy are important. If atomic materials are misused, life on this planet could be ended. Thus, the issue of nuclear reactors has raised some questions.

1. Should Canada sell nuclear reactors to other countries?
2. What controls should be put on nuclear materials and knowledge?

Nuclear energy: Three scenes
Before examining the details about nuclear energy, we will look at three different

situations. The first two fictional scenes take place in the future. The third is a real incident from the past.

To make your reading more useful, do the following exercise. More exercises of this kind follow the three scenes.

READING BETTER

1. **General ideas.** As you finish each scene, write in your notebook two major ideas that the scene tries to put across. Use your own words.

---

### Scene 1: Somewhere in the Middle East, 1980s

The terrorist leaders stood on the hilltop, 25 km from the centre of the city. They focused their binoculars on the centre of the city.

In the city, a car that contained a large suitcase was sitting in a public parking lot. At noon the suitcase exploded.

Within seconds the whole centre of the city disappeared from the face of the earth. The heat from the explosion set trees and wooden buildings on fire up to 7 km away. The heat was so intense that the outlines of people were found on walls—like shadows.

On the hill, the terrorist leaders stood up and watched as the heat from the bomb caused a giant windstorm. One of the terrorists turned to the woman called May and said, "I thought you said it would be a small one."

"It was," replied May. "Only one-tenth the size of the **Hiroshima** bomb. A tiny atomic bomb."

"We must steal more uranium and make another," said the man known as Supremo. "Let's attack the nuclear reactor that the Canadians built. We'll use the same method as last time."

Within a few days many of the survivors of the blast began to die. Radiation from the bomb had passed through their bodies like X-rays. They suffered slow, painful deaths.

### Scene 2: Somewhere in South America, 1980s

Ernesto Gonzales smiled with pleasure as he pressed the switch. He did not think he would ever get over the thrill of seeing lights come on in his home. He laughed. Outside his crops grew thick and green. In the kitchen, his wife Maria turned on a tap and clean, fresh water flowed out. This water and the water going to the fields came from a deep well. An electric pump forced the water out of the ground. The Gonzales family thought it was like a miracle.

Fifty kilometres away, in the city of Christabel, several new factories had opened. Jobs at the factories provided income for families who had always known poverty. The factories existed because, for the first time, there was electrical power to run them.

In this dry, flat country without rivers, coal, or oil, the electricity came from a CANDU nuclear reactor system. The uranium fuel for the reactors came from Canada. The reactor had been designed and built in Canada. The engineers making it work had been educated in Canada, too.

But the people whose lives had improved as a result of the power knew nothing about Canada. They simply thanked the miracle of electricity for their new life.

### Scene 3: India joins the nuclear club—with Canada's help

In May 1974, India exploded an atomic bomb. There was a great storm of controversy over the Indian A-bomb. In India headlines announced, "India Joins America, Russia, and China." Many Indians seemed to be proud of what their country had accomplished.

The bomb was exploded underground. It had the same power as 9 070 tonnes of TNT. The bomb was made from uranium that had been fuel in a Canadian reactor called CIR. This reactor had been in operation since 1956. Other Canadian nuclear reactors called RAPP I and II were also being built in India. They were designed to provide electricity in a country desperate for new energy sources.

Canada received a great deal of attention over the explosion. The prime minister of Pakistan at this time, Ali Bhutto, pointed to Canada as the source of India's ability to make the atomic bomb. Bhutto claimed that Canadians had not been strict enough in their agreement with India over the use of nuclear material.

The Canadian government seemed to agree. All sales of nuclear reactors and uranium to India were stopped. They were not to start again until India agreed not to use Canadian material in atomic bombs.

In 1976, all sales of Canadian uranium were stopped. Canada demanded promises from all countries that Canadian uranium would not be used in bombs. This freeze on sales was not lifted until early 1978.

India's bomb explosion caused fear throughout the world. Now that India had joined the nuclear club, would other countries soon follow? As more countries obtained the atomic bomb, would one nation finally use it? Would the world survive?

---

**READING BETTER**
1. a) **Make a list of the bad effects of nuclear energy as shown in Scene 1.**
   b) **Make a list of the good effects of nuclear energy as shown in Scene 2.**
   c) **Describe why, in Scene 3, Canada was upset by the explosion of India's first atomic bomb.**
   d) **In Scene 3, what did the Canadian government do after India exploded an atomic bomb?**

Facts about nuclear energy
The following facts will help you to understand more about nuclear energy. They will help you to take a stand on the questions facing Canadians and the world.

1. The following nations have built and exploded atomic bombs:

| | | |
|---|---|---|
| United States | China | Britain |
| Soviet Union | France | India |

2. The following nations are able to build atomic bombs, but so far, have not:

| | |
|---|---|
| Argentina | Italy |
| Australia | Japan |
| Austria | Netherlands |
| Belgium | Pakistan |
| Brazil | Poland |
| Canada | South Africa |
| Chile | Spain |
| Czechoslovakia | Sweden |
| Egypt | Switzerland |
| Hungary | West Germany |
| Israel | Yugoslavia |

3. Other nations, such as Iran, Libya, and Saudi Arabia, are able to buy the necessary experts and materials.
4. The following nations build and sell nuclear reactors:

| | |
|---|---|
| USA | France |
| USSR | West Germany |
| Britain | Canada |

### The fear of nuclear weapons

It is believed that any good university physics student can build an atomic bomb. In the United States, several students have proven that they could. The only thing missing has been uranium 235 or **plutonium 239**.

These elements can be found in the waste fuel of nuclear reactors. As more nuclear reactors are built, more uranium for bombs is available. As reactors are built and sold around the world, more countries have what is needed to make the bombs.

There is always a danger that desperate people will build a bomb. They may use their own reactors as the Indians did. They may steal the materials as the terrorists in Scene 1 did. Many concerned people fear that as more bombs are built, they may be used. Estimates show that by the year 1990, nuclear reactors could have produced enough material for 23 000 atomic bombs. This is more than enough to kill all life on earth.

An atomic explosion is caused when uranium 235 or plutonium 239 atoms are split quickly. This releases heat, light, X-rays, and various forms of deadly radiation. Some radiation lasts for years. Places where atomic bombs were tested in the 1950s are still not safe to visit.

### Nuclear reactors: Canada's achievements

The reactor is a way of controlling the splitting of atoms. There is no explosion. Yet deadly radiation is still produced. The reactors are built with many safety devices to prevent leaks. In addition, the waste uranium fuel from the reactors must be buried for hundreds of years in a safe place because of its radiation danger.

The Canadian-designed nuclear reactor is called CANDU. In the reactor **heavy water** (deuterium) becomes very hot. This heat is used to boil water, and make steam. The steam turns a generator, making electricity. Before **natural uranium** is put into a CANDU reactor, it is not harmful in small quantities. Canada has large deposits of natural uranium. Our country has enough to meet

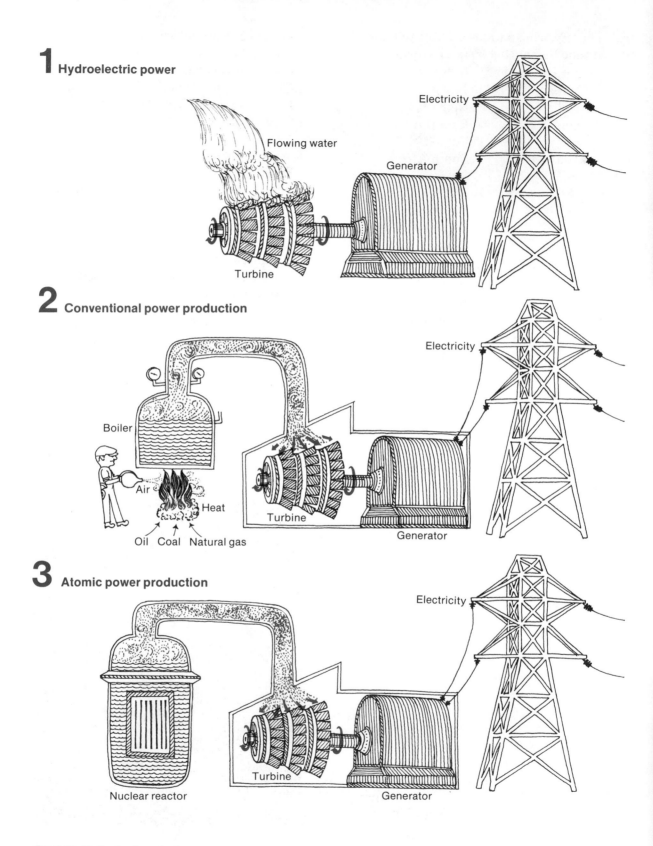

**1** **Hydroelectric power**

Electricity

Flowing water

Generator

Turbine

**2** **Conventional power production**

Electricity

Boiler

Air

Heat

Oil   Coal   Natural gas

Turbine

Generator

**3** **Atomic power production**

Electricity

Nuclear reactor

Turbine

Generator

**Fig. 3-10 Methods of producing power**

Source: D.R. Michelsohn, *Atomic Energy for Human Needs,* (New York: Julian Messner, 1976), p.118.

our needs for many decades. The waste products from CANDUs can be processed to provide materials for atomic bombs. However, this is an expensive and dangerous process.

## A brief history of nuclear energy in Canada

Canada, the United States, and Britain worked together during World War II to develop nuclear energy. As a result of this research, the US exploded two atomic bombs over the Japanese cities of Hiroshima and Nagasaki in 1945. Japan then surrendered, ending the war. Canada chose not to build atomic bombs.

In Canada, the first nuclear experiments were performed at Chalk River, 194 km from Ottawa. The first nuclear reactor to be operated outside the USA was built there in 1945. Other nuclear reactors were also built there. Chalk River became famous as a centre for nuclear research. Another research base, called the Whiteshell Nuclear Research Establishment, was built in 1963. It is located 100 km northeast of Winnipeg. At these two centres the CANDU nuclear reactors were perfected.

In addition to finding out more about nuclear reactors, these two centres produce **radioisotopes,** used in fighting cancer. Over 400 Canadian cancer treatment machines have been built in 40 countries.

Atomic Energy of Canada Ltd. (AEC) is a company set up by the federal government to run Chalk River and Whiteshell. This **crown corporation** co-operates with provincial power commissions to build nuclear generating stations. AEC is also in charge of foreign sales of CANDU.

CANDU's greatest success story so far has been the Pickering Nuclear Generating Station. Located just 10 km east of Toronto, four CANDU reactors are setting records. They have produced more electricity than any other nuclear generating station in the world. The success of

Ontario Hydro

**The Pickering Nuclear Generating Station in Ontario. How might such stations help other countries?**

487

Pickering has made the CANDU system one of Canada's greatest technical achievements.

In spite of Canada's success, there is still a great deal of debate over the use of nuclear energy. India's use of the CIR reactor to build an A-bomb has caused conflict over the question of sales.

QUICK QUIZ

These questions require short answers.
1. In what year did India join the nuclear club?
2. Why was Canada involved in the controversy over India's A-bomb explosion?
3. What does the CANDU reactor use for fuel?
4. Name three countries other than India that have bought CANDU reactors.
5. Where is the nuclear generating station that has set world records for electricity production located?

READING BETTER
1. In your own words, explain why nuclear weapons are feared.
2. What is a CANDU? How does it make electricity?

The nuclear debate: To sell or not to sell

Earlier in this section we saw what other nations can do with Canadian nuclear knowledge. The Indian explosion started a debate that still continues. Although the Canadian government has decided to keep selling the reactors, the debate is not over. A new government or a new world situation could produce a new decision. The opinions of Canadian voters could also influence government policy. What should be done? It is your turn to decide.

**The debate**

YES, LET'S SELL

CANDU reactor sales mean jobs for Canadians. In the 1970s, we sold CANDU reactors to Argentina and South Korea. Both nations agreed not to use any waste products for A-bombs. The sales of these reactors bring about $1.3 billion of business to Canadian factories. Canadian companies will also help build the reactors in the foreign countries. These companies employ about 25 000 Canadians. The foreign sales will help keep them working.

Canada should also keep on selling uranium to other countries. Our miners will then continue to have jobs. Besides, if we didn't sell uranium, cities like Karachi in Pakistan would have no electricity. They rely on our uranium to fuel their CANDU reactor. That reactor supplies all their power!

We should also sell our reactors because they show the world that Canada is an important nation. We should be proud that CANDU is recognized as one of the best and safest reactors in the world.

Another thing—let's not be stingy with our power. We are lucky to have coal, oil, natural gas, and water in this country. All these resources can be used to make electricity. But the rest of the world isn't always so lucky.

Some people fear that the nations that buy our reactors may misuse them. Canada is aware of the danger. That is why our country negotiates safeguards (see box) with these nations. Every reactor that is put in other countries is inspected by the International Atomic Energy Agency.

| Name | Location | Date of first power |
|------|----------|---------------------|
| NPD[1] | Ontario | 1962 |
| Douglas Point | Ontario | 1967 |
| Pickering A | Ontario | 1971-73 |
| Gentilly 1 | Quebec | 1971 |
| KANUPP[2] | Pakistan | 1971 |
| RAPP[3] 1 | India | 1972 |
| RAPP 2 | India | |
| Bruce A | Ontario | 1976-79 |
| Gentilly 2 | Quebec | 1979 |
| Point Lepreau | New Brunswick | 1980 |
| Cordoba | Argentina | 1980 |
| Pickering B | Ontario | 1981-83 |
| Wolsung 1 | South Korea | 1982 |
| Bruce B | Ontario | 1983-86 |
| Darlington | Ontario | 1985-88 |

[1]NPD—Nuclear Power Demonstration
[2]KANUPP—Karachi Nuclear Power Project
[3]RAPP—Rajasthan Atomic Power Project

Source: Atomic Energy Canada

**Fig. 3-11  CANDU power reactors—the record**

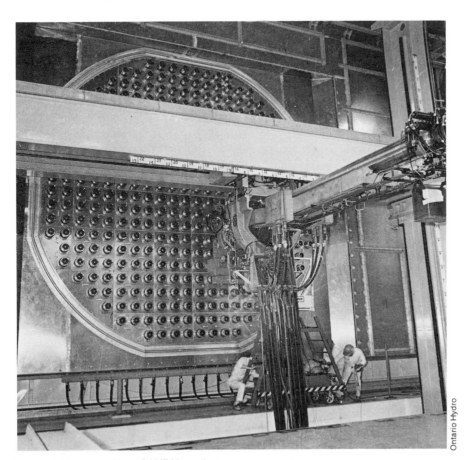

Ontario Hydro

**Fuel rods are placed in a CANDU reactor.**

> ### What are safeguards?
>
> Safeguards are usually promises not to use nuclear materials to make weapons. Canada says that any nations using its nuclear technology must do the following.
>
> 1. They must sign the *Nuclear Non-Proliferation Treaty*. This is a promise not to build atomic bombs.
> 2. They must promise never to use any Canadian material or technology for weapons. This covers CANDU reactors, uranium, and waste fuel.
>
> If any nation breaks these promises, Canada will stop all shipments of nuclear material. Canada may also demand the return of the materials. The matter may be sent to the United Nations for action.

NO, SELLING CANDU IS DANGEROUS

The CANDU reactor itself is not a threat to world peace. The people who may misuse it are the dangerous ones. When Canada sells a reactor to a nation, it is taking a chance. The nation may use the reactor to make weapons. Here are some reasons why reactors should not be sold to other countries:

1. Many countries that want to buy CANDU are not stable. Perhaps they have a long history of revolution, as Argentina has. Perhaps they are in conflict with their neighbours, as South Korea is. Whatever the case, these nations should not be given or sold anything that may be used to make bombs.
2. The president of South Korea may promise never to use the CANDU to build an A-bomb. But what about ten years later? Then a new president may not care about old promises. The new president may allow a bomb to be built with Canadian materials. For this reason safeguards are no good. They're just pieces of paper that can be ignored.
3. What can we do if another nation breaks promises? We do not have a big army, so we cannot fight. We cannot threaten to blast the other country because we do not have A-bombs ourselves. In fact, Canadians are opposed to war. The only thing we can do is appeal to the United Nations. Even that may not do any good.
4. The International Atomic Energy Agency (IAEA) was created to inspect nuclear reactors. This is supposed to stop the spread of nuclear weapons. The only problem is that the IAEA is too small. It has only 70 inspectors to cover the world.
5. We cannot be sure that other countries will not help our customers build bombs. France has sold plutonium-processing plants to countries with CANDUs. This French plant helps make the material that goes into bombs. A nation may get a reactor from Canada. It may use French equipment to get plutonium. From there it is only a small step to building an atomic bomb.

6. The more countries that own bombs or are able to build them, the greater the danger of a nuclear war.

My vote is to stop all sales to those parts of the world in which peace is threatened.

---

READING BETTER

1. In your own words, describe two or three general ideas given in each side of the debate.

ORGANIZING BETTER

1. Divide a page in your notebook into two columns. One column is for the *pros* of selling reactors, the other is for the *cons*.
In each column, list the main facts and arguments used to back up the point of view. Mark an X beside those reasons you agree with.

TAKING A STAND

1. Discuss: Should Canada sell nuclear reactors?
2. Write a class letter to your MP. Tell the MP the number of students in favour of nuclear reactor sales, and the number of students against the sales. Explain the reasons for each group's viewpoint. Ask the MP to respond to your letter.

RESEARCHING

1. The whole question of building nuclear generating stations in Canada has also caused public debate. Find out more about this issue in a library. Newspapers and magazines have printed many stories on the debate. Be sure, then, to check periodical indexes and vertical files for information.
Compile summaries of the *pro* and *con* arguments. Debate the topic in class.

Canada and nuclear energy: Summary

Nuclear energy may do much good for the world. It can also be a source of destruction. It is therefore important to have a good understanding of the issue.

Canada has produced an excellent nuclear energy system, CANDU. This system has been used to make electricity in Canada. It has also been sold to other nations. The Canadian government would like to sell more CANDU systems. However, there is always the danger that other countries will misuse them.

Canadian citizens have some influence over government policies on nuclear energy. They can express their opinions democratically, through votes or letters to MPs. Citizens may also join special interest groups, such as Pollution Probe, to help express their views.

The existence of humankind may be at stake in this issue. Where do you stand?

Conclusion

Many issues come up when nations deal with each other. This chapter has covered only a few of the issues. However, concerned people can learn more about them, and about Canada's foreign policies. Canadians can read newspapers and news magazines. They can watch TV news shows, join organizations, and attend special classes. Informed citizens can then take a stand and express their opinions to the Canadian government by voting or writing letters.

The world's concerns will not go away if we ignore them. We cannot pretend that they do not concern us. We are global citizens, so world issues will affect our lives.

READING BETTER

1. In this chapter there were three major case studies: Canada and the food crisis, Canada and the sea, and Canada and nuclear energy. In your own words, describe the main ideas expressed in each of these studies.

ORGANIZING BETTER

1. Make a list of the value conflicts that appear in each section of this chapter. (For example, nuclear energy: progress versus world peace.) Are the value conflicts similar in any cases?

2. Throughout this chapter you have decided what Canada's policy should be on a number of world issues. Make a list of the things you think the Canadian government should do. Examine the list carefully. Are you expecting the government to do too much? Also decide whether or not you have been consistent in your value decisions.

USING YOUR KNOWLEDGE

1. Suppose you were trying to explain to a friend from another country why world issues are of concern to Canada. Write a letter to your friend, giving reasons for Canada's concern.

SOLVING PROBLEMS

1. Review the structure and operation of the United Nations. How would you change it, if at all, to deal better with world concerns (such as the ones explored in this chapter)? Method: Create a committee of nations to improve the UN. Each person should represent one nation.
   a) Find out about your nation.
   b) Describe the main world concerns of your nation.
   c) Describe whether or not the UN is helping your nation at the present.
   d) How would your nation want to change the UN?

TAKING A STAND

1. Do you think that only government officials and experts should try to solve world problems? Or should ordinary citizens also become involved in solving the problems? Take a stand on this issue. Discuss it with your classmates, using facts to back up your viewpoint.

OR

Write a letter to the Minister of External Affairs. Express your opinion on one of the basic issues studied in this chapter.

RESEARCHING

1. In this chapter, we studied three world issues of concern to Canadians. Here are other world issues that involve Canadians.

| | |
|---|---|
| Human rights | Population control |
| Terrorism | Peace in southern |
| Free trade | Africa |
| Peaceful uses of | The arms race |
| space | The rights of Native |
| International trade | Peoples |
| Peace in the Middle | The energy crisis |
| East | Immigration |

Find information on one of these topics. In a report, describe the issue and outline the debate. Ask your classmates to discuss the issue and decide their own viewpoint.

## GLOSSARY

**CANDU.** Canadian Deuterium Uranium. A type of nuclear reactor designed and built in Canada.

**Colombo plan.** An international programme designed to aid national development.

**Commonwealth.** A group of nations freely associated for discussion on matters of common concern. The members recognize the Queen of the United Kingdom as the symbol of the association and head of the Commonwealth.

**Crown corporation.** A business that is owned by the government. Two examples are Air Canada and Atomic Energy of Canada.

**Foreign policy.** Courses of action adopted by government with regard to relations with other countries.

**Heavy water.** Also called deuterium. It is used in CANDU reactors.

**Hiroshima.** A Japanese city destroyed in 1945 by the first atomic bomb used in war. The US was responsible for the bombing.

**Malnutrition.** Poor nutrition, caused especially by an unbalanced diet.

**Natural uranium.** A mineral made up of two types of uranium—uranium 238 and small amounts of uranium 235. The second type causes the nuclear chain reaction to occur.

**Niacin.** A B vitamin found in foods high in protein.

**Outports.** Isolated fishing villages along Newfoundland's coast.

**Plutonium.** A radioactive metallic element. It is usually produced in nuclear reactors and may be used to make atomic bombs.

**Protein.** Part of certain foods that is essential to good health. It is found in meats, fish, grain, peas, and beans.

**Quota.** A limited share of the total.

**Radioisotopes.** Radioactive forms of a chemical element. They are often used in medical therapy and research.

**Thiamin.** A B vitamin found in such foods as grains, beans, egg yolks, and liver.

**Trawler.** A fishing boat that pulls a large net through the water.

**Twelve-mile limit.** The 12 miles in this limit are *nautical miles*. One nautical mile = 1.852 km. Fisheries Canada still officially uses the nautical mile measurement. The metric equivalent is not yet in use.

**World Bank.** An agency of the United Nations established in 1945 to make loans to member nations. The World Bank also gives advice on such matters as forming economic policies and development planning.

## Quick Quiz answers

### p. 7

1. It is about the union of Canada and the United States in 1995.
2. There were economic slowdowns.
3. The Union party. Its aim was to have Canada become part of the US.
4. They elected the Union party in November 1994.
5. They are to become states in "The United States of North America".

### p. 13

1. Any *two* of Halifax, Toronto, Winnipeg, Vancouver.
2. Eastsea.
3. They would be removed.
4. Some Canadian businesses would be ruined. They would be unable to compete with US businesses.
5. We would no longer have parliamentary government. It would become a Republic.
6. Some Canadian-born people were blaming immigrants for the lack of jobs.
7. Yes. He thought it would create more jobs in the West.
8. Yes. More than 90% of the voters voted for the Union Party.
9. They predicted that this former province would also seek union with the United States.
10. You may mention any item about jobs, trade, or wages.

### p. 17

1. It is the date on which Canada ceases to exist as an independent country.
2. Quebec leaves Canadian Confederation.
3. A poll was taken and then an election was held. The Union Party was voted into power.
4. She said that Canada had an identity of its own. It was a country that accepted all races and cultures.
5. Canada found that its problems were too big to solve on its own. The country could not find answers to its racial, economic, and regional problems.

### p. 31

1. The provinces—Newfoundland, New Brunswick, Prince Edward Island, Nova Scotia; parts of Quebec—the Eastern Townships and Gaspé Peninsula.
2. Lowlands, uplands, and highlands.
3. Parts of the mainland and islands that are submerged.
4. The temperatures are lower in summer and higher in winter than on the Prairies and in the Canadian Shield. Much precipitation falls— about 1 500 mm a year.
5. About 10%.
6. Any two of these: potash, iron, coal, oil, and gas.

7. Newfoundland.
8. Any one of these: the shipbuilding industry declined; free trade with the US ended; competition arose over timber and lumber shipments to Europe.
9. Any two of these: mining, fishing, manufacturing, tourism, hydroelectricity production.
10. It will prevent overfishing of Canada's coastal waters by foreign fleets.

### p. 35

1. Great Lakes Lowlands, St. Lawrence Lowlands.
2. Canadian Shield, Frontenac.
3. Humid.
4. Growing season.
5. Algonkians or Iroquoians.
6. Industrial or manufacturing.
7. Resources, transportation.
8. Land.
9. Local.
10. Mechanized.

### p. 44

1. Saskatchewan.
2. The Mexican border.
3. False. There are rolling hills and valleys.
4. There are no large bodies of water to act as a moderating influence.
5. 300 to 500 mm.
6. The Plains Indians.
7. Irrigation.
8. Athabaska Tar Sands.
9. The Qu'Appelle, North Saskatchewan.
10. In the 1890s.

### p. 50

1. The Cordilleras.
2. Any two of: Rocky Mountains, Columbia Mountains, Coastal Mountains, and Island Mountains.
3. The Fraser Delta.
4. Up to 2 500 mm.
5. Forestry, mining, and tourism.
6. The completion of the CPR.
7. Overfishing.
8. It is second only to Alberta.
9. Market gardening, vegetable and fruit growing.
10. Its position on the Pacific Ocean.

### p. 58

1. The 60th parallel of latitude.
2. About 60 000 people.
3. Any two of the following: cost, the hardships of environment, the needs of the Native Peoples.
4. The eastern part is mostly lowland. The west is mountainous.
5. In general, it is cold and dry.
6. Mining; also fur trading, fishing, tourism.
7. The climate is severe, and makes life difficult.
8. It increases the financial costs. It places physical strains on the workers.

9. Tundra.
10. It is land whose subsoil is permanently frozen.

## p. 66

1. False. They leave school at an earlier age than students in wealthy regions do.
2. True.
3. True.
4. True.
5. True.
6. True.
7. False. It is higher in the richer regions.
8. True.
9. False. Wages were lowest in the Atlantic region.
10. True.

## p. 71

1. False. Income tends to be higher in urbanized areas.
2. True.
3. False. A good climate can help a region's economy to thrive; a poor climate can create problems.
4. True.
5. False. Regions with natural resources tend to be wealthy.
6. True.
7. False. It helps the economy because the transportation of goods is easier.
8. True.
9. True.
10. True.

## p. 86

1. They set up a government and decided on rules to live by.
2. He stole food.
3. He thought that the majority of the survivors were ganging up on him and depriving him of his right to live.
4. He had stolen food and thus endangered the lives of people in the shelter.
5. He would be exposed to the deadly radiation.

## p. 97

1. True.
2. False. The BNA Act gives responsibility for the postal service to the federal government.
3. False. The prime minister usually chooses his Cabinet from among the elected MPs within his party.
4. True.
5. True.
6. False. The prime minister is a national, not a provincial, leader.
7. True.
8. False. Cabinet ministers are held responsible for *everything* their department does.

## p. 109

1. True.
2. False. The federal government was to be more important than provincial governments.
3. True.
4. False, At one time a council like the Senate did exist, but it was abolished.
5. True.
6. False. In general they do the same job in the provinces that the prime minister does in the country.
7. False. Three readings are required.
8. True.

## p. 132

1. Mr. Toomath thinks his situation is strange because he had always said that it is important for people to work. But now he is the one in the family without a job.
2. He went to a Canada Employment Centre (run by the federal government). He also tried some employment agencies (run by private business).
3. In Mr. Toomath's words, inflation means that the prices of products go up. Or, you pay the same price for a product, but the package is smaller, or the product is not as good.
4. The Toomaths need more money because inflation makes all sorts of prices rise. If the Toomaths do not get more money, they will have to spend less.
5. The swimming pool bothers Mr. Toomath because it seems a waste of money. He thinks that money spent on the pool could be used better elsewhere.
6. The money came from the federal, provincial, and municipal governments. These governments get their money from the taxpayer.
7. It provides recreation (people can work better if they feel refreshed). It also gives jobs to various people.
8. Any four of these will do: it provides Canada Employment Centres; it sends Mr. Toomath a weekly unemployment cheque; it provides public works such as hockey rinks, parks, etc.; it builds and maintains schools; and it provides rent controls.
9. Doreen cannot afford to buy or rent skis. She also cannot afford ski clothes.
10. He must decide whether to take the job at the auto supply store or whether to remain unemployed until a better job comes along.

## p. 137

| | |
|---|---|
| 1. Rise. | 4. Spending. |
| 2. Lose. . | 5. Spends, income. |
| 3. Rise, produce. | 6. Fall. |

## p. 140

| | |
|---|---|
| 1. i | 4. d |
| 2. f | 5. e |
| 3. c | 6. b |

7. g
8. a
9. h
10. j

**p. 143**

1. F
2. F
3. G
4. F
5. F
6. G
7. G
8. G
9. F
10. G

**p. 161**

1. Some people feel that laws and rules restrict their freedom.
2. The cars were racing down the highway at high speeds.
3. He failed history.
4. They were to do whatever they could get away with.

**p. 173**

1. Drunken driving.
2. He skipped class, and he did not do his homework.
3. She said that the neighbours have a right to hold outdoor parties. She also reminded her husband that the barbeque he had the night before was noisy. Also, the barbeque lighter fluid had a strong odour.
4. He did not believe in teenagers dating without a chaperone.
5. He threw a fire bomb into a store. A young girl was killed by the bomb.

**p. 242**

1. To prevent the English-speaking people from taking it over.
2. Riel.
3. Macdonald.
4. Macdonald.
5. Thomas Scott.
6. Ontario.
7. Quebec.
8. Manitoba.
9. An area in present-day Saskatchewan.
10. Duck Lake.

**p. 245**

1. Thompson.
2. Hopkins.
3. Thompson.
4. They felt that he had insulted Taché and that he had cheated the Indians in the Treaty of Manitoulin Island.
5. The Métis.

**p. 272**

1. The McGill boys had volunteered to join the army and they knew that French-speaking Canadians, in general, were not volunteering.
2. The government minister in charge of recruitment was an Orangeman who distrusted French-speaking Canadians.

3. 184 000 from Ontario, and 47 000 from Quebec.
4. 100 000.
5. Laurier.

**p. 357**

1. An economic nationalist.
2. Branch plant.
3. American.
4. Jobs for Canadians and taxes paid to our governments.
5. Americans from the parent plant get them.

**p. 373**

1. Continentalist.
2. Free trade.
3. General McNaughton.
4. b)
5. a)—Bennett.
   b)—Berger.
   c)—Lysyk.

**p. 386**

1. Indians and Inuit.
2. After 1759 Quebec was cut off from France. It thus developed its own way of life. Quebeckers were always ready to defend their language and culture.
3. The wilderness, the Native Peoples, and their own cultural backgrounds.
4. Loyalists.
5. Films, radio, TV.
6. Be successful in the USA.
7. CBC, National Film Board, Canada Council, or CRTC.
8. Multiculturalism.

**Canadian Culture Quiz p. 389**

1. Liona Boyd, Lise Payette, Karen Kain, Frank Shuster, Réne Simard, Anne Murray, William Shatner, Judy LaMarsh, Smoky Smith, Alice Munro, Frederick Banting, Patsy Gallant, Maurice Richard, Oscar Peterson.
2. Baseball, Corn flakes, computer, airplane, colour TV, nylon are *American*. All the rest were invented in Canada.
3. Guèvremont, Atwood, de la Roche, Mowat, Roy, Wiseman, Richler.
4. None of them—it was John A. Macdonald.

**p. 426**

1. No conscription.
2. France had been defeated, Britain was in danger.
3. Referendum.
4. Heavy losses in Normandy and Italy.
5. Louis St. Laurent.

**p. 488**

1. 1974.
2. Waste fuel from a Canadian gift reactor was used to make the A-bomb.
3. Natural uranium.
4. Pakistan, South Korea, Argentina.
5. Pickering, Ontario.

# Index

501